Cases in Management, Organizational Behavior and Human Resource Management

Fifth Edition

Randall S. Schuler
New York University

Paul F. Buller
Gonzaga University

WEST PUBLISHING COMPANY
MINNEAPOLIS/ST. PAUL NEW YORK LOS ANGELES SAN FRANCISCO

WEST'S COMMITMENT TO THE ENVIRONMENT

In 1906, West Publishing Company began recycling materials left over from the production of books. This began a tradition of efficient and responsible use of resources. Today, 100% of our legal bound volumes are printed on acid-free, recycled paper consisting of 50% new paper pulp and 50% paper that has undergone a de-inking process. We also use vegetable-based inks to print all of our books. West recycles nearly 27,700,000 pounds of scrap paper annually—the equivalent of 229,300 trees. Since the 1960s, West has devised ways to capture and recycle waste inks, solvents, oils, and vapors created in the printing process. We also recycle plastics of all kinds, wood, glass, corrugated cardboard, and batteries, and have eliminated the use of polystyrene book packaging. We at West are proud of the longevity and the scope of our commitment to the environment.

West pocket parts and advance sheets are printed on recyclable paper and can be collected and recycled with newspapers. Staples do not have to be removed. Bound volumes can be recycled after removing the cover.

Production, Prepress, Printing and Binding by West Publishing Company.

 TEXT IS PRINTED ON 10% POST CONSUMER RECYCLED PAPER    Printed with Printwise Environmentally Advanced Water Washable Ink

Contents

Preface

Cases in Management, Organizational Behavior, and Human Resource Management, Fifth Edition, was written to provide a single, comprehensive source of a variety of cases that have proven useful in many management, organizational behavior, and human resource management courses. As with the Fourth Edition, this casebook contains several "classic" cases such as "Dick Spencer", "Dowling Flexible Metals", "The Luggers Versus the Butchers", and "Peoples Trust Company". It also contains twenty-one new cases, many of which depict recent events at well-known companies. In total, this edition contains forty-six cases that we think provoke student interest and that you may find appropriate to use as a single text for a management, organizational behavior, or human resource management course taught entirely by the case method, or as a supplement to a textbook in one of these fields.

The cases involve a wide variety of organizational settings, from non-profit to service to manufacturing, from relatively small, entrepreneurial companies to large multinationals. Although we have categorized each case into a major section of management and organizational behavior by topic, many of the cases can be used flexibly to address other topics. As shown in the Instructor's Manual that accompanies the 5th Edition, nearly every case involves multiple management, organizational behavior and human resource management topics that can be analyzed and discussed. The cases included in this book can be analyzed by students having relatively little academic background and experience in management, organizational behavior, and human resource management as well as by those having extensive background and experience in these areas. Therefore, this casebook should be appropriate for all levels of management, organizational behavior, and human resource management courses, not just in business administration, but also in hotel administration, public administration, and other areas of administrative science.

This Fifth Edition of *Cases in Management, Organizational Behavior, and Human Resource Management* differs from the Fourth Edition in several respects. First, we have included twenty-one new cases. In doing so, we have added more comprehensive cases (e.g., "The Lincoln Electric Company" and "XEL Communications"), and more cases involving current topical issues such as globalization (e.g., "Using Leadership to Promote TQM"), ethics (e.g., "Salomon Brothers"), and managing diversity (e.g., "Managing Workforce Diversity: People-Related Issues at the Barden Corporation"). Second, we have added a number of cases involving well-known companies (e.g., "Apple Computer", "Nordstom", "American Express", and "Wang/Microsoft") to stimulate students' interest and involvement. Third, we have deleted a number of outdated cases in order to keep the casebook relevant and of reasonable length. Fourth, this edition has a new organization to better reflect current topics and issues of importance in management, organizational behavior and human resource management. For example, eleven cases involving international organizations and issues have been placed throughout the various sections of the book rather than in a separate section to better reflect the importance of globalization in all aspects of management, organizational behavior and human resource management.

A great many colleagues have been especially helpful to us in the preparation of this casebook. Several sent us some of their favorite cases and others made invaluable suggestions about the content of the book and the instructor's manual. We are most grateful to those individuals who provided us with their cases: Susan E. Jackson, Hrach Bedrosian, Allan Bird, and Suresh Kotha, New York University; Murray Silverman, San Francisco State University; Margaret E. Fenn, University of Washington; Jan P. Muczyk, The Cleveland State University; D. Jeffrey Lenn, George Washington University; Alan Hoffman, Bentley College; Robert P. McGowan and Cynthia V. Fukami, University of Denver; Vladimir Pucik, Nina Hatvany, and Craig C. Lundberg, Cornell University; Floyd G. Willoughby, Oakland University; Peter G. and Lynda L. Goulet, University of Northern Iowa; Jeffrey A. Barach, Tulane University; Dan Dalton, Indiana University; James C. Conant, California State University-Fullerton; Arthur D. Sharplin, McNeese State University; Joe Martochio, University of Illinois; Jerome H. Laubenstein, Aid Association for Lutherans; and Asbjorn Osland, George Fox College.

Special thanks go to Susan Schneider for providing us with several international cases she has developed. We also want to give special recognition to Richard D. Freedman and his colleagues at New York University for providing us with a number of high quality cases. Our appreciation also goes to Richard L. Daft and Kristen Dahlen for graciously providing the section on the use and application of cases.

The cooperation and assistance by the following publishers were also greatly appreciated: Elsevier Science; Kluwer Academic Publishers; Center for Professional Education, Arthur Andersen & Company; Case Development Center, University of Minnesota; Prentice-Hall, Inc.; North American Case Research Association; and West Publishing Company.

Finally, we wish to thank those with whom we have worked most closely during this project and who provided us with invaluable encouragement and support. Our editors, Sharon Adams Poore and Esther Craig, provided essential assistance from the very beginning to the very end. Kathy Rogers, Permissions and Rights Editor at West Publishing Company was also very helpful. We also thank Sandy Hank at Gonzaga University for her assistance in preparing the Instructor's Manual.

We hope that you will enjoy the 5th Edition of our casebook, and trust that you will find it useful in teaching management, organizational behavior, and human resource management. We welcome any comments and suggestions that will help us continue to improve the product.

RANDALL S. SCHULER
PAUL F. BULLER
June 1995

Guide to Case Analysis*

Students of biology, chemistry, and the physical sciences learn their fields through practicing and experimenting with theories and materials in the laboratory. As a student of organizational behavior and management, your laboratory will exist in the case problems and experiential exercises presented in this book. The cases and exercises provide the opportunity to experiment with real organizations in the classroom setting.

Management or organizational behavior, like any field, can be learned at three different levels: memorization, understanding, and application. Memorization is the lowest level of learning and involves the simple recitation of facts and simple concepts. Understanding involves deeper learning. It includes the ability to deal with relationships among concepts and to deal with concepts in different contexts. Application is the highest level of learning. Concepts have to be very well understood to apply them to the real world. Mastery of concepts sufficient to solve problems or to diagnose real organizational situations is a significant accomplishment. Learning to understand and apply concepts can be effectively and pleasantly accomplished through case study.

Cases and exercises do not replace the textbook and lectures. The management and organizational behavior textbooks, readings, and/or lectures provide a theoretical background. The material in this casebook is a supplement; it extends the learning process to the real world. The goal of studying management and organizational behavior with cases is to enable you to apply what is taught from a textbook to a real situation, a reconciliation of theory with life. Managers use theories and models in their day-to-day management of organizations. Often these models are intuitive and implicit. Sometimes they are explicit, just as in management textbooks. Whatever the nature of the theory or model they use, managers must react to situations relying on past experience and acquired skills to analyze and assess the issues and arrive at a solution. Case study develops your skill in analyzing problems and generating solutions based on your understanding of the theories and models of organization processes and behavior.

This book contains a variety of case materials and experiential exercises. The cases can be categorized by the educational objective of the instructor and the role of you, the student. The two educational objectives and the associated learning processes are summarized in Exhibit 1. The first type of case learning is theory application/illustration. In this type of case the problem or issue outlined in the situation has usually been solved, and it is your responsibility to analyze the outcome and its consequences. Cases selected for this type of analysis may not emphasize any problem, but present real-life situations that can be used to explain and illustrate theories and models of management and organizational behavior. The facts in the case may be focused toward specific theories, but seemingly irrelevant material will also be included. Sometimes you will be asked to evaluate the solution in the case and to propose an alternative solution if necessary. The second type of case educational objective is problem analysis. Cases used for this objective may be relatively complex. Your role will be to analyze and interpret the situation. You will have to sort out the facts of the case, determine the

---

*Reprinted from *Organizational Theory: Cases and Applications* by Richard L. Daft and Kristen M. Dahlen ©1984 by West Publishing Co. Reprinted with permission.

cause-and-effect relationships, and design a solution and plan for implementation. The primary goal is to solve the problem. The illustration of theories and models is not the primary goal of the case, but theories and models will be used to help identify alternatives and justify your solution.

	Theory Application/Illustration	*Problem Analysis*
Learning Focus	1. Understand concepts 2. Develop skill in use of concepts	1. Develop skill in identifying and analyzing problems 2. Develop skill in designing solutions and plans for implementation.
Learning Procedure	1. Identify examples of theories through relationships in case. 2. Determine inconsistencies with theory. Use concepts to evaluate behavior and predict outcomes.	1. Gather and interpret relevant facts, diagnose critical problems. 2. Use concepts to develop and support a solution and plan of action.

Exhibit 1.   The Educational Objective and Learning Processes Associated with Case Analysis

Another approach to learning management and organizational behavior is through experiential exercises. Experiential exercises engage you directly in the material. Cases require intellectual analysis of an external situation. By contrast, you become an ongoing participant in the situation when you are involved in an exercise. Experiential exercises require intellectual involvement and critical thinking, but are designed to also engage your real-life experience in the analysis. You are required to become involved in a situation, either in terms of an assigned role or as a participant observer. After the exercise is completed, the skills you will use to interpret your experiences are similar to those used with other case studies: problem analysis skills help you separate cause from effect and arrive at timely solutions, and theory application skills require you to recognize concepts and relationships in the context of the situation. A few of the exercises require role-playing in which individuals will be assigned specific identities within an organization situation. You will have the opportunity to test your analytical and conceptual skills in responding to your role and in discussing your interpretation of the unfolding drama.

As you develop your analytical and conceptual skills through cases and exercises, you will be able to master the understanding and use of personnel and human resource management. Many of the cases combine more than one objective. A specific case might be used to practice the application of theory, or to engage you in the identification and solution of the problem. Exercises can also be approached through problems to be solved or the application of theories and models. For any of these materials to enrich your learning experience requires your involvement. An integral part of the learning process is your commitment to preparing the analysis or application and becoming involved in class discussion. Remember, the cases serve a dual purpose: to develop your skills in problem solution and to increase your ability to apply

theory to real situations. To assist you in achieving these learning objectives, we sugg---
following steps as a guide to get you started.

Theory Application/Illustration

This casebook is intended to be used in conjunction with a textbook or a collection of readings that defines and outlines theories and models of organization. In studying the theories of personnel and human resource management, the cases enable you to see examples of the dimensions and relationships within the theories to be used when solving real problems. Applying theory to the case gives you a deeper understanding of how the theory works in the real world. Theory application enables you to relate the facts of the situation to theoretical prediction about processes. The cases and exercises provide you with practice in testing theories from your textbook or readings against the real world.

The application of theories and models to cases is an art that has to be developed through practice and creativity. The framework presented in Exhibit 2 illustrates the three steps required to move you through the process of theory application. The basic elements are identification, relationships, and inconsistencies.

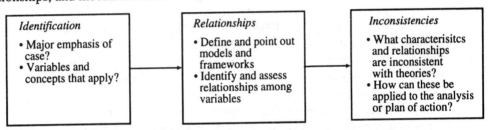

Exhibit 2. Steps in Using Cases for Theory Application/Illustration

Identification. What is the major emphasis of the case in terms of personnel and human resource management? The primary conceptual topic will be identified by the section heading under which the case appears. However, few cases are limited to one concept. Within the general topic area, what set of variables, ideas, and topics from the textbook are illustrated within the case? You must be familiar with the relevant theories and descriptions of management frameworks. Then you should review the processes described within the case, the interactions of the participants, and additional facts that may relate to the theories and models. Try to find as many illustrations of the theory as you can within the case.

Relationships. After identifying the specific concepts relevant to the case situation, describe the relationships among variables. Try to determine whether the predictions made by a theory are illustrated in the case. For example, do the number of rules and procedures reflect the organization's size and stage of development? Is the observed decision-making process what you would predict based on the level of uncertainty confronting managers? Is the organization's structure appropriate for the rate of change in the environment? Does internal organization culture reflect the values symbolized by top management? One test of an organizational theory is whether predicted relationships occur within organizations. By examining theoretical relationships you can understand cause-and-effect relationships and test whether the theory helps you understand the situation. If so, knowledge of one variable will enable you to predict and have knowledge of other variables. Understanding relationships is necessary for determining the impact of contextual factors on the organization under discussion.

Inconsistencies. When discussing relationships among variables, are there instances in which the relationships in the case are inconsistent with theoretical predictions? Perhaps formalization is not consistent with the organization size, or structure is not consistent with the environment. Situations in real life will not identically mirror theory from the textbook, although situations will be similar enough to theory to be useful in understanding the theory. Inconsistencies are an opportunity to challenge and refine your understanding of a theory. Perhaps a model applies only in certain situations. Perhaps other variables are at work that are overwhelming a specific relationship. Identifying inconsistencies and then digging into why they exist is an excellent way to both test and increase your understanding of the organizational theories and models. Occasionally there will be a case that defies theory, possibly presenting familiar variables with inconsistent results or outcomes. In your analysis, bring out these anomalies.

Problem Analysis

Problem analysis frequently requires greater involvement in the case than does theory application. Problem analysis includes and goes beyond the application of theory. Theory application can be accomplished without identifying and solving problems in the case. Problem analysis goes beyond theory by asking students to analyze the situation and propose a solution, as illustrated in Exhibit 3.

An important lesson in identifying and solving problems in a case is to realize that one reading of the case is not sufficient for fully understanding the issues presented. You should allocate your time so that at least two readings will be possible. The first time through, read to get an overall sense of the situation. You may initially assess all the variables involved, and the relative importance of each, and the nature and scope of the situation. After you interpret the facts of the organization, you will be able to move on to the following steps.

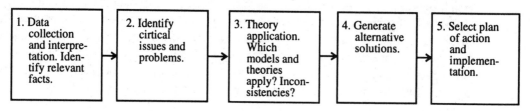

Exhibit 3. Steps in Using Cases for Problem Analysis

Data Collection and Interpretation. After carefully reading the case, make note of the data that will be useful in determining the state of the situation and the issues to be dealt with. The purposes of this step are to sort out irrelevant from relevant data and to develop a diagnosis of the current situation.

Critical Issues. After diagnosing and analyzing the facts of the situation, you will need to isolate the critical issues or problems to be solved. One way to think about problems is to look for factors that threaten the survival, goals, or performance of the organization or its major departments. Without identifying the real problem, any suggestion for solution will be inappropriate. Isolating the main problem can be quite frustrating, and you may never be absolutely certain you are correct. With careful attention, constant questioning, and practice, your skill at identifying critical issues will improve.

To begin with, think in terms of cause and effect; do not confuse the symptoms with the problem. Dig beneath the surface and determine if something more basic is generating the problem you have identified. For example, you may observe such things as intergroup conflict, a seemingly inappropriate organization structure, poor control, or lack of communication. But to conclude the problem is intergroup conflict or poor control is ignoring the roots or causes of these issues, and thus reduces your chances of finding a successful solution. After identifying the problem or issue, write it in a one-sentence statement that concisely conveys the main concern. By reducing your thoughts to one sentence, you force yourself to focus on a primary issue.

Theory Application. Having identified the critical issue, consider your analysis in light of the work you may have previously done with the theories and models that related to the case. Can the theories be used to understand the problem? Are the relationships clearer when viewed in light of the models? If the situation appears to be inconsistent with the theory, is this part of the problem? How can knowledge of the theory assist you in generating possible solutions?

Generating Solutions. Based on the issue or problem you have identified and the theories and models you have studied, brainstorm a list of possible solutions. In brainstorming you should write down every possibility. Do not evaluate the feasibility or rationality of each; just write them down. You should not limit yourself to the strict amount of information provided in the case, i.e., be creative in dealing with the situation.

Having generated a list of wide-ranging possibilities, review your problem statement and identify those alternatives that have a direct link with solving the problem. Combine similar suggestions and begin eliminating alternatives based on your earlier analysis of the situation: constraints of the organization, theoretical concepts, goals and objectives, interacting variables.

Selection of Course of Action and Plan for Implementation. Using your narrowed list of alternatives, begin a detailed analysis of each. Determine the criteria you will use in evaluating each solution. What requirements must a course of action meet? Are there cost constraints? What about timeliness? Resource availability? Are there constituents to consider? Future shock waves? List the pros and cons of each course of action in terms of the criteria you have specified. It may be necessary to make inferences and judgments based on the data provided in the case; this is encouraged as long as you also develop sound and logical arguments to support your interpretations.

The next step of the analysis is to select the best course of action based on the pros and cons and logical assessment of each alternative. You should state the specific steps you recommend and why. You should be sensitive to the arguments against your decision and should be prepared to refute any challenges to your reasoning. Be willing to take risks that can be supported by your analysis of the situation. Indeed, a bonus to solving problems in cases, compared with solving "real world" problems, is that you can take risks without having to answer for the consequences. Be creative and imaginative in developing your answers, but be aware that you will have to logically defend your solution.

Your recommendation should also include a plan for implementation. Consider personnel, time frames, and the sequence of events. In designing the implementation plan you will again be forced to consider your problem definition and analysis. Will your plan address the problem? What are the ramifications of implementing this plan? How will you address them? Many solutions die because no one considered how to introduce the solution or did not consider the possible roadblocks.

Conclusion

An observation you will make all too quickly when studying the cases in this book is that there is never enough information to make the right decision. You can't be certain you have identified the best answer. Other students may have developed different solutions and may present effective arguments for them. There is no perfect answer to a case problem. Each solution may be effective to some extent, but none will be 100 percent accurate. Moreover, no one ever has all the information that would be useful or desirable when analyzing a problem or making a decision. You will just have to make do with what you have, draw logical inferences and assumptions from the available data, and support your arguments with evidence found in the case and theory. Remember, you are being asked to deal with "reality," and there is a lack of information in the real world too.

As you progress through your course and the casebook, relate the material, concepts, and theory to your life beyond the classroom. Continue to develop and refine your analytical skills when viewing situations in which you live and participate every day. Look for examples of the theories and models in your own environment. In the classroom, be prepared for discussion, be involved, offer your insights, make constructive criticism, and expect to receive the same from your peers. The case method of learning is most effective when everyone is involved in the analysis and discussion and is willing to experiment with the application of theoretical concepts to the real world. Our intent in designing this casebook has been to challenge, stimulate, and facilitate your learning of management, organizational behavior, and human resource management. We also hope that you find this collection of case materials and exercises interesting, and that you can find the learning process enjoyable. Case problems provide a laboratory setting for your experimentation, and the laboratory is often the most exciting part of the learning process.

Part 1   Management and Leadership

Cases Outline

1. Custom Chip, Inc.*

I. Introduction

It was 7:50 on Monday morning. Frank Questin, Product Engineering Manager at Custom Chip, Inc. was sitting in his office making a TO DO list for the day. From 8:00 to 9:30 A.M. he would have his weekly meeting with his staff of engineers. After the meeting, Frank thought he would begin developing a proposal for solving what he called "Custom Chip's manufacturing documentation problem" – inadequate technical information regarding the steps to manufacture many of the company's products. Before he could finish his TO DO list, he answered a phone call from Custom Chip's human resource manager, who asked him about the status of two overdue performance appraisals and reminded him that this day marked Bill Lazarus' fifth year anniversary with the company. Following this call, Frank hurried off to the Monday morning meeting with his staff.

Frank had been Product Engineering Manager at Custom Chip for 14 months. This was his first management position, and he sometimes questioned his effectiveness as a manager. Often he could not complete the tasks he set out for himself due to interruptions and problems brought to his attention by others. Even though he had not been told exactly what results he was supposed to accomplish, he had a nagging feeling that he should have achieved more after these 14 months. On the other hand, he thought maybe he was functioning pretty well in some of his areas of responsibility given the complexity of the problems his group handled and the unpredictable changes in the semiconductor industry – changes caused not only by rapid advances in technology, but also by increased foreign competition and a recent downturn in demand.

II. Company Background

Custom Chip, Inc. was a semiconductor manufacturer specializing in custom chips and components used in radars, satellite transmitters, and other radio frequency devices. The company had been founded in 1977 and had grown rapidly with sales exceeding $25 million in 1986. Most of the company's 300 employees were located in the main plant in Silicon Valley, but overseas manufacturing facilities in Europe and the Far East were growing in size and importance. These overseas facilities assembled the less complex, higher volume products. New products and the more complex ones were assembled in the main plant. Approximately one-third of the assembly employees were in overseas facilities.

While the specialized products and markets of Custom Chip provided a market niche that had thus far shielded the company from the major downturn in the semiconductor industry, growth had come to a standstill. Because of this, cost reduction had become a high priority.

III. The Manufacturing Process

Manufacturers of standard chips have long production runs of a few products. Their cost per unit is low and cost control is a primary determinant of success. In contrast, manufacturers of custom chips have extensive product lines and produce small production runs for special applications. Custom Chip, Inc., for example, manufactured over 2000 different products in the last five years. In any one quarter the company might schedule 300 production runs for different products, as many as one-third of which might be new or modified products which the company had not made before. Because they must be efficient in designing and manufacturing many product lines, all custom chip manufacturers are highly dependent on their engineers. Customers are often first concerned with whether Custom Chip can design and manufacture the needed product *at all,* secondly with whether they can deliver it on time, and only thirdly with cost.

After designing a product, there are two phases to the manufacturing process. (See Figure 1.) The first is wafer fabrication. This is a complex process in which circuits are etched onto the various layers added to a silicon wafer. The number of steps that the wafer goes through plus inherent problems in controlling various chemical processes make it very difficult to meet the exacting specifications required for the final wafer. The wafers, which are typically "just a few" inches in diameter when the fabrication process is complete, contains hundreds, sometimes thousands of tiny identical die. Once the wafer has been tested and sliced up to produce these die, each die will be used as a circuit component.

If the completed wafer passes the various quality tests, it moves on to the assembly phase. In assembly, the die from the wafers, very small wires and other components are attached to a circuit in a series of precise operations. This finished circuit is the final product of Custom Chip, Inc.

Each product goes through many independent and delicate operations, and each step is subject to operator or machine error. Due to the number of steps and tests involved, the wafer fabrication takes 8 to 12 weeks and the assembly process takes 4 to 6 weeks. Because of the exacting specifications, products are rejected for the slightest flaw. The likelihood that every product starting the run will make it through all of the processes and still meet specifications is often quite low. For some products, average yield[1] is as low as 40 percent, and actual yields can vary considerably from one run to another. At Custom Chip, the average yield for all products is in the 60 to 70 percent range.

Because it takes so long to make a custom chip, it is especially important to have some control of these yields. For example, if a customer orders one thousand units of a product and typical yields for that product average 50 percent, Custom Chip will schedule a starting batch of 2200 units. With this approach, even if the yield falls as low as 45.4% (45.4% of 2200 is 1000) the company can still meet the order. If the actual yield falls below 45.4 percent, the order will not be completed in that run, and a very small, costly run of the item will be needed to complete the order. The only way the company can effectively control these yields and stay on schedule is for the engineering groups and operations to cooperate and coordinate their efforts efficiently.

---

[1]Yield refers to the ratio of finished products that meet specifications relative to the number that initially entered the manufacturing process.

Pre-production

• Applications Engineers design and produce prototype
• Product Engineers translate design into manufacturing instructions

Production

• Water Fabrication

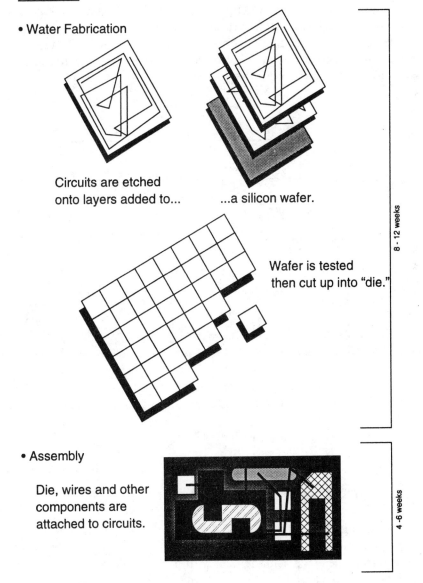

Circuits are etched
onto layers added to...   ...a silicon wafer.

Wafer is tested
then cut up into "die."

8 - 12 weeks

• Assembly

Die, wires and other
components are
attached to circuits.

4 -6 weeks

Figure 1. Manufacturing Process

IV. Role of the Product Engineer

The product engineer's job is defined by its relationship to application engineering and operations. The applications engineers are responsible for designing and developing prototypes when incoming orders are for new or modified products. The product engineer's role is to translate the application engineering group's design into a set of manufacturing instructions, then to work alongside manufacturing to make sure that engineering related problems get solved. The product engineers' effectiveness is ultimately measured by their ability to control yields on their assigned products. The organization chart in Figure 2 shows the engineering and operations departments. Figure 3 summarizes the roles and objectives of manufacturing, application engineering, and product engineering.

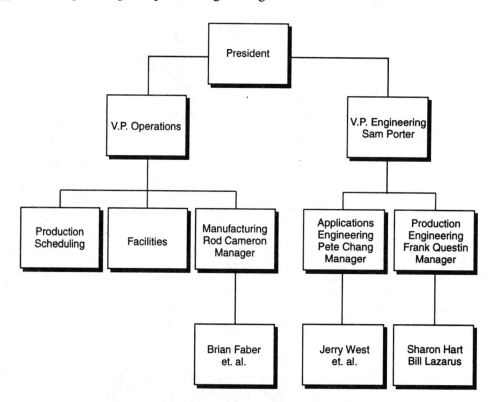

Figure 2. Custom Chip Inc. Partial Organization Chart

The product engineers estimate that 70 to 80 percent of their time is spent in solving day-to-day manufacturing problems. The product engineers have cubicles in a room directly across the hall from the manufacturing facility. If a manufacturing supervisor has a question regarding how to build a product during a run, that supervisor will call the engineer assigned to that product. If the engineer is available, he or she will go to the manufacturing floor to help answer the question. If the engineer is not available, the production run may be stopped and the product put aside so that other orders can be manufactured. This results in delays and added costs. One reason that product engineers are consulted is that documentation – the instructions for manufacturing the product – is unclear or incomplete.

Department	Role	Primary Objective
Applications Engineering	Design and develop prototypes for new or modified products	Satisfy customer needs through innovative designs
Product Engineering	Translates designs into manufacturing instructions and works alongside manufacturing to solve "engineering related" problems	Maintain and control yields on assigned products
Manufacturing	Executes designs	Meet productivity standards and time schedules

Figure 3. Departmental Roles and Objectives

The product engineer will also be called if a product is tested and fails to meet specifications. If a product fails to meet test specifications, production stops, and the engineer must diagnose the problem and attempt to find a solution. Otherwise, the order for that product may be only partially met. Test failures are a very serious problem, which can result in considerable cost increases and schedule delays for customers. Products do not test properly for many reasons, including operator errors, poor materials, a design that is very difficult to manufacture, a design that provides too little margin for error, or a combination of these.

On a typical day, the product engineer may respond to half a dozen questions from the manufacturing floor, and two to four calls to the testing stations. When interviewed, the engineers expressed a frustration with this situation. They thought they spent too much time solving short term problems, and consequently they were neglecting other important parts of their jobs. In particular, they felt they had little time in which to:

- **Coordinate with applications engineers during the design phase**. The Product Engineers stated that their knowledge of manufacturing could provide valuable input to the applications engineer. Together they could improve the manufacturability and thus, the yields, of the new or modified product.
- **Engage in yield improvement projects.** This would involve an in-depth study of the existing process for a specific product in conjunction with an analysis of past product failures.
- **Accurately document the manufacturing steps for their assigned products, especially for those which tend to have large or repeat orders.** They said that the current state of the documentation is very poor. Operators often have to build products using only a drawing showing the final circuit, along with a few notes scribbled in the margins. While experienced operators and supervisors may be able to work with this information, they often make incorrect guesses and assumptions. Inexperienced

operators may not be able to proceed with certain products because of this poor documentation.

V. Weekly Meeting

As manager of the product engineering group, Frank Questin had eight engineers reporting to him, each responsible for a different set of Custom Chip products. According to Frank:

> "When I took over as manager, the product engineers were not spending much time together as a group. They were required to handle operation problems on short notice. This made it difficult for the entire group to meet due to constant requests for assistance from the manufacturing area.
>
> I thought that my engineers could be of more assistance and support to each other if they all spent more time together as a group, so one of my first actions as a manager was to institute a regularly scheduled weekly meeting. I let the manufacturing people know that my staff would not respond to requests for assistance during the meeting."

The meeting on this particular Monday morning followed the usual pattern. Frank talked about upcoming company plans, projects and other news that might be of interest to the group. He then provided data about current yields for each product and commended those engineers who had maintained or improved yields on most of their products. This initial phase of the meeting lasted until about 8:30 A.M. The remainder of the meeting was a meandering discussion of a variety of topics. Since there was no agenda, engineers felt comfortable in raising issues of concern to them.

The discussion started with one of the engineers describing a technical problem in the assembly of one of his products. He was asked a number of questions and given some advice. Another engineer raised the topic of a need for new testing equipment and described a test unit he had seen at a recent demonstration. He claimed the savings in labor and improved yields from this machine would allow it to pay for itself in less than nine months. Frank immediately replied that budget limitations made such a purchase unfeasible, and the discussion moved into another area. They briefly discussed the increasing inaccessibility of the application engineers, then talked about a few other topics.

In general, the engineers valued these meetings. One commented that

> "The Monday meetings give me a chance to hear what's on everyone's mind and to find out about and discuss company wide news. It's hard to reach any conclusions because the meeting is a freewheeling discussion. But I really appreciate the friendly atmosphere with my peers."

VI. Coordination with Applications Engineers

Following the meeting that morning, an event occurred that highlighted the issue of the inaccessibility of the applications engineers. An order of 300 units of custom chip 1210A for a major customer was already overdue. Because the projected yield of this product was 70 percent, they had started with a run of 500 units. A sample tested at one of the early assembly points indicated a major performance problem that could drop the yield to below 50 percent. Bill Lazarus, the product engineer assigned to the 1210A, examined the sample and determined that the problem could be solved by redesigning the writing. Jerry West, the application engineer assigned to that product category was responsible for revising the design. Bill tried to contact Jerry, but he was not immediately available, and didn't get back to Bill until later in the day. Jerry explained that he was on a tight schedule trying to finish a design for a customer who was coming into town in two days, and could not get to "Bill's problem" for a while.

Jerry's attitude that the problem belonged to product engineering was typical of the applications engineers. From their point of view there were a number of reasons for making the product engineers needs for assistance a lower priority. In the first place, applications engineers were rewarded and acknowledged primarily for satisfying customer needs through designing new and modified products. They got little recognition for solving manufacturing problems. Secondly, applications engineering was perceived to be more glamorous than product engineering because of opportunities to be credited with innovative and ground breaking designs. Finally, the size of the applications engineering group had declined over the past year, causing the workload on each engineer to increase considerably. Now they had even less time to respond to the product engineer's requests.

When Bill Lazarus told Frank about the situation, Frank acted quickly. He wanted this order to be in process again by tomorrow and he knew manufacturing was also trying to meet this goal. He walked over to see Pete Chang, head of applications engineering (see Organization Chart in Figure 2). Meetings like this with Pete to discuss and resolve interdepartmental issues were common.

Frank found Pete at a workbench talking with one of his engineers. He asked Pete if he could talk to him in private and they walked to Pete's office.

Frank: We've got a problem in manufacturing in getting out an order of 1210A's. Bill Lazarus is getting little or no assistance from Jerry West. I'm hoping you can get Jerry to pitch in and help Bill. It should take no more than a few hours of his time.

Pete: I do have Jerry on a short leash trying to keep him focused on getting out a design for Teletronics. We can't afford to show up empty handed at our meeting with them in two days.

Frank: Well, we are going to end up losing one customer in trying to please an other. Can't we satisfy everyone here?

Pete: Do you have an idea?

Frank: Can't you give Jerry some additional support on the Teletronics design?

Pete: Let's get Jerry in here to see what we can do.

Pete brought Jerry back to the office, and together they discussed the issues and possible solutions. When Pete made it clear to Jerry that he considered the problem with the 1210A's a priority, Jerry offered to work on the 1210A problem with Bill. He said, "This will mean I'll have to stay a few hours past 5:00 this evening, but I'll do what's required to get the job done."

Frank was glad he had developed a collaborative relationship with Pete. He had always made it a point to keep Pete informed about activities in the Product Engineering group that might affect the applications engineers. In addition, he would often chat with Pete informally over coffee or lunch in the company cafeteria. This relationship with Pete made Frank's job easier. He wished he had the same rapport with Rod Cameron, the Manufacturing Manager.

VII. Coordination with Manufacturing

The product engineers worked closely on a day-to-day basis with the manufacturing supervisors and workers. The problems between these two groups stemmed from an inherent conflict between their objectives (see Figure 3). The objective of the product engineers was to maintain and improve yields. They had the authority to stop production of any run that did not test properly. Manufacturing, on the other hand, was trying to meet productivity standards and time schedules. When a product engineer stopped a manufacturing run, he was possibly preventing the manufacturing group from reaching its objectives.

Rod Cameron, the current manufacturing manager, had been promoted from his position as a manufacturing supervisor a year ago. His views on the product engineers:

> "The product engineers are perfectionists. The minute a test result looks a little suspicious they want to shut down the factory. I'm under a lot of pressure to get products out the door. If they pull a few $50,000 orders off the line when they are within a few days of reaching shipping, I'm liable to miss my numbers by $100,000 that month.
>
> Besides that, they are doing a lousy job of documenting the manufacturing steps. I've got a lot of turnover, and my new operators need to be told or shown exactly what to do for each product. The instructions for a lot of our products are a joke."

At first, Frank found Rod very difficult to deal with. Rod found fault with the product engineers for many problems and sometimes seemed rude to Frank when they talked. For example, Rod might tell Frank to "make it quick, I haven't got much time." Frank tried not to take Rod's actions personally, and through persistence was able to develop a more amicable relationship with him. According to Frank:

> "Sometimes, my people will stop work on a product because it doesn't meet test results at that stage of manufacturing. If we study the situation, we might be able to maintain yields or even save an entire run by adjusting the manufacturing procedures. Rod tries to bully me into changing my engineers' decisions. He yells at me or criticizes the competence of my people, but I don't allow his temper or ravings to influence my best judgment in a situation. My strategy in dealing with

Rod is to try not to respond defensively to him. Eventually he cools down, and we can have a reasonable discussion of the situation."

Despite this strategy, Frank could not always resolve his problems with Rod. On these occasions, Frank took the issue to his own boss, Sam Porter, the Vice President in charge of engineering. However, Frank was not satisfied with the support he got from Sam. Frank said:

"Sam avoids confrontations with the Operations VP. He doesn't have the influence or clout with the other VPs or the president to do justice to engineering's needs in the organization."

Early that afternoon, Frank again found himself trying to resolve a conflict between engineering and manufacturing. Sharon Hart, one of his most effective product engineers was responsible for a series of products used in radars — the 3805A— 3808A series. Today she had stopped a large run of 3806A's. The manufacturing supervisors, Brian Faber, went to Rod Cameron to complain about the impact of this stoppage on his group's productivity. Brian felt that yields were low on that particular product because the production instructions were confusing to his operators, and that even with clearer instructions, his operators would need additional training to build it satisfactorily. He stressed that the product engineer's responsibility was to adequately document the production instructions and provide training. For these reasons, Brian asserted that product engineering, and not manufacturing, should be accountable for the productivity loss in the case of these 3806A's.

Rod called Frank to his office, where he joined the discussion with Sharon, Brian and Rod. After listening to the issues, Frank conceded that product engineering had responsibility for documenting and training. He also explained, even though everyone was aware of it, that the product engineering group had been operating with reduced staff for over a year now, so training and documentation were lower priorities. Because of this staffing situation, Frank suggested that manufacturing and product engineering work together and pool their limited resources to solve the documentation and training problem. He was especially interested in using a few of the long term experienced workers to assist in training newer workers. Rod and Brian opposed his suggestion. They did not want to take experienced operators off of the line because it would decrease productivity. The meeting ended when Brian stormed out, saying that Sharon had better get the 3806A's up and running again that morning.

Frank was particularly frustrated by this episode with manufacturing. He knew perfectly well that his group had primary responsibility for documenting the manufacturing steps for each product. A year ago he told Sam Porter that the product engineers needed to update and standardize all of the documentation for manufacturing products. At that time, Sam told Frank that he would support his efforts to develop the documentation, but would not increase his staff. In fact, Sam had withheld authorization to fill a recently vacated product engineering slot. Frank was reluctant to push the staffing issue because of Sam's adamance about reducing costs. "Perhaps," Frank thought, "if I develop a proposal clearly showing the benefits of a documentation program in manufacturing and detailing the steps and resources required to implement the program, I might be able to convince Sam to provide us with more resources." But Frank could never find the time to develop that proposal. And so he remained frustrated.

VIII. Later in the Day

Frank was reflecting on the complexity of his job when Sharon came to the doorway to see if he had a few moments. Before he could say "come in," the phone rang. He looked at the clock. It was 4:10 P.M. Pete was on the other end of the line with an idea he wanted to try out on Frank, so Frank said he could call him back shortly. Sharon was upset, and told him that she was thinking of quitting because the job was not satisfying for her.

Sharon said that although she very much enjoyed working on yield improvement projects, she could find no time for them. She was tired of the application engineers acting like "prima donnas," too busy to help her solve what they seemed to think were mundane day-to-day manufacturing problems. She also thought that many of the day-to-day problems she handled wouldn't exist if there was enough time to document manufacturing procedures to begin with.

Frank didn't want to lose Sharon, so he tried to get into a frame of mind where he could be empathetic to her. He listened to her and told her that he could understand her frustration in this situation. He told her the situation would change as industry conditions improved. He told her that he was pleased that she felt comfortable in venting her frustrations with him, and he hoped she would stay with Custom Chip.

After Sharon left, Frank realized that he had told Pete that he would call back. He glanced at the TO DO list he had never completed, and realized that he hadn't spent time on his top priority – developing a proposal relating to solving the documentation problem in manufacturing. Then, he remembered that he had forgotten to acknowledge Bill Lazarus' fifth year anniversary with the company. He thought to himself that his job felt like a roller coaster ride, and once again he pondered his effectiveness as a manager.

2. Industrial Controls, Inc. Revisited*

Background and Philosophy of the Founder

Mr. Bauer had been a respected executive in one of the larger and most successful conglomerates. He rose to the position of Group Vice President, and his career in the company appeared promising. After all, he had an undergraduate degree in mathematics, a Harvard MBA, a good deal of experience in a large firm, and a history of success. Yet, approximately twenty-four years ago, Mr. Bauer elected to acquire a small firm engaged in manufacturing controls for a wide range of industrial machine controls, doing about $200,000 worth of business annually.

Mr. Bauer intended from the very beginning to expand his firm from a small company to a medium-size enterprise. This he wanted to accomplish through retained earnings and occasional loans in order not to dilute his ownership and control. In fact, Industrial Controls, Inc. did grow at an average rate of 20 per cent per year until 1974, when the company had sales in excess of $5,000,000 and employed 89 people (79 full-time and 10 part-time).

Evolution of the Firm

Stage 1. After acquiring Industrial Controls, Inc., Mr. Bauer hired a production manager. He selected a Mr. Dooley who had been a foreman in Mr. Bauer's former division at the multinational conglomerate and was known to him as a hard worker. Dooley did not have a college degree but had some electronic training in the Navy and took several evening courses at a local university.

Four years after acquiring Industrial Controls, Inc., Mr. Bauer availed himself of the opportunity to acquire another small firm (a four-man operation) owned and operated by a Mr. Cotton, an engineer who held several patents on equipment similar to that manufactured by Industrial Controls, Inc., but more sophisticated. Prior to forming his own company, Mr. Cotton had been employed as a sales engineer in a large firm in a similar line of business. Mr. Bauer also hired Mr. Cotton as the Chief Engineer and salesman. Mr. Cotton was given the opportunity to purchase a small interest in the firm and took advantage of it. Since that time, Mr. Cotton has been enlarging his stake in the firm, and currently is the second largest stockholder.

As long as the firm was small, these three individuals and the Sales Manager were able to manage the operations quite well. They worked out of the same office an a small building, saw each other frequently, remembered the details of day-to-day operations with minimum of policy, procedures, and paper work. There was even no need for an organizational chart or formal job descriptions.

Stage 2. There was nothing so unique in what Industrial Controls, Inc. was making and doing that could not be provided by any of a number of firms in the machine controls field. In fact, Industrial Controls, Inc. was in competition with small, medium-size, and large companies (in

---

*This case was prepared by Jan P. Muczyk, Senior Vice President and Professor of Management at Cleveland State University and is used here with his permission. © Jan P. Muczyk.

the last category the competition was foreign as well as domestic) when it came to producing and selling machine controls that had standard applications. Consequently, Industrial Controls had elected to carve out for itself a niche, viz., machine controls custom made to the specifications of a client and personalized service that the larger suppliers of more standardized equipment were not interested in providing. At this point in time, Industrial Controls, Inc. was dominant in one market niche. A product that the company purchased and continually improved for adjusting the tension on paper making equipment enjoyed an excellent reputation and was exposed to little competition.

Business continued to expand as the result of development of new and more complex lines of machine controls, and the operation was moved to a new and larger facility with individual offices for all corporate officers. Growth was further accelerated by the acquisition of several additional lines of related machine controls.

Up to this time, Mr. Bauer had been able to orchestrate the entire operation, i.e., he was the glue that held everything together and gave it direction. It just happened that at this juncture of the company's evolution, Mr. Bauer became increasingly involved in a number of time consuming community activities.

When the Sales Manager resigned, Mr. Cotton, because he liked selling above all else, was made the Vice President of Sales and Marketing. Mr. Daren, the Chief Development Engineer who reported to Mr. Cotton, was elevated to the position of Chief Engineer in charge of research and development as well as application engineering. Mr. Daren earned this promotion primarily on the basis of being a brilliant circuit designer. His human relations skills left much to be desired, but he probably would have left the firm if the promotion were denied him. Mr. Daren continued to do a considerable amount of R & D and application engineering after his promotion. Mr. Dooley remained as the Production Manager but had a much larger operation.

It must be kept in mind that in a company producing sophisticated industrial equipment to customer specifications which are at times incomplete because the customer isn't certain about what he wants, the interdependence between Sales, Production, and Engineering is considerable.

At this point in the company's evolution, a number of problem areas required attention. The inventory of components increased from $400,000 to $1,200,000 in one year. Although some of this increase was justified by the greater volume of business, the latter figure was deemed excessive. Engineering complained that it was not receiving accurate customer specifications from Sales as well as receiving late modifications of the specifications. Production was complaining that it was receiving inadequate engineering releases and not enough lead time for assembling and testing the equipment. Furthermore, Mr. Dooley argued that since most orders were customized, production inefficiencies and delays were inevitable. Mr. Dooley and Mr. Daren felt that Sales was not developing markets for more standardized items in larger quantities which in turn would ease the work-load for Engineering and Production alike. Sales and Production felt that Engineering was not giving them the support that was essential in this type of operation. When the Customer Service personnel needed assistance on a major equipment problem in the field, Engineering was reluctant to drop development and application work to assist with the problem. Customer Service personnel complained that Engineering was designing equipment that was difficult to service in the field. Sales believed that Engineering preferred to develop new product lines rather than perfect existing equipment.

Manufacturing personnel complained that they were not getting the amount of assistance from Engineering required to assemble a product either designed or modified by the Engineering Department. Customer complaints also started arriving at an increasing rate.

Stage 3. In light of rapid growth and increased complexity of the product lines, Mr. Bauer decided to reorganize. As a first step, he hired Mr. Cline as an assistant to the president in order to augment his time. Mr. Cline had considerable experience in several manufacturing plants, in a consulting firm, and taught marketing courses part-time at a local university. Soon after, Mr. Bauer assigned Mr. Cline the responsibility for corporate planning. He also separated the marketing functions from Sales and put Mr. Cline in charge of the former.

Mr. Bauer then hired a controller to assist in managing the accounting and financial aspects of the firm. Although Mr. Paves was a C.P.A. and had accounting experience, he was new to financial planning and control. Consequently, Mr. Bauer retained these responsibilities.

Since the product line had become more sophisticated and because the work load was now greater, Mr. Bauer appointed Mr. Hinds, who had formerly worked in the Engineering Department and had half-time responsibility for quality control, as a full-time Quality Control Manager reporting directly to him. Mr. Affermon was hired as a part-time Personnel Manager to establish personnel policy and handle personnel problems which had increased to the point that they were consuming a considerable amount of time of the operating personnel, including Mr. Bauer. Although Mr. Affermon had personnel administration experience in a larger firm, he was out of a job at the time he was hired by Industrial Controls, Incorporated. Mr. Dooley was given the title of Vice President of Manufacturing. Figure 1 reflects the organization at this juncture.

After a brief experience with the reorganization, Mr. Bauer concluded that something more fundamental had to be done in order to prepare his organization for future growth and to deal with the problems that were occupying his time.

Mr. Bauer believed, as did his fellow corporate officers, that a computer would aid them in a number of areas, such as processing sales orders, compiling an accurate bill of materials, controlling inventory, billing customers accurately, etc. The responsibility of integrating the new computer into company operations was given to Mr. Cline.

Mr. Bauer contemplated his future and that of the company. He concluded that he had the following choices:

1. He could sell his firm to one of the companies which in the past expressed an interest in buying Industrial Controls, Inc.
2. He could become a chairman of the board and leave the operating decisions to someone else. But who?
3. He could stay with the same management team and get more personally involved in the operations of the firm by divesting himself of his outside interests.
4. He could hire a new cadre of managers and remain as chief executive officer or become chairman of the board.

Mr. Bauer had a strong sense of loyalty to his present key personnel who played a large role in building the company. Consequently, he opted for the third alternative but decided to seek outside help to aid him in overcoming the present problems and preparing the company for future growth.

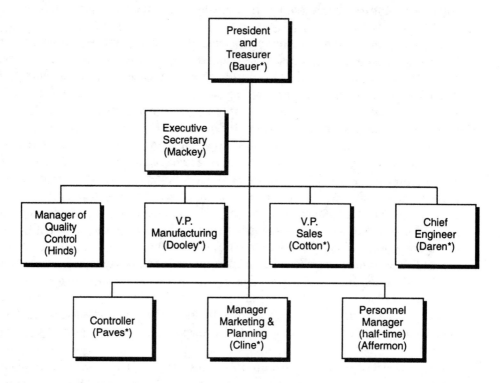

*represents members of the executive committee

Figure 1

Bring in Consultants

Mr. Bauer contacted two consultants who suggested performing a needs analysis first and a general approach to solving the firm's problems which would be made more specific after the needs analysis was completed. Messrs. Muzak and Ragu accepted the assignment and found that the motivation level of the managers and supervisors was very high. They worked long hours (including Saturdays and Sundays), but they were still getting behind. These men were seldom in their offices because of the day-to-day crises that came up. Cotton was on the phone with customers, prospective customers, manufacturer's representatives, and suppliers. Daren was designing and testing several pieces of equipment in order to make delivery dates. Dooley was on the shop floor helping the production people with their problems and expediting rush orders. Cline, instead of Affermon, was dealing with a number of personnel problems in addition to his other duties. Nobody had time to train his subordinates. Few people understood fully what Mr. Cline was doing, and no one knew what Mr. Affermon was doing.

Meetings were held frequently, but the consensus was that they were too long and at times unproductive. Personal conflicts were apparent between some people in Sales, Engineering, and Production who needed to interact in order to get the job done. A number of procedures that Mr. Bauer initiated were frequently ignored. In addition, some procedures that could have been routinized remained unnecessarily complex. Mr. Hinds proved to be an irritant to Engineering and Production, and even his subordinate questioned his competence.

In spite of the problems that have been identified, the company experienced rapid growth and was profitable every year of its existence.

During the needs analysis, two things left a special impression on the consultants. First, when the managers were asked by Mr. Bauer some time earlier to formulate action plans for next year, most of them had trouble beginning and completing them. Second, all of the managers genuinely wanted to improve their effectiveness.

The consultants concluded that they should present Mr. Bauer with a list of major problems, their priorities, and a concrete action program for dealing with these problems. In response to the consultants' recommendations, the management of Industrial Controls, Inc. decided to conduct a management development program starting with the members of the executive committee (see footnote on Figure 1 of the case for members of the executive committee). The consultants who conducted this program (Muzak and Ragu) were made available to the executive committee members during the program and for six months thereafter regarding any management problems that the managers might encounter.

After the executive committee went through the program, the supervisors and key staff persons were given a supervisory development program conducted by the same consultants. Once the executive committee and the supervisors completed their respective management development programs, interdepartmental (cross-function) teams were constituted to work on solutions to the most serious inter-departmental problems identified by the consultants. The teams were given deadlines by which they were expected to provide recommended solutions. The first problem to be addressed by Mr. Bauer and the rest of the executive committee was the clarification of organizational goals.

The consultants, with the assistance of the executive committee, persuaded Mr. Bauer to dismiss Mr. Affermon, and to put someone in charge of Mr. Hinds, who would be assigned simpler, non-supervisory tasks and duties. Mr. Cline, who was never accepted by most members of the executive committee, saw the writing on the wall and resigned. Mr. Bauer also initiated a search for a more seasoned and aggressive controller who would relieve him of many of the financial planning and control burdens and would provide Mr. Paves with much needed direction.

Mr. Bauer also intended to divest himself of many of his outside interests to devote most of his time to company matters, including the development of his subordinates.

The company is prospering financially, but the growth rate has slowed down. But before you give the consultants too much credit, remember that the company has grown rapidly and has been profitable since Mr. Bauer acquired it.

Stage 4. Mr. Bauer recognized that selling, installing, and maintaining systems (two or more of the more complex drives connected together) was interfering with the individual drive business because not many engineers and salesmen could handle the added technical complexity of systems, and the firm had difficulty freeing up the large number of engineering man hours required by the systems business. Mr. Bauer concluded that Cotton was not the person to head up corporate sales, but would probably enjoy heading up a Systems Division. Cotton had the technical expertise to handle systems and loved selling. Both Bauer and Muzak believed that he would do well as Vice President of a Systems Division. After Cotton was made Vice President of the Systems Division and authorized to assemble the necessary personnel, his second in command, McKeon, was made Vice President of Sales and Marketing. McKeon received a better offer shortly after his promotion and was replaced by Hiser. Mr. Schaefer, a competent and respected head of customer service who had reported to Cotton, was promoted to Vice President and placed in charge of field service and quality control.

During stage 4, numerous technological and economic environment changes impacted the machine controls industry. The demand for machine drives had stabilized, and any growth in a mature industry had to come at the expense of competitors. Moreover, the digital, microprocessor age (conventional drives are analog) had caught up with the machine controls industry. Lastly, two back-to-back recessions and a very strong dollar on top of a mature industry created fierce competition, with cut-throat pricing commonplace. The strong dollar made the purchase of off-shore components a must and necessitated joint ventures with European and Japanese companies. Joint ventures were also called for by the fact that Industrial Controls, Inc. had limited R & D capability. At this point foreign competition penetrated the U.S. market as never before.

In response to some of the aforementioned forces, Mr. Bauer had acquired a product in early stages of development as well as its inventor. This controller employed microprocessor technology and was capable of guiding metal cutting and welding equipment through the digital information programmed into it (numerical control). The product was successfully developed, and the first four generations, which constituted the state of the art in the metal cutting industry, gave Industrial Controls, Inc. a dominant position in this market for years. However, competition has increased substantially in this market niche as well as for the tension controller in the paper making business.

Mr. Bauer purchased two small competitors for their customers, especially the aftermarket business. Hence, he closed the production facilities of these firms. Since these firms had image problems before being acquired, an association of any nature with these firms constituted a mixed blessing. In order to get into the high end of the industrial drive business (in terms of technological sophistication as well as price), Industrial Controls, Inc. acquired a firm producing what are known as servo drives in order to establish a foothold in the high end of the drive business. This firm was plagued by a number of serious problems (new large orders were not being obtained, the product line was not being upgraded, and customer complaints were numerous and increasing) before acquisition, and the fact that it was located some 2,500 miles from the company that had bought it merely exacerbated the problems. This acquisition was integrated into the Industrial Controls, Inc. hierarchy as though it was just another plant location. The plant manager reported to Dooley. The chief engineer reported to Daren as well as the plant manager, the sales manager reported to Hiser as well as to the plant manager, etc.

Mr. Bauer also purchased a firm making a nascent product designed to improve the quality of die casting. This product was microprocessor based and appeared to offer considerable potential. This acquisition was treated as a separate company, however, but was located on the premises of Industrial Controls, Inc. The person from whom this company (product) was purchased, Dunn, became the president, and it was he who did the marketing and most of the selling of this product. Sales, however, were taking a long time getting off the ground.

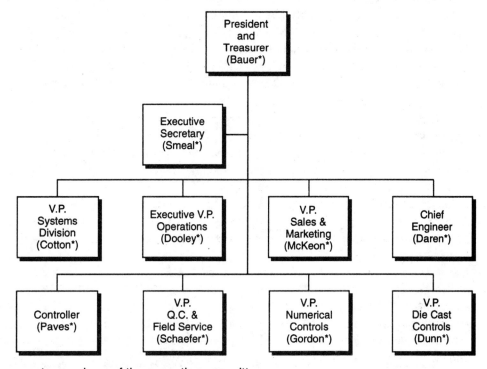

*represents members of the executive committee

Figure 2

Mr. Bauer acquired an industrial fabric cutting machine in the early stages of development and with serious unsolved technical problems. If Industrial Controls, Inc. could perfect this product, it had one large customer practically guaranteed. Mr. Cotton was placed in charge of completing the development of this product. Also, Mr. Bauer acquired another product in the early stages of development that operated on the sonar principle. The inventor joined the firm as well. If this product could be perfected, it would guide industrial machines, such as welding machines, in the same manner as lasers do, but at a considerably lower cost. Mr. Hiser was assigned the responsibility for bringing this product to market.

Industrial Controls, Inc. began deviating from its original marketing strategy by producing standard drives for inventory at the lower price end of the drive line. These drives were sold by distributors rather than manufacturer's representatives. This strategy worked out well after a good group of distributors was lined up. It took some time, however, to sign agreements with effective distributors, and initially the distributor policy was met with some suspicion by manufacturer's representatives. (Unlike manufacturer's representatives, distributors take ownership of the product that they sell.)

Industrial Controls, Inc. had a surprisingly broad product line of industrial drives. Only products at the extreme ends of a complete drive line were missing, and for good reason. The very inexpensive drives, known as AC inverters, weren't made because Industrial Controls, Inc. was located in a high labor cost area and probably could not make an adequate profit on this product. The most expensive servo drives with programmable position controllers (intelligent front end) were probably beyond the technical capability of Industrial Controls, Inc. engineers. In fact, much of the software engineering (computer programming) was being done under contract, but more and more inside personnel were acquiring these skills. A number of Industrial Controls, Inc. personnel frequently described the company as a manufacturing firm and not an engineering or a R & D firm. Figure 2 reflects the organizational structure at this point.

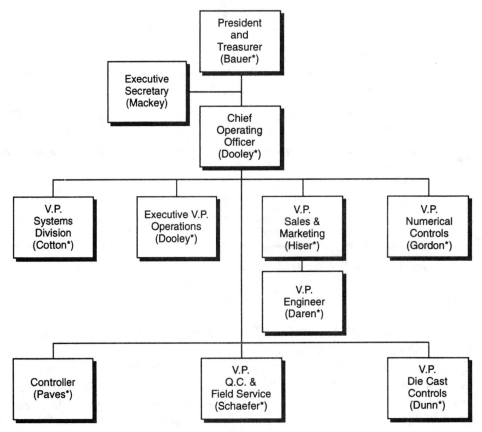

*represents members of the executive committee

Figure 3

Mr. Bauer was convinced that to continue growing he had to launch an aggressive acquisition program. He believed that being in a mature industry characterized by fierce competition, increasingly from off-shore firms, left him little choice. The limited R & D capability of his engineers merely reinforced his instincts.

Stage 5. After a hiatus of four years, Muzak was brought back as a consultant. He found a more sophisticated management this time around, especially with regard to planning acumen. Also, most organizational members were now familiar and comfortable with computers and Computer Assisted Design. The introduction of a new and more powerful central computer went quite smoothly.

Yet, problems existed. The backups to the Vice Presidents (the bench) needed considerable development as managers. Certain Vice Presidents still needed considerable improvement with regard to organization skills, human relations, coaching subordinates, and providing subordinates clear roles or expectations. Muzak was asked to work with managers in need of assistance on an individual basis in order to overcome their deficiencies, and he accepted the challenge. The firm needed to generate better marketing research data before launching a new product. Some new or redesigned products were sold before they were thoroughly debugged. Too many managers still avoided unpleasant decisions, especially personnel decisions. When subordinates did not execute their duties and assignments in a timely and satisfactory manner, too frequently negative consequences did not occur. Lastly, the company was reaching a size where the absence of a human resource development department was being felt.

Mr. Bauer was aware of the future impact of robotics on his business. When a group of developmental engineers in the field of medical diagnostic imaging did not follow their employer who left town, Mr. Bauer signed an agreement with these individuals with the intention of taking Industrial Controls, Inc. into the arena of vision robotics. If successful, this gamble would produce a technological quantum leap for Industrial Controls, Inc.

The firm was now organized largely along divisional lines with each division doing its own engineering, sales, and field service. Even manufacturing, which remained centralized for all products, had a group of four manufacturing engineers reporting to Dooley. Although Mr. Schaefer's group performed field service for products under Hiser's jurisdiction, it helped out the other divisions in an emergency. To complete the divisional organization scheme Mr. Bauer decided to place Mr. Daren's engineering group under Mr. Hiser, since Daren's engineers were now working mostly on the products under Hiser's jurisdiction. Mr. Bauer also decided that it was high time to designate an official number two person in the organization. Mr. Dooley was selected and given the title of Chief Operating Officer. He was chosen because of his organizational and human relations skills. Mr. Schaefer was given the added responsibility of determining when a new or redesigned product was sufficiently perfected to be shipped to a customer. Figure 3 represents the organization at this time.

At this point, the dollar had weakened considerably vis-a-vis the currencies of foreign competitors, orders for machine tools from Original Equipment Manufacturers (O.E.M.'s) were strong, and the economy was still in a prolonged recovery. The firm was still a closely held one, but now it was a subchapter "S" for tax purposes. But even without the benefits of a weak dollar and a strong economy, Industrial Controls, Inc. had prospered surprisingly well.

Stage 6. The product intended to improve the quality of die casting was sold back to Dunn, the developer of this technology. The West Coast operation was trimmed to the point where it remained only as a distribution and service center. Lastly, Mr. Bauer purchased an American subsidiary making industrial drives of a European corporation. The subsidiary was located approximately 150 miles from the parent and the acquisition doubled sales and personnel. The acquired firm is being managed as an independent subsidiary, at least for the immediate term.

Mr. Schultz, who headed up this operation for the European parent, was retained by Mr. Bauer to manage it as Vice President of Industrial Controls, Inc. (See Fig. 4.)

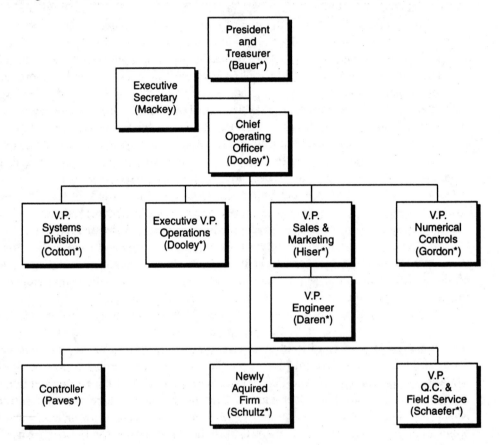

*represents members of the executive committee

Figure 4

3. Dick Spencer*

After the usual banter when old friends meet for cocktails, the conversation between a couple of University professors and Dick Spencer, who was now a successful businessman, turned to Dick's life as a vice-president of a large manufacturing firm.

"I've made a lot of mistakes, most of which I could live with, but this one series of incidents was so frustrating that I could have cried at the time," Dick said in response to a question. "I really have to laugh at how ridiculous it is now, but at the time I blew my cork."

Spencer was plant manager of Modrow Company, a Canadian branch of the Tri-American Corporation. Tri-American was a major producer of primary aluminum with integrated operations ranging from the mining of bauxite through the processing to fabrication of aluminum into a variety of products. The company had also made and sold refractories and industrial chemicals. The parent company had wholly-owned subsidiaries in five separate United States locations and had foreign affiliates in fifteen different countries.

Tri-American mined bauxite in the Jamaican West Indies and shipped the raw material by commercial vessels to two plants in Louisiana where it was processed into alumina. The alumina was then shipped to reduction plants in one of three locations for conversion into primary aluminum. Most of the primary aluminum was then moved to the companies' fabricating plants for further processing. Fabricated aluminum items included sheet, flat, coil, and corrugated products; siding; and roofing.

Tri-American employed approximately 22,000 employees in the total organization. The company was governed by a board of directors which included the chairman, vice-chairman, president, and twelve vice-presidents. However, each of the subsidiaries and branches functioned as independent units. The board set general policy, which was then interpreted and applied by the various plant managers. In a sense, the various plants competed with one another as though they were independent companies. This decentralization in organizational structure increased the freedom and authority of the plant managers, but increased the pressure for profitability.

The Modrow branch was located in a border town in Canada. The total work force in Modrow was 1,000. This Canadian subsidiary was primarily a fabricating unit. Its main products were foil and building products such as roofing and siding. Aluminum products were gaining in importance in architectural plans, and increased sales were predicted for this branch. Its location and its stable work force were the most important advantages it possessed.

In anticipation of estimated increases in building product sales, Modrow had recently completed a modernization and expansion project. At the same time, their research and art departments combined talents in developing a series of twelve new patterns of siding which were being introduced to the market. Modernization and pattern development had been costly undertakings, but the expected return on investment made the project feasible. However, the plant manager, who was a Tri-American vice-president, had instituted a campaign to cut expenses wherever possible. In this introductory notice of the campaign, he emphasized that cost reduction would be the personal aim of every employee at Modrow.

---

*This case was developed and prepared by Professor Margaret E. Fenn, Graduate School of Business Administration, University of Washington. Reprinted by permission.

Salesman

The plant manager of Modrow, Dick Spencer, was an American who had been transferred to this Canadian branch two years previously, after the start of the modernization plan. Dick had been with the Tri-American Company for fourteen years, and his progress within the organization was considered spectacular by those who knew him well. Dick had received a Master's degree in Business Administration from a well-known university at the age of twenty-two. Upon graduation he had accepted a job as salesman for Tri-American. During his first year as a salesman, he succeeded in landing a single, large contract which put him near the top of the sales-volume leaders. In discussing his phenomenal rise in the sales volume, several of his fellow salesmen concluded that his looks, charm, and ability on the golf course contributed as much to his success as his knowledge of the business or his ability to sell the products.

The second year of his sales career, he continued to set a fast pace. Although his record set difficult goals for the other salesmen, he was considered a "regular guy" by them, and both he and they seemed to enjoy the few occasions when they socialized. However, by the end of the second year of constant traveling and selling, Dick began to experience some doubt about his future.

His constant involvement in business affairs disrupted his marital life, and his wife divorced him during the second year with Tri-American. Dick resented her action at first, but gradually seemed to recognize that his career at present depended on his freedom to travel unencumbered. During that second year, he ranged far and wide in his sales territory, and successfully closed several large contracts. None of them was as large as his first year's major sale, but in total volume he again was well up near the top of salesmen for the year. Dick's name became well known in the corporate headquarters, and he was spoken of as "the boy to watch."

Dick had met the president of Tri-American during his first year as a salesman at a company conference. After three days of golfing and socializing they developed a relaxed camaraderie considered unusual by those who observed the developing friendship. Although their contacts were infrequent after the conference, their easy relationship seemed to blossom the few times they did meet. Dick's friends kidded him about his ability to make use of his new friendship to promote himself in the company, but Dick brushed aside their jibes and insisted that he'd make it on his own abilities, not someone's coattail.

By the time he was twenty-five, Dick began to suspect that he did not look forward to a life as a salesman for the rest of his career. He talked about his unrest with his friends, and they suggested that he groom himself for sales manager. "You won't make the kind of money you're making from commissions," he was told, "but you will have a foot in the door from an administrative standpoint, and you won't have to travel quite as much as you do now." Dick took their suggestions lightly, and continued to sell the product, but was aware that he felt dissatisfied and did not seem to get the satisfaction out of his job that he had once enjoyed.

By the end of his third year with the company Dick was convinced that he wanted a change in direction. As usual, he and the president spent quite a bit of time on the golf course during the annual company sales conference. After their match one day, the president kidded Dick about his game. The conversation drifted back to business, and the president, who seemed to be in a jovial mood, started to kid Dick about his sales ability. In a joking way, he implied that anyone could sell a product as good as Tri-American's, but that it took real "guts and know-how" to make the products. The conversation drifted to other things, but the remark stuck with Dick.

Sometime later, Dick approached the president formally with a request for a transfer out of the sales division. The president was surprised and hesitant about this change in career direction for Dick. He recognized the superior sales ability that Dick seemed to possess, but was unsure that Dick was willing or able to assume responsibilities in any other division of the organization. Dick sensed the hesitancy, but continued to push his request. He later remarked that it seemed that the initial hesitancy of the president convinced Dick that he needed an opportunity to prove himself in a field other than sales.

Trouble Shooter

Dick was finally transferred back to the home office of the organization and indoctrinated into productive and administrative roles in the company as a special assistant to the senior vice-president of production. As a special assistant, Dick was assigned several trouble-shooting jobs. He acquitted himself well in this role, but in the process succeeded in gaining a reputation as a ruthless head hunter among the branches where he had performed a series of amputations. His reputation as an amiable, genial, easygoing guy from the sales department was the antithesis of the reputation of a cold, calculating head hunter which he earned in his trouble-shooting role. The vice-president, who was Dick's boss, was aware of the reputation which Dick had earned but was pleased with the results that were obtained. The faltering departments that Dick had worked in seemed to bloom with new life and energy after Dick's recommended amputations. As a result, the vice-president began to sing Dick's praises, and the president began to accept Dick in his new role in the company.

Management Responsibility

About three years after Dick's switch from sales, he was given an assignment as assistant plant manager of an English branch of the company. Dick, who had remarried, moved his wife and family to London, and they attempted to adapt to their new routine. The plant manager was English, as were most of the other employees. Dick and his family were accepted with reservations into the community life as well as into the plant life. The difference between British and American philosophy and performance within the plant was marked for Dick who was imbued with modern managerial concepts and methods. Dick's directives from headquarters were to update and upgrade performance in this branch. However, his power and authority were less than those of his superiors, so he constantly found himself in the position of having to soft pedal or withhold suggestions that he would have liked to make, or innovations that he would have liked to introduce. After a frustrating year and a half, Dick was suddenly made plant manager of an old British company which had just been purchased by Tri-American. He left his first English assignment with mixed feelings and moved from London to Birmingham.

As the new plant manager, Dick operated much as he had in his troubleshooting job for the first couple of years of his change from sales to administration. Training and reeducation programs were instituted for all supervisors and managers who survived the initial purge. Methods were studied and simplified or redesigned whenever possible, and new attention was directed toward production which better met the needs of the sales organization. A strong controller helped to straighten out the profit picture through stringent cost control; and, by the end of the third year, the company showed a small profit for the first time in many years. Because he felt that this battle was won, Dick requested transfer back to the United States. The request was partially granted when nine months later he was awarded a junior vice-president title, and was made manager of a subsidiary Canadian plant, Modrow.

Modrow Manager

Prior to Dick's appointment as plant manager at Modrow, extensive plans for plant expansion and improvement had been approved and started. Although he had not been in on the original discussions and plans, he inherited all the problems that accompany large-scale changes in any organization. Construction was slower in completion than originally planned, equipment arrived before the building was finished, employees were upset about the extent of change expected in their work routines with the installation of additional machinery, and, in general, morale was at a low ebb.

Various versions of Dick's former activities had preceded him, and on his arrival he was viewed with dubious eyes. The first few months after his arrival were spent in a frenzy of catching up. This entailed constant conferences and meetings, volumes of reading of past reports, becoming acquainted with the civic leaders of the area, and a plethora of dispatches to and from the home office. Costs continued to climb unabated.

By the end of his first year at Modrow, the building program had been completed, although behind schedule, the new equipment had been installed, and some revamping of cost procedures had been incorporated. The financial picture at this time showed a substantial loss, but since it had been budgeted as a loss, this was not surprising. All managers of the various divisions had worked closely with their supervisors and accountants in planning the budget or the following year, and Dick began to emphasize his personal interest in cost reduction.

As he worked through his first year as plant manager, Dick developed the habit of strolling around the organization. He was apt to leave his office and appear anywhere on the plant floor, in the design offices, at the desk of a purchasing agent or accountant, in the plant cafeteria rather than the executive dining room, or wherever there was activity concerned with Modrow. During his strolls he looked, listened, and became acquainted. If he observed activities which he wanted to talk about, or heard remarks that gave him clues to future action, he did not reveal these at the time. Rather he had a nod, a wave, a smile, for the people near him, but a mental note to talk to his supervisors, managers, and foremen in the future. At first his presence disturbed those who noted him coming and going, but after several exposures to him without any noticeable effect, the workers came to accept his presence and continue their usual activities. Supervisors, managers, and foremen, however, did not feel as comfortable when they saw him in the area.

Their feelings were aptly expressed by the manager of the siding department one day when he was talking to one of his foremen: "I wish to hell he'd stay up in the front office where he belongs. Whoever heard of a plant manager who has time to wander around the plant all the time? Why doesn't he tend to his paper work and let us tend to our business?"

"Don't let him get you down," joked the foreman. "Nothing ever comes of his visits. Maybe he's just lonesome and looking for a friend. You know how these Americans are."

"Well, you may feel that nothing ever comes of his visits, but I don't. I've been called into his office three separate times within the last two months. The heat must really be on from the head office. You know these conferences we have every month where he reviews our financial progress, our building progress, our design progress, etc.? Well, we're not really progressing as fast as we should be. If you ask me we're in for continuing trouble."

In recalling his first year at Modrow, Dick had felt constantly pressured and badgered. He always sensed that the Canadians he worked with resented his presence since he was brought in over the heads of the operating staff. At the same time he felt this subtle resistance from his Canadian work force, he believed that the president and his friends in the home office were constantly on the alert, waiting for Dick to prove himself or fall flat on his face. Because of the constant pressures and demands of the work, he had literally dumped his family into a new community and had withdrawn into the plant. In the process, he built up a wall of resistance toward the demands of his wife and children who, in turn, felt as though he was abandoning them.

During the course of the conversation with his University friends, he began to recall a series of incidents that probably had resulted from the conflicting pressures. When describing some of these incidents, he continued to emphasize the fact that his attempt to be relaxed and casual had backfired. Laughingly, Dick said, "As you know, both human relations and accounting were my weakest subjects during the Master's program, and yet they are two fields I felt I needed the most at Modrow at this time." He described some of the cost procedures that he would have liked to incorporate. However, without the support and knowledge furnished by his former controller, he busied himself with details that were unnecessary. One day, as he describes it, he overheard a conversation between two of the accounting staff members with whom he had been working very closely. One of them commented to the other, "For a guy who's a vice-president, he sure spends a lot of time breathing down our necks. Why doesn't he simply tell us the kind of systems he would like to try, and let us do the experimenting and work out the budget?" Without commenting on the conversation he overheard, Dick then described himself as attempting to spend less time and be less directive in the accounting department.

Another incident he described which apparently had real meaning for him was one in which he had called a staff conference with his top-level managers. They had been going "hammer and tongs" for better than an hour in his private office, and in the process of heated conversation had loosened ties, taken off coats, and really rolled up their sleeves. Dick himself had slipped out of his shoes. In the midst of this, his secretary reminded him of an appointment with public officials. Dick had rapidly finished up his conference with his managers, straightened his tie, donned his coat, and had wandered out into the main office in his stocking feet.

Dick fully described several incidents when he had disappointed, frustrated, or confused his wife and family by forgetting birthdays, appointments, dinner engagements, etc. He seemed to be describing a pattern of behavior which resulted from continuing pressure and frustration. He was setting the scene to describe his baffling and humiliating position in the siding department. In looking back and recalling his activities during this first year, Dick commented on the fact that his frequent wanderings throughout the plant had resulted in a nodding acquaintance with the workers, but probably had also resulted in foremen and supervisors spending more time getting ready for his visits and reading meaning into them afterwards than attending to their specific duties. His attempts to know in detail the accounting procedures being used required long hours of concentration and detailed conversations with the accounting staff, which were time-consuming and very frustrating for him, as well as for them. His lack of attention to his family life resulted in continued pressure from both wife and family.

The Siding Department Incident

Siding was the product which had been budgeted as a large profit item of Modrow. Aluminum siding was gaining in popularity among both architects and builders, because of its possibilities in both decorative and practical uses. Panel sheets of siding were shipped in standard sizes in order; large sheets of the coated siding were cut to specifications in the trim department, packed, and shipped. The trim shop was located near the loading platforms, and Dick often cut through the trim shop on his wanderings through the plant. On one of his frequent trips through the area, he suddenly became aware of the fact that several workers responsible for the disposal function were spending countless hours at high-speed saws cutting scraps into specified lengths to fit into scrap barrels. The narrow bands of scrap which resulted from the trim process varied in length from seven to twenty-seven feet and had to be reduced in size to fit into disposal barrels. Dick, in his concentration of cost reduction, picked up one of the thin strips, bent it several times and fitted it into the barrel. He tried this with another piece, and it bent very easily. After assuring himself that bending was possible, he walked over to a worker at the saw and asked why he was using the saw when material could easily be bent and fitted into the barrels, resulting in saving time and equipment. The worker's response was, "We've never done it that way, sir. We've always cut it."

Following his plan of not commenting or discussing matters on the floor, but distressed by the reply, Dick returned to his office and asked the manager of the siding department if he could speak to the foreman in the scrap division. The manager said, "Of course, I'll send him up to you in just a minute."

After a short time, the foreman, very agitated at being called to the plant manager's office, appeared. Dick began questioning him about the scrap disposal process and received the standard answer: "We've always done it that way." Dick then proceeded to review cost-cutting objectives. He talked about the pliability of the strips of scrap. He called for a few pieces of scrap to demonstrate the ease with which it could be bent, and ended what he thought was a satisfactory conversation by requesting the foreman to order heavy duty gloves for his workers and use the bending process for a trial period of two weeks to check the cost savings possible.

The foreman listened throughout most of this hour's conference, offered several reasons why it wouldn't work, raised some questions about the record keeping process for cost purposes, and finally left the office with the forced agreement to try the suggested new method of bending, rather than cutting, for disposal. Although he was immersed in many other problems, his request was forcibly brought home one day as he cut through the scrap area. The workers were using power saws to cut scraps. He called the manager of the siding department and questioned him about the process. The manager explained that each foreman was responsible for his own processes, and since Dick had already talked to the foreman, perhaps he had better talk to him again. When the foreman arrived, Dick began to question him. He received a series of excuses, and some explanations of the kinds of problems they were meeting by attempting to bend the scrap material. "I don't care what the problems are," Dick nearly shouted, "when I request a cost-reduction program instituted, I want to see it carried through."

Dick was furious. When the foreman left, he phoned the maintenance department and ordered the removal of the power saws from the scrap area immediately. A short time later the foreman of the scrap department knocked on Dick's door reporting his astonishment at having maintenance men step into his area and physically remove the saws. Dick reminded the foreman of his request for a trial at cost reduction to no avail, and ended the conversation by saying that the power saws were gone and would not be returned, and the foreman had damned well better learn to get along without them. After a stormy exit by the foreman, Dick congratulated himself on having solved a problem and turned his attention to other matters.

A few days later Dick cut through the trim department and literally stopped to stare. As he described it, he was completely nonplussed to discover gloved workmen using hand shears to cut each strip of scrap.

4. Apple Computer, Inc.*

Apple Computer was formed in 1976 by Steven Jobs and Stephen Wozniak, who visualized a personal computer that could be used easily by anyone. Together, they created the Apple I. Setting up shop in Jobs' garage, they soon experienced sales beyond the garage's capacity. In the same year, A.C. Markkula was recruited as the company's first professional manager. With financing from Markkula and a group of venture capitalists, Apple Computer was incorporated on January 3, 1977.

As co-founder of Apple, Jobs' focus was on creating new and different products. He was the visionary responsible for Apple's reputation for innovativeness. Apple's mission was to change the world by bringing computers to the masses. Jobs' notion of "One person-one computer" became a central tenet of the Apple belief system.

In its first six years of business, Apple's earnings grew explosively from $793,000 to $76,714,000.[1] By 1983, Apple Computer had annual net sales of almost $1 billion, and 4,645 employees.[2]

The Microcomputer Industry

Apple Computer primarily produced microcomputers. This infant industry was characterized by the manufacture and sale of small desktop computers with microprocessors as central processing units. Apple's main competitors in this industry included IBM, Commodore and Atari. Competition was increasing. Both Hewlett-Packard and AT&T launched a personal computer and Commodore was planning to introduce a more advanced personal computer into the market. IBM's machines were the industry standard. Most PC makers made machines that were compatible with IBM. Apple did not. Its goal was to provide a machine "for the rest of us."[3] The differences between the Apple II and the IBM PC confused dealers and consumers who had to decide which one to buy, and software developers had to make software for two standards.

There were five major market segments in the industry: home, business, government, education and international sales. The home market included games and educational programs for children and programs for professionals who worked at home as well as hobbyists. The education market included programs used for educational purposes outside the home and was smaller than either the home or business market. The business market was by far the most profitable market and was predicted to grow faster than other segments. Exhibit 1 shows both 1984 and projected 1990 personal computer shipments by segment.

Apple Products and Markets

Apple focused its sales on the home and education markets and was the leader in the education market. Apple had two product lines, Apple II and the Macintosh. The Apple II line consisted of the Apple IIe and the Apple III. The Apple II family of computers represented the company's

---

* Reprinted with permission by the authors, Richard D. Freedman and Jill Vohr, Leonard N. Stern School of Business, New York University ©1992.

Exhibit 1 Worldwide Personal Computer Shipments by Market Segment

1984

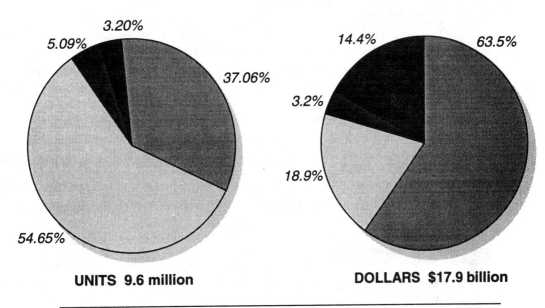

UNITS 9.6 million   DOLLARS $17.9 billion

1990

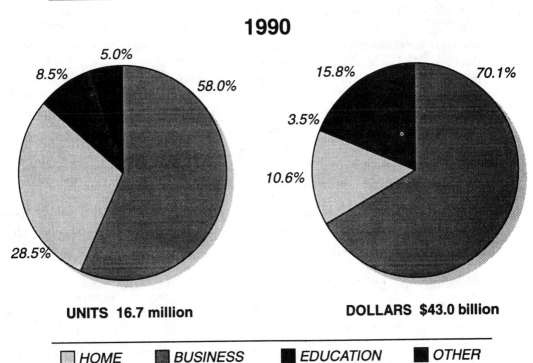

UNITS 16.7 million   DOLLARS $43.0 billion

☐ *HOME*   ◼ *BUSINESS*   ◼ *EDUCATION*   ◼ *OTHER*

Source: International Data Corporation, EDP Industry Report, August 30, 1985. Copyright ©1985 by International Data Corporation.

Exhibit 2

APPLE DIVISIONS

There are two major types of divisions within Apple — Product Divisions, responsible for the development, evaluation and manufacture of computer systems, software and peripheral devices, and Product Support Divisions, which handle marketing, distribution and post-sale product support. There are, in addition, a number of administrative departments in charge of overseeing Apple's day-to-day corporate activities.

PRODUCT DIVISIONS

PERSONAL COMPUTER SYSTEMS DIVISION (PCSD) is responsible for the Apple II and Apple III computer systems and is constantly working to refine and improve them. PCSD most recently introduced the Apple IIe, a significantly enhanced version of the Apple II.

PERSONAL OFFICE SYSTEMS DIVISION (POSD) designs and manufactures mass-storage devices for Apple computer systems. PSD unveiled Unifile and Duofile high-density floppy disk drives in late 1982 and continues to develop and produce both hard and floppy drives to support all Apple systems.

ACCESSORY PRODUCTS DIVISION (APD) produces all keyboards for Apple computers. It is also responsible for developing, manufacturing and marketing accessory products such as joysticks, cursors, numberic keypads and hand controllers. In addition, APD designs and markets a a variety of monitors, printers, modems and plotters.

MACINTOSH DIVISION (MAC) is pursuing a product line that promises to become the highest volume personal computer system of the '80s.

OPERATIONS DIVISION is responsible for most of the Apple's manufacturing activity. Other product divisions manufacture the initial prototype/pilot units and establish process procedures; products ready for high-volume production are then transferred to the Operations Division which manufactures in Dallas, Texas; Cork, Ireland; and Singapore.

PRODUCT SUPPORT DIVISIONS

NORTH AMERICAN SALES channels Apple's products to customers through field sales groups which service a larger dealer network. The division also handles direct sales to volume users and is responsible for the identification and penetration of major markets. Its highly successful National Accounts Program furnishes Fortune 1000 corporations with direct sales, installation, service, and support. Sales and marketing for the Far East, South Africa, Central and South America are handled by INTERCONTINENTAL SALES.

EUROPEAN DIVISION manages field sales and distribution activities throughout Europe, supporting the efforts of original equipment manufacturers (OEMs) and assisting other divisions in tailoring Apple Products to European markets.

COMMUNICATIONS DIVISION sees that sales prospects, investors and other parties interested in Apple receive whatever information they need. The division handles advertising and public relations activities, conducts market research and manages employee, investor and press communications.

MARKETS MARKETING group identifies and defines target markets for Apple and develops strategies for approaching them. The group also coordinates all proposed marketing activities to ensure that Apple's messages to each segment are clear.

ADMINISTRATIVE DEPARTMENTS

Many activities at Apple fall outside the neatly structured division, yet they are intimately associated with daily operations of the company. These activities report to Vice Presidents, just as the divisions do, and are lumped together under "Administration". Such operations include the following:

FINANCE DEPARTMENT monitors Apple's financial well-being. It provides accounting and cash management services to the company as a whole, at the same time working with each division to help prospect and manage expenses. Finance also oversees Apple's Management Information Services (MIS) computers that track all sales and inventories.

HUMAN RESOURCES safeguards and helps develop Apple's most valuable asset, its people. In addition to handling counseling, compensation and benefit programs, the department is responsible for staffing and training to ensure that Apple has the people it needs to reach its goals. Human Resources also provides the resources to assist employees in reaching personal and professions goals.

LEGAL SERVICES makes certain Apple complies with the law in all business operations. It also represents the company in legal disputes with individuals, businesses and the government. In addition, facilities and the Apple Education Foundation both now report to Legal Services.

Exhibit 3 Organizational Chart, 1983

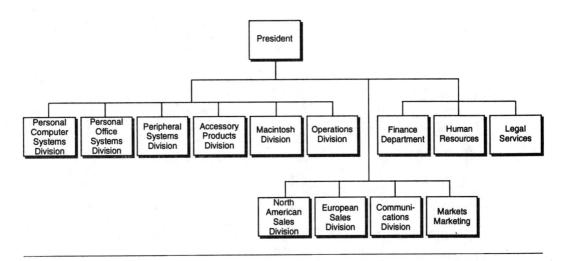

major revenue generator.[4] The Macintosh line consisted of Lisa (Macintosh XL) and the recently developed Macintosh. Macintosh had not yet been introduced to the market. Jobs personally headed its development.

Jobs believed that "Compatibility...was the noose around creativity".[5] It required conforming to a standard "out-of-date" hardware. Consequently, the Apple II family of products were incompatible with the Macintosh family of products. Apple sales people, who received regular feedback from the dealers, recognized that this incompatibility discouraged customers who did not want to invest several thousand dollars in an Apple computer and software only to discover that to move ahead technologically they would have to throw it out and start over.

Apple Management

To manage its products and marketing, Apple Computer had five product divisions responsible for the development, evaluation and manufacture of computer systems, software and peripheral devices, e.g. Macintosh. It also had four product support divisions which handled marketing, distribution and post-sale product support, e.g. North American Sales Division. In addition, there were a number of administrative departments in charge of overseeing Apple's day-to-day corporate activities, for example, the Finance Department.[6] Exhibit 2 provides a description of these divisions. Although Apple did not publish an organizational chart, Exhibit 3 represents what such an organization probably would have looked like.

The Early 1980s and John Sculley

Since 1981, Apple's market share relative to its industry competitors had steadily declined.[7] Apple attempted to enter the business market with its new Lisa and Apple III computers but the products failed to win acceptance and could not compete successfully with the IBM PC.

In May of 1983, Markkula retired from his posts as CEO and president but remained as director and consultant. Jobs hired John Sculley from PepsiCo where he had been the president

Exhibit 4 Organizational Chart, 1984

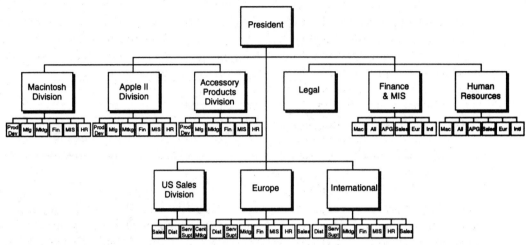

Source: Apple Computer interoffice memo, 1985.

of domestic operations and, before that, vice president of marketing. Sculley was hired for both his executive and marketing expertise. Considering Apple's new competitive pressures, choosing Sculley with his corporate experience as the company's new president was considered by Jobs to be "one of the most important decisions in Apple's history."[8]

Once Sculley joined the company, he had the following reaction:

> "As a member of the executive staff, I came away with a clear impression that there wasn't a common understanding of the company we were trying to build. In fact, there were many, competitive fiefdoms. A group called PCDS (Personal Computer Systems Division) was responsible for the development and marketing of the Apple II. Within that division was a smaller splinter group in charge of the Apple III. There was the Lisa computer division, and Steve's Macintosh team, which hadn't yet introduced a product."[9]

The Macintosh and Lisa teams were not getting along. The Macintosh people believed that once on the market their product would be better than Lisa and any other Apple product. They routinely referred to the Apple II people as "bozos" and were given perks such as free fruit juice and a masseuse to work the tense backs of the Mac engineers. The Apple II group resented this favoritism. They also resented that they had been moved to a building that was two and a half miles from the Apple campus. Furthermore, there was duplication of activities and resources within the company. Sculley recalls, "When I arrived, I found people all over the organization doing the same thing. Three or four home-marketing groups, for example, existed. Everyone had great ideas. But some structure was needed if people were to feel a greater sense of accountability."[10]

A Change in Structure

In December of 1983, Sculley reorganized management. His main change was to reduce the number of Apple product divisions to three; a division for Apple II products, another for the Lisa product and the development and production of the Macintosh, and an accessory products group. Each was responsible for its own functions and could be managed as "independent profit-and-loss centers". The organizational chart is presented in Exhibit 4. Sculley placed himself in charge of the Apple II group to "...learn how a product division worked."[11] He later gave this position to Del W. Yocam, a six-year Apple veteran. Jobs was placed in charge of the Macintosh division, but maintained his position as chairman of the board of directors.

Sculley hoped that the new structure would eliminate most of the overlap without causing massive layoffs.[12] Also, he did not want to be insulated from the organization.[13] He wanted many people reporting to him, both line and staff people, so he could "...assess all the pieces."[14] Sculley also installed tighter control policies and increased the market focus and level of discipline of Apple's managers. No longer did he have more than a dozen vice-presidents reporting to him, as was the case when he arrived. "Now there was a distinct hierarchy, with two powerful product divisions responsible for their own manufacturing, marketing, and finance and a small central organization for sales, distribution, corporate finance, and human resources - in essence, two companies, each reporting to Sculley and his staff, each competing with the other."[15]

New Apple Products

In 1984, Apple discontinued Apple III and Lisa and introduced a new product, the compact, portable Apple IIc. That same year, the Apple II division experienced record sales. It sold an estimated 800,000 Apple IIe's and portable IIc's and revenues that year nearly reached $1 billion.[16] The Macintosh was also introduced. In keeping with the company's new strategy, the Macintosh was promoted as an alternative business computer in a bold campaign to win space in offices at the expense of IBM, who's PCs dominated the business market. Despite the fanfare, the Macintosh failed to attract business customers, as had the Lisa and Apple machines before it. Its impressive graphics and ease of use, did not compensate business managers for its lack of power and software. Also, it was a closed machine in that it did not allow specialized add-on hardware and software. Jobs developed the machine this way because he wanted it to be as simple an appliance to use as a telephone; one complete package like any other appliance in the home. Yet this feature caused the computer to have limited applications. The business market sought machines that could be used with various hardware and software. Furthermore, Apple's image as an"...irreverent, hip, young company..." sustained a perception that the Macintosh was not a business computer. This discouraged professionals, most of whom were familiar with the maxim "No one ever got fired for buying IBM". Also, the Macintosh had fewer software programs written for it, 600 - 700 compared to the 3,000 programs that could run on IBM PCs and their clones.[17] Apple expected to sell 60,000 to 85,000 Macintosh's a month by late 1984, yet sales barely exceeded 20,000.[18] Still, an estimated 250,000 were sold by the end of 1984 which was more than the IBM PC had sold in its first year.[19] The division earned revenues of close to $500 million, but the cost of introduction and reorganization significantly reduced profits.[20]

A Changing Industry

In 1985 the microcomputer industry suffered its worst slump in over a decade. Many new computer products had been promised or rumored but were not yet available, causing consumers to delay purchases until they could evaluate the new machines. Also, the home market was saturated. Hobbyists and professionals who worked at home were pausing to "digest" their recently purchased systems and were not buying newer models.[21] Other potential home users did not yet see the need to have a computer in their homes, which made this market difficult to penetrate. The business market also experienced a decrease in sales. Businesses, concerned about an impending recession, delayed capital equipment purchases. Only one market, education, was still growing. Apple was still the dominant player in this segment. Unfortunately, it was smaller than either the business or home segments.

Consumer preference also changed. Service and how new products fit into an existing family of products had become more important. There was a growing demand for personal computers that could communicate and share information or that were tied together into cohesive information systems. It was estimated that this demand was growing at 30% a year; twice the rate of the overall industry.[22]

Apple focused its efforts on developing the Macintosh as an alternative business computer. In January, 1985, Apple introduced the "Macintosh Office" which consisted of the computer, a laser printer, a local area network called Appletalk, and a file server. The company's emphasis on gaining acceptance in the business market led it to finally acknowledge IBM's preeminence, which, in turn, led to a change in its competitive strategy. In the past, said marketing director Michael Murray, "we would have vowed to drive IBM back into the typewriter business where it belongs."[23] In 1985, according to William Gates, chairman of Microsoft Corp., Apple began to preach coexistence.[24] It now emphasized developing a comprehensive line of compatible computers that worked well with those made by other manufacturers. The company targeted the small and medium-sized businesses, accounting for 80% of personal computer sales, and tried to win several accounts from major corporations to be used as "showcase accounts".[25]

Despite these changes, Apple's efforts to sell Macintosh to businesses were making little progress and the company experienced its first quarterly loss. The Macintosh fell short of its 150,000 sales goal over the Christmas season by approximately 50,000.[26] Sales then declined to an average of 19,000 units a month; falling even further after that.[27] Sales of the Apple II, Apple IIe and the Apple IIc were also disappointing. The Apple II line of products was the company's cash cow, but in 1985 it was not bringing in the revenue it had in the past.[28] Although the company experienced stunning Christmas sales, the following quarters were worrisome. The company earned only $10 million on sales of $435 million for the three months following Christmas as compared with $46 million on sales of $698 million the previous quarter.[29] Apple had no back orders left over from Christmas, rather, it had inventory excess for the first time.

Internal Problems

Disappointing market performance was attributed to internal problems. Jobs and his director of engineering were missing schedules for crucial parts of the system. They were "...months behind with a large disk drive that would help Mac run sophisticated software programs for business and make it easier for users to share information."[30] In addition, Apple had no sales force with direct access to corporations. Unlike IBM which had 6,000 to 7,000 direct salespeople, Apple relied on 300 manufacturers representatives over whom they had no direct control. These representatives also sold the products of other manufacturers. In the early 1980's, Apple established a 60-person direct-sales staff. However, soon after, the staff began to experience conflict with the independent dealers who still provided most of Apple's revenue. The direct salespeople were accused of selling Macintoshes at lower prices than dealers, "elbowing" them out of markets.[31]

There also were marketing problems. The company failed to communicate a business image for the Macintosh to the market. A former Macintosh employee stated, "Mac was being perceived as a cutesy, avocado machine for yuppies and their kids, not as an office machine or as the technology leader that it is."[32] Jobs and Sculley disagreed over marketing strategy. Jobs believed that Apple should focus on technology; that this would be the motivating force behind purchases of computers. Sculley thought the focus should be on customer needs. Customer needs should determine the product, therefore, getting close to the market was of fundamental importance. Jobs complained that Sculley didn't understand the nuts and bolts of the business or how products were developed, and questioned Sculley's competence.[33]

These problems were heightened by conflicts between the Apple II and Macintosh Divisions. The members of the Apple product group, led by Del Yocam, were frustrated with Jobs' favoring the Macintosh product group.

> "According to several insiders, Jobs, a devout believer that new technology should supersede the old, couldn't abide the success of the venerable Apple II. Nor did he hide his feelings. He once addressed the Apple II marketing staff as members of the 'dull and boring product division.' "[34]

Jobs' intense involvement with the Macintosh project had a demoralizing effect on Apple's other divisions. The Apple group considered this intolerable favoritism, especially since their division was producing more than twice the revenues as the Macintosh division.[35] Apple had become "two different warring companies" and the internal competition was self-defeating. Sculley described his own perspective of the organization:

> "Initially, I saw Apple in PepsiCo terms. Frito-Lay and Pepsi-Cola could comfortably and successfully exist as separate entities under PepsiCo. The Apple II group could have its own factories and sales organization for the K-12 (kindergarten through 12th grade) education and consumer markets. Macintosh, with its own independent operations, targeted the university and business markets. What I didn't realize was that it wasn't working. The two groups became too competitive with each other. People were getting burned out."[36]

In February, 1985, Stephen Wozniak, designer of the Apple I and an engineer in Yocam's group, resigned.

Sculley was losing confidence in Jobs' ability to manage the Mac division.[37] When Jobs failed to order necessary parts for the Macintosh XL and Apple had to discontinue the product after having introduced it only three months earlier, Sculley became concerned.[38]

The organizational structure contributed to these management problems. As Sculley explained,

"the organization created two power bases and removed me from day-to-day operating decisions. I became more remote from the business. As chairman, Steve was over me. And as head of a product division, he was under me. He really had more knowledge about what was going on in the business than I did because all the information was coming up through the product divisions. They had all the power. The corporate staff basically became an impotent group, largely a financial organization."[39]

Sculley felt that he was losing control:

"It was nearly impossible to get the right information quickly when I needed it most. I was constantly surprised by new and disturbing findings, including the failure to order parts for the Macintosh XL. The management inexperience of many of Apple's key players as well as my own lack of experience in the personal computer industry should have been early warning signs that a decentralized organization wasn't suited for our volatile marketplace. It set up a system under which people would fight for what was best for their groups, not what was best for the company as a whole."[40]

According to middle managers at Apple, Sculley was in Jobs' shadow. He wasn't taking the action he needed to run the company. Jobs was making all the decisions and was being favored over all the other vice-presidents.[41] The board was also unhappy with the way Jobs was running the Macintosh division. They encouraged Sculley to exercise his authority as C.E.O and hire a new general manager to improve the Macintosh's sales.[42]

A New Organization without Jobs

In May of 1985, Sculley announced another reorganization. The three product divisions were consolidated into one called Product Operations. Exhibit 5 is an inter-office memo from Sculley introducing the new organizational structure to Apple's employees. The company was downsized in an effort to reduce operating costs. Advertising was reduced, factories were closed and the Lisa computer and some development efforts were eliminated. The direct sales force was dismissed except for those on established accounts. A total of 1,200 employees were laid off, 60% of whom were in manufacturing.[43] Other cutbacks were made across the organization except for R&D.

The other part of the reorganization called for bringing in a new general manager of the Macintosh Division to replace Jobs. Also, Jobs operating role in the company as chairman was taken away. On September 17, 1985, he resigned from Apple. Yocam was placed in charge of engineering, manufacturing and distribution and William V. Campbell became responsible for U.S. marketing and sales. Sculley imported two top-level executives to headquarters in California from Europe. Jean-Louis Gassee, head of Apple France, was promoted to replace Jobs as head of product development and Michael Spindler, a German national, who had been

Exhibit 5

APPLE COMPUTER INTER-OFFICE MEMO

Date: June 14, 1985
To: Board of Directors
From: John Sculley
Subject: Company Reorganization

The executive staff, key mangers and I have met almost daily over the past several weeks to develop a new organization. As you know, Apple has been a divisionalized company with several highly autonomous profit centers which have acted almost like stand-alone companies:

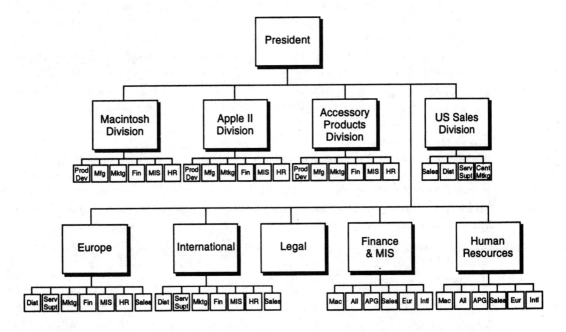

I am pleased to announce a new structure which is vastly simplified and organized around functions:

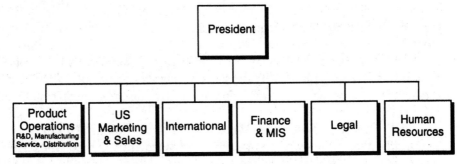

Source: Apple Computer Inc. 1985 Annual Report.

Exhibit 5 (cont.)

The new organization will reduce our breakeven point. It should also simplify internal communication of company objectives and allow for greater consistency in their implementation.

We have selected leaders of each functional area who have had considerable experience in their specialty and in managing people.

In the process of moving to this new organization, we will reduce the number of jobs at Apple by 1200. This is a painful and difficult decision. However, this streamlining will allow us to eliminate unnecessary job duplication in the divisional structure. (As shown in the organization chart, each division has had its own product development, manufacturing, finance, management information systems, and human resource staffs.)

The new organization would be more effective at providing products the marketplace wants and at providing them in a more timely manner. In addition to the greater effectiveness of the organization it should also be more efficient – making us more profitable on lower sales than would have been the case with the former organization.

The reorganization will be costly in the short run. We take such a strong step only because it is clear that the new organization and management team will vastly improve Apple's profitability for success as an industry leader.

Source: Apple Computer Inc. 1985 Annual Report

---

running European marketing and sales was promoted to head all of Apple's international operations. Apple became one of few companies to have two Europeans at the highest levels of senior management.

Apple International

Apple was an early market leader in Europe. Before 1983, the company expanded sales into Britain, Germany and France. Gassee led a successful marketing effort in France, and under his strong leadership, Apple achieved a high profile and a critical mass of buyers. However, Apple was not as successful in Britain and Germany. Competitors in the British education market shut out Apple. In Germany, the home market of hobbyists, where Apple products were most popular, never took off with the same popularity as it had elsewhere. Still, the company established a European headquarters in Paris with a staff of 45 people and built a production plant in Ireland.

Apple managed its international operations from California. This drew criticism from the European computer industry. Both Gassee and Spindler tried to convince Apple to pay more attention to growing markets abroad.

Enthusiast to Businessman

Following its 1985 reorganization, Apple began to adjust its products and marketing strategy to better fit the computer industry environment. Efforts were made to open up the Mac to third-party hardware and software companies. Product lines were filled out with equipment the consumer wanted, such as large disk drives, and more powerful versions of the machine itself. In late 1985, Apple successfully introduced desktop publishing, a method pioneered by the Macintosh for printing type-set-quality documents on the computer, was introduced with a strong response. "Some 50,000 Macintosh publishing systems were sold in 1986, and sales of the accompanying printers alone added about $150 million in revenues."[44] Excel, a spreadsheet program written by Microsoft Corp. for the Mac was also a success. Apple was now able to offer capabilities similar to IBM PC's running Lotus' 1-2-3 spreadsheet programs.

In January of 1986, Sculley began to pitch the Macintosh to Fortune 500 companies like General Electric, Eastman Kodak and Du Pont, and listened to their criticisms. He also expanded the number of business packages written for the Mac. Apple's marketing strategy focused more aggressively on the corporate market to win space in the office at the expense of the IBM. Simultaneously, the company slowly extricated itself from the unprofitable home computer market and lessened its dependence on sales to schools. Said Sculley, "We went after business because that's the biggest market with the highest profit and the fastest growth in the personal computer industry."[45]

In pursuing the business segment, Apple began to hire more employees with professional business backgrounds.

> "Early on, Apple tended to hire hackers and enthusiasts. For the last two years, they've taken on experienced professionals who were businessmen before they were Apple enthusiasts."[46]

The idea was that corporate managers would be more responsive to salespeople who were similar to them.

Apple's national salespeople were ordered to seek "highly visible reference accounts". The company received orders from Sea First Bank for 1,000 Macs, Federal Express for $5 million worth of machines, and commitments worth roughly $2.5 million apiece from General Motors, GTE, Honeywell and Motorola were made. In 1986, revenues from the sale of Macintosh products exceeded those of Apple II products. That following March of 1987, Apple introduced two new computers for the business market: the Macintosh SE and the Macintosh II. Both machines were "open"; the first to accommodate microprocessor boards made by outside companies.

> "The open design vastly increased the Macs appeal to businesses, since the extra boards let Macs work better in corporate computer networks, use bigger screens, and run software written for IBM computers. The Mac II had ten times the computing power of the first Mac."

These products attracted larger software houses that developed sophisticated applications for large business user.

Exhibit 6 Net Sales, Net Income and Number of Employees

	1982	1983	1984	1985	1986	1987	1988	1989
Net Sales (millions)	583.1	982.8	1515.9	1918.3	1901.9	2661.1	4071.4	5284.0
Net Income (millions)	61.3	76.7	64.1	61.2	154.0	217.5	400.3	454.0
Employees	3,400	4,645	5,382	4,182	5,600	7,228	10,836	14,517

The new Macintosh products and desk top publishing contributed to an expanded business market for Apple. Nearly half of Apple's sales and most of its profits came from selling personal computers and related products to business users. The company now offered product features that IBM did not offer that the business market highly valued.

Growth

Business market expansion resulted in a 30% increase in Apple's sales from 1901.9 million in 1986 to 2661.1 million in 1987.[47] Exhibit 6 shows net sales, net income and the total number of employees for years 1982 - 1989. Apple expected this rapid growth to continue, predicting a more than doubling of revenue to $10 billion annually by the early 1990s.[48]

As the number of employees increased, there was less time available for Sculley to devote to day-to-day operations.

> "As the bureaucracy continues to grow...there is a limit to how many engineers can walk directly into Sculley's office to pitch their ideas."[49]

Also, there were constant battles between Apple's sales, marketing and engineering departments. Upper managers were "...not all lined up facing in the same direction."[50] "The technical people didn't respect the marketing department, the marketing department was disorganized, and there was little possibility that we could afford all the projects it was working on."[51] These problems required even more of Sculley's time.

In an effort to centralize operations and involve Apple's senior management in day-to-day decisions, Sculley created a new position of Chief Operating Officer. (See Exhibit 7.) Yocam was given the position. Sculley hoped that this change would free up more of his time to spend on long-term planning. New high-level management positions included Vice-President of

Exhibit 7 Organizational Chart, 1988

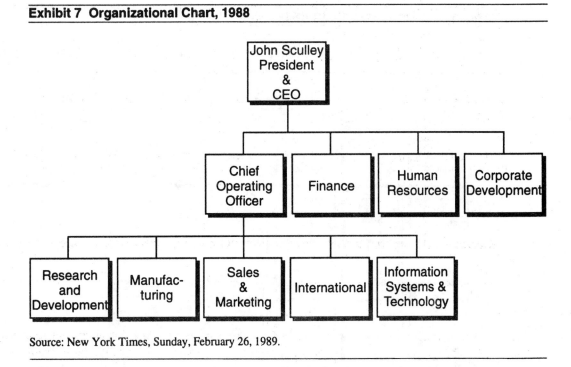

Source: New York Times, Sunday, February 26, 1989.

Advanced Technology and Vice-President of U.S. Sales and Marketing. Sculley doubled the size of Apple's field force and the number of employees grew to 10,836.[52]

International Growth

In 1987, international growth became a priority at Apple. The European market for PCs was expanding faster than the U.S. market. Apple depended on growth in markets abroad to cover up declining U.S. sales. Sculley said, "We were going to reduce our dependency in the U.S. consumer market, which meant sales growth in the international area would be important because otherwise people could feel Apple was failing."[53] Sculley turned to Michael Spindler, head of Apple's international division, to develop a strategy for growth in the European market. Spindler's strategy involved focusing more closely on the needs of corporate and other markets rather than home users. In order to appeal to these consumers, Spindler developed a business-like approach to the European market similar to the one Apple developed in the U.S. He brought more experienced computer industry professionals into Apple's older European subsidiaries and stressed a professional, corporate image from the start in newer ones.

Spindler reorganized Apple's European distribution network, which was geared more to individuals and small business buyers. He cut back the network and upgraded the remaining distributors to lure large corporate dealers who were accustomed to dealing with IBM. As Spindler explained,

> "We made a decision to take the distribution network down, and build it back up in quality rather than quantity. We put more emphasis on adding value, rather than just moving boxes."[54]

Exhibit 8 Organizational Chart, 1989

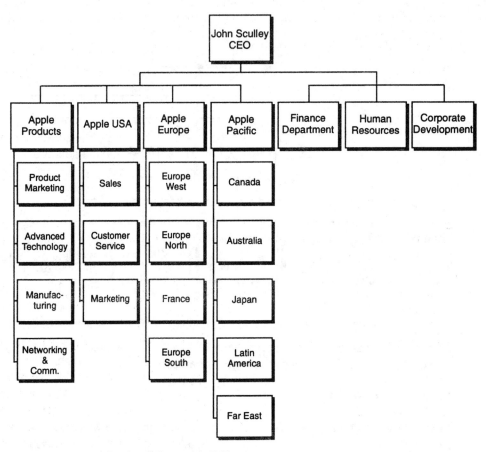

Source: New York Times, Sunday, February 26, 1989.

Spindler also championed a new "multi-local" approach to international subsidiaries. Most American multi-nationals simply cloned their U.S. operations overseas, selling the same products as were successful in the United States. According to Spindler, a "multi-local" approach meant "...you have a network model that adapts to local markets. You behave and act like a local company, yet you are within the network of the mother company back home. The whole world can thus become one big shopping cart for ideas and capital."[55]

An International Business Market Structure

By 1988, Apple had established strong markets in France, Canada and Australia. Major European companies such as France's Aerospatiale and Renault, Germany's Bayer and BASF and Britain's Plessey purchased a significant number of Macintosh machines. Apple gained 6% of the overall European market.[56] Apple Europe's revenues grew by 55%, faster than revenue growth for the entire company.[57] Apple experienced the same success in new markets such as Spain, Sweden, Holland, Belgium and Japan. Its Swedish subsidiary, developed in 1985, captured 15% of the business market in 1988.[58] Sales in Japan also took off as localized products were developed.

Apple's foreign operations now consisted of three manufacturing facilities in Ireland and Singapore and distribution facilities in Europe, Canada and Australia.[59] In October of 1988, European sales alone made up nearly one-third of total revenues for Apple.[60]

International growth spurred Apple to expand its European headquarters in Paris. The staff was increased by over 150 people.[61] "We can't do everything from the U.S. anymore; valuable things are happening in Europe," said Spindler.[62] A new corporate "account management" program was established which included several hundred corporate account specialists fanning out across the Continent. The proportion of European-made components used in Apple's Irish production plant was increased and Apple opened a $10 million R&D center in Paris that employed 50 engineers.[63]

This growth was accompanied by a realization that Apple's various markets were distinctly different and required different expertise. Apple responded by splitting its International Division into separate, autonomous Pacific and European units and creating the Apple USA division from what was formally known as U.S. Sales and Marketing. Exhibits 7 and 8 show the old and new Apple structures respectively. The four functional divisions were replaced by two, Apple Products and Apple USA, and the role of Chief Operating Officer was removed. Each division was headed by a president who reported directly to Sculley. Jean-Louis Gassee was placed in charge of Apple Products, responsible for all product development, manufacturing operations and marketing. U.S. sales and marketing, service and support and Apple's internal information systems operations were grouped into Apple USA. Sculley segmented this division's operations into business and education market units and a marketing support unit. Apple's International Division was split into Apple Europe and Apple Pacific. Michael Spindler was placed in charge of Apple Europe responsible for sales, service and marketing operations for primarily France, West Germany and Scandinavia. Del Yocam was placed in charge of Apple Pacific handling sales, service and marketing for Apple's current markets in Canada, Australia and Japan while investigating market opportunities in Pacific Rim and Latin American nations.

Notes

[1] Apple Computer Inc., Annual Report 1983.

[2] Ibid.

[3] Theresa M. Brady, "Apple Computer, Inc." Stern Business Strategy and Policy Readings 1989 - 1990, Second Edition (Copley Publishing Group, Massachusetts, 1989): p. 459.

[4] Apple Computer Inc., Annual Report 1983.

[5] Frank Rose, West of Eden: The End of Innocence at Apple Computer (Viking Penguin Inc., New York, 1989): p. 85.

[6] Apple Computer Library. 1992 Employee Orientation Packet.

[7] Theresa M. Brady, "Apple Computer, Inc." Stern Business Strategy and Policy Readings 1989 - 1990, Second Edition (Copley Publishing Group, Massachusetts, 1989): p. 454.

[8] Janet Guyon and Erik Larson, "New Apple Chief Expected to Bring Marketing Expertise Gained at Pepsi" The Wall Street Journal April 11, 1983: Section 2 p. 29;4.

[9] John Sculley, Odyssey: Pepsi to Apple...A Journey of Adventure, Ideas, and the Future (Harper & Row Publishers, New York, 1987): p. 142 - 143.

[10] Ibid.: p. 144.

[11] Ibid.: p. 143.

[12] Ibid.: p. 143.

[13] Ibid.

[14] Ibid.

[15] Frank Rose, West of Eden:: The End of Innocence at Apple Computer (Viking Penguin Inc., New York, 1989) p.166.

[16] Bro Uttal, "Behind the Fall" Fortune August 5, 1985: p.22.

[17] Theresa M. Brady, "Apple Computer, Inc." Stern Business Strategy and Policy Readings 1989 - 1990, Second Edition (Copley Publishing Group, Massachusetts, 1989): p. 462.

[18] Brian O'Reilly, "Growing Apple Anew for the Business Market" Fortune, January 4, 1988: p.37.

[19] Bro Uttal, "Behind the Fall" Fortune August 5, 1985: p. 22.

[20] Ibid.

[21] Theresa M. Brady, "Apple Computer, Inc." Stern Business Strategy and Policy Readings 1989 - 1990, Second Edition (Copley Publishing Group, Massachusetts, 1989): p. 457 - 458.

[22] Ibid.: p. 458.

[23] Felix Kessler, "Apple's Pitch to the Fortune 500" Fortune April 15, 1985: p. 54.

[24] Ibid.

[25] Ibid.

[26] Bro Uttal, "Behind the Fall" Fortune August 5, 1985: p. 22.

[27] Ibid.

[28] Theresa M. Brady, "Apple Computer, Inc." Stern Business Strategy and Policy Readings 1989 – 1990, Second Edition (Copley Publishing Group, Massachusetts, 1989): p. 462.

[29] Bro Uttal, "Behind the Fall" Fortune August 5, 1985: p.22.

[30] Ibid.: p. 22 – 23.

[31] Theresa M. Brady, "Apple Computer, Inc." Stern Business Strategy and Policy Readings 1989 - 1990, Second Edition (Copley Publishing Group, Massachusetts, 1989): p. 463.

[32] Bro Uttal. "Behind the Fall" Fortune, August 5, 1985: p.22.

[33] Ibid.: p. 23.

[34] Ibid.: p. 22.

[35] Ibid.

[36] John Sculley, Odyssey: Pepsi to Apple...A Journey of Adventure, Ideas, and the Future (Harper & Row Publishers, New York, 1987): p. 240.

[37] Ibid.

[38] Ibid.

[39] Ibid.

[40] Ibid.: p. 276.

[41] Frank Rose, West of Eden: The End of Innocence at Apple Computer (Viking Penguin Inc., New York, 1989) p. 229.

[42] Bro Uttal. "Behind the Fall" Fortune, August 5, 1985: p.22.

[43] John Sculley, Odyssey: Pepsi to Apple...A Journey of Adventure, Ideas, and the Future (Harper & Row Publishers, New York, 1987): p. 291.

[44] Katherine M. Hafner, "Apple's Comeback" Business Week, January 19, 1987: p. 85.

[45] Brian O'Reilly, "Growing Apple Anew for the Business Market" Fortune, January 4, 1988: p.37.

[46] Jane Sasseen, "Replanting Apples Across Europe" International Management October, 1988: p. 37.

[47] Apple Computer Inc., Annual Report, 1987.

[48] Brenton R. Schlender, "Apple Sets Plan To Reorganize into 4 Divisions" The Wall Street Journal, August 23, 1988: p. 2.

[49] Glenn Rifkin, "Getting to the Core of the New Apple" Computerworld February 1, 1988: p. 49.

[50] Ibid.: p. 48..

[51] Brian O'Reilly, "Apple Computer's Risky Revolution" Fortune May 8, 1989: p. 76-77.

[52] Apple Computer Inc., Annual Report, 1988.

[53] John Sculley, Odyssey: Pepsi to Apple...A Journey of Adventure, Ideas, and the Future (Harper & Row Publishers, New York, 1987): p. 282.

[54] Ibid.: p. 37.

[55] John Sculley, Odyssey: Pepsi to Apple...A Journey of Adventure, Ideas, and the Future (Harper & Row Publishers, New York, 1987): p. 328.

[56] Ibid.: p. 36.

[57] Jane Sasseen, "Replanting Apples Across Europe" International Management October, 1988: p. 36.

[58] Ibid.: p. 37.

[59] Phylles Fedderler and Thomas Wheelen, "Apple Computer Corporation 1987" Strategy Management and Business Policy, 3rd edition (Addison-Wesley Publishing Company Inc., Massachusetts, 1989): p. 547, 552.

[60] Jane Sasseen, "Replanting Apples Across Europe" International Management October, 1988: p. 36.

[61] Ibid.: p. 36.

[62] Ibid.: p. 36.

[63] Ibid.: p. 37.

Part 2   Ethics and Social Responsibility

Cases Outline

5. Salomon Brothers: "Apologies Are Bullshit"[1]*

> Discipline and integrity are vital. There isn't anything like a half-truth, either it's so or it isn't. Everything you say or do commits this firm. The main part of our discipline is truth. You'll be much more truthful here than in the rest of your life where you might have to tell white lies to get along.[2]
>
>   – John Gutfreund in a speech to new
>   Salomon employees, 1984

On February 21, 1991 Paul W. Mozer, Managing Director in charge of Salomon Inc.'s government securities trading desk, submitted a bid for Salomon of $3.15 billion, or 35% of the $9 billion five-year Treasury note auction offering amount (see Exhibit I for explanation of bidding procedures). Mr. Mozer also submitted two unauthorized customer bids, each at the 35% limit. One of the unauthorized bids was submitted in the name of "Warburg" for $3.15 billion. The other was submitted in the name of "Quantum Fund" for $3.15 billion. These bids circumvented a Treasury rule enacted seven months earlier specifically to curb Mr. Mozer's questionable bidding practices.[3]

The February 21 five-year note auction was subject to 54% proration, and thus $1.7 billion of those notes was awarded on each of the three bids. The $1.7 billion in notes awarded to each of "Warburg" and "Quantum" were initially placed into the customers' respective accounts and then "sold" to Salomon at the auction price. The customer confirmations for these transactions were suppressed following the instructions from Mr. Mozer.[4] As a result of the two unauthorized customer bids, Salomon effectively bid for 105% of the offering amount and purchased approximately 57% of the issue, thus exceeding the 35% purchase-limit rule.

The day after the auction took place, a representative of the Federal Reserve contacted Salomon's Government Trading Desk to inquire about the "Warburg" bid. Thomas Murphy – who was also a Managing Director and assistant to Mozer – advised the government official that the bid had mistakenly been submitted in the name of "Warburg" and should have been submitted in the name of Mercury Asset Management, an affiliate of S.G. Warburg & Co. Apparently unbeknownst to Mozer and Murphy, S.G. Warburg had in fact submitted a bid for $100 million in its own name in the February 21, 1991 auction.[5]

On April 17, 1991, the Treasury sent a letter addressed to Charles Jackson, a Senior Director of Mercury, reviewing the S.G. Warburg and "Mercury" bids.[6] The Treasury also sent copies of this letter to Mr. Mozer, as well as a representative of the Federal Reserve. The Treasury letter advised Mercury that, in the future, bids submitted by all subsidiaries of S.G. Warburg, including Mercury, would be treated as a bid from a single entity for purposes of the Treasury's 35% bid-limit rule.

When Paul Mozer received the letter, he apparently became concerned that the Treasury would learn from Mercury or S.G. Warburg representatives that neither of those entities had authorized Salomon's initial submission of a bid in "Warburg's" name, or its subsequent use of "Mercury" to identify the bid. Mr. Mozer contacted Charles Jackson and told him that

*Richard D. Freedman and Velvet V. Mickens, Leonard N. Stern Graduate School of Business, New York University, June 1993. Copyright © 1993 by Richard D. Freedman. Reprinted with permission.

Salomon had mistakenly submitted a bid in Mercury's name in the February 21 auction. Mr. Mozer requested that Mr. Jackson not embarrass Mozer with the Treasury and the Federal Reserve by responding to the Treasury's letter. The letter itself did not ask for a response. Paul Mozer also asked Nick Ritchie, Salomon's customer contact at Mercury, not to voluntarily report Salomon's "error" to the Treasury.

In late April 1991, Mr. Mozer approached his supervisor, John W. Meriwether, Vice Chairman of Salomon. Mozer showed Mr. Meriwether the Treasury's April 17 letter and indicated that he had submitted an unauthorized bid. At this time John Meriwether asked Mr. Mozer whether unauthorized customer bids had been submitted on other occasions. Mr. Mozer stated that February 21st was the only time an unauthorized customer bid had been intentionally submitted by the Government Trading Desk – a statement which was far from true. In fact, Mozer did not tell Meriwether that he had submitted a second unauthorized customer bid – the bid submitted in the name of "Quantum," in the same February 21 auction. John Meriwether told Mr. Mozer that he would have to bring the matter to the attention of Thomas W. Strauss, Salomon's President.

On April 29, 1991 Messrs. Strauss, Meriwether and Donald M. Feuerstein, Salomon's Chief Legal Officer, informed John Gutfreund (pronounced GOOD-friend), Chairman and Chief Executive Officer of Salomon Brothers, that Paul Mozer had admitted falsifying a customer's bid during an auction of five-year Treasury notes.

During this meeting the topic of terminating Mr. Mozer was never discussed. Nor did the participants discuss whether changes were necessary to guard against similar mistakes in the future. Instead, Vice Chairman John W. Meriwether defended Mozer, claiming that he had made a mistake. In reality, Mr. Mozer's February bid had been part of "a pattern of fraudulent conduct"[7] that continued even after he admitted it to his superiors.

Mr. Gutfreund has stated that the participants in the meeting decided that Mr. Mozer's conduct should be reported to government authorities and they discussed how this should be done. However, according to a statement issued by Salomon, "due to a lack of sufficient attention to the matter, this determination was not implemented promptly."[8] In fact, no final decision was made concerning the manner in which the matter would be reported to governmental authorities. Consequently, the four senior executives did not report Mozer's activities to the Federal Reserve Bank until August 1991, four months later.

As a result of their delayed action to the bond trading revelations, Messrs. Gutfreund, Strauss, and Meriwether resigned from their positions at Salomon. Mr. Mozer was fired. Months of government investigation followed and ultimately, Salomon agreed to pay $290 million for its actions, although it avoided the kind of criminal charges that have destroyed other securities firms.[9]

At the press conference in which he announced he was leaving the firm where he had worked for 38 years, Mr. Gutfreund was asked if he was sorry. He responded, "Apologies are bullshit."[10]

How did this top U.S. underwriter of securities reach this sorry state of affairs? A wide variety of explanations have been offered; from deficiencies in the ethics of the individuals involved to the absence of managerial controls to Salomon simply being a product of the times. This paper presents a historical perspective on Salomon Brothers and the Gutfreund era.

The Beginning

Salomon Brothers ("Salomon") was founded in 1910 by three brothers – Arthur, Herbert and Percy along with a clerk named Ben Levy. The company was primarily a bond-trading firm that made money by being on the winning side of its trades. In order to survive in what was then a marginal segment of the industry, Salomon had to provide rapid and superior service, and to obtain a reputation for honesty and integrity. Additionally, the firm risked its own capital to make money because it did not have fee-paying clients. The private company entered equities in the mid-1960's and investment banking in the early 1970's (see Exhibit II for description of investment banking functions).[11]

Salomon operated under a partnership structure which served to reinforce cohesiveness among its employees. With most of their net worth invested in the firm, partners put its overall health before their individual activities.[12] Battles over credit for deals and trades were minimal since compensation among partners was essentially equal. In addition, owning the firm motivated the partners to keep a close eye on expenses. This structure, among other things, helped the company remain successful despite the fact that the economy was undergoing significant changes which caused other firms to suffer losses. According to Salomon partner Abraham Eller:

> I think what helped make Salomon Brothers was not only the partners, but that the men they hired were hungry... We weren't the sons of rich men.[13]

The Economy of the 1970's

The years from the late 1960's through the 1970's were among the more troubled and dramatic periods in American history. The nation and the world suffered through two "oil shocks," which contributed to the decline of the American auto industry and threw the economy into alternating periods of inflation and recession. Additionally, chronic deficits had contributed to a weakening dollar. As a result, in 1971 President Richard Nixon imposed an array of restrictions on imports, instituted wage and price controls, and slashed the budget.[14]

Matters were further exacerbated when the Organization of Petroleum Exporting Countries (OPEC) boosted the price of oil at a time when the wage and price controls in America had already failed to take effect. The condition of the economy was being referred to as "stagflation," a combination of inflation and economic stagnation.[15]

The cheaper dollar and high interest rates had a dramatic impact on the capital markets and related areas. It meant that expansion-minded corporate managers who had the option of constructing new facilities or buying out the depressed stocks of companies chose to come down heavily on the buy side.[16] The stocks of capital goods manufacturers were sharply lower than the true value of underlying assets, and these companies became targets for acquirers with cash. In effect, the decline of the dollar resulted in the creation of a new merger and acquisition movement.[17]

This was a decade when many of the "rules" by which economists had lived for generations seemed to have been broken. At a time when the economy was generally sluggish and when, according to recognized economic theories, there should have been little or no inflation, prices were rising sharply.[18] As a result, many firms on Wall Street suffered losses. Salomon Brothers, on the other hand, remained profitable.

This success, however, would be greatly surpassed under the stewardship of John Gutfreund, Chairman and CEO of Salomon Brothers.

"The King of Wall Street"[19]

John Gutfreund grew up in the suburbs of New York City where his father was the owner of a trucking company, and a frequent golfing partner of William (Billy) Salomon, the son of one of the founders of the firm. Gutfreund graduated from Oberlin College in 1951, with a degree in English. After serving two years in the Army, he joined Salomon as a trainee in the statistical department in 1953.[20]

Once there, he advanced quickly into trading municipal securities where his trading skills and his ability to recognize investment opportunities were highly praised. He became a partner in 1963 and joined the Excutive Committee three years later. In 1978 – a year when Salomon purchased or sold over $500 billion worth of securities, and the firm's net worth rose to $208.7 million (see Exhibit III for a summary of the firm's financial performance) – he was named Managing Partner of the firm by Billy Salomon.[21] It is interesting to note that at this time, "thirteen of the twenty-eight partners had not been to college, and one hadn't graduated from the eighth grade. John Gutfreund was, in this crowd, an intellectual."[22]

Observers described Gutfreund as a "supremely self-confident, intellectual, ferociously competitive individual who was a throwback to the days on Wall Street when partnerships reigned and the personality of one man could dominate a firm."[23] He was also noted as being the most conservative member in the firm. In fact, Billy Salomon admired this trait in him and thought it would be a good example for the other members of the company.

Despite becoming Chairman and CEO of Salomon, Gutfreund was most at ease on the trading floor – the 41st floor which was known as "Power Central" – exchanging expletives with the traders who worked for him.[24] He spent most of his time at a large desk, overseeing one end of Salomon's gymnasium-sized bond trading room. "I get great pleasure from being on the floor. Salomon is a trading house and I was a trader."[25] In fact, he was probably the most accessible chairman of any concern on Wall Street. "The nitty-gritty of dealmaking, waging war with the weapons of quarters and eighths of a point were his joy."[26] To the Wall Street competition, Gutfreund "was the Salomon culture incarnate"[27] with his instructions to trainees to come to work ready to "bite the ass off a bear."[28]

However, there was another side to Gutfreund's leadership style. According to insiders,

> Gutfreund avoided confrontation and was slow to implement decisions. His business judgment was too often influenced by the people he liked at the firm. He had little time for budgets, planning, operations, technology or other critical details of management.[29]

Gutfreund himself acknowledged that he was not strong in managing his people. On one occasion he stated: "I'm too paternalistic. My problem is that I am too deliberate on people issues."[30] Rather than fire someone, he would move them to a backwater within the firm.[31] In the rare situations in which Mr. Gutfreund took tough internal action, it was only after much delay and under pressure from others.[32]

Michael Lewis, in his book *Liar's Poker,* captures the essence of why Gutfreund preferred to be on the trading floor, and appeared to avoid management:

> He [Gutfreund] loved to trade. Compared with managing, trading was admirably direct. You made your bets and either you won or you lost. When you won, people-all the way up to the top of the firm-admired you, envied you, and feared you, and with reason: You controlled the loot. When you managed a firm, well, sure you received your quota of envy, fear, and admiration. But for all the wrong reasons. You did not make the money for Salomon. You did not take risk.[33]

Despite his difficulties in the management arena, Gutfreund was the talk of the town and he was dubbed "The King of Wall Street"[34] by *Business Week* magazine because of his extraordinary success in taking advantage of the bull markets of the 1980's.

According to observers, Gutfreund was Salomon Brothers personified:

> For here was a man who was said to have stamped his personality onto an institution; his faults as well as his virtues were those of Salomon Brothers.[35]

The Economy of the 1980's

On October 6, 1979, the Chairman of the Federal Reserve, Paul Volker, announced that the money supply would cease to fluctuate with the business cycle; money supply would be fixed, and interest rates would float. In other words, interest rates were deregulated.[36] Some Wall Streeters feel that this event, "marked the beginning of the golden age of the bond man."[37] This shift in the focus of monetary policy meant that interest rates would move wildly. Importantly, bond prices move inversely to rates of interest. Allowing interest rates to swing widely meant allowing bond prices to swing widely. Prior to this announcement, bonds had been conservative investments, in which consumers invested if they did not want to delve into the stock market. After Volker's speech, bonds became a means of "creating wealth rather than merely storing it."[38]

Once interest rates were allowed to move freely, American consumers, governments and corporations borrowed money at a faster rate than ever before. This, in turn, meant that the volume of bonds increased substantially. That is, investors were lending money more freely than ever before. So not only were bond prices more volatile, but the number of bonds traded increased.

> A Salomon salesman who had in the past moved five million dollars' worth of merchandise through the traders' books each week was now moving three hundred million dollars through each day.[39]

The industry's revenues rose from $16 billion in 1980 to $51.8 billion in 1988.[40]

It was also a time when the mergers and acquisitions business came to the forefront of the industry, and the mortgage market became recognized as a major new segment of the capital markets. In addition, the marketplace itself was revolutionized by a new procedure sanctioned by the SEC that speeded the flow of securities from issuers to investors.

The Security and Exchange Commission's (SEC) Rule 415 was probably the most important change in the operation of the capital markets during the 1980's and served to further deregulate the industry. Enacted in 1982, the rule allowed a corporation to register in advance all the securities it intended to issue over the next two-year span (these registrations were known as "Shelf Registrations").[41] Then the corporation could offer any of them in literally a matter of hours. Therefore, a company might have in readiness an issue of, for example, $100 million in 20-year debentures, and bring it to market at a time when rates and acceptance seemed best.[42] Moreover, it could do so through an underwriter or institution selected at the last minute. This, of course, would subject the industry to even more intense competition.[43] Said one insider at the time, "We're moving from the traditional concept of marriage to one-night stands."[44] In order to succeed under Rule 415, underwriters had to "hone their sensitivity to the market,"[45] and be prepared to commit large sums of money on very short notice.

Under the new system's first full year of operation, "Shelf Registrations" accounted for 38 percent of all underwriting volume, and Salomon Brothers was the industry's leader.[46]

As a result of this deregulation and Rule 415, investment firms suddenly were free to invent and price new products. The protection of the Glass-Steagall Act, which had forbidden commercial banks to underwrite and distribute most securities, had all but disappeared. Foreign banks, in particular Japanese, began to underwrite U.S. securities. Giant financial houses emerged, offering across-the-board financial services.

These changes resulted in what Gutfreund termed "a perpetual storm of invention."[47] The number and complexity of products increased rapidly, while their life cycles decreased (often to a few days).

The Gutfreund Era

When he assumed control of Salomon, Gutfreund sought to take advantage of this economic growth and pursued a strategy of aggressive expansion, both in the services the firm provided for its customers, and in the role of the company in the global marketplace.[48] He saw the trend toward a common capital market worldwide. To support this growth he directed that offices be expanded and opened in London, Frankfurt, Tokyo and Zurich. In addition, he broadened the firm's foreign currency exchange operations.

Along with internationalization, he was aware of the significance of institutional dominance of the marketplace. He could see the key role of innovation and supported pioneering efforts in various fields. This included the establishment of a mortgage-backed securities division as well as the expansion of mergers and acquisitions. Gutfreund's efforts paid off handsomely. In 1985, the firm's peak year, Salomon brought in $760 million in pretax profits. In 1987, the company's capital reached $3.4 billion. Also, Salomon which traditionally traded only a few products, was trading well over 100 products by 1987.[49]

Despite this growth, Gutfreund realized that he needed additional capital resources in order to continue this path of expansion. In order to acquire the needed capital he arranged a buyout of Salomon Brothers by Philipp Brothers.

Deregulation of the Markets

In the late sixties, Wall Street started to shift from relationship banking – when a corporation gives most of its business to an investment banker it has known for years – to transactional banking – when investment houses compete for clients on a deal-by-deal basis. This shift was brought about as a result of the deregulation of the markets, and further solidified by Rule 415. The intensified competition to win deals reduced profit margins. The only way for investment houses to offset this decline was to increase their volume and to diversify into businesses which had higher margins.[50]

Firms, like Salomon, that had specialized in securities trading found that their skills at pricing stocks and bonds allowed them to effectively court corporate clients. Salomon's syndicate department, which organized underwritings, became efficient at undercutting their Wall Street rivals. The result of their success was that they became the most powerful entity within the firm.[51] John Gutfreund was the head of that department at the time.

Gutfreund and his colleagues were among the earliest to realize how much the investment banking field had changed by the late 1960's. The role and status of those bankers charged with raising funds and providing advice and liquidity to clients was evolving rapidly. Many of the exclusive relationships that had been common in earlier periods were breaking down. In the past, most companies had ongoing relationships with investment bankers which were handed down from one generation of the company to another. In the new, "fluid" atmosphere, corporations were willing to work with any reputable house that brought them new ideas.[52]

Philipp Brothers Corporation (Phibro)

In 1981, attempting to attain a more permanent source of capital, Gutfreund agreed to sell Salomon Brothers for $554 million to Phibro, an international house with revenues of $23.6 billion. Phibro traded more than 160 commodities in 45 countries and, therefore, was one of the world's largest commodities traders at that time.[53] "It was a marriage of Salomon's ingenuity with Phibro's cash."[54] The sale abolished Salomon's partnership structure and made the firm a publicly traded institution.

The buyout negotiations, however, were conducted in total secrecy, and was only revealed to Salomon's partners when negotiations were completed. It was a move that shocked all of Wall Street because Gutfreund had always stated that he would never deviate from the partnership structure of the organization.[55]

Gutfreund became chairman of the Salomon Brothers subsidiary and co-chief executive (along with the Philipp Brothers chairman, David Tendler) of the newly formed holding company Phibro-Salomon, Inc. As a result of the deal, Gutfreund received more than $30 million for his partnership shares.[56]

The access to Phibro's enormous capital resources enabled Salomon to deal in larger volumes, take larger risks and operate on lower profit margins. Said Gutfreund of the merger, "what we've done is leapfrog 20 years ahead. It explodes the size of our universe."[57] According to William Voute, a managing director at Salomon,

> We saw the size of the market expanding and the U.S. Treasury needs expanding. We had only in the neighborhood of $300 million in capital, and it was felt that this wasn't enough to bring us into the next century.[58]

However, it soon became clear that Gutfreund sold Salomon cheap. In the deal, Salomon received a price equal to slightly less than twice the firm's book value.[59] By comparison, Prudential Insurance paid more than twice book for Bache, and Shearson Loeb Rhodes received 3.4 times book from American Express, during the same year.[60] Still, the access to Phibro's capital resources enabled Salomon to deal in larger volume and operate on lower profit margins.

Shortly thereafter, the commodities markets experienced a downturn; the price of everything "from gold to crude oil tumbled".[61] This impacted seriously upon Phibro since it was the commodities market leader. In 1983, Salomon's traders earned $463 million before taxes, while Phihro's earned $307 million. Consequently, Salomon's traders demanded control over the combined company. Gutfreund lobbied the board of the holding company to be named sole chief executive officer since, as his argument went, "his Salomon Brothers unit was producing most of the company's profits".[62] Tendler also appeared before the board in an attempt to be appointed sole chief executive. However, on October 5, 1984 Gutfreund was named sole CEO and Tendler resigned.

Shortly thereafter the Philipp Brothers trading unit was reduced to one third its former size, and the name of the holding company was changed from Phibro-Salomon to Salomon, Inc.[63] According to Gutfreund: "I was never out to consciously usurp Tendler's power or run a commodities company. Unfortunately, it became my job to do that. Tendler played a weak hand. When you do that and you lose, you're out."[64]

The Good Years

Almost immediately, Salomon became the undisputed leader in a number of low margin-high volume businesses, such as the underwriting of corporate bonds and trading in government securities and large blocks of stock.[65] In 1984, the firm was worldwide leader in underwriting securities, raising over $150 billion. Trading and sales reached $2.4 trillion, and total capital of the Salomon Brothers group was $1.7 billion at the end of the year.[66]

Gutfreund recognized and cultivated Salomon's ability to evaluate value and risk of a wide range of securities. He had confidence in Salomon traders and was willing to back them up with his balance sheet.[67] As a result, Salomon pioneered and dominated the multi-billion dollar mortgage-backed securities market. While competitors hesitated, Salomon made hundreds of millions of dollars in fixed-income arbitrage.[68]

In order to accommodate this growth in businesses, Salomon opted to increase the size of its staff. The Salomon MBA training class of 1985 signalled the beginning of this influx of increasing numbers of employees into Salomon Brothers. That year the company hired 127 trainees – by far the largest training class in Salomon's history. The 1986 class was twice as large.[69] The ratio of support staff to professional at this time, was 5:1, so that 127 new members meant the company hired 635 additional support staff. This increase in employees was dramatic in a firm of slightly more than 3,000 people.[70]

According to insiders, "nothing bound [these new employees] to the firm, except money and a strange belief that no other jobs in the world were worth doing. There were no deep and abiding loyalties to Salomon Brothers."[71] Seemingly in support of this view, within three years, 75 percent of this new class left "the Brothers" (compared with previous years when after three years, on average, 85 percent of the class was still with the firm).[72]

It was an era of seemingly uninhibited growth, fueled by bull runs in the stock and bond markets. The firm, which had employed two thousand people in 1982, had six thousand people by 1987.

Infighting at "The Brothers"

See Exhibit II for a list of the Salomon Business Units.

As this corporate-wide growth increased, Salomon's traders, salespeople and investment bankers focused on their own operations rather than the firm as a whole. As one insider put it, "competing fiefdoms replaced interconnected businesses."[73] Another former employee said, "Organizational structure at Salomon was something of a joke. In fact, organizational charts were not allowed – they were too disruptive. Making money was mostly what mattered."[74]

Bond Traders and Salesmen

Traders are responsible for both proprietary and flow trading. Proprietary trading involved trading securities using Salomon's own capital and inventories for profit. Flow trading was trading to satisfy the needs of the clients. Traders must continuously monitor market conditions and alter their quotes so that they do not get stuck with unwanted inventory.

Traders spend much of their time under intense pressure trying to extract information about likely price movements of the securities they are responsible for from the price movements of related instruments. In trying to gauge market sentiment they work closely with salespeople who deal with their institution's customers.

The salesperson's job is twofold: on the one hand, he or she tries to uncover information about the types of securities that institutional investors are most interested in buying or selling; and on the other hand, the salesperson attempts to convince the bank's customers to buy the securities that the bank has already acquired through the activities of its traders. Thus, salespeople provide information to traders about the sentiment within the investment community as well as creating an outlet for the securities that traders have acquired.

A trader, who quotes bids and offers for securities on a continuous basis and accommodates incoming purchase and sale orders, places bets in the markets on behalf of Salomon Brothers. A salesman is the trader's voice to most of the outside world. The salesman speaks with institutional investors such as pension funds and insurance companies. The basic skills required for the two jobs are quite different. Traders require market savvy. Salesmen require interpersonal skills.

Salomon, more than any other concern on Wall Street, was run by traders. This was because traders were the people closest to the money. Because of this, the trader was the person whom people admired, watched and attended.

> The traders ruled the shop...A salesman's year-end bonus was determined by traders. A salesman had no purchase on a trader, while a trader had complete control over a salesman.[75]

The Salomon trading floor was unique. It had minimal supervision, minimal controls, and no position limits. That is, a trader could buy or sell as many bonds as he thought appropriate without asking.[76]

There were three bond groups within Salomon Brothers: governments, corporates, and mortgages.

The Arbitrage Group

Another factor in the growing intra-group turmoil was the status of the arbitrage group. Led by John Meriwether – thought by many within Salomon to be the best bond trader on Wall Street – the "arb" group was one of Salomon's great success stories of the late 1980's.

Meriwether was one of the first to recognize that futures provided almost unlimited leverage for buying and selling securities by taking advantage of small differences in price.[77] It was also an easy way to sell securities that the firm did not own. Although other firms also recognized this potential, "Salomon was the only concern to back the strategy from the outset with very large bets."[78]

As interest rates began fluctuating in the late 1970's and early 1980's, Meriwether's arb operation began earning enormous profits. In 1981, it made in excess of $100 million – one-third of Salomon's profits.[79] Senior management reacted by committing more of Salomon's capital to allow Mr. Meriwether to place bigger and bigger bets.

Since arbitrage was an unusual trading strategy, Meriwether did not recruit typical Wall Street employees; rather, he recruited his team from academia. His team was young —they ranged in age from twenty-five to thirty-two.[80] Most of them had Ph.D.'s in math, economics, and/or physics. "Because their backgrounds and businesses differed from traditional traders, the "arb" group took on an elite aura at Salomon."[81] In addition, in order to protect the group's competitive edge, members were highly secretive about strategy and earnings.[82]

According to insiders, senior management fostered this elitism. "Arbs" were promoted more quickly than others at Salomon. "Meriwether developed his own customized analytical systems with personal computers, while other departments had to work through a central mainframe computer."[83]

In 1990 Gutfreund made a deal with the "arb" group to increase the salaries of its traders in order to keep them from leaving the company. The corporate and government traders were not included in this arrangement. Salomon etiquette had been violated. Historically, traders, regardless of function, have been compensated similarly, be they treasury or mortgage traders.

> A single [agreement] had thrown into doubt not only the compensation system but also the long-standing pecking order within Salomon Brothers. Money was the absolute measure of one's value to the firm. Paying a mortgage trader much more than a treasury trader made the treasury trader feel unwanted.[84]

Interestingly, Paul Mozer's illegal bidding activity increased greatly after this compensation deal became known. He submitted two bids in late December, just a few days after learning of the deal. He did it again on February 7 and February 21, 1991.

These conditions helped cultivate a we-vs.-them attitude within the "arb" group. Members complained about the firm's excesses, the lackluster performance of many of its businesses, and Gutfreund's weak management. They felt their performance was subsidizing the rest of the firm.[85]

Mortgage Trading Department

With the possible exception of the "arb" group, during the 1980's the mortgage traders at Salomon were the most powerful group. This was because the mortgage department, which was formed in 1978, was the most profitable area of the firm. The group was led by Lewis Ranieri, "the Salomon legend who began in the mailroom, worked his way onto the trading floor, and created a market in America for mortgage bonds."[86]

> He [Ranieri] didn't mind hiding a million-dollar loss from a manager, if that's what it took. He didn't let morality get in the way. It was not that he lacked values, but he had a keen sense that at times the ends justified the means and an equally keen sense of his own interests.[87]

Once the mortgage department was initially formed, its group met with increasing hostility from other departments within the firm, particularly the corporate and government bond trading units, led by Bill Voute and Tom Strauss, respectively:

> The upshot of the hostilities between the mortgage department and the two other powers of Salomon, corporate and government bond trading, was that everything in the mortgage department was separate: mortgage sales, mortgage finance, mortgage research, mortgage operations, and mortgage trading.[88]

According to Ranieri, "the reason everything was separate was because no one in the firm would help us. They wanted us to fail."[89]

This attitude quickly changed. On September 30, 1981, Congress passed a taxbreak which allowed thrifts (i.e., savings banks, savings and loan associations, and credit unions) to sell all their mortgage loans in order to put their money to work for higher returns. Subsequently, the volume of outstanding mortgage loans increased from 700 billion dollars in 1976 to 1.2 trillion in 1981, and the mortgage market surpassed the combined U.S. stock markets as the largest capital market in the world.

As it so happened, Salomon Brothers had the only fully staffed mortgage department on Wall Street. As a result of this tax break, the department became a thriving monopoly.[90] Although there are no official numbers available, it was widely accepted at Salomon that Ranieri's traders made $200 million in 1983 (40 percent of the firm's revenues), $175 million in 1984, and $275 million in 1985.[91]

During the mid-1980's, the American mortgage market continued to grow faster than any other capital market in the world, making mortgage traders extremely powerful. As it was the best job on the Salomon Brothers trading floor, it was also quite possibly the best job on Wall Street since the Salomon trading floor dominated Wall Street.[92]

Further exacerbating intra-group hostilities was the fact that the mortgage department had a culture all its own – one based on food and practical jokes. For instance, each Friday was "Food Frenzy" day, during which all trading ceased while enormous amounts of food were consumed. Telling too was the group motto, "we don't work for Salomon Brothers, we work for the mortgage department."[93] Ranieri preserved this culture by hosting events from which government and corporate traders were strictly prohibited.

The Corporate Finance Group

The Corporate Finance Group advised corporations on financing needs and strategies for raising new equity. Relationships were generally long term and between Salomon's client relationship managers and the clients' Chief Financial Officers.

Members of the Corporate Finance Group are notably different from members of other groups within Salomon, particularly traders. They each have a big glass office, a secretary, a large expense account and lots of meetings with captains of industry.[94] The group services the corporations and governments that borrow money. But because they don't risk money, corporate financiers are considered "wimps" by traders.[95]

The Equities Group

Salomon Brothers was the leading underwriter of new-stock issues on Wall Street and one of the two or three top equity traders, but "inside Salomon Brothers the men from equities were second-class citizens."[96] This was because, comparatively speaking, equities made no money.

The equity department was not on the 41st floor, the principal trading floor, but rather on the 40th. This floor had low ceilings and no windows. In fact, the fortieth floor was "more remote from the all-powerful forty-first than mere geography can suggest."[97] A separate bank of elevators serviced the 40th floor. People conversed all day between the two floors and yet never laid eyes on each other.[98]

Trading equities had once been Wall Street's greatest source of revenues. However that died with the end of fixed stock brokerage commissions came on May 1, 1975, after which, commissions collapsed. Investors often switched to whichever stockbroker charged them the least. As a result, in 1976, revenues across Wall Street fell by approximately six hundred million dollars. To add insult to injury, the bond market exploded. "With the rise of the bond markets, the equity salesmen and traders had been reduced by comparison to small-time toll takers."[99]

More Problems

Bonuses and Compensation

At the end of each year the people on the Salomon trading floor also became occupied with "trading their careers."[100] This was because year-end bonuses were not tied directly to one's profitability, but rather to the perception of one's value by the Salomon Brothers compensation committee headed by Gutfreund. At Salomon, total compensation for non-managing directors averaged along the lines of 40% base salary and 60% bonus.[101] The 139 managing directors (approximately 2% of the firm's employees) could earn up to $150,000 in salary and well over $1 million in bonus. The process of determining bonuses was often contested and was frequently described as "political," too centralized, and not dependent enough on clear criteria.[102]

Consequently, although no one's total pay was permitted to drop more than 20% from year to year, year-end bonuses were highly subjective.[103] This constant upward pressure on a firm's compensation expense was less of a concern during the intense growth of the early 1980s, but in 1986 and 1987 when revenues and profits declined, the pressure to maintain high compensation levels remained.[104]

It would appear that Mr. Gutfreund's attitudes toward compensation were formed when Salomon was a partnership. In that type of system, traders were required to keep a substantial portion of their wealth in the firm. If the partner left the firm, he forfeited a portion of his investment. But after the Phillips merger, the partnership arrangement was dissolved. Therefore, when the new generation of traders produced millions for the firm, they demanded a percentage of the millions that they made for the company. Gutfreund had no intention of paying anyone "a cut."

Salomon's CEO openly criticized what he termed the considerable greed of the younger generation.[105] In a 1985 *Business Week* interview, he told the reporter, "I don't understand what goes on inside their pointy little heads."[106] These comments only served to anger his employees, since Gutfreund was the highest paid chief executive on Wall Street.

The inability of Salomon management to solve this compensation issue caused traders and senior executives to leave the company in ever increasing numbers. This was particularly true with mortgage traders, who had made a fortune for Salomon Brothers in 1984, while the firm as a whole had not done well. The competition was willing to pay them million dollar plus salaries, while Gutfreund was not.

In addition to the compensation issue, Salomon management was now faced with another problem: the traders who left Salomon provided the competition not only with trading skills and market understanding but also with a complete list of Salomon Brothers' clients. It is estimated that the transfer of skills and information cost Salomon hundreds of millions of dollars. And by allowing Salomon mortgage traders to leave and work for the competition, Salomon Brothers "let slip through its fingers the rarest and most valuable asset a Wall Street firm can possess: a monopoly."[107]

Installing Management Control

The year 1986 was a poor one for Salomon, and 1987 was worse as revenues ceased to grow and costs increased dramatically. Salomon's less than stellar performance got Mr. Gutfreund's attention. In 1986, a board of executives was established, consisting mainly of former traders. Above this layer Gutfreund created a new Office of the Chairman, in order to streamline decision making. To this office Gutfreund appointed Lewis Ranieri, Bill Voute, and Tom Strauss.

Gutfreund also wanted to name investment banking chief Jay F. Higgins to the new office. But when he indicated to Stanley B. Shopkorn – the head of equities – that he planned to appoint Higgins to the new office, employees witnessed a confrontation that "sent Gutfreund scurrying from the room."[108] The next day, Mr. Gutfreund announced that Shopkorn would also be a part of the chairman's office. The effort to streamline Salomon's leadership failed.

In addition to the formation of the OOC, task forces were created to evaluate which businesses were profitable and what to include in each business's strategic plan. As a result of their findings, Salomon's board of directors made three very important decisions. First, Salomon, the nation's largest underwriter of municipal securities would leave the municipal business. In addition, the firm would also vacate the commercial paper business, which dealt in short-term corporate securities. Lastly, the board decided to reduce the firm's head count by 12%, both in numbers of employees and dollars.[109]

Monitoring Costs

Another issue that had to be addressed was the fact that Salomon Brothers was the only major firm on Wall Street in the early 1980s with no system for allocating costs. Not only did this make budgeting and planning impossible, but it also gave unit heads license to spend whatever they could to build revenues. No measure was taken of the bottom line; people were judged by the sum total of the revenues on their trading books irrespective of what costs were incurred to generate those revenues. Net profits were not the focus. Trading managers were rewarded for indiscriminate growth. With trading revenues came glory and advancement at every level of the company. Gross revenues meant power.[110]

It is not surprising then, that costs were most out of control in the mortgage department, the place were there had been so much revenue. In fact, many mortgage traders felt that since they were underpaid – and Ranieri agreed with this assessment – the Salomon Brothers' expense account could be used to supplement their income. "We'd lend our telephone charge cards out to friends...people would use Salomon limos to take their wives shopping on the weekends."[111]

In 1986, Salomon's expenses increased 40 percent. Therefore in an effort to pare down Salomon's costs, Gutfreund appointed Don Howard, Citicorp's former Chief Financial Officer, to be the firm's CFO in 1988. He was to be responsible for monitoring the firm's nearly 20 billion dollars in daily transactions. Under his leadership a business unit approach was instituted within the organization. Under this arrangement, each business unit would have one head and would be responsible for its own financial support and systems development people. Additionally, each unit would have to submit budgets, business analysis reports, and business plans to the OOC. Semiannual forecasts of significant changes affecting the business would be prepared, as well as forecasts of anticipated performance for the next six months.

Management also developed new financial systems that could calculate profits for the new, complex products that the firm offered. Finally, a new revenue measurement system was defined that was intended to help senior management assess which businesses were profitable and where to allocate resources.

Despite this new emphasis on cost, Salomon management determined that new offices were needed to accommodate the increased staff. Therefore, the firm began construction of the biggest, most expensive real estate project to date in Manhattan. The company eventually discontinued the project at a cost of $107 million.

Good Intentions, Bad Implementation

It quickly became known that the Office of the Chairman was divisive. In essence it was a continuation of the battle between the three debt departments, with Strauss representing the government department, Voute representing the corporate department and Ranieri representing the mortgage department.[112] As an insider noted, "Around here you are in the Strauss family, the Ranieri family, or the Voute family. Few have been in more than one."[113] Ultimately, Strauss and Voute had Ranieri fired in 1987. Eventually the mortgage department was shut down.

Additionally, in order to cut costs, management fired or forced resignations of hundreds of accountants, computer programmers and other back-office technicians. This staff had provided an effective counterbalance to the firm's excesses of the 1980s. It had slowed some of the firm's growth by delaying new products that Salomon's back office was unable to support.

> The staff also rooted out problems before they erupted. For example, a routine audit discovered what could have been a major embarrassment to the firm: that it owned an interest in one of the largest brothels in Manila, the Philippines.[114]

In direct relation to the purging of the back-office staff is the fact that Salomon's control system should have detected Mr. Mozer's illegal trading activity by sending confirmations of trades to the clients in whose name they were made. A copy should have been sent to the salesmen responsible for those clients. And the trades should have shown up in internal sales reports. Mr. Mozer was able to avoid detection because Salomon's technology modernization program in the 1980s had become captive to the heads of its various operations, who were more concerned with controlling costs than having close scrutiny of their actions.[115]

The Revlon Assault

In the fall of 1987, corporate raider Ronald O. Perleman made an unsolicited, hostile bid for Salomon, backed by Drexel Burnham Lambert, Inc. It was the first time Wall Street had turned and attacked its own.[116]

There have been several theories as to why Perleman attempted to takeover Salomon. The one most frequently cited is that Drexel's junk bond king, and Perleman's true backer, Michael Milken, was taking revenge on Gutfreund. In early 1985 Milken went to Salomon's offices for a breakfast meeting with Gutfreund. Milken became angry because Gutfreund refused to speak to him as an equal. The meeting ended in a shouting match, with Milken being escorted from the building by security. In addition, Gutfreund excluded Drexel from all Salomon Brothers bond deals.[117]

To make matters worse, when Drexel found itself embroiled in an SEC investigation, a Salomon Brothers managing director mailed to Milken's clients copies of legal complaints (for extortion and racketeering) filed against Milken by three other clients.[118]

The relationship was further worsened by the fact that Drexel Burnham had replaced Salomon as Wall Street's most profitable investment bank in 1986. The company had made $545.5 million in profit on revenues of $4 billion, more than Salomon had ever made. It was making its fortune in junk bonds – a notion that was particularly disturbing to Salomon traders since they had failed to see how important junk bonds would become.[119]

Gutfreund had been aware for some time that, Minorco Corporation —Salomon's largest shareholder with a 14 percent interest – wanted to sell its holdings, but he had been slow to accommodate Minorco. Impatient, Minorco advertised its Salomon shares through other Wall Street institutions. Revlon Inc. was an interested buyer.

Even more alarming was the fact that, aside from the 14 percent share, Perleman wanted to buy an additional 11 percent stake in Salomon. If Perleman was successful, Gutfreund would no longer be in charge of "the Brothers."

The fact that Salomon was targeted for takeover personally hurt Gutfreund. "I see Salomon as occupying a special place in the financial system, and that was now in jeopardy."[120]

Taking action, Gutfreund found a friendly buyer to purchase the shares in question. He turned to an old friend of his, Warren E. Buffett, the chairman of Berkshire Hathaway Inc. Salomon sold Mr. Buffett $700 million in newly created convertible preferred stock, using the proceeds to buy the common stock Mr. Perleman had targeted. Not only did the stock pay 9 percent interest, it could be converted into common stock for $38 a share at anytime before 1996.[121] The result of the deal was that Buffett had little risk, but a huge potential profit. Salomon, on the other hand, was left with 109 million dollars less in capital and an annual bill of 63 million dollars for the dividends on Buffett's stock.

The Week The Stock Market Crashed

On October 12, 1987, an unknown board member of Salomon Brothers informed a *New York Times* reporter that the firm was planning to fire one thousand people. The news was completely unexpected by members of the company. Although employees were aware that a review of Salomon's businesses was underway, they were assured that everyone's job was safe.

That afternoon, two entire departments on the 41st floor, municipal bonds and money markets, were eliminated; 800 jobs were lost. Gutfreund told the press, and his employees, that he had intended to move carefully in determining who should be laid off. However, he felt that once the story hit the papers he had been forced to take quick action. Who leaked the story is still unclear since from his first day as a trainee to his last, a Salomon Brothers employee believes it is a cardinal sin to speak to the press.

Black Monday

When the stock market fell 508 points on October 19, 1987, Salomon Brothers lost $75 million in after-tax earnings for the month.[122] The firm's losses could have been mitigated however, by the fact that investors were taking money out of equities and putting it into the money markets. Had Salomon maintained their money market department, they could have taken advantage of this windfall. The decline in business after the crash occurred mainly in the equity markets. The one and only department that Salomon did not restructure was its equity department. In fact, the one glaring loss by Salomon occurred because the firm had agreed to purchase from the British government, and distribute worldwide, 31.5 percent of the shares in British Petroleum. Salomon lost more than 100 million dollars on this deal due to the crash.

As a result of the firm's losses, bonuses of top executives were cut. It was the first year since Salomon became public that bonuses actually declined. Gutfreund led the way by opting not to take a bonus at all. Instead, he received his $300,000 annual salary, plus $800,000 of cash deferred from 1984. However, in lieu of a bonus, he received 300,000 options for Salomon stock.[123]

Overall, for the year Salomon suffered its worst earnings performance of the decade, earning only $142 million, a 3.7 percent return on equity.[124] The firm experienced flat or declining revenues in many of its businesses. Compensation expenses had risen tremendously. And Salomon was shocked to learn that its work force had increased by 40% between January 1986 and June 1987. As the *New York Times* wrote on January 10, 1988, "Salomon became a glaring corporate victim of Wall Street's extended mad rush to expand."[125]

The company's financial position continued to decline in 1988. Salomon's net income was $280 million for the year. In reaction to Salomon's steady decline, Gutfreund admitted that fundamental changes should be instituted within the firm. He admitted that he and his executives had been slow to react to changes in the industry. He said, "the world changed in some fundamental ways, and most of us were not on top of it. We were dragged into the modern world."[126]

If Gutfreund recognized the need for fundamental changes within the firm, and sought to institute them, why did the Mozer incident occur?

EPILOGUE

On May 20, 1992, the U.S. Attorney's office for the Southern District of New York, the Antitrust Division of the U.S. Department of Justice and the SEC announced a resolution, without criminal charges, of their investigations into the Salomon Brothers illegal bidding. As a result, Salomon Brothers Inc. paid a total of $290 million: $100 million into a fund for the payment of private compensatory damage claims and $190 million to the United States for penalties and claimed damages and forfeitures. Salomon Brothers Inc. also agreed to an SEC injunction. Based on this resolution, the U.S. Federal Reserve Bank of New York announced its decision to retain Salomon Brothers' designation as a primary dealer.

The Federal Reserve Bank sanctioned Salomon by suspending the firm from trading activity with the Federal Reserve for two months, from June 1, 1992 until August 3, 1992.

Notes

1 Peter Grant and Marcia Parker, "Hurtling Toward Scandal," *Crain's New York Business* June 1-7, 1992, p. 20

2 Robert Sobel, *Salomon Brothers 1910-85: Advancing to Leadership* (Salomon Brothers Inc,1986), p. xi

3 Statement of Salomon Inc. submitted before the Securities Subcommittee, Committee on Banking, Housing and Urban Affairs, U.S. Senate, September 10, 1991: p. 19

4 Supplemental Report of Salomon, Inc. to the Federal Reserve Bank of New York, September 27, 1991, p. 10

5 Ibid.

6 Ibid., p. 11

7 Ibid.

8 Salomon Brothers Inc. press release, August 14, 1991, p. 3

9 Peter Grant and Marcia Parker, "Hurtling Toward Scandal," *Crain's New York Business* June 1-7, 1992, p. 3

10 Ibid., p. 20

11 Robert Sobel, *Salomon Brothers 1910-85: Advancing to Leadership* (Salomon Brothers Inc, 1986), p. 3

12 Ibid., p. 8

13 Ibid., p. 33

14 Ibid., p. 115

15 Ibid., p. 118

16 Ibid.

17 Ibid.

18 Ibid., p. 119

19 James Sterngold, "Too Far, Too Fast." *The New York Times Magazine,* January 10, 1988, p. 2

20 Robert Sobel, *Salomon Brothers 1910-85: Advancing to Leadership* (Salomon Brothers Inc, 1986), p. 83

21 Ibid., p. 98

22 Michael Lewis, *Liar's Poker* (W.W. Norton & Co., New York, 1989), p. 34

23 James Sterngold, "Too Far, Too Fast." *The New York Times Magazine,* January 10, 1988, p. 2

24 Ibid., p. 4

25 Ibid.

26 Ibid.

27 Ibid.

28 Michael Lewis, *Liar's Poker* (W.W. Norton & Co., New York, 1989), p. 59

29 Peter Grant and Marcia Parker, "Hurtling Toward Scandal," *Crain's New York Business* June 1-7, 1992, p. 3

30 Ibid., p. 6

31 Ibid.

32 Ibid.

33 Michael Lewis, *Liar's Poker* (W.W. Norton & Co., New York, 1989), p. 15

34 James Sterngold, "Too Far, Too Fast." *The New York Times Magazine,* January 10, 1988, p. 2

35 Michael Lewis, *Liar's Poker* (W.W. Norton & Co., New York, 1989), p. 59

36 Ibid., p. 35

37 Ibid.

38 Ibid., p. 36

39 Ibid.

40 Robert Sobel, *Salomon Brothers 1910-85: Advancing to Leadership* (Salomon Brothers Inc, 1986), p. 180

41 Ibid., p. 183

42 Ibid.

43 Ibid., p. 184

44 Ibid.

45 Ibid.

46 Ibid., p. 185

47 Ibid., p. 187

48 James Sterngold, "Too Far, Too Fast." *The New York Times Magazine,* January 10, 1988, p. 4

49 Ibid., p. 2

50 Ibid., p. 4

51 Ibid.

52 Robert Sobel, *Salomon Brothers 1910-85: Advancing to Leadership* (Salomon Brothers Inc, 1986), p. 170

53 Ibid., p. 171

54 Ibid., p. 174

55 James Sterngold, "Too Far, Too Fast." *The New York Times Magazine,* January 10, 1988, p. 4

56 Ibid.

57 Robert Sobel, *Salomon Brothers 1910-85: Advancing to Leadership* (Salomon Brothers Inc, 1986), p. 174

58 Ibid.

59 James Sterngold, "Too Far, Too Fast." *The New York Times Magazine,* January 10, 1988, p. 4

60 Ibid.

61 Ibid.

62 Ibid., p. 5

63 Ibid.

64 Ibid.

65 Ibid.

66 Ibid.

67 Ibid.

68 Ibid.

69 Michael Lewis, *Liar's Poker* (W.W. Norton & Co., New York, 1989), p. 38

70 Ibid.

71 Ibid.

72 Ibid.

73 Peter Grant and Marcia Parker, "Hurtling Toward Scandal," *Crain's New York Business* June 1-7, 1992, p. 6

74 Michael Lewis, *Liar's Poker* (W.W. Norton & Co., New York, 1989), p. 40

75 Ibid., p. 68

76 Ibid., p. 109

77 Peter Grant and Marcia Parker, "Hurtling Toward Scandal," *Crain's New York Business* June 1-7, 1992, p. 9

78 Ibid.

79 Ibid., p. 10

80 Michael Lewis, *Liar's Poker* (W.W. Norton & Co., New York, 1989), p. 15

81   Peter Grant and Marcia Parker, "Hurtling Toward Scandal," *Crain's New York Business* June 1-7, 1992, p. 10

82 Ibid.

83 Ibid.

84 Ibid.

85 Michael Lewis, *Liar's Poker* (W.W. Norton & Co., New York, 1989), p. 77

86 Ibid., p. 90

87 Ibid., p. 101

88 Ibid.

89 Ibid., p. 104

90 Ibid., p. 108

91 Ibid., p. 81

92 Ibid., p. 120

93 Ibid., p. 19

94 Ibid.

95 Ibid., p. 61

96 Ibid., p. 62

97 Ibid.

98 Ibid., p. 63

99 Ibid., p. 62

100 Ibid., p. 126

101 Peter Grant and Marcia Parker, "Hurtling Toward Scandal," *Crain's New York Business* June 1-7, 1992, p. 13

102 Ibid.

103 Ibid.

104 Ibid.

105 Michael Lewis, *Liar's Poker* (W.W. Norton & Co., New York, 1989), p. 127

106 Ibid., p. 132

107 Ibid., p. 136

108 Peter Grant and Marcia Parker, "Hurtling Toward Scandal," *Crain's New York Business* June 1-7, 1992, p. 7

109 Ibid.

110 Michael Lewis, *Liar's Poker* (W.W. Norton & Co., New York, 1989), p. 109

111 Ibid., p. 143

112 Ibid., p. 141

113 Ibid.

114 Peter Grant and Marcia Parker, "Hurtling Toward Scandal," *Crain's New York Business* June 1-7, 1992, p. 16

115 Michael Lewis, *Liar's,Poker* (W.W. Norton & Co., New York, 1989), p. 141

116 James Sterngold, "Too Far, Too Fast." *The New York Times Magazine,* January 10, 1988, p. 54

117 Michael Lewis, *Liar's Poker* (W.W. Norton & Co., New York, 1989), p. 208

118 Ibid.

119 Ibid., p. 211

120 James Sterngold, "Too Far, Too Fast." *The New York Times Magazine*, January 10, 1988, p.5

121 Michael Lewis, *Liar's Poker* (W.W. Norton & Co., New York, 1989), p. 225

122 James Sterngold, "Too Far, Too Fast." *The New York Times Magazine,* January 10, 1988, p.1

123 Ibid.

124 Michael Lewis, *Liar's Poker* (W.W. Norton & Co., New York, 1989), p. 245

125 James Sterngold, "Too Far, Too Fast." *The New York Times Magazine,* January 10, 1988, p.1

126 Ibid.

127 Statement of Salomon Inc. submitted before the Securities Subcommittee, Committee on Banking, Housing and Urban Affairs, U.S. Senate, September 10, 1991, p. 6

128 Company records.

129 Michael L. Goldstein, Strategic Decisions Conference, "Disequilibrium on Wall Street: The State of the Industry," May 31-June 1, 1989, New York.

EXHIBIT I

The Treasury Auction Rules – Pre-1990"[127]

Treasury rules prohibit a bidder at a Treasury auction from purchasing more than 35% of the total amount of the securities available on a competitive and noncompetitive basis for purchase by the public. Under the rules in effect before July 1990, the Treasury would award no more than 35% of the securities publicly available for purchase at the auction to any single bidder, but would recognize bids in excess of 35% of the public offering at any particular yield. Under those pre-July 1990 rules, a bidder might decide to submit a bid for more than 35% to increase its chances of being awarded the 35% maximum purchase amount in the event of proration — the process by which auction securities are divided proportionately among all bids at the highest yield accepted at the auction.

For example, if $10 billion in Treasury securities were being auctioned, a bidder might bid for $5 billion – 50% of the offering amount – at a particular yield. Under the pre-July 1990 auction rules, if the bids at that yield were prorated at a 70% rate, the bidder would have been awarded $3.5 billion in securities – the maximum award allowable – because the Treasury would have prorated the bidder's award based upon its entire $5 billion bid. If the bids at that yield were instead prorated at an 85% rate, the bidder still would have been awarded only the 35% maximum purchase amount, or $3.5 billion, because of the Treasury's 35% purchase-limit rule.

As a result of the proration process, Salomon, like other bidders, was from time to time awarded a smaller amount of the securities offered at a given auction than it hoped to purchase. In a July 1990 auction of 30-year bonds of the Resolution Funding Corporation, Mr. Mozer submitted a bid well in excess of 100% of the amount of bonds being auctioned, apparently in the hope of achieving a higher award in the event of proration. The Treasury viewed Mr. Mozer's conduct as inappropriate, and rejected Salomon's bid.

Following this auction, in July 1990 the Treasury announced changes in its auction rules.

The Treasury Auction Rules – Post-1990

Under the new rules, the Treasury does not recognize amounts tendered by a single bidder at any one yield level in excess of 35% of the amount of securities available at an auction for purchase by the public. Any bid submitted by a single bidder for an amount greater than the 35% limit at any one yield is reduced by the Treasury to the 35% amount. Thus, in the example given above, the bid for $5 billion of the $10 billion in securities being auction would be treated by the Treasury as a bid for $3.5 billion, and proration at 70% would result in an award of only $2.45 billion.

In announcing these rule changes in July 1990, the Treasury maintained its prior rule limiting the total actual purchases by any one bidder, at all yields, to 35% of the securities available for purchase by the public at an auction.

Paul Mozer was publicly critical of both the Treasury's new 35% bid-limit rule and the Treasury's actions in adopting the new rule without first consulting with primary dealers. He was critical of Michael Basham, Deputy Assistant Treasury Secretary for Federal Finance, who supervised auctions at the Treasury, and the new 35% bid-limit rule became known to many on Wall Street as the "Mozer/Basham" rule.

EXHIBIT II

Salomon Brothers Business Units – 1989[128]

Business Unit	Head of Unit
Domestic Equities	Shopkorn/Hackett
Domestic Fixed Income:	Meriwether
Domestic Corporate Debt	Hazeltine
Government Trading	Mozer
Mortgage Trading	Haupt
New York Arbitrage	Hilibrand/Rosenfeld
Firm Finance	MacFarlane
Foreign Exchange	Lipschultz
High Yield	Tyrse
Merchant Banking	Zimmerman
Real Estate	Manolis
Asset Management	Holland
Investment Banking	Higgins/Higdon
Fixed Income Sales	McIntosh
Research	Brock/Leibowitz
Support	Carp
Business Technology Org.	Dramis
Operations	Lambiase
Facilities Management	White
General Services	Wallace
Human Resources	Weihenmayer
Financial	Howard
London/Europe	Massey
Tokyo/Asia	Maughan

EXHIBIT III

Industry Profits by Market Segment[129]

Institutional	1986	1988
Sales & Trading	20%	12%
Underwriting	20	17
M&A Advisory, LBO Finance	20	33
Proprietary Trading	10	18
Retail		
Brokerage	13	-12
Asset Management	8	19
Other	9	12
Total	100	100

6. Roger Boisjoly and the Challenger Disaster: The Ethical Dimensions*

Preview for Disaster

On January 24, 1985, Roger Boisjoly, Senior Scientist at Morton Thiokol, watched the launch of Flight 51-C of the space shuttle program. He was at Cape Canaveral to inspect the solid rocket boosters from Flight 51-C following their recovery in the Atlantic Ocean and to conduct a training session at Kennedy Space Center (KSC) on the proper methods of inspecting the booster joints. While watching the launch, he noted that the temperature that day was much cooler than recorded at other launches, but was still much warmer than the 18 degree temperature encountered three days earlier when he arrived in Orlando. The unseasonably cold weather of the past several days had produced the worst citrus crop failures in Florida history.

When he inspected the solid rocket boosters several days later, Boisjoly discovered evidence that the primary O-ring seals on two field joints had been compromised by hot combustion gases (i.e., hot gas blow-by had occurred) which had also eroded part of the primary O-ring. This was the first time that a primary seal on a field joint had been penetrated. When he discovered the large amount of blackened grease between the primary and secondary seals, his concern heightened. The blackened grease was discovered over 80 degree and 110 degree arcs, respectively, on two of the seals, with the larger are indicating greater hot gas blow-by. Post-flight calculations indicated that the ambient temperature of the field joints at launch time was 53 degrees. This evidence, coupled with his recollection of the low temperature the day of the launch and the citrus crop damage caused by the cold spell, led to his conclusion that the severe hot gas blow-by may have been caused by, and related to, low temperature. After reporting these findings to his superiors, Boisjoly presented them to engineers and management at NASA's Marshall Space Flight Center (MSFC). As a result of his presentation at MSFC, Roger Boisjoly was asked to participate in the Flight Readiness Review (FRR) on February 12, 1985, for Flight 51-E which was scheduled for launch in April, 1985. This FRR represents the first association of low temperature with blow-by on a field joint, a condition that was considered an "acceptable risk" by Larry Mulloy, NASA's Manager for the Booster Project, and other NASA officials.

Roger Boisjoly had twenty-five years of experience as an engineer in the aerospace industry. Among his many notable assignments were the performance of stress and deflection analysis on the flight control equipment of the Advanced Minuteman Missile at Autonetics, and serving as a lead engineer on the lunar module of Apollo at Hamilton Standard. He moved to Utah in 1980 to take a position in the Applied Mechanics Department as a Staff Engineer at the Wasatch Division of Morton Thiokol. He was considered the leading expert in the United States on O-rings and rocket joint seals and received plaudits for his work on the joint seal problem from Joe C. Kilminster, Vice President of Space Booster Programs, Morton Thiokol.

*Journal of Business Ethics 8: 217 – 230, 1989. © 1989 Kluwer Academic Publishers. Printed in the Netherlands. Reprinted by permission of Kluwer Academic Publishers and the authors: Russel P. Boisjoly, Fairfield University; Ellen Foster Curtis, University of Lowell; and Eugene Mellican, University of Lowell.

His commitment to the company and the community was further demonstrated by his service as Mayor of Willard, Utah from 1982 to 1983.

The tough questioning he received at the February 12th FRR convinced Boisjoly of the need for further evidence linking low temperature and hot gas blow-by. He worked closely with Arnie Thompson, Supervisor of Rocket Motor Cases, who conducted subscale laboratory tests in March, 1985, to further test the effects of temperature on O-ring resiliency. The bench tests that were performed provided powerful evidence to support Boisjoly's and Thompson's theory: Low temperatures greatly and adversely affected the ability of O-rings to create a seal on solid rocket booster joints. If temperature was too low (and they did not know what the threshold temperature would be), it was possible that neither the primary or secondary O-rings would seal!

One month later the post-flight inspection of Flight 51-B revealed that the primary seal of a booster nozzle joint did not make contact during its two-minute flight. If this damage had occurred in a field joint, the secondary O-ring may have failed to seal, causing the loss of the flight. As a result, Boisjoly and his colleagues became increasingly concerned about shuttle safety. This evidence from the inspection of Flight 51-B was presented at the FRR for Flight 51-F on July 1, 1985; the key engineers and managers at NASA and Morton Thiokol were now aware of the critical O-ring problems and the influence of low temperature on the performance of the joint seals.

During July, 1985, Boisjoly and his associates voiced their desire to devote more effort and resources to solving the problems of O-ring erosion. In his activity reports dated July 22 and 29, 1985, Boisjoly expressed considerable frustration with the lack of progress in this area, despite the fact that a Seal Erosion Task Force had been informally appointed on July 19th. Finally, Boisjoly wrote the following memo, labeled "Company Private," to R. K. (Bob) Lund, Vice President of Engineering for Morton Thiokol, to express the extreme urgency of his concerns. Here are some excerpts from that memo:

> This letter is written to insure that management is fully aware of the seriousness of the current O-ring erosion problem ... The mistakenly accepted position on the joint problem was to fly without fear of failure ... is now drastically changed as a result of the SRM 16A nozzle joint erosion which eroded a secondary O-ring with the primary O-ring never sealing. If the same scenario should occur in a field joint (and it could), then it is a jump ball as to the success or failure of the joint ... The result would be a catastrophe of the highest order – loss of human life...
>
> It is my honest and real fear that if we do not take immediate action to dedicate a team to solve the problem, with the field joint having the number one priority, then we stand in jeopardy of losing a flight along with all the launch pad facilities.

On August 20, 1985, R. K. Lund formally announced the formation of the Seal Erosion Task Team. The team consisted of only five full-time engineers from the 2500 employed by Morton Thiokol on the Space Shuttle Program. The events of the next five months would demonstrate that management had not provided the resources necessary to carry out the enormous task of solving the seal erosion problem.

On October 3, 1985, the Seal Erosion Task Force met with Joe Kilminster to discuss the problems they were having in gaining organizational support necessary to solve the O-ring problems. Boisjoly later stated that Kilminster summarized the meeting as a "good bullshit session." Once again frustrated by bureaucratic inertia, Boisjoly wrote in his activity report dated October 4th:

> ... NASA is sending an engineering representative to stay with us starting Oct. 14th. We feel that this is a direct result of their feeling that we (MTI) are not responding quickly enough to the seal problem ... upper management apparently feels that the SRM program is ours for sure and the customer be damned.

Boisjoly was not alone in his expression of frustration. Bob Ebeling, Department Manager, Solid Rocket Motor Igniter and Final Assembly and a member of the Seal Erosion Task Force, wrote in a memo to Allan McDonald, Manager of the Solid Rocket Motor Project, "HELP! The seal task force is constantly being delayed by every possible means ... We wish we could get action by verbal request, but such is not the case. This is a red flag."

At the Society of Automotive Engineers (SAE) conference on October 7, 1985, Boisjoly presented a six-page overview of the joints and the seal configuration to approximately 130 technical experts in hope of soliciting suggestions for remedying the O-ring problems. Although MSFC had requested the presentation, NASA gave strict instructions not to express the critical urgency of fixing the joints, but merely to ask for suggestions for improvement. Although no help was forthcoming, the conference was a milestone in that it was the first time that NASA allowed information on the O-ring difficulties to be expressed in a public forum. That NASA also recognized that the O-ring problems were not receiving appropriate attention and manpower consideration from Morton Thiokol management is further evidenced by Boisjoly's October 24 log entry, "... Jerry Peoples (NASA) has informed his people that our group needs more authority and people to do the job. Jim Smith (NASA) will corner Al McDonald today to attempt to implement this direction."

The October 30 launch of Flight 61-A of the Challenger provided the most convincing, and yet to some the most contestable, evidence to date that low temperature was directly related to hot gas blow-by. The left booster experienced hot gas blow-by in the center and aft field joints without any seal erosion. The ambient temperature of the field joints was estimated to be 75 degrees at launch time based on post-flight calculations. Inspection of the booster joints revealed that the blow-by was less severe than that found on Flight 51-C because the seal grease was a grayish black color, rather than the jet black hue of Flight 51-C. The evidence was now consistent with the bench tests for joint resiliency conducted in March. That is, at 75 degrees the O-ring lost contact with its sealing surface for 2.4 seconds, whereas at 50 degrees the O-ring lost contact for 10 minutes. The actual flight data revealed greater hot gas blow-by for the O-rings on Flight 51-C which had an ambient temperature of 53 degrees than for Flight 61-A which had an ambient temperature of 75 degrees. Those who rejected this line of reasoning concluded that temperature must be irrelevant since hot gas blow-by had occurred even at room temperature (75 degrees). This difference in interpretation would receive further attention on January 27, 1986.

During the next two and one-half months, little progress was made in obtaining a solution to the O-ring problems. Roger Boisjoly made the following entry into his log on January 13, 1986, "O-ring resiliency tests that were requested on September 24, 1985 are now scheduled for January 15, 1986."

The Day Before the Disaster

At 10 a.m. on January 27, 1986, Arnie Thompson received a phone call from Boyd Brinton, Thiokol's Manager of Project Engineering at MSFC, relaying the concerns of NASA's Larry Wear, also at MSFC, about the 18 degree temperature forecast for the launch of Flight 51-L, the Challenger, scheduled for the next day. This phone call precipitated a series of meetings within Morton Thiokol; at the Marshall Space Flight Center; and at the Kennedy Space Center that culminated in a three-way telecon, involving three teams of engineers and managers, that began at 8:15 p.m. E.S.T.

Joe Kilminster, Vice President, Space Booster Programs, of Morton Thiokol began the telecon by turning the presentation of the engineering charts over to Roger Boisjoly and Arnie Thompson. They presented thirteen charts which resulted in a recommendation against the launch of the Challenger. Boisjoly demonstrated their concerns with the performance of the O-rings in the field joints during the initial phases of Challenger's flight with charts showing the effects of primary O-ring erosion, and its timing, on the ability to maintain a reliable secondary seal. The tremendous pressure and release of power from the rocket boosters create rotation in the joint such that the metal moves away from the O-rings so that they cannot maintain contact with the metal surfaces. If, at the same time, erosion occurs in the primary O-ring for any reason, then there is a reduced probability of maintaining a secondary seal. It is highly probable that as the ambient temperature drops, the primary O-ring will not seat; that there will be hot gas blow-by and erosion of the primary O-ring; and that a catastrophe will occur when the secondary O-ring fails to seal.

Bob Lund presented the final chart that included the Morton Thiokol recommendations that the ambient temperature including wind must be such that the seal temperature would be greater than 53 degrees to proceed with the launch. Since the overnight low was predicted to be 18 degrees, Bob Lund recommended against launch on January 28, 1986 or until the seal temperature exceeded 53 degrees.

NASA's Larry Mulloy bypassed Bob Lund and directly asked Joe Kilminster for his reaction. Kilminster stated that he supported the position of his engineers and he would not recommend launch below 53 degrees.

George Hardy, Deputy Director of Science and Engineering at MSFC, said he was "appalled at that recommendation," according to Allan McDonald's testimony before the Rogers Commission. Nevertheless, Hardy would not recommend to launch if the contractor was against it. After Hardy's reaction, Stanley Reinartz, Manager of Shuttle Project Office at MSFC, objected by pointing out that the solid rocket motors were qualified to operate between 40 and 90 degrees Fahrenheit.

Larry Mulloy, citing the data from Flight 61-A which indicated to him that temperature was not a factor, strenuously objected to Morton Thiokol's recommendation. He suggested that Thiokol was attempting to establish new Launch Commit Criteria at 53 degrees and that they couldn't do that the night before a launch. In exasperation Mulloy asked, "My God, Thiokol, when do you want me to launch? Next April?" Although other NASA officials also objected to the association of temperature with O-ring erosion and hot gas blow-by, Roger Boisjoly was able to hold his ground and demonstrate with the use of his charts and pictures that there was indeed a relationship: The lower the temperature the higher the probability of erosion and blow-by and the greater the likelihood of an accident. Finally, Joe Kilminster asked for a five-minute caucus off-net.

According to Boisjoly's testimony before the Rogers Commission, Jerry Mason, Senior Vice President of Wasatch Operations, began the caucus by saying that "a management decision was necessary." Sensing that an attempt would be made to overturn the no-launch decision, Boisjoly and Thompson attempted to re-review the material previously presented to NASA for the executives in the room. Thompson took a pad of paper and tried to sketch out the problem with the joint, while Boisjoly laid out the photos of the compromised joints from Flights 51-C and 61-A. When they became convinced that no one was listening, they ceased their efforts. As Boisjoly would later testify, "There was not one positive pro-launch statement ever made by anybody." (Report of the Presidential Commission, 1986, IV, p. 792, hereafter abbreviated as R.C.)

According to Boisjoly, after he and Thompson made their last attempts to stop the launch, Jerry Mason asked rhetorically, "Am I the only one who wants to fly?" Mason turned to Bob Lund and asked him to "take off his engineering hat and put on his management hat." The four managers held a brief discussion and voted unanimously to recommend Challenger's launch.

Exhibit 1 shows the revised recommendations that were presented that evening by Joe Kilminster after the caucus to support management's decision to launch. Only one of the rationales presented that evening supported the launch (Demonstrated erosion sealing threshold is three times greater than 0.038" erosion experienced on SRM-15). Even so, the issue at hand was sealability at low temperature, not erosion. While one other rationale could be considered a neutral statement of engineering fact (O-ring pressure leak check places secondary seal in out board position which minimizes sealing time), the other seven rationales are negative, anti-launch, statements. After hearing Kilminster's presentation, which was accepted without a single probing question, George Hardy asked him to sign the chart and telefax it to Kennedy Space Center and Marshall Space Flight Center. At 11 p.m. E.S.T. the teleconference ended.

Aside from the four senior Morton Thiokol executives present at the teleconference, all others were excluded from the final decision. The process represented a radical shift from previous NASA policy. Until that moment, the burden of proof had always been on the engineers to prove beyond a doubt that it was safe to launch. NASA, with their objections to the original Thiokol recommendation against the launch, and Mason, with his request for a "management decision," shifted the burden of proof in the opposite direction. Morton Thiokol was expected to prove that launching Challenger would not be safe (R.C., IV, p. 793).

The change in the decision so deeply upset Boisjoly that he returned to his office and made the following journal entry:

> I sincerely hope that this launch does not result in a catastrophe. I personally do not agree with some of the statements made in Joe Kilminster's written summary stating that SRM-25 is okay to fly.

Exhibit 1. MTI Assessment of Temperature Concern on SRM-25 (51L) Launch

---

- Calculations show that SRM-25 O-rings will be 20° cooler than SRM-15 O-rings
- Temperature data not conclusive on predicting primary O-ring blow-by
- Engineering assessment is that:
  - Colder O-rings will have increased effective durometer ("harder")
  - "Harder" O-rings will take longer to "seat"
- More gas may pass primary O-ring before the primary seal seats (relative to SRM-15)
- Demonstrated sealing threshold is 3 times greater than 0.038 erosion experienced on SRM-15
- If the primary seal does not seat, the secondary seal will seat
- Pressure will get to secondary seal before the metal parts rotate
- O-ring pressure leak check places secondary seal in outboard position which minimizes sealing time
- MTI recommends STS-51L launch proceed on 28 January 1997
- SRM-25 will not be significantly different from SRM-15

Joe C. Kilminster, Vice President
Space Booster Programs

The Disaster and its Aftermath

On January 28, 1986, a reluctant Roger Boisjoly watched the launch of the Challenger. As the vehicle cleared the tower, Bob Ebeling whispered, "We've just dodged a bullet." (The engineers who opposed the launch assumed that O-ring failure would result in an explosion almost immediately after engine ignition.) To continue in Boisjoly's words, "At approximately T+60 seconds Bob told me he had just completed a prayer of thanks to the Lord for a successful launch. Just thirteen seconds later we both saw the horror of the destruction as the vehicle exploded."

Morton Thiokol formed a failure investigation team on January 31, 1986 to study the causes of the Challenger explosion. Roger Boisjoly and Arnie Thompson were part of the team that was sent to MSFC in Huntsville, Alabama. Boisjoly's first inkling of a division between himself and management came on February 13 when he was informed at the last minute that he was to testify before the Rogers Commission the next day. He had very little time to prepare for his testimony. Five days later, two Commission members held a closed session with Kilminster, Boisjoly, and Thompson. During the interview Boisjoly gave his memos and activity reports to the Commissioners. After that meeting, Kilminster chastised Thompson and Boisjoly for correcting his interpretation of the technical data. Their response was that they would continue to correct his version if it was technically incorrect.

Boisjoly's February 25th testimony before the Commission, rebutting the general manager's statement that the initial decision against the launch was not unanimous, drove a wedge further between him and Morton Thiokol management. Boisjoly was flown to MSFC before he could hear the NASA testimony about the pre-flight telecon. The next day, he was removed from the failure investigation team and returned to Utah.

Beginning in April, Boisjoly began to believe that for the previous month he had been used solely for public relations purposes. Although given the title of Seal Coordinator for the redesign effort, he was isolated from NASA and the seal redesign effort. His design information had been changed without his knowledge and presented without his feedback. On May 1, 1986, in a briefing preceding closed sessions before the Rogers Commission, Ed Garrison, President of Aerospace Operations for Morton Thiokol, chastised Boisjoly for "airing the company's dirty laundry" with the memos he had given the Commission. The next day, Boisjoly testified about the change in his job assignment. Commission Chairman Rogers criticized Thiokol management, "... if it appears that you're punishing the two people or at least two of the people who are right about the decision and objected to the launch which ultimately resulted in criticism of Thiokol and then they're demoted or feel that they are being retaliated against, that is a very serious matter. It would seem to me, just speaking for myself, they should be promoted, not demoted or pushed aside."

Boisjoly now sensed a major rift developing within the corporation. Some coworkers perceived that his testimony was damaging to the company image. In an effort to clear the air, he and McDonald requested a private meeting with the company's three top executives, which was held on May 16, 1986. According to Boisjoly, management was unreceptive throughout the meeting. The CEO told McDonald and Boisjoly that the company "was doing just fine until Al and I testified about our job reassignments." McDonald and Boisjoly were nominally restored to their former assignments, but Boisjoly's position became untenable as time passed. On July 21, 1986, Roger Boisjoly requested an extended sick leave from Morton Thiokol.

7. Propmore Corporation Case - Situation I*

Overview

Don Bradford was on the fast track at the Propmore Corporation. But he wished he could slow things down a bit, given several hard choices he had to make.

Propmore Corporation was a good place to work. It had sales of about $500 million per year, a net profit margin of 5 percent, and a return on equity of 15 percent. Propmore made several key components used by the aerospace industry and consumer goods market. It was a leader in its field. The company was organized by product divisions, each reporting to the Executive Vice-President. Its operations were decentralized, with broad decision-making capability at the divisional level. However, at the corporate level functional departments (Purchasing, R&D, Personnel, and Marketing) set company policy and coordinated divisional activities in these areas. Propmore was financially successful, and it treated its people well, as Don Bradford's experience showed.

After earning his MBA four years ago from a respected state university, Don quickly rose through the ranks in Purchasing. At age 31, he holds the prestigious position of Manager. (See organizational chart.) Before joining Propmore, Don earned a B.S. in engineering and worked for three years in the aerospace industry as a design engineer. During his first three years at Propmore, Don was a buyer and received "excellent" ratings in all his performance appraisals.

As Purchasing Manager, Don enjoyed good working relationships with superiors and subordinates. He was accountable directly to the Division General Manager and, functionally, to the Corporate Vice-President of Procurement, Mr. Stewart. His dealings with these people were always amiable and he came to count upon them for technical guidance, as he learned the role of Divisional Purchasing Manager. Don had several staff assistants who knew the business of buying and were loyal employees. He had done a good job of handling the resentment of those passed over by his promotion to manager, and he had developed a good deal of trust with the buying staff. At least he thought he had – until Jane Thompson presented him with the first in a series of dilemmas.

Jane Thompson, age 34, had been with Propmore for ten years. She had a B.A. in English Literature and two years experience as a material expediter before coming to Propmore. Initially hired as a purchasing assistant, Jane became a buyer after two years. She enjoyed her job and the people she worked with at Propmore. In four years of working with Don, Jane had come to admire and respect his approach to management. She appreciated his sensitive yet strong leadership and saw him as an honest person who could be trusted to look after the interests of his subordinates.

But the dilemma with which Jane now presented Don made him wonder whether he had the skill to be a manager in a major division.

---

*This case was developed by Dr. Peter Madsen and Dr. John Fleming. Arthur Anderson & Co. thanks the authors for their substantial contributions to the PACE Program. Dr. Madsen is the Executive Director and Senior Lecturer at the Center for Advancement of Applied Ethics, Carnegie Mellon University. Dr. Fleming is a Professor of Management for the University of Southern California. Arthur Andersen & Co. also thanks Mr. Harry Goern, Vice President of Procurement for Alcoa for his input and thoughtful reviews. Reprinted with permission of Aurhur Andersen & Co., SC.

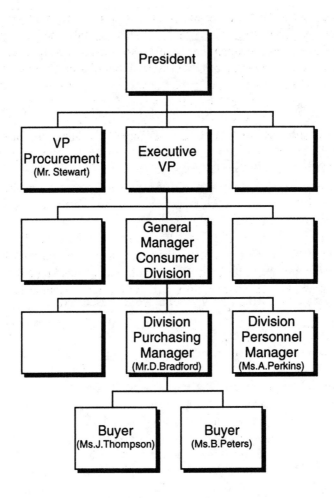

A Luncheon Harassment

After a two hour purchasing meeting in the morning, Bill Smith, an Airgoods Corporation Sales Representative, had invited Jane Thompson to lunch. They left at noon. An hour and a half later, Jane stormed into Don Bradford's office, obviously upset. When Don asked what was wrong, Jane told him in very strong terms that Bill Smith had sexually harassed her during and after the luncheon.

According to Jane, Bill made some sexual comments and suggestions toward the end of the meal. She considered this to be offensive and unwelcome. Jane, however, told Bill to take her back to the office. He attempted to make light of the situation and said he was only joking, but on the way back he made some further comments and several casual physical contacts to which she objected. When they arrived at the company, Bill was embarrassed and tried to apologize. But Jane entered the office before he could finish.

Jane demanded that the Airgoods Corporation be taken off the bidder list for the raw material contract and that Airgoods' President be informed of the unseemly and illegal behavior of one of his salesmen. She would also consider taking legal action against Bill Smith through the Equal Employment Opportunity Commission for sexual harassment. Also, Jane stated she would investigate suing the Propmore Corporation for failure to protect her from this form of discrimination while she was performing her duties as an employee of the company. At the end of this outburst, Jane abruptly left Don's office.

Don was significantly troubled. Jane played a critical role in getting bids for the raw material contract. He needed her. Yet he knew that if he kept Airgoods on the bidder list, it might be difficult for her to view this vendor objectively.

Don was somewhat concerned about Jane's threat to sue Propmore but doubted that she had a very good case. Still, such an action would be costly in legal fees, management time, and damage to the company's image.

Don wasn't sure what to do about the bidder list. Airgoods had an excellent record as a reliable vendor for similar contracts. Propmore might be at a disadvantage if Airgoods was eliminated. On the other hand, Don firmly believed in standing behind his subordinates.

At this point, he needed more information on what constitutes sexual harassment and what policy guidelines his company had established. He examined two documents: the EEOC Definition of Sexual Harassment (Appendix 1) and the Propmore Corporation's Policy HR-13, on Sexual Harassment (Appendix 2).

APPENDIX 1 : SITUATION I

EQUAL EMPLOYMENT OPPORTUNITY COMMISSION DEFINITION OF SEXUAL HARASSMENT

"Unwelcome sexual advances, requests for sexual favors and other verbal or physical contact of a sexual nature constitute sexual harassment when (1) submission to such conduct is made either explicitly or implicitly a term or condition of an individual's employment, (2) submission to or rejection of such conduct by an individual is used as the basis for employment decisions affecting such individual, or (3) such conduct has the purpose or effect of unreasonably interfering with an individual's work performance or creating an intimidating, hostile or offensive working environment."

"Applying general Title VII principles, an employer, employment agency, joint apprenticeship committee or labor organization (hereinafter collectively referred to as 'employer') is responsible for its acts and those of its agents and supervisory employees with respect to sexual harassment regardless of whether the employer knew or should have known of their occurrence."

– EEOC guideline based on the Civil Rights Act of 1964, Title VII

APPENDIX 2 : SITUATION I

THE PROPMORE CORPORATION POLICY HR-13

POLICY AREA: Sexual Harassment

PURPOSE: The purpose of Policy HR-13 is to inform employees of the company that The Propmore Corporation forbids practices of sexual harassment on the job and that disciplinary action may be taken against those who violate this policy.

POLICY STATEMENT: In keeping with its long-standing tradition of abiding by pertinent laws and regulations, The Propmore Corporation forbids practices of sexual harassment on the job which violate Title VII of the Civil Rights Act of 1964. Sexual harassment on the job, regardless of its intent, is against the law. Employees who nevertheless engage in sexual harassment practices face possible disciplinary action which includes dismissal from the company.

POLICY IMPLEMENTATION: Those who wish to report violations of Policy HR-13 shall file a written grievance with their immediate supervisors within two weeks of the alleged violation. In conjunction with the Legal Department, the supervisor will investigate the alleged violation and issue his or her decision based upon the findings of this investigation within 30 days of receiving the written grievance.

Propmore Corporation Case - Situation II

Gathering More Information

Don Bradford had met Bill Smith, the Airgoods Corporation Salesman, on several occasions but did not feel he really knew him. To learn more about Bill, Don talked with his other key buyer, Bob Peters. Bob had dealt with Bill on many contracts in the past. After Don finished recounting the incident concerning Jane, Bob smiled. In his opinion, it was just a "boys will be boys" situation that got blown out of proportion. It may have been more than a joke, but Bob did not think Bill would do something "too far out." He pointed out that Bill had been selling for ten years and knew how to treat a customer.

Don's next step was a visit to the division personnel office. In addition to going through Jane's file, he wanted to discuss the matter with Ann Perkins, the division's Human Resource Manager. Fortunately, Ann was in her office and had time to see him immediately.

Don went over the whole situation with Ann. When he had finished his account, Ann was silent for a minute. Then she pointed out that this was a strange sexual harassment situation: it did not happen at the company, and the alleged harasser was not a member of the Propmore organization. The extent of the company's responsibility was not clear.

She had heard of cases where employees held their companies responsible for protecting them from sexual harassment by employees of other organizations. But the harassment had taken place on company premises, where some degree of direct supervision and protection could have been expected.

Ann filled out a slip authorizing Don to see Jane's personnel file. He took the file to an empty office and went through its contents.

There were the expected hiring and annual evaluation forms, which revealed nothing unusual and only confirmed his own high opinion of Jane.

Then Don came to an informal note at the back of the file. It summarized a telephone reference check with the personnel manager of Jane's former employer. The note indicated that Jane had complained of being sexually harassed by her supervisor. The personnel manager had "checked it out" with the supervisor, who claimed "there was nothing to it." The note also indicated that Jane was terminated two months after this incident for "unsatisfactory work."

Don returned to his office and called his functional superior, Mr. Stewart, to inform him of the situation. Mr. Stewart was the Corporate Vice-President of Procurement. He had known Bill Smith personally for a number of years. He told Don that Bill's wife had abandoned him and their three children several years ago. Although Bill had a reputation for occasional odd behavior, he was known in the industry as a hard-working salesperson who provided excellent service and follow-through on his accounts.

Propmore Corporation Case - Situation III

A Telephone Call

Don felt he needed even more information to make a thorough investigation. He contemplated calling Bill Smith. In fairness to Bill, he should hear his version of what happened during the luncheon. But he knew he was not responsible for the actions of a non-employee. Furthermore, he wondered if talking to Bill would upset Jane even more if she found out? And would it be a proper part of an investigation mandated by company policy?

As Don considered his options, the phone rang. It was Bill Smith's boss, Joe Maxwell. He and Bill had talked about the luncheon, he said, and wanted to know if Jane had reported anything.

"Don, I don't know what you know about that meeting," said Joe, "but Bill has told me all the facts, and I thought we could put our heads together and nip this thing in the bud."

Don wasn't sure if this call was going to help or hinder him in his decision making. At first, he felt Joe was trying to unduly influence him Also, he wasn't sure if the call was a violation of Jane's right to confidentiality. "Joe, I'm not sure we should be discussing this matter at all," said Don. "We might be jumping the gun. And what if Jane—"

"Wait, wait," Joe interrupted. "This thing can be put to rest if you just hear what really happened. We've been a good supplier for some time now. Give us the benefit of the doubt. We can talk 'off the record' if want. But don't close the door on us."

"Okay," said Don, "let's talk off the record. I'll hear Bill's version, but I won't reach a conclusion over the phone. Our policy requires an investigation, and when that's complete, I'll let you know our position."

"Gee, Don," said Joe, "I don't think you even need an investigation. Bill says the only thing that went on at lunch was some innocent flirtation. Jane was giving him the old 'come on,' you know. She was more than friendly to him, smiling a lot and laughing at his jokes. Bill saw all the signals and just responded like a full-blooded male."

"You mean Jane was the cause of his harassing her?" Don asked.

"No, he didn't harass her," Joe said with urgency in his voice. "He only flirted with her because he thought she was flirting with him. It was all very innocent. These things happen every day. He didn't mean any harm. Just the opposite. He thought there was a chance for a nice relationship. He likes her very much and thought the feeling was mutual. No need to make a federal case out of it. These things happen – that's all. Remember when you asked out one of my saleswomen, Don? She said 'no,' but she didn't suggest sexual harassment. Isn't this the same thing?"

"I don't know. Jane was really upset when she came to me. She didn't see it as just flirting that went on," said Don.

"Come on, Don," insisted Joe. "Give her some time to calm down. You know how women can be sometimes. Maybe she has PMS. Why don't you let things just settle down before you do anything rash and start that unnecessary investigation? I bet in a couple days, you can talk to Jane and convince her it was just a misunderstanding. I'll put someone else on this contract, and we'll forget the whole thing ever happened. We've got to think about business first, right?"

Joe Maxwell's phone call put things in a new light for Don. If it was only innocent flirtation, why should good relations between Propmore and Airgoods be damaged? Yet he knew he had an obligation to Jane. He just wasn't sure how far that obligation went.

8. Baksheesh*

It was the middle of the night. My legs and neck ached as I stood up in the aircraft, but, as a young man about to start his first expatriate assignment, I was thrilled to be in East Africa. Outside, the air was hot and against the night sky the terminal building was floodlit. A small crowd of people moved out towards the aircraft, eager to meet relatives who had been to Europe on business, expats back for another tour of duty and, most important of all, to receive supplies of fresh food, newspapers, and other goods from Europe.

The General Manager of the local company, Mr. Lagarde, stood there on the tarmac to welcome me. He was French, in his early fifties, and had spent the last fifteen years as an expatriate in Africa, moving from country to country every three or four years. He seemed friendly enough and spoke to me in fatherly tones. I was far younger than he and had only worked for the company a year. I thought that he might resent my university background and early promotion to line responsibility overseas, but I also realized that he desperately needed a willing subordinate to manage an investment program to repair and rebuild the company's facilities, which had fallen into disrepair.

The local company marketed oil products in the country and used its storage facilities in the port for trans-shipment to neighboring countries as well. The oil storage tanks which sat between the small two-story office block and the Red Sea were built in 1936, but since the closure of the Suez Canal, they had been little used. The company had run down its operations and was only just profitable. It was wholly owned by one of the oil majors but was fully autonomous in day-to-day operations. With about one hundred local staff and three expatriates, it was too small to receive much attention from the parent company other than an annual review of the business plan. In 1983, an unexpected upturn in business had put new demands on the facilities which no longer met the appropriate safety standards. I was sent out for eighteen months or so with a mission to patch up the damage and update the facilities where necessary.

To meet my objectives, storage tanks, pumps, and pipework would need to be replaced section by section in order to keep the depot operational. The work would have to be done by local contractors as the company only employed a small maintenance crew of semi-skilled workers, and I would depend on these contractors to do their work properly and finish on time. I was pleased when, in the first couple of weeks, a number of them came to see me in my office. As they had no offices and ran their business from their cars, they would turn up at any time and would sit outside waiting for me to arrive. They would come in, usually alone, introduce themselves, and sit down. I explained to them that each section of the work would need to be bid for and that I would contact them soon.

Sapid Guedi must have been the fifth such contractor to come and see me. He told me that his firm had worked for my company for many years and hoped that we would have a long and fruitful relationship. He reached into his pocket and pulled out a gold chain which he held out to me as a "gift for my lady."

I was shocked. I had imagined this scene many times but felt unable to respond. This was "baksheesh," not a bribe relating to a particular job or contract, but a token offering which, he

---

*This case was written by Tom Delay, M.B.A., under the supervision of Susan Schneider, associate professor, for purposes of classroom discussion. INSEAD © 1988. All rights reserved.

hoped, would win him my favor. Eventually, I thanked him but explained that I could not accept his gift which, in any case, was not necessary. He replied, "but your predecessor took my gifts."

Suddenly I felt quite alone. I had assumed that my colleagues would turn away baksheesh but now I wasn't sure. I said no again, led him out of my office, then sat back and thought about my position. I was flattered that my position justified such treatment but was upset that he thought I might accept his gift. I realized that I would have to establish a position of principle in order to avoid this problem in the future.

Within the company I felt that I could trust no one. Guedi had made me realize that my expatriate colleagues could possibly be taking bribes. A couple of days later, the General Manager came into my office and asked me to consider a particular contractor for a forthcoming job, explaining that he had been "recommended by a Minister." He was probably quite honest and his story was probably true, but I had a lingering doubt in my mind. I never told him what had happened with Guedi and, more generally, we never discussed the subject of bribery.

Two months or so later, I had settled down in both the country and the company. I had moved into a small apartment in town away from my colleagues but close to a number of other expatriates. I had a small jeep to get me around and had built up an active social life. I did have some problems when the Port Police began to stop and search the jeep on my way into work every day, but I had learned to be patient and they gave up after a week. I later found the Guedi arranged this "stop and search" to put me in my place. Other contractors had, apparently, heard that I was "clean" and I got no more offers of baksheesh.

At work, things were going well, and I had established a good rapport with the clerical staff and the manual labor out in the depot. Some of them, in fact, seemed more able and enthusiastic than the local managers. In the morning the office was simply chaotic with suppliers running around chasing lost invoices and the local managers running around chasing their staff. In the afternoons, however, the managers would get their jobs done with some help from the expatriates. These able young men were being managed by four local managers who could barely read and write. Amongst the four was a man called Ismail Farah. He was the ringleader and had ambitions of being promoted to the post of Operations Manager, a job which had always been done by an expatriate. Previous General Managers had considered him for the post but none had recommended him, despite the company's declared policy of promotion for nationals wherever possible. I wondered why.

Before leaving for Africa I was told that two of the last three General Managers had had nervous breakdowns which had caused them to be repatriated but I was also told that these were caused by "age" in one case and "marital problems" in the other. The standard of living of the expats in the country was not high, but there was no particular hardship to explain why two previously successful managers should crack up in this way. I was told that one of them would come to the office at night and work through the company's accounts. On one occasion, he was found sitting on the floor in tears by his secretary when she arrived in the morning. If life outside the company were not responsible, what within it could cause this level of anxiety?

I stood on the quay in the Port late one night, watching our men couple up hoses to a tanker which had to discharge oil into the storage tanks. As I looked down the quay I could see someone walking up towards me. It was Ismail. He came up, and we chatted for a few minutes before he started to tell me about his career and how he had been overlooked for promotion. I pointed out that I had not discussed his position with the General Manager but that the company would promote nationals whenever possible. It was a weak reply, but it was honest.

Ismail was the most talented of the four local managers, but I didn't know him well enough to form any other opinion. He seemed pleased that I would discuss the matter with him and hoped that we would "be good friends." He started to talk about the past, about how the country had broken away from colonial rule, and about the company's development through this time. Eventually, he started to talk about the first of the General Managers who had had a nervous breakdown. He smiled and appeared to mock the man's misfortune. "That man was trouble to me. He was a racist and he was weak. He treated us like children so we behaved like children. We would make mistakes in our work that he could never find and it drove him crazy."

I was stunned. I must have looked quite shocked too, because he went on to say, "Don't worry, you'll be all right, you are my friend." This time I went to see the General Manager. We talked about Ismail and his past which, it transpired, had been well documented in appraisal reports. He had the support of a minister within the government which prevented us from firing him. There was nothing we could do.

Eventually, I had come to terms with both internal and external threats and had learned to be cautious in my dealings. I had good working relationships with a number of contractors and no problems dealing with the local authorities. When the Chief of Port Police came to see me in my office, I assumed that his visit was a courtesy call.

He sat down and, after a few minutes' discussion, started to explain that his mother was ill and needed health care he could not pay until he received his pay at the end of the month. "Could you, as a personal favor, lend me the money until the end of the month?" I had had similar requests before and knew that the story was almost certainly a fabrication. "I'm sorry, I would help you if I could, but I have no money in this country." He leaned across the desk and beckoned me forward so that he could whisper into my ear, "But I know that you have money in your account file in the bank." I felt quite sick. I had lied, and he knew it. Although his request was clearly extortion, I felt guilty. I stood up, told him that he must have made a mistake, and led him out of my office. Later that day I went to see the bank manager. As upset about the leak in confidential information as I had been, he gave me an overdraft so that, from that day on, I never did have any money in the bank.

As work in the Port depot progressed, we decided to invest in a small office block out at the airport to house the aviation manager and the fifteen staff responsible for fueling European airlines as they stopped over en route to and from the Indian Ocean. It would be a small, single-story Arab-style building, and it had been designed by a young French architect, resident in the country, who reckoned that it would cost about $200,000 to build. Five contractors had bid for the construction work, and I had awarded the contract to the lowest bidder, subject to planning approval being granted. To get the approval, the architect had completed the necessary forms and had submitted them in the company's name to the Ministry of Public Works six weeks beforehand. We hadn't received any reply in writing when Abdi Issa, officer in charge of planning at the Ministry, called me by phone. "I have a few queries about the drawings you submitted with the planning application forms for your new airport office; nothing serious, the sort of thing we should discuss around the table. Could you come in and see me tomorrow morning in my office'?" I wondered, now what?

9. The Marketing Campaign at ChemCorp*

Jim Wallace stood at the window of his 8th floor office looking out over a city about to be engulfed by dusk. He had just come back from a meeting with Art Jackson, President of ChemCorp, an agricultural chemical and fertilizer company. Unlike other meetings with Art, this one left Jim with a feeling of uneasiness.

Art had proposed that Jim, in his position as Vice President of Sales, develop a sales campaign for AgriCoat, a pesticide to be shipped from Western Fertilizers and Chemicals, a California company. The President had asked that this project be given top priority because of its importance to both ChemCorp and its parent company, CCA. But the circumstances surrounding the request made it difficult for Jim to start designing the campaign right away. He struggled to find the reasons for his reluctance.

Background of ChemCorp

ChemCorp was founded in the early 1920s by two chemical engineers as a small chemical company with a focus on the market in the southeastern part of the United States. With a limited product line but a reputation for quality and service, it became a very successful company, weathering both the Great Depression and World War II. The booming post-war economy found ChemCorp poised for expansion within the emerging agricultural industry in the Southeast. Agricultural cooperatives and larger farmers became the primary customers who fueled its growth as they came to rely on ChemCorp to meet their needs.

The small core of managers who had guided the company through its early period gave way to a new group of managers in the 1950s who brought new sophistication to both production and marketing. ChemCorp expanded its production capacity by building new plants in a number of small towns in the Southeast. An aggressive marketing strategy was inaugurated through a well-trained sales force, an expanded product line, and a substantial research and development program designed to create products suited to the needs of farmers. Growth never clouded ChemCorp's fundamental mission of retaining a reputation for product quality and customer service.

Art Jackson became president 10 years ago, the first outsider to take over the reins of the company. Well-established in the industry as a divisional vice president of a major chemical company, Art found a new home at ChemCorp. He quickly surrounded himself with a new executive group and set his sights on consolidating the position of ChemCorp as a regional leader in the agricultural chemical industry.

Four years ago, ChemCorp was taken over by CCA, a diversified conglomerate headquartered in the Northeast. CCA was searching to expand its portfolio of small and medium companies with excellent cash flow and established market share in the agricultural industry. ChemCorp was a prime candidate to round out a new CCA division which already included two other small chemical and several agricultural product companies. While reluctant initially

---

*This case was written by D. Jeffrey Lenn, School of Government and Business Administration, The George Washington University. Key names and facts within the case have been disguised to protect the confidentiality of sources.

to sell, the ChemCorp board took Art's advice that the price was right. CCA's promise to maintain an arms-length management relationship while providing capital infusion was important also in the board's decision. They sold to CCA with the understanding that top management would stay and the thrust of the business would be maintained.

Jackson's forecast had been correct. CCA was liberal in its capital expenditure policy as it approved a large initial capital budget proposed by the President. This led a full revamping of the ChemCorp plants with the latest in technology built into the production process. The inclusion of ChemCorp in a national division provided the basis for further integration into a broader marketing strategy in which ChemCorp was expected to play a major role over the next few years.

Jim Wallace's Career at ChemCorp

Jim started as a chemical engineer with ChemCorp right out of college. He worked in the production side for nearly 7 years but became a little frustrated with the highly technical aspects of his job. When an opening in the sales department came up, he jumped at it. His first two years were rocky ones as he just met his sales quota each year. He found that his engineering training had not equipped him very well to handle the day-to-day contacts with customers. While he could help them understand the technical characteristics of the products, he was not always sure just how to convince them to buy these products.

But he worked hard, and with the help of an excellent regional sales manager, began to learn how to couple his product knowledge with customer knowledge to become a highly successful salesman. When a regional manager's position opened up, his own manager recommended him highly. Jim proved his ability in this new position because of his sales expertise and his management experience. An earlier stint as an engineering manager had helped set the stage for this success.

Five years ago, when Art Jackson had reorganized, he had chosen Jim as his new Vice President of Sales. The CEO saw in Jim someone with executive talent. He had fine experience in the field and an excellent reputation with key customers and the sales force. He had acquired good product knowledge through his years in engineering. And most of all, he had developed a good sense of the importance of overall corporate objectives with his exposure to both sales and production. Art recognized that the informal grooming process for executive talent in ChemCorp had produced a fine candidate for this position.

Jim took to the position nicely. Sales volume increased as well as the customer base during his tenure. He worked hard to shape the sales force into a cohesive unit through his hiring practices, a new incentive program, and a personal touch, where he was in touch with top producers on a quarterly basis. His department developed a new sense of pride which led to even greater productivity.

Jim fostered a good working relationship with the engineering department. He worked closely with them to develop new products which were responsive to farmers' needs for fertilizers and pesticides. One of these new products, Gro-Go, was developed nearly three years ago in response to growers' concerns about environmentally safe products. Gro-Go was a breakthrough in a market which was now demanding pesticides which could both control insects and not be harmful to the ultimate consumer. In its first two full years on the market, Gro-Go established itself as a strong product with an excellent future.

At 42, Jim recognized that he had become a successful executive. His relationship with Art made him a key member of the ChemCorp executive team. His hard work and full commitment to his staff had increased his stature within the sales department as well as within other departments. He was pleased with his ability to forge a career which incorporated both production and sales skills rather than simply being defined as a narrow advocate of one or the other of the corporate functions. He was optimistic about his future career.

The Meeting with Art Jackson

Jim was puzzled by the hastily arranged meeting with Art Jackson. He was disturbed by the CEO's manner as they sat across the large oak desk in Art's office. Art's words seemed to be more carefully chosen than usual as he explained that the CCA Group Vice President had called yesterday with a proposal for ChemCorp.

The proposal detailed that ChemCorp would add AgriCoat, a pesticide produced by Western Fertilizers and Chemicals, another subsidiary of CCA on the West Coast, to its product line. The CCA Vice President indicated that the full inventory of AgriCoat would be shipped within the next two weeks and ChemCorp should be prepared to sell it to its customers over the next six months. It suggested that AgriCoat might be heavily discounted or coupled with other promotions to move it quickly into the market in light of such a short time horizon.

While Art was covering some of the financial details, Jim sifted through his knowledge of AgriCoat. He originally had considered adding it to the ChemCorp line but decided that another pesticide would be better suited to his market. His decision to develop Gro-Go had been prompted by customer interest in the environmental aspect. Art had been supportive of this decision even though he recognized that the research and development costs would be higher. Jim's strategy had paid off in terms of the sales figures for Gro-Go. Thus, Art's acceptance of the current CCA proposal was all the more surprising because it appeared that AgriCoat would be in direct competition with Gro-Go.

As Jackson started to outline some of his own ideas about a sales campaign, Wallace interrupted: "But Art, why the big push for AgriCoat now? Sales for Gro-Go are excellent, and we are just beginning to see the early signs of our campaign to build its image as a pesticide which is effective while safe. Introducing AgriCoat would work at cross purposes with what my sales force is doing right now."

Art stumbled a little as he explained the importance of the AgriCoat campaign. Then he paused and looked Jim in the eye: "I wasn't supposed to tell you this, but we have worked together too long not to be honest with each other. CCA staff has found out from inside sources that the U.S. Government has decided from confidential studies that a number of pesticides should be banned from the market. These studies show a direct link between these pesticides and cancer in laboratory animals. The implication is that they also cause cancer in human beings. AgriCoat is one of these pesticides."

"CCA will join with other chemical companies to appeal the ban but expects that it will be unsuccessful. Western is already in shaky financial condition with a heavy inventory of AgriCoat. A California newspaper has leaked a state environmental agency report which questions the safety of this product in particular. Sales have begun to drop off, so CCA has decided that Western will discontinue production of AgriCoat in a week and ship their full inventory to us for marketing here. The Group Vice President estimates that the federal ban will finally take effect in six months. In the meantime, there is little likelihood of much controversy here in our market as nobody knows anything about AgriCoat."

The CEO moved quickly to the point of the meeting: "Jim, I know that the arms-length relationship with CCA has been beneficial to ChemCorp. Now it is time that we begin to see ourselves as part of the larger company by assuming some of the burden from another subsidiary. You are in charge of this operation and I have full confidence that you will be successful.

"We need tell nobody else about the real reason for taking on AgriCoat. Let's just position it as part of our product line. I can understand your difficulties in light of the strength of Gro-Go, but this is only temporary. We really have no choice on this one, as it comes from the top. Your work on this campaign will be important to me and to CCA. This is a big one for your career as well. Those guys at headquarters will be watching us on this one.

"Remember, Jim, we have to move it! In fact, that might be a good start on your campaign with the sales force – 'Move it!' I will need a general outline of your campaign by tomorrow morning so I can call CCA. We can finalize the details by the end of the week."

The Decision on the AgriCoat Campaign

Having called home to say he would be working late, Jim settled down to review the CCA proposal. He began to think through a strategy for the campaign with Art's words of "Move it!" echoing in his ears. He realized that marketing in a highly competitive industry took a lot of creativity. But there was something which nagged at him on this campaign. He had always been able to overcome his uncertain feelings in the past and work out a successful strategy. But there was some deep uncertainty about this one, something which he could not put a label on.

Part 3   Strategy, Planning and Organizational Culture

Cases Outline

10. American Express*

It was 1977 when James D. Robinson III became chairman and CEO of the profitable charge card, travelers checks and finance company, American Express Corporation (Amex). For 30 years Amex had maintained a string of increased earnings, "The Record" as it was called.[1] This record was considered so significant that maintaining it became a primary goal of the company. This was not a simple task. Amex's three core businesses were experiencing problems. The company "...managed to maintain 'the Record' into the mid-1970's only by resorting to fancy accounting."[2] The earnings of Amex's property/casualty insurance company, Fireman's Fund, were volatile. Amex's second core business, American Express International Bank, suffered losses in 1977 when it experienced a significant reduction in its return on assets.[3] Also, several major loans to Third-World countries made the threat of loan defaults a serious concern. Amex's largest sector, Travel Related Services (TRS) was prospering. However, its business of credit cards and travelers checks was mature and did not seem to offer much growth potential. Furthermore, its rivals, Visa and Master Charge, were applying competitive pressure by entering into the business travel market. Citicorp's recent purchase of Carte Blanche, another credit card company, was also threatening.

Jimmy Threesticks

Robinson had gained a reputation for hard work and fast solutions in his early years on Wall Street. "Jimmy was a white-shoe (version of) what makes Sammy run," said Abram Claude Jr., who supervised him for a time at Morgan Guaranty Trust Co. "He just ate up problems and spit them back at you. He became almost a chore for me as a manager."

Adds Paul Hallingby Jr., who oversaw Robinson at the investment bank White, Weld & Co., "I've never, ever seen someone work so hard."[4] In 1970, Howard Clark Sr., Amex's chairman at the time, wanted Robinson at Amex. Clark knew all about Robinson. "Everybody in town wanted to hire him when he came out of Harvard (Business School),"[5] said Clark, who also knew Robinson's father. The 54 year old Clark approached Robinson and said he planned to retire at 60 and that Jim would have a chance to succeed him.[6]

True to his word, when Clark retired in 1977, he left Robinson in charge. Yet, despite Robinson's achievements, the nickname, Jimmy Threesticks, still stuck with him. It derived from James III and the prevalent conception that his success was predetermined by his father's wealth and influence. His great-grandfather and grandfather had been bankers in Atlanta and the family was wealthy, prestigious and aristocratic. Although Robinson clearly benefitted from some powerful family friends, he did not like to be thought of as one whose success was handed to him on a platter as if it was a birthright.[7] Consequently, he continued to struggle to prove his management abilities. Now that he was responsible for managing Amex, he had the opportunity. What was he going to do?

---

*Written by Richard D. Freedman and Jill Vohr, Leonard N. Stern School of Business, New York University, Copyright © 1991 by Professor Richard D. Freedman. Reprinted with permission.

Lou Gerstner and TRS

Robinson devised two strategies to stimulate growth. "Plan A was to find a major new line of businesses...and plan B (was to)...hire Lou Gerstner to revive the TRS business."[8]

Amex's core business, TRS, comprised of the American Express card, travelers checks and a variety of products and services sold to cardholders. Before Robinson became CEO of Amex, he ran TRS and Lou Gerstner was hired as his younger advisor. Gerstner graduated from Dartmouth, with an engineering degree, and Harvard Business School. People who knew Gerstner referred to him as serious and driven, "a guy in a hurry."[9] In a cover story, the *Institutional Investor* described him as having "...the methodical, research and planning approach consistent with his Harvard MBA and ten years as a McKinsey and Co. consultant."[10]

Gerstner performed a variety of studies for Robinson. Robinson explained that Gerstner "...moved into the position of kind of (a)...spiritual as well as (a)... professional sounding board...Lou was someone in whom I had confidence to brainstorm with. He is insightful, excellent at summarizing things and laying out the key alternatives or issues."[11] In 1978, when Robinson was promoted to CEO, he placed Gerstner in charge of TRS.

> "Gerstner quickly transformed the card business, which was overwhelmingly based on the U.S. green card, into a rainbow of different products around the world. He created a successful corporate product by combining the card with Amex's money-losing travel-agency business to offer companies a unified system to monitor and control travel expenses...(He)...also expanded the overseas card business changing the focus from serving international travelers to going after purely domestic business in other countries. Perhaps most important,...(He)... fundamentally redefined the green card, positioning it for use not merely for business travel but for any purchase its customers wanted to make. This allowed dramatic expansion on two fronts: new sorts of card members (such as women and graduating college students) and new merchants (boutiques and department stores at first and now practically everything from gas stations to hardware stores).

> (Gerstner)...codified the TRS business proposition into eight principles, generally management platitudes such as staying close to the customer and valuing employees. But also on the list are the key ideas that differentiate American Express from the pack: that it will offer premium, top-of-the-line products and that quality service will be its principal competitive weapon. It's no accident that his principles resemble the Ten Commandments. Like a missionary, Gerstner has had them translated into fourteen languages, and he has just mailed desk cards with the principles to the homes of all 44,000 TRS employees."[12]

McGraw-Hill

Robinson's Plan B, to hire Lou Gerstner at TRS, proved successful. His Plan A, to find a new line of business, was more complicated. Robinson had to consider what kind of company Amex should become. Some possible business areas were travel, financial services, insurance or communications. Still uncertain what future direction was appropriate for Amex, Robinson decided that he would diversify the company and transform it into what he called a "broadly defined service company".[13] He began this diversification using what *Fortune* called a "classic acquisition strategy".[14] He considered several different types of diversifications including companies in the entertainment, communications, financial, and insurance businesses. Attempts were made to buy the Walt Disney and Philadelphia Life Insurance Companies, but they were not successful. To help guide the process, Amex developed a new department, the Office of Strategic Program Development (OSPD), "to act as a catalyst and to develop and evaluate opportunities for new and important sources of earnings."[15]

In 1979, Robinson and the OSPD considered McGraw-Hill, the publishing and information services company, for their next acquisition attempt. Amex had developed its own highly sophisticated data and communications services in its recent tie with Warner Communications. McGraw-Hill, better known for its publishing of educational texts, was also profitably involved in selling specialized information through magazines and financial and data base services.

The acquisition never took place. Harold McGraw-Hill, the company's chairman, declined Amex's offer. Amex did not take no for an answer and continued to pursue the company, announcing a tender offer. McGraw was angered and went on the offensive publishing an open letter in major newspapers throughout the country questioning "the morality of the travelers cheque because Amex didn't pay any interest on their funds" and questioning whether it was appropriate for Amex to own *Business Week,* that published articles on the company, and Standard and Poor, which rated its bonds.[16] Amex threatened to sue McGraw-Hill for libel. These hostilities brought a quick end to Amex's takeover attempts, leaving the company publicly embarrassed. President Roger H. Morley resigned, taking the brunt of the blame. Robinson remained unscarred and Amex managed to maintain its "Record".

A Vision

Robinson liked to surround himself with brilliant people - visionaries. He worked best as a catalyst for innovative ideas, translating them into practical strategies. When his long time friend, Salim Lewis, an investment banker, described the future financial services industry as being dominated by large companies able to offer a wide range of financial services - stock brokerage, real estate, insurance, lending, etc., Robinson's vision of Amex changed. He realized that Amex's move into a major new line of business meant an expansion into financial services. His "broadly defined service company" became a financial service company. Lewis suggested that the acquisition of Shearson Loeb Rhoades, a large, profitable brokerage firm, could make Amex one of the first of these large financial service institutions.[17]

Shearson

Shearson was one of the most profitable brokerage houses in the nation. Under the leadership of Sanford Weill, Shearson had grown through a process of numerous acquisitions during the seventies. Connie Bruck of *The New Yorker* described the company as having "...scavenged up Wall Street for weakened firms, swallowing up one after another"[18] and as a "...paradigm of cost consciousness (acquiring each of its firms) at a bargain-basement price, disbanding the firm's back office, and stripping away other redundant employees"[19] One longtime Shearson employee commented that "The genius of Shearson was that one and one always equalled one and a half, never two."[20]

Robinson and the OSPD began to explore the possibility of acquiring Shearson. There were several issues to consider. One was whether the two companies' customers were compatible. Amex's travelers checks and credit card customers were essentially buying security and convenience. Would the same customers be interested in the risky buying and trading of securities? Would Amex customers buy a wider variety of financial services if the company acquired Shearson? Robinson and the OSPD reasoned that because Amex provided financial services primarily through their credit cards, and 70% of the financial assets in the country were held by card holders, Shearson's products and services could be sold to Amex card holders and Amex's cards could be sold to Shearson's clientele.[21]

Another consideration was the apparent cultural and operational differences between the two companies. Shearson was a younger and smaller company that concentrated on efficiencies in its back office operations. It was also entrepreneurial with open lines of communications to the environment. It was "sharp toothed"[22] with a "hard-sell hustle".[23] Conversely, Amex was mature, conservative and formal. Connie Bruck described Amex as "the imperial corporation" as exemplified by its "...concerns with titles and lines of authority, its intensely political atmosphere, its formidable public relations apparatus, its endless deluge of memos, and its readiness to convene numerous meetings for almost any reason, no matter how trivial."[24] A Shearson executive remarked, "We always thought of the American Express people as overly planned, overly staged, overly bureaucratic. We saw ourselves, on the other hand, as the tough guys, very smart who were marching to our own drummer, who made decisions by the seat of our pants."[25] Shearson was involved in the volatile brokerage business, very different from the more stable credit services business central to Amex. The company's profit swings could mar Amex's steady growth record. Also, Shearson's salaries and bonuses were far greater than Amex's corporate pay scale.

Despite these differences, expectations and events in the financial services industry finally led Amex to make the acquisition. Financial market activity was expected to increase significantly following the Reagan administration's loosening of regulations controlling financial institutions, and its encouragement of investment activity in general. Also, In March of 1981, Prudential Insurance Co. purchased Bache Securities forming the large, wide-ranged financial services company Lewis had envisioned and setting an example for Amex. A move into Shearson's brokerage business became that much more appealing and important. Robinson was emphatic with respect to the merger and the OSPD agreed. That following June, Amex purchased Shearson Loeb Rhoades Inc. for $930 million, and with it, acquired Sandy Weill and Peter A. Cohen.[26]

Sandy Weill was the quintessential self-made entrepreneur, Brooklyn-born, cigar smoking, charming, yet ruthless and tenacious. Peter Cohen was Weill's sidekick, his detail man and number cruncher. Weill took over Roger H. Morley's position as president of Amex and he and Robinson placed Cohen in charge of Shearson. Weill, however, had difficulty conforming to Amex's structured management regimen. Robinson had given him "...a three-page memo defining the limits of his authority...(Yet) Weill was unable or unwilling to alter his free-wheeling style and instead of working through organizational channels to get something done, he tended to just go and do it."[27] Despite these conflicts, Amex's merger with Shearson proved to be profitable. In 1983, Shearson's profits rose a spectacular 40% and revenues 37% over the previous year.[28]

A Changing Wall Street

In the mid-eighties, the expectations of increased financial activity were realized. Deregulation gave many financial institutions the opportunity to involve themselves in additional financial activities. Baby boomers began to spend and invest their substantial mid-life incomes. Wall Street entered a bull market and financial service institutions began to experience rapid growth and profitability.

Cohen's Vision

In 1981, when Robinson made Cohen CEO of Shearson, at 36, he was the youngest head of a major Wall Street firm. He continued to operate as he had while working for Weill. He was methodical, fastidious and pragmatic. Cohen's friends had thought of him as short of the imagination and vision needed to create a great institution. As CEO of Shearson, however, Cohen now had a vision. He wanted Shearson to become an investment banking powerhouse. In order to realize his vision, Cohen tried to build an investment banking arm, but with little success. Then Cohen discovered what he called "a once-in-a-lifetime opportunity": Lehman Brothers.[29]

Lehman Brother Kuhn Loeb

Lehman Brothers had been an influential investment banking house since its founding in 1850. However, internal conflicts between its traders and investment bankers had weakened the company. Cohen saw a promising connection between Shearson and Lehman. He recognized the value of the Lehman partners. Having been reared in the old school of "relationship banking", they had developed a network of longtime clients who were worth a wealth of business.[30] Lehman had managed to maintain many of these blue-chip clients. A merger with Lehman could bring its partners' clients and trading expertise to Shearson, but only if its partnership remained intact. Cohen asked that the majority of partners sign a contract preventing them from working for a competitor in the three years following the merger. Fifty-seven agreed to sign and Shearson acquired Lehman for $360 million in 1984.[31]

Wall Street was skeptical. Lehman Brothers had a reputation of elegance, old-line tradition, and hauteur. In comparison, Shearson was considered a "tacky wire house", parochial and homely.[32] Lehman's dining room was a virtual display of grandiosity, with everything from the finest Havana cigars for partners and their guests to Renoirs and Picassos hanging on the walls. By contrast, Shearson occupied a thrifty space at the World Trade Center. The companies' cultures differed as well. Lehman was an investment banking house driven by big deals and egos. Shearson was a retail securities brokerage - tightfisted and controlled. Still Cohen, with Robinson's blessing, set out to show Wall Street that despite the differences, the two companies were compatible.

Cohen and the Shearson Lehman contingent put together a long-term strategic plan. Under the plan, the company would "try to regain the ground Lehman Brothers had lost by concentrating on areas in which Lehman and Shearson had excelled as separate firms. They would also solicit business from giant corporations instead of smaller companies that had been a Lehman specialty."[33] To Cohen's dismay, however, the Lehman investment bankers had little idea how to go after new clients. They had been accustomed to waiting for longtime clients to bring in business. Said Sherman Lewis, who Cohen had placed in charge of Lehman, "For all that's been made of the difference between the Shearson and Lehman cultures, this was the one real difference."[34]

Cohen worked hard to motivate the Lehman partners to adapt to Shearson's aggressive culture. He awarded bonuses for the pursuit of new business. When the Lehman partners were reluctant to lure customers from other Wall Street houses, the response they received was "This is our plan. Do it." Within six months, his efforts began to pay off. Despite Wall Street's skepticism, Cohen had his investment bankers out hustling for business and getting it. Thomas W. Strauss, a managing director of rival Salomon Brothers, said of Shearson, "They have demonstrated that the merger worked."[35]

The Financial Supermarket

The acquisition of Lehman Brothers represented a uniting of Robinson and Cohen's vision for Amex. They both believed that the global marketplace had arrived and that within the next decade it would be dominated by a handful of giant firms offering the gamut of financial services to a wide range of customers.[36] In other words, a financial supermarket. Lehman Brothers was vital to their shared vision. The acquisition expanded Amex's financial offerings by bringing Shearson into the business of primary securities.

Robinson looked to Shearson as a primary vehicle for fulfilling his financial supermarket vision. Shearson was Amex's main connection to the burgeoning activities on Wall Street. However, he also moved Amex toward this vision through the company's acquisition of Swiss-based Trade Development Bank (TDB) founded by Edmond Safra, well known for his financial connections and reputation among the very wealthy.

Safra, TDB's chairman, was a legend - a reclusive Lebanese-born banker who had brought in close to $5 billion in deposits for TDB.[37] He specialized in personal banking and was highly respected by immensely wealthy people who trusted him to handle their money. "Edmond is a guy who sits in an office all day alone and who has always controlled his own destiny," said Cohen, who had once worked for Safra. Cohen assisted in the TDB deal by bringing Safra to American Express for negotiations. Robinson sought TDB for its exclusive, wealthy niche and Safra for his elite clientele, international connections and personal banking expertise. According to the *Institutional Investor*, the deal "...was supposed to marry Safra's private banking savvy to Amex's then-wobbly international banking arm (its American Express Bank) and give the then Shearson Lehman Brother's asset managers access to a rich market."[38]

Robinson had other goals for Amex as well. He wanted to build on the company's existing strengths. He followed the TDB acquisition by another of Investors Diversified Services (IDS) of Minneapolis in 1984, a mass-market financial planning and investment company. IDS marketed an array of annuities, life insurance and mutual funds to middle America and was attractive to Robinson because it would, as he said,"...open up the savings and investment side of the equation, where we correctly anticipated growth. Whether consumers spent with the card or saved with IDS, American Express had a chance to win."[39] One security analyst acclaimed the acquisition a "masterstroke" for it got "Amexco's toe, if not their entire foot into the middle-income market."[40]

Robinson also worked to develop synergies. He had Shearson bankers approach TDB clients for business, TDB bankers approach Shearson clients for business, Shearson securities sold to investors who were customers of other Amex divisions, and American Express Cards and life insurance sold to everyone. From 1982 to 1987, billions of dollars in life policies were sold to American Express cardholders and customers of Shearson, TDB and IDS.[41] Pretax profits on life insurance sales to card members alone were $45 million in 1985.[42] Robinson implemented a synergy plan he called "One Enterprise".

> "Amex, he (Robinson) said, is 'one enterprise', a collection of companies that sell different brands to different consumers but are united in the same goal of making money for the same shareholders. (He required) senior executives to identify two or three promising One Enterprise synergy projects in their annual strategic plans and work on them during the year. He made it a corporate policy to evaluate every manager and professional employee on their contributions to One Enterprise, and then handed out extra bonuses to senior executives who did their bit for the cause."[43]

Robinson supervised middle managers to make sure that they too cooperated. He had a monthly report developed on the status of each "One Enterprise" project, which was circulated among the company's top 100 executives. His measures proved successful, for roughly 10% of Amex's net income in 1986 came from capitalizing on synergistic opportunities.[44] One analyst from Paine Webber commented that "American Express management is better at finding new pockets of growth and exploiting them than any financial company I'm aware of."[45]

Robinson contributed to the success of TRS by, as he describes, "accelerating the focus of quality."[46] During Gerstner's development of the 8 commandments, Robinson was emphasizing service. As described by John Paul Newport, Jr. of Fortune Magazine, "Service has two components at American Express. The first is quality. While it may sound like a cliche, management really does insist that the company (TRS) strive to deliver the highest quality of service possible. The second and more daring element has to do with change. Robinson demands that employees not merely anticipate change but also reach out to embrace it before it overpowers them.[47] Said Robinson, "Change is going to happen, and we should be excited by that. We should be out there helping change to happen so that we can be the first to take advantage of it."[48]

TRS earnings grew 17% a year compounded and return on equity increased to 28% in 1988. With $800 million in profits, TRS would have been the third largest financial services company in the U.S. if it were an independent firm.[49] Said Paine-Webber analyst, Rodney Schwartz, "TRS has been more profitable by a mile than any other large financial services company I can think of."[50]

Gerstner's success in running TRS had made him a likely candidate for the number 2 spot under Robinson. In 1983, however, Weill was made president. Friends described Gerstner as frustrated during this period, that he began to consider seriously some of the job offers he was getting as his success became known.[51] "He talked to some of us quietly and privately about frustrations and aspirations," a friend recalled. Despite his frustrations, however, "He hunkered down. He knew that the core business he was running was still the family jewel."[52]

The Loss of Safra

All of American Express was not doing as well as TRS. In late 1983, Fireman's Fund suffered combined losses of $452 million, forcing Amex to pump in $230 million in fresh capital which ended their 35-year unbroken string of earnings gains.[53] Robinson fired the subsidiary's top management, and with his blessing, "...the Amex board sent Weill to San Francisco to fix Fireman's Fund. The assignment removed Weill from the mainstream of management."[54]

Safra, who was Amex's largest shareholder, was infuriated. *Institutional Investor* remarked that (he) "...felt deceived about the woes of Amex's Fireman's Fund subsidiary which sorely damaged the value of the stock he had accepted at TDB's sale."[55]

Safra also was having difficulties adjusting to Amex's style of management. He was unable to function within the rigid framework of a multinational conglomerate. "American Express officials found Safra remote; he was reluctant to leave Geneva for forays to American Express headquarters in New York and was disinclined to adjust to the firm's memo-and-meeting style of business."[56] Cohen tried to mediate the clash in styles between Robinson and Safra. He explains,

> "I used to say to Jim, 'If you understand what Edmond is and you create the environment for him to be himself here, it can work. But if we impose upon him the bureaucracy and surround him with all the things that are alien to him, it will never work.'..And unfortunately, I don't think Jim fully understood what I meant when I said that. And visa versa, I said to Edmond, 'You know, you're going to have to come to board meetings occasionally, you're going to have to play the game a little bit.' But it turned out to be, 'I don't want to play the game.'"[57]

In December, 1984, Safra resigned as chairman of the TDB-American Express Bank.

A Plan for Amex

Amex continued to experience difficulties.

> "It was still digesting its acquisition of Lehman, TDB and IDS, and Fireman's Fund was still reeling from unexpected losses... The board asked for a review of the company's strategy, and Robinson assigned the task to Weill. Weill organized a presentation of the plans for each of the divisions, but the board wasn't satisfied. It wanted an overall strategy for the corporation. 'Sandy just gulped,' recalls a participant. It was back to the drawing board, and a series of meetings were held at the Plaza hotel in New York attended by Weill, Gerstner, Cohen, IDS chief Harvey Golub and William McCormick, who at the time was running Fireman's Fund along with Weill, and other executives. They debated organization, marketing and financial goals as they tried to hammer out a single coherent mission for American Express. Robinson wasn't there for most of the meetings but would join them for dinner later."[58]

As head of corporate planning, Gerstner presented the results of the brainstorming to the board in the Spring of 1985. His plan was a success. It included specific criteria, however, that excluded Fireman's Fund.   → *clever: edges Weill out*

"As Gerstner saw things, Amex should aim to be first, second or third in market share in any business it was to be in and control its own distribution channels. That way the company could differentiate its own products from the competition. Fireman's Fund did not meet these criteria. It was eighth in the property/casualty market, it had only a 1 percent market share, and it worked entirely through independent agents. Institutional business such as Fireman's did was seen as less attractive than efforts aimed at individuals, in which there is more opportunity for cross-marketing different products. And most important, Gerstner set out a target of 18 to 20 percent return on equity and 12 to 15 percent average annual earnings growth for each division. Even in good years, Fireman's Fund fell far below these targets, and Amex shortly decided to sell."[59]

The Loss of Weill

Weill had been unhappy with Amex's management style. "Moreover, he plainly (had)... not (been) satisfied with just being president and (had) pressed for the additional post of chief operating officer."[60] Robinson was not responsive. So, "... Weill carefully remained within the bounds of his job, (but) he openly chafed under Robinson's direction."[61]

When Weill was assigned to Fireman's Fund, he immersed himself in the project of turning the company around. He became "...enamored of (the company's)...prospects (and)... was itching to run his own company again."[62] Upon hearing that Amex was planning to sell the troubled company, Weill made a bid to buy it. The board rejected his bid and Weill resigned. In October, 1985, Amex sold 58% of Fireman's Fund to the public, which turned out to be the largest public stock offering ever made on Wall Street. It sold an additional 15% in May of 1986.[63]

The Financial Super Market and Shearson

Shearson's acquisition of Lehman Brothers in 1984 significantly changed the company's nature. "Now, with Lehman's investment-banking franchise and inestimable cachet, Shearson was making a bid to break into the elite Wall Street club - the 'bulge bracket', or first-tier securities firms."[64] Cohen set out to prove that Shearson Lehman could live up to the style of Lehman Brothers. Shearson moved to the World Financial Center in New York and built its own Shearson Lehman executive dining room that "rivalled its Lehman forerunner in elegance."[65] Cohen too began to change. He no longer managed Shearson with "compulsive vigilance".[66] He now began to "...(give) himself over to the far more chimerical high-profile and high margin world of investment banking."[67] Robinson supported Cohen's transition. He said that he "encouraged Peter to establish his contacts around the world in banking, in government and in business."[68]

Both Robinson and Cohen believed that a global presence was necessary and that it should be sizable. Shearson began its international expansion before acquiring Lehman. It acquired L. Messel, a middle-sized securities firm in London. By the end of 1989, Shearson had opened branches in 9 countries across Europe, Asia, the Far East and Australia. Expansion occurred domestically as well. In late 1987, Shearson acquired E.F. Hutton Group Inc., one of the nation's largest retail brokers that was experiencing severe organizational problems.

"It was a perfect strategic move, inasmuch as it would enable Shearson to go from third place as a retail power to a spot where it could vie with Merrill Lynch for No. 1. Of all the expansions Shearson was undertaking, this was the most justifiable, since it involved the firm's core, historic business. There were no dissenters, or even doubters, on the American Express board, and Robinson was strong in his support."[69]

Shearson also moved into the business of merchant banking. It took substantial equity positions in deals, such as leveraged buyouts (when public shares of a company are bought in an acquisition financed largely by debt and collateralized by the company's assets) and bridge loans (loans that span the interval between a deal's closing and the placement of its debt with buyers). Thus Shearson

"moved from a traditional role as an intermediary to the far more dramatic one of principal. Shearson and its Boston Company private-banking and asset-management subsidiary both invested hundreds of millions of dollars in junk bonds. Shearson also acquired twenty-eight per cent of a high-flying Los Angeles life-insurance company, First Capital, which maintained an enormous junk-bond portfolio. And Shearson's primary real-estate subsidiary, Balcor was now moving aggressively into construction lending - a somewhat anomalous business for a Wall Street securities firm, even in the freewheeling, improvisational eighties."[70]

Cohen's vistas were widening as rapidly as Shearson's. Cohen had been frugal. He had continued to drive a Buick station wagon long after he became a multimillionaire. However, by 1989, through Shearson, he owned three Gulfstream jets, one lined with ultrasuede in a style created by Ralph Lauren's interior designer. Flight attendants were asked to regularly brush the lining. Under Cohen's direction, Shearson Built a conference center at the ski resort town of Beaver Creek, Colorado. When Karen, Cohen's wife, noticed that other neighboring chalets could be seen from the conference center's windows, she directed that full-grown evergreen trees be planted. The center ended up costing Shearson $25 million.

Cohen built Shearson toward his vision of "a securities-industry titan - the biggest in retail brokerage and one of the foremost in investment banking and capital markets, here and abroad."[71] His reign at Shearson was characterized by "an ethos of limitlessness: that there was, and should be, no limit to resources, no limit to businesses in which to invest, no limit to the sublime market conditions of the mid-eighties. 'The view was that you had to be in every market doing everything with every product, because you didn't want to miss the pot of gold'" said J. Tomilson, the co-head of investment banking at Shearson.[72] A Shearson executive remarked that "Peter was always saying, 'Here is the opportunity - let's take it'. Shearson did not miss one opportunity - some opportunities were related to our core businesses, and some not."[73] Another Shearson executive said, "The question that most would ask was not 'What is in the best interests of the firm?' but 'What does Peter want?'"[74]

Gerstner's Vision

The success of Gerstner's strategic plan for Amex guaranteed him presidency in 1985 following Weill's resignation. Gerstner had finally achieved the number 2 spot he had long hoped for. He still held the chairman position at TRS and was also officially responsible for the corporate finance and planning functions and IDS. Shearson and American Express Bank reported to Robinson. Robinson began to turn his attention to outside policy issues such as trade and international debt. There were even rumors that he was angling for a job in Washington.[75] This left Gerstner in charge of more of the daily operations of the company.

During this time, Gerstner developed his own unique vision for the Amex Corporation that did not place Shearson at the center of a financial supermarket. Gerstner believed that computer services was destined to be Amex's core business. He visualized high-priced, high-quality service, and computer services fit that vision better than financial services. "In the data-processing area, Amex (was)...already the fifth-largest provider of computer services in the country. 'It is a high-profit, high-cash-flow, rapidly growing business,' said Gerstner, 'And it is a business that relies on a couple of things we know very well: customer service and technology.'"[76] Gerstner considered First Data Resources to be the company at the center of computer services at Amex. He developed a clear strategy for FDR that aimed to capitalize on its strengths. "The company wants to take its expertise in billing and customer-record keeping and move into other industries....If Amex makes another large acquisition, (Gerstner said)...it will most likely be a computer company."[77]

Symbiosis or Autonomy

In the mid-eighties, Robinson emphasized service and "One Enterprise". Yet he focused most of his energy toward global issues like solving the Third World debt crisis which had cost Amex in lost reserves from bad Latin American loans. He was chairman of the United Way of America and the New York City Partnership, a prominent corporate sponsor of minority housing and employment projects. During this time, Gerstner was emphasizing synergy and information management. He concentrated on developing Amex's computer services. Cohen, on the other hand, was trying to build Shearson into the biggest, most powerful financial firm on Wall Street. And, according to Bruck, he wasn't building Shearson for the greater glory of the American Express empire, but "qua Shearson" and was glad to have resources of American Express behind him. He had resisted Robinson's entreaties for synergy "...and Shearson had remained stubbornly isolationist. His desire was not for symbiosis but for even-greater autonomy,...to pursue his vision...with a minimum of interference."[78] Cohen was required to participate in Amex's strategic planning sessions. One participant in these planning sessions recalls Cohen as "blasé, bored, just not interested. His attitude was that you could not plan for a securities firm as you would for other industries. Peter would say, 'You guys, don't give me that crap. This (Shearson) is a *real* industry, this is a *tough* industry, this isn't selling traveller's checks.'"[79]

Gerstner was growing more frustrated with Cohen and Shearson as time went on. Shearson's erratic earnings were obscuring TRS's enormous success. Said Henry Duques, the president and CEO of Information Services Corporation, "While earnings at TRS, under Lou, were growing at fifteen per cent, year after year, Shearson's earnings were up one quarter, down another, and it was disturbing when the market valuation of American Express stock was so affected by Shearson's ups and downs. So Lou would ask Peter for numbers, and ask him some probing questions. But Peter's response was 'Don't try to pin me down. I can't manage it (Shearson) the way you do - it's a different business. The market goes up and the market goes down. And if it goes up next month I could make a hundred million.'"[80]

Gerstner argued to Robinson that Shearson's strategy should be subjected to the kind of rigorous review experienced by other parts of Amex. Robinson treated Shearson differently than Amex's other divisions. He did not supervise the company's activities as intently and allowed Cohen significant leeway. Bruck describes Robinson's light supervision of Cohen as "attributable to his belief in decentralization, and to his "hands-off style."[81] Robinson, himself, acknowledges that he may have sometimes given subordinates what looked like too much latitude. But, he said, "if that's what their personalities require to be the most turned-on, dynamic contributors to American Express, that's an easy price to pay."[82]

Robinson considered Cohen to be one such dynamic contributor. Bruck describes Robinson as having "believed so intensely in Cohen's prowess that he willingly suspended disbelief. Even today,...Robinson speaks about Cohen (with)... the echo of thrall."[83] Some believed that Cohen had become overzealous, too confident to the point of being condescending and abrasive. But Robinson seemed to overlook these quirks. One Robinson associate said that although many people, including Robinson's wife, Linda, criticized Peter, "..Jim really was his booster, I think he was mesmerized by him."[84]

Under Cohen's direction, Shearson had provided Amex a significant boost. The company's record earnings in 1986, $341 million, were a blessing to Amex during its recovery from its Fireman's Fund's losses.[85] With Shearson, Amex was sharing in the money that everyone was making on Wall Street. A Robinson associate commented that "Jim wanted to build a great financial-services company that would be the biggest or one of the biggest in the world, and Shearson was critical to that strategy."[86]

Fortune and Fame

Despite the rising tensions between Cohen and Gerstner, the company was doing extremely well. Amex had tripled its revenues between the years of 1979 and 1987[87] and earned an average return on shareholders' equity of better than 15% a year.[88] It was the first to top $1 billion a year in income in 1986 and was responsible for more than $298 billion in other people's money.[89] The press surrounding Robinson, Cohen and the Shearson-Amex empire was equally as glowing. In January of 1988, a *Business Week* cover story on Robinson declared that he had "...transformed the company...(into)...the unrivalled colossus of financial services...(having led)...what is widely considered the most successful financial services diversification drive of the 1980's."[90] Cohen's press was also stunning. There were few publications that had not glorified him as a "wunderkind" or a "legend".[91] In 1987, *Euromoney* named him Banker of the Year. In 1988, following the E.F. Hutton acquisition, *Institutional Investor* released a cover story on him. Its title read, "Today Hutton, tomorrow..." The article compared Cohen to such Wall Street legends as "Andre Meyer, Sidney Weinberg and Robert Lehman."

The Safra Affair

When Edmond Safra resigned as chairman of the TDB and American Express Bank, he agreed, at the request of Amex, to not found a new Swiss bank until March, 1988. Months later, Amex suspected that Safra was hiring away TDB employees in preparation for his re-entry into Swiss banking. Amex feared that when Safra returned to Swiss banking, he would reclaim his former customers. The company considered Safra's activities as unfair competition and tried to protect itself through legal action. Despite these efforts, in the summer of 1988, Safra opened a new bank at the site of his old one in Geneva.

Only two weeks later, Safra was upset to find several published articles linking him to the Mafia, South American drug traffickers, the CIA, the Iran Contra scandal and drug money laundering. These articles attacked Safra's reputation and threatened his business. Safra conducted his own investigation and determined that Amex was behind the smear campaign. Eventually, he confronted Robinson on the telephone and later at a meeting in Safra's Manhattan apartment. Robinson claimed that he would be "dumbfounded" if he found out his people had anything to do with the smear and that he would check into the matter.[92]

Several links suggested that Harry L. Freeman, Executive Vice President of Amex, likely was in charge of the scandal. He had hired Susan Cantor and Antonio Greco to investigate Safra's dark side and was alleged to have trumped up the illegal connections. A month later, in the summer of 1988, Amex admitted to the campaign to ruin Safra's reputation and made a public apology for what Robinson called "an unauthorized and shameful effort to use media to malign...(Safra)..."[93] Amex paid $8 million to Safra and charities he selected as penance.[94]

Robinson received little criticism for the scandal. He was able to escape the blame partly because Freeman retired after the company's public apology and became the scapegoat. Robinson's reputation of escaping blame for his company's errors has earned him the description "slicker than teflon".[95] Public relations people like Robinson's wife, Linda, who owns her own public relations firm, call this "damage control".[96]

"An Albatross Named Shearson"[97]

The 1987 stockmarket crash brought the end of the Bull Market and Shearson's earnings reflected this change, dropping severely in 1988. Securities analysts contended that Shearson was spread too thin to excel in any one area of its highly cyclical industry. "All of a sudden, they've got more businesses than they can handle.'"[98] It seemed that Cohen had overreached. Some believe that he had inflated a highly profitable retail brokerage outfit into a full-service investment house that did absolutely everything but excelled in nothing. As the financier, Michael David-Weill described it, "We are only as good as the times we are in."[99] The glory years were over and Cohen and Shearson's glory would end with them.

A string of devastating setbacks befell Shearson. The company's net worth had been severely diminished by the E.F. Hutton acquisition and the "junk-bond" market collapsed. These and other losses destroyed Shearson's financial profile. The company's losses began to affect Amex's balance sheet and Robinson took notice.

First, Shearson damaged its own and Amex's reputation by representing a British firm, Beazer P.L.C., in its hostile bid for Pittsburgh's Koppers Company in the spring of 1988. Although Beazer and Shearson eventually won control of Koppers, the battle was a rough one. Pittsburgh residents, including the mayor and civic leaders, were incensed. Wall Street disapproved. It was not appropriate for a reputable investment bank to be a principal in a hostile takeover. Residents were televised burning and cutting their American Express cards in half. Remnants were mailed to Robinson, who had a difficult time handling the public ridicule, especially since Shearson, and not Amex, was to blame. The incident infuriated Robinson, who began to question his trust in Cohen's management capabilities.[100] He forbade Shearson from backing any more hostile deals.

Shearson also failed to back F. Ross Johnson's attempt to acquire RJR Nabisco from its shareholders in late 1988. This incident was detailed in the best-selling book by Burrough and Helyar called "Barbarians at the Gate".[101] Shearson made an embarrassingly low first bid, and was easily beaten out by Kohlberg Kravis Roberts and Company. The defeat cost Shearson more than $200 million in potential fees and led to a loss of credibility. Shearson had been out-classed. Robinson was, again, furious. Johnson was one of Robinson's closest friends and Cohen had fumbled the merger out of Johnson's hands. Shearson was humiliated and was labeled inept by the press.

Other embarrassments occurred. Shearson's Boston Company, a monetary management subsidiary, was caught having overstated its 1988 earnings by $30 million. Cohen had to fire Boston Company president, James N. VonGermeten, for the scandal, and Chief Financial Officer, Joseph F. Murphy, resigned. Amex's earnings were subsequently reduced by $30 million as the company admitted to the blunder.

In *Barbarians*, Burrough and Helyar blamed Cohen for the failed RJR deal and described him as having flawed judgement and bad demeanor.[102] Shearson had become a liability to Amex, and Cohen, an embarrassment. On January 29, 1990, Robinson fired Cohen. Amex absorbed the rest of Shearson and discovered the company to be a patchwork of dozens of investment houses sloppily stitched together. *Business Week's* cover story titled "The Failed Vision" described its own interpretation of why Robinson's dream never materialized.

> "The plans of one-source delivery of various financial services and cross-selling to AmEx's various customers never materialized. In many ways the product mix and clientele became so varied that customers and executives alike were confused."[103]

Robinson spent the next few months cutting the unwieldy Shearson down to a more manageable size.

what is net?

Shearson showed net loss this year

Total Revenues for American Express Company Divisions 1977 - 1982 (millions of dollars)

	1977	1978	1979	1980	1981	1982	1983	1984	1985	1986	1987	1988	1989
Travel Related Services	792	993	1,239	1,661	2,175	2,516	2,889	3,620	4,226	5,951	5,607	6,854	8,357
International Banking Services American Express Bank '83-'89	381	516	706	930	1,068	1,025	1,437	1,548	1,568	1,685	1,733	1,738	2,100
Insurance Services	2,253	2,556	2,719	2,914	3,104	3,356	601	740	659	-	-	-	-
American Express Information Services	-			-	-	-	-	-	-	-	384	447	660
Investment Services/Shearson Lehman Brothers '83-'89	-	-	-	922	1,016	1,318	1,826	2,280	3,246	4,600	*6,749	*10,529	*12,501
IDS Financial Services	-	-	-	-	-	-	-	1,576	2,201	2,395	1,360	1,557	1,934
Other and Corporate	27	32	33	35	22	14	(6)	82	166	330	342	108	193
Adjustments and Eliminations	(7)	(21)	(30)	(36)	(94)	(136)	(149)	(204)	(216)	(309)	(213)	(338)	(698)
Consolidated	3,446	4,076	4,667	6,426	7,291	8,093	6,598	9,642	11,850	14,652	15,962	20,895	25,047

*Includes Hutton

Notes

1. Saul Hansel, "What's in the Cards for Lou Gerstner?," *Institutional Investor* December, 1988, p. 51.
2. Anthony Bianco, "Do You Know Me? An Intimate Profile of Jim Robinson, CEO of American Express," *Business Week* January 25, p. 75.
3. Peter Z. Grossman, ."James D. Robinson, III Takes Charge," *Best of Business Quarterly 9,* no. 2 (Summer 1987), p. 90.
4. Anthony Bianco, "Do You Know Me? An Intimate Profile of Jim Robinson, CEO of American Express," *Business Week* January 25, p. 75.
5. Ibid.
6. Ibid.
7. Ibid, p. 74.
8. Saul Hansel, "What's in the Cards for Lou Gerstner?," *Institutional Investor* December 1988, p. 51.
9. Ibid, p. 51.
10. Ibid, p. 50.
11. Ibid, p. 51.
12. Ibid, p. 52, 55.
13. Peter Z. Grossman, "James D. Robinson, III Takes Charge," *Best of Business Quarterly* 9, no. 2 (Summer 1987), p. 90.
14. John Paul Newport Jr., "American Express: Service that Sells," *Fortune* November 20, 1989, p. 80.
15. Peter Z. Grossman, "James D. Robinson, III Takes Charge," *Best of Business Quarterly* 9, no. 2 (Summer 1987), p. 90.
16. Ibid, p. 87.
17. Ibid, p. 90.
18. Connie Bruck, "Undoing The Eighties," *The New Yorker* July 23, 1990, p. 56.
19. Ibid, p. 58.
20. Ibid.
21. Peter Z. Grossman, "James D. Robinson, III Takes Charge," *Best of Business Quarterly* 9, no. 2 (Summer 1987), p. 89.
22. Anthony Bianco, "Do You Know Me? An Intimate Profile of Jim Robinson, CEO of American Express," *Business Week* January 25, p. 76.
23. "Not Doing Nicely, American Express and its Broker, Shearson Lehman," *The Economist* February 3, 1990, p. 84.
24. Connie Bruck, "Undoing The Eighties," *The New Yorker* July 23, 1990, 56.
25. Ibid.
26. *Business Week,* March 19, 1990, pg.110.
27. Anthony Bianco, "Do You Know Me? An Intimate Profile of Jim Robinson, CEO of American Express," *Business Week* January 25, p. 76.
28. Connie Bruck, "Undoing The Eighties," *The New Yorker* July 23, 1990, p. 58.
29. Monci Jo Williams, "Shearson Lehman: The 'Mismatch' May be Working," *Fortune,* March 31, 1986, p. 33.
30. Anthony Bianco, "Do You Know Me? An Intimate Profile of Jim Robinson, CEO of

American Express," *Business Week* January 25, p. 76.

31. Joe Queenan and Tatiana Pouschine, "The Peter Principle," *Forbes* July 10, 1989, p. 41

32. Connie Bruck, "Undoing The Eighties," *The New Yorker* July 23, 1990, p. 58.

33. Monci Jo Williams, "Shearson Lehman: The 'Mismatch' may be Working," *Fortune,* March 31, 1986, p.33.

34. Ibid.

35. Ibid.

36. Connie Bruck, "Undoing The Eighties," *The New Yorker* July 23, 1990, p. 57.

37. Lenny Glynn, "Edmond Safra Targets Geneva," *Institutional Investor* March 1988, p. 154.

38. Ibid.

39. John Paul Newport Jr., "American Express: Service that Sells," *Fortune* November 20, 1989, p. 84.

40. Ibid.

41. Monci Jo Williams, "Synergy Works at American Express," *Fortune* February 16, 1987, p. 79.

42. Ibid.

43. Ibid, p. 80.

44. Ibid, p. 79.

45. Ibid, p. 80.

46. John Paul Newport Jr., "American Express: Service that Sells," *Fortune* November 20, 1989, p. 80.

47. Ibid, p. 80.

48. Ibid, p. 82.

49. Saul Hansel, "What's in the Cards for Lou Gerstner?," *Institutional Investor* December 1988, p. 50.

50. Ibid.

51. Ibid.

52. Ibid, p. 56,59.

53. Connie Bruck, "Undoing The Eighties," *The New Yorker* July 23, 1990, p. 62.

54. Anthony Bianco, "Do You Know Me? An Intimate Profile of Jim Robinson, CEO of American Express," *Business Week* January 25, p. 77.

55. Lenny Glynn, "Edmond Safra Targets Geneva," *Institutional Investor* March 1988, p. 154.

56. Ibid.

57. Ibid, p. 154, 156.

58. Saul Hansel, "What's in the Cards for Lou Gerstner?," *Institutional Investor* December 1988, p. 59.

59. Ibid.

60. Anthony Bianco, "Do You Know Me? An Intimate Profile of Jim Robinson, CEO of American Express," *Business Week* January 25, p. 76.

61. Ibid.

62. Saul Hansel, "What's in the Cards for Lou Gerstner?," *Institutional Investor* December 1988, p. 59.

63. Jaques Lowe, "Fireman's Fund: Who's in Charge Here?," *Institutional Investor* August, 1986, p. 104.
64. Connie Bruck, "Undoing The Eighties," *The New Yorker* July 23, 1990, p. 58.
65. Ibid.
66. Ibid, p. 59
67. Ibid.
68. Ibid.
69. Ibid, p. 60.
70. Ibid, p. 60-61.
71. Ibid, p. 57.
72. Ibid, p. 62.
73. Ibid, p. 61.
74. Ibid.
75. Saul Hansel, "What's in the Cards for Lou Gerstner?," *Institutional Investor* December 1988, p. 51.
76. Ibid, p. 59, 61.
77. Ibid, p. 61.
78. Connie Bruck, "Undoing The Eighties," *The New Yorker* July 23, 1990, p. 57, 61.
79. Ibid.
80. Ibid.
81. Ibid, p. 71.
82. John Paul Newport Jr., "American Express: Service that Sells," *Fortune* November 20, 1989, p. 89.
83. Connie Bruck, "Undoing The Eighties," *The New Yorker* July 23, 1990, p. 62.
84. Ibid, p. 57.
85. Ibid, p. 62.
86. Ibid.
87. Anthony Bianco, "Do You Know Me? An Intimate Profile of Jim Robinson, CEO of American Express," *Business Week* January 25, p. 78.
88. John Paul Newport Jr., "American Express: Service that Sells," *Fortune* November 20, 1989, p. 80.
89. Anthony Bianco, "Do You Know Me? An Intimate Profile of Jim Robinson, CEO of American Express," *Business Week* January 25, p. 72.
90. Ibid.
91. Connie Bruck, "Undoing The Eighties," *The New Yorker* July 23, 1990, p. 56.
92. Brian Burrough, 'The Vendetta: How American Express Orchestrated a Smear of Rival Edmond Safra," *The Wall Street Journal* September 24, 1990.
93. Connie Bruck, "Undoing The Eighties," *The New Yorker* July 23, 1990, p. 65.
94. Brian Burrough, 'The Vendetta: How American Express Orchestrated a Smear of Rival Edmond Safra," *The Wall Street Journal* September 24, 1990.
95. Allan Sloan, "Being Slicker Than Teflon at American Express," *Los Angeles Times March 5, 1990, p. D5.*
96. Ibid.
97. Kurt Eichenwald, "An Albatross Named Shearson," *The New York Times* July 15, 1990, p. F1.

98. Ibid.

99. Connie Bruck, "Undoing The Eighties," *The New Yorker* July 23, 1990, p. 58.

100. Ibid, p. 63-65.

101. Ibid, p. 68.

102. Ibid.

103. John Meehan and Jon Friedman with Leah J. Nathans, "The Failed Vision," *Business Week* March 19, 1990, p. 111.

11. The Boston YWCA: 1991*

In the summer of 1991 Mary Kinsell, Controller and Chief Financial Officer for the Boston YWCA, briefed her successor, Carolyn Rosen, and Marti Wilson-Taylor, the YWCA's new Executive Director. Deeply aware of the organization's financial crisis, Kinsell noted that the past 20 years had created many difficulties for the once-predominant Boston YWCA. Especially pressing was the need to seek out new sources of funding because of significant cuts in federal funding to non-profits, increased demand and competition in the fitness and day-care industries, and increased real estate costs. In addition, the YWCA faced questions about how to deal with several aging YWCA buildings, located in prime neighborhoods of Boston but unmodernized and slowly deteriorating. Ms. Kinsell warned, "The Boston YWCA is like a dowager from an old Boston family that has seen better days: it is 'building rich' and 'cash poor.' Leveraging equity from its buildings is difficult and making operations generate enough cash flow to maintain the buildings seems almost impossible." The YWCA must now meet these challenges or it will be forced to cut back its activities, and may even face bankruptcy.

The First 100 Years

The Young Women's Christian Association (YWCA) is a non-profit organization whose original mission was "To provide for the physical, moral, and spiritual welfare of young women in Boston." For more than twelve decades it has done just that: meeting the changing needs of women in the community by providing services, opportunities, and support in an environment of shared sisterhood.

In 1866, a group of affluent women formed the Boston Young Women's Christian Association to rent rooms to women and children whom the Industrial Revolution had forced to leave their failing farms for work in city factories. Not only were their working conditions deplorable, but their living conditions consisted almost entirely of unsafe slums and unsanitary tenements. The Boston YWCA offered a clean, safe alternative to these living conditions, as well as recreation, companionship, and an employment referral network for women. The success of the facility led to the opening of the Berkeley Residence (40 Berkeley Street, Boston) in 1884, with accommodations for 200 residents and an employment and training bureau. It also housed the first YWCA gymnasium in America, a crucial part of its mission to "empower women through fitness, health care, and independent employment opportunities." At this early date in the YWCA's history, most of the funding for the YWCA's facilities and services was raised by wealthy women patrons both through their family connections and from among their friends and acquaintances. From its inception, the YWCA, unlike the larger, more well-known, and more aggressive YMCA, which easily garnered bank loans and donations, had to struggle to fund its projects.

In the ensuing decades, the Boston YWCA opened The School of Domestic Science to train women as institutional housekeepers and managers, and started a secretarial training

---

*This case was prepared by Donna M. Gallo of Boston College and Professors Barbara Gottfried and Alan N. Hoffman of Bentley College. Copyright © 1992 by Donna M. Gallo, Barbara Gottfried, and Alan N. Hoffman. Reprinted by permission of the authors.

program, and other training and educational programs for women. In 1911, the Boston YWCA became affiliated with the other YWCAs in the United States. By this time, the YWCA was no longer merely a philanthropic association run by upper class women for women of a lower class, but an association of working women meeting the needs of other working women in the home and in the marketplace. Nevertheless, the continued support of wealthy patrons was crucial to the YWCA's viability as a community resource.

In the early 1920s, the "Y" initiated a capital campaign under the slogan "Every Girl Needs the YWCA" to raise funds for another building. Over one million dollars in contributions was received by subscription from donors of both the middle and upper classes, and in 1927 ground was broken at the corner of Clarendon and Stuart Streets for the Boston YWCA's new headquarters. The new building, including recreational facilities, a swimming pool, class-rooms, meeting rooms, and offices for the staff, was dedicated in 1929 and has served as headquarters for the association ever since.

During World War II, the YWCA contributed to the war effort by sponsoring educational lectures and forums such as "Fix-It-Yourself" for the wives of servicemen, offering housing to women doing war work, and providing recreation and entertainment to men and women in the armed services. During this time the YWCA continued to be managed and funded primarily by women, for women.

After the war, YWCA administrators made a concerted effort to reach out to immigrant women. An interracial charter was adopted at the national convention which called for the integration and participation of minority groups in every aspect of the association, the community, and the nation. In addition, rapid postwar population growth in the suburbs west of Boston led to the opening in 1964 of the West Suburban Branch of the "Y" in Natick, Massachusetts, 20 miles west of Boston. The Natick "Y" focused its energies on the needs and wants of suburban women and their children. Additionally, advocates formed a lobbying group, the YWCA Public Affairs Committee, to focus on the areas of housing and family planning, and to call attention to the needs of those women, especially mothers, who were not being met by traditional social service organizations.

Throughout its first 100 years, the Boston YWCA, staffed and funded almost entirely by women, worked to empower women by helping them take charge of their lives, plan for their futures, and become economically independent and self-supporting.

Recent History

> In 1866, the Boston YWCA became the first YWCA in the nation. Today we are part of the oldest and largest women's organization in the world, serving all people regardless of sex, race, religion, or income. Our One Imperative is the elimination of racism.
>
> *Mary L. Reed —Former Executive Director, 1986*

The 1960s were a time of social and cultural upheaval, especially with regard to civil rights, the movement whose goal was equality for all races. In support of the civil rights movement, the YWCA made a commitment to fight racism and integrate its programs and services at every level, initiating a special two-year action plan in 1963. The operating budget for the plan provided for two staff members and support services to become more involved with other community groups working in the areas of fair housing, voter registration, and literacy programs. In 1967, the YWCA's first black President, Mrs. Robert W. Clayton, was elected at the National Convention. In 1968 the Boston YWCA opened Aswalos House in Dorchester, Massachusetts, especially to meet the needs of women in the inner city. As a fitting ending to the 1960s, the One Imperative "to eliminate racism wherever it exists and by any means necessary" was adopted and added to the statement of purpose as the philosophical basis for the YWCA in coming years.

Although fighting racism remained important, in the 1970s the YWCA shifted its attention to issues raised by the changing roles of women in American society. The 1960s and 1970s were decades of the revival and growth of the feminist movement in the United States and throughout the world. The social and political arena in which the Boston and other YWCAs were operating was changing rapidly. More and more women were working outside the home while raising children. The number of women living at or near the poverty level was on the rise. Classes and programs at the YWCA had to be redesigned to meet changing demands. For instance, the "Y" offered instruction in survival skills for urban living; but more radically, because non-traditional jobs for women were on the rise, in 1977 the "Y" launched its first non-traditional training program, funded by the federal government, to train women to work in the construction industry. Thus, in the 1970s, federal, state, and local governments became increasingly involved in social welfare, whereas in the past these needs had been met by private charitable and voluntary organizations. At the same time that the YWCA began to rely more on government funding and less on private donations, the YWCA's Board of Directors in the 1960s and 1970s changed to reflect the racial and class diversity of the women in the communities the YWCA served. While the new Board members helped the YWCA respond effectively to the immediate needs of the inner city community, they lost touch with the monied constituency that had formerly been the YWCA's base of support, and that monied constituency in turn shifted its attention and support to other causes. See Exhibit 1 for the YWCA's organization chart.

The Changing Environment

The late 1970s saw a dramatic rise in the number of unwed mothers, teen pregnancies, and teen parents. At the same time, more and more state and federal funds became available for social programs. and many non-profits directed their energies to establishing themselves as vendors or service providers to win government contracts. The Boston YWCA became a major vendor in the areas of child care, employment training, teen services, and domestic abuse programming. As a result of the YWCA's strong advocacy efforts, major federal and state contracts were awarded to the YWCA for further study of issues related to teen pregnancy. However, the YWCA's redirecting of its efforts toward securing government funding significantly eroded its base of private support, especially among those upper crust women who had, for generations, been the primary source of funds for the YWCA in Boston, and the YWCA, which had for a long time been one of a few non-profits, became one of many contending for the same funds.

As the decade came to a close, the outlook for the Boston YWCA began to shift. Given the community's growing need for services and their own aging facilities, the management team of the Boston YWCA realized they would have to make some tough decisions about

Exhibit 1

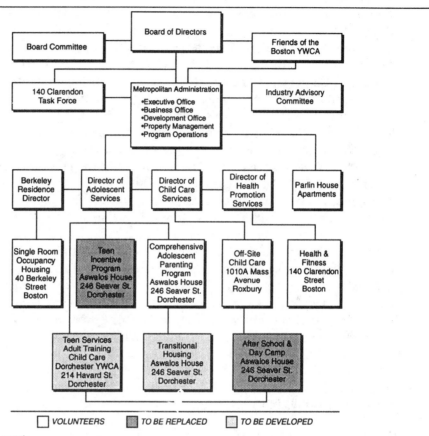

Source: Boston YWCA records.

allocating funds that were beginning to get more scarce. If they were to decide that a major outlay of cash or large loans for facilities were necessary, they would have to pull funds from the programs and services the association provided to the community at a time when the need for community services was greater than ever and funds for these services were scarcer than they had been for some time. However, if the YWCA's management team continued to allocate funds for services and programs while making only minimal allocations for facility maintenance, they risked incurring the cost either of major repairs further down the line, or the serious deterioration of their major assets. Though the management team did not want to lose sight of the YWCA's commitment to the women and children in the community, the "Y's" financial crisis would require foresight, careful planning, and some hard choices.

The Economic Crunch

In the early 1980s the need for social services grew, increasing the number of nonprofit organizations competing for the same funds. At the same time the Reagan Administration cut back federal funding, and non-profits were forced to go back to raising funds through private donations, grants, bequests, and the United Way. The mid-1980s, however, were prosperous years, especially in the Boston area. Individuals and companies gave more generously than in past years to non-profits, and in response to the limited availability of federal funds for social services during the Reagan era, non-profits increasingly directed their resources to funding everything from homeless shelters and food pantries to drug and alcohol rehabilitation centers.

However, the economic downturn in late 1987 immediately cut into the funding flow for non-profits. Corporations and the general public became more discerning about where they directed their charitable contributions. Many people lost their jobs; a high-debt lifestyle caught up with others: in short, people's disposable income dropped off. It became increasingly difficult to raise the funds necessary to keep up the facilities and to provide the services the community continued to demand. As the economy worsened, the need for services increased proportionately and at a more rapid rate than the Boston YWCA had ever witnessed. At the same time, the YWCA had to contend both with its old "mainstream" image in the face of the proliferation of more "chic" non-profits such as homeless shelters, battered women's shelters, or "safe houses," and with the growing misperception of the YWCA as an organization run primarily by women of color for women of color.

The climate for the banking industry in Boston during the late 1980s also altered dramatically. Many banks were in financial trouble and those that had lent freely in the mid-1980s now scrutinized every loan request and rejected a large majority of those they received. Funds for capital improvements and construction were not looked upon favorably by most Boston area banks; and money to fund new projects and large renovations became nearly impossible to obtain. These negative trends have only worsened so far in the 1990s, as the YWCA faces the absolute necessity of making some hard decisions regarding the allocation of its shrinking resources.

Sources of Funding

Revenue for the Boston YWCA comes from three sources:

1. **Support Funds** – funds from the United Way of Massachusetts Bay, contributions, grants, legacies, and bequests.
2. **Operating Revenue** – money from program fees, government-sponsored programs, membership dues, housing and food services.
3. **Non-Operating Revenue** – income from leasing of office space to outside concerns, investment income, and net realized gain on investments.

Exhibit 2 shows the percentage each has contributed to total revenue for the past five years. From 1985 to 1989 the United Way accounted for 70 – 80% of the support funds revenue. But like all non-profit organizations in the late 1980s, the United Way was under fire for its operational procedures and found itself in a fiercely competitive fundraising environment. The United Way anticipated a 30% drop in fundraising for 1991, which would affect all the agencies it funded, including the Boston YWCA (see Exhibit 3). At the same time, operating revenues for the YWCA dropped off in 1990 as well, so that more, rather than less support funding was needed to operate. Since support funding is expected to continue to decrease in the next three to five years, the Boston YWCA must discover new sources of funding to maintain its services and meet its operational expenses. The financial statements for the Boston YWCA are shown

EXHIBIT 2   Percentage Breakdown – Sources of Funding: Boston YWCA

	Years					
	1990	1989	1988	1987	1986	1985
Source of funding						
Support funds	33%	24%	21%	23%	22%	22%
Operating revenue	54%	63%	67%	65%	66%	67%
Non-operating revenue	13%	13%	12%	12%	12%	11%

in Exhibits 4 and 5.

FACILITIES

In 1987, the Boston YWCA was operating from four facilities in neighborhoods of Boston and one in a Natick, a western suburb of the city. During 1987, the Boston Redevelopment Authority, a commission that oversees all real estate development in the city, awarded a parcel of land to the YWCA for $1.00 on which to build a new facility as part of the city's redevelopment plan. The new facility would replace the old Dorchester YWCA, Aswalos House, which a grant would then convert to transitional housing for unwed mothers and their children. Since the YWCA now had a new parcel of land, and other existing facilities in need of maintenance records and repair, the management team embarked on a three-year study to analyze its programs and services, and its properties. Most importantly, they decided to implement an aggressive renovation schedule designed to modernize all facilities, to protect the value of the YWCA's major assets, its buildings.

As part of this renovation, repair, and maintenance program, the association's management team had to perform a thorough review of its programs and services. The programs most beneficial to the agency in terms of revenue and those the community had the greatest need

EXHIBIT 3   Detailed Analysis of YWCA Funding Revenues 1991: Boston YWCA

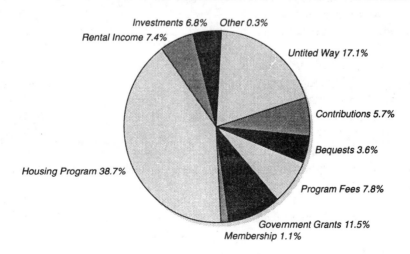

Investments 6.8%   Other 0.3%
Rental Income 7.4%
Untited Way 17.1%
Contributions 5.7%
Bequests 3.6%
Program Fees 7.8%
Housing Program 38.7%
Government Grants 11.5%
Membership 1.1%

EXHIBIT 4 Statement of Support and Revenue, Expenses, Capital Additions, and Changes in Fund Balances: Boston YWCA (June 30, 1991)

Years Ending June 30	Current Fund	Plant Fund	Endowment Fund	1991 Totals	1990 Totals
Support and Revenue					
Support					
United Way	$ 703,643	—	—	$ 703,643	$ 713,500
Contributions and grants	233,624	—	—	233,264	197,700
Legacies and bequests	150,386	—	—	150,386	537,540
	1,087,293	—	—	1,087,293	1,488,740
Operating Revenue					
Program fees	320,611	—	—	320,611	355,170
Government-sponsored programs	471,615	—	—	471,615	411,050
Membership	45,674	—	—	45,674	71,579
Housing and food service	1,589,587	—	—	1,589,587	1,586,553
	2,427,487	—	—	2,427,487	2,424,352
Non-operating revenue					
Rental income	302,641	—	—	302,641	298,036
Investment income	278,982	—	—	278,982	244,244
Net realized gain on investments	41,392	—	—	41,392	2,308
Other revenue	7,967	—	—	7,967	43,790
	630,982	—	—	630,982	588,358
Total support and revenue	4,145,762	—	—	4,145,762	4,461,450
Expenses					
Program services					
Aswalos House	250,621	14,782	—	265,403	384,776
Berkeley Residence	1,053,131	86,465	—	1,139,596	1,054,106
Cass Branch	1,216,544	128,673	—	1,345,217	1,394,075
Child Care	422,411	2,030	—	424,411	344,011
Harvard	6,132	—	—	6,132	—
	2,948,839	231,950	—	3,180,789	3,176,968
Supporting services					
General and administration	632,657	15,364	—	648,021	793,861
Fundraising	287,448	6,981	—	294,429	135,978
	920,105	22,345	—	924,450	929,839
Total expenses	3,868,944	254,295	—	4,123,239	4,106,807

EXHIBIT 4 Statement of Support and Revenue, Expenses, Capital Additions, and Changes in Fund Balances: Boston YWCA (continued)(June 30, 1991)

Years Ending June 30	Current Fund	Plant Fund	Endowment Fund	1991 Totals	1990 Totals
Excess (deficiency) of support and revenue over expenses before capital additions	$ 276,818	(254,295)	—	22,523	354,643
Capital Additions					
Grants	106,495	38,985	—	145,480	314,798
Investment income	—	5,529	65,598	71,127	68,018
Net realized gain on investment transactions	—	—	72,577	72,577	63,874
Write-off of deferred charges	—	—	—	—	(305,312)
Loss on sale of asset	—	—	—	—	(11,856)
Total capital additions	106,495	44,514	138,175	289,184	129,522
Excess (deficiency) of support and revenue over expenses after capital additions	$ 383,313	$ (209,781)	$ 128,175	$ 311,707	$ 484,165
Fund balances, beginning of year	$1,379,040	$1,486,053	$3,042,128	$5,907,221	$5,423,056
Transfers between funds					
Plant acquisition	(274,155)	274,155	—	—	—
Principle repayment on loan payable to endowment fund	(143,841)	143,841	—	—	—
Permanent fund transfer	346,908	(346,908)	—	—	—
	(71,088)	71,088	—	—	—
Fund balances, end of year	$1,691,265	$1,347,360	$3,180,303	$6,218,928	$5,907,221

for had to be assessed for future expectations of growth and space requirements. New programs would have to be accommodated and those programs that were no longer financially feasible or in demand would have to be eliminated. The management team planned to complete their research and decision-making prior to implementing any expansion or renovation of the buildings.

West Suburban Program Center

When the YWCA expanded, and opened a branch in Natick, Massachusetts, a suburb located 20 miles west of Boston in 1964, it bought a building which quickly became inadequate to the YWCA's needs, and in 1981 the center moved to a new facility. The resources for women at

EXHIBIT 5 Balance Sheet: Boston YWCA (June 30, 1991)

Years Ending June 30	Current Fund	Plant Fund	Endowment Fund	1991 Totals	1990 Totals
Assets					
Current assets					
Cash	$ 137,469	66,292	—	203,761	110,684
Cash in escrow and security deposits	40,642	—	—	40,642	37,932
Accounts receivable (less allowance for doubtful accounts of $3,500 in 1991 and $2,687 in 1990)	102,334	—	—	102,334	166,245
Supplies and prepaid expenses	54,452	—	—	54,452	73,613
Total current assets	334,897	66,292	—	401,189	388,474
Pooled investments	1,793,198	—	3,180,303	4,973,501	4,755,252
Land, buildings, and equipment, net	—	2,147,155	—	2,147,155	1,869,963
Deferred charges	—	349,638	—	349,638	349,638
	1,793,198	2,496,793	3,180,303	7,470,294	6,994,853
Total assets	**$2,128,095**	**2,563,085**	**3,180,303**	**7,871,483**	**7,383,327**
Liabilities and Fund Balances (Deficit)					
Current liabilities					
Current maturities of long-term notes payable	—	18,979	—	18,979	17,524
Accounts payable and accrued expenses	254,757	—	—	254,757	201,581
Deferred revenue	182,073	—	—	182,073	202,717
Total current liabilities	436,830	18,979	—	455,809	421,822
Long-term notes payable, less current maturities	—	1,196,746	—	1,196,746	910,443
Loan payable to endowment fund	—	—	—	—	143,841
Total liabilities	436,830	1,215,725	—	1,652,555	1,476,106
Fund balances (deficit)					
Unrestricted					
Designated by governing board to function as endowment	1,507,135	—	—	1,507,135	1,453,867
Undesignated	(101,933)	—	—	(101,933)	(354,084)
Total unrestricted	1,405,202	—	—	1,405,202	1,099,783
Restricted—nonexpendable	286,063	223,798	3,180,303	3,690,164	3,545,183
Net investment in plant	—	1,123,562	—	1,123,562	1,262,255
Total fund balances	1,691,265	1,347,360	3,180,303	6,218,928	5,907,221
Total liabilities and fund balances (deficit)	**$2,128,095**	**2,563,085**	**3,180,303**	**7,871,483**	**7,383,327**

this branch were designed to serve its suburban constituency, and included programs for women re-entering the job market after years of parenting, training programs for displaced workers, spousal and family abuse programs, divorce support groups, and counseling for women suffering from breast cancer. However, in 1988, after much research and years of restructuring the services offered at the West Suburban Program Center, its inability to support itself financially through its operations led to a decision to close down the facility.

Aswalos House

Aswalos House, located in Dorchester, Massachusetts, an urban center within the jurisdiction of the City of Boston, was originally opened in 1968. Until 1989, it housed an After School Enrichment Program and a Teen Development Program that offered training for word processing and clerical work, and GED preparation courses. Later, Aswalos House added a program for teen mothers.

In 1989, the receipt of a $100,000 Department of Housing and Urban Development (HUD) grant transformed Aswalos House into transitional housing for teenage mothers and their children, and existing programs were transferred to other facilities. Originally the programs were to be transferred to the new Dorchester Branch planned for the parcel acquired from the City of Boston. However, that parcel was never developed because development costs were estimated at $1.5 – $2 million, but the YWCA was only able to raise $300,000. Consequently, the parcel of land was returned to the City of Boston.

The new Aswalos House for teen mothers opened in October 1990, and provided transitional housing for ten mothers and their children. Prospective occupants have to be between sixteen and twenty and demonstrate severe financial need. Counseling services are provided, and a staff case worker arranges for schooling and job training for the teenagers. In addition, a staff housing advocate coordinates permanent housing for the mothers and their children.

Half the expense of running the facility is covered by a federal grant to the Boston YWCA. The remaining half is made up by fees paid by the teen mothers from their welfare income, and by contributions from the United Way and private donations.

YWCA Child Care Center

The YWCA Child Care Center is rather inconveniently located in downtown Boston on the fringe of the commercial district, and is rented rather than owned by the YWCA. To be licensed as a day-care center in the Commonwealth of Massachusetts, it had to undergo extensive renovations. The owner of the property contributed a substantial portion of the cost of the renovation work, and the balance of the expense was covered by a private grant so that no loans were necessary to complete the project.

The center, a licensed pre-school, provides day care for 50 children at fees of $110 a week per toddler and $150 a week per child for children under 3. Some scholarships are available for families who are unable to pay. When the center first opened, many of its clients were on state funded day-care vouchers. Participation has now dropped considerably, however, because a significant percentage of state-funded day-care vouchers were cut from the state budget. To compensate for the loss of clients, the center went into the infant care business, caring for children from 6 months to 2 years, but it continues to run at less than capacity.

The Berkeley Residence

The Berkeley Residence was opened in 1884 in downtown Boston to serve as housing for women of all ages. Originally there was housing for 100 residents, an employment and training bureau, and a gymnasium, the first in the country for women. In 1907, 35 rooms and a meeting hall were added to the facility.

In 1985 the Berkeley Residence was cited by Boston's Building Code Department because it did not meet current safety and fire codes of the city or the Commonwealth. Major repairs and renovations estimated at $1 million were necessary to bring the building up to health, safety, and legal standards. In 1986, a construction loan for the full amount was secured at 10% interest amortized over 25 years. Once the project was completed, payments would come to approximately $100,000 annually. Work began in 1988. Repairs were needed to the infrastructure of the building, and included a conversion from oil heat to gas, a sprinkler system and smoke detector system wired throughout the building, new elevators, as well as many other repairs and maintenance work of a less costly nature. Tenants were not displaced during construction, a major concern at the beginning of the project's planning stage.

After completion of the renovation work in the spring of 1991, the facility now rents 215 rooms, which provide long-term and short-term housing for women of all ages. The Berkeley Residence offers inexpensive rent and meals, an answering service, and maid service. Other services located at the facility include a referral network for jobs and services, social services, tourist information, and emergency services. The building is open and staffed 24 hours a day, 7 days a week, providing safe, secure housing at reasonable rates for single women in the city.

Boston YWCA Headquarters at 140 Clarendon Street

Constructed between 1927 and 1929, the headquarters for the Boston YWCA is advantageously located at the corner of Clarendon and Stuart Streets, on the edge of one of the city's most prestigious retail districts, Newbury and Boylston Streets and Copley Place, in the heart of Boston's Back Bay business district. The area offers the finest in upscale retail stores and desirable office space, including the John Hancock Building and the Prudential Center. The Clarendon Headquarters, a 13-story brick and steel building, sits on approximately 13,860 square feet of land and includes approximately 167,400 square feet of space. It currently houses the YWCA administration offices, the Parlin House Apartments, the Melnea Cass Branch of the YWCA, and several commercial tenants. The Melnea Cass Branch operates health and fitness facilities, which include a swimming pool, and employment training programs. The Parlin House Apartments occupy floors 9 – 13 and comprise studio, one- and two-bedroom apartments rented at market rates.

The building has not been significantly renovated since its completion in 1929, and no longer complies with city and state building codes. In 1987, the building elevators desperately needed repairs at an estimated cost of $270,000. The building also now needs a new sprinkler system to ensure the safety of its residents and tenants and to bring the building up to code. The Parlin House Apartments also require major renovations to achieve an acceptable standard of safety, appearance, and comfort. The Apartments currently use common electric meters, and need to be rewired so tenants can control the electricity to their individual units, and pay accordingly. The YWCA's administrative offices also require improvements and repairs.

The health and fitness facilities also require significant repairs, updating, and renovation.

Old, dreary locker rooms are unattractive to current and potential members, and a larger men's locker room is needed to accommodate male members. In addition, to keep up with new trends in the fitness industry, the YWCA needs to refurbish its space for aerobics classes and purchase new weight training equipment. During this time, the YWCA has also been forced to close the pool for repairs, and the pool building itself needs significant exterior work. Cost estimates for the work on the pool and pool building are in excess of $200,000. At the same time, a decrease in demand for health and fitness clubs and an increase in competition in both the day-care and health and fitness industries has had a negative impact on revenues for this facility.

Because the YWCA's Clarendon headquarters is in such a state of disrepair, it has become very costly to maintain and operate the building. In years past, the Board of Directors has chosen to funnel their scarce available resources into their programs rather than into general repairs and maintenance of the facilities, with the result that the building at 140 Clarendon Street is currently running at a net loss in excess of $200,000 a year.

In 1988 a certified appraiser valued the Clarendon property at $16 million dollars. (However, the real estate market in the Boston area has since declined significantly.) The Boston YWCA's Board of Directors then sought a $7 million dollar loan for the proposed renovations from several major Boston area banking and financial institutions, but most of these institutions did not respond favorably to the loan request. While there were a number of valid reasons for the banks' refusing to loan the YWCA the funds necessary for the renovations, including the YWCA's own uncertainty about how the changes would impact revenues, the fact that the YWCA is a women's organization without connections in the "old-boy" network of the banking establishment contributed to the YWCA's lack of financial credibility. Finally, although the Clarendon building's excess value would cover the loan-to-value ratio, the banks raised serious questions about whether the YWCA's existing and potential cash flow could meet the debt service obligation.

The executive committee of the Boston YWCA is now faced with a serious dilemma. It must decide what to do with a deteriorating facility that not only serves as its headquarters, but also as a flagship of services offered by all the area YWCAs. After several years of study, review, and debate they are considering the following options for the Clarendon headquarters.

1. Sell the building with a guaranteed leaseback for its facilities and offices.
2. Sell the building to an interested local insurance company and rent space for the administrative offices in a nearby office building.
3. Bring in an equity partner to fund the renovations for a percentage of ownership in the facility.
4. Continue with minimal renovations and operate as they have in the past.

Increasing Competition in Fitness Services

In 1989, the management team of the Boston YWCA hired a consulting firm to review their Health Promotion Services division, housed at 140 Clarendon Street, one of the YWCA's primary sources of both operating revenue and expense, and to assist them in finding ways to enhance this branch of their services. The consultants surveyed current, former, and potential members about the strengths and weaknesses of the YWCA's Health Promotion Services including appearance, cleanliness, scheduling, products (i.e., equipment, classes, swimming pool, etc.), and overall management of the facility. This study also noted that there is considerable competition from the following vendors in the area of health and fitness:

- Bally's Holiday Fitness Centers
- Healthworks
- Fitcorp
- Boston Sports
- SkyClub
- The Mount Auburn Club
- Nautilus Plus
- Fitness International
- Fitness First
- The Club at Charles River Park
- Mike's Gym
- Fitness Unlimited
- Gold's Gym

The health club marketplace is, for the most part, a standardized industry in terms of the products and services offered at the various facilities. Most clubs offer free weights, weight equipment, exercise and aerobics classes, locker rooms, and showers with towels available. During the 1980s many new health clubs opened and the health club market became increasingly competitive. These clubs went to great expense to promote elaborate grand openings and fund extensive advertising campaigns to attract new members. The consultants' study found that fifteen other health and fitness facilities within the city are in direct competition with the YWCA. However, the YWCA does fill a unique niche because it is affordable, strongly emphasizes fitness in a non-competitive and non-commercial environment, appeals to a diverse cross-section of people, and is conveniently located. Other clubs are perceived as more commercial and competitive than the YWCA, with a greater emphasis on social interaction and frills such as saunas, racquetball and squash courts, eating facilities, etc. A comparison of the YWCA's Health Promotion Services to other health clubs in the city shows the YWCA to be in a price range somewhere between the commercial clubs and the no-frills gymnasiums. The commercial clubs range from $800 – $1200 a year, plus a one-time initiation fee of from $100 – $1200; the no-frills gymnasiums range from $300 – $400 per year; and the YWCA costs between $420 and $600 a year, plus an annual membership fee of $35.

The YWCA is comparable in size to the competition, but its space is not as well laid out as at other clubs. Most of the other clubs are air-conditioned but the YWCA isn't and its membership drops significantly during the summer months, while for other clubs summer is the peak season. The YWCA also ranks behind the top four clubs in cleanliness, and members note that its dreary atmosphere contributes to their sense of its uncleanliness. The YWCA's weight-lifting equipment and weight machines are not quite up to the standards of the competition and the YWCA lacks the staffing and supervision other clubs provide. On the other hand, the YWCA can boast a swimming pool, an indoor track, and day care. Only one other club has a pool that comes close in size to the YWCA's, and only two other clubs offer indoor tracks or day care.

According to the consultants' study, current users of the YWCA's Health Promotion Services joined because the YWCA is convenient, provides a caring environment that promotes interaction, and is relatively inexpensive. A current user profile revealed that members are generally seeking a health and fitness experience for themselves as individuals rather than a social atmosphere, and that what mattered to them additionally were sensible class schedules, adequate staffing, staff communication with the members, timely information, affordable pricing, an atmosphere without pressure, and an open, caring, and diverse environment. The complaint most often cited among current users was the lack of communication with members with regard to scheduling changes for classes, changes in the hours of operation, class cancellations, pool closings, and changes in procedures and policies of the club. Other factors that concerned current members were: the lack of cleanliness, dreary appearance, small men's locker room, poor management of the staff, poor management of class capacity, inadequate maintenance of equipment, poor scheduling, poor layout of the facility, and the lack of public relations and advertising to attract new members.

Former members were also surveyed to determine why they did not renew. Their reasons mirrored the complaints of current members:

- Poor communication with members
- Equipment breakdowns
- Untimely equipment repairs
- Poor upkeep/cleanliness
- Poor ventilation
- Dreary appearance
- Dissatisfaction with staff (no personal attention)
- Rigid schedules
- Lack of air conditioning
- Overall deterioration of the facility

The study also concluded that marketing and promotion of the Health Promotion Services are minimal, with little effort put into attracting new members, making it nearly invisible in the community.

Marti Wilson-Taylor, the new Executive Director, and Carolyn Rosen, the new Chief Financial Officer, quickly realized as they took control of the Boston YWCA in 1991 that several major decisions concerning the YWCA's physical facilities and programs and services had to be made. However, first and foremost, it was necessary for them to determine the strategic direction of the YWCA for the remainder of the decade. In an environment of increasing competition and shrinking resources, the challenge facing them is great.

12. XEL Communications, Inc.*

As he was turning into the parkway that curves around his company's plant, Bill Sanko, President of XEL Communications, glanced at a nearby vacant facility that once housed a now-defunct computer manufacturer. Over the next few months, in May, 1995, XEL would be moving into this building. While this move was a sign of how far XEL had come in the last ten years, Bill considered that they might have met the same fate as the previous tenant. He also wondered whether they would be able to sustain the same culture that enabled the company to succeed in a rapidly changing, highly competitive industry. At the same time, he realized that change could also create opportunities.

After parking and completing the short walk to his office, Bill grabbed a copy of today's *Wall Street Journal*. One article which caught his attention was entitled, "Baby Bells Lobby Congress for Regulatory Freedom." As one of many suppliers of telecommunications equipment to the Regional Bell Operating Companies (RBOCs), this development posed some interesting issues for XEL Communications. If the RBOCs were allowed to pursue their own manufacturing (which they are currently prohibited from doing), how would this affect XEL's existing contracts? As telephone and cable companies develop more strategic alliances and partnerships, would this provide an opportunity for XEL? At the same time, it appeared that the telecommunications industry was now becoming a global industry in which developing countries are allowing outside companies the ability to establish and maintain telecommunications services. What role could XEL play in this rapidly growing market?

The Telecommunications Industry

A decade after the breakup of the telephone monopoly, the prospect of intense competition driving the telecommunications industry was creating some interesting scenarios.[1] The AT&T of old was the model for the telecommunications company of the future. "You're going to see the re-creation of five or six former AT&Ts – call them 'full-service networks' – over the next five years or more," said Michael Elling, first vice president at Prudential Securities. Marketing and capital-equipment dollars are invested more efficiently if distribution is centralized, he continued."It could be that U S WEST, Time Warner, and Sprint get together. It could be that Bell Atlantic, Nynex and MCI get together. It could be that GTE, AT&T and a few other independents (local providers not affiliated with a regional Bell) get together."The inevitability of such combinations was matched by the uncertainty over what form they would take. A business known for its predictability had suddenly found itself unpredictable. "I think you can't rule anything out in this industry anymore," says Simon Flannery, a vice president at J.P. Morgan Securities. "All the rules of the game are up for review." In most cases, telecommunications systems transmitted information by wire, radio, or space satellite. Wire transmission involved sending electrical signals over various types of wire lines such as open wire, multipair cable, and coaxial cable. These lines could be used to transmit voice frequencies, telegraph messages, computer-processed data, and television programs. Another somewhat related transmission medium that had come into increasingly wider use, especially in telephone communications, was a type of cable composed of optical fibers. Here, electrical signals converted to light signals by a laser-driven transmitter carried both speech and data over bundles of thin glass or plastic filaments. Radio communication systems transmitted electronic signals in relatively narrow frequency bands through the air. They included radio navigation and both amateur and commercial broadcasting. Commercial broadcasting consisted of AM, FM, and TV broadcasting for general public use. Satellite communications allowed the exchange of television or telephone signals between widely separated locations by means of microwaves — that is, very short radio waves with wavelengths from 4 inches to 0.4 inches, which corresponded to a frequency range of 3 to 30 gigahertz (GHz), or 3 to 30 billion cycles per second. Since satellite systems did not require the construction of intermediate relay or repeater stations, as did ground-based microwave systems, they could be put into service much more rapidly.

Not only had the mode of delivery changed, but also the content. Modern telecommunications networks not only sent the traditional voice communications of telephones and the printed messages of telegraphs and telexes, they also carried images — the still images of facsimile machines or the moving images of video in video conferences in which the participants could see as well as hear each other. Additionally, they carried encoded data ranging from the business accounts of a multinational corporation to medical data relayed by physicians thousands of miles from a patient.

The U.S. telecommunications services industry was expected to continue to expand in 1994.[2] Revenues were expected to rise about 7.7 percent, compared with a 6 percent increase in 1993. In 1994, revenues generated by international services increased about 20 percent, and local exchange telephone service was expected to rise by 3 percent. Sales of domestic long distance services were expected to grow more than 6 percent in 1994, depending on overall growth in the economy. Value-added network and information services were to climb an estimated 15 percent in 1994. Revenues from cellular mobile telephone services were to increase 39 percent in 1994; satellite service revenues in 1994 were to grow nearly 25 percent.

Local telephone services were provided by about 1,325 local telephone companies (telcos), including 7 Regional Bell Operating Companies (RBOCs), telcos owned by GTE, Sprint (United Telecom and Centel franchises), and independent local telephone companies. Many of these small, local companies operated as rural telephone cooperatives. Long distance service was provided by AT&T, MCI, Sprint, WilTel, Metromedia Communications, Litel Telecommunications, Allnet, and more than 475 smaller companies.

In 1993, the local exchange telephone companies were confronted with increasing competitive pressures in certain local services they had monopolized for decades. In response to these pressures, and to possible future competition from cable TV companies and others for local exchange telephone service itself, the RBOCs stepped up their campaign to obtain authority to enter the long distance and telecommunications equipment manufacturing businesses, and to offer video programming services.

The major long distance carriers, meanwhile, focused their attention on wireless technologies and made plans to work with or acquire companies in the wireless market. This would enable them to provide long distance services to cellular users and possibly to develop a more economical local access network to reach their own subscribers. Internationally, the large service providers continued to make alliances and seek out partners in efforts to put together global telecommunications networks and offer the international equivalent of the advanced telecommunications services available in the U.S. domestic market.

In terms of policy developments that affect the telecommunications industry, the Clinton Administration had focused its attention on the national telecommunications infrastructure, or the "information superhighway." Bills were introduced in both houses of Congress that addressed this and other key telecommunications policy issues. There was broad consensus that the Federal Government should not finance the construction of a national network. Rather, the Government was being urged to help promote competition in network access, advance interconnection and interoperability standards, see that customers would have access to new services provided over the digital infrastructure at reasonable rates, and support pilot projects for applications in education and health care. Under proposed legislation, the digital infrastructure would be extended to tap information resources at libraries, research centers, and government facilities. Congress was to consider major telecommunications legislation in the future and would then face how it would resolve the contentious issues involved that concerned so many large and powerful interests. There were also signs that some states would also open up their exchange and local service markets to competition.

Cable TV companies were likely to become another group of competitors the local telephone companies would face in the near future. Cable companies already had connections with 60 percent of U.S. households, and cable facilities extended into areas where another 30 percent of the households were located. New digital and fiber optic technologies would allow them to provide telephone services over their networks, something cable companies already were doing in Britain.

XEL Communications: The Beginning

XEL Communications was born not only with an opportunity but with a challenge as well. Bill Sanko started with General Telephone and Electronics (GTE) as a product manager after spending six years in the U.S. Army.[3] He was chosen in 1972 to help establish the GTE Satellite Corporation. After he was successful with this enterprise, GTE then selected Bill for another startup business called Special Service Products in 1980.

The Special Service Products division was established to manufacture certain telecommunications products to compete with small companies who were making inroads into GTE's market. These products ranged from voice and data transmission products to switches customized to specific business needs. After two previous failures, it was GTE's third (and perhaps final) try at starting such a division. Company officials granted Sanko almost full autonomy to build the division, including recruiting all key executives, establishing a location in Aurora, Colorado, a rapidly growing region east of Denver, and in designing the division's overall operating philosophy.

By 1984, the division realized its first year of break-even operations, but it wasn't enough to win over GTE executives. Despite its initial success and the prospect of a fast-growing market, SSPD found itself heading toward orphan status in GTE's long-range plans.[4] After divestiture in telecommunications, GTE opted to concentrate primarily on providing telephone service rather than hardware. (GTE has subsequently divested all of its manufacturing divisions.) "Even though we were doing the job expected of us in building the business," Sanko said, "GTE's and SSPD's strategic plans were taking different directions." They opted to close the division. Sanko lobbied and ultimately persuaded GTE to sell the division.

The result was an action as unlikely as it was logical. On July 3, 1984, appropriately one day before Independence Day, Sanko and fellow managers from SSPD signed a letter of intent to buy the division from GTE. Two months later, the bill of sale was signed and XEL Communications Inc. became an independent company. Sanko gathered a group of managers and raised the money – some through second mortgages on homes. GTE loaned Sanko and his colleagues money, and the rest was supplied by venture capitalists. In fact, just before the new company was scheduled to begin operations, one of the banks backed out of the arrangement. According to Julie Rich, one of the co-founders and Vice President for Human Resources, "we didn't have any money lined up from September to December of 1984. Making the first payroll for a company of 180 employees was one of the major challenges. Christmas that first year was particularly lean."

The financing was eventually arranged, and XEL was underway. Sanko reflected on the perils and rewards of leaving the corporate nest to seek one's fortune: "In the end, it was the right thing to do, but it wasn't an easy decision to make. After 17 years with GTE, I had achieved vice president status; and I was more than a little nervous about leaving the corporation."[5]

Early Years

One of the more interesting exercises in starting any new company is what to name it. John Puckett, Vice President for Manufacturing and also one of the original founders, recalled: "We did a lot of brainstorming about what to call this new company – including taking initials from the original founders' names and seeing what combinations we could come up with. Usually, they didn't make a whole lot of sense. We finally decided on XEL which is a shortened version of excellence."

More than simply naming the company, one of the key concerns for XEL Communications was whether their customers would stay with them once they were no longer part of GTE. Not that XEL has ever exactly been an abandoned child. GTE may have kicked XEL out the door in 1984, but it remains XEL's biggest customer, with GTE Telephone Operations accounting for about 35 percent of the company's total business. In fact, the relationship between the two companies continues to be close and mutually beneficial. Ever the proud parent, GTE recognized XEL as its Quality Vendor of the Year in both 1987 and 1988, and as a Vendor of Excellence in subsequent years.

At first, all XEL produced was a handful of products for GTE. Even so, the company showed a profit in its first year of independent operation. "We were off to a better start than you might expect, just because we had always had a certain independence," says Sanko. "We had our own engineers, we were a non-union shop (unlike most of the other divisions of GTE at the time), we had installed our own computer systems, and we were out here in Colorado, on our own. We were doing things differently from the start, and so we just continued."

Weaning itself from GTE was a corporate goal entirely dependent on new product development, and XEL spent over 10 percent of its revenues on R&D. That focus on development would not likely change: The XEL product line is custom manufactured and therefore constantly evolved and changed as customers' needs changed. "Running a small company has a lot of challenges," Sanko says. "But one of the major advantages is being able to respond to the market and get things done quickly. Here we can respond to a customer requirement."

XEL's Products and Markets

For example, XEL sold products that facilitated the transmission of data and information over phone lines. Driving the need for XEL's products was the fact that "businesses are more and more dependent on the transfer of information," as Bill Sanko noted. In addition, more businesses, including XEL, were operating by taking and filling orders, for example, through electronic data exchanges. Instead of dialing into inside salespeople, businesses often accessed databases directly.

XEL's products performed a number of functions that allowed businesses to incorporate their specific telecommunications needs into the existing telephone "network" functions such as data exchanges. XEL had a diverse product line of over 300 products that it manufactures. Some of its major products included:

- Fibre Optic Terminal Products
- Coaxial Business Access
- Analog Voice Products
- Analog Data Products
- Digital Data Products
- Digital Transmission
- Telecom Maintenance Products

XEL's products would, for example, translate analog information into digital transmissions. Adapting electronic information for fiber optic networks was another area of emphasis for XEL, as was adapting equipment to international standards for foreign customers.

One of XEL's strengths was its ability to adapt one manufacturer's equipment to another's. Often, it was the bits and pieces of telecommunications equipment that XEL provided to the "network," that allowed the smooth integration of disparate transmission pieces. XEL also sold central office transmission equipment and a full range of mechanical housings, specialty devices, power supplies and shelves.

"Business customers and their changing telecommunications needs drive the demand for XEL's products. That, in turn, presents a challenge to the company," said Sanko. Sanko cited the constant stream of new products developed by XEL – approximately two per month – as the driving force behind its growth. Industry-wide, product life cycle times were getting ever shorter. Before the breakup of the Bell System in 1984, transmission switches and other telecommunications devices enjoyed a 30-to-40 year life. In 1995, with technology moving so fast, XEL's products had about a three-to-five year life.

In terms of its customers, XEL sold to all of the Regional Bell Operating Companies as well as such companies as GTE and Centel. Railroads, with their own telephone networks, were also customers. XEL's field salespeople worked with engineers to satisfy client requests for specific services. Over a period of time, a rapport was built up with these engineers, providing XEL with new product leads.

With all the consolidations and ventures in telecommunications, one may suspect that the overall market would become more difficult, but Sanko believed "out of change comes opportunity. The worst-case scenario would be a static situation. Thus, a small company, fast to respond to customer needs and able to capitalize on small market niches, will be successful. Often, a large company like AT&T will forsake a smaller market and XEL will move in. Also, XEL's size allows it to design a product in a very short time."

Interestingly, Sanko was watching pending federal legislation proposing to open up local telephone services to companies other than the regional Baby Bells. Consequently, said Sanko, "we need to expand our market and be prepared to sell to others as the regulatory environment changes." Sanko believed legislation would be signed in the near future that would set the groundwork and time tables to open local telephone monopolies to competition. The recent joint venture between Time Warner and U S WEST also signalled that telephone and cable companies would be pooling their resources to provide a broader array of information services.

As for the future, Sanko saw "a lot of opportunities we can't even now imagine."

The XEL Vision

In addition to the issue of developing products and maintaining customer loyalty, XEL also had to deal with a number of important "people" issues. "We had good, sound management practices right from the beginning," Sanko said. "We were competing with small companies who did not have the control systems, discipline and planning experience that we had gained as part of GTE. Coming from a large arena, we could start from the top down and tailor the procedures to our needs, rather than, as many small businesses do, have to start developing controls from the bottom and then apply them – hopefully in time."[6]

Yet, while bringing such experiences from GTE proved to be quite valuable, there were also a number of thorny issues which emerged.The first one involved people. As with any transition, there were those people that the owners wished to bring on to the new team and those whose future, for whatever reasons, was not with this new organization. "We were fortunate that personnel from GTE worked in tandem with us in this people transition phase," noted Julie Rich. "We spent a great deal of time talking people through it."

There were other critical human resource issues as well. One of the first ones was the design of the benefits package for the people. Under GTE, XEL had a traditional benefits package with little employee selection. To be competitive as well as cost effective, Julie needed to design a package that had to be reduced from 42% of overall payroll costs to 30%. She also wanted to create a package that was flexible and allowed the individual some latitude. "One approach we instituted was to allow individuals to have an allowance for total time off as opposed to so many days for sick leave, vacation, and the like. Its primary purpose was to bring down costs. And while it did succeed in this regard, we did have occasions in which people were coming to work sick rather than use this time."

Another approach was to institute a cafeteria plan of benefits in which the individual would select the specific benefits they would like to receive as part of an overall package. "The cafeteria approach was just beginning to be discussed by organizations at this time (1984)," noted Julie. "We felt there were a great deal of pluses to this approach; and it allowed the employee some discretion."

One critical issue that XEL wanted to address was developing a culture that would distinguish them from others and would also demonstrate that they were no longer a division of a large corporation. So, beginning in 1985 and carrying over into 1986, Julie Rich did a lot of reading and research on changing culture. By 1986, a first draft of these ideas and principles were developed (Exhibit 1). Julie reflected on this initial effort: "Once we developed 'XEL's Commitment to XEL-ENCE,' we printed up a bunch and hung them on the walls. However, nothing changed. You also have to realize that this company is largely comprised of engineers and technicians; and for them, a lot of this visioning was foreign."

By late 1986 and early 1987, the senior management team felt that a change agent was needed to help them deal with the issue of managing culture. An outside party was brought in; and his philosophy was that corporate vision should be strategically driven. This approach was warmly received by Bill Sanko; and through a series of monthly meetings, he worked with senior management.

His first effort was directed at getting the team to determine what their core values were and what they would like the company to look like in five years. Bill made an effort to develop a first draft of such a statement. In addition, other members of the senior team made similar efforts. "It was interesting," Julie notes, "Even though we each had a different orientation and background, there was a lot of consistency among the group." The team then went off-site for several days and was able to finalize the XEL Vision statement (Exhibit 2). By the summer of 1987, the statement was signed by members of the senior team and was hung up by the bulletin board. Again, Julie reflects: "The other employees were not required to sign the Vision statement. We felt that once they could really buy into it then they were free to sign it or not."

Julie then described their approach to getting the rest of the organization to understand as well as become comfortable with the XEL Vision: "Frequently, organizations tend to take a combination top-down/bottom-up approach in instituting cultural change. That is, the top level will develop a statement about values and overall vision. They will then communicate it down to the bottom level and hope that results will percolate upward through the middle levels. Yet it is often the middle level of management which is most skeptical, and they will block it or resist change. We decided to take a "cascade" approach in which the process begins at the top and gradually cascades from one level to the next so that the critical players are slowly acclimated to the process. We also did a number of other things — including sending a copy of the vision to the homes of the employees and dedicating a section of the company newspaper to communicate what key sections of the vision mean from the viewpoint of managers and employees."

Unlike the first vision statement which was hung on the wall but not really followed, this new vision statement has sustained and reinforced a corporate culture. Julie believed that employee involvement in fashioning and building the statement made the real difference, as well as the fact that XEL made significant use of teams in all facets of its business, including decision making. For example, in 1990, XEL was experiencing some economic difficulties. The employees were brought into meetings and were told the business was in trouble, and were asked for ideas on how to deal with the downturn. The employees discussed the problem and decided to try a four-day work week rather than lay off anyone. After a few months, the economic difficulties continued and the employees reluctantly decided to lay off 40% of the workforce. The work teams were asked if they wanted to be involved in deciding who would be laid off. They declined to participate in these tough decisions, but were still clearly concerned about the decisions themselves. In fact, Julie recalls being visited by a number of production workers during this time. "There was one particular fellow who knew that a coworker had a family, and that he would suffer a great deal of hardship if he was to be laid

---

Exhibit 1

XEL'S COMMITMENT TO XEL-ENCE

XEL Communications, Inc. is a customer oriented supplier of high quality transmission system products and services to telecommunications service providers with emphasis on the effective application of emerging digital technologies.

XEL provides its customers with products which allow them to offer competitive special service features to the end users while improving system operating efficiencies.

To achieve our commitment to XEL-ENCE:

Our customers needs shall always come first.

Profitability ensures a return to our investors, company growth, and team member rewards.

High ethical standards are maintained in all corporate relationships.

On time individual commitments are a personal pledge.

Superior performance through teamwork achieves rewards and advancement.

Customers, employees, and suppliers are team members to be treated with respect and dignity at all times.

---

off," Julie remembers, "This fellow came in to my office and asked that he be laid off instead of his coworker. That's when I knew the employees believed in and shared our vision." Eventually, virtually all of the laid off production workers were hired back.

In a strange way, the business crisis of 1990 moved the teams along more quickly than they might have developed in times of profit. Like many businesses using work teams and facing downsizing, XEL laid off a number of middle managers who were not brought back when business improved. When tough decisions needed to be made, the work teams no longer had managers to fall back on.

When teams, or managers, are making decisions, it is routine for the XEL Vision statement to be physically brought into the discussion, and for workers to consult various parts of the statement to help guide and direct decisions. According to Julie, the statement has been used to help evaluate new products, to emphasize quality (a specific XEL strategic objective is to be the top quality vendor for each product), to support teams, and to drive the performance appraisal process.

The XEL Vision was successfully implemented as a key first step; but it was far from being a static document. Key XEL managers continually re-visited the statement to ensure that it became a reflection of where they want to go, not where they have been. Julie believed this was a large factor in the success of the vision. "Our values are the key," Julie explains, "They are strong, they are truly core values, and they are deeply held." Along with the buy-in process, the workers also see that the statement is experimented with. This reflected the strong entrepreneurial nature of XEL's founders – a common bond that they all share. They were not afraid of risk, or of failure, and this spirit was reinforced in all employees through the vision itself, as well as through the yearly process of revisiting the statement. Once a year, Bill Sanko sat with all employees and directly challenged (and listened to direct challenges) on the XEL Vision. Since 1987, only two relatively minor additions have altered the original statement (see Exhibit 2).

Human Resource Management at XEL

Julie Rich was pleased as she scanned the recent article in *Business Week* which mentioned XEL's efforts to use team-based compensation.[7] It mentioned that, once they instituted this system, average production time has been slashed from 30 days to 3, and waste as a percentage of sales has been cut in half. "We have certainly come a long way."

Julie was heavily involved in the development of XEL's first vision statement, and she chuckled about the reaction from others: "Being the non-engineer in an outfit that is predominantly made up of technical people, they looked at me like they thought I was crazy. This 'touchy-feely' vision and values statement was about as foreign to them as it could get. Yet, once they saw the linkage to XEL's strategy and direction, it began to catch on." In many ways, Julie was an unusual HR manager. Not only did Julie believe HR to be a strategic issue for XEL, Julie herself was one of the owners of the business. Where HR was often relegated to a "staff" function, Julie was clearly a "line" manager at XEL. Julie felt very comfortable working closely with technical managers, and carried the entrepreneurial spirit as strongly as her colleagues.

Once the vision statement had been finally developed, Julie and others soon turned their attention to the issue of managing the new culture within XEL. A key ingredient of this process was changing the mindset of the employees. In the GTE days, individuals had discrete jobs and responsibilities which were governed by specific policies and procedures. "We wanted to instill a sense of ownership on the part of employees," Julie noted. When asked when she knew that the culture was working, she replied, "One day, a work team was having a meeting. The team leader was agitated, and was speaking harshly to one of the team members. One of the other workers stood up and confronted the team leader, saying that his treatment of the worker was not consistent with The XEL Vision." The worker, and her team leader, still work on the same team at XEL.

The HR system at XEL was unusually well-integrated. The team-based work system created a great deal of intrinsic motivation, and opportunities for employee voice and influence were in abundance. The workers participated in hiring decisions, and XEL used a 360 degree performance appraisal system. Production workers were appraised by peers and also appraised themselves. The compensation system used a three-pronged approach: profit-sharing to encourage teamwork, individual and team-based merit to encourage quantity and quality of performance, and skill-based pay to encourage continuous improvement. In one quarter in 1994, the 300 production workers were paid an average of $500 each in profit-sharing. When workers mastered a new task, they had the opportunity to earn an additional 50 cents per hour.

Exhibit 2

THE XEL VISION

XEL will become the leader in our selected telecommunications markets through innovation in products and services. Every XEL product and service will be rated Number One by our customers.

XEL will set the standards by which our competitors are judged. We will be the best, most innovative, responsive designer, manufacturer and provider of quality products and services as seen by customers, employees, competitors, and suppliers.*

We will insist upon the highest quality from everyone in every task.

We will be an organization where each of us is a self-manager who will:

- initiate action, commit to, and act responsibly in achieving objectives
- be responsible for XEL's performance
- be responsible for the quality of individual and team output
- invite team members to contribute based on experience, knowledge and ability

We will:

- be ethical and honest in all relationships
- build an environment where creativity and risk taking is promoted
- provide challenging and satisfying work
- ensure a climate of dignity and respect for all
- rely on interdepartmental teamwork, communications and cooperative problem solving to attain common goals**
- offer opportunities for professional and personal growth
- recognize and reward individual contribution and achievement
- provide tools and services to enhance productivity
- maintain a safe and healthy work environment

XEL will be profitable and will grow in order to provide both a return to our investors and rewards to our team members.

XEL will be an exciting and enjoyable place to work while we achieve success.

---

* Responsiveness to customers' new product needs as well as responding to customers' requirements for emergency delivery requirements has been identified as a key strategic strength. Therefore, the vision statement has been updated to recognize this important element.

** The importance of cooperation and communication was emphasized with this update of the Vision Statement.

Finally, each unit shared a bonus based on meeting a quarterly goal, such as improving on-time delivery. The average reward was 4.5% of payroll, with top teams earning up to 10% and lagging groups getting nothing. Employee response to the compensation system was generally positive. "The pay system doesn't stand alone," said Julie. "It's only in support of the teams."[8]

Julie did a lot of background reading in the management literature as well as exploring what other companies were doing. Unfortunately, she found that them was little to go on. "That is when, in working with John Puckett, vice-president for manufacturing, we began to see that self-directed work teams could give them a distinct competitive advantage — resulting in better quality products that could be delivered in a timely manner."

A key step in the development of self-directed teams was to create an open organization. The first step was to take a look at the physical layout of the work environment. One experience remains vivid for Julie: "I remember that on one particular Friday, John was toying with the idea of how to better organize the plant. One worker approached John and told him to take the weekend off and go fishing. John, initially hesitant, decided to do so; and over one weekend, the workers came in and, on their own, redesigned the entire floor. On Monday, John returned and found that they had organized themselves in various work cells — each devoted to a particular product group. Teams were then organized around this cellular production and began to set their own production goals and quality procedures."

XEL's Strategic Planning Process

The business telecommunications market was rapidly changing and evolving in 1995 — creating an ideal business climate for XEL.[9] Working with local telephone companies and others, XEL designed and manufactured equipment that "conditioned" existing lines to make them acceptable for business use.

As a means of positioning themselves for products and markets in a rapidly changing environment, XEL engaged in a strategic planning process on an annual basis. Exhibit 3 provides an overview of this process. As Bill Sanko noted: "Since there are such rapid changes taking place and new products being constantly introduced, we needed to tie what we're doing back to the strategic elements — quality, responsiveness, cost."

The strategic planning process began in August of each year with the senior management team listing strategic issues and taking on key assignments. For Bill, his key assignment began with assessing key external factors. Taking on such an assignment provided him an opportunity to step back and look at the bigger picture.

"I hope that legislation pending will deregulate local telephone companies. This will open up local telephone services to companies other than the regional Baby Bell. At present, AT&T has almost 60% hold in the market with respect to long distance but deregulation will allow the local companies to enter the global market. Major telephone companies have been downsizing in the recent past to cut down on costs by developing products and installing services that require less maintenance and, therefore, less people to maintain them. With this trend, we hope to get business from our present customers seeking help to develop such products for them."

Another key industry trend which was constantly monitored is technology. The pace at which the technology was moving had reduced the product life cycle from 40 years to less than 5 years. Bill noted the example of fiber optic products, which is a very hot area in today's

Exhibit 3. XEL Planning Cycle

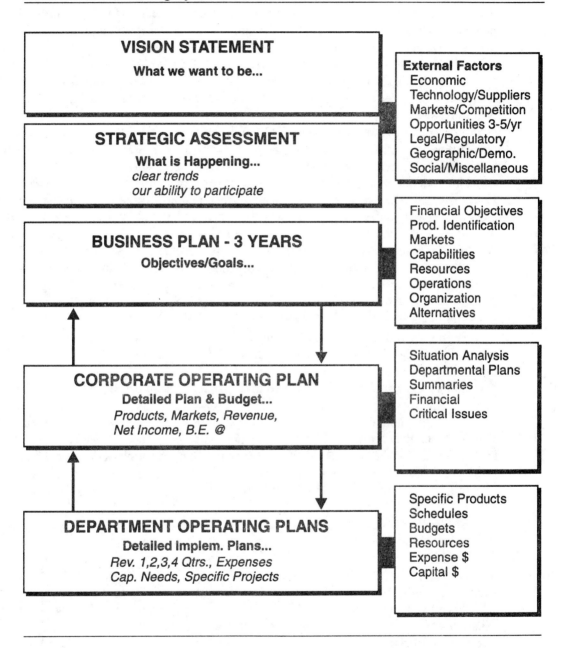

market; XEL was trying to compete with other companies with respect to building fiber optic products. Other areas in which it was trying to find opportunities for a small company was the emerging personal communications systems market.

With the industry trend data as a beginning, the senior team then spent the ensuing months in developing plans around the key strategic issues. This would then entail capturing data on key competitors and assessing their strengths and weaknesses relative to XEL. "Some of these data are available due to public disclosure requirements," according to Bill Sanko," but data on private competitors are particularly difficult to get — due to the competitive nature of the business; we get a lot of information through trade show contacts."

Throughout this entire process, the XEL team needed to keep a focus on those critical success factors that would determine their performance. Essentially, they involved: innovativeness, skilled sales force, quality, investing in automation, effective pricing, and, above all, responsiveness.

Another key goal was to achieve a 20% improvement in margin by year end 1994 and to strive to reach 25% by December 1995 and 30% by December 1997. This goal is one that was particularly sensitive among the senior management team since it involved two critical variables: pricing coupled with achieving economies of scale in the manufacturing plant. Previously, achieving such a goal was parceled out among the respective groups: marketing and sales, operations, finance and the like. Unfortunately, this activity was frequently tabled in the face of day-to-day activities. It was then decided that a cost reduction team needed to be formally structured to address this goal. As such, XEL decided to hire an engineer, a technician, and a buyer from outside the organization to constitute the team. Its primary responsibility was to examine the pricing of products and costs, and to target core products for the purpose of achieving 25% improvement in margin by December of 1995. The team reported primarily to the vice president of manufacturing, John Puckett.

In terms of overall financial performance, XEL has been profitable. It's revenues increased from $16.8 million in 1992 to $23.6 million in 1993 and $52.3 million in 1994 – over a three-fold increase in three years.

Another key issue that was identified in the strategic planning process was how much to invest in R&D – given the rapid pace of technology development that is taking place in this industry. XEL's goal was to invest 10% of its sales in R&D. "We have come to realize that we grew faster than last year's plan," according to Bill Sanko, "and we need to invest more in engineering as a means of keeping pace. Our goal is to have one-third of our revenue in any given year come from products introduced in the past two years." This would also involve investing its R&D efforts into new technologies as cable TV converges with telecommunications.

Aside from investment in new technologies, the other key strategic issue that was identified in the planning process was penetration into international markets. XEL was seeking to do business in Mexico in order to build data networks that are critical in upgrading Mexico's infrastructure. It has also looked for business opportunities in countries such as Brazil, Chile, Argentina, Puerto Rico, and the Far East. As a means of focusing responsibility for this effort, XEL tapped Malcom Shaw, a new hire of XEL who is fluent in Spanish and has prior marketing experience in South America, to lead this international expansion effort.

As all of the above issues indicate, the formal strategic planning process was a critical ingredient of XEL's way of doing business. "Strategic planning makes you think about how to invest for the future," Bill emphasized. "The role of the CEO is really to keep a viewpoint of the big picture — not to micro-manage the operation." To reinforce this last point, it should be noted that Bill Sanko had a personal tragedy in June of 1992, in which he was involved in a serious auto accident — the car in which he was traveling was broad-sided by another auto. "Even while I was out of the office for an extended period of time," noted Bill, "the fact that we had a formal strategic plan and an annual operating plan gave us the guidance to continue business as usual." As the planning process moved forward, Bill's goal was to have their 1995 strategic plan ready for the November meeting of the Board of Directors. As Julie noted, "We don't just look for 'programs,' but for ideas for the long-term."

XEL's Markets

The marketing and sales functions for XEL closely reinforced the earlier emphasis on being responsive and oriented to customer's needs. Don Bise, vice president of marketing, came to XEL with diverse experience, having moved around in nine previous firms. "The culture here at XEL is much less structured than some other organizations where I worked before," Don reflected, "I feel much more comfortable in a stand-alone company as opposed to being a branch or subsidiary of a large firm."

Unlike many companies in which the marketing approach is to have product managers dedicated to certain product segments or accounts, XEL's sales managers worked closely with the engineers in addressing customer needs. "The difficulty with having the sales manager or the engineer working solely with the customer is that their particular perspectives may differ," noted Don. "By having both the engineer and the sales manager working with the customer, we have cut down on the communications difficulties and have been able to develop a more realistic pricing and delivery schedule. At the same time, by having the engineer present, he is able to understand their specific needs or can steer them towards a reasonable solution to what they are trying to achieve. This has gone a long way to create great customer loyalty and repeat business. In addition, we have been able to manage our overall costs better. Our marketing expenses are typically 6-7% of sales which is low compared to a number of companies."

In terms of XEL's marketing strategy, a number of external developments have reshaped its approach. "Traditionally, in a market as concentrated as the telecommunications industry, the customer has tremendous buying potential and tries to leverage this as much as possible. With more players coming into this market, coupled with downsizing on the part of the Regional Bell Operating Companies, we are trying to develop a portfolio approach to make us less dependent on a few key accounts. As a result, XEL must introduce new products for traditional as well as new accounts. This means that XEL must pay a great deal of attention to technology."

To meet this goal, marketing worked closely with the engineering group – not only in the sales area but also in new product development. Specific market opportunities included the convergence of telephony with cable, personal communication services based on radio expertise, and business access in developing countries. To reach these market segments, Don Bise noted that XEL was exploring several avenues.

One approach was the OEM (Original Equipment Manufacturer) market in which XEL built the product according to another's specification. GTE's Airfone, which allowed airline passengers to place calls and receive calls, was a three-way venture in which XEL manufactured the electronics for the phone and did final assembly and test. This venture was quite profitable for XEL; they shipped about 300 Airfones a day out of their plant in 1995. A second approach was to build customized units for voice and data transmission in the industrial market. Exhibit 4 provides an example of XEL's approach to this market.

Exhibit 4

AN OVERVIEW OF OUR PRODUCTS AND SERVICES

XEL Communications offers complete product selection for voice and data applications. Products include a complete line of both voice and data channel units for D4, 9004, D448, and DE-4 channel banks. We have expanded our product line to include intelligent DSTs, 11 equipment, and 2B1Q systems.

XEL pioneered the development of the multifunctional, modular approach to transmission card design — the X-Card. This concept uses a basic board (such as a line amplifier) and through modular "build-ons," adds specific functions resulting in a custom-performance card. Customers specify their requirements and XEL assembles, tests, and ships the solution on a single board.

In 1990, XEL introduced a new line of channel units to address the needs of customers who use D448 T-Carrier Systems. These channel units incorporate our years of special service design experience to provide many unique units that reduce installation time and eliminate the needs for external equipment and units.

As part of XEL's product family, our 2B1Q system provides service for two 4-wire customers on a single pair of wires (3 pair gain) while still providing unique (patent pending) testing features.

A third avenue, one that offered a great deal of future potential is the international market. This is an area that Don was particularly excited about: "Clearly the growth path is international as developing regions are looking to upgrade their telecommunications infrastructure to spur economic growth. To do this, both voice and data transmission are key. What XEL can do is take something that we are familiar with and use it in areas they aren't familiar with. For example, in one particular country, we found that we can take one of our channel units and plug it into their system-providing an instant upgrade to their current capabilities." Yet going international was not without its risks. "We would prefer to begin by developing a niche in international markets with our existing equipment. This would minimize some of the up-front risks. As the international side of the business begins to take off, we realize we will need to have a local in country partner and will need to have some local manufacturing content."

To successfully compete in the future, Don felt that XEL should "go where they ain't." XEL needed to seek out niches where there was very little or no competition, keep its cost low, and price accordingly. He felt that their traditionally strong customer base, the major telephone companies, was using its buying power to telegraph the prices they would accept. At the same time, they were cutting down their list of vendors quite extensively.

Financial Considerations

Turning from the ever-present spreadsheet on his desktop computer, Jim Collins, vice-president of finance, reflected on the key financial considerations facing XEL. "Coming from another company to XEL, I soon found out that the culture here is quite different. There is indeed a sense of empowerment and teamwork. People set their own goals; and the engineers make a serious commitment to the customer."

In addition to the formal strategic planning process, financial planning at XEL involved a 3 year top-down plan with input from the bottom-up. According to Jim, "I interface a great deal with marketing and sales and develop costs. My goal is to ensure that there aren't a lot of surprises. We also tend to manage by percentages." Jim was asked whether XEL was experimenting with implementing some form of activity-based accounting. He noted that they reviewed it in 1993 and decided that they weren't ready. Yet, they do plan to implement a modified activity-based accounting system in 1995. "We tend to look at the major drivers of cost in this business. There is an overall operations review once a month among the senior management team in which there is open dialogue; and we explore a number of key operational issues."

Yet the financial picture for XEL has not always been rosy. "In addition to the costs associated with the separation from GTE, there were three years where we lost money — part of this was due to our dependency on GTE as it was going through its own consolidation as well as a new product introduction which didn't fly." Again, Jim Collins remarked: "those two setbacks were a bitter pill to swallow. We now try to make our financial projections more realistic – even somewhat on the conservative side. We also set targets by market segments."

Although there was pressure to raise cash by going public, Jim felt that this wasn't realistic for XEL. "We really don't want analysts setting constraints for our business — rather we tend to look for cash infusions from strategic partnerships and alliances." Both Bill Sanko and Jim Collins were actively involved in negotiating these partnerships, particularly in the international arena. "Above all," Jim commented, "we need to stay focused, develop a plan, and get realistic input."

Quality Management at XEL

One of the critical success factors that was identified in the strategic planning process and was imbedded throughout XEL was the focus on responsiveness to customers. When XEL was in its initial stages, cycle time – the period from start of production to finished goods — was about six weeks. That left customers disgruntled and tied up money in inventory.[10] XEL's chain of command, moreover, had scarcely changed since the GTE days. Line workers reported to supervisors, who reported to unit or departmental managers, who reported on up the ladder to Sanko and a crew of top executives. Every rung in the ladder added time and expense. "If a hardware engineer needed some software help, he'd go to his manager," Sanko says. "The manager would say, 'Go write it up.' Then the hardware manager would take the software manager to lunch and talk about it. We needed everybody in the building thinking and contributing about how we could better satisfy our customers, how we could improve quality, how we could reduce costs."

Soon after XEL drafted its vision statement, John Puckett, vice president for manufacturing, redesigned the plant for cellular production, with groups of workers building whole families of circuit boards. Eventually, Sanko and Puckett decided to set up the entire plant with self-managing teams. By 1988, the teams had been established; and the supervisory and support staff was reduced by 30%.

The RIF (Reduction in Force) was achieved by a number of avenues. In 1990, there was a downturn in business and workers went to a four-day work week in order to avoid layoffs. Unfortunately, the downturn continued and production workers, supervisors, and supports staff were laid off. Workers were asked for cost-saving ideas. Some workers moved to trainer roles. One worker was moved to Industrial Engineering while another became the manager of facilities.

Unlike other plans where workers are incented to provide cost saving ideas and suggestions, there was no such direct financial incentive at XEL. As Julie recalled, "We were in a

Exhibit 5.   XEL Communications, Inc.
Process Solder Defects

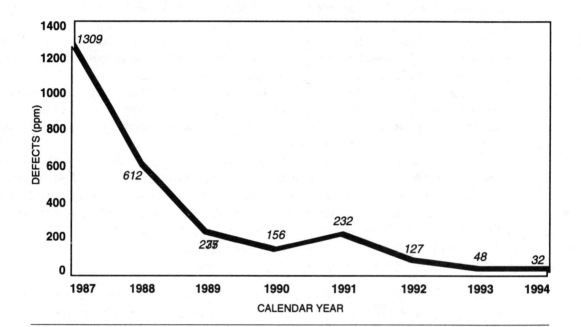

Exhibit 6. XEL Communications, Inc.
Scrap/Rework (in $Thousands)

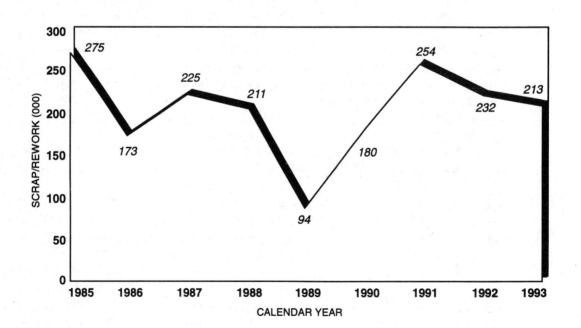

total survival mode — the only payoff was that the doors stayed open." Eventually, the teams and the quality strategy took hold and a turnaround was achieved. Virtually all laid-off production workers were rehired. The supervisory and support staff were not. This is a testament to the strength of the team system at XEL.

XEL rebuilt itself around those teams so thoroughly and effectively that the Association for Manufacturing Excellence chose the company as one of four to be featured in a video on team-based management. Dozens of visitors, from companies such as Hewlett-Packard, have toured through their facility in search of ideas for using teams effectively.

On the shop floor, colorful banners hung from the plant's high ceiling to mark each team's work area. Charts on the wall tracked attendance, on-time deliveries and the other variables by which the teams gauge their performance. Diagrams indicated who on a team was responsible for key tasks such as scheduling.

Every week, the schedulers met with Production Control to review what needed to be built as well as what changes needed to be made. The teams met daily, almost always without a manager, to plan their part in that agenda. Longer meetings, called as necessary, took up topics such as vacation planning or recurring production problems. Once a quarter, each team made a formal presentation to management on what it had and hadn't accomplished.

As for results, XEL's cost of direct assembly dropped 25%. Inventory had been cut by half; quality levels rose 30% (Exhibits 5 and 6). The company's cycle time went from six weeks to four days and was still decreasing (Exhibit 7). Sales have also grew to $52 million in 1994, up from $17 million in 1992. Above all, according to John Puckett, these self-directed work teams must be guided by customer focus (Exhibit 8). In order to facilitate this, customers frequently came in and visited with the team. By clearly understanding their customers' needs the teams were able to respond rapidly with a high quality product. At the same time, XEL team members went and visited with their key suppliers.

Another key issue for manufacturing involved establishing certain procedures while retaining a certain degree of flexibility. Part of this involved the strategic issue of entering global markets. As firms go global, meeting ISO 9000 standards for quality becomes critical. "To meet these standards, several things have to take place," John noted."We have to have a structure that defines the process; then we need to document and have solid procedures in place." In addition, John felt that manufacturing for international markets would also mean building manufacturing capabilities closer to those markets, which entailed a whole host of environmental issues and labor laws. Developing alliances would also be critical since XEL could not afford to run it all.

In terms of integration with other parts of XEL, John briefly sketched out the overall process. "Basically, most of manufacturing is driven off of the financial and market plan. We start with a three year plan which is converted in terms of the demands on facilities. My staff then develops models which reflect product development and product mix. The budget then sets the baseline for new product development. Here, at XEL, we tend to plan on the low side and are fairly conservative. Currently, we target two new products per month and produce in low volume for beta testing. This allows us to carefully manage costs."

As for future issues, John was struggling with the XEL goal of improving margins by 25% by December of 1995. "This is going to be a real challenge for my operation since we have to maintain a short cycle time as the business grows without a lot of excess inventory. We instituted a just-in-time (JIT) system several years ago, and we are currently turning our

Exhibit 7. XEL Communications, Inc.
           Cycle Time Reduction, 1984-94

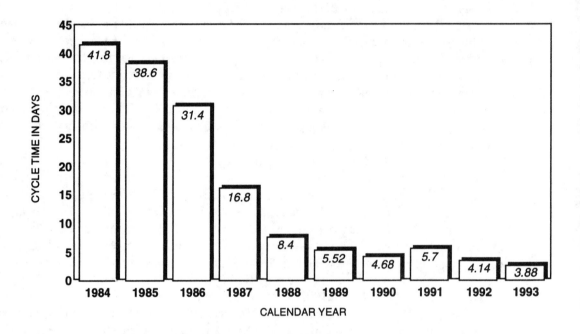

Exhibit 8. XEL Communications, Inc.
           Customer Returns, Component Level, All Causes

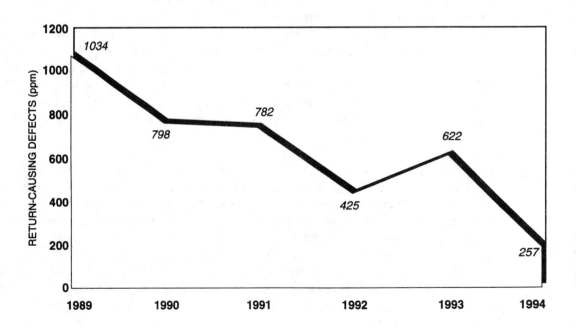

**Exhibit 9. XEL Communications, Inc.
          WIP Annual Inventory Turns 1985-94**

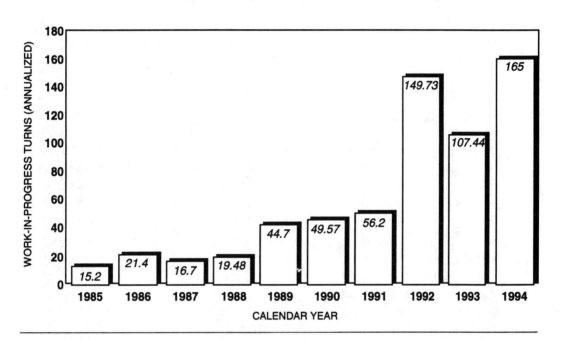

inventory about 7 or 8 times, which is close to our benchmarks relative to the best in our business (Exhibit 9). Supply chain management is really critical for us."

Another issue John faced was maintaining the culture which had been instituted through the team-based training. "While the current teams have pretty much gelled in terms of feeling comfortable with setting their targets and self-managing, orienting new members becomes a challenge. We are exploring some form of built-in orientation which would involve two weeks of internal training."

John also faced an even greater concern: skilled workers. "I think one of the serious deficiencies in our current U.S. educational system is vocational and occupational education. People have simply not been prepared. There is a misconception that there is a shortage of jobs in this business. They are dead wrong. One of my difficulties is finding qualified workers. As a basic assembler, you aren't going to become rich and put down a deposit on a BMW. But it provides a nice steady income – particularly for two wage earning families." John felt that there needed to be a stronger work ethic for those entering the labor force. "We need to understand how to transfer those hard skills that are needed as well as the concept of holding a job. Part of this should involve more industry-level involvement in changing the overall mind-set of what is needed for today's workers. I would like to create an environment in which people really enjoy working here."

The strategic need for skilled workers drove XEL's involvement in a Work Place Learning Skills program, funded by the Department of Education. When XEL began training workers in quality tools, managers noticed that the training was not having as great an effect as it might have. Upon further investigation, the managers discovered that some workers were having difficulty not only in making calculations, but also in reading the training materials. Using the

Exhibit 10. XEL Communications, Inc.
Productivity, 1989-94

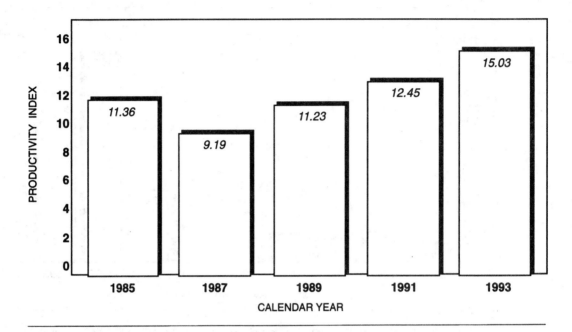

DOE grant, and working with Aurora Community College, which is located near the plant, XEL developed a basic skills training program which is now used as a template by DOE for worker training across the United States. The program, not surprisingly, was designed by an employee task force made up of managers and workers. The task force used a questionnaire to ask employees which courses they would be interested in taking. Participation in the program was not mandatory, but a measure of its success is that 50% of employees participated in the program on their own time. Courses were offered on site for convenience, and included "soft" skills such as communication and stress management. On December 1, 1994, XEL was awarded a three year DOE grant to expand and continue the training, and to scientifically evaluate the effects of the training on such outcomes as productivity and ROI. Julie believed that these training programs were consistent with other Human Resource policies of XEL, such as skill-based pay. More than that, Julie stated, "The Work Place Learning Skills program is consistent with our XEL vision." As further testament to these efforts, XEL's overall workforce productivity continues to improve (Exhibit 10).

Maintaining Innovation

In a climate that is constantly undergoing rapid change, staying ahead of the competition is the name of the game. For XEL, this meant that cross-functional relationships were key. One critical link in this process was the role of new product development. Terry Bolinger, vice-president of engineering, described how this process worked: "Here at XEL, engineering is involved from start to finish. Rather than have a large marketing staff that is out there making calls or picking up new pieces of information, we deliberately have a small group. The engineers do a lot of traveling at XEL – going out in the field and working directly with the customers."

As for its commitment to innovation, XEL allocated approximately 10% to 12% of sales to R&D. Terry noted that, for the current year, he spent below this amount. When pressed why, he commented: "I guess I am hesitant to spend up to this amount since I don't want to grow my engineering group too fast. A few years back, we went through some cutbacks due to a number of factors; and I am somewhat gun-shy about that experience. I know we are running at about the 10% level; and Bill keeps pressing me about this. But I would rather proceed somewhat cautiously."

In order to create a climate to allow his people to innovate, Terry noted that he was careful not to create a management system that bogged everything down. "Our process of setting priorities is fairly free-form. While we are typically running 50 projects at one time, we don't do much formal scheduling. We went through a time in which a lot of formal planning and presentations were done. Unfortunately, we spent too much time in meetings and too little in what I considered the search and discovery process." While Terry was comfortable with this loose form of management, he laughed that others were not so at ease. "I see Bill Sanko stroll the office periodically; and I know that he is often perplexed with how this works – coming from his engineering background. I just say 'trust me' and he is pretty good at accepting it."

In addition to this loose form of project management, Terry tried to motivate his engineers in other ways. "I also try to give them interesting assignments which will challenge them. They are also allowed to work at odd hours – many come to work on weekends or at night. In a number of cases, I will simply send them to work at home where they can be relaxed. If they need some particular equipment, I will get it for them with little or no questions asked. Also, they periodically like to travel just to get out of the office; and field calls to customers or potential customers is a way getting them charged up." There were also periodic in-house seminars with professors from various universities who would come and brief them on new technological advances. In a sense, Terry was trying to recreate the college environment within XEL.

As XEL continued to grow, Terry saw several issues that were critical for his group: "First is the issue of how do I improve time to market without sacrificing quality; second, how do I speed up product development; and third, how do I respond extremely fast to new technology developments?" As he prepared his departmental plan for the strategic planning meeting, he also shared some concern about the opening of the second building. While he clearly needed more space for his people, the ease with which an engineer could go over to manufacturing or marketing and sales if he or she had a question or needed some information would be hard to replace.

XEL's Future

Ironically, the most serious current issue for XEL came from its own success, namely growth. XEL had increased its labor force by 50% and had doubled its revenues in the last year, and was experiencing some associated growing pains. Hiring sufficient workers was difficult, and assuring that the new workers will "fit" the XEL culture was hindered because of the pressures to add staff. The teams, who normally hired their own replacement workers, were less able to participate in the hiring process since they were under great pressure to produce and satisfy their customers.

Another example of the pressures of growth occurred in the skills training program. Originally, team members were scheduled to teach the classes. Unfortunately, as pressures for production increased, more and more team members canceled their training classes. As a solution, trainers were hired from local community colleges, and the team members acted as their partners to assure the course content was job-related.

Growth increased pressure to satisfy customer demands, increased pressure on the culture via the increased size and complexity, and created additional financial pressures. As a high-technology company, XEL faced the challenge of using technology to help the company be more effective. XEL would use its annual strategic planning process to determine its priorities, what measures it will use to assess its results, and which feet to hold to the fire.

Having finished reading the *Wall Street Journal* article, Bill Sanko made a note to have a copy made for the next managers' meeting, which was scheduled for every other Thursday. He also wondered what the new session of Congress would bring – now that the Republicans appeared to be in solid control.

Since XEL was in the process of beginning its annual strategic planning process, Bill thought that a useful exercise for the next managers' meeting would be to have everyone list and prioritize the key strategic issues facing XEL over the next three to five years. At the same time, he wondered whether it would be possible for XEL to maintain its entrepreneurial culture while it managed rapid growth.

Endnotes

1. *Financial World*, October 11, 1994.
2. 1994 University of Michigan Economic Forecast
3. *Denver Business Journal*, June 17, 1994, p. 12.
4. *Rocky Mountain Business Journal*, July 1, 1985.
5. *Colorado Business*, July 1990.
6. *Rocky Mountain Business Journal*, July 1, 1985.
7. *Business Week*, November 14, 1994, p. 62
8. Ibid., p. 62.
9. *Denver Business Journal*, April 15, 1994.
10. *Inc.* September 1993, p. 66.

13. Goldman Sachs/Lehman Brothers*

The Modern Investment Banking Industry

The investment banking industry has changed dramatically over the past twenty years. The most apparent manifestation of this change has been a shift from relationship banking to transactional banking. Relationship banking exists when a company establishes a relationship with a bank that handles most of its business, generally over an extended period of time. Transactional banking exists when a company is involved with many investment banks that compete for its business on a deal by deal basis.

A deal is any exchange of assets, such as stocks, bonds and parts or all of companies, between investment banks that sell them for their owners and those who buy them. The environment of investment banking had become turbulent and the volume of activity had greatly increased. Deal-making replaced banking as the more profitable investment banking activity. Because the number and profitability of deals increased and buyers and sellers became less certain with respect to exchange rates, the trust between companies and banks, the foundation for relationship banking, became difficult to maintain. Corporations began to "shop" for the best deals. Thus began the era of transactional banking.

Banks became more competitive and expanded and innovated their products and services. The investment banking industry became more specialized and segmented. Bank partners feared a drop in the value of their own particular share and many resigned. Firms that were, subsequently, deficient in capital went public in order to broaden their financial bases. This increase in competition and activity caused an explosive growth in investment banking firms. Firms increased capital and human resources to support their growth. All these changes required new management techniques, especially in the area of deal making.

Deals and Deal-Making

Deals are made quickly to minimize competition and to avoid complications from fluctuating exchange rates. Deals are also unique. Each requires information and assistance from endless possible combinations of internal and external sources. When a deal is made, it requires participation, cooperation and support internally across several product and service specialized departments and externally from industry experts and companies that provide different related services. Firms do not operate independently, rather they depend on outside sources for information and services. The boundaries of firms have become much more porous, meaning that the flow of information in and out of the firm has increased. Internally, employees are uncertain as to whether their efforts towards a deal will secure that deal and whether they will be compensated for their work. Interdependence and a spirit of sharing and trust is crucial. These issues require new management techniques that encourage cooperative behavior and support an organizational structure that is flat and flexible rather than hierarchical and rigid.

Written by Richard D. Freedman and Jill Vohr, Leonard N. Stern School of Business, New York University. Copyright © 1991 by Professor Richard D. Freedman. Reprinted with permission.

The Management of Deal-Making

The transition from relationship banking to transactional banking has required an accompanying transition in organizational structure and management in their book, *Doing Deals*, Robert G. Eccles and Dwight B. Crane suggest how these structures and management systems should develop. They argue that because the heart of investment banking is the making of a deal, it follows that those at lower levels of the firm who are involved in deal-making are best equipped to formulate the firms operational strategy. This process of grass-roots strategy formulation requires" a self-designing organization in which organizational structure is determined by those who develop the business strategies within the broad parameters of organizational design established by top management."[1]

Top management has the responsibility of overseeing the formulation process and making sure that employees do not pursue that which may be in their individual interest but not in the long-term interests of the firm. According to Eccles and Crane, this environment requires management to impose tight control systems including reports on calling activity, evaluations from customers, internal cross-evaluations within and between departments and measures of financial outcomes. A structure that is flexible enough to "roll with the deals" and a management system that supports this flexibility while keeping it in tight check will provide an environment well suited for the modern investment banking industry.

Lehman Brothers

Lehman Brothers, once the longest surviving continuing investment banking house, fell to its demise in April 1984 when it was sold to Shearson/American Express. Yet, only several months before, the company ranked as one of Wall Street's largest investment banking houses, more profitable than it had been at any point in its long history. The firm had a capital base of close to $250 million and incomes for its partners of over $2 million. The sudden decline in profits that led to Lehman's sale was unexpected.

The company had experienced a similar setback in 1969 when Robert (Bobby) Lehman died unexpectedly causing chaos in the leaderless Lehman Brothers.

> "His patrician calm, his absolute, unquestioned rule,...(and) his ability to spot promising enterprises early...gave security and structure to the fractious partnership." Bobby had a management style that seemed to work for Lehman: "For years, Bobby Lehman had enjoyed watching the competition among his partners almost as much as he enjoyed watching his stable of beloved horses race. Lehman Brothers had a long tradition of encouraging independence among its bankers, but as long as Bobby was alive, there was someone with the authority to police warring fractions." [2]

Bobby Lehman's death provoked partners to resign, depleting capital resources. The firm was losing money at an annual rate of $9 million as it struggled to find a new leader and regroup.

Lehman Brothers turned to one of its partners, Peter G. Peterson. Peterson came from a long history of success. He was president of Bell and Howell at the age of 34 and Secretary of Commerce under President Nixon. Felix Rohatyn, an investment banker who had worked with Peterson said that the Lehman Board members "wanted Pete to help settle the place down and the same time establish corporate relationships. He took over, and, in a short time, he did an absolutely brilliant job."[3] He reorganized the company, cutting down staffs to reduce costs and bringing in new business to expand capital resources. Over his ten years as Chief Executive Officer, he had managed to engineer successful mergers, first with Abraham and Company and then Kuhn Loch.

Peterson was an attractive man with a trim figure, a deep voice and a deliberate manner, all of which conveyed authority. He possessed an "ambassadorial" management style and his "dazzling" approach was marked by considerable intelligence and aggressive preparation. He was the archetypical Washington insider, referring to Kissinger as "Henry" and Buchwald as "Art". His strengths came from his numerous contacts with clients, competitors, governments, the press and public. Peterson was considered Mr. "Outside", spending much of his time representing Lehman to external constituencies. However, he was not considered as successful an inside man. He gave little attention to his partners and even less to other employees, and did not play an active role in the management of the business. His associates felt that he was insensitive to people. Partner Stephen W. Bershad described what he thought of Peterson's management style.

> "...He would set his mind on something and see nothing else. He would walk down the hall with a stack of letters, read the mail, write replies and just throw them over his shoulder, assuming someone would be there to pick them up. He would call partners at all hours, summon them to ride uptown in his chauffeured Oldsmobile and then ignore them as he talked on the telephone or scanned a memorandum. Many partners thought him self-centered, haughty, unfeeling, uncaring." Eric Gleacher, another partner, felt that a major shortcoming of Peterson's was his "failure to create a sense of teamwork across the firm – it was absent when he arrived, as well as when he departed. Lehman was held together strictly by money, blood money."[4]

Unfortunately, Peterson was unaware that many of his partners respected him but did not like him. One such partner was **Lewis Glucksman**.

Lewis Glucksman was considered Mr. "Inside". He managed the day-to-day business of the firm. All of the departments reported to him, and his knowledge of Lehman Brothers was vast. Glucksman was a trader, unlike Peterson who was a banker, and had a very different management style:

> "He arrived at his desk before 6 A.M., his tie already loosened. Soon, his trousers would be sprinkled with cigar ash, his hands blackened by newsprint from ripping out newspaper articles to review with 'my team' as he liked to refer to his staff. He almost always ate lunch at his desk on the trading floor instead of in Lehman's elegant 43rd-floor partners' dining room. Instead of a windowed office overlooking New York's East Side waterfront, he had private quarters off the trading floor that were windowless and cramped. It was dubbed "the chart room" because Glucksman, who loves boating and fishing, had hung navigational charts on the walls. On the trading floor, Glucksman worked in a glass-walled office known as "the fishbowl," where his people could see him, feel his presence, hear him bellow

profanities, watch his round face redden with rage, see him burst the buttons on his shirt or heave something in frustration, watch him hug or kiss employees to express appreciation. 'Lew managed people...through a combination of fear and love'."[5]

Instead of pictures of fish or navigational charts, Peterson's office walls were hung with signed lithographs and autographed photographs from, no doubt, highly prestigious, very close friends of his. He was particularly conscious of proper dress and behavior and was engaged in an elaborate social life. Glucksman concerned himself primarily with Lehman Brothers, spending most of his days at work or dining alone in a Chinatown restaurant.

Glucksman, prior to his elevation to Co-C.E.O., had grown resentful of Peterson. He felt that Peterson was arrogant and condescending and that Peterson considered him to be a lowly trader. A history of conflict between bankers and traders in the investment banking industry had developed into a war of stereotypes at Lehman Brothers. Bankers were perceived by traders as elitist snobs, ivy-leaguers, who took long lunches, fawned over clients and did not work too hard. Traders were frequently perceived by bankers as under-educated and crude robots, *hic et nunc* types. These stereotypes perpetuated a rift between the two groups that was most accurately portrayed by Peterson and Glucksman's relationship. Peterson, in Glucksman's opinion, spent too much time "cultivating clients over expensive meals, dropping names, worrying about his own press notices, behaving as if investment banking were still about the old-school relationships rather than market-responsive transactions."[6] Glucksman was concerned that Peterson was greedy; that he had plans to sell Lehman Brothers before he would be required to start selling his shares back and that he distributed the firm's profits unfairly. 60% of the stock was allocated to Peterson's "banker group" which contributed less than 1/3 of the firm's profits.

From Peterson's perspective, Glucksman wanted more recognition and managerial freedom to make decisions. Peterson felt pressure to assuage Glucksman. He believed that Glucksman was a vital asset to the firm and responsible for much of its success in trading. "Lew built commercial paper into an $18 to $20 billion business. Even his more ardent critics will tell you that he was one of the best in the business at credit analysis."[7] It was these features that eventually convinced Peterson to promote Glucksman as his Co-C.E.O.. Peterson believed he was doing a favor for Glucksman. He felt that the promotion had played a part in the transformation of Glucksman. He congratulated himself for helping him become a calmer executive, losing 70 lbs and rehabilitating a wardrobe once dominated by light suits and wide ties. Glucksman, however, was insulted by the move: "It was a slap in the face,...Another example of Pete's unwillingness to let go when his interests were outside the business."[8] What Glucksman really wanted was for Peterson to announce plans to step down. In July of 1983, Glucksman's resentment of Peterson had grown to such and extent that he decided to use his powers as Co-CEO to remove Peterson from the company altogether. Following his promotion, Glucksman met with Peterson to ask if he could run the business alone, suggesting that Peterson leave by September 30th. Although Peterson had not planned on leaving the company so soon, considering his options and the likelihood that he would secure excellent financial terms,he decided to accept Glucksman's request. He announced his resignation to a stunned board on Monday, July 25, 1983.

Glucksman intended to bring peace and equity to Lehman Brothers, but his reign was instead characterized by dissension and upheaval that began with Peterson's surprise announcement to the Board. The board felt understandably deceived and insecure as their firm's fate was decided without their consultation. No sooner was Glucksman at the helm when major changes began to occur. He reorganized the leadership of the firm, "shuffling jobs around and making enemies."[9] He reallocated profits, increasing bonuses for "his team", the trader group, and decreasing those for bankers. He similarly redistributed the firm's shares. He was accused of buying off key partners who could have blocked his actions and brought in new partners, established in the field, at income rates that partners resented because they felt it hurt their equity positions. Key partners began to leave. Internal turmoil increased. Business turned down in a negative market and serious capital problems arose. Even Glucksman was affected by the downturn. To some he began to appear more like Peterson. "He had very little time to say good morning."[10] Many were outraged by what they perceived as "Glucksman's lust for power, his unwillingness to consult the board on an issue vital to the health of the partnership."[11] He seemed to manage the company as if he were trying to right past wrongs.

> "He allocated bonuses and the distribution of shares based not on what partners had traditionally received or on their status within the firm; rather, he strove to make decisions on what he said were 'the merits' of each partner's performance. In fact, many banking partners believed his decisions were too personal, meant to settle old scores. They believed that Glucksman was not controlling his demons."[12]

Still others criticized the board for being "preoccupied with their bonuses and their shares,"[13] in what represented personal avarice and petty coalitions rather than the best interests of Lehman Brothers.

After less than a year under Glucksman's management, the unsettled Lehman Brothers merged with Shearson/American Express.

Goldman Sachs and Company

Goldman Sachs and Company, a New York investment banking firm, was so successful that each of its seventy-five partners earned $5 million per year in 1984. Their earning could not be casually explained in terms of sales and commissions. It was something else; a unity of beliefs, values, and ethics throughout the entire organization. In the words of John Whitehead when he was co-chairman:

> "There are some things about Goldman as an institution that make it unique: its team spirit, the pride in what we do, the high standard of professionalism, the service orientation...That's the essence of Goldman's culture, the things that have made us what we are, and I would say that culture has been the key to our success."[14]

This culture did not just happen. It was the long-term result of the joint leadership of John Weinberg and John Whitehead, who had been a part of the firm since the late 1940s and succeeded C.E.O. Gus Levy when he died in 1976. Their co-commitment to traditions, loyalty to the corporations they serve and subordination of their own individual egos through power sharing and teamwork for the good of the firm have worked to generate and maintain the culture that has been the key to Goldman's success. Throughout the company's organizational levels, there had been a well-forged emphasis on entrepreneurial aggressiveness, self-effacing team-work, a shared knowledge of what the business would and would not do, homegrown talent, and, moreover, a commitment to serving the customer above all other interests. The *espirit de corps* was so strong that one partner noted, "if you polled people here and asked them why they work so hard, they would probably say that there's nothing else in their lives that gives them nearly the charge that their work does."

At Goldman Sachs, and other investment banking firms, greed is prevalent. Yet, during the Weinberg and Whitehead era, this greed was channeled in such a way that it worked for and benefited the entire firm. There was no backstabbing or selfishness; no "star system". Rather, it was "all for one and one for all."[15]

The thrust of the Goldman culture was its indomitable team spirit. Partners and staff "gang tackled" problems with a near mania for interdepartmental and interpersonal communication and coordination. Credit was given "loud and clear" to everyone who participated.

To assure the acculturation of the teamwork and other values at Goldman Sachs, the organization "grew" its own talent with entrenched recruitment and training programs. The thirty individuals who were given jobs with Goldman Sachs one year (over 1,500 applied) were the ones with brains, humor, motivation, confidence, maturity, and needless to say, an inclination to play on the team. Once a young person was hired, he or she usually spent a career with the same department. Therefore, all departments within Goldman Sachs had a deep bench of expertise with viewpoints that were similar.

Of course, inbreeding can and does cause insularity, but again, unlike other organizations, this too benefited Goldman Sachs. The firm took pride in its aloofness and was not even interested in how its competition was doing things. Outsiders were rarely brought into the organization, and the great majority of the firm's seventy-five partners had been with the company for ten to twenty years.

Weinberg and Whitehead had distinct traditions in doing business. To them, service and loyalty to the Goldman Sach's customer were paramount. They strictly adhered to certain standards about who the company would do business with. Clients must have had sound management of their operations, produce only high-quality goods and services, show profits for all their businesses, and also benefit the public in some way. Other such standards included Goldman Sach's refusal to underwrite any dealing involving nonvoting stock (a violation of the belief that shareholders should have voting rights) and its refusal to participate in unfriendly tender offers.

The culture at Goldman Sachs emphasized a unique "loose-tight" management style, where the organization is rigidly controlled at the top concerning operational procedures and overhead, yet, each department is allowed autonomy concerning entrepreneurship and inno-vation. The effectiveness of this management approach has been reflected in the success of the company. In 1984, the company's profit margins were the widest in the investment banking industry. Over recent years, however, changes in the investment banking industry have caused threads of the culture to unravel.

The hypergrowth of leading investment banking firms and the 1987 market crash has provoked Goldman Sachs to behave in ways that are not congruent with its culture. The firm has hired and fired numerous employees. Homegrown talent and lifetime employment are no longer basic characteristics of Goldman Sachs. Once, a new employee was expected to rise through the ranks to ensure complete adoption of the company's value system. Now, newcomers are starting as partners. In order to bring in experience to lead new areas of growth, the company has hired prominent employees from other firms and placed them immediately in key positions.

Goldman Sachs called in the Delta Consulting Group in response to growing concerns over internal tensions and resentments. Eleven current and former partners discussed, among other issues, ego and greed problems, a generation gap with respect to values and a rise in staff defections.

The greed that once drove the company towards unified excellence, now seems to be causing internal problems. A new kind of greed has emerged within the company. Increased hiring has brought in a large number of younger employees who have riot had the time to absorb the culture that discourages individualistic greed and encourages loyalty and teamwork. This new generation of Goldman employees has a selfish greed that could erode the team spirit that has kept Goldman together.

In hiring experts from the industry to fill high level positions before they have been properly acculturized, Goldman Sachs has introduced yet another breed of greed - an inflated sense of self and an enormous need for recognition. This greed is especially dangerous since it is among those who are leading the company.

These changes have not gone unnoticed by others at Goldman Sachs.

> "In one comment that the (Delta Group) study highlighted,...a partner said, 'The greediness of people is the one thing I dislike the most of what I see.' Another partner said: 'In the old days, when you became a partner, you would feel free to give your wallet to another partner to hold for safe-keeping. I do not think it is that way today.'..."[16]

The nature of greed is not the only cultural aspect that has been affected. Goldman Sach's hasty hiring and neglect of appropriate acculturation has destroyed the mechanism for its insularity. Outsiders are being brought into the organization all over the place.

> "Two examples: Commodities veteran Daniel Amstutz left a 25-year career at Cargill to lead Goldman's commodities department, Michael Mortara left Salomon Brothers to help lead Goldman's mortgage-backed securities department just two years ago."[17]

Nearly half of Goldman Sach's employees have been there less than three years. For Goldman, where inbreeding has been of key importance to its cultural maintenance, this could introduce problems. "It's unbelievable" laments one Goldman department head, "I have the 'twos' (two-year veterans of the firm) teaching the 'ones'."[18] How to train and infuse these new comers with Goldman ideals is a problem for management. Whether these employees have the maturity or judgement to handle the responsibilities of their positions, especially in turbulent market environments, and the loyalty that years with the firm cultivates is a concern for many at Goldman Sachs. Managing a larger "family" has made integrating individuals within teamwork settings difficult. H. Frederick Krimendhal, the Goldman partner in charge of operations and administration, concedes that "Everyone is uncomfortable with the rate of growth. We all feel that if we don't keep expanding, we'll lose our position. But if we keep growing at a certain rate, we'll lose control."[19] "The traditional answer to growth has been to separate producers from managers," reasons Goldman vice president Peter Mathias, "But for our business, if managers aren't in close touch (with the markets) they lose credibility."[20] One way to manage the rapid growth and turbulent conditions would be to impose bureaucratic devices, such as high formalization. However, this would be self-defeating because it would decrease flexibility.

There has been a growing resentment amongst the older generation of Goldman employees. They have given their lives to the company with the hope of winning one of the precious partnership spots that they now see newcomers filling. This has left them understandably bitter, and has led to numerous staff defections and early retirements. Two partners agreed: "We lost ten people who have been here three to five years who we thought would be stars/producers".[21]

Hypergrowth and market decline have also disrupted some business traditions at Goldman Sachs, and with them, the company's fundamental nature. Black Monday (October 19, 1987) forced Goldman into widespread layoffs. This was an unprecedented move for the company. "There is a slight feeling that the contract with employees has been broken."[22] Another partner commented: "Goldman Sachs used to be paternalistic. Now we've become tougher in a more competitive world. Some would even say we've become ruthless."[23] In 1989, Weinberg ended the tradition of refusing to represent a hostile bidder in a takeover attempt. The profitability of these takeovers and the threat of competition made them difficult for the company to resist.

Hypergrowth has also placed capital pressures on Goldman Sachs that might make its remaining a partnership infeasible. Whether it can maintain the capital resources for its continued growth without going public is uncertain. "At current profit levels, Goldman would fetch as much as $4 billion in the stock market, thus it could raise perhaps $500 million by selling a big minority stake of its equity to the public."[24] However, in doing so, Goldman might lose the lucrative lure of partnership that is believed to play a large role in its mystique. "You'd have the headhunters all over this place if we announced the end (of partnerships),"[25] acknowledges Krimendhal.

Even Goldman's integrity has been in question. The resignations of Senior stock trader, Robert Freeman, after having pled guilty to a charge of insider trading, and partner Lewis M. Eisenberg, after his secretary filed a sexual harassment suit, clearly has soiled Goldman's pristine reputation. The company has also had problems incorporating women and minorities into their work force. They claim that they find it difficult to recruit successfully among these groups and that is why there is an absence of women and minorities in their top management positions. These groups have also had problems assimilating. In 1990, five women quit Goldman in order to form their own "boutique" investment firm. The women wanted to pursue their dreams of entrepreneurship that Goldman seemed unable to fulfil.

Problems of acculturation have not arisen unchallenged by Goldman Sachs. They have hired consultants to advise them on management techniques and developed programs designed to integrate new arrivals into their corporate culture and to generate a sense of involvement. These include management and leadership seminars and orientation programs. "Classroom exercises range from a Goldman Sachs culture game – akin to Trivial Pursuit – to role playing. Sample question: What was the first issue Goldman Sachs ever did? (Answer: one for United Cigar Manufacturing Co.) In role playing, different teams represent Goldman's competitors and discuss their various strengths and weaknesses and what they imply for the strategy of the home team – Goldman."[26] Goldman answers the problems of growth and control with the same ideal its maintained from day one – teamwork. "When the firm's new investment banking chief, Geoffrey Boisi, organized a seminar recently for the client-coverage group, he invited Red Auerbach, president of the Boston Celtics to address the name-tag-decked, 270-strong gathering on 'winning'".[27]

Teamwork has, indeed, continued to triumph at Goldman. By making an effort to give the lowliest associate as sense of belonging, enlisting their participation in decisions and keeping them well posted on developments affecting the firm, resentment has been alleviated. Also, training has stressed specialization as well as a basic understanding of general issues, so teams can form and disband efficiently and flexibly.

Although Goldman's hiring of experts outside their firm has caused resentment and acculturation problems, it has also supported the company's growth. As products have become more specialized, new expertise has kept the company head to head with its competitors in a fast paced race.

It seems that the evolution of the Goldman Sach's culture has done little to jar the company's top position. For the first six months of this year, the firm accumulated $29.5 billion in deals and a market share of 14.2%. Teamwork, training and loyalty are still prevalent. The firm continues to be cautious about expanding into new areas. This tradition has afforded them protection from losses other firms have incurred in junk bonds and bridge loans. "Our approach is dull", concedes Vice Chairman Robert E. Rubin, "But it's not a bad way to run a business, (and) we have been working for some time to make sure we are there with new products and to stay on the cutting edge."[28] Trail-blazers they may not be, but this has not had a negative effect on their profitability.

In November 1990, Senior Partner and Chairman, John L. Weinberg, will be succeeded by Robert E. Rubin and Stephen Friedman, both Vice Chairmen of the firm's management committee. The three men expect that the working environment at Goldman will not change and Rubin and Friedman will continue to encourage the traditions and culture at Goldman in the face of industry changes and accompanying turmoil. Thus, a challenge facing Goldman Sachs is to maintain its culture by finding individuals suited for it, while simultaneously reinforcing the culture for those already within the organization.

Notes

1. Robert G. Eccles and Dwight B. Crane, Doing Deals (Boston: Harvard Business School Press, 1988). P. 49.
2. Ken Auletta, 'The Fall of Lehman Brothers". *New York Times Magazine*, (Part 1, February 17, 1985), p.36.
3. Ibid, p. 40.
4. Ibid, p. 34.
5. Ibid, p. 33.
6. Ibid, p. 30.
7. Ibid, p. 33.
8. Ibid, p. 30.
9. Ibid, p. 59.
10. Ken Auletta, "The Fall of Lehman Brothers". *New York Times Magazine* (Part 2, February 24, 1985), p. 36.
11. Ken Auletta, "The Fall of Lehman Brothers". *New York Times Magazine* (Part 1, February 17, 1985), p. 60.
12. Ibid, p. 92.
13. Ken Auletta, 'The Fall of Lehman Brothers". *New York Times Magazine* (Part 2, February 24, 1985), p. 39.
14. Beth McGoldrich, "Inside the Goldman Sachs Culture," *Institutional Investor* (January 1984): 53-67.
15. Ibid.
16. Alison Leigh Cowan, "An Exercise in Introspection Lets Goldman Bare Its Soul". *The New York Times*, (January 25, 1990), p. D1.
17. Jack Willoughby, "Can Goldman Stay on Top?". *Forbes* (September 18, 1989), p. 154.
18. Henny Sender, "Too Big for Their Own Good". *Institutional Investor*, (February,1987). p. 63.
19. Ibid.
20. Ibid., p. 64.
21. Alison Leigh Cowan, "An Exercise in Introspection Lets Goldman Bare Its Soul". *The New York Times*, (January 25, 1990).
22. Ibid.
23. Ibid.
24. Jack Willoughby, "Can Goldman Stay on Top?". *Forbes*, (September 18, 1989). p. 154.
25. Henny Sender, "Too Big for Their Own Good". *Institutional Investor*, (February,1987). p. 63.
26. Ibid., p. 65.
27. Henny Sender, "Too Big for Their Own Good". *Institutional Investor*, (February,1987). p. 64.
28. Jon Friedman, "How Playing the Tortoise Paid off For Goldman Sachs". *Business Week*, (May 7, 1990), p. 131.

Part 4   Organizational Structure & Design

Cases Outline

14. Kidder, Peabody & Co. in 1994*

In January 1994, Kidder, Peabody named Orlando Joseph Jett, 36, as the recipient of the Chairman's Award, signifying that he was the outstanding employee of the year, in recognition of his performance as head of its government bond desk. 1993 was a good year for Kidder and Jett's best year. To reward Jett for the impressive profits he produced, he received the second largest bonus in the firm; $9 million. Jett said he was proud to be recognized by the firm for his trading performance. In his acceptance speech, he drew an analogy between trading and war, emphasizing the need for members of the firm to work together to be successful.[1] One member of the audience, John Liftin, described Jett's address as a "winning-is-everything speech".[2]

Joseph Jett

Background

For Jett, receiving the Chairman's Award seemed to mark the culmination of a long journey from his politically conservative middle-class origins. Jett grew up in Wickliffe, Ohio a small town near Cleveland. His father was a strict disciplinarian who emphasized education – Jett and his siblings were expected to receive good grades and were punished if they did not. Jett was not allowed to play team sports because his father believed that it was a trap.[3]

Jett felt he did not fit in when he attended high school because of his successful focus on academics and the fact that he did not speak black slang.[4] He would frequently clash with other black students, confronting them with his conservative views on affirmative action. In one instance he described walking onto a basketball court, taking the basketball and announcing, "It's time that we as a people stop making baskets and start making A's."[5]

After high school he won a scholarship to MIT[6] where he earned a bachelor's degree in 1980 and a master's degree in 1982 in chemical engineering.[7] He landed his first job at General Electric's plastics division in Selkirk, New York.

He felt stifled by his job, he wanted more responsibility and the opportunity to lead. He decided that engineers would, "always be order takers"[8] in the corporate world, so he left GE and entered Harvard Business School (HBS) in 1985.

Jett states that he went to HBS with the intention of returning to GE once he had completed his MBA. While there however, he decided to pursue a career in trading. He identified with the students who had worked on Wall Street prior to attending Harvard because of their drive and energy.[9] He explained, "It was the lure of objectivity, not big money. There is a purity to the markets. It is the place to be judged by an objective standard, how much you make. It was a place, I was sure, where I would not be judged by race, but by my performance, objectively measured. I have turned down jobs that were based on race. That sort of affirmative action has the same effect that welfare has on poor people. Affirmative action is welfare for the middle class."[10]

He obtained his first position in finance as a summer intern at Ford Motor Company

*This case was prepared by Richard D. Freedman and Jennifer Burke, Stern School of Business, New York University, November 1994. Reprinted by permission.

working for the group that managed Ford's short-term cash. Although Harvard states that Jett finished his coursework, HBS did not award him an MBA.[11] This detail did not prevent him from beginning his career in trading at Morgan Stanley. He started as a trainee and later became a junior trader. In an effort to fit in, he says he was "loud and brash"[12] which alienated his colleagues. He was laid off in less than two years.

It took him six months to find his second job, at CS First Boston. In order to correct what he felt were his mistakes at Morgan Stanley, he tried to change the way he carried himself. He said, "I felt I simply could not allow a personality. I became very dry. My God, did I become a dry quiet, dull person."[13]

He didn't last long at First Boston. He explained that his dismissal in early 1991 was because the firm discovered he was looking for work at Kidder, Peabody. Former colleagues at First Boston say he was let go because of lackluster performance and for having presented a resume that exaggerated his experience; particularly his experience as a trader at Morgan Stanley.[14]

Jett Joins Kidder

After six month of unemployment, Kidder hired Jett as a government bond trader (see Appendix I for an explanation of trading) in the Fixed Income Division about April 1991.[15] Government bond trading is considered to be one of the most straightforward kinds of securities trading, stressing a knowledge of yield curves and mathematics. It was a good place for someone with limited trading experience to start. This seemed to be a lucky break for Jett who had no prior experience trading government securities. Jett described the position as his "dream job"[16] and said he worked 12 hour days and then studied at home after hours to learn the job. He was determined to succeed.

At the end of 1991 he received a $5,000 bonus (a slap in the face by Wall Street standards) along with a warning that if he did not improve his profitability he would be dismissed. It seemed as if Jett was in the process of failing once again. In response, he removed the furniture from his apartment and slept on the floor. He did this, he says, to punish himself for his failure at First Boston and for his unsatisfactory performance at Kidder.[17]

The Turnaround

In 1992 he experienced a complete turnaround. Suddenly Jett was very profitable for the firm and at the end of the year he received a $2 million bonus. Edward Cerullo, Chief of the Fixed Income Division and the number two executive at the firm, noticed Jett's performance. Jett continued to impress management as he entered the next year. As his monthly profits grew, he was allowed to make larger and larger trades, risking more and more of the firm's capital. Before Jett's arrival, $20 million in annual earnings was the best record for the Government Desk, yet in 1993 his profits ranged from $5 to $10 million per month. Apparently, Jett's supervisors believed that he had invented a new trading technique which had transformed the government bond desk into a powerful money-making asset for the firm.

In March, 1993, Jett was promoted to head the Government Desk where he had been a trader for the past two years. He would fill a vacancy created by Melvin R. Mullin who had been promoted to head up the derivatives trading desk. Mullin, Jett's former boss and the man who had trained Jett, recommended to Cerullo that Jett take his place citing Jett's outstanding performance as a bond trader.

Cerullo and Michael A. Carpenter, CEO of Kidder, Peabody met early in 1993 to review a list of possible promotions. Cerullo had been watching Jett's profits and slowly increasing the size of the trades Jett was allowed to make. Cerullo championed Jett's promotion because Jett was disciplined and, "had a high-energy level, he was very execution-oriented, and he had a drive to succeed."[18] Cerullo and Carpenter decided to promote Jett to head the Government Bond Desk in March of 1993.

Jett, who had joined Kidder only 26 months ago with no prior experience trading government bonds, now had direct responsibility for 32 people and a great deal of authority. Jett's performance and money-making ability continued to impress management and at the end of 1993 he was promoted to Managing Director.

Jett had turned the tide of his unfortunate beginnings on Wall Street. For 1993, Jett's trading activities had generated more than $299 million in profits[19] and accounted for more than one-quarter of the Fixed Income Division's operating profits.[20] This was the performance that led to Jett being honored with the Chairman's Award, and receiving the $9 million bonus.

Kidder, Peabody

Kidder's Acquisition by GE

Kidder was acquired by GE in 1986 for $600 million, as a means of increasing their presence in the then booming financial markets. GE's 1986 Financial Report explains the reason for the acquisition, "Kidder adds value to the Company's financial portfolio in other ways. It gives [GE Capital Corp.] access to a valuable new distribution network in addition to helping create and market new securities. And, by introducing its clients to GECC, it can pave the way for creative financings that combine the talents for both groups."[21] It was expected that Kidder would benefit from the access to GE Capital's "highly sophisticated marketing, systems, and international capabilities."[22] In addition, Kidder was expected to use its Wall Street expertise to find deals for GE Capital and to share its knowledge of Wall Street with GECC.

Kidder reported directly to GE Capital, the huge financial services arm of GE. Having the backing of such a large parent was seen by many Wall Street observers as giving Kidder a major advantage over those competitors without a large industrial parent. Relative to other investment houses that lacked such a sponsorship, Kidder had access to GE Capital's tremendous capital base. Those firms that operated under the traditional partnership, such as Goldman, Sachs, rely upon their partners' capital, which is no match for GE Capital's resources.

Partnerships are operated by their owners. Partners are selected from the traders and investment bankers that work for the firm, or are recruited away from other firms. Partners determine the firm's overall investment strategy and consequently the level of risk to which their strategy will expose the firm. Generally, partnerships take a more conservative investment approach because they are, in essence, investing their own money. The culture and compensation system ties the partner's financial gains to the long-term well-being of the firm. Partners generally leave most of their bonuses in the firm's capital account, where it is reinvested to generate more growth for the firm. In other words, it encourages deferring short-term gains (i.e., large cash bonuses) in favor of the long-term rewards of partnership. Employees working for firms like Goldman, strive to gain partnership status because of the lucrative payoff they will gain upon retirement, when they cash out of the partnership.

In a firm like Kidder, the traders are employees. Thus, their future financial well-being is not so closely tied to the firm's. Since Kidder's traders were not trading with their own money, they were more open to riskier trading strategies because this could mean bigger short-term profits for the firm resulting in bigger annual bonuses for the trader.

In addition, Kidder's management was under intense pressure from GE to produce big profits and to demonstrate rapid growth. As a result, senior management at Kidder chose to adopt a relatively risky investment strategy leveraging itself significantly more than many of its competitors on Wall Street. Had Kidder been a free-standing partnership, it is less likely that the firm would have chosen such a risky strategy.

The opportunities for synergy and increased revenues that GE anticipated when it acquired Kidder turned out to be less lucrative than expected. Since its acquisition of Kidder, GE had to invest considerable effort and resources into making the firm a serious player on Wall Street. In the late Eighties and early Nineties, GE provided Kidder with approximately $500 million of capital infusion in response to Kidder's business problems. In April of 1994 the fixed income market soured and GE again had to infuse Kidder with $200 million in capital funding[23] to save the firm.

When GE acquired Kidder, they expected to gain access to Kidder's "insider" knowledge about Wall Street. Over time however, as GE Capital realized that Kidder did not possess any more knowledge about Wall Street than GE Capital did, the relationship soured. GE Capital employees became disparaging toward Kidder's "stuffed-shirt" behavior increasing the cultural rift. Kidder was expected to bring GE Capital in on big deals. But, rumor had it that GE Capital forced Kidder out of these deals once Kidder initiated them. This, of course, had a negative effect on the morale of Kidder professionals.

General Electric

Under Jack Welch, Chairman and CEO, GE developed a broad diversification strategy that had proven highly successful. Businesses in the GE portfolio had to be number 1 or number 2 in their global market,[24] and demonstrate a high growth rate (generally double-digit revenue and profit growth). If a business' performance did not meet expectations, Welch would "fix, close, or sell" the unit.[25]Over the prior ten years, GE sold off almost two dozen major businesses that were worth $11 billion and employed tens of thousands of people.[26]

Under Welch's direction, GE was transformed from a rather slow and steady "blue-chip" institution, growing at about the same rate as the U.S. GNP, into a high-powered growth organization that became a Wall Street favorite. By any financial measure the firm has turned in outstanding results; for the 10 years 1981 - 1991 GE earnings grew at an annual rate of more than ten percent (to $4.4 billion of earnings on revenues of $60 billion), which was one-and-one-half times the GNP's growth rate for the same period.[27]

In order to accomplish this feat, Welch adopted his strategy of diversification and then set about changing the culture of the organization. He diversified into three main types of business; Services (financial, information, and television), Technologies (aerospace, aircraft engines, medical, and plastics), and Manufacturing (appliances, power systems, motors, and transportation systems). He slashed overhead and decentralized the organization – reducing layers of management and pushing decisions down the hierarchy. GE eliminated the, "entire second and third echelons of management."[28] This meant that the fourteen Strategic Business Units (SBU's) now reported directly to the three most senior people in the organization, which included Jack Welch, CEO, Edward Hood, Vice Chairman, and Lawrence Bossidy, Vice Chairman.[29]

This was a sea-change for a historically bureaucratic culture like GE's. Traditionally, the norm was for employees to push decisions up the hierarchy. Referring most major decisions up the chain of command had been ingrained in the culture long before Welch took over. This "cultural habit" probably had its roots in GE's historical focus on manufacturing, especially those operating in rather stable environments, such as dishwashers and lighting.

In order to bring about the cultural shift, Welch emphasized a philosophy of leadership, not management. In other words, he pushed his employees to become more autonomous, in the hopes that they would take responsibility for their actions and decisions. This was intended to increase GE's ability to respond to the demands of the many different markets it operated in. Welch sums up his philosophy:

> The old organization was built on control, but the world has changed. The world is moving at such a pace that control has become a limitation. It slows you down. You've got to balance freedom with some control, but you've got to have more freedom than you've ever dreamed of.[30]

Management Team

For the first three years that GE owned Kidder, they left Kidder executives to run the business. There were troubles with the Kidder unit from the first day that GE completed its acquisition of Kidder; Siegel, a Kidder trader was found guilty of insider trading and, as a result, management and controls at Kidder were seriously questioned. Other problems followed and in 1989, Welch decided that a manager with strategic and general management skills would be better suited to take on the tremendously difficult task of straightening out Kidder's many problems.

Welch appointed Michael A. Carpenter to the position of CEO of Kidder, Peabody. Carpenter, a personal friend of Welch's, came from GE's Chairman's Office where he handled strategic issues. Prior to joining GE, Carpenter had worked for many years as a consultant, but he had no prior experience on Wall Street. In fact, he was not licensed to run a brokerage firm by the SEC from January 1989 through March 1993.[31]

Consistent with GE's growth requirements, Welch wanted to see strong profit growth from Kidder. There was a good deal of resentment among the ranks at Kidder that an "outsider" had been appointed to lead the firm. Carpenter had to work to gain the acceptance of the Kidder employees while striving to achieve the growth Welch demanded of Kidder. Carpenter knew he had to find a way to make Kidder a leader in at least one market and identified the mortgage-backed securities (MBS's) as the market segment where Kidder would make its mark. He developed a strategy that emphasized aggressive underwriting in MBS's and sought to control costs. Welch supported this strategy and helped finance it through a large standby credit line made available to Kidder by GE.

As one industry expert pointed out, the impact of these decisions had many implications for the way that the firm developed over the next few years. Through the focus on MBS's and on improved profitability in the rest of the fixed income division, Kidder suddenly became very trading oriented. In a certain sense, Carpenter's strategy was spot on, because the fixed income markets were in a bull market for much of the Eighties and early Nineties. There were two weak links in Carpenter's strategy; one was the infrastructure (systems and controls) needed to support a heavy-trading environment and the other was the need for traders with sufficient skill and experience. As a result, Kidder often promoted less experienced traders into positions of responsibility (relative to their competitors).[32]

When a firm like Kidder underwrites an issue of a given security, they agree to sell an issuer's security to the public. The practice of underwriting requires that the underwriting firm buy any unsold inventory of the security from the issuer. This can expose the firm to substantial risks, particularly if the value of a security is sensitive to changes in market interest rates (e.g., bonds) or other variables.

Under Carpenter, Kidder's overall standing improved from the rank of 10th largest underwriter of all new debt and equity issues in 1990, to 4th in 1993. This was largely driven by Kidder's aggressive underwriting in the MBS sector. In 1989 Kidder underwrote roughly 5% of new MBS issues, this shot up to almost 15% in 1990. By September of 1994 Kidder was the number one MBS underwriter controlling almost 25% of the market and holding a very large inventory in MBS's.[33] It is noteworthy that none of Kidder's competitors challenged their bid for ownership of the MBS market. Competitors did not see MBS as an attractive market because of their inherent low liquidity. Some industry observers even take the perspective that Kidder's competitors took advantage of Kidder's strategy and began dumping their MBS inventory on Kidder.[34]

Kidder, like many of its competitors financed much of its underwriting activities with debt. As of the end of 1993, Kidder was so highly leveraged that every $1 of equity was supporting $93 of assets.[35] Compared to the industry average of $1 equity to $27 assets, they had taken a very high risk position. According to one source, a 3.2% decline in the value of its portfolio could have wiped out Kidder's entire net worth.[36]

Cerullo, who reported to Carpenter, was largely credited with turning Kidder around. It was through his direction of the Fixed Income Division, that Kidder became the lead player in MBS underwriting. His division was not only Kidder's most profitable business (in percentage terms), but also the firm's largest contributor to operating profits (in dollar terms). In 1993, Cerullo was responsible for managing $100 billion in assets, $20 billion in daily transactions, $1 billion of earnings, and about 750 people, including traders.[37] Cerullo was given a great deal of latitude in running the Fixed Income Division, which he operated out of a separate building from the rest of Kidder.

Over time, Cerullo's responsibilities grew. One former trader explains, "Anytime something new came along, whether a new futures or derivatives product, Ed was given responsibility. Gradually he was just given responsibility for everything [in the Fixed Income Division]."[38] Because his division produced the majority of the firm's profits, Cerullo was "given something akin to carte blanche to run his own show."[39]

Cerullo relied on a number of reports to keep himself up-to-date with the activities of his many traders. These reports included inventory reports, Profit & Loss statements, control reports, and risk management reports.[40] In order to strengthen the system of checks and balances in the Fixed Income Division, Cerullo had also hired a separate risk manager, financial analyst, and compliance officer just for his Division.[41] His risk manager was David Bernstein, Manager of Business Development. He was considered to be Cerullo's right-hand man; responsible for risk management as well as trouble shooting.

Traders had a variety of perceptions about Cerullo's management style. Joseph W. Cherner, a former top trader at Kidder said, "Ed is an extremely gifted manager...Ed is not easily fooled. He's very skeptical, very thorough, very street smart."[42] Another former Kidder trader described Cerullo's style like this, "If [he] thinks someone is doing a good job, he gives them absolute carte blanche. He's a very trusting person."[43]

On the whole, traders summed up the culture under Cerullo as 'produce or perish'. Traders were expected to produce profits for the firm, or be fired. Former fixed-income traders were so leery of reporting losses to Cerullo, that they would often under-report profits in order to build up a reserve for use in months when they had a loss.[44]

One authority attributes the high pressure culture at Kidder to their practice of principle trading. The firm uses its own capital to trade, the practice can be highly profitable, but it is also highly risky. He describes traders as, "superstar gunslingers. They're like baseball players who are free agents – they're trying to maximize their income in the short term. The firms have encouraged this because they have made so much money."[45]

Control at Kidder

For Wall Street firms, issues of compliance and control are serious business. There are a number of important federal laws that have been enacted to insure a stable and orderly market. These laws are enforced through a variety of government regulations and company controls designed to insure compliance (see Appendix II for an explanation of government regulations). Furthermore, without appropriate controls traders could expose firms to disastrous losses.

The Chief Financial Officer (CFO) at Kidder, like most of its competitors, is a special management function which includes among its responsibilities oversight of compliance and controls. Richard O'Donnell, Kidder's CFO commented in April 1994, "I've got great comfort, as the person who signs off on our numbers, knowing that my corporate parent is devoted to total compliance."[46] He went on to explain that GE's financial auditors were "swarming" all over Kidder, to insure that their controls were better than their competitors.[47]

Kidder is subject to external audits by GE's corporate auditors every 18 months. Kidder also relies on an automated accounting/control system as well as internal audits by Kidder accountants. In addition to accounting-based controls, Kidder, like other firms, relied upon management to insure compliance. As Chief of the Fixed Income Division, Cerullo was ultimately responsible for the performance and actions of the traders that worked under him. It was Cerullo's responsibility to understand his trader's practices and trading techniques. Cerullo, as head of the division, set the tone for compliance practices in his division.

The Event

Beginning of the End

Early in 1994, the computer system began having difficulty keeping up with the volume of trades that Jett was making.[48] Specialists were called in to fix the computer system. What the Information Systems (IS) specialists found was astounding; during Jett's tenure with Kidder he had entered $1.7 trillion in trades into the Kidder system (this is almost one-half of the total dollar value of Treasury securities currently estimated to be held in private hands).[49] The IS specialists discovered that none of Jett's trade deals were ever consummated. This meant that while no securities had ever changed hands, the profits associated with these allegedly fictitious trades had been accounted for as income on Kidder's books.

Once the computer specialists realized the gravity of the situation they called in the accountants, and senior executives, including Cerullo, to investigate. Cerullo's aide, David Bernstein began an in-depth audit and found a "distortion" totaling $300 million on Jett's trading book.[50] In mid-March 1994, Cerullo notified Carpenter about the situation and asked for dedicated resources to investigate the matter further.

By early April, the findings of Kidder's investigation validated their initial fears and showed that the problem would significantly impact Kidder's profitability for 1993 and 1992. The week of April 11, Carpenter notified Welch that the problem would likely affect Kidder's profitability and would result in a major loss of capital. As the accountants continued to dig, the magnitude of the problem grew; Kidder claims Jett had created some $350 million[51] in false profits and had hidden approximately $85 million in real losses.[52] Kidder officials notified regulators at the Securities and Exchange Commission (SEC) and the New York Stock Exchange that it expected to report a major loss of capital.

Jett traded government strips, which involves separating the bond's principal and interest components into two separately traded issues. Jett would enter into "forward" contracts that would join the principal and interest components together again at a later date (called "recons"). Instead of settling when these forward contracts came due, Jett would roll them over, allegedly leaving the profit on the books.[53] In order to keep the system going, Jett allegedly had to continually increase the value of his portfolio, meaning the system operated much like a pyramid scheme. This could explain the tremendous volume of trades in early 1994.

On Thursday April 14, Jett was summoned to a meeting of senior Kidder executives to answer questions regarding the matter of his questionable trades. Jett denied that his trading practices created false profits, he explained that in response to the firm's efforts to slash assets, he was using a hedging strategy.[54] Kidder attorney, John Luftin, described Jett's behavior at the meeting, "He was subdued, polite, quiet, civil. He was not the same person that gave that speech in January [at the Chairman's Award ceremony]."[55]

The following Sunday, Cerullo sent Jett a letter notifying him that he was dismissed from the firm. That evening, General Electric issued a press release stating that it would have to reduce its after-tax profits for 1993 by $210 million because of the false trading profits reported by Jett.[56] The firm also froze approximately $8 million of Jett's assets which were held in various accounts at Kidder.[57]

Controls and Jett

GE's last audit of Kidder's books was at the end of 1992. This audit, GE says, concentrated on mortgage derivatives and government options to insure the firm was hedging their risk properly. According to GE, "the Treasuries desk was not involved" in this audit.[58] This might explain why GE did not find Jett's irregular trades, which dated back to early 1992.

Kidder's internal auditors reviewed Jett's trading desk twice in 1993, but according to the Lynch Report (a review of the Jett incident performed for GE by its outside counsel) the auditors were inexperienced, and Jett misrepresented his desk's activities to the auditors.[59]

Former Kidder traders described Kidder's accounting system as unsophisticated.[60] Zero-coupon bonds (the type of bond Jett traded) were tracked in the system by price rather than yield. This practice overstated the profits of the securities from the time they are entered into the system. Furthermore, tracking such a security by price does not provide an accurate valuation in a dynamic marketplace. This is because the value (or price) of the bond fluctuates with changes in the market interest rate. In the words of one former Kidder trader, Robert Dickey, "You can make a temporary profit, but its not real."[61]

Employees had raised questions about Jett's trading practices as far back as 1992. Hugh Bush, a trader who worked alongside Jett raised question's about Jett's sudden profitability with supervisors. He believed Jett was mismarking or misrecording his trading positions. The practice of mismarking is illegal and carries heavy penalties by the SEC for the firm and the trader if discovered. Bush was fired for what Kidder described as an unrelated reason, immediately after raising these questions and Cerullo never investigated Bush's accusations.[62]

In May 1993, a Kidder accountant realized that there was a defect in the system's set-up. Charles Fiumefreddo suggested that the accounting system be changed to correct this flaw. The change Fiumefreddo suggested would have exposed Jett's alleged irregular trading activities. Jett is purported to have opposed this change and it was never implemented.[63]

In late 1993, Brian Finkelstein, another Managing Director at Kidder, questioned how Jett could be so profitable in light of the Government Desk's historical profitability. He spoke with Bernstein, Cerullo's right-hand man, about his concerns. The Lynch Report states, "According to Finkelstein, Bernstein also stated that Cerullo was aware of Jett's trading activities."[64] There is no mention in the Lynch Report as to whether the issue of possible wrong-doing on Jett's part was ever investigated.

It is interesting to note that soon after the Jett scandal erupted, two other Kidder traders were fired for allegedly hiding losses. In April, Kidder fired Neil Margolin for purportedly hiding $11 million in losses on a bond-derivatives transaction, and in June Peter Bryant was fired for alleged hiding losses totaling $6 million on a number of options trades.[65]

A History of Control Issues - Kidder Management

According to former Kidder traders, Kidder management practices differ from those of other firms. Kidder executives, according to Kidder traders, don't spend much time on the trading floor. This is in sharp contrast to the practices of other firms' makers, who see it as their duty to verify the reports generated by the audit and control functions. Some firms go so far as to plant spies on the trading floor to watch for any irregular or odd trading activity.

One fixed-income manager at another firm commented, "It's a general manager's responsibility to know what your trading practices are. [Cerullo] should never have had to rely entirely on secondary sources, including the firm's accounting department. You have to rely on your own direct questioning as a manager, no matter how senior you are."[66] Another manager remarked, "The top of the firm didn't understand the business".[67]

One former Kidder trader, Mark Pinto, commented that Cerullo, "didn't care how profits were made."[68] In fact, the Jett scandal was not the first issue of questionable practices in the bond department. In 1985 there was a deal involving the sale of bonds from Kidder to a Texas thrift institution. Kidder allegedly took a 29% profit ($6.3 million) when the maximum profit allowable under regulatory guidelines for this type of trade was 5%. Cerullo was involved in this deal, and in 1990 Kidder settled the matter by agreeing to pay $3.7 million just before the case went to arbitration.

In another instance in 1988, a Kidder trader in Cerullo's division, Ira Sakrstein, took advantage of a pricing error made by CS First Boston. The error cost First Boston $1.1 million according to an investigation by the National Association of Securities Dealers (NASD). After the investigation, NASD fined both Kidder and Cerullo for failing to reverse the trade later. Furthermore, once NASD had released its findings in the matter, Kidder balked at refunding First Boston the $1.1 million.[69]

Perhaps more significant than any of these events were comments made by a former Kidder trader when questioned about his trading activities while working for Cerullo. Walter Mihailovich quit his trading job with Kidder to join a rival firm and left Cerullo with an options position that began to accumulate losses due to market movements. According to former traders, what followed exemplifies to what lengths Cerullo would go to avoid posting a loss to his books.[70]

Cerullo accused Mihailovich of erroneous record-keeping and called in GE's legal counsel and auditors. In the course of a subsequent investigation, Mihailovich explained to the auditors that traders working under Cerullo in the fixed-income area were "given latitude in working with the back office to mark their own closing positions."[71] Former traders explained that this practice gives traders more flexibility to work with different market closings. In addition, it can help traders make the books look better.[72]

Another issue that was raised by the media some time after the Jett scandal erupted centered around licensing of senior managers. *Fortune* pointed out that Carpenter was not licensed to manage a broker-dealer until March 1993, yet he had been running the firm since January of 1989.[73] If a firm or individual fails to register with the SEC (i.e., get licensed) they can be fined up to $50,000 or suspended from the securities business.

Management Comments

On a purely technical basis, it was an accounting loophole in Kidder's system that made Jett's alleged trading practices possible. Carpenter commented, "Is this a sloppy firm that doesn't care about risk management and controls? No way. No way. We are very diligent about it." He went on to say, "There is no system in the world that cannot be beaten by somebody that is determined to game it."[74]

Cerullo and Mullin (Jett's first boss at Kidder) both claim that they relied on internal reports to keep tabs on their traders, including Jett. According to the Lynch Report, one of the reasons they didn't catch Jett's irregular trading activities was because the Kidder accounting system doesn't distinguish between realized profits (resulting from the sale of securities) and unrealized profits (resulting from increases in the value of securities in inventory).[75]

Cerullo commented about the Jett affair, "To hang me with the responsibility, singularly or solely, for detecting or not detecting this is unreasonable. This isn't one guy running the department with a lot of spies running around." As regards his responsibilities as a supervisor, Cerullo says that the internal controls he developed and implemented, "meet industry standards".[76]

Jett Comments

Jett and his lawyers have remained steadfast in their position that Jett is innocent. Jett claims that he filed his trades every day, and that his trading positions were monitored regularly by his superiors.[77]He also pointed out that Kidder's management felt sure enough of his trades to report them as profits in their financial statements.[78]

Jett comments, "Kidder has presented no factual evidence, so it became necessary to destroy the character of the person they were accusing. They have done it in spectacular fashion. They are very, very good at that. It is basic crisis management. Put all the blame on one person. It becomes necessary to destroy that person's credibility through the media."[79]

Industry Experts Comment

David Beim, Professor, Columbia Business School:
> "I think that people are sometimes driven to this by the way that Wall Street firms, or at least some Wall Street firms, compensate their people, and I think there's an important lesson to be drawn for managements of Wall Street firms about compensation policy."[80]

Samuel Hayes, Professor of Investment Banking, Harvard:
> "I can't believe others didn't know about [Jett's alleged trading activities]"[81]

Roy C. Smith, Professor of Finance, NYU, Salomon Center:
> "I think [Jett] stumbled upon a way to make money on the firm's computers, and probably thought (at least at first) that the money was real. Lots of people must have known what his trading strategy was, though few figured out how much trading had to be done downstream to keep the game going. It is telling, I think, that $8 million of the $9 million paid to Jett was still in his brokerage account when the dam broke. If he was trying to cheat Kidder, why leave the money where it could be frozen?"[82]

The Sale of Kidder, Peabody

Although Kidder, Peabody was able to liquidate Jett's trading portfolio at an $8 million profit (despite expectations of a $25 million loss), Kidder experienced large losses on its fixed income trading positions in 1994 and has been, "merged out of existence"[83] with rival PaineWebber Group Inc. taking over selected businesses and GE Capital "warehousing" the left-over assets (primarily MBS's)[84] . GE will receive common and preferred Paine Webber stock estimated to be worth $670 million.[85] GE will now hold one seat on Paine Webber's board and a 25% stake in the company.[86] This allows GE to maintain a presence on Wall Street without the responsibility of actively managing a Wall Street firm.

Roy C. Smith, Professor of Finance at NYU's Salomon Center, points out that while the Jett affair, "was embarrassing and revealed management and control problems,...it was the unrelated losses in MBS's that seriously destabilized the firm leading to its sale."[87] This view was later supported in a *Wall Street Journal* article, "Kidder, Peabody's most severe financial strain stemmed from its huge portfolio of mortgage-backed bonds," which were hit very hard with the interest rate hikes. This essentially paralyzed the firm by deflating the value of its tremendous MBS portfolio thereby crippling Kidder's ability to underwrite new MBS business.[88]

As explained earlier, Carpenter's strategy of becoming number one in MBS's was a highly risky strategy, given the low liquidity and high volatility of these securities. As interest rates rose, Kidder took huge losses on their MBS portfolio and by the first quarter of 1994 they needed GE to step in with a capital infusion to keep the firm solvent.

Where Are They Now

Joseph Jett is currently under investigation by the U.S. Attorney, the SEC, and the New York Stock Exchange. He faces possible criminal charges and Kidder is suing him. In addition, he may face other civil sanctions.

Michael A. Carpenter was forced to resign from his post on June 22, 1994. This was largely due to the loss of confidence that the Jett scandal caused among clients and lenders.

Edward A. Cerullo was forced to resign on July 22, 1994, just one day before the Lynch Report was released. Although the Lynch Report did not find any wrong-doing on Cerullo's part, the report questioned his supervision. Cerullo is currently under investigation by the U.S. Attorney, the SEC and the NYSE, and may face civil sanctions.

Melvin R. Mullin was forced to resign on August 3, 1994. He is under investigation by the U.S. Attorney, the SEC and the NYSE, and may face civil sanctions.

David Bernstein was demoted for his "incorrect analysis [which] contributed to the failure to detect Jett's trading abuses."[89]

Appendix I

Trading[90]

Some firms, like Kidder, Peabody, are Primary Dealers. They have the right to buy government bonds directly from the Federal Reserve. In exchange for this privilege, they are required to make a market in government securities. This means they must provide access to government securities for the rest of the market, selling from their own inventory or buying from a seller when they cannot match up market buy and sell orders externally. This insures that the market operates efficiently and fairly for all participants. In exchange, the Primary Dealers have the opportunity to corner the market on a given issue (i.e., buy up all inventory for an entire issue and become the sole source for that issue), giving them the opportunity to make additional profit on that issue.

Primary Dealers utilize traders to carry out the buying and selling of securities. Traders are allocated a certain amount of the firm's capital with which to carry out their trading activity. Traders set the prices at which they are willing to buy or sell a given security. In the process of making these trades they are trying to generate profit for the firm. As a trader proves his/her ability to trade profitably, they are often allowed to take larger positions; that is, they are able to risk more of the firm's capital base. Essentially, traders working for one firm are competing against other traders at other firms.

Traders operate in an extremely fast-paced, high-pressure market environment. This requires an aggressive, highly self-confident personality combined with an ability to live with high-risk situations. To be successful traders must be facile with mathematics, have a very strong knowledge base about the securities they trade, and understand how changes in the economy will impact that security.

Traders generally specialize in one type of security. For example, in the case of Kidder's Government Desk, the traders specialize in government debt instruments. Within this area there are three basic sub-specialties based upon the maturity of the debt instrument - Treasury Bills (maturity of one year or less), Treasury Notes (maturity of one year to ten years), and Treasury Bonds (maturities longer than ten years).

The head of a desk, also called a trading manager, sets the strategy for the firm by determining the level of risk their traders may expose the firm to – called a risk position. This is a dynamic process, and the manager may change his/her instructions frequently to insure fit between the firm's strategy and the current market situation. The manager must have an in-depth knowledge of all the different maturities within the security they manage in order to develop a successful strategy for the firm.

Both traders and trading managers are paid a salary plus bonus. Bonuses often exceed the trader's salary. The bonus a trader receives is based on the trader's profitability for the year. A trading manager's bonus is based upon the profitability of his/her desk for the year. In 1993, another Kidder trader – Michael Vranos received more than $14 million as a bonus for his trading. Cerullo, the head of the Fixed Income Division received at least $15 million (some estimate it at $20 million) in bonuses for 1993.

Appendix II

Controls - An Industry Perspective

Given the large amount of capital that traders work with, and the nature of a reward system that focuses almost exclusively on profitable performance for traders, traders can be faced with great temptation to cheat. Therefore, the issue of controls is very important in managing traders. These controls are designed to insure that traders work with the legal strictures of the highly regulated securities industry and the objectives, policies, rules and procedures of the firms that employ them.

The Securities Act of 1933 was passed to protect investors by requiring the full disclosure of relevant information relating to the issue of new securities. The Securities and Exchange Act of 1934 was enacted to establish the Securities and Exchange Commission (SEC). The SEC's main purpose was to administer the 1933 Act, by insuring that the relevant facts are disclosed by firms seeking to raise funds in the securities exchanges, Over-The-Counter (OTC) trading, brokers, and dealers (such as Kidder).

The SEC's primary responsibility is to oversee the securities market. The SEC shares its oversight responsibilities with other regulatory agencies, such as the Federal Reserve. The Fed is responsible for the health of the US financial system, and enacts regulations to insure an orderly and stable securities market.

Because the securities market is so big, the SEC delegates much of the day-to-day responsibility for oversight of trading to secondary exchanges (e.g., NYSE). In addition, much of the securities industry is self-regulated through professional organizations such as the National Association of Securities Dealers (which oversees OTC trading).

One of the SEC's responsibilities is to make sure that firms such as Kidder insure compliance with regulations through adequate controls on their trading floors. In order to increase pressure on these firms, the SEC has recently been placing greater emphasis on the responsibility of supervisors in insuring that traders do not engage in any illegal transactions. In may cases over the last few years, supervisors have been fined or otherwise censured if a subordinate is found guilty of illegal trading activities.

Investment houses take this very seriously, and have devised a number of ways to insure compliance. Most firms rely upon a combination of close supervision by management and computerized systems to track trader's activity and their ensuing profits/losses. Since these methods are often not enough, some firms, such as Goldman, Sachs, have made ethical standards a part of their cultural norms. Others, like Bear Stearns Co., employ in-house spies on the trading floor to investigate oddly priced or risky trades.

The penalties for being found guilty of illegal trading activities range from fines to being barred from working on Wall Street for a few years to life. The much publicized Milken case is one instance where a trader was barred from trading securities for life. In other instances, traders and/or their supervisors have been fined $5,000 or more.

Notes

1. Sylvia Nasar with Doug Franz, "Fallen Bond Trader Sees Himself as an Outsider and a Scapegoat", New York Times, June 5, 1994, p. A28.
2. James Kim, Micheline Maynard, "Intense Trader Played to Win / Accused of Falsifying $350 Million in Bond Trades at Kidder", USA Today, April 25, 1994, p. 3B.
3. S. Nasar with D. Franz, "Fallen Bond Trader Sees Himself as an Outsider and a Scapegoat", New York Times, June 5, 1994, p. A28.
4. S. Nasar with D. Franz, "Fallen Bond Trader Sees Himself as an Outsider and a Scapegoat", New York Times, June 5, 1994, p. A28.
5. S. Nasar with D. Franz, "Fallen Bond Trader Sees Himself as an Outsider and a Scapegoat", New York Times, June 5, 1994, p. A28.
6. Martin Walker, "Lynching on Wall Street", The Guardian, July 11, 1994, p. T2.
7. J. Kim, M. Maynard, "Intense Trader Played to Win/Accused of Falsifying $350 Million in Bond Trades at Kidder", USA Today, April 25, 1994, p. 3B.
8. S. Nasar with D. Franz, "Fallen Bond Trader Sees Himself as an Outsider and a Scapegoat", New York Times, June 5, 1994, p. A25.
9. S. Nasar with D. Franz, "Fallen Bond Trader Sees Himself as an Outsider and a Scapegoat", New York Times, June 5, 1994, p. A28.
10. M. Walker, "Lynching on Wall Street", The Guardian, July 11, 1994, p. T2.
11. J. Kim, M. Maynard, "Intense Trader Played to Win / Accused of Falsifying $350 Million in Bond Trades at Kidder", USA Today, April 25, 1994, p. 3B.
12. S. Nasar with D. Franz, "Fallen Bond Trader Sees Himself as an Outsider and a Scapegoat", New York Times, June 5, 1994, p. A28.
13. 13 S. Nasar with D. Franz, "Fallen Bond Trader Sees Himself as an Outsider and a Scapegoat", New York Times, June 5, 1994, p. A28.
14. S. Nasar with D. Franz, "Fallen Bond Trader Sees Himself as an Outsider and a Scapegoat", New York Times, June 5, 1994, p. A28.
15. J. Kim, M. Maynard, "Intense Trader Played to Win / Accused of Falsifying $350 Million in Bond Trades at Kidder", USA Today, April 25, 1994, p. 3B.
16. S. Nasar with D. Franz, "Fallen Bond Trader Sees Himself as an Outsider and a Scapegoat", New York Times, June 5, 1994, p. A28. 17
17. S. Nasar with D. Franz, "Fallen Bond Trader Sees Himself as an Outsider and a Scapegoat", New York Times, June 5, 1994, p. A28.
18. Laurie P. Cohen, Aliz M. Freedman, and William Power, "Growing Mess, Kidder's No. 2 Man Comes Under Scrutiny In Trading Scandal", Wall Street Journal, May 2, 1994, p. Al, AS.
19. S. Nasar with D. Franz, "Fallen Bond Trader Sees Himself as an Outsider and a Scapegoat", New York Times, June 5, 1994, p. A28.
20. Sylvia Nasar, "Kidder Scandal Tied to Failure of Supervision", New York Times, August 5, 1994, p. Al, D3.
21. General Electric Financial Statements, Year ended 1986, p. 14.
22. Roy C. Smith, "Comeback, 'The Restoration of American Banking Poser in the New World Economy", (Boston, Harvard Business School Press: 1993), p. 113.

23. Sylvia Nasar, "The Case for a Sale of Kidder", New York Times, September 6, 1994, pp. D1, D7.24

24. Thomas W. Malnight & Francis J. Aguilar, "GE - Preparing for the 1990s", (Boston, President and Fellows of Harvard College; 1989), p. 332-333.25

25. Noel M. Tichy and Stratford Sherman, "Control Your Destiny or Someone Else Will", (New York, Currency and Doubleday: 1993), p. 14.26

26. S. Nasar, "The Case for a Sale of Kidder", New York Times, September 6, 1994, pp. D1, D7.

27. N. M. Tichy and S. Sherman, "Control Your Destiny or Someone Else Will", (New York, Currency and Doubleday: 1993), p. 13.28

28. Thomas W. Malnight & Francis J. Aguilar, "GE - Preparing for the 1990s", (Boston, President and Fellows of Harvard College; 1989), g. 334.29

29. Thomas W. Malnight A Francis J. Aguilar, "GE - Preparing for the 1990s", (Boston, President and Fellows of Harvard College; 1989), p. 334 & 349.30

30. N. M. Tichy and S. Sherman, "Control Your Destiny or Someone Else Will", (New York, Currency and Doubleday: 1993), p. 21.

31. Terence P. Pare, "Jack Welch's Nightmare on Wall Street", Fortune, September 5, 1994, p. 40.

32. This paragraph is based upon comments from Roy C. Smith in correspondence with Professor R. Freedman, November 27, 1994.

33. Sylvia Nasar, "The Case for a Sale of Kidder", New York Times, September 6, 1994, pp. D1, D7.

34. Roy C. Smith, November 27, 1994 in correspondence with Professor R. Freedman.

35. T. P. Pare, "Jack Welch's Nightmare on Wall Street", Fortune, September 5, 1994, p. 40.

36. T. P. Pare, "Jack Welch's Nightmare on Wall Street", Fortune, September 5, 1994, p. 40.

37. Sylvia Nasar, "Sells Supervisor at Kidder Breaks Silence", New York Times, July 26, 1994, p. D14.

38. L P. Cohen, A. M. Freedman, and W. Power, "Growing Mess, Kidder's No. 2 Man Comes Under Scrutiny In Trading Scandal", Wall Street Journal, May 2, 1994, p. Al, AS.

39. L. P. Cohen, A. M. Freedman, and W. Power, "Growing Mess, Kidder's No. 2 Man Comes Under Scrutiny In Trading Scandal", Wall Street Journal, May 2, 1994, p. Al, A8.

40. Sylvia Nasar, "Jett's Supervisor at Kidder Breaks Silence", New York Times, July 26, 1994, pp. Dl, D14.

41. S. Nasar, "Jett's Supervisor at Kidder Breaks Silence", New York Times, July 26, 1994, pp. D1, D14.

42. Douglas Frantz with Sylvia Nasar, "The Ghost in Kidder's Money-Making Machine", New York Times, April 29, 1994, p. D1, D4.

43. D. Frantz with S. Nasar, "The Ghost in Kidder's Money-Making Machine", New York Times, April 29, 1994, p. D1, D4.

44. L P. Cohen, A. M. Freedman, and W. Power, "Growing Mess, Kidder's No. 2 Man Comes Under Scrutiny In Trading Scandal", Wall Sheet Journal, May 2, 1994, p. Al, A8.

45. Michael Siconolfi, "Kidder Firing May Indicate Further Woes", Wall Street Journal, April 25, 1994, p. A3, AS.

46. M. Walker, "Lynching on Wall Street", The Guardian, July 11, 1994, p. T2.

47. M. Walker, "Lynching on Wall Street", The Guardian, July 1 1, 1994, p. T2.

48. S. Nasar with D. Franz, "Fall Bond Trader Sees Himself as an Outsider and a Scapegoat", New York Times, June 5, 1994, p. A28.

49. Floyd Norris, "Market Watch, Fools Profits: Just How Dumb Was Kidder?", New York Times, August 7, 1994, Section 3, p. l.

50. M. Siconolfi, "Bond Epic, How Kidder, a Tiger In April, Found Itself The Prey by December", Wall Street Journal, December 29, 1994, p. Al, A4.

51. S. Nasar with D. Franz, "Fallen Bond Trader Sees Himself as an Outsider and a Scapegoat", New York Times, June 5, 1994, p. A28.

52. S. Nasar, "Kidder Scandal Tied to Failure of Supervision", New York Times, August 5, 1994, p. Al, D3.

53. M. Siconolfi, "Bond Epic, How Kidder, a Tiger In April, Found Itself The Prey by December", Wall Street Journal, December 29, 1994, p. Al, A4.

54. M. Siconolfi, "Bond Epic, How Kidder, a Tiger In April, Found Itself The Prey by December", Wall Street Journal, December 29, 1994, p. Al, A4.

55. J. Kim, M. Maynard, "Intense Trader Played to Win / Accused of Falsifying $350 Million in Bond Trades at Kidder", USA Today, April 25, 1994, p. 3B.

56. S. Nasar, "Kidder Scandal Tied to Failure of Supervision", New York Times, August 5, 1994, p. Al, D3.

57. S. Nasar, "Kidder Scandal Tied to Failure of Supervision", New York Times, August 5, 1994, p. Al, D3.

58. Gary Weiss, "What Lynch Left Out", Business Week, August 22, 1994, p. 61.

59. G. Weiss, "What Lynch Left Out", Business Week, August 22, 1994, p. 60.

60. L P. Cohen, A. M. Freedman and W. Power, "Growing Mess, Kidder's No. 2 Man Comes Under Scrutiny In Trading Scandal", Wall Street Journal, May 2, 1994, p. Al, AS.

61. L P. Cohen, A. M. Freedman and W. Power, "Growing Mess, Kidder's No. 2 Man Comes Under Scrutiny In Trading Scandal", Wall Street Journal, May 2, 1994, p. Al, A8.

62. L P. Cohen, A. M. Freedman, and W. Power, "Growing Mess, Kidder's No. 2 Man Comes Under Scrutiny In Trading Scandal", Wall Street Journal, May 2, 1994, p. Al, AS.

63. F. Norris, "Market Watch, Fools Profits: Just How Dumb Was Kidder", New York Times, August 7, 1994, Section 3, p. l.

64. G. Weiss, "What Lynch Left Out", Business Week, August 22, 1994, p. 60.

65. M. Siconolfi, "Bond Epic, How Kidder, a Tiger In April, Found Itself The Prey by December", Wall Street Journal, December 29, 1994, p. Al, A4.

66. S. Nasar, "Jett's Supervisor at Kidder Breaks Silence", New York Times, July 26, 1994, p. D1.

67. M. Siconolfi, "Bond Epic, How Kidder, a Tiger In April, Found Itself The Prey by December", Wall Street Journal, December 29, 1994, p. Al, A4.

68. Alix M. Freedman, Laurie P. Cohen, and Michael Siconolfi, "Kidder Trading Controls Drew Scrutiny Well Before Jett", Wall Street Journal, May 6, 1994, p. C1.

69. A. M. Freedman, L P. Cohen, and M. Siconolfi, "Kidder Trading Controls Drew Scrutiny Well Before Jett", Wall Street Journal, May 6, 1994, p. C1.

70. A. M. Freedman, L P. Cohen, and M. Siconolfi, "Kidder Trading Controls Drew Scrutiny Well Before Jett", Wall Street Journal, May 6, 1994, p. C1.71

71. A. M. Freedman, L P. Cohen, and M. Siconolfi, "Kidder Trading Controls Drew Scrutiny Well Before Jett", Wall Street Journal, May 6, 1994, p. C1.72

72. A. M. Freedman, L P. Cohen, and M. Siconolfi, "Kidder Trading Controls Drew Scrutiny Well Before Jett", Wall Street Journal, May 6, 1994, p. C1.

73. T. P. Pare, "Jack Welch's Nightmare on Wall Street", Fortune, September 5, 1994, p. 40.

74. D. Frantz with S. Nasar, "The Ghost in Kidder's Money-Making Machine", New York Times, April 29, 1994, p. D1, D4.75

75. G. Weiss, "What Lynch Left Out", Business Week, August 22, 1994, p. 60.

76. L. P. Cohen, A. M. Freedman, and W. Power, "Growing Mess, Kidder's No. 2 Man Comes Under Scrutiny In Trading Scandal", Wall Street Journal, May 2, 1994, p. Al, A8.

77. M. Walker, "Lynching on Wall Street", The Guardian, July 11, 1994, p. T2.

78. M. Walker, "Lynching on Wall Street", The Guardian, July 11, 1994, p. T2.

79. M. Walker, "Lynching on Wall Street", The Guardian, July 11, 1994, p. T2.

80. Television Show: "Inside Business" 6:30 pm ET, May 8, 1994, Transcript #210

81. J. Kim, M. Maynard, "Intense Trader Played to Win", USA Today, April 24, 1994, p. 3B.

82. Roy C. Smith, November 27, 1994 in correspondence with Professor R. Freedman.

83. Brett D. Fromson, "GE Sells Its Loss-Plagued Kidder Unit; Paine Webber Acquires Remnants of Brokerage", Washington Post, October 18, 1994, p. C1.

84. B. D. Fromson, "GE Sells Its Loss-Plagued Kidder Unit; Paine Webber Acquires Remnants of Brokerage", Washington Post, October 18, 1994, p. C1.

85. Douglas Frantz, "For GE, Sale Was Fast and Cheap", New York Times, October 18, 1994, p. D6.

86. Douglas Frantz, "For GE, Sale Was Fast and Cheap", New York Times, October 18, 1994, p. D6.

87. Roy C. Smith, November 27, 1994 in correspondence with Professor R. Freedman.

88. M. Siconolfi, "Bond Epic, How Kidder, a Tiger In April, Found Itself the Prey by December", Wall Street Journal; December 29, 1994, p. A1, A4.

89. S. Nasar, "Kidder Scandal Tied to Failure of Supervision", New York Times, August 5, 1994, p. Al, D3.

90. Primary Source for this Appendix: Salomon Bros. Training Materials for Trading

91. Stephen Taub and David Carey with Andrew Osterland and David Yee, "The Wall Street 100", Financial World, July 5, 1994, Vol. 163, No. 14.

92. Zvi Bodie, Alex Kane, Alan J. Marcus, "Investments", (Boston, EL: Irwin, 1993), p. 101 - 102.

93. Zvi Bodie, Alex Kane, Alan J. Marcus, "Investments", (Boston, Bi: Irwin, 1993), p. 101 - 102.

94. Zvi Bodie, Alex Kane, Alan J. Marcus, "Investments", (Boston, Ed.: Irwin, 1993), p. 101 - 102.

95. Michael Siconolfi, "Kidder Firing May Indicate Further Woes", Wall Street Journal, April 25, 1994, p. A3.

15. The Plaza Inn*

David Bart, General Manager of the Plaza Inn, had just finished reading a letter from Jean Dumas, President of the prestigious Relais & Chateaux, a French hotel association of which the Plaza Inn was a member. In the formal and polite tone of the French language, the president stated that the last inspection had determined that the service levels of the Plaza Inn did not measure up to the Relais and Chateaux standards. Moreover, the letter noted that the Front Desk and Reservations, two critical guest contact departments, received the worst ratings among all of the Relais and Chateaux member properties. The letter concluded that unless the management of the Plaza Inn could submit a plan for guest service improvement and pass the next inspection scheduled in six months, the Relais and Chateaux would "regrettably be forced to withhold the Plaza Inn's membership."

Background

Located within walking distance of the Country Club Plaza and the Crown Center districts of Kansas City, the Plaza Inn is a 50-room hotel modeled after the boutique hotels of Europe. The Inn's intimate atmosphere and unobtrusive service attract business and leisure travelers alike.

Built in the 1920s in the classic Victorian style and meticulously renovated in 1985, the Inn occupies a place on the National Register of Historic Places. Guest rooms are decorated in the best country manner with antique furnishings and oriental rugs discretely coupled with the most modern leisure and business amenities. Luxurious terry cloth robes and marbled baths, for examples, awaited the weary guest. The Plaza Inn also boasts two gourmet restaurants: the romantic, nationally acclaimed St. Jacques with an award winning wine list, and the more casual Andre's bar and bistro. In addition to its overnight guests, the restaurants have an established local clientele.

Nostalgia prompted Andre Bertrand and Tim Boyle, two successful Kansas City entrepreneurs and real estate developers, to purchase the Plaza Inn in 1983. They entered into a partnership with Antoine Fluri, a Swiss hotelier who soon assumed the position of the Inn's general manager. In addition to the three general partners the Inn is owned by approximately 20 limited partners.

"One of the Ten Best New Inns"

Under the charismatic direction of Antoine Fluri, the Inn quickly established a national reputation. In 1987, Travel magazine voted the Plaza Inn among the "ten best new inns." A loyal clientele included such famous people as former French President Valery Giscard D'Estaing, Senator Danforth, and Susan Sontag, to name a few. Antoine Fluri also negotiated the Inn's membership in the prestigious, world-renowned Relais and Chateaux association. The existing hotels in the immediate area: a Marriott, a Holiday Inn, and a Hilton gave the Plaza Inn virtually no competition for the upscale traveler.

---

*Written for class discussion by Craig Lundberg, Cornell University, based on field research by Monika Dubaj. This case does not purport to illustrate either effective or ineffective managerial practices. Reprinted with permission.

Despite the success of the Inn, in early 1989 Antoine Fluri sold his share to the remaining two partners and left the Inn citing, "irreconcilable differences" as the reason. A year later, he opened his own restaurant in the Country Club Plaza District.

To continue to promote the European image of the Inn, the owners hired a French couple from Normandy, Marc and Nicole Duval, to replace Antoine Fluri. However, the Duvals soon proved to lack knowledge about European hospitality practices as well as management expertise. They abused their position and power, and within a short time succeeded in alienating many of the Inn's clientele and most of its staff. Under their management, the Inn rapidly incurred heavy financial losses. Alarmed by the practices of the Duvals, the owners looked for new management for the Inn. In December 1989, David Bart was hired as the new general manager. A native of Missouri, he had a solid hotel management background in the middle west, most recently including several years as controller at the headquarters of a large chain hotel.

As David Bart assumed the direction of the Inn in early 1990, he faced several challenges, including steadily declining hotel occupancy and revenues. Many of the regular clientele complained that the Inn had not been the same since Antoine Fluri left. Moreover, contrary to optimistic expectations, the Inn was also losing business to a 300-room, upscale Ritz-Carlton hotel which had just opened a few blocks down the street, and was offering introductory room rates as low as $75. Finally, toward the end of 1990 demand also declined as a national recession began to set in.

Given the poor performance of the hotel, David Bart immediately proceeded to cut costs, which included the elimination of several staff positions. In the Food and Beverage Department (F&B), two of the three restaurant managers were eliminated. St. Jacques and Andre's were to be run by the F&B director with the assistance of only one restaurant manager. In the Rooms Department, Bart eliminated the position of PBX operator, and transferred the responsibility of answering the phone directly to the front desk. Finally, the front office manager position was eliminated, and the front desk staff came under the supervision of the sales manager. Thus, the Inn began to operate with a lean management and staff group. All operating departments, with the exception of F&B, were headed by one person and with no administrative support. Even Bart himself did not retain a secretary.

The Front Desk

The end of David Bart's first year at the Plaza Inn was marked by the outbreak of the Gulf War. During the first quarter of 1990, occupancy hit an all time low of just 40%. However, business finally began to pick up in April. This increase in demand was especially hard for the front desk. The reception area, consisting of an elegant antique concierge-type desk, was too small to be staffed by more than one person at a time. Consequently, only one front desk receptionist was scheduled per shift. With no PBX operator and no secretarial staff, this meant that the front desk receptionist was responsible for not only providing guest service, but also for answering the telephone, taking messages for the management staff, and booking room and restaurant reservations. Moreover, the sales office was not connected to the computerized Property Management System (PMS), and consequently the sales and catering managers relied on the front desk to check availability and block and update group reservations. Similarly, the housekeeping department was not computerized, and the front desk was charged with the preparation of housekeeping room assignments each morning and evening as well as with the tracking and updating of room status in the PMS. Bart believed that the front desk should perform a central function in the operation of the Inn. Rather than computerize the housekeeping, sales and catering departments, and train the managers to utilize the PMS, Bart preferred the front desk to oversee those activities. This, he believed, allowed for greater consistency and control.

With only one person scheduled per shift, the front desk receptionist had to juggle the telephone, coordinate department activities, and take care of guest needs in the personalized manner that was the trademark of the Inn. On busy days, guests checking in or out were rudely interrupted by the ringing telephone, or alternatively, callers were put on hold for lengthy periods of time while the front desk receptionist helped a guest.

The inability to efficiently expedite phone calls and respond to guest needs became worrisome not only from a guest service perspective, but also from a potential revenue loss standpoint. Room reservation calls usually hung up if they remained on hold for more than two minutes. Moreover, under the pressure to answer the phone and help a guest at the same time, the front desk receptionists frequently underquoted rates, mixed up arrival dates and booked rooms on sold out nights. Cancellation requests were not handled correctly with the consequence that some guests were billed for reservations that they had canceled. One of the front desk receptionists commented: "It's extremely difficult to make a room sale when I constantly have to ask the customer to hold because I'm trying to pick up the other five lines that are ringing. What is more important: making a $130 room reservation for two nights or taking a message for one of the managers?"

Reinstatement of the Front Office Manager

Lost revenues and customer complaints about front office service finally convinced David Bart of the need to reinstate the position of the front office manager. A manager was needed to monitor the rooms inventory and ensure that no revenues were lost due to uncanceled reservations and unreleased room blocks, to coordinate activities between the departments, and to train the front office staff consisting of front desk receptionists and valets/bellhops. However, to minimize costs, Bart decided that the front office manager would also work three shifts per week at the front desk as a receptionist.

In February 1991, Bart offered the position of front office manager to Ms. Claire Ruiz, who had been working as a front desk receptionist since 1989. The promotion worked out well. Claire knew the job thoroughly and was genuinely interested in hotel management. She was able to effectively combine her managerial duties with the three shifts at the front desk.

Cooperation between the departments soon increased significantly. Claire believed that the Inn would never be able to afford the specialized and extensive front office staff of a larger hotel, and thus its ability to deliver high quality customer service depended on mutual cooperation between all employees. Consequently, when things got busy, she had the front desk ask other departments for support. For example, if the switchboard was busy, reservation calls were transferred from the front desk to accounting or sales. Even the general manager himself got called on to help the valets park cars or assist guests with luggage although he clearly preferred being in his office going over reports and records.

The New PBX Position

While other managers were willing to help out, they also had their own duties to tend to and weren't always available. Since occupancy remained strong, Claire convinced the general manager to reinstate the PBX position. However, Claire's idea was to have the PBX operator function as an extension of the front desk. A PBX station was set up in an unoccupied reception area in the lobby, and with the exception of checking guests in and out, the PBX operator performed the same duties and was compensated at the same rate of pay as the front desk receptionist. This additional support allowed the front desk to provide more efficient and gracious service to the Inn's guests, and improve their room selling ability. Despite the continuing recession and competition from the Ritz-Carlton, 1991 proved to be a year of record high occupancy and revenues for the Plaza Inn.

In August 1992, Claire left the Plaza Inn to pursue a graduate degree in hotel management at an eastern university. David Bart believed that the situation at the front desk was under control, and did not plan to fill the vacant position of front office manager. The front desk staff once again would be indirectly supervised by the sales manager.

It wasn't long, however, before the same problems Claire had worked so hard to resolve cropped up again. With the start of the school year, the front desk staff were no longer as flexible in terms of scheduling, and the PBX operator was called on to fill vacant shifts at the front desk. More often than not, there was only one person scheduled to work in the front office, and guest service began to suffer again. One day, for example, David Bart discovered that a recently hired front desk receptionist frequently told clients that the hotel was sold out because she was too busy to take a reservation.

Bart believed that there was no one at the front desk capable of being promoted to the position of front office manager. However, he also thought that it would be difficult to hire an outsider who would be willing to work the three shifts at the front desk for the modest salary he was willing to offer (most managers at the Plaza Inn were paid $5,000 to $7,000 less than other Kansas City hotels). Thus, Bart was relieved to learn that Laura Dunbar, who had previously worked at the Plaza Inn as a front desk receptionist, was interested in the position.

A New Front Office Manager

In addition to her experience at the Plaza Inn, Laura had worked as a concierge at one of the convention hotels in downtown Kansas City for several years. She had left the Plaza Inn for a secretarial position that offered more pay than the front desk position at the Inn. However, she missed the excitement and pace of the hospitality industry, and accepted the front office manager position in December 1992 with enthusiasm.

Despite her extensive connections with other Kansas City hotels, as well as the Kansas City Concierge Association, Laura soon found that one of her biggest challenges was the hiring and retaining of the front desk staff. The difficulty of hiring qualified employees forced Laura to work more than three shifts at the front desk. This left her with little time for planning and managing the front office operation. Short-staffed, she sometimes found herself working as much as 30 days in a row without a day off. In addition, the PBX position had not been filled on a regular basis for several months. Laura noticed that the front desk receptionists were not very attentive to the guests and were unable to meet guest expectations of a personalized, concierge-type service. Guest comment cards frequently included negative observations regarding front desk service; in fact, one guest commented that it seemed to him that the front desk receptionists "Were responsible for doing everything with the exception of bartending and bussing the tables in the restaurants."

Laura believed that David Bart was reluctant to hire a full-time PBX operator due to financial constraints. She also felt pressured to meet the front office payroll budget, which had been prepared by Bart and which she felt had been grossly underestimated. In a bimonthly management staff meeting, Laura suggested to the F&B director that perhaps the restaurant should assume responsibility for managing their own reservations and inquiries, so as to free up the front desk staff to improve guest service and sell more rooms. However, the F&B director was quick to point out that the evening restaurant manager was called on to assist with rooms-related issues on a daily basis, and replaced the evening front desk receptionist so that she could take a break. The restaurants, he asserted, could not afford to create a position just to take reservations and answer inquiries.

Laura felt especially pressured with managing the front desk operation on the weekends. During the week she felt she could call on the other managers for help, whether it was to park a car or take a reservation. On the weekends, however, the only manager on duty was the restaurant manager, and he was often too busy with the restaurant to help with rooms issues. The Manager on Duty (MOD) program (in which all department managers rotated in being at the Inn on call and in charge Friday and Saturday nights) that had been established the prior spring at the initiation of Bart, had been a tremendous help; however, it had been canceled when the Inn had hit the slow summer period. David Bart was not in on the weekends, and Laura felt he somehow forgot that the hotel existed on weekends, not to mention that it usually ran at full occupancy.

By mid-fall, Bart agreed with Laura that there was a definite need to reinstate the MOD program, as well as the PBX position. However, Bart thought that Laura herself had reduced her role of front office manager to that of a front desk receptionist. She seemed to him to surround herself with employees who were either not flexible or not qualified enough, and thus was left to fill a lot of shifts at the front desk herself. This didn't leave her with any time to oversee the operation of the front desk, and to ensure everything was in order. She still hadn't even finished writing up job descriptions for the Inn which he had told her to do two months ago. Bart wondered if the problems at the Front Desk stemmed from Laura's rather shy personality, or perhaps from her lack of management expertise. It appeared that she was unable to articulate her needs to him and other managers. Perhaps he needed to give her more direction, however, this was contradictory to his belief that each manager should assume the responsibility of defining his or her own role consistent with the objectives of the Inn. The weakness he saw in the front office manager was of growing concern to David Bart. Clearly, it was a key position in the operation of the Inn, and required a highly competent, proactive individual.

As he thought back to the ultimatum he had received from the president of Relais and Chateaux, the general manager wondered what he should do. Perhaps he should look for an experienced manager to head the front office, even if it meant paying a much higher salary. Perhaps he just needed to shake Laura up. Perhaps the situation would just straighten itself out. David Bart reached for a copy of the Inn's organization chart (Figure 1), perhaps a major structural change was needed. Perhaps....

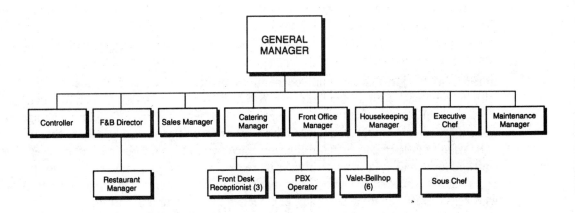

Figure 1: Organizational Chart, The Plaza Inn - 1993

16. Dowling Flexible Metals*

Background

In 1960, Bill Dowling, a "machine-tool set-up-man" for a large auto firm, became so frustrated with his job that he quit to form his own business. The manufacturing operation consisted of a few general purpose metal working machines that were set up in Dowling's garage. Space was such a constraint that it controlled the work process. For example, if the cutting press was to be used with long stock, the milling machines would have to be pushed back against the wall and remain idle. Production always increased on rain-free, summer days since the garage doors could be opened and a couple of machines moved out onto the drive. Besides Dowling, who acted as salesman, accountant, engineer, president, manufacturing representative, and working foreman, members of the original organization were Eve Sullivan, who began as a part-time secretary and payroll clerk; and Wally Denton, who left the auto firm with Bill. The workforce was composed of part-time "moonlighters," full-time machinists for other firms, who were attracted by the job autonomy which provided experience in setting up jobs and job processes, where a high degree of ingenuity was required.

The first years were touch and go with profits being erratic. Gradually the firm began to gain a reputation for being ingenious at solving unique problems and for producing a quality product on, or before, deadlines. The "product" consisted of fabricating dies for making minor component metal parts for automobiles and a specified quantity of the parts. Having realized that the firm was too dependent on the auto industry and that sudden fluctuations in auto sales could have a drastic effect on the firm's survival, Dowling began marketing their services toward manufacturing firms not connected with the auto industry. Bids were submitted for work that involved legs for vending machines, metal trim for large appliances, clamps and latches for metal windows, and display racks for small power hand tools.

As Dowling Flexible Metals became more diversified, the need for expansion forced the company to borrow building funds from the local bank, which enabled construction of a small factory on the edge of town. As new markets and products created a need for increasingly more versatile equipment and a larger workforce, the plant has since expanded twice until it is now three times its original size.

In 1980, Dowling Flexible Metals hardly resembles the garage operation of the formative years. The firm now employs approximately thirty full-time journeymen and apprentice machinists, a staff of four engineers that were hired about three years ago, and a full-time office secretary subordinate to Eve Sullivan, the Office Manager. Their rapid growth has created problems that in 1980 have not been resolved. Bill Dowling, realizing his firm is suffering from growing pains, has asked you to "take a look at the operation and make recommendations as to how things could be run better." You begin the consulting project by interviewing Dowling, other key people in the firm, and workers out in the shop who seem willing to express their opinion about the firm.

*This case was prepared by Floyd G. Willoughby, Oakland University, Rochester, Mi. © 1980 by Floyd G. Willoughby. Reprinted by permission.

Bill Dowling, Owner-President

"We sure have come a long way from that first set-up in my garage. On a nice day we would get everything all spread out in the drive and then it would start pouring cats and dogs – so we would have to move back inside. It was just like a one-ring circus. Now it seems like a three-ring circus. You would think that with all that talent we have here and all the experience, things would run smoother. Instead, it seems I am putting in more time than ever and accomplishing a whole lot less in a day's time.

"It's not like the old days. Everything has gotten so complicated and precise in design. When you go to a customer to discuss a job you have to talk to six kids right out of engineering school. Every one of them has a calculator – they don't even carry slide rules anymore – and all they can talk is fancy formulas and how we should do our job. It just seems I spend more time with customers and less time around the shop than I used to. That's why I hired the engineering staff – to interpret specifications, solve engineering problems, and draw blueprints. It still seems all the problems are solved out on the shop floor by guys like Walt and Tom, just like always. Gene and the other engineers are necessary, but they don't seem to be working as smoothly with the guys on the floor as they should.

"One of the things I would like to see us do in the future is to diversify even more. Now that we have the capability, I am starting to bid jobs that require the computerized milling machine process tape. This involves devising a work process for milling a part on a machine and then making a computer process tape of it. We can then sell copies of the tape just like we do dies and parts. These tapes allow less skilled operators to operate complicated milling machine without the long apprenticeship of a tradesman. All they have to do is press buttons and follow the machine's instructions for changing the milling tools. Demand is increasing for the computerized process tapes.

"I would like to see the firm get into things like working with combinations of bonded materials such as plastics, fiberglass, and metals. I am also starting to bid jobs involving the machining of plastics and other materials beside metals."

Wally Denton, Shop Foreman, First Shift

"Life just doesn't seem to be as simple as when we first started in Bill's garage. In those days he would bring a job back and we would all gather 'round and decide how we were going to set it up and who would do it. If one of the 'moonlighters' was to get the job either Bill or I would lay the job out for him when he came in that afternoon. Now, the customers' ideas get processed through the engineers and we, out here in the shop, have to guess just exactly what the customer had in mind.

"What some people around here don't understand is that I am a partner in this business. I've stayed out here in the shop because this is where I like it and it's where I feel most useful. When Bill isn't here, I'm always around to put out fires. Between Eve, Gene, and myself we usually make the right decision.

"With all this diversification and Bill spending a lot of time with customers, I think we need to get somebody else out there to share the load."

Thomas McNull, Shop Foreman, Second Shift

"In general, I agree with Wally that things aren't as simple as they used to be, but I think, given the amount of jobs we are handling at any one time, we run the shop pretty smoothly. When the guys bring problems to me that require major job changes, I get Wally's approval before making the changes. We haven't any difficulty in that area.

"Where we run into problems is with the engineers. They get the job when Bill brings it back. They decide how the part should be made and by what process, which in turn pretty much restricts what type of dies we have to make. Therein lies the bind. Oftentimes we run into a snag following the engineers' instructions. If it's after five o'clock, the engineers have left for the day. We, on the second shift, either have to let the job sit until the next morning or solve the problem ourselves. This not only creates bad feelings between the shop personnel and the engineers, but it makes extra work for the engineers because they have to draw up new plans.

"I often think we have the whole process backwards around here. What we should be doing is giving the job to the journeymen – after all, these guys have a lot of experience and know-how – then give the finished product to the engineers to draw up. I'll give you an example. Last year we got a job from a vending machine manufacturer. The job consisted of fabricating five sets of dies for making those stubby little legs for vending machines, plus five hundred of the finished legs. Well, the engineers figured the job all out, drew up the plans, and sent it out to us. We made the first die to specs, but when we tried to punch out the leg on the press, the metal tore. We took the problem back to the engineers, and after the preliminary accusations of who was responsible for the screw up, they changed the raw material specifications. We waited two weeks for delivery of the new steel, then tried again. The metal still tore. Finally, after two months of hassle, Charlie Oakes and I worked on the die for two days and finally came up with a solution. The problem was that the shoulders of the die were too steep for forming the leg in just one punch. We had to use two punches (see Exhibit 1). The problem was the production process, not the raw materials. We spent four months on that job and ran over our deadline. Things like that shouldn't happen."

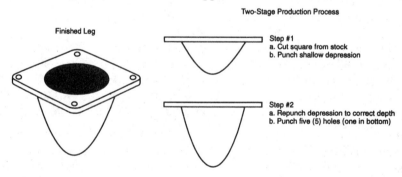

Exhibit 1

Charlie Oakes, Journeyman Apprentice

"Really, I hate to say anything against this place because it is a pretty good place to work. The pay and benefits are pretty good and because it is a small shop our hours can be somewhat flexible. If you have a doctor's appointment you can either come in late or stay until you get your time in or punch out and come back. You can work as much overtime as you want to.

"The thing I'm kind of disappointed about is that I thought the work would be more challenging. I'm just an apprentice, but I've only got a year to go in my program before I can get my journeyman's card, and I think I should be handling more jobs on my own. That's why I came to work here. My Dad was one of the original 'moonlighters' here. He told me about how interesting it was when he was here. I guess I just expected the same thing."

Gene Jenkins, Chief Engineer

"I imagine the guys out in the shop already have told you about 'The Great Vending Machine Fiasco.' They'll never let us forget that. However, it does point out the need for better coordination around here. The engineers were hired as engineers, not as draftsmen, which is just about all we do. I'm not saying we should have the final say on how the job is designed, because there is a lot of practical experience out in that shop; but just as we haven't their expertise neither do they have ours. There is a need for both, the technical skill of the engineers and the practical experience of the shop.

"One thing that would really help is more information from Bill. I realize Bill is spread pretty thin but there are a lot of times he comes back with a job, briefs us, and we still have to call the customer about details because Bill hasn't been specific enough or asked the right questions of the customer. Engineers communicate best with other engineers. Having an engineering function gives us a competitive advantage over our competition. In my opinion, operating as we do now, we are not maximizing that advantage.

"When the plans leave here we have no idea what happens to those plans once they are out in the shop. The next thing we know, we get a die or set of dies back that doesn't even resemble the plans we sent out in the shop. We then have to draw up new plans to fit the dies. Believe me, it is not only discouraging, but it really makes you wonder what your job is around here. It's embarrassing when a customer calls to check on the status of a job and I have to run out in the shop, look up the guy handling the job, and get his best estimate of how the job is going."

Eve Sullivan, Office Manager

"One thing is for sure, life is far from dull around here. It seems Bill is either dragging in a bunch of plans or racing off with the truck to deliver a job to a customer.

"Really, Wally and I make all the day-to-day decisions around here. Of course, I don't get involved in technical matters. Wally and Gene take care of those, but if we are short-handed or need a new machine, Wally and I start the ball rolling by getting together the necessary information and talking to Bill the first chance we get. I guess you could say that we run things around here by consensus most of the time. If I get a call from a customer asking about the status of a job, I refer the call to Gene because Wally is usually out in the shop.

"I started with Bill and Wally twenty years ago, on a part-time basis, and somehow the excitement has turned into work. Joan, the office secretary, and I handle all correspondence, bookkeeping, payroll, insurance forms, and everything else besides run the office. It's just getting to be too hectic – I just wish the job was more fun, the way it used to be."

Having listened to all concerned, you returned to Bill's office only to find him gone. You tell Eve and Wally that you will return within one week with your recommendations.

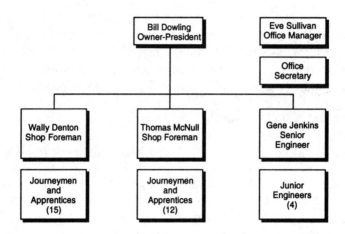

Exhibit 2. Dowling Flexible Metals Organizational Chart

17. Sunday at Al Tech*

Saturday, August 14, 1982, 9 p.m.

George Hayes, Assistant to the President at Star Manufacturing, Inc., was sitting in his motel room in a small city near Chicago with his feet propped up on the bed recalling the events which had prompted his being there. On Thursday, only two days earlier, he had attended a meeting of the top managers at the Star corporate headquarters on the east coast. The day's agenda centered on his analysis of the recent performance of the company's various divisions. One in particular, Al Tech, was receiving an unusual amount of attention that day.

George had the numbers on the table next to him. Sales, net income, and return on investment (ROI) for Al Tech were down from the previous year and below budgeted performance levels. The results were somewhat understandable given the unexpected severity of the current economic downturn and Al Tech's sensitivities to such conditions. Just when George had felt the meeting was about to adjourn, the president asked him for more details concerning Al Tech's new expansion and equipment acquisition plans. George knew those numbers all too well. He had reviewed them prior to Star's approval of the project. He had even been sent to the equipment manufacturer for a first-hand look at the technology and accompanying manpower and facilities requirements. George recalled that this had been the trip which had caused him to miss the tenth birthday of his twin daughters.

The meeting had continued with George reporting that the building addition at Al Tech was nearing completion and the equipment was scheduled for installation during the month of October. The management group then had briefly discussed Al Tech's forecast for the year beginning in January 1983, the first full year the new equipment would be operational. Several forecasts had been prepared, each based on different assumptions concerning the utilization of the new technology. The most pessimistic forecast – utilizing less than 50 percent of the new capacity and having no new product lines – still resulted in overall profit performance for the division which was better than that from 1981 or from the current year's adjusted projections.

George had also reported that if the most optimistic forecast were attained, Al Tech would become one of the corporation's most profitable divisions. Though marketing new product lines would require development time and the acquisition of experience with the new technology, it was still plausible to expect some sales of new products by the end of the upcoming year.

George's mind wandered. Al Tech had been his pet project for the last four years. He had first heard of the company while attending his ten year college reunion in Illinois over four years ago. George's former fiancee, Julie, who had broken their engagement to marry Ben Brown, introduced him to her husband at the reunion. Ben had just been promoted to Personnel Manager at Al Tech. George recalled, however, that Ben wasn't certain how long he would be able to retain that position as the Carter family, who owned the firm, wished to sell it to

*Lynda L. Goulet and Peter G. Goulet, Instructor and Associate Professor, respectively, University of Northern Iowa. Reprinted by permission. Copyright © 1983, 1984. All rights reserved. This case describes a hypothetical company based on a composite of several actual experiences in a similar industrial setting.

settle an estate. Only the Vice-President of Sales, Stuart Carter, was a family member. The President, Russell Wainscott, had been hired several years earlier when the founder of the company retired. Following the founder's death, everyone in the family except Stuart wanted the firm to be sold, for cash rather than for stock in another firm. George remembered the many hours of work and travel time he had invested analyzing this potential acquisition for Star Manufacturing. The work had all come to fruition in late 1978 when Star purchased Al Tech from the Carter family estate.

A door to a nearby room slammed shut. George was jarred back to thoughts of the last few minutes of last Thursday's meeting at Star. At long last Star's President made it clear why Al Tech had been the focus of attention. Russell Wainscott, who had been retained as the General Manager at Al Tech after the acquisition, had been severely injured in a car accident and would be hospitalized for an unknown, though substantial, period of time. George was to assume responsibility for the division as its Acting General Manager until Wainscott was able to assume his duties again.

George slipped into bed early, knowing Sunday would be a very long day. He had made arrangements to spend the day at Al Tech alone, preparing for his first week as GM. Before going to sleep he felt both apprehension and excitement. Finally he would have the opportunity to get the line management experience he needed to advance his career. However, with line responsibility, especially under these circumstances, comes high visibility. George nervously drifted off to sleep.

Sunday, August 15, 8 a.m.

The keys to the Al Tech office building and the GM's office were in the box at the motel desk when George went to breakfast. A note from Wainscott's secretary, Barbara Curtis, was in a manila envelope with the keys. It read:

> Mr. Hayes:
>
> As you requested in your Friday telephone call, all the managers prepared memos relating any problems under their responsibility which must be resolved in the near future. Five of the memos are in envelopes on Rusty's [Wainscott] desk. Richard Simcox told me he would slip his memo under the office door as he wasn't able to complete it before I left Friday. In addition, I prepared a summary of Rusty's agenda for next week with some explanations of any meetings to the best of my knowledge. Finally there is a stack of mail on the desk. Some of it is left over from before the accident and some arrived since then. I hope this is satisfactory. I'm looking forward to working for you in Rusty's absence and will arrive early Monday morning to help you begin your first week.
>
> (Signed) Barb Curtis

Sunday, August 15, 9 a.m.

When George arrived at the office he found the following items awaiting his attention:

Memos from managers (Exhibits 1 – 6)
Agenda for the week of the sixteenth (Exhibit 7)
Correspondence (Exhibits 8 – 17)

Before he began working George scribbled on a piece of paper and added that to the pile on top of his desk (see Exhibit 18).

Place yourself in George Hayes' position. Plan your activities for the week of August 16. What meetings must be held? When? With whom? What decisions must be made? When? Which decisions can be delegated? To whom? A note on Al Tech appears below to provide you with additional background. An organizational chart is also provided as Figure 1.

A Note on Al Tech

Al Tech is a vertically integrated firm which converts aluminum billets (cylindrical ingots of aluminum) into aluminum extrusions which are then converted into finished products. Aluminum extrusions are produced by hydraulic presses which force billets heated to just below the melting point through profile dies of hardened steel. The hot extrusions run out onto long tables for cooling. These extrusions are cut to length, heat treated, and machined through various operations, typically in punch or brake presses, to produce the constituent parts for numerous products. Al Tech makes extrusions for its own lines of windows, storm sash, patio doors, screens, and extension ladders.

The major suppliers for Al Tech are companies which provide the aluminum billets, flat glass, and screen cloth. Al Tech's customers include nearly 500 firms, though their major source of revenue derives from about twenty manufacturers of recreational vehicles (RVs) and manufactured housing (MH) and two chains of discount retailers who purchase the ladders for sale under private labels.

The major investment to which Al Tech recently committed itself is a series of machines which electrostatically paint extrusions. The equipment requires a facility with a forty-foot ceiling as the extrusions are painted while suspended vertically. Al Tech's new installation will allow it to paint extrusion lengths among the longest that can be painted in any U.S. facility. Aluminum is very difficult to paint successfully because the paint doesn't adhere to the surface easily. Though painted aluminum also scratches easily, it must still be painted before machining to achieve necessary economies.

There is a great deal of demand for painted aluminum products because painting both colors the surface and prevents the unsightly oxidation of the bare metal characteristic of aluminum. Anodizing also accomplishes these purposes and produces a harder, more durable finish than that achieved with painting. However, the cost of anodizing is so high as to be prohibitive for almost all uses but curtain walls for high-rise office buildings and high-valued decorative products. Painting also offers a greater variety of colors and finish textures than anodizing.

Al Tech built its paint facility for internal use. However, with this facility and its extrusion operation, it felt it could develop demand for high-margin custom-extruded, custom-painted parts for current as well as new markets.

Exhibit 1

From: Ben Brown
To: George Hayes
Date: August 13, 1982

George:

Looking forward to working with you for a while – too bad it had to be under these circumstances. Barb passed your message along and I guess there are several issues we need to discuss pretty soon.

1.   Sam Howarth, one of our designers, has been suspected of the "appropriation" of minor amounts of company materials for a long time. Two weeks ago, Dick Simcox inadvertently caught him piling some obsolete screens into his car. These screens probably would have been sold for scrap. Dick, Rusty, and I decided to let him take some vacation time until we decided what to do about it. We'd have fired him on the spot but the truth is he is a good designer and our designers are underpaid and turnover is terrible. Howarth has been with the firm for over fifteen years and is responsible for a couple of innovations that have been really profitable. His vacation time will run out at the end of the week so some decision must be reached by the 20th.

2.   The new paint process equipment is scheduled for delivery and installation during October. I have placed an ad for a supervisor in that department and I have an application in hand for a good man. He used to supervise a line that painted cabinets for TV sets. The problem is that one of our assembly supervisors wants the job. Dick tried to convince her to stay in assembly but she's being a hard-nose about it. She is not qualified for this job from the standpoint of having run a paint room. She probably could be trained eventually but we don't know how good a job she would ever do. It will also delay us for a long time if we go this route. As I see it all she really wants is the money or the prestige associated with the new position. What she doesn't understand, or won't accept, is that the higher wages for the paint room job reflect the level of skill required. She says she'll cause some trouble if she doesn't get the job this week but none of us knows what she means by "trouble." The final kicker is that this is our only female manager at any level.

3.   You probably aren't aware of this, but every year Al Tech has a company party for its employees and their spouses. I have been in charge of the arrangements for the last few years. It's next Saturday at the local Elks club. Some of the people around the office have wondered if it wouldn't be wise to postpone it because of Rusty's accident. My feeling is that it's a bit late to cancel. Besides, it'll be months before Rusty can get back on his feet

again. The Carter family started the tradition fifteen years ago and Stuart hates to see it abandoned. Al White thinks it's an awful waste of money but Dick says it's a real morale booster for his workers. I need to know about this no later than Monday afternoon.

4. One final thing, and this is a real winner. Somewhere in Rusty's pile of stuff there should be a copy of a letter from our receptionist. I'll just let you read it for the pure joy of the moment. When you have gotten off the floor let me know and we'll talk about it. By the way, she officially works for me.

Exhibit 2

From: Aaron McClosky
To: George Hayes
Date: August 13, 1982

Welcome aboard.

The fellows in engineering have been busy working up some new designs to expand our product lines. Stu Carter, Dick Simcox, and I have been going around for months trying to decide what to do with the extra capacity of the new paint line. We're all in agreement that the window and door lines will go on first. I guess you've got the figures on this, too. There is a lot of demand for white and brown frames on both the RV and MH window lines and the margins are a good deal better than for the unpainted units. However, I believe we'd better develop some new products quickly if we want to get above the low capacity utilization our current products will provide. Dick thinks there's no real problem here because he feels we can land a lot of contract painting jobs. As far as I know Stu hasn't even tried to check out that possibility.

I'm having one of the designers collect some of our more promising designs. She should have them ready for you by Monday. We've been working on the designs for a line of picture frames, some designer curtain rods, and a dynamite set of shower doors. For the last several years there has been talk around the sales office of redesigning our lines for the retail market but we never seem to get anywhere on this. Just when the designers get excited about a new product design, it seems like Stu comes up with a variation on our windows that the mobile home guys just "have to have." By the time that's taken care of the new products get lost in the shuffle. I sure hope that doesn't happen with the paint line ideas.

We really ought to move on this business so my department can develop prototypes by year end. After that it'll take at least six months to work out the bugs, let the dies, and get into production.

Exhibit 3

From: Albert White
To: George Hayes
Date: 8/13/82

Mr. Hayes:

Having just recently corresponded with you at headquarters concerning the latest quarterly report, I am certain you are well aware of our current position. This week I have been reviewing the updated estimates for the fourth quarter. In doing so I have been reminded of a potential problem to which you should be alerted. The details are attached but I have summarized the situation below. [Attachment not shown.]

On July 28, Stuart Carter got an order for 10,000 window units with storms and screens and 1000 patio doors. [Attachment shows this order to be worth just under $300,000.] The customer, a new one for us, is a large condominium developer with units in five states. The order was to be delivered by November 5. Normally an order of this size would be greatly appreciated. However, these units are all non-standard product for us. Though assembly will not be a problem, the glass will be. For some reason we cannot find any way to cut the glass without a great deal of waste. The upshot of this is that in figuring the costs on this order, given the price Stuart quoted, we would be selling the whole order at about break-even.

Rusty and I talked about this situation and decided that one solution to this problem might be to try to resell the order using painted extrusions from the new line. We sent Stuart back to the customer and the developer said he would let us know this Wednesday if the order would be changed. By changing to painted windows we were able to quote a price that covered us for the painting and the excess waste and provide a profit. However, there is a catch. The customer is willing to wait a bit longer to give us a chance to operationalize the paint line, as he is in the design stage of the development. However, he wants a penalty clause in the order in case we are late in delivering under the revised order. If for any reason the equipment isn't ready to go on time we will either have to pay a penalty or have the extrusions painted outside. Either way, we would lose about $10,000 on the order if the revised quote is accepted and the paint room isn't ready by November.

Exhibit 4

From: Stu Carter
To: George Hayes
Date: August 13

Sorry I won't be in town when you arrive at Al Tech. I've had a big sales trip planned to meet with several of our major window customers in the South. Rusty wanted me to drum up some firm orders for the new painted metal lines since we're going to be going on line soon. He was apparently concerned our customers wouldn't order the more expensive, painted products, given the recession. I told him not to worry, though, as the expensive stuff usually sells OK anyway, especially in the South where the economy isn't as hard hit.

Barb was lucky to catch me before I left. I'll be swinging on back through Cincinnati for the Manufactured Housing Suppliers Show, then home for the big party!

Oh, before I forget, sooner or later you're bound to hear about it. In fact, the lawyer was going to meet with Rusty this week. While I was on the road recently the Groves kid broke into my office. I know he rifled my desk because the drawers were an awful mess. I don't care what he says he was after, he's had it in for me ever since I fired his dad from the sales force a year ago. How did I know his old man, Marv, would end up marrying my secretary! I have a good notion to fire her when I get back. Marv Groves went over my head to McClosky, insisting he could sell more to the chain stores if we had more retail lines. I told Marv to keep his nose out of the design department and when he didn't I finally fired him. Those guys in design would spend all their time on the new stuff instead of helping me out on the window lines. The MH guys are always hot for slick-looking new window designs. Now McClosky is convinced that the new paint line was put in just so his department could have some fun.

Gotta run.

Exhibit 5

From: Charles Weber
To: George Hayes
Date: 8/13/82

Mr. Hayes:

Ms. Curtis suggested I prepare a memo to advise you of any problems I may be encountering in Purchasing. I foresee two areas of concern.

First, it will be necessary for me to locate long-term reliable sources of supply for the paint facility. We have temporary sources for the materials we need for the forecasted window and door production through December. Beyond that we need to be concerned about the demands of any new product lines and/or contract paint work. We also have not accounted for the condominium order, should it require painting.

Second, I have been hearing some rumors that two of our major aluminum suppliers may be cutting back production further. In the last major recession several of the "majors" shut off some potlines [smelting equipment] to artificially tighten supplies so they could raise prices even in a period of slack demand. This strategy worked well last time, so I suspect the rumors may be true. I may know more by the middle of next week. One of our suppliers will have their regional sales manager in the area on the pretext of training a new territory representative. You might wish to join us on the morning of the 18th, should you be available.

The last time billets were in short supply both of our contract suppliers instituted a very restrictive policy before supplying us with metal. For each pound of aluminum we wished to purchase we had to turn in a pound of scrap at the going price. Obviously, we could not keep up such a practice for very long without severe production cutbacks. Otherwise, we would be forced into the spot market to fill our remaining needs. To anticipate this possibility it might be wise to begin stockpiling our scrap. This will hurt our quarterly cash flow, but may help protect our supply of new metal. The next regular scrap pickup is scheduled for Friday the 20th.

Just a reminder, the engineers from the paint equipment company will be here Tuesday. It might be a good time for you to learn more about the new facility firsthand.

If I can be of any additional help, please don't hesitate to ask.

Exhibit 6

From: Dick Simcox
To: George Hayes
Date: August 14, 1982

Just before shutdown on Friday I got a phone call from one of our large customers. Apparently Stu had left on his sales trip already, and due to the urgency of the call, his secretary transferred the call to me. Here's the trouble. Our trucks just delivered a shipment of our new hexagonal windows to our biggest MH customer. These babies were right on spec, exceeded federal standards by a mile – the designers did a bang-up job. These are the most expensive windows we make because of the unusual shape. The tooling is incredible and glass-cutting is a real chore. I was real proud of assembly when I inspected these before loading. My supervisor, Judy Mills, did a great job on this. I sure wish she'd get off her horse about this paint job; I need her here. Anyway, the bums wouldn't accept delivery of the order. They told the driver the latch was on the wrong side. What's more like it is that their business is really off and they stopped producing the model that uses the hex windows. The driver's bringing them back this weekend.

What's got me worried is that this was just the first batch. The order was for three times what we shipped. We got a big set of tools and hired and trained a guy just for this product, hoping to get some more customers for it next year. If we could get in touch with Stu we could get him to see the customer at the show this week. The next batch was already started but I canceled them on Friday night until we find out what gives here. Not filling this order will do some damage to our sales targets for the quarter.

What worries me most is that this could be a trend. If all our customers are hurting now, how are we going to sell the painted stuff? We've been counting on the higher margins there to offset some volume declines in other products. Rusty's been worrying about this, too. He told me just last week. But Stu is convinced there's no problem. Seems to me we ought to be out looking for some contract painting. It'll be a bad Christmas for a lot of our people if we have to cut back in the last quarter.

I can free up an hour or two any time after 10 a.m. Monday if you need me.

Exhibit 7

From: Barbara Curtis
To: George Hayes
Date: August 13, 1982

Below is a summary of Rusty's agenda for the week of August 16.

1. Luncheon with Alan Holtman at noon on Monday.
    Mr. Holtman is the attorney retained by Al Tech. The subject of the meeting is the trespass, breaking and entering charge pending against Mitchell Groves, age 16, stepson of Stu Carter's secretary.

    On July 31, the boy was apprehended inside our office building after he set off the silent alarm. He claims to have been looking for proof that his stepmother was having an affair with Stu. They both deny this. When the police searched the boy, they found nothing in his possession belonging to Al Tech. The Groves think the situation can and should be worked out at home, though they want the boy to pay for damages. Stu seems to want to press for prosecution.

2. Tuesday, 11 a.m. to 3 p.m. meet with Janice Schulcraft and Dennis Sanchez. These are the engineers from the paint equipment manufacturer. The subject of their visit concerns the finalization of the delivery and installation plans. Rusty had planned a tour of the building addition, now almost completed, lunch, and then a briefing session to include Messrs. Weber, White, and Simcox.

3. Wednesday, 7:45 a.m.
    Rusty had reservations to leave O'Hare for Cincinnati for the MH Suppliers Show, returning Friday after dinner. He was to meet Stu upon his arrival.

4. Saturday, 6 p.m. to midnight, annual party, Elks club Rusty was to deliver a short speech after dinner.

Exhibit 8

Unopened letter dated August 12, 1982:

Dear Mr. Wainscott:

Our office has on file your plans for the construction of an addition to your facility on Eleventh Street, including the remodeling of the south-side entrance. You may be aware of the fact that last Monday, August 9, the City Council approved proposed building code modifications which go into effect immediately.

One section of the revised code may impact on your current construction. This notification is intended to provide you with some warning that, as filed, your new premises may not pass inspection. It is to your benefit to discuss this situation with your architect and your general contractor as soon as possible.

Enclosed is a copy of the changes in the code as approved by the council [Enclosure not shown.] If my office can help you in interpreting these changes or in answering any other questions, please let me know.

Sincerely,
(Signed) Stanley Lerner, City Engineer

Exhibit 9

Manila envelope containing petition: August 2, 1982

We the undersigned request that the management of Al Tech repair the employees' parking lot. Many of us damaged our tires and suffered wheel alignment problems after last winter from the deep ruts, potholes, and frost heaving problems. We also request that in fall the apples from the trees by the lot be swept up regularly so the lot is not an obstacle course to walk through.

[253 signatures followed]

Exhibit 10

Unopened letter dated August 10, postmarked New York:

Dear Mr. Wainscott:

For the past two years you have supplied our chain of stores with your aluminum extension ladders. Let me express to you again how pleased we all are here with the high quality and timely delivery of this product. It continues to be a strong item for us.

In light of recent and expected changes in both demographics and the economic climate, we have redefined our corporate merchandising strategy. It is our intention to provide more variety in home improvement products and hardware. To implement this strategy we are seeking reliable suppliers in such product lines to provide our chain with private label merchandise. We would be interested in talking with you about the possibility of contracting for an exclusive line of windows, doors, and porch enclosures.

Since this may require some rethinking of your firm's priorities, I have decided to approach you directly rather than contacting your sales department. We are very anxious to proceed and I am hopeful we can expand our already cordial business relations further. I am planning to be in Chicago for a regional meeting on the 19th of this month. If you will be available it would be no trouble for me to drive out to your office on the 20th to discuss this in more detail. If you wish to get together at that time please call my office by the 18th.

Sincerely,
(Signed) John Colby
Vice President,
Merchandising

Exhibit 11

Letter postmarked August 9, addressed to "Al Teck." Letter was handwritten and is reproduced verbatim below:

To the man who runs things at Al Teck,

I was at your factory a few weeks back to get a job that was in the Want Ads. The boss woodn't hire me. Over the week end I seen my sister inlaw She says I can sue your place cause I am pertecked class. To be nice I give you one more chance befor I get a loyer.

Marie Grace

Exhibit 12

Letter dated July 23, 1982, opened by Wainscott:

Dear Mr. Wainscott:

County General Hospital is vitally concerned with the increasing number of job-related accidents occurring in our community. In an attempt to ameliorate this trend we have added a Safety Consultant to our hospital staff. His job is to suggest specific improvements which can be implemented with minimal expense in offices and factories in our community.

The services of our Safety Consultant will be made available to local businesses under one of two programs: a per-diem consultation to our charitable contribution plan. The per-diem rate is $500. The charitable contribution plan is based on the actual savings accruing to each firm through the reduction in expenses from reduced insurance costs and direct company-borne medical costs. If your company institutes any of the improvements suggested by our Safety Consultant, rather than pay the per-diem expense you may elect to contribute 10 per cent of the first year's actual dollar savings to our hospital.

We at County General sincerely believe this program will benefit both the community and the businesses that are so critical to its welfare. Please feel free to make an appointment with me at your earliest convenience so we can confer on this matter.

Respectfully,
(Signed) Michael Franz, Administrator
County General Hospital

Exhibit 13

Unsigned, handwritten note, no date, found on the floor near the office door on Sunday morning:

To the new Acting General Manager

Sir, the foremen here at Al Tech got together after quitting time on Friday and talked about the situation since Rusty's accident. We're sure you're a good guy and all or the company wouldn't have sent you. We just want you to know that we think Dick [Simcox] should have gotten the job. It didn't need to go to an outsider.

Exhibit 14

Letter dated August 4, 1982, opened by Wainscott, postmarked St. Louis:

Dear Rusty,

It's about that time again. We need to make plans for this year's holiday break. Some of the others want to spend the week after Christmas lolling on the beaches in either southern California or Florida. I'm partial to the Gulf side of Florida because my in-laws are in the area, and my kids could spend the week with them. Do you have any preferences?

This sure was one heck of a good idea. I don't remember exactly whose it was though – it's been three years now. Doesn't really matter. Since all the divisions are shut down for the holidays anyway and the only thing going on is inventory, we general managers might as well enjoy ourselves. Besides, last year Frank said our gossip about HQ really helped him when it came time to put together the report on closing down his Kirksville plant. Knowing how the guys at HQ felt about things saved him a couple of months time.

Well, give me a call as soon as possible so we can finalize our plans and make reservations. Say hi to your good-looking wife for me.

(Signed) Jonas [Calder, General Manager, Metal Stampings]

Exhibit 15

Envelope, hand addressed to Mr. Hayes:

I have been a bookkeeper in the Accounting Department for eight years and heard about your temporary assignment to Al Tech on Friday morning. My parents are retired and vacation in Florida during the winter. Their two-bedroom home is located about a mile from our office at 2132 Elm St. It's near an elementary school. I called my folks over the lunch hour and they offered to rent the house to you for $250 a month. They are leaving after Labor Day and won't be back until Easter. It's really a good deal as two-bedroom apartments in town are scarce and rent for about $350 a month. Let me know early in the week if you are interested.

Dotty Simmons

Exhibit 16

Handwritten note from Ben Brown, clipped to the letter below, dated August 11:

Rusty:

This is a xerox of a letter I just got today from Joyce Riley, the new receptionist. I don't know what you want to do about this, but we should talk about it on Friday, the 13th (unless you want to meet at the Olympus Club Saturday).

Ben

Dear Mr. Brown:

Since you are both my boss and the Personnel Director, I felt it was right to mention a problem I'm having to you. I feel I am being harassed on my job.

When I interviewed for work here I asked if it was all right to moonlight and you said I could use my own time as I wished. The truth was that I had a job then, and still do, working Friday and Saturday nights at the Olympus Club on Sycamore Street. Sooner or later you're bound to hear it so I'll tell you now that I work there as an exotic dancer.

It seems some of the workers who know I work in the factory told a couple of the office people about my moonlighting and several of them came to see me at work. The club was really busy the last couple of weekends. Now rumors are all over the place about me. I know it's true because I overheard some of the workers in the lunchroom talking about drawing straws to see who gets to bring paperwork over to the office from the factory. Some of our office people must even have told customers who call here, because visitors to our office have said a few things to me. I'm not really complaining about what they say to me or how they look at me. I'm used to that. But what happened recently really bothers me.

A woman called here two days ago, wouldn't say who she was, and accused me of all sorts of things with her husband. I finally got over that and then yesterday another woman called and said I was a loose woman who shouldn't be allowed to work in an office where nice husbands worked. She said if I didn't quit my job she'd tell the other wives and get me fired. I enjoy my work but I don't play around with married men and I don't want to give up either job. Can you help me?

(Signed) Joyce Riley

Exhibit 17

Letter dated August 4, 1982, opened by Wainscott:

Dear Mr. Wainscott:

In preparation for the coming year the Board of Education has voted its continuing support for our Career Day program at Central High School. Your firm's participation last year was appreciated and we hope you will again donate your time and effort to help ensure the success of this year's program.

Career Day is scheduled for Friday, January 7, 1983, from 9 o'clock to 4 o'clock. This year the Board has decided to cancel all classes for the day so the participating firms will have more space for displays and meetings than we had last year.

We need your response by August 20 so we may make the necessary arrangements. Thank you for your cooperation in our efforts.

Sincerely,
(Signed) Robert Wood, Superintendent of Schools

Exhibit 18

Note written to himself by George Hayes when he arrived in the office:

Catch 8:30 p.m. United flight from O'Hare on Friday for our anniversary on Saturday – get present.

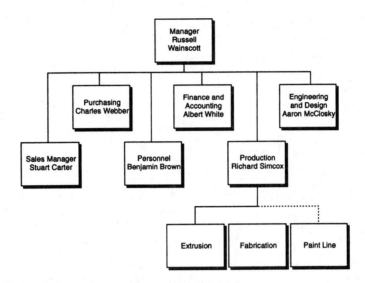

Figure 1. Organization Chart – Al Tech Division

Part 5   Organizational Control, Power and Conflict

Cases Outline

18. Traveler Import Cars, Incorporated*

Background

Randy Traveler had been a partner in Capitol Imports, one of the most prosperous foreign car dealerships in greater Columbus, Ohio, selling expensive European automobiles. His wife, Beryl, a holder of an MBA degree from a respected private university, was a consultant specializing in automobile dealerships.

In 1979, Randy and Beryl decided to go into business for themselves. Since between the two of them they had four decades of automobile dealership experience, they elected to acquire their own dealership. With some luck, they obtained a dealership selling a brand of Japanese cars that had become known in the United States for its very high quality. Randy became president and Beryl executive vice-president.

Evolution of the Firm

Stage 1. After obtaining the Japanese dealership, Randy and Beryl decided to locate it approximately two miles from Capitol Imports. The decision was made on the basis of immediate availability of a suitable facility. This location, however, was several miles from a major shopping area of any kind, and the closest automobile dealership was Capitol Imports. Furthermore, the location was approximately three miles from the nearest interchange of a major interstate highway. Nonetheless, the dealership was located on a busy street within easy access to half a dozen upper-middleclass-to-affluent neighborhoods with residents predisposed to purchasing foreign automobiles with a high quality image.

A number of key employees were enticed by Randy and Beryl to leave Capitol Imports and join Traveler Import Cars. Stuart Graham, who was in charge of Finance and Insurance at Capitol Imports, became general manager at Traveler Import Cars. Before specializing in finance and insurance, Graham was a car salesman. Several mechanics and car salesmen also left Capitol Imports to join Traveler Import Cars. As a rule, the policies and procedures that pertained at Capitol Imports were relied on at Traveler Import Cars, Inc. for the first five years of operations.

No one at Traveler Import Cars was unionized, but the mechanics were given everything that unionized mechanics received at other dealerships in order to remove the incentive to unionize. By everything, it is meant direct compensation, indirect compensation (fringe benefits), and work rules.

Randy and Beryl viewed their dealership as a family. This was in some measure due to the fact that the dealership was part of a Japanese Corporation (which viewed its employees as family), and partly due to the beliefs that Randy and Beryl shared about organizations. Randy and Beryl made every effort to involve subordinates in day-to-day decision-making. As tangible evidence of her commitment to democratic leadership, Beryl decided to introduce a quality circle into Traveler Import Cars, Incorporated. This was done by selecting five

*Copyright © 1984 by Jan P. Muczyk, Professor of Management, College of Business Administration, The Cleveland State University. Reprinted by permission.

non-supervisory employees (one from each part of the organization) to meet once a month with Beryl and Stuart Graham in order to discuss problems, possible solutions, and implementation strategies. No training whatsoever regarding quality circles was provided anyone involved with the so-called "quality circle," and this includes Beryl and Stuart.

Stuart Graham, on the other hand, was a benevolent autocrat, although he tried to create the facade of a democratic leader because he understood well Randy and Beryl's leadership preferences. Most employees agreed with Randy and Beryl that Traveler Import Cars was a family. Furthermore, most employees felt free to voice an opinion on anything to Randy, Beryl, and Graham, or to any other supervisor or manager, for that matter.

Stage 2. As long as the dealership was small everything went well, largely because Randy and Beryl made all key decisions, provided daily direction to supervisors and managers (including the general manager – Stuart Graham, who should have been running the dealership on a day-to-day basis), and resolved problems through face-to-face communications with the involved individuals. As the dealership grew and prospered, it generated enough money for growth. Expanding the dealership rapidly was impractical because of the limited allotment of cars due in large measure to the so-called "voluntary" import quotas by the Japanese car manufacturers. The demand for these cars was so great that cars were even sold from the showroom floor, leaving at times few models for new customers to view.

The first acquisition that Randy and Beryl made was a car leasing company, which they located next to the dealership. Randy elected to spend most of his time building up the car leasing company, leaving the operations of the dealership to Beryl. The second acquisition consisted of another car dealership located approximately ten miles from the original one. The new dealership sold another make of Japanese cars and an expensive European make. The newly acquired dealership was located in the midst of automobile dealerships on a main road, but was housed in inadequate facilities and beset by many problems. Beryl became the chief operating officer of the second dealership as well. Soon after acquiring the second dealership, Randy and Beryl decided to construct new facilities adjacent to the existing ones.

Stage 3. The newly acquired dealership created a great deal of additional work for Beryl, but she understood and accepted that reality because she and Randy knowingly acquired a business that had been plagued by problems prior to acquisition. What bewildered and frustrated Beryl was the fact that the operation of Traveler Import Cars, Inc. took so much of her time as well as physical and psychic energies. After all, it has been five years since she and Randy purchased that dealership. Many key supervisory and managerial personnel now have five years of experience with the dealership, yet the task of running Traveler Import Cars is just as consuming at this time as it was when the dealership was new. Frequently, Beryl would tell one of the managers to do something, but it wouldn't get done. Decisions were reached at management meetings, but they did not get implemented. Programs were initiated, but were frequently permitted to drift and disappear. Important deadlines were being missed with increasing frequency. Mechanics and salesmen were coming to work late and taking excessive lunch breaks with greater frequency. Beryl knew that these problems were not due to insubordination or lack of motivation. Yet, if she did not directly oversee implementation of an important decision, it did not get implemented.

In order to relieve herself of some of the work load, Beryl hired two experienced managers. In order to justify their salaries, however, they spent half of their time at Traveler Import Cars and the other half at the newly acquired dealership. The newly hired managers had good ideas, yet Beryl was working just as hard as ever, and the problems that motivated Beryl to hire two experienced managers remained practically unchanged. In spite of the problems, the dealership grew as rapidly as the increase in the quota of cars that was allotted to the dealership by the manufacturer permitted. In addition, Traveler Import Cars began wholesaling parts to service stations and car repair shops, and started to lease cars in direct competition with the leasing operation managed by Randy. Although an organizational chart did not exist, it would look like Figure 1, if Randy and Beryl bothered to construct one.

About this time, Randy and Beryl's marriage had come undone, and Randy remarried a lady considerably his junior. Even so, Beryl and Randy maintained their business relationship, and were able to work together professionally without visible acrimony. Beryl now had more money than she knew what to do with, and was about to make much more because the newly acquired dealership was being turned around rapidly, largely due to Beryl's considerable talents, the new facility, and the rapidly recovering economy. Yet Beryl no longer wanted to work as hard as she had in the past.

Beryl understood that Stuart Graham lacked the right stuff to be general manager of a car dealership in a metropolitan area, and she approached Randy on the matter. His response was: "Stuart Graham is too valuable of an asset because Traveler Import Cars, Inc. had generated a $500,000 after tax profit last year. He must be doing something right."

Even though Beryl had been a consultant to automobile dealerships for twenty years, she decided nonetheless to retain a consultant. Beryl was fortunate to contact a particularly astute consultant by the name of J. P. Muzak. Her request was that Muzak straighten out the quality circle, which she felt wasn't living up to her expectations. Muzak, however, was reluctant to get involved unless he was permitted to conduct a thorough needs analysis before selecting any kind of intervention strategy. Beryl, after thinking the matter through, assented to Muzak's proposal. The organizational needs analysis relied on confidential structured interviews with all the managers, supervisors, and select non-supervisory personnel. The summary of Muzak's organization needs analysis follows.

Possible Problem Areas

Goals. Although general goals (such as providing the best customer service possible) exist at the organizational level, many individuals report that what is expected of them, in terms of specific and measurable objectives, isn't clearly defined. It is difficult to make a superior happy if the subordinate isn't sure just what it is that the boss wants.

Also, there does not appear to be a philosophy for setting goals. For example, should goals and objectives be imposed unilaterally by the superior on the subordinate, or should the goals and objectives be set jointly between the superior and subordinate?

Organizational Structure. The organizational structure in a number of instances appears to be confusing. Specifically, a number of individuals appear to be reporting to two or more superiors. Irma Krupp reports to David Chapel and Stuart Graham. Tom Tucker reports to Sam Carney and Stuart Graham. Charles Spikes reports to Tom Tucker, Sam Carney, and Stuart

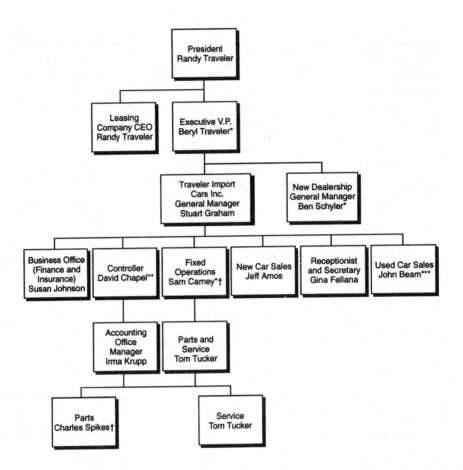

* These individuals spent approximately one-half of their time at Traveler Import Cars and one-half at the new dealership.

**David Chapel is the controller for Traveler Import Cars, the new dealership, and the leasing company. He spends about one-half of his time at Traveler Import Cars and one-half at the new dealership.

***John Beam frequently is asked by Randy Traveler to assist with matters pertaining to the leasing company.

+ Sam Carney owned and operated his own small business prior to joining Traveler Import Cars, Inc. Charles Spikes was a supervisor at a local office of a national automobile parts distributor before coming to work for Traveler Import Cars, Inc.

Figure 1. Organizational Chart of Traveler Import Cars, Inc.

Graham. John Beam had Susan Johnson's jobs before he became manager of used cars. David Chapel believes that he reports to the two general managers, to Beryl, and to Randy. Gina Fellana appears to report to everyone.

There is the perception that few managers know what they can do on their own authority and what they must get approved and by whom.

Communications. There appear to be too many meetings and they do not seem to be as productive as they could be. On this point there is a consensus.

A paper flow problem exists in several areas. The Accounting Office at times does not receive properly filled out forms from the Business Office. It appears that Susan Johnson does not have the time to fill out carefully and on a timely basis all the forms and attend to her other finance and insurance duties. The Accounting Office at times does not receive the necessary paper work from New Car Sales. The Parts Department at times doesn't receive on a timely basis the necessary information from New Car Sales.

Some individuals complain that their superiors do not keep them informed. Everything is a secret.

Training and Development. A number of individuals have risen through the ranks into supervisory and managerial positions. Since these individuals have never received formal managerial training, the void must be filled by coaching. In a number of cases, the void has not been filled by coaching, and these persons are learning through trial and error – an expensive and time-consuming way of learning, indeed.

The consensus is that the computer equipment is adequate to the task, but the operators need additional training to realize the potential of the equipment. The mechanics receive the latest training from the manufacturer.

Performance Appraisal. Many people reported that they do not receive a periodic formal appraisal. Thus, their need for performance feedback is frustrated.

Wage and Salary Administration. Numerous individuals have reported that it is the subordinate who has to initiate a wage or salary increase. Most individuals report that they would like to see the superior initiate wage and salary action at least annually. Moreover, a number of individuals are not sure on what basis they are remunerated. The absence of a systematic periodic performance appraisal is responsible, in part, for this perception.

Discipline. In a number of instances, individuals arrive late, take extended lunch breaks, and violate rules with impunity. This creates a demoralizing effect on others.

Control System. The financial control system at the top of the organization appears to be satisfactory. The operational control systems in the rest of the organization are problematic.

Morale. While there is still the feeling that the organization is a family and the best place the employees have ever worked, the feeling is starting to diminish.

Sundry Problems.

1. Quality circle may need restructuring along traditional lines.
2. The time it takes to make decisions should be shortened.
3. The organization has difficulty implementing decisions that have been made.
4. Lack of follow-up presents serious problems.
5. Policies and programs are permitted to drift and disappear (motivator board is an example).
6. Managers may not be delegating enough.
7. New car salesmen do not always turn customers over to the Business Office, resulting in loss of revenue to the dealership.

8. Service desk is crucial and it has been a revolving door.

At a meeting, Muzak presented the findings of his needs analysis to the management team of Traveler Import Cars, Inc., and a discussion ensued regarding each of the possible problem areas. Randy Traveler did not attend since he relegated the operation of the dealership to Beryl. At the end of the discussion, the management team agreed that all the problems uncovered by Muzak were real and, if anything, understated.

Muzak did not present at the meeting his assessment of the potential of the key managers. This he did in a private discussion with Beryl. In summary, Muzak concluded that Stuart Graham was too set in his ways to change. Moreover, he displayed too much emotion publicly, and lacked the respect of his subordinates. Jeff Amos was considered by his subordinates to be a nice guy, but was indecisive, lacked firmness, was manipulated by subordinates, and did not enjoy the respect of his subordinates. Tom Tucker was probably in over his head in his present position. He was only a high school graduate, he was not a mechanic, was unsure of himself, and lacked the confidence of his subordinates. Lastly, he was quite impulsive. His previous experience was as a service desk writer (the person to whom the customer explains the car problems and who writes the work order). All the other managers and supervisors were thought to possess the necessary potential which could be realized through training and experience.

19. Managerial Systems Ltd.*

Introduction

It had been a rough week for Managerial Systems Ltd. By Thursday, MSL's president, Ken Long, had received upsetting phone calls from consultants Phil Mercer, Ray Terrell, and Fred Sargent concerning client difficulties. He had also talked at length with Karen Webster about conflicts between her personal and professional lives. Crises always seemed to come in avalanches. Tomorrow's staff meeting promised to last the entire spring day, ruining any plans Ken had for sailing.

Managerial Systems Ltd.

Managerial Systems Ltd. was a behaviorally based consulting organization focused on helping client companies improve the effectiveness of managerial systems through the application of sophisticated behavioral science technologies. (Exhibit 1 briefly explains the basics of behavioral consulting). MSL consultants worked with client organizations to help define needs and then identify the proper methods for satisfying those needs. (Exhibit 2 lists the types of services provided in the past.) All MSL consultants had at least a master's degree in the behavioral sciences and most had obtained a doctorate in a related field. Many had worked in the behavioral area in either private practice or with institutions prior to joining MSL. (Exhibit 3 is a selected biography of representative consultants' backgrounds.)

MSL incorporated in 1977 when Ken Long, the president, resigned his professorship at a prominent southern business school in order to devote his full time to the company. In the past four years MSL had expanded to ten consultants, two research assistants, and five support staffers. MSL's primary clients had been in the petrochemical industry. However, attempts to implement a strategy of diversification had begun this year.

The diversification into other industries presented something of a problem for MSL. MSL's consulting expertise had been developed and proven in the petrochemical field. But potential clients questioned how well that expertise would translate to their specific types of problems. To help overcome these questions, Ken had decided to concentrate in three areas related to the prior experience of MSL. These included flow process plants, e.g., petrochemical, energy services and equipment companies, and banking. Ken anticipated no major problems transferring techniques from one industry to the others. This was because MSL tailored each behavioral intervention to a client's particular set of needs.

*This case was written by Molly Batson and Nancy Sherman under the supervision of Associate Professor Jeffrey A. Barach, A. B. Freeman School of Business. This case has been prepared as a basis for class discussion rather than to illustrate effective or ineffective administrative practices. Copyright 1982 by the School of Business, Tulane University. Reproduced with permission.

Exhibit 1. Description of Organizational Development (OD)

Organizational Development (OD) is a process by which behavioral science principles and practices are used in an ongoing organization in a planned and systematic way. It is utilized to attain such goals as developing greater organizational competence while improving the quality of work life and the organization's effectiveness. (Effectiveness refers to setting and attaining appropriate goals in a changing environment.) OD differs from other planned change efforts such as the purchase of new equipment or floating a bond issue to build a new plant, in that the focus includes the motivation, utilization, and integration of human resources within the organization and is focused on total system change.

OD is a vehicle for helping organizations adjust to accelerated technological enrichment, group team-building, or management by objectives. OD may use specific techniques, but only after the relevance and utility of a special technique has been clearly demonstrated by careful diagnosis. Interventions or techniques can be grouped in ten basic classifications:

– Individual consultation (counseling-coaching) usually involving a change agent in a one-on-one helping interaction with a single client.
– Unstructured group training involving individuals in a group lacking specific task purpose except that of understanding individual or group dynamics.
– Structured group training including management and group development courses structured to change participant attitudes, convey knowledge, or develop skills.
– Process consultation involving small groups or work teams identifying and solving common problems.
– Survey-guided development, involving collection of data about client work-group or organizational functioning and feeding back data to work groups to use in problem solving.
– Job redesign involving altering the tasks, responsibilities, interactions patterns, or the technical and physical environment intrinsic to the work itself.
– Personnel systems involving implementation through traditional personnel functions.
– Management information and financial control systems involving tracking and evaluating employee or work-group performance.
– Organizational design involving a structural change in organizational authority and reporting relationships.
– Integrated approaches including more than one of the methods described above.

Source: Edgar F. Huse. *Organization Development and Change,* 1980.

Exhibit 2. Consulting Services Rendered to Clients – 1980

Organizational Development initiation, planning, and execution
Managerial effectiveness training
Supervisory skills training
Organizational team-building
Organizational diagnostic surveys
    – Organizational climate
    – Employee attitude assessment
    – Specific areas of concern
Managerial expectations clarification
    – Goal setting
    – Organizational dissemination
    – Individual superior-subordinate clarifications
Performance feedback enhancement
    – Establishing organizational systems
    – Expectations setting/feedback skills training
Development of organizational systems
    – Progressive discipline
    – Managerial communications
    – Work system redesign
    – Managerial succession system
Employee Assistance Programs
    – Individual managerial counseling
    – Employee psychological services
    – Alcoholic/drug abuse program
    – Assisting terminated and retiring employees
Effective planning and implementation of organizational changes
EEO Audit simulation
EEO Assimilation Programs
Research Studies
    – Attrition problems
    – Employee acceptance/rejection of anticipated change
    – EEO-related employee attitudes
    – Organization-wide training systems
Workshops on special topics
    – Management of stress situations
    – Assimilation of new managers
    – Problems faced by temporary supervisors
    – Successful specific conflict resolution
Facilitating development of overall top management goals

Exhibit 3. Selected Biographies of MSL Consultants

Karen Webster,	30, MBA from Tulane University, BA, psychology, had been with MSL for four years. Prior to joining MSL, Karen worked in a managerial capacity in private business. Her consulting expertise was primarily in management and supervisory development.
Fred Sargent,	55, had been with the firm for three years, joining MSL upon completion of a doctorate in Adult Education. He spent twenty-five years in the Army and rose to the rank of Colonel. During his military career, Fred held many managerial positions, planning and implementing numerous training programs. He also earned an MBA from Syracuse University while in the Army. His Army experiences carried over easily in behavioral consulting where Fred focused on development and execution of organizational needs analysis and management training programs.
Ray Terrell,	32, received his Ph.D. in clinical psychology following a master's degree in counseling. He had joined MSL on a part-time basis one and a half years ago while continuing to teach at a local university. Small group facilitation had been Ray's specialty within MSL.
Phil Mercer,	36, had been with MSL on a part-time basis for a year. He continued to teach in the Social Work Department at a local university. His academic credentials included an MSW, an MPH, and a Ph.D. in Human Ecology, a discipline which works against exploitation of the environment. This degree strongly reflected Phil's personal values. He spent many years "throwing rocks at big business from the outside" but had never been a part of that world. He went into consulting to learn more about how big business works and to help improve conditions for people working in the system.

Ken wanted each consultant to bring in at least one new client by the end of the year. Each consultant was asked to make contacts in new companies and arrange a presentation of MSL's array of services to management. Several of the consultants expressed their feelings of uneasiness in taking on a sales role. They felt they lacked sufficient experience to decide which companies and executives to approach as potential clients. Once they managed to make contact, the consultants were worried about how to make an effective presentation. To alleviate these concerns, Ken had begun training the consultants in sales techniques. The consultants were taught basic sales techniques tailored to MSL's particular marketing needs.

Long felt it was important for MSL's consultants to have divergent backgrounds both academically and professionally. However, he insisted that potential consultants have a fundamental belief in the benefits of a capitalistic society. When hiring consultants he discussed at length how the individual felt about working for major oil companies. If there was a wide gap in the beliefs of MSL and the consultant, Ken would refuse to hire them. He felt the strains of working to improve a system one did not believe in would be detrimental to the consultant's working abilities and effectiveness. Ken encouraged the consultants to come to him to talk about any problems they were having on the job. He felt this minimized the changes of a consultant working him/herself into a corner over an issue.

Ken emphasized the importance of doing a thorough job with a client company. Many times a client company would bring in MSL to solve a specific problem that management had isolated. MSL wanted to gather their own data in order to determine the validity of management's point of view and to find out if there were any additional problems related to the ones indicated. MSL was prepared to walk away from a contract if management refused to allow them to do the necessary research or if management wanted their services for any reason other than to improve working conditions.

The Dilemmas

Phil Mercer

Phil had just completed a large project on the reasons for the engineer attrition rate for a major oil company. The report and final recommendations would be ready the following week. Phil was quite pleased with the results. He attributed the success of the project to the agreement of management to release the report and the final recommendations to the engineers. The engineers took this as a sign that management was making a serious effort to correct many of the problems they faced at work. Therefore, they cooperated fully and candidly with Phil in the interviewing process.

Phil called Mr. Spencer, the Vice-President of Personnel, Engineering, to inform him of the date the report would be ready. He also inquired about distributing the report to the engineers. Mr. Spencer said the report would not be released as planned. A two-page summary of it would be made available. The recommendations would be omitted.

This upset Phil. He had given his word to the engineers that they would receive copies of the report and the recommendations. He reminded Mr. Spencer of management's promise to release it. All the positive effects of the promised release would be negated and the engineers' attitudes would sour. Phil questioned the wisdom of such a move. Mr. Spencer blamed the change in plans on MSL's failure to stay within the contracted budget. He said there were insufficient funds available to copy the report. Phil was at a loss on what to reply, so he terminated the conversation, promising to call again in the next few days.

Phil reviewed his alternatives. He could try again to convince Mr. Spencer to release the results regardless of the costs involved. He thought this would be fruitless based on the previous conversation. Phil considered going directly to the engineers and giving them the report and the recommendations without management's approval. After all, they had been promised a copy of the report and he could provide it verbally anyway. He also thought about going to someone higher in the company who could countermand Spencer's decision.

Phil called Ken to talk about the situation. Ken suggested that Phil bring up the issue at tomorrow's staff meeting. Before hanging up Ken mentioned that the company had contacted him about another consulting job. He wanted Phil to think about whether or not MSL should accept the job in light of the situation with Mr. Spencer.

Fred Sargent

Hugh Cavanaugh was the Operations Manager of a medium-sized petrochemical refinery located on the Louisiana coast. The refinery was part of a large, well-known energy concern. Cavanaugh was from the traditional school of management ("seat of the pants" or "we've always done it this way"). At sixty-two, his physical condition was excellent, considering his recovery from open-heart surgery two years earlier. Although every other member of the Management Committee supported the Plant Manager's initiation of MSL's organizational development (OD) efforts within the refinery (which included supervisory training, team-building, and EEO development work) Cavanaugh thought OD was a waste of time. He reportedly said, "Young turks come in and try to change the organization when they don't even understand its history ... besides, the refinery was maximizing production capacity way before all this new OD rubbish came up." Cavanaugh constantly refuted the OD effort along with other organizational changes. He was against the massive computerization then underway, and blatantly expressed his feelings throughout the refinery. As Operations Manager with thirty-seven years of experience, Hugh was in a potentially powerful position on the Management Committee. As a result, his negative attitude hindered the effectiveness of the Management Committee in the change process.

Dennis Kline, the refinery's young, aggressive Plant Manager, was a strong supporter of OD and realized its potential for improving the refinery's productivity. He had been in his present position for one year and one of his first actions had been to initiate the OD effort with MSL's assistance. This was a good way to revitalize the workforce while improving the bottom line. The OD effort would help him gain the respect of the refinery employees by demonstrating his concern for their working environment. Hugh had been his only obstacle to implementing the OD effort. He had tried to energize Hugh by utilizing him as a leader to work decisions and assume responsibility for part of the OD effort. Kline figured that if Cavanaugh felt ownership of the ideas and participated in them from their inception, he would realize their value and be won over. However, Cavanaugh refused to get involved in any way and stonewalled all of Kline's efforts over the entire year. Kline had tried everything short of firing Hugh.

Fred Sargent, MSL's senior consultant working with the Management Committee, knew that the members of the committee recognized Hugh's biases against OD, but they really did not have the professional insight and objectivity to see that he had no capability for change. Some of the committee members had blinders on due to their longtime friendship and respect for Hugh. As a result, the whole Management Committee was having a difficult time accepting the realities of the situation. But it was quite obvious to Sargent, based on his past consulting experience, that as long as Cavanaugh was a forceful member of the Management Committee, MSL's OD efforts could never reach their full potential.

Should Fred work with the Management Committee to accept the fact that Hugh would never change, he would be the catalyst for Hugh's encouraged early retirement. This would then allow Sargent to facilitate the OD process. But, if Fred was linked to Hugh's encouraged retirement, he might be labeled as a "hit man," which could inhibit his ability to work with the

Management Committee and other members of the refinery organization. They might see Fred's actions as part of a conspiracy to do some housecleaning and thus find working through behavioral dilemmas with him quite threatening. In addition, the loss of Cavanaugh could be detrimental to the refinery's operations. His position as Operations Manager was a subtle link in labor negotiations currently underway as a result of a recent wildcat strike. Cavanaugh was well-respected by his subordinates, and quite effective in the technical aspects of his job which gave him influence on the union negotiations. It was Fred's feeling that Cavanaugh's work was his life and crucial to his survival, both psychologically and financially.

Feeling extremely frustrated, Fred approached George Davenport, Process Division Manager, Management Committee member, and a longtime friend of Hugh Cavanaugh. George was in his early sixties, but, unlike Hugh, had been able to adjust to organizational changes quite well. He was able to see the potential benefits of OD and could look at the situation from a broad perspective.

Fred:	George, I'm really concerned about the slow progress of the Management Committee in this recent OD effort concerning EEO and team building. What do you see as the barrier?
George:	I seem to be having the same feelings that things are moving rather slowly. If only we could get Hugh on board ... I think things would take off. I've tried to talk to him about the value of the OD efforts, but I can understand his objections. After all, our past experience with consultants billing themselves as OD experts has not been too good. They cost an arm and a leg and talk in generalities, never touching on our specific problems. However, your company has tailored its efforts to our specific needs. Also, Hugh's knowledge and understanding of company history can't be matched – even by the Plant Manager! He really feels outside consultants aren't qualified to facilitate changes in the organization.
Fred:	But, George, everyone else on the committee seems able and ready to accept the OD efforts. Hugh is living in the past. He's dug in his heels and won't budge.
George:	Well, I do know he's too valuable not to have on the Management Committee at this point.

Fred Sargent was in a bind and didn't know what to do. If he didn't take any immediate action and chose to buy time, hoping to either change Hugh Cavanaugh or wait for his scheduled retirement, the entire OD effort might be doomed. Cavanaugh would do everything in his power to stop the effort, if not through the Management Committee, then verbally throughout the refinery. Another option for Sargent was to take on the biggest challenge of his career and spend all his time trying to change Hugh Cavanaugh. If he could somehow work it so Cavanaugh received full credit for part of the OD effort and was recognized by corporate headquarters for this accomplishment, he'd have no choice but to go along with the continuation of the effort.

Other options open to Fred include convincing Dennis Kline to "force" Hugh's early retirement with all the usual fanfare; going to corporate headquarters Human Resources Vice-President or the Vice-President of Refining (who were both strong OD supporters) and explaining the situation; going to Hugh directly and asking him to retire; slowly showing the Management Committee in a calculated way that Hugh was damaging the refinery's effectiveness; or creating a scandal in order to get Hugh fired if he refused to retire.

Fred decided that the next step would be to bring his dilemma to MSL's monthly staff meeting for discussion.

Karen Webster

Karen had several problems at work to think about that night. She usually discussed things with her husband, Jack, in order to put things into a better perspective. The weekly staff meeting was coming up and she wanted to be prepared to present her dilemmas as clearly and concisely as possible to the other consultants to get their opinions.

Karen joined MSL at its inception and had been very active in helping the company to reach its current size and in building its good reputation. She was the only woman consultant for several years. MSL did most of its consulting in flow processing plants and many of the plant managers were products of the "Good Ole Boy" syndrome. They had grown up in the back country and had been taught that women stayed at home. There were few, if any, women working in the plants because of the rough nature of the work. Karen found that it was difficult to get the managers to accept her as a professional, knowledgeable consultant. She had to prove herself time and again. She found that she couldn't allow her clients to think of her as a woman first and a consultant second. Her professional reputation had been built with these men through much hard work and continuing efforts to educate them.

After working for MSL for five years, Karen and Jack had decided to begin a family. A lot of thought had gone into this decision. Karen had no plans to stop working after the baby was born. This opened several areas of potential conflict between raising the baby and Karen's career. However, after carefully evaluating the situation, she began planning her projects so any traveling would be completed by the end of her seventh month of pregnancy. Back in December she had confirmed plans for an eight-day team-building session at a plant seventy-five miles away. She planned to commute every other day. This session would be the culmination of almost a year of hard work.

Several days ago the client company had contacted Karen and stated that the session would have to be pushed back. The new dates coincided with the end of the eighth month of her pregnancy. She was very concerned about this change. The thought of having to drive to and from the plant every other day was not pleasant. She also disliked the idea of staying at the plant for the entire week. She knew Jack would be upset if she were gone from home so late in her pregnancy. She would tire more easily and would not be as effective as usual. However, she had made a commitment to the client to complete the team-building process. Karen felt very strongly about fulfilling her obligations to MSL and to her career.

Karen considered her options. On some projects it would be possible to bring in another consultant to complete the training. However, this was not the case with team-building. Team-building's purpose was to improve the effectiveness and performance of people who work together closely on a regular basis. Because of the difficulty and time necessary to build a close, trusting relationship between the consultant and the group, it would be impossible for another consultant to take over. She could also go back to the client company and try to convince management to allow the original dates to stand. She could refuse to do the training now and try to complete it after she returned to work.

As Karen talked with Jack she voiced these possibilities and wondered how the other consultants would react to her situation. She was worried about the impact cancellation would have on her career and professional reputation. There was even a possibility that MSL would lose the client if she canceled. How would her decision affect Ken's decisions to hire other women consultants? Karen wanted to get some feedback from the other consultants at the staff meeting before making her decision.

Ray Terrell

Back at MSL's New Orleans office on the morning of the monthly staff meeting, Ray Terrell's mind began to wander. Only twenty-four hours ago he had been in Dallas, Texas, in the midst of a tension-filled Management Committee meeting and a potentially explosive discussion with Bill Matthews, Vice-President of Refining – Southwest Region for a major energy concern. Ray had decided that this was an issue to be discussed by the entire MSL professional staff, as it had serious implications for MSL's future. He began to jot down notes in preparation for the meeting....

During the first quarter of this year, Ray had become involved in an OD effort at one of the company's Southwest Region refineries located in Corpus Christi, Texas. Terrell, representing MSL, spent approximately three weeks in the data-gathering phase of the OD process, which included employee-consultant interviews in all refinery divisions. According to MSL's standard practice, prior to conducting the employee interviews, Ray had assured the employees that any information obtained during the interviews would be kept confidential. The Management Committee was aware of this practice but had no explicit confidentiality agreement with MSL. MSL had no formalized written statement on the subject of confidentiality in their signed contracts due to their philosophy of tailoring each OD effort to the particular client. It was strongly believed by all MSL consultants that their current practice was in the best interest of the client organization, the individual, and the consulting firm. This was based on the premise that a consulting organization's ability to collect accurate data about individuals and corporations was critical to successful performance. Effective data-gathering depended on trust that the information would not be used to the possible detriment of the individual unless clearly indicated up front.

Upon completion of the data-gathering phase, Ray compiled his results into a written document and presented it to the refinery's Management Committee which included Bill Matthews as an Ex Officio member. The report emphasized a heavy concern for race relations as expressed by black wage earners in particular. Ray had stated, in a broad general sense, that blacks felt mistreated given their seniority and the jobs they got in relation to other refinery workers with similar seniority. He supported this racial concern by stating that blacks felt they were not receiving as adequate career counseling and development as white workers were (both in technical areas and otherwise) so that blacks could compete for higher level positions. Ray's report concluded with recommended action steps which specified supervisory training in EEO awareness and counseling skills as the first steps. In addition, Ray would undertake an intensive study and revamping of the company's employee training program and practices.

Following Ray's presentation, Plant Manager Ron Gallagher called for a discussion. The EEO issue was of great concern to the entire committee, given an impending Department of Labor audit within a few months. Negative audit results could cause significant delay in the expected promotions of Ron (to a headquarters divisional V-P position) and Bill Matthews (to President of the corporation's small Chemical Division) at the end of the year. It was obvious to Ray that he had hit one of the company's most vulnerable spots. This meant that chances for successful implementation of his recommendations were even greater than he had expected. As a result, MSL could probably count on at least six months of steady billing. This would definitely please Ken.

The Management Committee discussion did not seem to be accomplishing anything. It was apparent the members were quite uncomfortable with the topic of EEO in addition to being defensive of their own subdivisions' nondiscriminatory posture. Finally Bill Matthews spoke. He congratulated Ray on his effective presentation, reiterated his deep concern for the findings, and stated that he was all for immediate action. However, it would be essential for the Management Committee to find out exactly who had expressed these concerns so that steps could be taken to rectify their situation right away. After all, Ray and MSL were working for management. Of course, his major concern was for the employees, but there was the upcoming audit to consider, since EEO charges or possible lawsuits could easily result in a prolonged audit and bad publicity. Once the situation was under control, the problem as a whole could be tackled.

When Matthews finished there was an awkward silence in the room. Ron Gallagher made an attempt to neutralize the situation by acknowledging the refinery's potential racial problem and admitting that blacks never came to any of the refinery's social gatherings.

Terrell could not believe that Matthews had the nerve to ask for identification of his information sources in front of the entire Management Committee! He was even more enraged that no one had objected to the request. Terrell did not know how to respond. As a management consultant he did have a responsibility to management, but had Matthews overstepped the professional boundary? This company was currently MSL's largest client, having produced the majority of projects and billing days throughout MSL's short history. If this situation got out of control, there was the possibility that the relationship would be severed. This could be devastating to MSL since their diversification strategy targets for this quarter had not been realized. At this point MSL was relying heavily on its current clients to produce further projects in other areas of their organizations. This vertical penetration marketing strategy had worked very well with almost no specific sales effort on the part of MSL consultants and now seemed crucial to the firm's immediate survival.

Since all refinery divisions were represented on the Management Committee would Ray be putting MSL's immediate financial future on the line if he did not divulge his information sources? Additionally, if Gallagher and Matthews did get those promotions into the upper echelons of the company, would he be jeopardizing MSL's future with the entire corporation and MSL's reputation in the industry? Finally, one of his goals as an MSL consultant was to improve organizational effectiveness. If he gave the Management Committee the information Matthews wanted, he could be the catalyst needed for the refinery to address the racial concerns affecting the organization's effectiveness.

Ray's mind raced through his confused thoughts. Matthews would be expecting an answer. Ray decided to hold his tongue for the moment and told the Management Committee he'd be in touch with them at their meeting next week.

The Staff Meeting

Ken opened the staff meeting with a brief discussion of the various projects in progress. He then asked the consultants if they had any problems they wanted to discuss. Four hands shot up and Karen, Phil, Ray, and Fred then presented the problems confronting them. Once the initial recitals had been made, Ken recommended a fifteen-minute coffee break so everyone could digest the problems they had just heard about. He asked the group to think about possible courses of action for each situation, the pros and cons of each, and what their final recommendations would be.

20. Control from Afar*

Background

Westways Utility Services is a company whose operations are limited to the northwest region of the United States. While they do have other minor interests, their main business is providing telephone service. As a public service, they are subject to rather close scrutiny by state utility commissions. Westways' companies actually come under the jurisdiction of three different western states.

Public telephone companies are watched very closely, especially with respect to quality of service. In most states, one of the primary methods of assessing the quality of telephone service is through the "customer service index." There is a relatively complicated formula for determining this number. It is really a combination of factors. Among other things it includes the number of customer complaints about service outages (telephones not working for one reason or another) per hundred lines in use.

The customer service index also includes the number of complaints which are made directly to the public utility commission by customers. This happens rarely but is considered a serious matter. Only a few complaints of this nature will cause the "customer service index" to be very low. A complaint of this nature usually indicates one of two things. First, a customer has received very poor service over a long length of time. For one reason or another, this telephone just never seems to work properly. Another reason for a direct complaint to the public utility commission is an inability of the telephone company to fix a problem to the satisfaction of a customer. Suppose, for example, that a customer has complained about "noise" on the line. The customer feels that almost every time that he is on the telephone there is static or background noise or something of that nature. The telephone company, however, tells the customer that they have tested the line and can find nothing wrong. Businesses are usually more likely to make complaints directly to the public utility commission.

There are a couple of reasons for this. First, as you would expect, continuing problems are ordinarily more serious for a business. For many individuals a telephone out of order is an inconvenience. For commercial concerns, some of which may rely on their telephone service for nearly all their business, bad telephone service is more than inconvenient. There is a second reason also. Frankly, most individuals do not realize that they can complain directly to the public utility commission about poor service.

There is another major factor which is included in the customer service index. Most utility commissions occasionally (usually once a month) test telephone equipment. They do this by installing automatic dialing equipment in a telephone office. This device dials a certain number of calls. Suppose, for example, that the device dials 100 numbers. Obviously, if all 100 numbers are completed, then the service would appear to be reasonable. On the other hand, if several of the calls are not completed, then there is evidence that something is wrong with the telephone company's equipment.

It should be noted that 100 telephone calls is very few. In the average telephone central office (the location where these calls take place) hundreds of thousands of calls would be made

---

*This case was prepared by Dan Dalton, Indiana University, and is used here by permission.

each day. The principle of the automatic dialer, however, is like checking for the quality of light bulbs in a manufacturing company. In order to assure the quality of light bulbs, you do not have to plug in every light bulb that is manufactured. You might, however, select a random sample of light bulbs to test. If all the light bulbs you check work as they should, there is some evidence that the entire batch of light bulbs is all right. On the other hand, if you select 100 light bulbs to check and seven of them do not work, that is strong evidence that something is seriously wrong.

These three measures – number of customer complaints, complaints to the public utility commission, errors on the automatic dialing devices – are combined to form the "customer service index." The combination of these factors is adjusted so that 100 is a perfect index. It indicates an extremely high level of customer service. Anything less than 94/95 is cause for concern. A customer service index less than 94 would be a very serious matter which would require immediate action. Telephone companies are very sensitive about this number. It is ordinarily calculated every month. It is an important number. It is likely to be brought up, for instance, when a telephone company asks for an increase in rates for its service or if the telephone company wants to expand its services. Opposing groups may argue that the current service is poor (based on the customer services indexes) and therefore question whether an increase in rates or a service expansion should be allowed.

The Meeting

"Thank you for your attendance on such short notice. I'll tell you why I called this meeting," remarked Adrienne Parkins, vice-president of operations for Westways Utility, to a group of operations officers. "Quite frankly, I am not pleased with last quarter's reports from the northern divisions of this state. Our operations in the other states are reasonable, even good at times. I have been watching the customer service indexes from our northern divisions and they are abysmal. The customer complaints are way out of line with our guidelines; the overall customer service index is low by any standards," continued Ms. Parkins.

"Well, as you know, the majority of our facilities in that region are remote equipment locations. We typically have one supervisor per five or six locations. The day-to-day operations are handled by a few nonmanagerial employees without direct supervision," offered Dale Jorgensen, a company general manager. "The obvious solution is to put a first-level supervisor at each site. Presumably, the performance of the workers, especially the completion of our routine preventive maintenance will be improved by closer supervision," finished Mr. Jorgensen. "As you know, the key to maintaining service indexes at acceptable levels is our routine preventive maintenance. You have to catch problems before they happen."

"Well," countered Ms. Parkins, "I am not going to continue to pay those people to merely babysit that equipment, to put out fires as problems are reported. I want that routine preventive maintenance done and I want it done right. I know that there are no supervisors on those shifts. Frankly, I am hesitant to put a supervisor on shifts with so few people. In fact, I will not hear of adding first-line supervisors to those remote sites. We would probably be talking about a dozen or so supervisors. I cannot justify that expense," concluded Ms. Parkins.

Several people present at the meeting argued that short of putting new first-line supervisors at the currently unsupervised locations, there was no way to assure the quality necessary to improve the customer service indexes in the region.

To this Ms. Parkins replied, "In the near future, Westways Utility intends a major expansion in the northern division. In order to finance that, we will ask for rate increases. It should be clear that we will have an uphill battle all the way if our service indexes do not improve dramatically. I will not authorize new supervisors for the remote locations. Nonetheless, I want improvement in the quality of our services in those regions."

21. Suntory*

Mr. Tanaka, the production manager in charge of Royal 60 whiskey, sat reflecting on the forecasted demand provided to him by the marketing department. He wondered about the impact of this increase on the production line, and what this meant in terms of gearing up for increased production. Demand of Suntory's upscale Royal 60 whiskey was expected to increase rapidly. Over the next two years it was expected to grow over 40 percent. Forecasts predicted even more dramatic growth for the two years following that. The questions that preoccupied Mr. Tanaka were: (1) whether the current production capacity was sufficient, and (2) whether major changes would be required to meet this growing demand.

Marketing and Product Image

Royal 60 was one of a line of whiskeys marketed by Suntory in Japan. Its specific target market was the urban, upper-middle class Japanese manager. Over the years Suntory had built a cultural ambiance around Royal 60 that conveyed a feeling of understated European class: a drink for men who were quietly self-assured, who were neither rich nor by any means poor, who were somewhat cosmopolitan, but not overly so, and who appreciated the good things in life.

Part of Royal 60's distinctive product image was its packaging, which included a ribbon fastening cap to bottle. It was a distinctive feature not found on most domestic or imported brands of whiskey. The ribbon was perceived to make the whiskey more European by implying an association with European brandies and cognac which came similarly packaged. It also suggested Old World craftsmanship and elegance: the type of detail not found in a product that the average consumer would buy.

Production, Bottling, and Packaging

At Suntory, whiskey was produced using processes that were fairly standardized in the industry. Except for some automation, the method currently in use was similar to the one that had been in practice for centuries. The process essentially involved three stages. During stage one, whiskey mash was fermented and then distilled. This stage was automated at Suntory. In the second stage, distilled spirit was placed in wooden casks and then stored in large warehouses for anywhere from five to thirty-five years. From time to time, testers sampled the distilled spirit to check for proper color and taste. When the distilled spirit reached an appropriate level of maturity, processing moved into the third stage. During this stage, spirits of various ages were blended together to achieve the right color and taste. Royal 60, representing one such blended product line, was one of Suntory's higher quality brands.

After blending, the bottling of Royal 60 proceeded through a series of semi-automated and automated steps. The bottling process began with the sterilization of bottles in a hot water bath. Once sterilized, bottles were then filled with blended whiskey, capped and passed on to the

*This case was written by Allan Bird and Suresh Kotha, both from the Stern School of Business, New York University. This case was prepared as basis for class discussion rather than to illustrate either effective or ineffective handling of administrative situations. Reprinted with permission.

labeling area where gold colored labels were applied automatically. The bottles then proceeded to the most labor-intensive step in the process – the tying of the distinctive ribbon to the Royal 60 bottle. The fastened caps were secured to the bottle by means of a hand-tied ribbon which was attached to the bottle by means of a machine-sealed wax stamp. Finally, the bottles were put into boxes and prepared for shipping to distributors.

Exhibit 1. Steps in Tying Ribbons on Royal 60

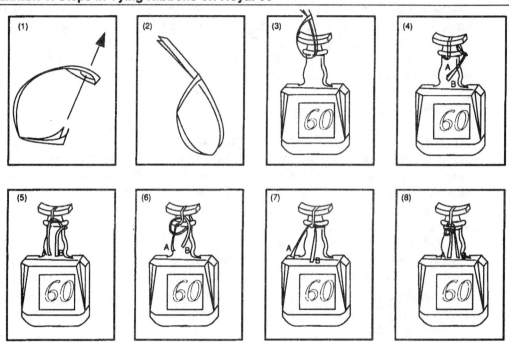

Problems and Concerns

A quick review of the Royal 60 bottling line by Tanaka revealed that the ribbon-tying phase of the line represented the slowest-moving part of the process. With rapidly increasing demand it was apparent that productivity improvements in the ribbon-tying phase were essential if Suntory was to increase production levels without raising production costs. With this under-standing, Tanaka began to examine the ribbon-tying process in more detail. He noticed that ribbons were tied manually on an assembly line of twenty workers (all women) during the stage prior to shipment. The manual process took eight steps, as shown in Exhibit 1. A ribbon was folded in half and then tucked back through the fold to form a loop. The loop was next hooked over the left side of the bottle and the top of the cap. It was then wrapped around the bottle, from back to front. At the front, one end was passed through the initial loop from the inside, while the other end was passed through the loop from the outside. The two ends were then drawn tight, and the second end was tied around the first in a half-clove hitch. Employing this procedure, a line worker tied an average of three and a half bottles per minute. This translated into an average line speed of seventy bottles per minute.

From his detailed examination, it was clear to Tanaka that the ribbon-tying line was experiencing no major problems. He was aware that his workers were consistently meeting schedules and there was no known delay in product shipment in the past. However, he noticed differences in the knot sizes, resulting from the way they were tied. At that moment he was not sure whether these differences mattered. But he suspected that they did detract from the bottle's overall appearance. Further, two other things concerned him: (1) there were no standards or established specifications for the knot tying process, and (2) no final quality inspection of the product was undertaken before it was shipped.

Later during a conversation with Sato of the production research department, Tanaka learned that the placement of the knot varied as a result of worker inexperience, fatigue, or occasional worker inattention. Since it was the last operation before boxing, it was hard to catch mistakes. Even when an off-center knot could be identified and corrected, the adjustment took time, thus further slowing down the line. Also according to Sato, one of the most difficult aspects of the work for new employees was learning how to properly set the loop so that it would stay anchored and centered. If drawn too tightly, the loop tended to pull the knot to the left of center. If not drawn tightly enough, the loop would loosen, thus shifting the knot to the right of center. It currently took nearly sixty days for a new line worker to reach the average level of proficiency at this task. In addition, Sato noted that the resulting off-center knot did detract from the bottle's overall appearance. However, he did point out that he was not aware of any complaints from the marketing department.

According to Sato a complete automation of the ribbon-tying process was impossible. Automation of the process up to step 7 (see Exhibit 1) was certainly feasible, though it would require a sizable capital investment. However, Sato warned that it would still be necessary to retain workers to perform steps 7 and 8. Nonetheless, with automation the total number of workers on the line could be reduced. The production department estimated that each machine could on the average process six bottles a minute. Tanaka was aware that, given the current budgetary pressures, senior management was not inclined to provide major funds for this product line.

Tanaka's investigations led him to focus increasingly on the current production facility capacity to keep up with rising demand. The main bottleneck was the ribbon-tying operation – the slowest phase of the bottling line operation. In addition, there was no space on the current line to expand the number of workers; nor was it clear that automation would be economically justifiable given the fact that it would still be necessary to retain workers to complete the final stages of the tying process. Given Tanaka's conservative nature and the fact that the optimistic forecasts provided by the marketing department might never materialize, it seemed to him more prudent to wait before making major changes.

Enter the Violets

In the meantime, Tanaka decided to approach the Quality Control (QC) circle named as Violets[1] on the ribbon-tying line to see what they could come up with. A previous QC circle had recommended the use of pre-glued ribbon (see Exhibit 2b). The standard, pre-glued loop

---

[1]The Violets consisted of eight workers on the ribbon-tying line ranging in age from 19 to 56 years, with an average age of about 37 years. This recently formed group met once a week to discuss ways to increase productivity and improve the quality of the final product.

had cost 78.2 per unit as opposed to 14.7 per unit for the pre-folded variety (see Exhibit 2a) and resulted in a sixteen percent productivity increase, thus more than offsetting the added cost. Perhaps, Tanaka hoped, the Violets could find ways to increase productivity that would serve, at the very least, as a short-term response to demand pressures.

After meeting with Mr. Tanaka, the circle began to discuss ways to increase productivity. They felt strongly that occasional defects and problems related to the centering of ribbon knots were symptomatic of inefficiencies in the ribbon-tying process and that steps to remove these inefficiencies could both improve quality and, more importantly, raise productivity.

During one of their meetings it was suggested they experiment with a preset loop (see Exhibit 2c) rather than use a pre-glued ribbon. After some experimentation on the production line, the group proposed that pre-folded ribbons be glued in two places, thus facilitating the early part of the tying process (i.e., forming the ribbon into a loop). Also the use of a pre-set loop would make centering automatic, thereby reducing the amount of time it took new workers to get up to speed. They began exploring this possibility by surveying workers on the line as to what the ideal loop size should be (see Exhibit 3 for results of the survey). Based on these findings the circle decided on a loop size of 160 mm.

While the cost of pre-set loop ribbons would remain unchanged, the members predicted a slight increase in line speed resulting from this change. While making the knot tying process easier, the pre-set loop would also reduce some of the problems associated with sizing and centering of the knots. Thus, as part of a three-month test run, an order was placed for 50,000 such pre-set loop ribbons. The loop size was specified as 160 mm with a tolerance of plus or minus 2 mm.

In using these ribbons it was found that the line speed did increase to 74 bottles per minute, with individual workers tying an average of 3.7 bottles per minute. This represented a 5.7 percent increase in a line productivity. But it was not without its problems.

New Concerns

While the new pre-glued ribbons were being tested on the line, members of the quality circle sampled ribbons received to check if they met specifications. They randomly selected 480 ribbons from a consignment of 9,300 ribbons for measurement (see Exhibit 4 for results of this survey).

Exhibit 2. Types of Ribbons Used on the Ribbon Tying Line for Royal 60

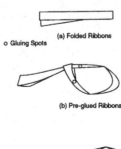

o Gluing Spots   (a) Folded Ribbons

(b) Pre-glued Ribbons

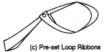

(c) Pre-set Loop Ribbons

Exhibit 3. Histogram of Survey Results for Preferred Loop Size

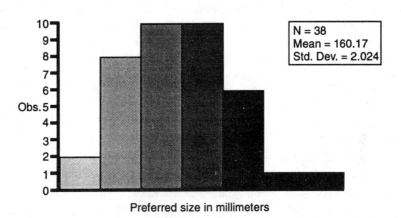

Preferred size in millimeters

A survey of line workers indicated that there were also problems with ribbon quality. On some ribbons there was too much glue which caused the ribbons to stick together occasionally. It was also painful to the fingers when the glue hardened. Workers also complained about the look of the ribbons, some of which seemed to have been crushed during transportation.

The identification of variations in loop size extending outside the specifications encouraged the circle to examine how ribbons were produced by the supplier. They learned that their supplier wove fibers into ribbon, winding the ribbon onto large spools. The spools were then taken to a cutting room where they were measured, but to a uniform length and tied into bundles. The bundles were then delivered by the supplier to fifty housewives. These women formed the pre-set loop ribbons by folding the pre-cut ribbon in half, measuring 160 mm from the fold on a ruler, forming a loop, and then gluing the loop at the appropriate spot. Ribbons were then tied in bundles of 100 and picked up by the supplier for delivery to Suntory. In an effort to understand the process better, a member of the QC circle sampled twenty pre-set ribbons from each housewife working for the manufacturer. The results from 6 representative housewives are shown in Exhibit 5.

The members discussed these new concerns at the next Violets Circle meeting with Tanaka. Had they created more problems than they had solved? True, they had achieved a productivity increase. But their actions created a whole range of additional concerns that needed to be dealt with immediately.

Tanaka, returning to his office from this latest meeting with the QC members, focused his thoughts once again on the ribbon-tying process. He was not sure what to do next. He wondered if there had been any value in involving the Violets. While he was contemplating more changes, he wondered how the marketing people would react if he recommended doing away with the ribbon tying process completely.

Exhibit 4. Histogram of Loop Size from Random Sampling

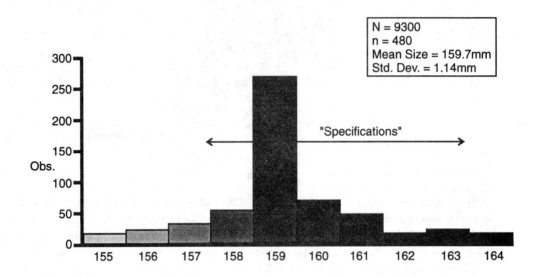

Exhibit 5. Breakdown by Housewife of Random Sampling Results

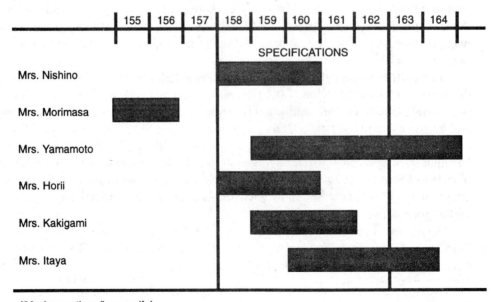

(20 observations/housewife)

22. Conflict Management*

Area Manager John H. was surprised and astounded by the conversation he had just heard – if you could call it a conversation! He could hardly believe that two of his key managers could be involved in such a bitter feud. One accused the other of trying to undermine his department by stealing his best people and the other accused in rebuttal that the other manager was simply finding excuses for his bad management. There had been accusation and counteraccusation followed by hot denials and bitter recrimination. He finally decided there was nothing to be gained by further outbursts and sent both men back to their departments. This, he hoped, would give them a cooling off period and himself a chance to try and sort it all out.

It wasn't unusual for Technical Development and Product Engineering to have these differences, but they rarely took on such a heated aspect. John's thoughts turned to Ralph, Manager of Technical Development. He had come highly recommended by the president of another division. He had been very successful in development work and seemed well suited to this assignment. In his six months on the job he had reorganized several sections and initiated new projects. It wasn't spectacular but it appeared competent from all John could see. There had been a few gripes that he was too aloof and reserved, but that was natural in view of the man he had replaced. It always took a little time for these management transitions to settle down. It appeared Ralph was aware of his problem since he had inserted a new manager under him (Frank) who was effective in personal relationships. It was too early to tell how that was working out but it seemed a wise move.

John knew there were problems, however. He had talked with Personnel after the recent Opinion Survey and learned the morale in Ralph's group was down from its usual mark. There seemed to be more employee apathy, more lateness and absences, and more transfer requests. This latter was the most surprising since there were few such requests usually. It was odd to find morale at such a low ebb since the group was well knit and had strong group identity. Personnel had talked informally with a few of the people and their view was (1) the work load was too low and they didn't feel meaningfully utilized and (2) they felt their present management was too distant and reserved.

It was difficult to put these in perspective. From Ralph's viewpoint the low work load was directly traceable to the "game" George was playing. He contended one of George's people would request a "sizing" for a particular job. His people would carefully give cost, technology, and schedule estimates, but then nothing happened. One of his people would call over to find out where the work requisition was and would be told the job had been canceled by George. His manager would be offered a much smaller job – provided they transferred the people key to the former job request – "to help keep your people busy." When this finally came to Ralph's attention he "hit the roof" and this is what led to the recent confrontation. George's views varied greatly, hence the hot argument.

George had been in the department longer than Ralph. He was known as an effective, "hard-nosed" manager who got the job done. He was ambitious and had grown rather rapidly over the last two years. He was adaptable as shown by the fact that he had made the transition

---

*This case was prepared by James C. Conant, School of Business Administration and Economics, California State University, and is used here with his permission. Copyright © James C. Conant.

from Chemistry to Product Engineering. The Product Engineering Department had a poor reputation prior to George's moving over and he had been instrumental in changing its image to a very positive one. As a result the department had grown considerably under George. All in all it was a good record.

George contended Ralph was an inefficient manager, with too much fat in his organization, who was unwilling to cut back to a reasonable level. As a result Ralph was pricing himself out of the business. He had to cancel jobs because the costs were prohibitive. George laid some of the blame on the previous manager, Henry, claiming it was Henry's doing that caused the lab to reach the present ridiculous size. George felt Ralph should reevaluate his situation and curtail the department size and become competitive again. If the cost problem had merit as an argument it could go back to Henry. There was nothing to indicate Ralph's costs were out of line with past history.

George freely admitted to wanting several of Ralph's people. He felt they would be better placed and better utilized in his area, but he hotly denied he had "played any games" to get them. The pressure of the new releases had caused a backlog in his department and he could use expert help.

John wondered why George steadfastly refused to use the Technology group. He was slipping schedules and the overtime costs would eventually overtake the claimed excessive costs of Ralph's group. He wasn't in any serious trouble as yet and might be gambling he could pull his chestnuts out by the transfer of a few key people. If this was his gamble he might be trying to force Ralph's hand.

John decided he had better talk to Henry in order to clarify this matter further. After that was concluded he sorted out the following impressions. Henry had no love for Ralph. He felt it was still his "shop" and Ralph was doing a poor job of taking over. On the other hand Henry supported Ralph's contentions about George. He indicated he had similar problems in the past and had called him on it a number of times. He flatly denied that the group was too large and indicated it would function well if George didn't feel he had to save the managership of all operations necessary to his function. The conversation left John more puzzled than edified.

Well, there it was. All made good points. If George is correct an overhaul is in order and Ralph should get his costs in line. If Ralph is right George must be stopped from disrupting the department and risking full project success for the sake of his own gain. In all probability both have valid points and the problem will be how to respond appropriately to both managers.

Ralph's Viewpoint

Ralph was transferred into this division after several successful projects in Engineering Development. He came highly recommended by the president of another division, under whom he had worked, and was deemed a candidate for higher management in the near future.

There was little doubt about his technical competence. He was informed and innovative. He preferred small groups to large, complex ones, and this was a partial reason for giving him this assignment. Higher growth would depend on his ability to handle larger groups. For this reason the job had been enlarged to encompass additional functions. This meant Ralph had a substantially larger group to manage than his predecessor.

Although Ralph never commented on his reaction to this change in operations for him, he appeared a little overwhelmed by it. He spent considerable time in his office planning and integrating the various functions. He only rarely met with the Lab people and had staff meetings on an irregular basis. It must be emphasized he had been in the job only about six months and still was getting his feet on the ground.

He had never been much of a delegator. Some of this was by temperament and some from the nature of the reward structure. He had been heard to comment: "I do my business in the halls. When I run into the Division President and he asks about my project I can get away with maybe one 'I don't know' and after that I'm known as an 'I don't know guy.'" The result was a tendency to know details that usually are reserved for subordinates. The new job stretched him to the point that he had greater difficulty doing this, but it may account for the inordinate amount of time he spent in his office.

In his approach to others he was direct and confronting. People knew where they stood, and in general their comments indicated they liked this style of managing. He was aware he interacted somewhat stiffly with others and this had occasioned the insertion of Frank at the Lab level. In addition he was planning to change some of the procedures Henry had instituted, and he felt Henry would be an obstacle to these plans. Frank would be a major factor in assuring that the new procedures went as smoothly as possible.

His relationship to Henry was cordial but distant. He had no particular dislike for Henry, but felt the group could be more effectively organized. He was in the process of developing these plans when the problem broke.

His relationship with John, the Director, was essentially OK as far as one could tell. On the whole his "clout" with John was undeveloped, as was his impact on his peers. He seemed to be regarded as an unknown quantity – perhaps something of a threat in view of his reputation.

He was disappointed with the way the meeting turned out. He didn't like shouting matches but he wasn't going to stand by and have George put him or his Lab group down. He was sure they were effective and as soon as he completed some of the new project planning he knew their work load would be more than adequate. He was familiar with people trying the kind of thing George was doing and the only way to avert it was through direct confrontation. He only wished he could better predict John's reaction.

Henry's Viewpoint

Henry was an "old timer" and had been the Lab's Manager for many years. He was affable and outgoing, walking the shop regularly and on a first-name basis with virtually everyone in the Lab. It had been his assignment to create and staff the Lab, and over the several years he managed it he exercised care in the selection and placement of the staff. It had been generally conceded the Lab was staffed with topnotch people.

The Lab group had strong ties with one another. There were a few who had turned down promotions in order to remain with the group. That it was not all one big happy family was indicated by a few dissidents who felt they had been passed over for promotion. On the whole, however, they worked well together and enjoyed a favorable reputation by all concerned.

As Henry had indicated, George had tried to lure some of his better talent away during the recent past. Henry learned of these rather quickly because of his close relationship to the group and he effectively aborted each of these. George had finally given up on this and had gone to outside recruiting for the talent he wanted. This meant a slower indoctrination process for him and slowed down his growth potential. It was Henry who first became aware that George was up to his "old tricks."

He probably should have gone to Ralph with the information about George but he felt at odds with Ralph's methods. He resented the staff role into which he had been put, even though medical advice was the basis for the move. He sensed that Ralph was planning changes and he had not been consulted. When Frank was brought in he felt even more resentful. He regarded his assignment as a "make work" one and did not feel meaningfully utilized. He still felt a strong proprietary interest in the Lab group and would take whatever measures he could to prevent its disruption.

Given a choice of choosing between Ralph or George he would choose Ralph, and eventually this choice had to be made. In his meetings with John he had been fully candid regarding George's tactics and hoped this once John would put a stop to them. He did it more to ensure the Lab remaining intact than because of Ralph. He certainly didn't want to see the Lab destroyed after all the years he'd spent building it to its present state.

George's Viewpoint

George was dynamic, energetic, and technically proficient. He had taken over the Product Engineering group when it was regarded with disfavor and had steadily built into its present respectable state. He had ambition and sought to enlarge his sphere of influence whenever possible. He viewed the situation in this way. "I like this environment. It is highly fluid and I have a lot of freedom to do things the way I believe they should be done. I get reprimanded when I make a mistake – and that's only fair as far as I'm concerned. My attitude is to take over and operate any group I can. If I'm successful it will soon come under my jurisdiction. I keep pushing until I'm told to stop by someone who can make it stick."

This had been George's method of operation as long as he had been a manager. It had paid off handsomely for him, and from the Company's standpoint they had benefited too. His group was well-managed, competently staffed, and morale was at least as good as one could find in the Division. His people were loyal to him and respected his ability. He had considerable "clout" because of his past success and had more than the usual influence with the Director.

He had no personal antipathy for Ralph. He was anxious to secure some of the key Lab people and honestly believed they would be more effective in his organization. He felt this would be better for the Company and would provide the people with greater opportunities for growth. There was some accuracy to the latter, but the former was a matter of opinion.

As he regarded the Lab group he felt they were overstaffed and underutilized. He didn't think Ralph was effective in moving to reorganize the department and felt the people were fair game for his managerial approach.

(It was interesting to this observer that direct methods were never utilized. The ground rules permitted making offers to people in other departments, through promotions, raises, etc. Why George never did was unclear.)

George felt he was an effective manager, better than his peers (possibly including the Director). He felt Ralph was running a country club and that it needed effective management. If possible he wanted to absorb the Lab into his operation, but that would require a restructuring of the organization. Since the Lab served many groups in addition to his, his functions would have to be broadened, an unlikely move at this time.

He was taking a calculated risk in not using the Lab for some of his immediate jobs because he might well get into a last minute "crunch" and, failing to meet schedule, lose some of the ground he had gained. On the other hand if he could secure some key people, he could come in on schedule and be in a position to take over other Lab functions that would arise later. In the meantime it would appear as if the Lab was not as necessary because of the low work load. He, at this time, was the major user of the Lab – although this was not always the case. This depended on the development cycle, which was at a low ebb for other groups, but would probably pick up fairly soon.

All in all George was satisfied with his progress and felt he had a good chance at the Director's job when John was promoted. He wasn't happy about this current situation with Ralph, but felt he could weather it and perhaps make Ralph appear foolish or somewhat less competent. It would be a good time for a put-down, his being new and all. The last meeting with John left him uncertain as to where each stood. He was sure he had not heard the last of the situation.

Part 6 Human Resource Management

Cases Outline

23. Precision Measurement of Japan: A Small Foreign Company in the Japanese Labor Market*

Precision Measurement of Japan (PM-J) is a joint venture company between Takezawa** Electric Company (TEC), a Japanese electrical equipment manufacturing company, and Precision Management, Inc. (PMI), a Minnesota-based manufacturer of measurement devices. Major markets for these devices are chemical processes, pipelines, aircraft and aerospace and power generation. As a multinational corporation, PMI is faced with the problem of penetrating the Japanese market before one of its Japanese competitors perfects the various gauges and shuts the U.S. company out of the Japanese market. In order to penetrate the Japanese market, PMI has entered into a business relationship with TEC, thus forming a quasi-Japanese company, PM-J. This step was intended to increase PMI's credibility with the Japanese, and to forestall a Japanese competitor from using its protected domestic market to work out bugs, employ economies of scale, undercut PMI's pricing scheme, and generally take over the world instrument market. This would seriously, perhaps fatally, affect PMI's visibility.

The Problem

The problem faced by his company, according to Joe Smith, president of PM-J, is that the Japanese instrument companies are becoming more visible and are developing broader product lines which may directly affect PM-J's market share. Corporate PMI headquarters is genuinely concerned that the Japanese long-term plan is to capture and dominate the world instrument markets just as they have taken over camera, automobile, video recorder and other high-tech markets. The instrument market could be the next Japanese strategic industry.

Currently, the Japanese tend to dominate only their domestic instrument markets, says Smith. This could change by working their familiar strategy. This is accomplished by closing the Japanese markets to foreign competition, acquiring volume and experience in domestic markets, and basing foreign marketing on that experience.

The usual Japanese strategy is to either (1) obtain licenses for advanced technology from other companies (usually from the United States) and then improve the technology and market it alone or (2) use some company's proven distribution to establish a market base and then go it alone. Both of these approaches save considerable time and expense to the Japanese company, thus freeing resources and capital for quick and effective marketing of the new and/or improved technology. Smith reports that two competitors gained real substance in this manner.

After penetrating the foreign markets with this strategy, excellent service and responsive-

*This case was prepared by James C. Scoville (with the assistance of Christine Hoffman and Eliyahue Stein), Carlson School of Management, Case Development Center, University of Minnesota. Reprinted with permission.
**I am also indebted to referees who commented on the case. One of their suggestions was a brief guide to pronunciation of the Japanese names in this case. In general, each vowel merits a syllable: thus, "Tah.Keh.zah.wah." The only exception is when "i" serves as a "y," as in the name of Keio ("Kayo") University. All "sh" combinations in this case are pronounced as in "shoe."

ness from the Japanese companies are generally reported. The Japanese will, no doubt, continue their patient, persistent way of presenting high-technology, high-performance products which are backed by quality service. Even though they gain market position slowly, says Smith, once the Japanese establish accounts their outstanding customer relations and excellent service record often mean they keep the accounts; the non-Japanese are then in a position of lost accounts and a declining market share.

Objective

PMI wishes to establish a permanent position in the Japanese domestic market. Additionally, it would be preferable that any Japanese competition be retarded by PMI's establishment of a strong sales and manufacturing posture in Japan. To acquire and maintain a market share in the instrument industry, PMI must establish credibility as a viable company; this it sought to do by combining with TEC. By establishing PM-J, PMI is demonstrating a long-term commitment and significant investment in Japan. In its efforts to capture the Japanese market, PM-J is faced with two overriding questions:

1. Is it possible to hire a sufficient number of qualified sales engineers (preferably newly graduated) to increase sales, establish quality accounts, and achieve a reasonable profit growth?
2. In what manner might PM-J increase its market position and distribution in the Japanese market?

The answers to these questions are complicated by a variety of socioeconomic factors unique to Japan.

The Country

Japan has a small amount of inhabitable land located on a number of mountainous islands, with few natural resources but abundant human resources. Pressured by the need to import almost all raw materials, including 100% of all oil, the Japanese economy grew at phenomenal rates during the 1960s and 1970s. During this period, Japanese industrial products moved from a reputation as cheap and flimsy to a position known for quality and reliability. This achievement was attained in part through protective import practices and a coordinated industrial strategy featuring cooperation between major manufacturing groups and the government, especially through activities of the Ministry of International Trade and Industry (MITI).

The Company

Precision Measurement, Inc. was founded in the mid-1960s to produce a wide range of measurement and instrumentation equipment. Over the years, the company has remained at the forefront of this industry and continues to this day to pursue cutting edge research. In recent years, the company's financial strength has been sustained by a classic "cash cow" – a gauge for measurement of flow and pressure. The success of this gauge relies on two factors – (1) very fine and precise machining of high quality material to strict quality standards and (2) an ingenious application of elementary principles of physics. Neither of these constitutes a substantial barrier to Japanese competition: machining materials to high standard is straightforward; even the casewriter's late 50's high school physics allows him to understand the way the gauge works!

Staffing Implications

To penetrate the Japanese domestic market, an optimal staffing pattern must be generated which would yield the desired sales capability. (Manufacturing takes place in the United States, with the gauge being modified to the customer's needs in Japan by production engineers and technicians.) PM-J's president supplied a table (Exhibit 1) of desired staffing patterns from the beginning of 1985 through 1987, which focuses on their probable staffing needs. Although PM-J found it very difficult to hire the eight engineers who presently represent the company, it is now faced with the need to engage seven more in just two and one-half years.

Engineering Labor Markets in Japan

The nature of Japanese labor markets, particularly for professionals and managers, directly affects attainability of the staffing patterns outlined by the company. Modern, large Japanese organizations generally hire people as they finish school for "lifetime employment." The employee then receives a traditional training which consists of considerable job rotation and general training which develops broad skills; the employee, therefore, expects a pay system based primarily on length of service with the company rather than job specific performance. Thus, PM-J's competitors would typically hire engineers on completion of university training and employ them until their early to mid-50s. Then, as is the practice with many managers, the senior employees are transferred to subsidiaries, client organizations, smaller plants, or less demanding jobs.

A small company like PM-J cannot easily compete in the labor market because it cannot guarantee its own survival for the career lifetime of the employees. Small organizations are more likely to go out of business and are, even if they survive, less likely to obtain a major share of the product market. This fact does little to instill confidence in the new graduate who expects lifetime employment as a condition of employment. The same weakness generally applies to foreign companies in Japan. They often do not share a commitment to lifetime employment, traditional pay systems, or a long business presence in Japan. This image, formed

Exhibit 1. Projected Staffing Patterns, 1985 – 7

		April 1985	end 1985	end 1986	end 1987
Administration		5	5	5	5
Secretarial/Clerical		5	5	5	5
Engineering					
Sales & Marketing	3	8	11	13	15
Engineering Services Group	3				
Production	2				
Production Technicians		2	3	3	3
		20	24	26	28

by some foreign companies that came to Japan and then laid off many people or totally withdrew, is widespread among Japanese professionals.

PM-J has generally been unable to recruit the immediate postgraduate because it is both small and foreign. This has necessitated acquiring its engineering force in various ad hoc ways, predominantly relying on recommendations from its joint venture partner, TEC. While not optimal, it has at least allowed the company to develop a skeleton staff.

The first two columns of Exhibit 2 show the name and recruiting source of engineers currently employed by PM-J. The third and fourth columns show the salaries of these people (millions of yen per year) as compared with the average pay of employees of the same age and education in large companies in Japan. The final column shows each employee's job perform- ance evaluation as reported by company president Smith. Exhibit 2 clearly demonstrates that PM-J's hiring pattern has strongly deviated from the stereotypical post-university hire/lifetime employment pattern of Japanese industry in general.

Alternatives to the Current Situation

Given the staffing and recruiting patterns of Japanese industries and the staffing dilemmas faced by PM-J, what alternative plans of action are available to a small, foreign company which will promote its slated objectives of expanded sales and increased market share? If PM-J is to predominate in the Japanese market, what alternatives to its current pattern of hiring mid-career engineers could move the company toward hiring newly-graduated qualified engineers? Are there changes occurring in the Japanese labor culture which might benefit PM-J if the company recognizes and adapts the changes to fit its needs?

Attracting Younger Engineers

How might PM-J increase its hiring ratio of younger engineers directly out of school? Will it be as difficult to hire new graduates in the future as previous experience suggests? The latter situation seems to be loosening a bit as professors' influence in directing students has declined. Indeed, some students are more willing to consider employers other than just the very largest and more traditional Japanese companies. Furthermore, the typical lifetime employment pattern seems to be eroding as some younger professionals with relatively recent dates of hire move to new companies after only three or four years of employment. Organizations like The Recruit Center (a major recruiting and placement organization providing extensive published information on companies as prospective employers) and "headhunters" are supporting these changes in employment patterns by publicizing employment opportunities and company characteristics. Young professionals in engineering and other technical fields are beginning to rely on such data in making career decisions.

The advantages of this alternative, i.e., to employ personnel agencies, are straightforward. First, PM-J could more readily advertise the benefits and opportunities it is able to provide to career-minded professionals via the agencies and headhunters, as third parties, can confer as they present the company as a stable organization that demonstrates Japanese characteristics. Third, recruitment agents are financially motivated to match employers and employees; PM-J can capitalize on this by requesting younger, well-educated, technically qualified engineers who have a potentially longer career life with the company.

The principal disadvantages of personnel agencies are their high cost to the small

Exhibit 2. Sales and Support Force, Spring 1985

Name	Source	Annual (million yen) including bonuses	Average Pay at large companies* (million yen)	Performance Evaluation
Sato	small company experience, recommended by the general manager of PM-J	9.5	9.7	55% effort rating; lower segment on performance
Suzuki	formerly a representative for PM-J	7.3	5.8	80%
Takahashi	TEC (age: late 40s)	7.3	7.2	75-85%
Watanabe	Nihon Medical(age: early 50s), recommended by a classmate who is now a professor	9.5	9.5	very high
Tanaka	junior high school education plus 20 years in the instrumentation sales business; answered an ad in a trade journal			N/A
Ito	TEC (age: 32)	5.8	5.8	90%
Kobayashi	new university graduate	2.9	3.0	N/A
Saito	TEC (age; about 40)	6.3	6.3	very high
Yamamoto	TEC (age: mid 40s)	8.4	7.8	very high

*Equal to 18 months salary in the average large company, no housing or other allowances figured in. The extra six months' pay reflects the average level of bonuses in Japan. At present, large Japanese companies pay roughly 2 months' salary as a bonus three times a year (late spring, late summer and at the Christmas – New Year's season).

Source: Japan Institute of Labor Statistical Reports.

organization, in terms of money and CEO time. Further caveats must be noted: graduates of the best Japanese universities and engineering programs (University of Tokyo and Keio University) would probably not be interested in employment agencies, because they would most likely be recruited by the large domestic companies via contacts with university professors. Likewise, headhunters would be less able to lure young new hires from large companies to work for a smaller foreign-based firm. Additionally, if PM-J accepted a large proportion of graduates from second and third tier universities, it would be unable to generate a level of credibility which a workforce of "better" educated employees from top-rated universities would confer.

Attracting Female Engineers

One intriguing labor market strategy might be to get women into PM-J's labor force as sales engineers. A growing number of women are enrolled in engineering programs of Japanese universities. Their employability, at least in principle, should be enhanced by equal opportunity legislation recently passed by the Diet (Japan's Parliament). More distant observers, including some at the corporate offices of PMI, have occasionally brainstormed about job redesign and the use of women engineers; U.S.-based students may almost think this a natural option.

Practical reaction at PM-J, however, stresses that the acceptability of women in many Japanese work roles is not immediately forthcoming, as the tale related in Exhibit 3 amply suggests. Moreover, it will be even longer in coming within the industrial setting where men are almost exclusively employed and where evening entertainment of customers is an expected job component.

Engineers vs. Salespeople

A variant on the idea of increasing the number of engineers at PM-J is to reduce the company's reliance on engineers by employing non-technically-trained salespeople; the sales component of the engineers' positions would be eliminated or substantially decreased. After all, engineers don't do all the selling in the United States; rather, they provide technical backup and design work after the salesperson has made the pitch.

Exhibit 3. Prospects for Female Engineers

The actual and potential roles of women in Japanese society and work-life are undoubtedly changing. The increasing proportions of female students at universities is one index of this change and is directly related to PM-J's problems. Between 1970 and 1980, the female enrollment ratio more than doubled from 9.6% to 20.1%. In spite of this upsurge, the number of female engineering graduates in all fields remains very small; 1981 engineering graduates included 1,143 women as compared to 73,631 men.

Numbers alone fail to tell the full tale of how difficult it could be to employ women successfully in PM-J's sales engineering positions, where they would have to call on and entertain male customers. A recent event described in Labor Trends in Japan, 1983, may illuminate the employability of women in Japan today.

"A minor scandal erupted in 1983 with the publication of confidential employment guidelines of one of Japan's major bookselling chains employing 2,000 persons, over half of them women, in 28 outlets. The manual told office managers to guard against hiring certain types of women. Among these were women who wore glasses, short women (under 4 ft., 8 in.), ugly women and those with country bumpkin-like attributes. Educational criteria for exclusion included college drop-outs and graduates of four-year universities ("too head-strong"). Also to be avoided were potentially troublesome women, including those who belong to political or religious organizations since they would not be able to easily change their way of thinking, those whose fathers are university professors or whose husbands are teachers or writers, and women who take an interest in legal affairs or who could otherwise be argumentative, such as those who belonged to school newspaper clubs. Another group which should not be hired, according to the manual, are women with complicated family situations or chronic illnesses. Lastly, presumably since their conduct might not be above suspicion, women who have changed jobs more than once, divorcees, single women renting their own apartments, and women who respect "passionate artists" such as Van Gogh should be passed over. (Labor Trends in Japan, 1983)

Perhaps it is feasible to explore hiring graduates of technical high schools and vocational schools for sales, following the example set when Tanaka was hired (Exhibit 2). This could be accomplished by multiple testing (less restricted in Japan than in the United States, and increased training to identify and qualify strong sales candidates. In fact, PMI in the United States and other organizations in Japan succeeded in using a combination of both occupations in marketing products.

By using non-engineering salespeople, PM-J could easily expand its labor force with younger employees. Unfortunately, the company is small and foreign; in reducing the perceived qualifications of its salesforce it will suffer a further loss of credibility conferred on employees holding an engineering degree from a respected university.

Maintaining Status Quo

Staying with the status quo is another strategy. PM-J could continue using mid-career people. Most of these employees have been recruited from the joint venture partner, TEC. This method is relatively inexpensive, because the initial recruitment, selection, and training costs are absorbed by TEC since the engineers began employment there. An advantage of this method is that the engineers with 25 to 30 years' experience have far more business contacts than do fresh graduates. The principle disadvantage is that one cannot be certain that the TEC engineers are quality employees. After all, why should TEC give up its best people to PM-J and retain the marginal employees for its own use? It's quite conceivable that the joint venture could be receiving some of the less productive TEC personnel. This also perpetuates the current dilemma of a salesforce in its early to mid-50s, which does not assist the company's image, credibility, or ability to capture the difficult Japanese market.

A further complication in PM-J's reliance on TEC's transferred employees is that many mid-career professionals may be loyal to their previous employer; this will not result in a highly motivated salesforce which will be prepared to endeavor diligently to promote a new employer in the market.

Supplementing the Status Quo

Another strategic option is to supplement the status quo (hiring mid-career professional engineers) with headhunters and/or employment agencies such as the Recruit Center. Headhunters are more prevalent in the Japanese labor market recently, and many Japanese companies report some successes in employing their services. Even though such agencies and headhunters are quite expensive and time-consuming, they do represent one means in filling gaps created by internal rotations of employees or vacancies resulting from terminated employees. Perhaps the most likely recruit from headhunting would be in the 28- to 30-year-old range who is making a career move. Although not fresh from school, these engineers would still be relatively recent university graduates with respectively longer career lives ahead of them. This would tend to stabilize PM-J's engineering and salesforce turnover while simultaneously conferring the credibility to be gained from the honored university degree.

Toward an Appraisal of These Options

The likely success of these various strategies clearly depends on the prospective state of the Japanese engineer labor market. PM-J's hiring success will be directly enhanced by any developments which reduce the number of engineers absorbed by the rest of Japanese industry and by its ability to gain credibility as a stable "Japanese" company. Indirect effects are also possible.

For example, it's likely that any developments which loosen the supply of male engineers will make it even more difficult for female engineers to be accepted, especially in sales. Thus, a reliable forecast of engineering labor market conditioned in Japan is central to any strategy recommendation to PM – J.

Future Labor Market Developments

Effects of an Aging Workforce

The Japanese labor force and population has aged in recent years, pressuring the social insurance and retirement systems, similar to the U.S. situation. This has led the government to explore postponing pension age from about 60 to 65. The Japanese employment system for engineers (among other professions) initially moves employees in the 50 to 55 age range to secondary employment (within the firm) or to other employers.[1] Since the government has made early pension less likely, it seems that in coming years more men will seek longer second careers. As noted, this would dampen women's employability. It would also increase the availability of engineering resources to a company like PM-J.

The Decline of New Workers

The declining number of young people entering the labor market and the declining pool of new engineering graduates implies that small companies like PM-J are more likely to be squeezed out of the market. Based on present hiring patterns, 80% of the graduates of the top 10 Japanese engineering schools would be recruited and absorbed by a select group of employers consisting of the largest domestic and foreign organizations. This tightening of the youth market decreases the viability of a strategy aimed at hiring fresh graduates into small, foreign companies.

Foreign Product Competition and the Japanese Labor Market

One must consider the labor market effects of opening Japanese product markets to foreign competition. If Japan concedes to growing pressure from its allies to reduce import tariffs and trade barriers, who will be hit hardest? Which Japanese industries will be hurt by a policy of greater import penetration into Japan? First of all, it is not probable that agriculture will be hit heavily. Even though Japanese food prices are three to six times the world level, it's unlikely that the government would chance eroding its support base among small farmers. This is due to the fact that import restriction policies have supported the relatively large agricultural population who have in turn faithfully supported the incumbent government party, the Liberal Democrats, since the late 1940s.

Are import penetration liberalizations for non-agricultural products apt to affect big companies like Matsushita, Hitachi, or Asahi? These firms run the Japanese "economic

---

[1]The age-related pay system (nenko), plus the common decline of productivity after a certain age older workers tend to become more and more expensive rapidly.

miracle" and are closely tied to government policy through the coordinating activities of the Ministry of International Trade and Industry. Such an alliance between government and big business is likely to forestall serious import impacts on the key companies. Thus, won't any opening of Japanese markets to U.S. imports probably be designed to have the most impact on items produced by smaller businesses? As these smaller businesses cut back on employment, won't they have the effect of loosening the labor market exactly where PM-J is located (in terms of company size)?

Political considerations aside, it is also true that small-scale industry in Japan has much higher labor costs (relative to larger enterprises) than in the United States or Germany (another major trading country), as seen in Exhibit 4. Increased foreign product-market competition and a resulting loosening of the smaller-company labor market would increase a surviving small foreign company's ability to recruit and retain qualified employees.

Exhibit 4. Relative Labor Costs in Manufacturing by Size of Enterprise

Number of Employees	Japan (1985)	USA (1977)	West Germany (1977)
1-9	136		N/A
10-49	129	102	97
50-99	124		101
100-499	108	92	102
500-999	97		99
1000 and more	100	100	100

Source: Toward a More Vital Society, Japan Federation of Employers Assns., 1985

To the extent that Japanese trade policy is liberalized, PM-J should be more successful on all fronts in trying to hire engineers in competition with Japanese firms. On the other hand, the staffing demands of other foreign firms which either expand or enter Japan as a result of this trade policy liberalization will have to be taken into account.

Product Market Issues

Having considered some major human resource dynamics affecting PM-J's penetration into the Japanese market, it is necessary to review what product market considerations are relevant to the company's success of PM-J in the Japanese market.

Standards are most frequently mentioned as problems or barriers by would-be American importers of technical equipment. Japanese standards are simply not the same as the United States' and are very difficult to understand or change. With respect to the "cash cow gauge," PM-J spent six or seven years on the standards acceptance process.

The biggest issue regarding the product market is the prospect for increased penetration of imports into the Japanese market. Japanese government policy on this is evolving. During the spring of 1985, as PM-J grappled with the strategic issues, Prime Minister Nakasone undertook his famous shopping trip, urging all Japanese to spend 25,000 additional yen on foreign goods. Whether this will help sell PM-J's product is doubtful, since its principal applications are industrial. But if it becomes easier for foreign firms to bid on government jobs (pursuant to GATT agreements), PM-J might see a direct sales payoff in major government projects.

Issues from this Case

There are at least two preliminary issues for the student to address in this case.

First, Is TEC doing its job? Are they providing qualified people to the joint venture, PM-J, or are they "dumping" marginal employees who are past their peak performance and on the downslide?

The second preliminary issue that the student should address is whether PM-J's pay scale is appropriate. Data in Exhibit 2 provide comparisons with big companies' pay levels.

The Longer-Run Labor Market Strategy Options

The student should identify the risks, benefits and costs of various alternatives (including staffing options) against the backdrop of various "states of the world." Those states of the world will be dominated by the degree to which government policy changes so that PM-J (or more radically, a lot of foreign competition) is able to penetrate domestic markets in Japan. Some engineering labor market strategies will be higher risk and lower risk, with higher and lower costs and payoffs, depending what one thinks will happen to, the engineering labor market and PM-J's ability to penetrate the product market. Although Japanese government policies on foreign access to markets may dominate the scene, other things that will impinge upon the labor market should be considered:

- the aging population
- shortages of youth entering the labor force
- increased numbers of people (early to mid-50s) seeking longer second careers
- increased number of women seeking positions
- changing Japanese culture and labor markets

Considering the case as a whole, the basic issue can be starkly posed: How should PM-J attempt to recruit enough people to permit an effective penetration of the Japanese product market on which the survival not only of PM-J, but of its parent PMI, may depend?

24. Bringing HR into the Business*

Mike Mitchell left the Bank of Montreal to become vice president of human resources at the North American branch of the Swiss Bank Corporation (SBC) in the autumn of 1993. It was a move up for him in terms of status, responsibility, monetary compensation and challenge. Of these, it was the challenge that was most intriguing to Mitchell. In his mid-30s, he saw this as perfect time to take a risk in his career. He realized that if he succeeded he would establish a prototype that could be marketed to other firms. In addition, success could lead to further career opportunities (and challenges). While he had a general idea of what he wanted to do and had gotten verbal support from his superiors, the senior vice president of human resources and the president of SBC, North America, the details of exactly what he was going to do and how he was going to do it, remained to unfold.

In 1992 the parent company of SBC (a $110 billion universal bank) headquartered in Basel, Switzerland decided it needed a clearer statement of its intentions to focus its energies and resources in light of the growing international competition. Accordingly, it crafted a vision statement to the effect that the bank was going to better serve its customers with high quality products that served their needs rather than just those of the institution. While the North American operation was relatively autonomous, it was still expected to embrace this vision. The details of its implementation, however, were in local hands. For the human resources side, the hands became those of Mitchell.

While Mitchell had spent some time in human resources at the Bank of Montreal in New York, the bulk of his work experience was as an entrepreneur in Monteal, Canada. It was this experience that impacted his thinking the most. Thus when he came to the SBC, his self-image was a business person who happened to be working in human resources. It was in part because of this image that his stay at the Bank of Montreal was brief: human resources was still a bit too conservative for his style. Too many of his ideas "just couldn't be done." In interviewing with the top managers at SBC, however they warned him of the same general environment. He thus knew he would have to go slow to change almost 1000 employees including his own department of 10 employees, but he really didn't know what this meant. He knew, however, that he wanted to reposition and "customerize" the HR department at SBC. He knew that this was necessary to connect the HR department to the business.

He identified the four major aspects for his program to reposition and customerize the HR department so that it could become current with the state of the art and practice and so that it could be connected to the business (and develop a customer-focus attitude). The four aspects included: gathering information; developing action agendas; implementing those agendas; and then evaluating and revising those agendas.

Gathering Information. Finding out how things are involves asking the customers, diagnosing the environment and asking the HR department itself. From the customers Mitchell learns the nature of the business strategy and how HR generally can fit with or, help that strategy. He also learns what they now get from the HR department, what would be the ideal, and how the

---

*This case was prepared by Randall S. Schuler, who expresses his appreciation for the cooperation of Michael Mitchell.

ideal could best be delivered. This analysis is done for each activity in HR as well as the entire department and the staff. From the environment Mitchell learns what other companies are doing with their HR departments and their HR practices. He looks at competitors and those in other industries in order to see the possibilities for the entire department and for each HR activity. From the HR department he learns how they see themselves in relation to servicing their customers; their knowledge of strategy; how they think the customers perceive the department; and their desire to improve, to be the best or whatever they want.

Developing Agendas. Making agendas based upon this information is the second aspect of Mitchell's plan. This involves feeding the information back to the HR department and letting them draw up plans (agendas) for resolving any discrepancies between what they are doing and what their customers want. But in order for the department to do this they really need to determine a vision of themselves what they want to be vis-a-vis themselves and the rest of the organization. They also need to determine if their current ways of operating and its current structure are sufficient to move ahead. If not, then the HR department needs to get themselves reorganized. This can be occurring while they are developing the agendas. The HR department may need to get new skills if they are to be successful in implementing their new vision (especially if they decide to be current and customer-oriented). Once the vision starts taking shape and the agendas drawn up, the HR department can establish a game plan for how they will get their agendas implemented. They then need to get line approval for moving ahead with the implementation. Top management and line managers immediately impacted should give approval.

Implementing the Agendas. This third aspect involves the HR department going out and meeting with the customers to discuss the agendas. While this aspect will involve responding to specific needs of the line managers, it may also involve selling the line managers on other activities. Now that the HR department is being more strategic and customer-oriented, they will begin to develop programs that go beyond the regular administrative activities and services that it generally provides the line managers. These will be based upon the ideas of the HR department. They will get these ideas upon their knowledge of the strategy, the competitors, what other successful firms are doing and their knowledge of HR practices. Because these services are new, they will need to be sold to their customers, at least at first. Once successful they will develop a demand of their own. So in addition to implementing the specifically agreed upon agendas and contracts, this aspect will include developing and implementing (and selling) new programs.

Evaluating and Revising. Part and parcel of the agenda setting is the development of contracts. These specify what will be delivered to the customer. The customer then has the right to appraise the work delivered. Based on these appraisals by the line managers, the agendas become evaluated. Revisions and adjustments can then be made for improvements the next time around. The contracts, however, may not be the only way to appraise the work of the HR department. Other criteria may be used (although they could be put into the contract) based on the desire of the HR department. Such criteria could include the reduction in turnover from better selection procedures or an increase in the number of new ideas or innovations from a change in the HR practices to facilitate the innovative strategy of the business.

Implications for the HR Department

There are several implications for the HR department (Mitchell and his staff) in their efforts to reposition and customerize.

1. A major one is the need for the HR department to be re-oriented. Its mind set has to be strategic and customer-oriented.
2. The HR department needs to become a constant gatherer of information: from the internal environment and the external environment. They need to know the opportunities and the possibilities for HR practices and how to implement these ideas with and for the line managers. Consequently, they need to know the competition, the business strategy and how the competition can be beat in relation to the current assets of the company and those that they could or need to develop.
3. The HR department needs to identify what level of excellence they want to attain. In doing so they will identify the speed and quality at which they will be a strategic player and fulfill their managerial and operational roles.
4. HR managers and staff will need to work closely with the line managers in designing systems to get them the needed services and information. They will need to work with the line managers to develop contracts by which the HR department will be evaluated by the line managers.
5. The HR department will be changed so that there is more of a generalist rather than a specialist orientation. There will be a greater team orientation also.
6. Things will never be the same. This goes for the HR department and the entire competitive marketplace. This means that the HR professionals in the department will be always on the go, gathering, servicing, evaluating, revising and most of all listening. And because the business will be changing all the time, the HR department will need to always be changing what it delivers. Nonetheless the opportunities for making things better and the company and its people more competitive and successful are endless and challenging!

Implications for the Line Managers

There are also several implications in the repositioning and customerization program for line managers.

1. The line managers need to work closely with Mitchell and his staff to gather information on what is now happening and what is desired. Line managers will also have to share their views on the strategy of their business with Mitchell. Together, they become partners in the business. The line managers need to be willing to accept a new role being played by Mitchell and his HR staff.
2. The line managers need to work closely with the HR staff in developing the agendas for action. They need to be willing to spend time with the staff to look at each of the HR activities now being provided by the HR department.
3. The line managers need to work with the HR staff in appraising the success of the HR efforts. They do this through the development and use of the contracts established with the staff.

4.   The line managers need to be ready to talk with and listen to Mitchell, his staff as they propose new programs to improve the chances for gaining competitive advantage through the use of human resources.

The Benefits from the Partnership

The results of this partnership may be well worth the costs involved in the changes necessary to ensure repositioning and customerization. As far as Mitchell is concerned, there are several products from a repositioning and customerization program. They include:

- enhancing the quality and responsiveness of the HR department
- developing the HR department in terms of new jobs (skillwise), providing new excitment and building commitment to the company's mission, goals and strategies
- HR becoming linked with the business
- HR becoming integrated with the corporate strategy
- HR becoming market or customer-oriented and gains a flexibility to respond to and anticipate changes
- criteria being developed by which to evaluate and revise the behaviors of the HR department
- HR gaining an ability to develop and use HR practices to gain competitive advantage
- HR gaining an awareness of the potential ways different HR practices can be done by constantly monitoring what other successful companies are doing
- HR becoming more keenly aware of the internal and external environment
- standard products of the HR department being provided more efficiently
- new products and services being developed
- software being developed as a way to deliver the new products
- new services and products being sold outside the company
- the HR department changing dramatically and consequently becomes an example for the rest of the company regarding change
- the HR department becoming a place where everyone wants to work
- HR's services and products becoming sought after

Discussion Questions

1.   Who are the customers of Mitchell and his HR staff?
2.   What must Mitchell do in order for his staff to be able to do the things necessary to reposition and customerize?
3.   Do you think that the line managers will cooperate with Mitchell and his staff? What will it take to see that they do? What would be their reasons for resisting a partnership with the HR department?
4.   Develop a matrix with projects, dates, milestones and people involved (i.e., HR, line managers and employees) for Mitchell and his staff.

25. The Tall Pines Hotel and Conference Center*

Gordon McGregor sorted through his morning mail to find the report from Natalie Sharp about the open house sponsored by the hotel for job applicants. With the sounds of hammering and the smell of fresh paint all around, he was eager to get a picture of his new staff as he neared the opening of the hotel in about two months. He pushed aside samples of carpeting left by a subcontractor this morning to read the five-page report from Natalie.

As hotel manager, Gordon was faced with the last of the major hurdles in getting Tall Pines open – the filling of about 315 positions ranging from bellhops and butchers to clerks and chambermaids. The grand opening scheduled for May first made it imperative to bring his full staff on board and get them trained and operational quickly. He had brought in most of his managerial and supervisory staff over the past six months. Many had come from other hotels in the nationwide chain. Some he had worked with in other parts of the chain in his fifteen years in the system, so there was a sense of excitement about being together as a team to create something brand new. Today marked the beginning of the final phase of his plan to manage his own hotel successfully.

The Tall Pines Hotel

Gordon had been involved in the planning of the hotel for about two years. Corporate management had selected the site four years ago on the basis of a careful study by its market research staff of the southeastern part of the United States. They were interested in launching a new concept in hotels and had chosen the city of Riverton (pop. 95,000), located in the suburbs of Roosevelt City, a major city in the Southeast. The entire metropolitan area had grown dramatically since the early 1960s to a total population of about 1.9 million, with further growth forecast for the next fifteen years before a leveling off would occur.

Riverton comprised about half the area and two-thirds the population of one of the counties that surrounded Roosevelt City. Growth in population, wealth, and industry had been concentrated in the suburban counties, although there was new interest in the revitalization of the old downtown area. Riverton had been especially aggressive in its plan to attract new industry with the creation of an economic development committee, which had been successful in enticing a number of high-technology firms to open offices or build small facilities within the city limits. Many offices had moved from Roosevelt into the suburbs to take advantage of lower taxes, new buildings, and a pool of skilled workers. Shopping centers, restaurants, and housing developments mushroomed to meet the demands of the population shift.

Corporate management saw the opportunity to fill a niche in the suburbs because of lack of hotel and conference space. They purchased an eighteen-acre tract on a major highway that entered Roosevelt City from the south on the west side of Riverton. It was to be developed as a campuslike setting with the preservation of two major pine groves and the expansion of a natural lake. The hotel had been constructed in line with these plans to include 350 rooms, two swimming pools, three restaurants, small shops, and a small exercise and weight room. An outdoor jogging trail was being completed as well. The conference center was built to cater to

---

*Reprinted by permission of D. Jeffrey Lenn, George Washington University, 1986.

corporate meetings with secretarial services, teleconferencing facilities, and even access to personal computers. The entire facility was oriented toward comfortable stays of extended periods as well as overnight lodging.

An architect of national reputation had designed the building to become a focal point for the surrounding area. Twin towers jutted through the pines to provide the foundation for a five-story atrium. The glass enclosure provided light and freshness to the restaurants and public space below. The building was striking as viewed from the interstate in both directions, standing boldly against the horizon and rising from the pine groves. Tall Pines was a particularly appropriate name for the entire center, which could act as a comfortable retreat from both city activity and corporate life.

The building had also been controversial. The Riverton Board of Architectural Review was besieged by complaints about the design. But support from the city council and the mayor dissolved the opposition quickly. Projections of a $3.8 million payroll and annual tax bills of $350,000 for the city and $420,000 for the state made the entire project highly appealing. The board voted unanimously to accept the architectural plans.

Natalie Sharp, Director of Personnel

Last November, Gordon had hired Natalie Sharp to become his director of personnel. She had worked for two other hotel chains after college and then been hired three years ago to help with the opening of a new one-hundred-room hotel in the Southwest. She had done an outstanding job of staffing this hotel set in the center of an older city undergoing major renovation. Corporate management was enthusiastic about her potential and had urged Gordon to consider her for the job. Two days of interviews at Tall Pines confirmed this potential as well as the experience he needed in opening a new hotel.

Natalie was given the responsibility for the entire staffing process, although Gordon had made it clear that his department managers had the final authority for those working in their departments. Supervisory personnel were hired with Natalie confirming managerial decisions and working out job descriptions, salaries, and other specifics for each position.

Her major task was the recruitment and hiring program for the bulk of the staff to ready the hotel for opening on May first. She and Gordon had met in the middle of January to review her plan. She had worked closely with the state Department of Employment Services as well as Riverton's Employment Options Office to arrange for a Job Fair on February fifteenth. Held at a local school on a Saturday, the fair was designed to attract candidates and provide a screening session and even some first-round interviews. Tall Pines would provide a good package of benefits on top of a competitive wage:

- Blue Cross/Blue Shield
- Paid vacation (after one year)
- Pension plan (vested after seven years)
- On-site job training
- Educational benefits

Natalie had convinced Gordon that although minimum wage would be the controlling factor for many entry-level positions, the promise of raises in six months was needed as an inducement for retention of good employees.

Natalie believed that the primary pool of candidates would be found in Roosevelt City and Riverton. The figures provided by a local government agency supported her belief that a number of people would apply for the various positions to be filled.

Local Unemployment Rates*	
Metropolitan area	3.7%
Roosevelt City	8.1
Riverton	5.0
All suburbs	3.7
*December figures.	

An advertising campaign directed toward the larger metropolitan area, coupled with state and city support, should yield at least double the number of candidates needed for each position. Natalie had shown Gordon a series of articles in the Metro Star, the major daily, about a large hotel opening last year in the center of Roosevelt City. Over 11,000 applications were made for 350 positions; the articles included pictures of long lines of people trying to get through the door for interviews. Tall Pines would find an eager group ready to work at its hotel.

The Disappointing Report

The note of optimism of last month was missing from the short report on yesterday's Job Fair. Just over 200 people had applied for the 315 positions. Of these, only 75 had been screened and interviewed. Most had little experience in the hotel business but seemed capable of on-the-job training. The applicants were mostly from the surrounding towns in the county and Riverton, with a few from Roosevelt City.

Natalie had done an informal survey of her small cadre of interviewers late in the afternoon. Applicants had concerns about wage scales and transportation. Unskilled workers with some experience found it difficult to believe that they would start at minimum wage, saying that they could get more at many fast-food chains. Three employees from Big Tex, a regional hamburger chain, had come to the fair together and reported that the chain had just upped starting salaries for counter help to seventy-five cents above minimum wage. Natalie's follow-up call to Big Tex, as well as her conversation with a representative of the county chamber of commerce, had confirmed that many employers were offering hourly wages in excess of minimum wage simply to fill empty positions.

The concerns about transportation were more difficult to bring into focus. Natalie pieced together a picture of Tall Pines being out of the way for most people using public transportation. A few asked about whether the hotel planned to provide bus transportation into Roosevelt City. It had taken them nearly an hour from home with a transfer from a subway stop onto a bus, which dropped them off about three blocks away. Riverton residents indicated that it took thirty minutes to get over from the east side of the city, which meant crossing the interstate because the bus route ended there. Location clearly was a factor in keeping applicants away.

The Stream of Telephone Calls

Gordon's optimism about his gala opening was suddenly deflated by this report. Natalie's conclusion was concisely stated in one sentence:

> I have arranged another Job Fair in ten days with the hope that our results will be better this time.

He wondered whether there would be enough candidates for the remaining positions and whether there would be enough time to train them after all of the necessary personnel paperwork had been completed.

His thoughts were interrupted by a call from his secretary indicating that a reporter was on the line from the Riverton Telegram, asking questions about the Job Fair. He directed the call to Natalie's office. A call from the Metro Star was also redirected. But he did take a call from the Riverton mayor's office to assure them that the hotel had the hiring situation under control with the opening still set for May first. Later in the afternoon, the director of one of the associations scheduled to hold a conference at the hotel during the first week called to ask about the opening. Bad news travels fast! thought Gordon as he hung up with another set of assurances to the anxious director.

Natalie sailed into the office to report on the two phone calls from the press. Both had received information about the disappointing turnout at the Job Fair and were interested in both the reasons and the impact on the opening. She thought that it would be difficult to assess the impact of the publicity until the morning editions were out. Gordon suggested a breakfast meeting with the hotel's top staff to discuss the problem and work toward a solution.

The Breakfast Staff Meeting

Both papers covered the story with short articles hidden away in the second sections. The Telegram headline read:

NEW HOTEL NEEDS 240 WORKERS

It briefly described the low turnout at the Job Fair with a listing of the positions still available. A quote from Natalie indicated that another fair would be held in the near future. The story was done in a generally favorable light with emphasis on new business within Riverton, which the hotel should attract.

The Star headline was more critical:

NEW SUBURBAN HOTEL SURPRISED
TO FIND FEW APPLY FOR 315 JOBS

The new twin towers were pictured along with a sheet from the fair that listed the jobs available at the hotel. Natalie was quoted about the continuing search to be carried out as well as the types of benefits offered by Tall Pines. A representative of the Roosevelt City Office of Job Services was quoted: "It's not so much that people here won't look in the suburbs; it's that once you cross over that city line, there is a mental barrier about being away from home. Employers have to offer good jobs, good transportation, and a lot of encouragement to get people to apply." A union office spokesman wondered whether people were discouraged because Tall Pines is a nonunion hotel. A man who had been offered a second interview at the fair indicated that he would rather work close to his home in Roosevelt City, but had been out of work for four months and needed the job.

Gordon and Natalie agreed that neither article gave a negative perspective on hotel management, but questions could be raised about postponement of the opening. Clearly, it was important to follow up with the Riverton mayor's office as well as meeting planners who had scheduled the hotel opening for May and June to assure them that the situation would be under control. Contact with the Roosevelt City Office of Job Services was mandatory now.

At the meeting, Gordon asked Natalie to review her report as well as the press clippings for the assembled department heads. They both answered a number of questions about the Job Fair and the type of applicants at the fair. Gordon suggested that they delay the discussion about the future until later in the meeting so that all of the facts surrounding the problem could be sorted through carefully. It became clear that many departments could operate for the first two weeks in May on a reduced staffing pattern using supervisory personnel to fill in. But a full staff was essential to accommodate the anticipated increase in business.

The meeting then turned to a brainstorming session to help Natalie develop a strategy for attracting people who would be good candidates to fill the remaining positions. The group agreed that four areas merited further consideration:

- *Advertising campaign*
  Directed particularly toward Roosevelt City and Riverton with focus on benefits of working at Tall Pines.
- *Upgrade of wage scale*
  Additions to minimum wage for entry-level jobs in order to be competitive.
  Necessity for incentive pay to retain good employees.
- *Transportation system*
  Necessity for assistance to workers coming from both Riverton and Roosevelt City in particular because of their reliance on public transportation.
- *Cooperation with public agencies*
  Cultivation of relationships with a number of agencies to identify other applicant pools.

Gordon asked Natalie to make use of these ideas in the development of a plan to fill the 240 remaining positions. He assured the managers that he would call them the next day with a finalized plan to meet the objective of full staffing by May first. In the meantime, he would handle the public relations aspect of the issue through his office. The meeting adjourned with an agreement that any hotel was only as good as its personnel.

Reflections Over Lunch

As manager of Tall Pines, Gordon enjoyed a number of prerequisites unavailable in other jobs. Today, he was delighted to initiate one of those – access to the best meals from the hotel kitchens. Jack Sanders, the sales and convention manager, wheeled in a cart of delectable dishes prepared by one of the French chefs interviewing for the position as head chef. Expecting to join Gordon for lunch, he set a small table for two and uncorked a bottle of wine. As he settled into one of the chairs and pulled out his napkin, Gordon interrupted: "Sorry, Jack. This is a working lunch for me with all of this hiring mess on my mind. You're welcome to take a plate back to your office, but I need to be alone to get a handle on this situation." Jack excused himself, a full plate and wineglass in hand, while Gordon settled into his chair.

The meal was excellent, with the wine chosen for its appropriate balance with the food. Gordon thought about his fortunate managerial situation – no fast-food lunches, no traveling throughout the week, and no narrow job responsibilities. All of these were left behind for any hotel manager. There was a sense of excitement about what lay in store for him both here at Tall Pines and within the larger national organization as it expanded.

But the past day had drowned out much of that excitement. What seemed so close to completion was now filled with a number of questions. Could Tall Pines attract a good staff? Could they be trained and on the job by May first? How costly was it going to be to pay a competitive wage? Could he instill within the staff a sense of pride about Tall Pines? Could the hotel open on May first?

The smell of paint, the carpet samples, and even the faint sound of hammers now came into fuller focus as he asked the last question. Where had he gone wrong in the development of his plan to open the hotel? Why didn't he foresee a potential problem about staffing earlier? Getting the right people seemed like the easiest of his plans to implement. Now it looked like an impossible task. With a cup of coffee in hand, he moved back to his desk to begin the process of solving the problem he faced.

26. A Broader View Seizes More Opportunities*

Don English, corporate vice president in charge of human resources, is now finally able to take a pause from the continuous stream of fire fighting activity he has been engaged in since he came to Bancroft ten years ago! Like many of his colleagues in other firms, Don's knowledge of human resource management came as much from doing it as anything else.

His constant fire fighting activity tended to keep him pretty narrowly focused. Because of his workload, he rarely read personnel journals or attended professional conferences. However, recently, things have been easing up. He has been able to recruit and train almost all the division managers in charge of human resources. Now they can do most of the fire fighting, at least that's what Don is planning on. And he has been doing more reading than ever before. Of course, Dan has not been totally out of touch with the rest of the world or the growing importance of human resource management planning. When he started filling the slots for division personnel managers he made sure that it was a learning experience for him. Don always required job candidates to prepare a one hour talk on the state of research and practice in different areas of personnel, e.g., selection, appraisal, compensation and training. He would even invite MBA candidates who had no course work in personnel and ask them to relate their field of interest to human resource management.

Don is planning to become the chief executive officer of Bancroft or some other firm of similar or larger size within the next five to seven years. He thinks he can achieve this if he remains in human resources and does an outstanding job. He will have to be outstanding by all standards, both internal and external to the firm. From his interviews during the past three years, Don knows that it is imperative to move human resources in a strategic direction while at the same time doing the best possible job with the "nuts and bolts" activities.

During a moment of reflection, Don begins to scratch some notes on his large white desk pad. In the middle is Bancroft. To its left are its suppliers and to its right are its customers. In his head are all the human resource practices he is so familiar with. He has a hunch that there must be a way to use the firm's expertise in performance appraisal and training to help Bancroft be more effective. Bancroft has been learning tremendously from its five-year drive to improve quality but during the past year, quality gains have slowed. Bancroft must continue to improve its quality, but large internal quality gains are becoming more and more difficult as Bancroft climbs the learning curve. Don wonders: How can he help Bancroft experience the excitement of seeing large gains in quality improvement again? Don circles the list of suppliers and begins to formulate a plan that will improve his chances of becoming CEO. He now seeks your advice in exactly what to do and how to go about doing it.

Discussion Questions

1. Let's assume that Don has gotten the approval from his boss to help Bancroft's suppliers. Should he work with them all or decide to just start with one or two and see how it goes?
2. If Don can do anything to help his suppliers with their human resource management activities, what should he focus on the most?
3. Should Don actually go into the suppliers and do their HR work or should he train the suppliers' HR professionals at Bancroft?

*This case was prepared by Randall S. Schuler, Stern School of Business, New York University.

27. Northeast Data Resources, Inc.*

George Wellington closed the door behind him and slumped into his desk chair with an air of resignation. He had just returned from a meeting of the Executive Committee of Northeast Data Resources where personnel layoffs had been decided upon. As a director of personnel at NDR, he realized that he would be responsible for both developing the process by which the layoffs would take place and assisting the managers responsible for the actual implementation. It wasn't a pleasant task, particularly in light of the human resources program that he had begun to implement over the past four years.

Wellington pulled out a pad of paper from the top desk drawer and began to scribble notes. He had found that in times of pressure it was best to get some perspective on the situation before taking action. The drastic character of this situation required a review of the growth of Northeast Data Resources from its inception in 1969 to the present. It was the first crisis the young company had been forced to face.

Background of the Company

In 1969, four young engineers formed a partnership to form the basis of NDR. Three of them had worked for a large, national data-processing company. They had recognized the high potential in the computer industry particularly for a product which filled a vital need in this growing field. Another engineer working in a research program with a large university was asked to join them because of his expertise in the computer field.

Jack Logan was the prime mover of the new company. He had been working for nearly five years on a project within the large company to develop ways to protect its computer systems from being copied by competitors. The primary objective in this project was to ensure that a customer would have to purchase the entire system rather than being able to make use of a number of different systems. Jack saw the opportunity to sell a service to customers that would do just the opposite – provide a mechanism that would link various competing systems into an integrated unit.

He and a colleague, Charlie Bonner, developed a "black box" which had the capacity to connect at least two types of computer systems already on the market. They had worked in Jack's basement over a two-year period to perfect this instrument. Another six months of testing found that it was very effective. The two other engineers had begun to work with them in order to expand the box to tie together three other systems with which they had experience.

The four men decided to strike out on their own and found that their innovation and daring paid off. The first two years were both exhilarating and demanding. NDR subcontracted the production of the black box to a small manufacturing company while the partners divided responsibilities between marketing and continuing research. Jack and Charlie carried the marketing and organizational functions while George Miller and Al Grant worked to streamline the instrument itself.

---

*This case was prepared by D. Jeffrey Lenn, School of Government and Business Administration, The George Washington University. It is not meant to be an example of effective or ineffective personnel and human resource management but an example for teaching and discussion purposes. Reprinted by permission.

Early success in securing contracts with some key customers and fears about loss of the exclusive information about the unpatented invention led to a decision to go into full production. An old plant was leased and renovated and workers were hired to begin the process of building the black box for distribution. Within two years the company had grown from four partners to nearly 100 people. By 1976 NDR had expanded to about 700 people and had become the focus of attention for a number of investors. The invention, now dubbed Omega I, had become a product competitors emulated but with little success.

Logan assumed the responsibilities of chairman and president with Bonner as executive vice-president in charge of operations. Miller and Grant stayed in the lab with more interest in research and development, being willing to act more in advisory capacity on managerial decisions.

Logan saw the need to consolidate and expand the overall operations of the company. Production and distribution now overflowed into three buildings separated by nearly ten miles. He negotiated a contract with the economic development committee of Newbury, a New England town about forty miles away, to help construct a new building to house headquarters and plant. The town agreed to help NDR through reduced taxes, water, and sewage hookups at a minimal charge, arrangements with local banks to secure a loan for construction of the plant, and development of a federal grant to train new workers at the plant. In exchange, NDR agreed to move its entire operation to Newbury within the next two years. It helped Newbury in its search for new industry while assuring NDR of a secure base of operations for the future.

The Newbury headquarters was only forty miles from the old facilities so NDR lost few of its present staff because of the change. But the growth in business demanded an increase in personnel. Engineers with sophisticated skills in computer science were hired to expand the system capability. Often, international engineers were the only ones available and the importation of English and Australians with a spattering of Europeans gave an international flair to the small company. New factory workers from Newbury and surrounding towns were hired so that the production shifts could be expanded from one to two. The training grants secured by the town helped to equip new workers and the integration with more experienced workers moved smoothly. Empty managerial slots required hiring from the outside mostly. A new vice-president of manufacturing came from a large industrial company in the Midwest. The new vice-president of finance had a solid resume which included most recently financial experience with a large conglomerate but before that two stints with growing companies much like NDR. The staffing of the growing company proceeded professionally.

Future of the Company

The phenomenal growth of NDR in old industrial New England rivaled the computer companies developing in California's Silicon Valley. The workforce had evolved from 4 in 1969 to 100 in 1971, 700 in 1976, and 1,350 by 1982. Sales increased from two small initial contracts in 1969 of $75,000 to nearly $59 million by 1982. In 1975, NDR went public and was listed on the New York Stock Exchange in 1980. The opening price of 7 moved to between 8 and 9 and hovered there in 1981. But a feature article in a national stock advisory report about NDR led to an upward move in the summer in 1982 to 15. Even without paying a dividend in its thirteen years of existence, it had become an attractive investment.

Logan had taken time during the summer of 1982 to begin the process of strategic planning.

Convinced that he and his executive committee could and should do this alone, he decided not to engage outside consultants to develop a costly set of plans. His projection was that the computer industry would grow nearly ten times in size over the next decade. Conservatively the company could expect to hold its share of the market which meant a doubling of sales in five years to $120 million and up to $210 million by 1992. Expansion was the key to maintaining market share and holding its own against the handful of competitors which had begun to appear by 1982.

In shaping the strategy, Logan began to map out a new marketing plan which would guarantee NDR's position in the national market instead of the eastern market alone. He saw new customer possibilities in the fields of insurance, financial institutions, and state and local governments. He negotiated an option to buy the factory of a watch company moving South. Its building was about thirty-five miles away in the heart of another old industrial New England town with a pool of skilled workers available to be retrained. He began to develop some ideas about how many new staff would be needed and the kind of capital necessary to finance this expansion.

George Wellington's Career at NDR

George stopped his writing and reviewed the rapid growth of NDR up to this point. He remembered vividly his first few months at the company in 1977. He had moved to a nearby town to retire in the serenity of New England. His career had begun immediately after completing his MBA from a leading eastern university where he had concentrated on management and personnel. He had begun work in the personnel area with a major corporation located in New York. Six years in the field had led him next into marketing and then strategic planning with another company. The last seven years had been with a prestigious consulting firm in New York where he had focused on a variety of problems for a host of clients. His decision to retire had been prompted by a dislike for traveling and a desire to settle down in the area where his children had located.

While retirement continued to bring part-time consulting work, George still found the travel excessive. But his ideas of relaxation in retirement quickly exposed his own need to be fully active in business to be happy. His search for a part-time job was successful as Jack Logan met him at a Chamber of Commerce luncheon in Newbury and hired him as a consultant to help with the transition from the old to the new facilities. He remembered the challenges associated with coordinating not only the efforts of NDR personnel but outside contractors and town officials as well.

The flawless nature of the transition into the new plant made the president recognize that he needed George full-time. Wellington agreed to stay only another six months as a special assistant to Logan. He carried out a variety of projects for Logan and quickly became an integral part of the management team at NDR.

The president called in George one day and showed him an organization chart which he was reworking. "George, I know that your six months are nearly up but I need you around here on a permanent basis. I just don't know where to put you on this chart. How about becoming director of personnel for NDR? That is the only important position which we haven't filled here in the past few months and it would allow me to have you close at hand for help on those big decisions."

George asked for some time to think through his decision and within a week agreed to a full-time position. While Logan still saw personnel as a somewhat unnecessary staff function, there would be a chance for George to help him understand the importance of human resources to this company.

Wellington began immediately to develop a plan for human resources at NDR. Logan encouraged him but wasn't excited about the use of the term "human resources." "I don't understand why you have to complicate this whole business of personnel with a new name. Why not still use the old 'personnel' for the department?" Logan asked. George saw a futile battle in this naming process so he clearly defined his function as that of director of personnel.

His plan for that function at NDR had three major elements:

The Program

Gathering Employee Information. He had his staff develop a file on each employee with a record of hiring date, previous experience and employers, salary, job title, etc. This was stored in a computer so that he could have rapid recall for evaluation.

Performance Appraisal System. He developed a new appraisal system which incorporated a three-page form to be completed twice a year by immediate supervisors. The annual review was tied to salary and bonus decisions. He experimented with it in two engineering sections over a two-year period and then was able to get Logan to mandate it for all of NDR beginning in 1981. The results from the 1981 – 82 year were compiled and filed for future use.

Personnel Policy Manual. In 1981, a new personnel policy manual was developed that detailed the policies and procedures as well as benefits for all personnel at NDR. There was some initial negative reaction by those who had enjoyed a variety of benefits from the early days of the company. But the imprint of Logan on the manual quelled the complaints and ensured uniformity in the policies.

EEO and Affirmative Action (AA) Program. The highly technical character of the NDR business and its presence in a small New England town made both EEO and AA difficult to pursue. A visit to Wellington by an EEO field investigator regarding the case of a former worker led him to move quickly to formulate this program. The data was gathered on minority hiring and promotion and then a plan designed for increasing the percentage of minorities in all categories and the number of women in management in particular. Logan resisted the immediate implementation of the program with the argument that the Reagan administration would soft-pedal civil rights in employment so that business people did not need to worry. George accepted this decision with reluctance but got an agreement to update the plan periodically as well as pursue informally a goal of more integration of the workforce.

Management Development Program. The rapid growth of NDR created many new managerial positions. Hiring from the outside became one method by which to increase the number of managers, but George believed that the key to the company's future lay in developing them from within. He negotiated a contract with a professor of management at a local university to design and teach a course in management for selected employees. George and the professor team-taught a six-week course for twenty middle level managers in 1980. Its success led to an offering three times a year to both managers and potential managers.

The Staff

George became director of personnel in the spring of 1979. He selected four professionals and two secretaries to work with him. Two professionals came from outside of NDR and two from within. All four had human resources management experience but needed more training. One was encouraged to enter an MBA program on a part-time basis with a concentration on human resource management. The other three were sent to local and national seminars to upgrade skills and understanding in the various areas of HRM. But at the heart of their training was George Wellington, drawing on his vast experience and encouraging his younger colleagues to learn through experimentation and discussion.

The Office Location

The final design of the NDR headquarters had not been decided when George became a consultant to the project so he had taken primary responsibility for the design of the corporate office area. Later, as director of personnel, he negotiated some changes in the office assignments so that personnel was located at one of the major entrances and exits of the building. It was a primary thoroughfare for engineers and managerial personnel arriving in the morning and leaving at night. It was also a stop along the way to the new cafeteria that had just opened.

George had chosen this location for a reason. He felt that human resources departments must have high visibility and availability. Being in the middle of a key thoroughfare allowed people to recognize the central function of personnel in the operation of NDR. It encouraged questions about policies and procedures. It also gave the HRM staff the chance to get to know all of the managers and professionals within a short period of time. This provided instant recognition and a capacity to deal with problems on a much more personal basis. George himself was always at his desk working before most of the staff arrived and usually left after 6:00 p.m. This gave him considerable visibility with managerial personnel who often worked late.

The images of the first few years were succeeded by thoughts about the past two months with his staff. He had begun to engage them in the planning process by asking them to think about NDR for the next five years. He had sketched out the growth projections of Logan and then provided some parameters within which to think about staffing. Each of his professional staff was to develop a short presentation on four consequences for HRM:

1. Impact on the size of our workforce.
2. Impact on the mix of skills needed in the workforce.
3. Impact on the recruitment efforts from outside NDR and development efforts from within.
4. Impact on the working conditions within the company itself, both physically and organizationally.

The first meeting four weeks ago had produced some very good reports. With one exception, the four had done a lot of homework and some imaginative thinking about the future with regard to how HRM plans would fit into the NDR overall strategic plan. George had collated and refined the projections and redistributed them to the professional staff asking for further thought and more specific targets for the next five years. He asked for input for his own report to the president, which he had hoped would be ready by December 1982.

The Present Dilemma

That work had now come to an abrupt halt although he had not alerted the staff to the discussion taking place within the executive committee until the day before. Logan's projections about the future had been overly optimistic.

Two weeks ago, Logan had asked George to meet him at 8:00 p.m. He laid out a report on the results from the first quarter of this fiscal year and then a chart which traced the sales of the last nine quarters. The last two quarters showed a significant decline. Logan indicated to George that, "The decline is now a trend and not simply a blip on the screen as I had thought." The loss of five key contracts totaling nearly $5 million dollars over the past six months plus the entry of a new competitor in the southeastern market had been responsible for the dramatic sales drop. At the same time, profits had suffered as well because of the increased expenses from a decision to increase the size of the engineering and financial service departments. The president admitted that his projections had been too optimistic and that something had to be done immediately. The cash flow problem had emerged as the most important pressure in this situation. The budget had to be pared while efforts to increase revenue were intensified.

George studied the figures carefully and agreed reluctantly to both the conclusions and recommendations reached by Logan. The two men took some time to sort through the various options available but it always came back to drastic cuts in personnel. He urged Logan to call a meeting of the executive committee in the morning and provide the data to them with encouragement to diagnose the problem and solutions to it. He argued that any solution must be a product of consensus of the committee.

The meeting caught everybody by surprise as they had accepted the president's projections of growth despite a temporary decline in sales. Two weeks of intensive debate among the executives led to the meeting this morning which defined the exact personnel cuts to be made. It was agreed that twenty-five others from various departments would be laid off within the next two weeks. In addition, fifteen new marketing and sales personnel would be added as soon as possible to carry out a new marketing thrust aimed at a different market segment.

There had been heated discussion about the exact number to be laid off and hired, with considerable friction between the vice-presidents of production, engineering, and marketing. The blame for the crisis was shouldered by Logan who asked that the executives recognize that they had to work together to resolve this problem if the future of NDR was to be assured. Wellington as the director of personnel was given the task of coordinating the identification of the people to be laid off although the actual decision would rest in the hands of the three vice-presidents. There were no criteria for the decisions although all agreed that loyal and trusted employees who had been with NDR for a number of years should be released only as a last resort.

The Director's Responsibility

The acrimonious debate of the morning still echoed in George's ears that afternoon. He tore the pages on which he had been writing off the pad and began a new one as he started to determine how the layoffs should be handled. It was a far cry from the exuberance with which he had begun the process of developing a five-year human resource plan just two months ago. Cutbacks in personnel demanded the same precision and careful thought in planning and action as hiring and promotion. There was less excitement about retrenching than growing because it affected the livelihood of so many people.

George jotted down the important questions in three different areas as he mapped out his thinking on this problem.

1. *The Layoffs*
   • Criteria to be used?
   • Data available on employees?
   • Impact of EEO and AA on decisions?
   • Severance pay and benefits?
   • Procedure for layoffs?
2. *The New Hires*
   • Skills needed in marketing and sales?
   • Available resources for positions?
   • Salary and benefit package?
   • Procedure for hiring?
3. *The HRM Plan*
   • Immediate impact on HRM five-year plan?
   • What if only temporary reversal of growth trend? (Commitments to rehire or not?)
   • Impact on employee morale now and in future?

George recognized that he had a lot of work to do. He struggled to regain his sense of professionalism as he began to detail the options available to each of the questions. His days as a consultant and manager had given him little experience in the arena of layoffs. But Logan had given him the responsibility and he knew that the future of NDR would depend heavily on how it handled this crisis.

28. Frost, Inc. in Britain*

Frost, Inc. is a small manufacturing company with a single location near Grand Rapids, Michigan. Chad Frost, the grandson of the founder and current CEO, has moved the company during the 1980s from an old line manufacturing facility to a highly progressive, technologically sophisticated company. It employs the latest in CAD-CAM technology. It is now able to be one of the lowest cost producers of the highest quality door moldings and trim serving the manufacturing enterprises of the Midwest. The automobile companies are its biggest and most demanding customers. They want and get cost, quality and timeliness of delivery from any supplier.

Frost, Inc., has been able to survive and even prosper in this highly competitive and demanding industry of supplying the automobile industry by combining high technology with high involvement human resource management practices. Frost is famous in the Midwest for offering employment security to its employees if they commit themselves to flexible job assignments and retraining. Frost operates in a very open environment with few secretaries and few secrets. Being in the western part of Michigan has enabled Frost to attract a workforce dedicated to hard work and without the need to be represented by a union.

Over the past two years Frost has been supplying Nissan USA with door moldings and trim for its facilities in Tennessee. Nissan has been so impressed that it is now asking Frost to become a sole supplier for its new plant in Sunderland, England. While Chad Frost knows that the automobile business is a worldwide industry, he has no particular experience in operating internationally. He does acknowledge, however, that this is an opportunity that comes around only once. He further acknowledges that with his consulting arm, Amprotech, which specializes in advising firms seeking to automate their operations, he has the technological know-how to set up a plant anywhere. One of the major questions he has, however, revolves about how he would staff the operation and whether or not he could find the type of employee in England that he has found in western Michigan. He is convinced that Frost must do business in Britain.

Discussion Questions:

1. Should Frost be concerned with staffing the British operation?
2. Should all employees be recruited from Britain?
3. Who should determine the type of staffing practices Frost should pursue in Britain?
4. Would he be better off seeking a partner for a joint venture? What are the issues he needs to consider in forming an International Joint Venture (IJV)?

---

*This case was prepared by Randall S. Schuler, Stern School of Business, New York University.

Part 7 Managing Diversity

Cases Outline

29. Managing Workforce Diversity: People-Related Business Issues at the Barden Corporation*

Background

The largest segment of the business at the Barden Corporation is the Precision Bearings Division. It manufactures high precision ball bearings in a range of sizes for machine tools, aircraft instruments and accessories, aircraft engines, computer peripherals, textile spindles, and medical and dental equipment. Presently, the division employs about 1,000 people, which includes a marketing department and a small corporate staff. It was founded during World War II to manufacture the special bearings needed for the Norden bombsight. It has been non-union since that time (which gives you a hint about the culture). The following description is told by Mr. Donald Brush, Vice President and General Manager of the Precision Bearings Division.

Reporting directly to me is a small staff comprising a manufacturing manager, a quality manager, an engineering manager, a director of manufacturing planning, and a director of industrial relations. We meet together several times a week to discuss current problems, as well as short- and long-range opportunities and needs. On alternate weeks we augment this group by including the supervisory personnel who report to the senior managers listed above. I might interject here that all supervisors meet with hourly employees on either a weekly or bi-weekly basis to review specific departmental successes and failures, and otherwise to keep employees informed about the business and to encourage ownership of their own jobs. The managers themselves meet on call as the Employee Relations Committee to discuss and recommend approval on a wide range of issues that include the evaluation and audit of hourly and salaried positions, as well as the creation or modification of all divisional personnel policies.

A few words about our Personnel (or Industrial Relations) Department: (You will notice that the term "Human Resources" does not yet roll off our tongues easily, but we understand what it means.) There are six employees who together provide the basic services of employment, affirmative action, employee activity support, labor relations, interpretation of the plethora of federal and state laws, benefits administration, wage and salary administration, records preparation and maintenance, cafeteria supervision, and so on. There are, in addition, two people who coordinate our rather extensive training activities.

As presently organized, the Medical Department comes under the supervision of the director of industrial relations. Its authorized staff includes a medical director, the manager of employee health and safety (who is an occupational health nurse), a staff nurse, a safety specialist, and secretary/ clerk.

The development and execution of plans and programs, including those of a strategic nature, almost invariably involve the active participation of Personnel. And that's how we want it to be. On the other hand, the Personnel Department doesn't run the business. By this I mean they don't hire or fire, promote, or demote. They don't write job descriptions or determine salaries or wages, etc., etc. All these things are done by the line managers with the Personnel

---

*This case was prepared by Randall S. Schuler who expresses his appreciation for the cooperation of Donald Brush.

Department providing a framework to insure consistency and that all actions are appropriate to company goals. You might say that Personnel is our "Jiminy Cricket" – they are there for advice, consent and, importantly, as a conscience.

During the past several months we have been running into many issues that are affecting the very essence of our business: growth, profits, survival, and competitiveness. Because the issues involve our human resources, we call them people-related business issues. Would you please give us your experience, expertise, and suggestions as to how we can solve them? Thanks! The following briefly describes the nature of each of the four issues.

Issue: Recruiting and Training New Hourly Employees

The need to recruit and train approximately 125 new hourly workers to respond to a surge in business in a high cost of living area at a time when the unemployment rate is no more than 2.5% is very challenging. By mid-1989 it had become evident that we had an opportunity to significantly increase our business. In order to achieve otherwise attainable goals, we have to increase our hourly workforce by a net of about 125 employees (that is, in addition to normal turnover, retirements, etc.) in one year. I have asked Personnel to test the waters, recognizing the unemployment in the Danbury labor market has reached an unprecedented low of about 2.5%.

Issue: Safety and Occupational Health Issues

The need to create a heightened awareness by the workforce for safety and occupational health considerations is very important. This is an evolving mission born of a dissatisfaction on our part about "safety as usual." Over the years, Barden employees have assumed that, because we are a metal working shop, people were just going to get hurt. But we cannot afford to have people get hurt and miss work anymore. Yet, as our workforce ages, the employees seem to get out of shape and become more injury and illness prone.

Issue: Spiraling Health Costs of an Aging Population

The spiraling health costs of an aging and sometimes out-of-shape workforce are very costly. All employers face this. Barden's problem is a little unique in that hourly employees tend to stay with the company and retire from the company. For example, we still have several employees whose careers began with us 45 years ago shortly after the company was founded. Our average age approaches 45 for employees and their dependent spouses. Generally, our jobs do not require much physical effort, and it's easy to become out of shape and overfed. As a consequence, they get sick, use hospitals, and have accidents.

Issue: New Machines and the Development of Qualified Workers

The technological evolution of increasingly complex machinery and related manufacturing equipment and the development of trained workers to operate and maintain these machines and equipment, are important facts of life. This process is unceasing and requires a good deal of planning for both the short and the long run. For example, where will we be next year or five years out in order to remain competitive in terms of cost, quality, and service? Buying and rebuilding machines is part of the story. Running them efficiently is quite another. As you know, modern equipment of this sort requires operational people who are not only knowledgeable about the turning or grinding of metals, but also conversant with computerized numerical controls. The employee who sets up and operates a $500,000 machine must be well-trained. Yet having trained people is getting more difficult.

Summary

Mr. Brush knows that these four people-related business issues all reflect the increasing diversity of the workforce. Because of this, he knows that these issues will be around for a long time. Therefore, he requests that you provide him with action plans that can offer long lasting solutions (if at all possible!). He would also appreciate having any more facts related to the four issues identified.

Exhibit 1. Precision Bearings Division

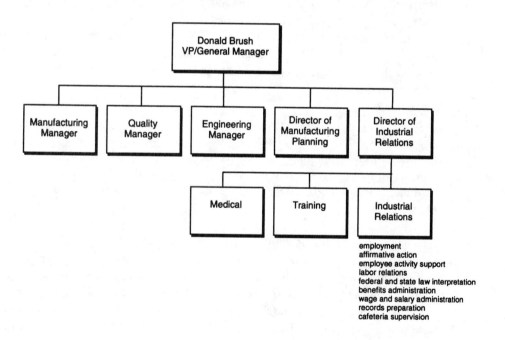

employment
affirmative action
employee activity support
labor relations
federal and state law interpretation
benefits administration
wage and salary administration
records preparation
cafeteria supervision

30. Propco, Inc.*

Allied Technologies Corporation (ATC)

Founded in 1918, Allied Technologies is a diversified designer and manufacturer of advanced technology products, and is one of the largest private employers in the state of Rhode Island. Headed by Joseph R. Wagner, the company is comprised of 10 operating units. These units conduct their businesses within four principal industry segments or lines of business – Marine Systems, Construction, Power, and Motor Parts. During 1991, the major business units within these four segments held, in most instances, rankings of either number one, two, or three in their major lines of business.

Revenues for 1991 totaled $16,427 million, with an operating income of $892 million. Non-U.S. operations accounted for 41% of sales in 1991, while U.S. Government business comprised 23% of sales.

Historically, at least half of ATC's revenues were derived from the military sector. Cuts in defense budgets for marine products (e.g., submarine engines, screw propellors, and environmental control systems), both in the U.S. and in other developed countries, have reduced requirements for military submarines and ships and related equipment from U.S. suppliers. Total U.S. defense spending peaked in 1985, and current budget requests indicate a further 4 percent decline in spending by 1993.

Wagner stated:

> "Beyond the problems in the military business, the plant closings and layoffs are intended to make the company more efficient. We have begun a transformation more profound and more potent than any single event in the corporation's recent history...sadly, though, 13,900 jobs must be eliminated in order to attain this efficiency."

Consequently, according to many experts, diversification of their operations into non-military marine areas is one of the most promising strategies for survival. In fact, ATC is following a diversification strategy. ATC has grown from a narrowly focused marine company in the 1970s with revenues of less than $2 billion, to what is today a $16 billion enterprise. Based on 1991 sales, the firm is one of the largest U.S. industrial companies, and one of the tenth largest U.S. exporters.

According to Wagner,

> "We have built the Company in order to be profitable in the face of declining Pentagon expenditures; the firm is reducing its reliance on defense contracts. We are now selling more products overseas. The Company is very strong and viable."

---

*This case was written by Richard D. Freeedman, Stern School of Business, New York University. Reprinted with permission. This case is based upon a real situation, certain facts have been changed and the names of the corporations and the names and titles of individuals have been disguised.

But some of ATC's operating units – such as Propco – whose primary task was to develop and construct military equipment, have suffered extensive financial losses because of the reductions in the military budget in the post-cold-war era.

Overall, the Corporation's earnings for the first nine months of 1991 were down 65 percent from the equivalent period of 1990. In 1991 ATC suffered its first annual operating loss in three decades in 1991.

Propco

Propco was the creation of a 1929 consolidation of HLL Vessels and the Excelsior Screw Propeller Company. At that time, Propco was the largest manufacturer of marine propellers in the world. Its specialty was the development and construction of screw propellers for submarines. A major risk to submarines is their location by enemies using instruments that detect the sounds and signals they make. Propellor screws are a major source of such "noise." Consequently the design and manufacture of better screw propellers is a significant issue in submarine development. Propco is renowned for its leadership in screw propellor development.

Although the advent of the jet age did not eliminate ocean-travel, it did reduce their commercial business and require that the company acquire other types of businesses. In the 1950s, with the development of an electronics group and a new engineering group, the division diversified into other marine and space systems especially in the defense industry.

At present, under the leadership of Malden K. Ruhn, Propco is a leading domestic producer of a number of Marine Systems products. Its major production programs include engine controls, environmental controls, marine-engine controls and propellers for commercial and military boats.

The Marine Systems business is affected by many different factors: rapid changes in technology; lengthy and costly development cycles; heavy dependence on a small number of products and programs; changes in legislation and in government procurement and other regulations and procurement practices; licensing or other arrangements; substantial competition from a large number of companies; and changes in economic, industrial and international conditions. In addition, the principal methods of competition in the Marine Systems business are price, delivery schedules, product performance, service and other terms and conditions of sale. Consequently, in times of recession and reduced government spending, firms heavily involved in the production of these systems must seek to reduce production and cut costs in order to remain profitable.

One primary way in which the company sought to cut spending is through employee layoffs. In 1991, Propco had a workforce of approximately 14,000 people, 3.2 percent of which were minorities. As of January 1, 1993, the firm's employees totaled 10,000 with just under 1.1 percent comprised of minorities.

Corporate Re-structuring

In 1991 there was a sharp decline in ocean traffic, construction and engine production. This marked the first time that ATC's core commercial markets simultaneously hit the bottom of their industry cycles. In addition, government reassessments of the military threat from the former Soviet Union – and efforts to reduce the U.S. deficit – resulted in fewer defense procurement contracts being awarded.

Consequently, in early1992, ATC management announced that it would eliminate 15,297 jobs, including 8,143 in Rhode Island, by the end of 1994. At the time of this announcement, the Company had over 50,000 employees based in Rhode Island. The proposed cuts represent over 7.5 percent of the over 100,000 workers employed worldwide by the sprawling company – virtually all parts of the company will be affected. The largest job losses will be in the divisions which produce defense products.

According to CEO Wagner,

> "The corporation is embarking on a sea of change that will produce a leaner, tougher-minded company capable of enduring the current recession, and seizing opportunities as they arise in the future. The harsh reality is that a shrinking military budget means fewer orders for the company's military marine equipment and sophisticated electronics."

The goal of the restructuring plan is to reduce costs by $1.2 billion a year by 1994 in order to improve the company's financial performance. The Company has said that the layoffs would save $500 million a year; closing plants will add another $400 million by early 1993 and improvements in design, engineering and manufacturing will add an additional $500 million in projected savings.

Repercussions for Propco Employees

As part of the reorganization announcement by ATC, Propco was instructed to lay off 925 employees. According to corporate spokespeople, most of the reductions are being accomplished through severance and enhanced early retirement programs. The official statement released by Propco's public relations department is:

> "We understand the difficulties that our employees are under during this time of restructuring, however, it is in Propco's long-term interests to become a much leaner and more flexible organization. In order for our Company to compete effectively and efficiently, we must cut costs where possible. It is our understanding that the reorganization will be completed soon."

But while ATC executives emphasize the necessity for the layoffs and paint a positive picture of the Corporation's recent balance sheet performance, Propco employees appear to be much more pessimistic about this latest round of employee firings. Below are the comments of some of Propco's former and current employees who have witnessed, and experienced, the effects of the restructuring program.

Vincent S.

(Vincent is a White, 33-year-old Operations Center Manager at Propco. He received his MBA in Operations by attending school at night while working for the company. Vincent is married and is the father of newborn twins. He has been with the company for six years.)

Propco has been laying off people for close to two years now. Each new quarter we receive fewer Marine Systems orders. Unfortunately, this leads to another round of layoffs. It's not that our people don't know how to project orders. Look, the entire industry is suffering and our customers have had to cut back, most times at the last minute. They have to look out for their bottom line, just like we do.

It's frustrating. It's frustrating as hell. My men look to me for answers as to when this is all going to end, but I know little more than they do about future economic performance. Of course morale is very low. "Was the last layoff the last?" is the most unanswered question among the guys. Every time a new wave of layoffs comes around you can feel the tension. People barely speak to each other, and no one wants to speak to me. You can see the fear in people's eyes.

I'm scared too. I'm not really afraid of losing my job. I'm afraid that someone is going to take their anger out on me. Every time my boss calls a meeting I'm scared that I have to lay off more men. In December I had to layoff 50 people - right after Christmas. I was told that would be the last of the reduction from my unit. But two weeks ago I was told to reduce my numbers by another 20 men. You have no idea how hard it is to tell a man who is old enough to be your father, that he's fired. It really is hard. Men have cried and begged for their jobs. Let me tell you, I don't sleep well at night when I have to do this. I don't park my car in the employee parking lot when I lay people off. Some of the manager's cars have been scratched or dented after they lay off people. Telling people who have worked for a company for 20 or 30 years that they are no longer needed is one of the hardest things I have had to do in my life. I hope this all ends soon.

These constant layoffs have been really hard on everyone here. At first the unions took a hard-line stance – an "us vs. them" mentality. But after the fourth round of layoffs they decided to cooperate in order to make the firm more competitive. They know that in the long run this is what's best. Because union leadership decided to cooperate, we were able to adopt many Japanese-style manufacturing models. This has not prevented layoffs, but it has resulted in a more accurate determination of the number of employees that should be dismissed.

The bottom line is that everyone wants Propco to remain competitive so that when things get better, corporate headquarters will keep Propco in Rhode Island.

The layoffs have caused the level of distrust between the hourly employees and senior management to increase a great deal. Hourlys think management is incapable of saving the company; is not making any sacrifces (for example they recently received bonuses), and, the hourly workers think management sees them as process components instead of human beings. Senior management thinks that hourlys are incapable of understanding the market situation; are not helping to regain competitiveness; and are spoiled union babies. I'm sort of in the middle of all this since I'm not a part of senior management, and I'm not an hourly employee. I'm the guy that gets the job of actually laying off my workers.

Richard C.

(Richard is a White, 48-year-old Manager of Central Purchasing. He received his undergraduate degree in Finance from an Ivy League university. He is married and a father of three teenagers. Richard has been with the company for 27 years.)

I was laid off right before Christmas. I can honestly say that I had no idea whatsoever that I would be let go. I mean, I have been with Propco for 27 years. It's home to me, and the people there are my family. Or so I thought. I guess I got too complacent. You figure, "I'm part of management. I make $85,000 a year. I'm secure." Do you know that my boss wouldn't even look me in the eye when he told me? I really thought we were friends. We used to be a team in the company golf tournaments. I'm sure it was hard on him, but at least he still has his job.

At first they offered me an early retirement package last November. The package included a payment of $15,000 and, get this, 3 months of medical before my benefits would run out. At first I turned the package down, but my boss told me that if I didn't take it I would be fired anyway. Some choice.

I understand that the economy is in a recession, but you figure that if you put in as much time as I did with a company, nothing will ever happen. You'll retire and receive a good pension. Now I'm mailing out resumes and cover letters, something I never thought I would have to do again. Propco is a great company to work for; I loved it there. But apparently the feeling was not mutual. Do you know that the company did not give me any career counseling? At least the hourly workers get that.

What went wrong? Who knows? I guess the company screwed up. It's not my concern now. The only thing on my mind now is how to take care of my family. My wife works, but we need to have a second income. I made some connections with other firms in the industry while I was at Propco. Hopefully something comes through soon.

Carl G.

(Carl is a 35-year-old, African-American former screw propeller grinder. He was employed at Propco for 12 years. Carl has taken courses toward an undergraduate degree in Sociology from a local university. He is divorced.)

Yeah, I was a grinder at Propco for 12 years before the layoff. I made $15.22 an hour to grind metal off of a military screw forging. Sounds really hard, but it was just manual labor; a lot of lifting and hard work, but it was easy once you got used to it. I have to say, though, that most of the unit's grinders were Black. I used to hear some of the White union guys joking and calling our area "the plantation," saying what we did was "slave labor". They weren't lying. I was there for 12 years and I never could seem to get promoted out of that area. Most of the time, new Black guys were put in our area. Not to say that Propco has a lot of Black workers – they don't. That's a different story though, but it seems strange to me that a company that is 15 minutes from Hartford and 50 minutes from New Haven has so few minorities in their plant.

Out of the ten Blacks in my section, four have been laid off. You see, union people know when they will be laid off because its done by seniority. Those people with the most years don't have worry. But since most of the Black guys are what they call "recent hires," they are the first to be fired. You know the old saying. That's the name of the game.

What was it like to be Black at Propco? Well, you never quite feel comfortable there. You feel like what you are, an outsider. The foreman watches you all the time. He's never as easy with you as he is with the White guys. He checks your time card. He calls you at home to make sure that's where you are, when you call in sick. When the rest of the guys go play golf, you're never invited. They just assume you don't know how to play. Or else they just don't want you around. When there's some kind of party, either you're not invited, or they invite you at the last minute. The White guys talk to you when they want to know how to do something. Otherwise, for the most part, they act like you're not there. There are some White guys who are cool; they try to get to know you. But for the most part, you are looked down at, even though they are doing the same kind of work.

The Black guys in my area were lucky though, because we had each other. We laughed and talked and told stories. We did our own thing. We covered for each other, and helped out when someone fell behind. We had our own parties. We went out together. We helped each other.

Propco has diversity meetings all the time. They say they're trying to find ways to hire more minorities and women. I haven't seen any real progress. It seems more like talk to me. Sometimes I think that they only had the Blacks that they did there because of the government contracts. You see, whenever you do work for the government, you have to have a certain number of minorities. It could be that Propco only hired the minorities that it did because of that.

Don't get me wrong, Propco is a pretty good company to work for. You get health, dental, a savings plan, and free education. Even after the layoff my benefits will last for one year. Also, the union gave us job counseling and assistance. I received one week's pay for every year of employment as severance pay. But, there is no doubt that a lot of people in management are prejudiced. I used to hear jokes all the time about minorities. You know, sexual jokes, stupid jokes, that type of thing. Usually you try to ignore it. It's hard.

I guess I'm lucky. I just found another job. Most everyone I know is still looking. Maybe things are getting better.

Samuel L.

(Samuel is a White, 36-year-old foam machinist. He recently received a B.A. in Psychology from a local college by attending night school. He is married and has two children. Samuel was employed at Propco for 14 years.)

I knew it was coming, but I prayed that the economy would get better before it was my time to get the pink slip. In a way it's a relief that it finally happened. Every time layoffs were announced, I couldn't sleep. I couldn't eat. I yelled at my family. I was very difficult to live with. The waiting got to be too much. Even being at work was hard. The guys walked around like someone had just died. It was real uneasy there. Guys who used to be friends, barely spoke to each other. I guess it was the tension. Everyone looked at each other like they were enemies. Like the next guy would take their jobs from them. It was really rough.

I was a foam machinist at Propco; I put a regional blade spar into a die machine and injected high pressure foam that forms a X-10 screw shape. Big deal. I doubt that I can find another job doing the same thing. Not that I would want to, but what else can I do? I have a degree, but what do you do with it? Psychology. What a useless degree unless you go back to school. I can't do that now. I guess I'm lucky since my wife makes a pretty good salary and she can support the family until I can find another job.

I made good money at Propco – $15.35 an hour. But management sure as heck makes a lot more. And you don't see too many of them getting laid off. It's always the same. Management gets paid a lot of money to "manage", but the people who actually do the work get $15.00 an hour. Then when management messes up the company, they fire the people who work and keep the people who think. Does this make any sense to you? They could fire a couple of "thinkers" and save more money than if they fired twenty of us. But, hey, what do I know? I'm just an hourly.

Race relations at Propco? What about it? There were a few Black guys there – not a whole lot though. I never had any problem with them. They were just like any of the other guys to me. I mean they worked hard. Everyone at Propco did. I heard a few guys telling race jokes. But they told other kinds of jokes too. You know, like jokes about Polish people; Italian people; women, sex. The people who told those jokes were jerks. I don't have a problem working with Black people. As long as the guy does his work, he's all right with me.

The Black guys sure did stick together. They ate lunch together. Clocked in and out together. I guess I understand. There just weren't that many of them. I'm sure I would be like that too. But you know, the Italian guys were sort of like that too. Strength in numbers I guess.

I feel sorry for all of us now. I know that the economy has been bad, but Allied Technologies is a rich company. It's huge. Something else could be done. They could work with the Governor; maybe negotiate tax breaks. They could try lots of things. You're damn right I'm angry. I worked at that place for 14 years. And what do they do for me? They fire me to save themselves.

Steven H.

(Steven is a 38-year-old, African-American Division Manager at one of Allied Technologies Corporation's other operating units. Prior to his present position, he was assigned to corporate headquarters where he had frequent interaction with Propco managers. He has an engineering

degree from an Ivy League university and advanced studies in business and Human Resources. He has been with the company for eight years. Steven is married.)

Out of over 3,000 people at Propco, there are only 81 Black salaried workers. When I say salaried, that includes clerks, buyers and secretaries, as well as unit managers. Out of that 81, only seven are actually managers of people. And after the next round of layoffs, I expect that number to drop. Black managers are an endangered species here at Propco, and in fact throughout ATC.

It's just a fact that Black salaried workers have a higher propensity of getting laid off. Propco's culture – like other ATC operating units – is one of institutional racism. For example, in one of their units there are 400 employees. Only 15 of those people are Black. That was last October. Now I understand that there is only one Black salaried employee. And he's there because somebody high up likes him.

The bottom line is that Black employees at Propco don't have a support network. There is a lot of nepotism there, so that when it comes time to layoff salaried workers, those who don't have real friends often find themselves on the unemployment line. Face it, people don't lay off their friends and family. This situation generally applies to salaried workers, since hourly workers are laid off based upon seniority.

To further exacerbate matters, it is difficult for Black employees to take additional training and education classes that would assist in making them more competitive. I am not saying that these individuals are not already highly qualified. Management does not tend to hire minorities unless they are superior achievers. It is just that it is essential for a manager's career to always look like he is trying to improve his leadership skills.

But then again even education is no safety net. Here is a classic example. There was a Black employee at Propco who had started as an hourly and had worked his way up to a position as a $40,000 a year manufacturing engineer. When his mentor left, he was demoted back to an hourly worker as a dispatcher. And this guy had an engineering degree. It goes without saying that he left Propco.

Is Propco consciously racist? I tend to think so. I can't tell you how many diversity meetings friends of mine have attended where someone from upper management would say, "we can't find qualified minority candidates to fill our positions." That whole argument is ridiculous. Propco participates in a program where minority college students are given summer internships at the Company. They are also assigned a mentor from the management ranks. These kids are not dumb. Their grade point averages are in the 3.3 range. How many are with the Company now? None. This is despite the fact that over 90 percent of the interns get superior ratings on their summer performance. I think this speaks for itself.

I believe that something has to be done to address the racist mentality around the entire Corporation. I hate being the one that has to defend my race all of the time, but there are very few others that care. I'm doing what I can, but I can't fix the problem alone.

Do I see a future for myself here? ATC is doing great things. I think that if I hang in here long enough, I can make a difference. I want to help qualified minorities – not just Blacks – get into these large firms. ATC has a lot to offer employees. But if it gets too tough for me, I don't think I'll have a problem finding another position somewhere else.

Propco's Human Resource Policies

The ATC Human Resources Department has issued policy statements over time regarding layoffs, diversity and minorities that the company indicates are the basis for its layoff decisions. All divisions have to rigorously adhere to these policies. All of them have been developed with the direct involvement and approval of the CEO, Joseph E. Wagner. Wagner has given numerous speeches stressing the importance of diversity in corporate life in general and ATC in particular. ATC donates considerable money to civil rights organizations and Wagner himself has received several humanitarian awards.

It is the position of Allied Technologies Corporation to hire qualified candidates regardless of race, creed, color, sex or ethnic origin. We have an ongoing diversity program in place in which we hope to devise ways to introduce more minorities and women into our businesses. For the past two years the Company has participated in an internship program in which minority college students are given the opportunity to work in some of our business units during the summer. It is our hope that the students will learn from, and enjoy, their intern experience and consider working for ATC upon graduation.[1]

As far as industry standards are concerned, the Company is on an even keel with other firms of it's size when it comes to the number of minority employees that it employs.

There is a concerted effort on the part of the executives at ATC to hire the best people for the job, and that is what we do.

In laying off union workers, we adhere to the union contract and lay them off in order of seniority.

---

[1] NOTE: As of now, Propco does not have any of the former interns in its employ, although some have graduated from college.

31. Promotion to Police Sergeant*

Until recently selection of candidates for promotion to police sergeants at State University was done unsystematically. Job analysis was not the foundation for selection decisions but rather intuition and subjective judgments. The presence of a legal imperative and a desire to make better and more objective selection decisions resulted in a program to develop new promotion procedures.

State University is a large university with eight campuses spread throughout the state. Each campus has its own police department. Although the eight campuses are fairly autonomous and independent, there is a central administration group which coordinates certain functions, including personnel. Legally the police departments are responsible for their selection and promotion decisions; they are not governed by the personnel group in central administration nor by the campus-based personnel departments. But the chiefs recognize that their expertise is limited and so they regularly seek advice and guidance from the campus and central administration personnel departments.

The eight campuses differ from each other in many ways, including size (from 4,000 students at the smallest campus to 30,000 students at the largest campus), location (both urban and rural), and age or time in existence (from as young as ten years to as old as more than 100 years). Corresponding to these differences among the campuses are differences in the composition, philosophies, and histories of the police department, each run by its own police chief. Of particular importance in 1983 was an ongoing rivalry between two large departments, one in the northern part of the state and the other in the southern part of the state; each was vying for recognition as the "best."

Despite competition among the departments, all eight police chiefs recognized the value of pooling their resources to maintain a single promotion procedure (or test) for selecting sergeants. By having a single procedure, a rank-ordered list of all university police officers qualified for promotion could be developed and made available to all campuses. Each list had a two-year life. During these two years, whenever a vacancy for sergeant came up on any of the eight campuses, the people at the top of the list had first priority for promotion. Approximately twenty vacancies occurred during a list's two-year life, and usually about 150 of the 250 police officers met the minimum requirements for promotion (i.e., two years of college credits, two years' police experience, and completion of a state-sponsored management training course).

Because of the attractive small selection ratio, the police chiefs wanted to improve their selection procedures so that the twenty vacancies were filled with the very best of the 150 eligible police officers. Accordingly, the university agreed to pay for a consultant to work with the police and personnel groups to design a high-quality promotion procedure for sergeants. They hired Gerri Smith from a prestigious consulting firm specializing in selection.

---

*This case was prepared by Susan E. Jackson, New York University. The example used is for teaching purposes and is not meant to be an example of effective or ineffective management practice. Reprinted with permission.

Getting Started

As with previous consulting assignments of this type, Ms. Smith knew that the development of a new promotion procedure would take time and involve several components. These components, beginning with job analysis, are outlined in the sequence through which Ms. Smith proceeded. This outline is shown in Exhibit 1.

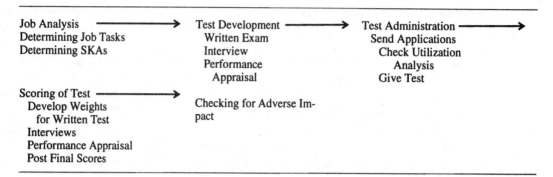

Exhibit 1. Components of the Promotion Test Developed by Ms. Smith

Job Analysis

In 1979, six of the eight police departments had hired a firm to conduct job analyses of all jobs within their departments. The method the firm had used appeared to be the critical incident technique (CIT), but it was difficult to tell for sure because the documentation of the job analysis procedures had been retained by the consulting firm. The police chiefs contacted the firm after Ms. Smith pointed out to them that this documentation would be critical should they ever need to defend in court decisions they made using the results of the job analysis. Unfortunately, the particular consultant they had worked with four years ago was no longer with the firm and the documentation was nowhere to be found.

Neither Ms. Smith nor the police chiefs had anticipated this problem. They had hoped to have their promotion list ready in four moths. If they did a job analysis, they knew they might have to wait six or seven months before seeing that list. After discussing the matter at length, the chiefs decided that in the long run it was in their best interest to collect systematic, up-to-date job analysis information, so they asked Ms. Smith to get started.

Phase I: Determining Job Tasks

Usually Ms. Smith likes to use an extended CIT method of job analysis but in this case it was not practical. To do so, she would have had to travel to eight locations that were hundreds of miles apart from each other. Both time and budget constraints ruled this out. Therefore, Ms. Smith decided to combine features of the CIT and GOJA methods. This creative solution was possible because the Uniform Guidelines recognize that there is no one best method of job analysis. As long as the method used provided information about the importance, frequency, difficulty, and trainability of one's job tasks, it would probably hold up to the scrutiny of the courts.

Ms. Smith conducted the job analysis for sergeants as follows: First, she asked each police department to send copies of the job descriptions for all of their sergeants. These gave her a general working knowledge of what the job of sergeant involved. Next, she developed a form that she would send to each sergeant to fill out. This form asked the sergeant to list all of his or her job duties and then, for each duty or task, to rate how frequently it was performed relative to other duties, how important it was to the job overall, how difficult it was to perform, and the amount of training that would be needed to teach someone to perform the duty. This form was sent to each sergeant, who filled it out and then reviewed it with his or her commanding lieutenant. If the lieutenant felt any qualifications or changes were needed, these were noted in a designated space. Both the sergeant and lieutenant then signed the form to indicate they had reviewed it together. Finally, the chief reviewed the form, added any comments he felt were appropriate, and signed it. The original copy of the form was kept by the campus police department and a photocopy was sent to Ms. Smith.

Using the information from the completed forms, Ms. Smith generated a list of eight job domains, which she believed, based on the data she had collected, represented the tasks relevant to the job of a sergeant. Then, for each domain, she listed all of the specific tasks that she felt belonged to the domain. For each task, she recorded the corresponding ratings of frequency, difficulty, importance, and trainability (FDIT ratings). This list of domains and tasks was then sent back to twelve randomly chosen sergeants and three lieutenants who reviewed it. Ms. Smith asked these reviewers to study the list she had generated and evaluate whether the domains made logical sense to them and whether the tasks within each domain belonged there. They returned their suggestions for revision to Ms. Smith in writing. She then finalized the list, which is shown in Exhibit 2.

Phase 2: Determining Skills, Knowledge and Abilities (SKAs)

Now that the major job tasks had been identified, Ms. Smith needed to determine the SKAs required to perform those tasks. Then methods of assessing applicants' relevant SKAs could be designed for use as a selection test.

To find out which SKAs were important for performing a sergeant's job, Ms. Smith went back to the experts – the sergeants and lieutenants. In order to record their judgments in a systematic way, Ms. Smith designed a simple matrix for the job experts to complete. The headings on the eight columns of the matrix were the names of the domains generated in Phase 1 of the job analysis. The labels for the seventeen rows of the matrix were names of abilities, knowledges, and skills that she believed someone might need to perform well as a sergeant.

This domain's X abilities matrix was sent to all sergeants and lieutenants along with a list of the tasks that belonged in each domain and definitions of each ability. The job experts completed the matrix by indicating the importance of each ability for performing the tasks in each demain. Using these ratings, Ms. Smith determined the nine SKAs that were most important to assess in order to predict performance as a sergeant (see Exhibit 3).

Exhibit 2. Job Domains for the Position of Police Sergeant

| | | Average Ratings | | | |
		F	D	I	T^a
Domain:	Law enforcement activities including patrolling, investigating, apprehending.	6.2	5.8	6.3	5.1^b
Sample tasks:	1. responding to call for crime in progress 2. cultivating sources of street information				
Domain:	Adaptability to the job, including completing work in a timely manner, attention to detail, willingness to assume accountability for one's work.	6.4	3.3	5.7	4.0
Sample tasks:	1. accepting orders or assignments 2. keeping up-to-date files				
Domain:	Dealing with the public.	6.7	4.9	5.2	4.1
Sample tasks:	1. referring citizens to other agencies 2. interviewing witnesses				
Domain:	Personal appearance and demeanor.	6.7	2.7	5.3	2.9
Sample tasks:	1. physical fitness activities 2. maintenance of uniform and equipment				
Domain:	Supervision and leadership.	4.7	6.4	4.8	6.7
Sample tasks:	1. working with a rookie or new transfer 2. supervising an investigation				
Domain:	Report writing.	5.9	4.6	5.5	5.1
Sample tasks:	1. writing up findings for an ongoing investigation 2. writing descriptions of events that occurred during on-site call				
Domain:	Teamwork, including working with other professionals both inside and outside of the department.	5.4	5.1	5.7	4.3
Sample tasks:	1. requesting assistance from other officers 2. teaching knowledge and skills to other officers				

[a]F = Frequency of task performance; D = Difficulty; I = Importance; T = Trainability.

[b]Ratings were made using a scale of 1 to 7. Values shown are means obtained by averaging across all items in the domain.

Exhibit 3. SKAs Assessed by the Sergeant's Promotional Exam

| Skills, Knowledges, & Abilities | I^b | Exam Component in Which SKA Was Assessed[a] | | |
		Written	Interview	Performance
1. Knowledge of State and Federal Law	6.7	X	X	X
2. Knowledge of Local Procedures and Regulations	6.6	X		X
3. Writing Ability	5.2	X		X
4. Communication Skills	5.8		X	X
5. Reasoning Ability	5.0		X	X
6. Skill in Interpersonal Relations	6.1		X	X
7. Knowledge of General Management Principles	5.4	X		
8. Reading Ability	4.9	X		
9. Leadership Skills	4.8		X	X

[a]An "X" indicates the ability was assessed by that component of the exam.
[b]I = Importance rating of the ability. The value shown is a mean obtained by averaging the importance ratings of the ability for all job domains.

Test Development

The police refer to the process through which sergeants are selected as the Sergeants' Promotional Exam (SPE). Traditionally, SPE has three components: a written exam, an interview, and an evaluation of past performance. These three components have always been used by the university police departments and they are typically used by city and state police departments as well. The police chiefs wanted Ms. Smith to maintain the three components of SPE, but they were eager to have the content of each component revised and updated. So, the major questions were: (1) Which SKAs should be assessed by each component? and (2) How exactly should each SKA be measured?

In deciding how to design the SPE, Ms. Smith kept several things in mind:

First, she knew that written tests were more likely than interviews and performance ratings to have impact against minorities, especially blacks and Hispanics. Second, she was wary of interviews because she knew they are difficult to standardize and make reliable. Third, she preferred to assess as many SKAs as possible using the most job-related method possible, which in this case was the performance appraisal. Finally, she knew that each of the three methods at her disposal (written test, interview, performance ratings) had both strengths and weaknesses, so the best strategy would be to measure all SKAs using more than one method, if possible.

The three components of the SPE Ms. Smith designed are described in detail below. Throughout these next sections, reference is made to a Task Force. This Task Force was organized to assist Ms. Smith with her task of developing the tests. It consisted of three chiefs and two lieutenants.

The Written Exam

During Phase II of the job analysis, seventeen SKAs had been rated for their importance to a sergeant's job performance. Of these, nine were judged to be relatively high in importance. Five of the nine were judged to be appropriately assessed in a written exam: reading skills, writing skills, knowledge of basic management principles, knowledge of state and federal laws, and knowledge of university regulations and procedures as described by the local General Orders manual. The two skill areas had been rated as relatively less important than the three knowledge areas, so the proportion of test items devoted to each skill or knowledge area was adjusted to reflect the importance ratings.

Usually, the most difficult part of developing a written test is writing the test items. Fortunately, the Task Force had the advantage of being able to obtain potential items from a state agency that maintained a bank of thousands of test items for law enforcement exams. Upon request, this agency randomly selected a total of 400 items relevant to the SKAs to be assessed on the exam. Each member of the Task Force then reviewed all 400 questions and noted any objections they had. At a group meeting, the Task Force discussed their evaluations of the 400 items. Their goal was to select a total of 100 of the best items. The decision rule they used to eliminate items from the pool of 400 was to eliminate any item to which any member of the Task Force had objections. This reduced the pool to fewer than 200. Finally, redundant items were eliminated and the final 100 items were chosen to fit the goal of distributing items across the five knowledge and skill areas according to the relative importance of the areas.

As already noted, one disadvantage of written tests was that minorities tend to score lower than whites, resulting in adverse impact for selection decisions based on written tests. Test experts now realize that a major source of unfairness in written tests is that often the reading skill needed to take the test is higher than the skill needed to do the job in question. To decrease the potential for unfair discrimination, any written tests used for selection should be checked to ensure that the readability level of the test is equal to or below the readability level of written materials typically encountered in the job. Therefore, as the last step in developing the written test for the SPE, Ms. Smith conducted readability analyses of the test and of samples of department memos, regulation manuals, legal documents, and correspondence taken directly out of the record files of current sergeants. This analysis showed the reading skill needed to take the test was somewhat less than the skill needed to read materials from the sergeant's actual files.

The Interview

In the past, the police department interviewed only candidates who passed the written test. This practice meant that the chiefs had to decide on a cut-off point to define what a passing score would be for the written exam. They had always found this to be an extremely difficult judgment to make and wanted to avoid making that judgment this year. Their solution to the problem was to allow everyone to go through the interview process and not use the written test as a hurdle. This solution fit the chiefs' philosophy that someone who does well in the interview should be able to have that compensate for a low score on the written test, but it creates a practical problem: How could they interview approximately 100 candidates spread throughout a large state in a manner that everyone perceived to be standardized and fair, without incurring prohibitive expenses?

Ideally, it seemed that fairness and standardization could be best attained by having only one interview board (or panel), rather than having one panel at each of the eight campuses. But this would mean unbearably high travel costs – either the board members would have to travel around the state, or applicants would have to travel to the board. The Task Force decided the only practical solution was to set up two interview boards, one in the northern half of the state, and one in the southern half. This solution presented a real challenge to Ms. Smith who had to develop an interviewing procedure so sound it could not be attacked as possibly giving an unfair advantage to candidates in either half of the state. Ms. Smith realized that this challenge could be met only with a structured interview conducted by trained interviewers.

The first order of business was to solicit volunteers to serve as interviewers. The chiefs believed the interviewers should represent the following: the Affirmative Action officers from central administration, the general university community, the local communities by which the campuses were surrounded, the state law enforcement agencies, and their own departments. The group included the people to whom the chiefs felt most directly accountable, the people to whom the chiefs wished to demonstrate the credibility of their departments, and the people for whom the chiefs felt their departments should serve as role models. The Task Force was given the responsibility of creating two interview boards. Each board was to have one member to represent each of the five groups listed above.

After the interview boards were set up, Ms. Smith arranged a one-day training session for the interviewers. Her objectives for this training session were as follows:

- Develop a set of four or five questions that would be used for all interviews.
- Develop standards to use in evaluating candidates' responses to each question.
- Generate consensus among the interviewers about what they were to accomplish with the interview process.
- Give the interviewers an opportunity to role play an interview session.
- Develop an appreciation among the interviewers of the seriousness of their task and the problems inherent in accomplishing it (e.g., rater errors and biases, primacy and recency effects, and possible boredom and fatigue).

In order to accomplish these objectives, Ms. Smith did several things. First, prior to the training session she identified five SKAs (based on her job analysis) that could potentially be assessed in an interview. For each of these SKAs, she asked a few lieutenants to suggest interview questions that would tap the SKAs. Using these suggestions, she generated a list of about twenty potential interview questions. She sent this list, along with a short manual on interviewing and a job description for sergeants, to all members of the interview boards. The interviewers were asked to review this material prior to the training session.

At the training session, Ms. Smith reviewed several principles of interviewing and explained her objectives to the board members. She explained her belief that the only way to accomplish the objectives was for the interviewers to spend the day communicating and problem solving together. She turned over to them the task of selecting four or five questions that they all agreed were appropriate, and for which they were able to specify standards to be used in evaluating the candidates' responses. The interviewers struggled for several hours with this task, which they were surprised to find so difficult. By the end of the day, they had developed four questions they could all live with and a conviction that the interview process would be standardized and fair. At the end of the day, one of the interviewers – a twenty-year veteran of a large city's police department – admitted to Ms. Smith that he came to the training session believing the day would be a waste of time because there was nothing he didn't already know about interviewing. To his surprise he came away feeling that every interview board should go through a similar process before they began evaluating candidates, especially since their evaluations can strongly influence the careers of young officers.

Performance Appraisals

The third component of the SPE was a performance appraisal of each candidate. Ms. Smith was happy to learn that the department already had a good performance appraisal procedure that was used for promotion decisions. The system worked as follows: For each candidate, all of the department officers who knew the candidate (this was typically three or four people) filled out a detailed appraisal form. The appraisal form accessed seven domains of job performance. For each performance domain, eight to twelve specific tasks were listed. The officers evaluated the candidate's performance of each task using a ten-point rating scale. These ratings were averaged and multiplied by ten to yield one overall performance score.

Administering the SPE

At the same time the three test components were being developed, Ms. Smith and the Task Force were planning for the administration of the tests. Only internal applicants were allowed to take the SPE, so the recruiting process was simple. All university police officers were sent a letter that described the testing procedures in detail. An application form was sent with this letter instructing all interested persons to apply by a particular date.

Although it was routine practice for the department to use only internal recruiting for the SPE, the chiefs always felt obliged to justify this practice. The major argument against the practice of internal recruiting was that it would perpetuate any existing underrepresentation of minority groups. To counter this argument, the chiefs sent a utilization analysis to the university's AAP officer, who compared this information to their routinely collected availability data. Because the police department had an aggressive recruiting program for entry-level positions, this comparison usually revealed that minority groups were not underrepresented in the pool of potential internal applicants.

The written exam was scheduled for a Saturday morning, and the police chiefs were all instructed to take this into account when assigning duties during that period. All interviewing was conducted the week after the written test. The officers completed their performance appraisals during that week also. Candidates were told the final list of total scores would be posted three weeks after the date of the written test.

Scoring the SPE

Final SPE scores were created by adding together the weighted scores from each component. The written test was weighted 50 percent, and the interview and performance appraisal were each weighted 25 percent. The final list of promotion candidates consisted of a rank ordering of everyone who had completed all three phases of the SPE based on the overall scores. This list was posted in each of the eight campus police departments along with a notice encouraging all applicants to speak with their chief to obtain detailed feedback.

The chiefs chose to weight the written test more heavily than the interview and performance appraisal primarily because they and their patrol officers all believed the written test was the most objective component of the SPE, and thus was the least subject to the criticism that favoritism determined the scores. Initially, the chiefs had suggested to Ms. Smith that the performance appraisal be weighted only 10 percent because it was the component believed to be the most subjective. However, Ms. Smith countered that the performance appraisal was the most job-related component and therefore was probably the most valid predictor. The 50-25-25 weighting system was eventually agreed upon to take into account these and other similar types of concerns.

Checking for Adverse Impact

As noted previously, this university's police departments viewed themselves as leaders in the field of law enforcement practice. Consequently, they were particularly concerned about maintaining a force that was balanced with respect to the races and sexes. Recall that it was primarily this concern that led the departments to use a compensatory selection model rather than use the written test as a hurdle and therefore have to impose an arbitrary cut-off score for that component.

Exhibit 4. Analysis to Check for Potential Adverse Impact

Test Component	Asian (n-23)[a]	Black (n=37)	Hispanic (n=11)	Am. Indian (n=3)	White (n=71)	Males (n=118)	Females (n=27)
	% of Subgroup Who Are Among the Top 20 Candidates						
Written	(5)[b]22%	(2) 5%[c]	(1)9%[c]	(1)33%	(11)15%	(14)12%	(6)22%
Interview	(6)26%	(3) 8%[c]	(1)9%[c]	(0) 0%[c]	(10)14%	(16)14%)	(4)15%
Performance Appraisal	(5)22%	(5)14%	(0)0%[c]	(1)33%	(9) 13%	(15)13%	(5)19%
	% of Subgroup Who Are Among the Top 30 Candidates						
Written	(7)30%	(7)19%	(2)18%	(1)33%	(13)18%	(22)19%	(8)30%
Interview	(7)30%	(6)16%	(2)18%	(1)33%	(14)20%	(24)20%	(6)22%
Performance Appraisal	(5)22%	(6)16%	(2)18%	(2)67%	(15)21%	(25)21%	(5)19%

[a]n = indicates the total number of job applicants in the subgroup.

[b]Values in parentheses represent numbers of applicants.

[c]Indicates that adverse impact defined by the 80% rule exists for the subgroup in comparison to the majority group (whites or males).

Ms. Smith believed that when management is sincerely concerned about the potential discriminatory effects of their selection procedures, the best guarantee for preventing unfair discrimination is information. Therefore, her last task for the police department was to conduct numerous analyses that illustrated the effects certain types of policies could have on their selection process. For example, one analysis involved computing adverse impact figures (using the 80 percent rule and a computer) under the assumption that the top ten, twenty, or thirty candidates, respectively, would eventually be promoted from their list. This analysis revealed that strong adverse impact against blacks would occur if only the top ten candidates were promoted, that using the top twenty candidates would cause less adverse impact, and that no adverse impact would occur if the top thirty candidates were promoted (see Exhibit 4). Similarly, Ms. Smith demonstrated the adverse impact of each of the three components of the SPE and the effects that changing the weighting system would have with respect to adverse impact. Because adverse impact was associated only with the written test, the adverse impact of the total SPE was directly affected by the weight given the written test – the higher the weight of the written test, the more adverse impact of the SPE overall. To reduce the potential adverse impact of the SPE, the weight of the written test should be reduced.

Ms. Smith concluded her consulting assignment with the police chiefs. It is now up to them to fairly utilize, evaluate, and update the promotion procedures Ms. Smith helped them design. What problems, challenges, and issues face the police chiefs in carrying out the procedures developed by Ms. Smith?

32. Nissan Motor Co., Ltd.*

One afternoon of late November, 1988, Mr. Sasaki, Director of Europe Group of Nissan Motor Co., was busy signing Christmas and New Year cards in his office in headquarters in Tokyo. He felt the pile of cards became much higher than the previous year. "This should be because of our recent development in Europe. Now we have Nissan Motor Iberica in Barcelona, Nissan Italy in Rome, and a factory in U.K. has just started operation. It looks that these two years have flown away, keeping us very busy with working for those projects."

Speaking to himself with a satisfied smile, Mr. Sasaki started to look back at Nissan's European operations. Though satisfied, he worries about future development of and some fundamental problems in two subsidiaries in Spain and Italy, wondering what lessons could be learned for other overseas operations and what were the implications for future "globalization."

The Company

Nissan Motor Co., Ltd. was established in 1933. The company has always been strongly overseas oriented and set up its first plant outside Japan in Mexico as early as 1966. And even today it is the only Japanese automobile company that has its own manufacturing base in Europe.

This is not only because the company always has been the second to Toyota in the domestic market. They recognized the necessity to be close to the market in order to better satisfy customer needs, to get integrated in and to contribute to the local economy. Therefore, Nissan is aiming at a whole process localization – to be an "insider" through all the operations from R&D to sales.

Nissan has dramatically increased its presence in Europe these last few years. Several international economic and market environment have promoted this trend: yen appreciation, trade friction, increasing competition, and European common market integration. Reacting to those changes, Nissan has clearly positioned its strategy for "Internationalization" and further "Globalization." The company intends to go beyond export and partly overseas manufacturing, to exploit cost advantage, to establish various activities abroad, and to integrate them horizontally.

Corporate Culture

Nissan does not have a strong corporate culture. As it was established through mergers of some companies during 1910 to 1930, Nissan has no clear "founder." This is an obvious difference from the other Japanese overseas oriented companies like Sony, Honda or Matsushita, whose corporate cultures are directed or affected by strong characters of founders.

*This case was prepared by Ayako Asakura, MBA student, under the supervision of Susan Schneider, associate professor, INSEAD, as a basis for class discussion rather than to illustrate either effective or ineffective handling of an administrative situation. All rights reserved. Reprinted with permission.

This gives freedom to the organization. People are not bound by a certain philosophy, policy or image of the founder and hence the company. Also that the top management positions are totally open to all the employees helps to create motivation.

On the other hand absence of a strong philosophy or visible embodiment of the founder makes it difficult to unite the whole company, to provide a clear sense of direction, and to keep on moving forward. This also causes weakness in their external image. Nissan has enjoyed a good reputation for its high technology, but it is relatively declining with other competitors catching up. Apart from this Nissan lacks a special image in the Japanese market.

Having recognized this point, in January 1987 Nissan, for the first time stated a clearly written "Corporate Philosophy." On the first page of the 1987 annual report it says, "Nissan – growing and changing to meet the needs of today's customers." The company printed this on a business card-size card, distributed to every employee.

This statement is translated in languages of each country where Nissan has plants, offices, or subsidiaries. The translation is not a literal one. It is aimed to express the core policy and objectives and rewritten in a way that the idea would be best implemented in each situation and cultural environment.

Policy Towards Overseas Operations

Nissan's policy towards overseas operations is not rigid. Taking many different situations into consideration, the company has a "clear end and loose means" policy. There is no standardized way. As far as it is in line with the realization of Nissan's objectives, it allows a certain amount of autonomy to each plant or subsidiary and lets them seek for the best way, depending on situations. For example, while the Mexico plant is in a typical Japanese style, the American one in Smyrna, Tennessee, is run in an American way with American top management. The British plant in Sunderland, which is to start operation this autumn (1988) is to be half-British, half-Japanese style.

This variety depends on many factors such as the locations, the form (green-field investment or joint venture), preceding history, technological level, product, human resource availability, target market, and so on.

With its long history of overseas business and operations, the company points out two issues as keys to success. One is to be an insider in the markets wherever they are present. Another is to promote globalization of the headquarters in Japan. In order to understand the development and the situation of overseas operations of Nissan, here are two good examples in Europe: Nissan Motor Iberica and Nissan Italia.

Nissan Motor Iberica S.A. (MISA)

Nissan Motor Iberica is a manufacturing and distribution company, 70% owned by Nissan Motor, and within its management control.

1. History

Motor Iberica dates from as early as 1920 (older than Nissan) and since then it has been a leading commercial vehicle manufacturer in Spain. But the company has a complicated history.

Ford Motor Co. came to Cadiz in 1920, moved to Barcelona three years after, and set up Ford Motor Iberica S.A. in 1929. It became a 100% Spanish equity in 1954, but soon Massey Ferguson, a Canadian agricultural equipment company, bought 36% of its shares. With the declining situation of the main business, Massey Ferguson sold its equity in Motor Iberica to Nissan Motor Co. in 1980.

At that moment Nissan was seeking opportunities to gain better access to European markets and was thinking of building a plant in Spain. Unfortunately, this was just after GM invested in Spain and Spanish government, being afraid of excess capacity, did not permit Nissan's green field investment project. So for Nissan this chance of holding equity in a local company was considered to be a very timely alternative.

Thereafter, Nissan has increased its share to 55% in 1982, to 70% (i.e., 2/3 equity is necessary to hold the practical management leadership in Spain). And the name was changed to Nissan Motor Iberica S.A. in 1987 to show a new identity of the company.

Nissan has introduced new product lines step by step: Patrol (diesel engine, 4WD) in 1983; Vanette (van and coach) in 1985; and Trade (heavy van) in 1987. They also have trucks (Ebro) and derivative big vans.

Nissan has tried to consolidate the business. In 1986 a joint venture was started with Kubota Ltd. and all the tractor business (both manufacturing and sales) was transferred. Since then the number of factories and subsidiaries spread in Spain has also been decreased from 18 to 8 (five plants and three manufacturing subsidiaries).

2. Nissan's Policy Towards Nissan Motor Iberica

The company policy towards overseas business is very well expressed in MISA's situation. Nissan does not think that any standardized way would apply to various environments and treats each operation in a case-by-case way. It leaves "how to do" to each operation or subsidiary.

In the case of Nissan Motor Iberica the main objective is to bear a strategic role in European business. Each country (and EEC as a whole) is more protective than the United States to automobile imports with tight tariffs and quotas demanding a high ratio of local procurement. Therefore, it is critical to have a manufacturing base within Europe and to be treated as a European company. And Motor Iberica meets these conditions quite well.

Nissan pays much respect to the existing identity of Motor Iberica. A Japanese staff says, "We are the late-comer. Here they already have a long history and experience in business, high level of technological skills, well-respected corporate culture and good human resources. We should adapt to Motor Iberica, respecting their culture and the way of business."

3. Change Under Nissan and the Present Situation

Based on this policy, Nissan remains in very small presence in the management of Nissan Motor Iberica.

Organization. When Nissan increased its share in the capital to 55%, one of the existing managers of Motor Iberica became Chairman. Even after acquisition of 70% equity and change of the company's name, from the viewpoint of competence, personality, image, and opinion towards outside relationships with Nissan, Nissan had not done much to change the way of business in Motor Iberica.

The supreme decision maker is the management committee, consisting of Chairman, Company Secretary, Managing Director, and General Manager in charge of technology. With the former two Spanish and the latter Japanese, Nissan has the practically equal power over the business. Besides them, however, all Japanese are in positions of coordinator, advisor or assistant. There are nine Japanese working together in the plant for manufacturing, quality control or design sector. A Japanese says, "In a 6000 employee company, there are only 16 Japanese. We are only 0.3!" And all the directors of seven departments (Manufacturing, Production Planning and Control and Purchase, Design, Finance, Controller, Sales and Personnel) are Spanish. In addition, the company sends Spanish employees (mainly foremen) to train in Japan for better understanding of the Japanese manufacturing system.

The personnel system was kept in a Spanish way. Even through the process of plants and subsidiaries consolidation, every decision and procedure to streamline the organization was initiated by the Spanish manager. Many workers left the company, but most of them were guaranteed employment by the new plant owners or economically compensated for.

Communication. Spanish is the "official language" in the whole company. Papers are written and meetings are conducted in Spanish. Communication between the headquarters is directly done by Spanish managers in English and not necessarily through Japanese.

Outside Relationships. Towards suppliers the company decreased 1000 suppliers to 400, but it is far more compared to the average of 200 in Japan. This is due to two situations. One is that to make this variety of commercial vehicles with more varied components, more suppliers are needed than for ordinary cars. The other is the long history of the Spanish automobile industry. Since foreign car makers (Ford, GM, etc.) came to Spain from quite early days, local suppliers were of high level, used to dealing with car makers, and very reliable.

Nissan Motor Iberica is totally an "insider" in Barcelona, Spain. This facilitates the relationships between the government of both countries and Catalonia. So the company does not have the disadvantage of being a foreign-owned company. It does not need to follow troublesome procedures and a long time to go through governmental requirements as is the case in most other countries.

Internal Acceptance and Effect. Nissan's taking over of management has been well accepted by the employees. According to one Japanese, "As they know Japan through its good quality products like TV, camera, computers, automobiles or audio equipments, it looks they already have a good image of Japan. They mostly feel proud to join manufacturing Japanese products." Especially after the name change of the company the consciousness of working for Nissan has increased. For example, in plants, although it is not forced, some workers started to wear uniforms printed with the company's name.

Also, the Spanish Chairman shows that there is no ceiling for the promotion of Spaniards in the organization. Since the time Nissan took control over 70% of the shares, not a single director left the company.

4. Perceived Differences, Problems, and Approach

Although transition into "Nissan" has been quite smooth, Japanese expatriates perceive that some phenomena in the organization are quite different from that of Japan.

Basic Attitude to Work. A Japanese describes the difference of working attitudes of the Spanish as follows: "People follow the instructions as given, and judgment is totally up to managers. It is necessary to give detailed directions or procedures often in written forms. This is difficult and painstaking for the Japanese, who are used to communicating verbally, not necessarily specify the job with written documents, leave some ambiguity, 'Let's do it together' and 'Let it happen from the bottom' way. They often do not get to work until they totally understand and agree to the logic of the job. But once they agree to it, they do a very fine job."

In Spain the scope of each person's responsibility is very clearly defined, sometimes to the extent that it gets too limited. To make their jobs more efficient, they will need to see the total flow and to have more consideration for their backward and forward operations. This is true both in plants and in offices.

Internal Communication. With this kind of basic mentality, it is not surprising the horizontal communication among departments is not done well. Spanish managers do not discuss each other's job, thinking it is even impolite to "interfere" with others' business.

To make matters worse the office and plant are separately located (within a 15-minute drive). In the office there is only a limited organization of around 50 people: Chairman, Managing Director, Personnel Department, and some staff and secretaries (including two Japanese).

To improve horizontal communication in the office some parts of the walls are glass instead of nontransparent materials. "We thought it would be too drastic to change the office into a Japanese styled office (open office landscape) and risk to create a source of hostility. So we decided to leave it almost as it was. This was also responding to the space constraints," says a Japanese, who has been here more than four years.

On the other hand, MISA is building another office near the existing one. This is purely for the Chairman, President, and one Japanese assistant to the President. One reason is space constraint, another is to use the new office as a guest house. (Actually this new office is a house.) There is a concern, however, that this movement might hinder internal communication.

Role of the Japanese. The Japanese are working as advisors, assistants, or coordinators. They are only helping and complementing Spanish managers. In effect, however, they bear an important role to connect those fragmented parts of the company, as pointed out above, through business and social interactions. (It is difficult and does not make sense to rigorously separate business and social talk for the Japanese, especially when they are abroad and in small numbers.)

Labor Mobility. As is often the case in Western countries, there exists a belief and perhaps a fact that the better you are, the more often you change companies. It is difficult to accumulate internal human resources and build up relationships to cover all the company's business. Fortunately, MISA has at present very efficient directors. Six of seven are internally trained people. Under these directors, however, there is a lack of human resources. Therefore, how to retain people inside and how to recruit and integrate new people from outside are critical, important issues.

New Corporate Policy. Translation of the "company philosophy" statement made public by the headquarters in January 1987 is now available to all employees in MISA. The printed statement is put up on the wall. With this, Nissan is trying to get the people to understand the policy of "customer satisfaction first." "The word 'customer' should be interpreted in a broad sense. This leads to respect and satisfaction of not only buyers or consumers, but also of all the people around you who are working together."

Relationships with Headquarters. At the moment, there is no conflict nor serious problem between MISA and the headquarters in Tokyo. But in general, it is very important and difficult to make the local situation understood well, especially when more commitment or resources are needed, and the overseas operations have to persuade the headquarters to upgrade their priority.

Nissan Italia S.P.A.

Nissan Italia is a distributor and after-service (repair and part sales) company. Sixty-four percent of the share is owned by Nissan Motor Co. and the rest by Nissan Motor Iberica.

1. History

The company, named EBRO, was first founded as a joint venture of an Italian company and Motor Iberica in February 1978 for commercial vehicle sales and after-services. After the name change to Nissan Motor Iberica S.A. (1987), in January 1988 Nissan Motor Co. purchased 49% of the local share (the rest was owned by Nissan Motor Iberica) and changed its name to Nissan Italia S.P.A., and in March increased its share to 64%. Therefore, Nissan Motor is now fully in control of Nissan Italia. The mission given to Nissan Italia in the Nissan group is to cover a very protective Italian market from the sales and service side.

It is not, however, their first footing into the Italian market. Already in 1980 Nissan started a joint venture with Alfa Romeo, but it turned out to be very difficult to control the company, because Nissan had only 50% of the share, and the practical personnel decision was made by Italian managers and the company in Italy. Therefore, Nissan could not take the initiative of the business and annulled the joint venture in 1987. So it was after this experience that Nissan set up Nissan Italia as a new base for the Italian market. Now Nissan Italia sells cars, not only imported from Japan, but also those produced by Nissan Motor Iberica in Spain and from November 1988 also those in a new factory in Sunderland, U.K.

Concerning parts supply, there are two routes: 73% (in 1987) are from Barcelona (the parts manufactured by Nissan Motor Iberica) and the rest are from the Nissan Motor Parts Center in Amsterdam (the parts imported from Japan).

2. Localization – Change to Nissan Italia

Based on Nissan's basic policy of "clear end and loose means," and because of its evolution, Nissan Italia is a very Italian company. As seen in the organization and the communication, here the Japanese are adjusted to the local ways.

Even after March 1988, when Nissan increased its share in the company, there has not been any drastic change. Mr. Arai, President of Nissan Italy, says,

> I did not give any speech to address "new President's declaration." This is not a change of that kind. I have been with them a while and nothing would suddenly change. The base of this company is "Italy." Furthermore, without any formal words the people understand Nissan's intention. In the meantime, maybe when we will move to the new office,[1] I will say a word.

It is obvious, however, that Nissan conveyed a clear message that it is going to be more seriously engaged in a longer term development in the Italian market through this company. And there are also some other signals to show the company's determined will as seen below. From part of the original company this change is very well accepted, because the company is given a chance to jump from a small business to a medium one.

3. Present Situation

Organization. The organization remains very "local." Although the board consists of three Spanish directors and four Japanese, in practice only the President and his assistant are Japanese and one director and one manager are Spanish. Mr. Oyama, the Japanese assistant, is sent over only in September 1988.

Mr. Arai, President, is a veteran about Italy with his 18 years experience as a government official in the Japanese Ministry of Foreign Affairs, as a businessman in a big Japanese trading company, and in Nissan. (He has been with Nissan since the joint venture with Alfa Romeo.)

As this shows, the organization is not a "Japanese managers with Italian subordinates" structure but is very open to the local people up to directors. The people are given responsibilities; for example, Italian staffs fly to Amsterdam or Japan for meetings.

Communication. Italian is always used in the company, as both Spanish managers and the Japanese are fluent in Italian, but externally the official language is English. At the moment, the communication between the headquarters and Nissan Italia is mainly done through Japanese, but it will change as English is more used by both sides, i.e., headquarters and Italian staff. In order to improve communication efficiency and to increase the internationality of the company, English lessons for the Italian staff have been started, which will also help to promote the open mentality of the organization.

The company has a very open atmosphere in spite of the individually separated office style. The door of the President's office is almost always kept open and people come in to talk with Mr. Arai. He says, "I don't like to use first name to call each other, because it sounds to me too casual. But of course I don't mind other people doing it among themselves." And it is true

---

[1]Nissan Italia is now going to have a new head office with warehouse facilities.

that this is only a matter of his taste, and relationships with Italian employees seem very warm.

Japanization. There is no particular effort to Japanize the company. There have been, however, naturally some changes throughout the history of Nissan's increasing share and, hence, control in the company. Mr. Arai described the change so far as "Phase 1."

> Up to now Nissan has done everything it can to help this company: invest in the facilities, send the people, finance the capital, and introduce the passenger cars (before the company was dealing only in commercial vehicles). Phase 1 is the visible change from the top. Now in Phase 2 the company should change by itself based on these preparations.
>
> What I expect from them is to have the participation mentality and to propose their ideas voluntarily to the company.
>
> There are some variances among people's attitude depending on the department. The sales people are quite participative and give their feedback from the field although they are paid on salary basis and not on commissions. This is partly because sales results are, being quantitative and obvious, easier to use for control and motivation.
>
> Compared to them, people in the office or in the warehouse are relatively passive and do not take the initiative. As their jobs are more difficult to evaluate objectively and quantitatively, this is understandable. But I would like them to change their working mind gradually.

Dealer Relationships. Dealer relationships in the case of sales network business are something equivalent to the supplier relationships in the manufacturing. Nissan Italia's dealers are multi-franchisers with contracts with several car manufacturers except Fiat. They sell various kinds of cars. Being independent from Nissan, they are difficult to control. Mr. Arai says,

> They are profit-oriented dealers. But I would like to change our relationships and develop a more longer term one.
>
> For this purpose Nissan Italia makes efforts to improve communication with them, to make them understand Nissan's policy and products superiority and to ask for dealers' cooperation, for example, hold meetings, increase advertisement budget and so on. And in the future, we would also like to have our own exclusive dealer network.

4. Perceived Problems

Working Style. Mr. Arai says, "Here the manager should give every instruction to get things done. You cannot expect the employees to act positively or manage voluntary activities like QC (Quality Circles). Especially the people in the workshop (repair and after-service) who rarely do overtime."

Personnel. Labor mobility is also a big problem to the human resource management. The better a manager is, he tends to move to another company, and this makes it difficult to plan in-house training, to keep good people, and to accumulate the expertise. "But on the other hand we enjoy some merits of this mobility, too. That is, we can recruit experienced people from outside whenever necessary," says a Japanese manager with a bitter smile.

5. Expatriate Situation

Until September 1988, Mr. Arai has been the only Japanese in the company, with Mr. Oyama sometimes coming to Rome on a long business trip basis. Both of them do not seem to have any difficulty working and living here thanks to their language ability and personalities. Here some points are given by Mr. Arai as general comments about the expatriate situation.

Inconvenience about Business Schedule. The difference of working hours, i.e., the time lag and the difference in working hour length, causes the expatriates to work very long – the early morning or late night telephone call to home, coming to the office on weekends, local holidays or during summer vacation, which is much longer here than in Japan.

Another thing is that they are expected to be attendants for Japanese managers or clients when they make a visit. They should play a role of "perfect" attendant: driver, interpreter, tourist guide, and shopping advisor all at the same time, from morning to night. This is especially the case in big cities like Paris, London, or Rome.

Japanese Circle. In every city with more than a certain amount of Japanese population, there is a Japanese Association. So in Rome, but compared to Milan, where many companies situate, the Japanese population in Rome is small and hence not many activities are going on in the Japanese circle.

According to Mr. Arai, "If you try to maintain a Japanese lifestyle or to stick together with the Japanese, then you might have a problem to adjust to the foreign life and people. But as far as you try to get accustomed to a new environment, there would be no problem."

And there are not many Japanese restaurants, either. "Anyway Rome (and any Italian cities?) is a bit different from other cities in terms of the food internationality. There are not many foreign food restaurants. For example, generally fancy French restaurants are appreciated as the best cuisine and can be found in any big international cities. But it seems that Italians mock at French cooking which 'damages natural and original taste of food with heavy sauce.' People are just as happy with their own Italian food," says Mr. Oyama, who also loves Italian food.

Children's Education. Last but not least, today perhaps the biggest issue for Japanese expatriates is children's education.

Many foreign cities have Japanese schools of either full-time or complementary depending on the Japanese population. However, as the Japanese society is very education-conscious, many parents want children to enter a good company, a good university, a good high school ... Therefore at the "critical" age for high school or junior high school, many children (and with their mothers) are sent back to Japan.

What is very interesting and shows a particular aspect of Japanese society is that this tendency is stronger for boys; there are many boys going back home to prepare for good universities while there are more girls going to local schools at various levels and staying abroad longer. Since the Japanese working world is still a rather male society with lifelong employment, it is thought that boys should equip themselves with high education for their own future happiness, i.e., employment, marriage, and so on.

Back at Headquarters

Looking at the current situations in Nissan Motor Iberica and Nissan Italia, Mr. Sasaki is quite pleased with their evolution so far as the first phase. At the same time, however, he realized some difficult problems. Most of them are not new, they come up more or less every time Nissan tries to develop business abroad. Therefore, to solve these problems would take a long time, and more than that the solution itself is still not clear.

There are some common points for both subsidiaries. First, human resource management is of concern. As a whole, Nissan has kept the local identity of each subsidiary and retained most of the personnel. There seems no hostility nor problem for adjustment. But there is a very fundamental difference among employees' working mentality which has puzzled Japanese managers, i.e., local staffs are not very participative and communication within the company (especially horizontal communication among functions and operations) is rather poor. Also, high job mobility restrains them from accumulation of expertise and planning for human resource management.

"What can we do to motivate them and make them participate? Would the Japanese way of management with regard to motivation and incentive systems work?"

This first question leads to the second question, which is more fundamental. "How far could or should we reinforce Japanization in foreign subsidiaries? Where is the optimal balance?"

"And what is the role of Japanese expatriates and the headquarters?" Mr. Sasaki knows expatriates' frustration toward headquarters very well and recognizes the necessity of head-quarters' globalization. "Expatriate managers are 'sandwiched' in between demands from the headquarters and the local subsidiary. They need our understanding and support in terms of money, people, technology, and human network and its mental support. But we cannot afford to respond to all of their needs due to the shortage of resource, especially at this time of rapidly expanding overseas business. First of all, we should at least be better prepared to use English to facilitate communication between foreign subsidiaries. And more fundamentally to raise good human resources able to cope with international operation. This will be a real long-term job."

And another question is how to train employees for globalization strategy? For example, now Nissan sends a few employees to business school, mostly in the United States. "Would we rather send someone to Europe, too, as our presence in Europe has very much increased? Then which school'?"

The last question in his mind is about human resource management. How to respond to expatriates' problems both in a working situation and a general private life situation? How can the headquarters support their job? How far should the company support them for their children's education or maintenance of houses they leave in Japan?

But, Mr. Sasaki was brought back to Nissan's policy at the end: "clear end and loose means." "Maybe there is no right answer to be generalized, and we should try to think out in each context."

Part 8   Motivation and Performance

Cases Outline

33. The Lincoln Electric Company, 1989*

> People are our most valuable asset. They must feel secure, important, challenged, in control of their destiny, confident in their leadership, be responsive to common goals, believe they are being treated fairly, have easy access to authority and open lines of communication in all possible directions. Perhaps the most important task Lincoln employees face today is that of establishing an example for others in the Lincoln organization in other parts of the world. We need to maximize the benefits of cooperation and teamwork, fusing high technology with human talent, so that we here in the USA and all of our subsidiary and joint venture operations will be in a position to realize our full potential.
>
> *George Willis*
> *Former CEO, The Lincoln Electric Company*

The Lincoln Electric Company is the world's largest manufacturer of arc-welding products and a leading producer of industrial electric motors. The firm employs 2,400 workers in 2 U.S. factories near Cleveland and an equal number in 11 factories located in other countries. This does not include the field sales force of more than 200. The company's U.S. market share (for arc-welding products) is estimated at more than 40 percent.

The Lincoln incentive management plan has been well known for many years. Many college management texts make reference to the Lincoln plan as a model for achieving higher worker productivity. Certainly, the firm has been successful according to the usual measures.

James F. Lincoln died in 1965 and there was some concern, even among employees, that the management system would fall into disarray, that profits would decline, and that year-end-bonuses might be discontinued. Quite the contrary, 24 years after Lincoln's death, the company appears as strong as ever. Each year, except the recession years 1982 and 1983, has seen high profits and bonuses. Employee morale and productivity remain very good. Employee turnover is almost nonexistent except for retirements. Lincoln's market share is stable. The historically high stock dividends continue.

A Historical Sketch

In 1895, after being "frozen out" of the depression-ravaged Elliott-Lincoln Company, a maker of Lincoln-designed electric motors, John C. Lincoln took out his second patent and began to manufacture his improved motor. He opened his new business, unincorporated, with $200 he had earned redesigning a motor for young Herbert Henry Dow, who later founded the Dow Chemical Company.

Started during an economic depression and cursed by a major fire after only one year in business, the company grew, but hardly prospered, through its first quarter century. In 1906, John C. Lincoln incorporated the business and moved from his one-room, fourth-floor factory

*Copyright Arthur D. Sharplin, Waltham Associates, Inc., Austin, Texas. Reprinted from *Managing Human Resources* 5th Edition, Randall S. Schuler. Reprinted with permission.

to a new three-story building he erected in east Cleveland. He expanded his work force to 30 and sales grew to over $50,000 a year. John preferred being an engineer and inventor rather than a manager, though, and it was to be left to another Lincoln to manage the company through its years of success.

In 1907, after a bout with typhoid fever forced him from Ohio State University in his senior year, James F. Lincoln, John's younger brother, joined the fledgling company. In 1914 he became active head of the firm, with the titles of General Manager and Vice President. John remained president of the company for some years but became more involved in other business ventures and in his work as an inventor.

One of James Lincoln's early actions was to ask the employees to elect representatives to a committee which would advise him on company operations. This "Advisory Board" has met with the chief executive officer every two weeks since that time. This was only the first of a series of innovative personnel policies which have, over the years, distinguished Lincoln Electric from its contemporaries.

The first year the Advisory Board was in existence, working hours were reduced from 55 per week, then standard, to 50 hours a week. In 1915, the company gave each employee a paid-up life insurance policy. A welding school, which continues today, was begun in 1917. In 1918, an employee bonus plan was attempted. It was not continued, but the idea was to resurface later.

The Lincoln Electric Employees' Association was formed in 1919 to provide health benefits and social activities. This organization continues today and has assumed several additional functions over the years. In 1923, a piecework pay system was put in effect, employees got two weeks paid vacation each year, and wages were adjusted for changes in the Consumer Price Index. Approximately 30 percent of the common stock was set aside for key employees in 1914. A stock purchase plan for all employees was begun in 1925.

The Board of Directors voted to start a suggestion system in 1929. The program is still in effect, but cash awards, a part of the early program, were discontinued several years ago. Now, suggestions are rewarded by additional "points," which affect year-end bonuses.

The legendary Lincoln bonus plan was proposed by the Advisory Board and accepted on a trial basis in 1934. The first annual bonus amounted to about 25 percent of wages. There has been a bonus every year since then. The bonus plan has been a cornerstone of the Lincoln management system and recent bonuses have approximated annual wages.

By 1944, Lincoln employees enjoyed a pension plan, a policy of promotion from within, and continuous employment. Base pay rates were determined by formal job evaluation and a merit rating system was in effect.

In the prologue of James F. Lincoln's last book, Charles G. Herbruck writes regarding the foregoing personnel innovations:

> They were not to buy good behavior. They were not efforts to increase profits. They were not antidotes to labor difficulties. They did not constitute a "do-gooder" program. They were expressions of mutual respect for each person's importance to the job to be done. All of them reflect the leadership of James Lincoln, under whom they were nurtured and propagated.

During World War II, Lincoln prospered as never before. By the start of the war, the company was the world's largest manufacturer of arc-welding products. Sales of about $4,000,000 in 1934 grew to $24,000,000 by 1941. Productivity per employee more than doubled during the same period. The Navy's Price Review Board challenged the high profits. And the Internal Revenue Service questioned the tax deductibility of employee bonuses, arguing they were not "ordinary and necessary" costs of doing business. But the forceful and articulate James Lincoln was able to overcome the objections.

Certainly since 1935 and probably for several years before that, Lincoln productivity has been well above the average for similar companies. The company claims levels of productivity more than twice those for other manufacturers from 1945 onward. Information available from outside sources tends to support these claims.

Company Philosophy

James F. Lincoln was the son of a Congregational minister, and Christian principles were at the center of his business philosophy. The confidence that he had in the efficacy of Christ's teachings is illustrated by the following remark taken from one of his books:

> The Christian ethic should control our acts. If it did control our acts, the savings in cost of distribution would be tremendous. Advertising would be a contact of the expert consultant with the customer, in order to give the customer the best product available when all of the customer's needs are considered. Competition then would be in improving the quality of products and increasing efficiency in producing and distributing them; not in deception, as is now too customary. Pricing would reflect efficiency of production; it would not be a selling dodge that the customer may well be sorry he accepted. It would be proper for all concerned and rewarding for the ability used in producing the product.

There is no indication that Lincoln attempted to evangelize his employees or customers – or the general public for that matter. Neither the chairman of the board and chief executive, George Willis, nor the president, Donald F. Hastings, mention the Christian gospel in their recent speeches and interviews. The company motto, "The actual is limited, the possible is immense," is prominently displayed, but there is no display of religious slogans, and there is no company chapel.

Attitude Toward the Customer

James Lincoln saw the customer's needs as the raison d'etre for every company. "When any company has achieved success so that it is attractive as an investment," he wrote, "all money usually needed for expansion is supplied by the customer in retained earnings. It is obvious that the customer's interests, not the stockholder's, should come first." In 1947 he said, "Care should be taken... not to rivet attention on profit. Between 'How much do I get?' and 'How do I make this better, cheaper, more useful?' the difference is fundamental and decisive." Willis, too, ranks the customer as management's most important constituency. This is reflected in Lincoln's policy to "at all times price on the basis of cost and at all times keep pressure on our cost..." Lincoln's goal, often stated, is "to build a better and better product at a lower and lower price." "It is obvious," James Lincoln said, "that the customer's interests should be the first goal of industry."

Attitude Toward Stockholders

Stockholders are given last priority at Lincoln. This is a continuation of James Lincoln's philosophy: "The last group to be considered is the stockholders who own stock because they think it will be more profitable than investing money in any other way." Concerning division of the largess produced by incentive management, he wrote, "The absentee stockholder also will get his share, even if undeserved, out of the greatly increased profit that the effciency produces."

Attitude Toward Unionism

There has never been a serious effort to organize Lincoln employees. While James Lincoln criticized the labor movement for "selfishly attempting to better its position at the expense of the people it must serve," he still had kind words for union members. He excused abuses of union power as "the natural reactions of human beings to the abuses to which management has subjected them." Lincoln's idea of the correct relationship between workers and managers is shown by this comment: "Labor and management are properly not warring camps; they are parts of one organization in which they must and should cooperate fully and happily."

Beliefs and Assumptions about Employees

If fulfilling customer needs is the desired goal of business, then employee performance and productivity are the means by which this goal can best be achieved. It is the Lincoln attitude toward employees, reflected in the following comments by James Lincoln, which is credited by many with creating the success the company has experienced:

> The greatest fear of the worker, which is the same as the greatest fear of the industrialist in operating a company, is the lack of income ... The industrial manager is very conscious of his company's need of uninterrupted income. He is completely oblivious, evidently, of the fact that the worker has the same need.

> He is just as eager as any manager is to be part of a team that is properly organized and working for the advancement of our economy... He has no desire to make profits for those who do not hold up their end in production, as is true of absentee stockholders and inactive people in the company.

> If money is to be used as an incentive, the program must provide that what is paid to the worker is what he has earned. The earnings of each must be in accordance with accomplishment.

> Status is of great importance in all human relationships. The greatest incentive that money has, usually, is that it is a symbol of success... The resulting status is the real incentive... Money alone can be an incentive to the miser only.

There must be complete honesty and understanding between the hourly worker and management if high efficiency is to be obtained.

Lincoln's Business

Arc-welding has been the standard joining method in shipbuilding for decades. It is the predominant way of connecting steel in the construction industry. Most industrial plants have their own welding shops for maintenance and construction. Manufacturers of tractors and all kinds of heavy equipment use arc-welding extensively in the manufacturing process. Many hobbyists have their own welding machines and use them for making metal items such as patio furniture and barbecue pits. The popularity of welded sculpture as an art form is growing.

While advances in welding technology have been frequent, arc-welding products, in the main, have hardly changed. Lincoln's Innershield process is a notable exception. This process, described later, lowers welding cost and improves quality and speed in many applications. The most widely-used Lincoln electrode, the Fleetweld 5P, has been virtually the same since the 1930s. The most popular engine-driven welder in the world, the Lincoln SA-200, has been a gray-colored assembly including a four-cylinder continental "Red Seal" engine and a 200 ampere direct-current generator with two current-control knobs for at least four decades. A 1989 model SA-200 even weighs almost the same as the 1950 model, and it certainly is little changed in appearance.

The company's share of the U.S. arc-welding products market appears to have been about 40 percent for many years. The welding products market has grown somewhat faster than the level of industry in general. The market is highly price-competitive, with variations in prices of standard items normally amounting to only a percent or two. Lincoln's products are sold directly by its engineering-oriented sales force and indirectly through its distributor organization. Advertising expenditures amount to less than three-fourths of a percent of sales. Research and development expenditures typically range from $10 million to $12 million, considerably more than competitors.

The other major welding process, flame-welding, has not been competitive with arc-welding since the 1930s. However, plasma-arc-welding, a relatively new process which uses a conducting stream of super heated gas (plasma) to confine the welding current to a small area, has made some inroads, especially in metal tubing manufacturing, in recent years. Major advances in technology which will produce an alternative superior to arc-welding within the next decade or so appear unlikely. Also, it seems likely that changes in the machines and techniques used in arc-welding will be evolutionary rather than revolutionary.

Products

The company is primarily engaged in the manufacture and sale of arc-welding products – electric welding machines and metal electrodes. Lincoln also produces electric motors ranging from one-half horsepower to 200 horsepower. Motors constitute about 8 to 10 percent of total sales. Several million dollars have recently been invested in automated equipment that will double Lincoln's manufacturing capacity for 1/2 to 20 horsepower electric motors.

The electric welding machines, some consisting of a transformer or motor and generator arrangement powered by commercial electricity and others consisting of an internal combustion engine and generator, are designed to produce 30 to 1,500 amperes of electrical power.

This electrical current is used to melt a consumable metal electrode with the molten metal being transferred in super hot spray to the metal joint being welded. Very high temperatures and hot sparks are produced, and operators usually must wear special eye and face protection and leather gloves, often along with leather aprons and sleeves.

Lincoln and its competitors now market a wide range of general purpose and specialty electrodes for welding mild steel, aluminum, cast iron, and stainless and special steels. Most of these electrodes are designed to meet the standards of the American Welding Society, a trade association. They are thus essentially the same as to size and composition from one manufacturer to another. Every electrode manufacturer has a limited number of unique products, but these typically constitute only a small percentage of total sales.

Welding electrodes are of two basic types: (1) Coated "stick" electrodes, usually 14 inches long and smaller than a pencil in diameter, which are held in a special insulated holder by the operator, who must manipulate the electrode in order to maintain a proper arc-width and pattern of deposition of the metal being transferred. Stick electrodes are packaged in 6- to 50-pound boxes. (2) Coiled wired, ranging in diameter from .035" to 0.219", which is designed to be fed continuously to the welding arc through a "gun" held by the operator or positioned by automatic positioning equipment. The wire is packaged in coils, reels, and drums weighing from 14 to 1,000 pounds and may be solid or flux-cored.

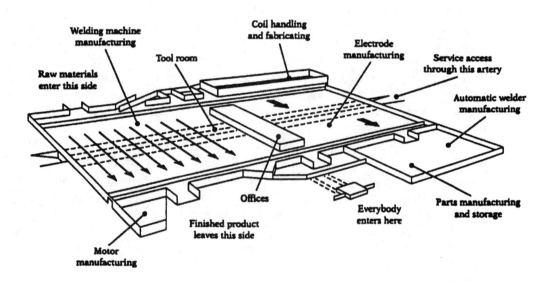

Figure 1. Main Factory Layout

Manufacturing Processes

The main plant is in Euclid, Ohio, a suburb on Cleveland's east side. The layout of this plant is shown in Figure 1. There are no warehouses. Materials flow from the half-mile long dock on the north side of the plant through the production lines to a very limited storage and loading area on the south side. Materials used on each work station are stored as close as possible to the work station. The administrative offices, near the center of the factory, are entirely functional. A corridor below the main level provides access to the factory floor from the main entrance near the center of the plan. *Fortune* magazine recently declared the Euclid facility one of America's 10 best-managed factories, and compared it with a General Electric plant also on the list:

> Stepping into GE's spanking new dishwasher plant, an awed supplier said, is like stepping "into the Hyatt Regency." By comparison, stepping into Lincoln Electric's 33-year-old, cavernous, dimly lit factory is like stumbling into a dingy big-city YMCA. It's only when one starts looking at how these factories do things that similarities become apparent. They have found ways to merge design with manufacturing, build in quality, make wise choices about automation, get close to customers, and handle their work forces.

A new Lincoln plant, in Mentor, Ohio, houses some of the electrode production operations, which were moved from the main plant.

Electrode manufacturing is highly capital intensive. Metal rods purchased from steel producers are drawn down to smaller diameters, cut to length and coated with pressed-powder "flux" for stick electrodes or plated with copper (for conductivity) and put into coils or spools for wire. Lincoln's Innershield wire is hollow and filled with a material similar to that used to coat stick electrodes. As mentioned earlier, this represented a major innovation in welding technology when it was introduced. The company is highly secretive about its electrode production processes, and outsiders are not given access to the details of those processes.

Lincoln welding machines and electric motors are made on a series of assembly lines. Gasoline and diesel engines are purchased partially assembled but practically all other components are made from basic industrial products, e.g., steel bars and sheets and bar copper conductor wire.

Individual components, such as gasoline tanks for engine-driven welders and steel shafts for motors and generators, are made by numerous small "factories within a factory." The shaft for a certain generator, for example, is made from raw steel bar by one operator who uses five large machines, all running continuously. A saw cuts the bar to length, a digital lathe machines different sections to varying diameters, a special milling machine cuts a slot for the keyway, and so forth, until a finished shaft is produced. The operator moves the shafts from machine to machine and makes necessary adjustments.

Another operator punches, shapes and paints sheetmetal cowling parts. One assembles steel laminations onto a rotor shaft, then winds, insulates and tests the rotors. Finished components are moved by crane operators to the nearby assembly lines.

Worker Performance and Attitudes

Exceptional worker performance at Lincoln is a matter of record. The typical Lincoln employee earns about twice as much as other factory workers in the Cleveland area. Yet the company's labor cost per sales dollar in 1989, 26 cents, is well below industry averages. Worker turnover is practically nonexistent except for retirements and departures by new employees.

Sales per Lincoln factory employee currently exceed $150,000. An observer at the factory quickly sees why this figure is so high. Each worker is proceeding busily and thoughtfully about the task at hand. There is no idle chatter. Most workers take no coffee breaks. Many operate several machines and make a substantial component unaided. The supervisors are busy with planning and record keeping duties and hardly glance at the people they "supervise." The manufacturing procedures appear effcient – no unnecessary steps, no wasted motions, no wasted materials. Finished components move smoothly to subsequent work stations.

Appendix A includes summaries of interviews with employees.

Organization Structure

Lincoln has never allowed development of a formal organization chart. The objective of this policy is to insure maximum flexibility. An open door policy is practiced throughout the company, and personnel are encouraged to take problems to the persons most capable of resolving them. Once, Harvard Business School researchers prepared an organization chart reflecting the implied relationships at Lincoln. The chart became available within the company, and present management feels that had a disruptive effect. Therefore, no organizational chart appears in this report.

Perhaps because of the quality and enthusiasm of the Lincoln workforce, routine supervision is almost nonexistent. A typical production foreman, for example, supervises as many as 100 workers, a span-of-control which does not allow more than infrequent worker-supervisor interaction.

Position titles and traditional flows of authority do imply something of an organizational structure, however. For example, the Vice-President, Sales, and the Vice-President, Electrode Division, report to the President, as do various staff assistants such as the Personnel Director and the Director of Purchasing. Using such implied relationships, it has been determined that production workers have two or, at most, three levels of supervision between themselves and the President.

Personnel Policies

As mentioned earlier, it is Lincoln's remarkable personnel practices which are credited by many with the company's success.

Recruitment and Selection

Every job opening is advertised internally on company bulletin boards and any employee can apply for any job so advertised. External hiring is permitted only for entry level positions. Selection for these jobs is done on the basis of personal interviews – there is no aptitude or psychological testing. Not even a high school diploma is required – except for engineering and sales positions, which are filled by graduate engineers. A committee consisting of vice presidents and supervisors interviews candidates initially cleared by the Personnel Department. Final selection is made by the supervisor who has a job opening. Out of over 3,500 applicants interviewed by the Personnel Department during a recent period fewer than 300 were hired.

Job Security

In 1958 Lincoln formalized its guaranteed continuous employment policy, which had already been in effect for many years. There have been no layoffs since World War II. Since 1958, every worker with over two year's longevity has been guaranteed at least 30 hours per week, 49 weeks per year.

The policy has never been so severely tested as during the 1981-83 recession. As a manufacturer of capital goods, Lincoln's business is highly cyclical. In previous recessions the company was able to avoid major sales declines. However, sales plummeted 32 percent in 1982 and another 16 percent the next year. Few companies could withstand such a revenue collapse and remain profitable. Yet, Lincoln not only earned profits, but no employee was laid off and year-end incentive bonuses continued. To weather the storm, management cut most of the nonsalaried workers back to 30 hours a week for varying periods of time. Many employees were reassigned and the total workforce was slightly reduced through normal attrition and restricted hiring. Many employees grumbled at their unexpected misfortune, probably to the surprise and dismay of some Lincoln managers. However, sales and profits – and employee bonuses – soon rebounded and all was well again.

Performance Evaluations

Each supervisor formally evaluates subordinates twice a year using the cards shown in Figure 2. The employee performance criteria, "quality," "dependability," "ideas and cooperation," and "output," are considered to be independent of each other. Marks on the cards are converted to numerical scores which are forced to average 100 for each evaluating supervisor. Individual merit rating scores normally range from 80 to 110. Any score over 110 requires a special letter to top management. These scores (over 110) are not considered in computing the required 100 point average for each evaluating supervisor. Suggestions for improvements often result in recommendations for exceptionally high performance scores. Supervisors discuss individual performance marks with the employees concerned. Each warranty claim is traced to the individual employee whose work caused the defect. The employee's performance score may be reduced, or the worker may be required to repay the cost of servicing the warranty claim by working without pay.

Compensation

Basic wage levels for jobs at Lincoln are determined by a wage survey of similar jobs in the Cleveland area. These rates are adjusted quarterly in accordance with changes in the Cleveland area wage index. Insofar as possible, base wage rates are translated into piece rates. Practically all production workers and many others – for example, some forklift operators – are paid by piece rate. Once established, piece rates are never changed unless a substantive change in the way a job is done results from a source other than the worker doing the job.

In December of each year, a portion of annual profits is distributed to employees as bonuses. Incentive bonuses since 1934 have averaged about 90 percent of annual wages and somewhat more than after-tax profits. The average bonus for 1988 was $21,258. Even for the recession years 1982 and 1983, bonuses had averaged $13,998 and $8,557, respectively. Individual bonuses are proportional to merit-rating scores. For example, assume the amount

Figure 2. Merit Rating Cards

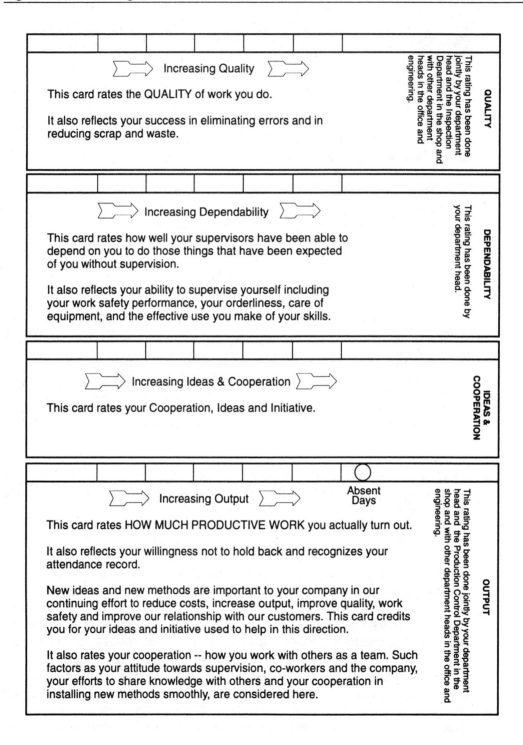

Increasing Quality

This card rates the QUALITY of work you do.

It also reflects your success in eliminating errors and in reducing scrap and waste.

QUALITY — This rating has been done jointly by your department head and the Inspection Department in the shop and with other department heads in the office and engineering.

Increasing Dependability

This card rates how well your supervisors have been able to depend on you to do those things that have been expected of you without supervision.

It also reflects your ability to supervise yourself including your work safety performance, your orderliness, care of equipment, and the effective use you make of your skills.

DEPENDABILITY — This rating has been done by your department head.

Increasing Ideas & Cooperation

This card rates your Cooperation, Ideas and Initiative.

IDEAS & COOPERATION

Increasing Output   Absent Days

This card rates HOW MUCH PRODUCTIVE WORK you actually turn out.

It also reflects your willingness not to hold back and recognizes your attendance record.

New ideas and new methods are important to your company in our continuing effort to reduce costs, increase output, improve quality, work safety and improve our relationship with our customers. This card credits you for your ideas and initiative used to help in this direction.

It also rates your cooperation -- how you work with others as a team. Such factors as your attitude towards supervision, co-workers and the company, your efforts to share knowledge with others and your cooperation in installing new methods smoothly, are considered here.

OUTPUT — This rating has been done jointly by your department head and the Production Control Department in the shop and with other department heads in the office and engineering.

set aside for bonuses is 80 percent of total wages paid to eligible employees. A person whose performance score is 95 will receive a bonus of 76 percent (0.80 x 0.95) of annual wages.

Vacations — very limited timing

The company is shut down for two weeks in August and two weeks during the Christmas season. Vacations are taken during these periods. For employees with over 25 years of service, a fifth week of vacation may be taken at a time acceptable to superiors.

Work Assignment

Management has authority to transfer workers and to switch between overtime and short time as required. Supervisors have undisputed authority to assign specific parts to individual workmen, who may have their own preferences due to variations in piece rates. During the 1982-1983 recession, 50 factory workers volunteered to join sales teams and fanned out across the country to sell a new welder designed for automobile body shops and small machine shops. The result – $10 million in sales and a hot new product.

Employee Participation In Decision Making

Thinking of participative management usually evokes a vision of a relaxed, non-authoritarian atmosphere. This is not the case at Lincoln. Formal authority is quite strong. "We're very authoritarian around here," says Willis. James F. Lincoln placed a good deal of stress on protecting management's authority. "Management in all successful departments of industry must have complete power," he said, "Management is the coach who must be obeyed. The men, however, are the players who alone can win the game." Despite this attitude, there are several ways in which employees participate in management at Lincoln.

Richard Sabo, Assistant to the Chief Executive Officer, relates job enlargement/enrichment to participation. He said, "The most important participative technique that we use is giving more responsibility to employees. We give a high school graduate more responsibility than other companies give their foremen." Management puts limits on the degree of participation which is allowed, however. In Sabo's words:

> When you use participation, put quotes around it. Because we believe that each person should participate only in those decisions he is most knowledgeable about. I don't think production employees should control the decisions of the chairman. They don't know as much as he does about the decisions he is involved in.

The Advisory Board, elected by the workers, meets with the Chairman and the President every two weeks to discuss ways of improving operations. As noted earlier, this board has been in existence since 1914 and has contributed to many innovations. The incentive bonuses, for example, were first recommended by this committee. Every employee has access to Advisory Board members, and answers to all Advisory Board suggestions are promised by the following meeting. Both Willis and Hastings are quick to point out, though, that the Advisory Board only recommends actions. "They do not have direct authority," Willis says, "And when they bring up something that management thinks is not to the benefit of the company, it will be rejected."

Under the early suggestion program, employees were awarded one-half of the first year's savings attributable to their suggestions. Now, however, the value of suggestions is reflected in performance evaluation scores, which determine individual incentive bonus amounts.

Training and Education

Production workers are given a short period of on-the-job training and then placed on a piecework pay system. Lincoln does not pay for off-site education, unless very specific company needs are identified. The idea behind this latter policy, according to Sabo, is that everyone cannot take advantage of such a program, and it is unfair to expend company funds for an advantage to which there is unequal access. Recruits for sales jobs, already college graduates, are given on-the-job training in the plant followed by a period of work and training at one of the regional sales offices.

Fringe Benefits and Executive Perquisites

A medical plan and a company-paid retirement program have been in effect for many years. A plant cafeteria, operated on a break-even basis, serves meals at about 60 percent of usual costs. The Employee Association, to which the company does not contribute, provides disability insurance and social and athletic activities. The employee stock ownership program has resulted in employee ownership of about 50 percent of the common stock. Under this program, each employee with more than two years of service may purchase stock in the corporation. The price of these shares is established at book value. Stock purchased through this plan may be held by employees only. Dividends and voting rights are the same as for stock which is owned outside the plan. Approximately 75 percent of the employees own Lincoln stock.

As to executive perquisites, there are none – crowded, austere offices, no executive washrooms or lunchrooms, and no reserved parking spaces. Even the top executives pay for their own meals and eat in the employee cafeteria. On one recent day, Willis arrived at work late due to a breakfast speaking engagement and had to park far away from the factory entrance.

Financial Policies

James F. Lincoln felt strongly that financing for company growth should come from within the company – through initial cash investment by the founders, through retention of earnings, and through stock purchases by those who work in the business. He saw the following advantages of this approach:

1. Ownership of stock by employees strengthens team spirit. "If they are mutually anxious to make it succeed, the future of the company is bright."
2. Ownership of stock provides individual incentive because employees feel that they will benefit from company profitability.

3. "Ownership is educational." Owners-employees "will know how profits are made and lost; how success is won and lost... There are few socialists in the list of stockholders of the nation's industries."
4. "Capital available from within controls expansion." Unwarranted expansion would not occur, Lincoln believed, under his financing plan.
5. "The greatest advantage would be the development of the individual worker. Under the incentive of ownership, he would become a greater man."
6. "Stock ownership is one of the steps that can be taken that will make the worker feel that there is less of a gulf between him and the boss... Stock ownership will help the worker to recognize his responsibility in the game and the importance of victory."

Until 1980, Lincoln Electric borrowed no money. Even now, the company's liabilities consist mainly of accounts payable and short-term accruals.

The unusual pricing policy at Lincoln is succinctly stated by Willis: "At all times price on the basis of cost and at all times keep pressure on our cost." This policy resulted in the price for the most popular welding electrode then in use going from 16 cents a pound in 1929 to 4.7 cents in 1938. More recently, the SA-200 Welder, Lincoln's largest selling portable machine, decreased in price from 1958 through 1965. According to Dr. C. Jackson Grayson of the American Productivity Center in Houston, Texas, Lincoln's prices increased only one-fifth as fast as the Consumer Price Index from 1934 to about 1970. This resulted in a welding products market in which Lincoln became the undisputed price leader for the products it manufactures. Not even the major Japanese manufacturers, such as Nippon Steel for welding electrodes and Osaka Transformer for welding machines, were able to penetrate this market.

Substantial cash balances are accumulated each year preparatory to paying the year-end bonuses. The bonuses totaled $54 million for 1988. The money is invested in short-term U.S. government securities and certificates of deposit until needed. Financial statements are shown in Table 1. Figure 3 shows how company revenue was distributed in the late 1980s.

How Well Does Lincoln Serve Its Stakeholders?

Lincoln Electric differs from most other companies in the importance it assigns to each of the groups it serves. Willis identifies these groups, in the order of priority ascribed to them, as (1) customers, (2) employees, and (3) stockholders.

Certainly the firm's customers have fared well over the years. Lincoln prices for welding machines and welding electrodes are acknowledged to be the lowest in the marketplace. Quality has consistently been high. The cost of field failures for Lincoln products was recently determined to be a remarkable 0.04 percent of revenues. The "Fleetweld" electrodes and SA-200 welders have been the standard in the pipeline and refinery construction industry, where price is hardly a criterion, for decades. A Lincoln distributor in Monroe, Louisiana, says that he has sold several hundred of the popular AC-225 welders, which are warranted for one year, but has never handled a warranty claim.

Perhaps best-served of all management constituencies have been the employees. Not the least of their benefits, of course, are the year-end bonuses, which effectively double an already average compensation level. The foregoing description of the personnel program and the comments in Appendix A further illustrate the desirability of a Lincoln job.

Table 1. Condensed Comparitive Financial Statements ($000,000)*

Balance Sheets

	1979	1980	1981	1982	1983	1984	1985	1986	1987
Assets									
Cash	2	1	4	1	2	4	2	1	7
Bonds & CDs	38	47	63	72	78	57	55	45	41
N/R & A/R	42	42	42	26	31	34	38	36	43
Inventories	38	36	46	38	31	37	34	26	40
Prepayments	1	3	4	5	5	5	7	8	7
Total CA	121	129	157	143	146	138	135	116	137
Other assets**	24	24	26	30	30	29	29	33	40
Land	1	1	1	1	1	1	1	1	1
Net buildings	22	23	25	23	22	21	20	18	17
Net M&E	21	25	27	27	27	28	27	29	33
Total FA	44	49	53	51	50	50	48	48	50
Total assets	189	202	236	224	227	217	213	197	227
Claims									
A/P	17	16	15	12	16	15	13	11	20
Accrued wages	1	2	5	4	3	4	5	5	4
Accrued taxes	10	6	15	5	7	4	6	5	9
Accrued div.	6	6	7	7	7	6	7	6	7
Total CL	33	29	42	28	33	30	31	27	40
LT debt	—	4	5	6	8	10	11	8	8
Total debt	33	33	47	34	41	40	42	35	48
Common stock	4	3	1	2	0	0	0	0	2
Ret. earnings	152	167	189	188	186	176	171	161	177
Total SH equity	156	170	190	190	186	176	171	161	179
Total claims	189	202	236	224	227	217	213	197	227

Income Statements

	1979	1980	1981	1982	1983	1984	1985	1986	1987
Net Sales	374	387	450	311	263	322	333	318	369
Other Income	11	14	18	18	13	12	11	8	9
Income	385	401	469	329	277	334	344	326	377
CGS	244	261	293	213	180	223	221	216	239
Selling, G&A**	41	46	51	45	45	47	48	49	51
Incentive bonus	44	43	56	37	22	33	38	33	39
IBT	56	51	69	35	30	31	36	27	48
Income taxes	26	23	31	16	13	14	16	12	21
Net income	30	28	37	19	17	17	20	15	27

*Column totals may not check and amounts less than $500,000 (.05) are shown as zero, due to rounding.
**Includes investment in foreign subsidiaries, $29 million in 1987.
***Includes pension expense and payroll taxes on incentive bonus.

Figure 3. Revenue Distribution

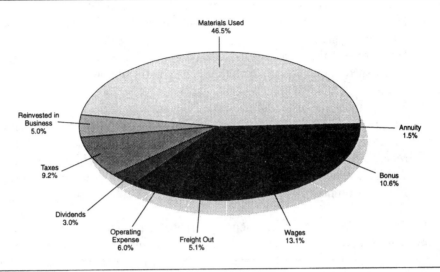

While stockholders were relegated to an inferior status by James F. Lincoln, they have done very well indeed. Recent dividends have exceeded $11 a share and earnings per share have approached $30. In January 1980, the price of restricted stock, committed to employees, was $117 a share. By 1989, the stated value, at which the company will repurchase the stock if tendered, was $201. A check with the New York office of Merrill Lynch, Pierce, Penner and Smith at that time revealed an estimated price on Lincoln stock of $270 a share, with none being offered for sale. Technically, this price applies only to the unrestricted stock owned by the Lincoln family, a few other major holders, and employees who have purchased it on the open market. Risk associated with Lincoln stock, a major determinant of stock value, is minimal because of the small amount of debt in the capital structure, because of an extremely stable earnings record, and because of Lincoln's practice of purchasing the restricted stock whenever employees offer it for sale.

A Concluding Comment

It is easy to believe that the reason for Lincoln's success is the excellent attitude of the employees and their willingness to work harder, faster, and more intelligently than other industrial workers. However, Sabo suggests that appropriate credit be given to Lincoln executives, whom he credits with carrying out the following policies:

1. Management has limited research, development, and manufacturing to a standard product line designed to meet the major needs of the welding industry.
2. New products must be reviewed by manufacturing and all producing costs verified before being approved by management.
3. Purchasing is challenged to not only procure materials at the lowest cost, but also to work closely with engineering and manufacturing to assure that the latest innovations are implemented.

4. Manufacturing supervision and all personnel are held accountable for reduction of scrap, energy conservation, and maintenance of product quality.

5. Production control, material handling, and methods engineering are closely supervised by top management.

6. Management has made cost reduction a way of life at Lincoln, and definite programs are established in many areas, including traffic and shipping, where tremendous savings can result.

7. Management has established a sales department that is technically trained to reduce customer welding costs. This sales approach and other real customer services have eliminated nonessential frills and resulted in long-term benefits to all concerned.

8. Management has encouraged education, technical publishing, and long range programs that have resulted in industry growth, thereby assuring market potential for the Lincoln Electric Company.

Sabo writes, "It is in a very real sense a personal and group experience in faith – a belief that together we can achieve results which alone would not be possible. It is not a perfect system and it is not easy. It requires tremendous dedication and hard work. However, it does work and the results are worth the effort."

Appendix A: Employee Interviews

Typical questions and answers from employee interviews are presented below. In order to maintain each employee's personal privacy, fictitious names are given to the interviewees.

Interview 1

Betty Stewart, a 52-year-old high school graduate who had been with Lincoln 13 years and who was working as a cost accounting clerk at the time of the interview.

Q: What jobs have you held here besides the one you have now?
A: I worked in payroll for a while, and then this job came open and I took it.
Q: How much money did you make last year, including your bonus?
A: I would say roughly around $25,000, but I was off for back surgery for a while.
Q: You weren't paid while you were off for back surgery?
A: No.
Q: Did the Employees Association help out?
A: Yes. The company doesn't furnish that, though. We pay $8 a month into the Employee Association. I think my check from them was $130.00 a week.
Q: How was your performance rating last year?
A: It was around 100 points, but I lost some points for attendance for my back problem.
Q: How did you get your job at Lincoln?
A: I was bored silly where I was working, and I had heard that Lincoln kept their people busy. So I applied and got the job the next day.
Q: Do you think you make more money than similar workers in Cleveland?
A: I know I do.
Q: What have you done with your money?

A: We have purchased a better home. Also, my son is going to the University of Chicago, which costs $13,000 a year. I buy the Lincoln stock which is offered each year, and I have a little bit of gold.

Q: Have you ever visited with any of the senior executives, like Mr. Willis or Mr. Hastings?

A: I have known Mr. Willis for a long time.

Q: Does he call you by name?

A: Yes. In fact he was very instrumental in my going to the doctor that I am going to with my back. He knows the director of the clinic.

Q: Do you know Mr. Hastings?

A: I know him to speak to him, and he always speaks, always. But I have known Mr. Willis for a good many years. When I did Plant Two accounting I did not understand how the plant operated. Of course you are not allowed in Plant Two, because that's the Electrode Division. I told my boss about the problem one day and the next thing I knew Mr. Willis came by and said, "Come on, Betty, we're going to Plant Two." He spent an hour and a half showing me the plant.

Q: Do you think Lincoln employees produce more than those in other companies?

A: I think with the incentive program the way that it is, if you want to work and achieve, then you will do it. If you don't want to work and achieve, you will not do it no matter where you are. Just because you are merit rated and have a bonus, if you really don't want to work hard, then you're not going to. You will accept your 90 points or 92 or 85 because, even with that you make more money than people on the outside.

Q: Do you think Lincoln employees will ever join a union?

A: I don't know why they would.

Q: So you say that money is a very major advantage?

A: Money is a major advantage, but it's not just the money. It's the fact that having the incentive, you do wish to work a litter harder. I'm sure that there are a lot of men here who, if they worked some other place, would not work as hard as they do here. Not that they are overworked – I don't mean that – but I'm sure they wouldn't push.

Q: Is there anything that you would like to add?

A: I do like working here. I am better off being pushed mentally. In another company if you pushed too hard you would feel a little bit of pressure, and someone might say, "Hey, slow down; don't try so hard." But here you are encouraged, not discouraged.

Interview 2

Ed Sanderson, a 23-year-old high school graduate who had been with Lincoln four years and who was a machine operator in the Electrode Division at the time of the interview.

Q: How did you happen to get this job?

A: My wife was pregnant, and I was making three bucks an hour and one day I came here and applied. That was it. I kept calling to let them know I was still interested.

Q: Roughly what were your earnings last year including your bonus?

A: $45,000.00

Q: What have you done with your money since you have been here?

A: Well, we've lived pretty well and we bought a condominium.

Q: Have you paid for the condominium?

A: No, but I could.

Q: Have you bought your Lincoln stock this year?

A: No, I haven't bought any Lincoln stock yet.

Q: Do you get the feeling that the executives here are pretty well thought of?

A: I think they are. To get where they are today, they had to really work.

Q: Wouldn't that be true anywhere?

A: I think more so here because seniority really doesn't mean anything. If you work with a guy who has 20 years here, and you have two months and you're doing a better job, you will get advanced before he will.

Q: Are you paid on a piece rate basis?

A: My gang does. There are nine of us who make the bare electrode, and the whole group gets paid based on how much electrode we make.

Q: Do you think you work harder than workers in other factories in the Cleveland area?

A: Yes, I would say I probably work harder.

Q: Do you think it hurts anybody?

A: No, a little hard work never hurts anybody.

Q: If you could choose, do you think you would be as happy earning a little less money and being able to slow down a little?

A: No, it doesn't bother me. If it bothered me, I wouldn't do it.

Q: Why do you think Lincoln employees produce more than workers in other plants?

A: That's the way the company is set up. The more you put out, the more you're going to make.

Q: Do you think it's the piece rate and bonus together?

A: I don't think people would work here if they didn't know that they would be rewarded at the end of the year.

Q: Do you think Lincoln employees will ever join a union?

A: No.

Q: What are the major advantages of working for Lincoln?

A: Money.

Q: Are there any other advantages?

A: Yes, we don't have a union shop. I don't think I could work in a union shop.

Q: Do you think you are a career man with Lincoln at this time?

A: Yes.

Interview 3

Roger Lewis, a 23-year-old Purdue graduate in mechanical engineering who had been in the Lincoln sales program for 15 months and who was working in the Cleveland sales office at the time of the interview.

Q: How did you get your job at Lincoln?

A: I saw that Lincoln was interviewing on campus at Purdue, and I went by. I later came to Cleveland for a plant tour and was offered a job.

Q: Do you know any of the senior executives? Would they know you by name?

A: Yes, I know all of them – Mr. Hastings, Mr. Willis, Mr. Sabo.

Q: Do you think Lincoln salesmen work harder than those in other companies?

A: Yes. I don't think there are many salesmen for other companies who are putting in 50 to 60-hour weeks. Everybody here works harder. You can go out in the plant, or you can go upstairs, and there's nobody sitting around.

Q: Do you see any real disadvantage of working at Lincoln?

A: I don't know if it's a disadvantage but Lincoln is a spartan company, a very thrifty company. I like that. The sales offices are functional, not fancy.

Q: Why do you think Lincoln employees have such high productivity?

A: Piecework has a lot to do with it. Lincoln is smaller than many plants, too; you can stand in one place and see the materials come in one side and the product go out the other. You feel a part of the company. The chance to get ahead is important, too. They have a strict policy of promoting from within, so you know you have a chance. I think in a lot of other places you may not get as fair a shake as you do here. The sales offices are on a smaller scale, too. I like that. I tell someone that we have two people in the Baltimore office, and they say "You've got to be kidding." It's smaller and more personal. Pay is the most important thing. I have heard that this is the highest paying factory in the world.

Interview 4

Jimmy Roberts, a 47-year-old high school graduate, who had been with Lincoln 17 years and who was working as a multiple-drill press operator at the time of the interview.

Q: What jobs have you had at Lincoln?

A: I started out cleaning the men's locker room in 1967. After about a year I got a job in the flux department, where we make the coating for welding rods. I worked there for seven or eight years and then got my present job.

Q: Do you make one particular part?

A: No, there are a variety of parts I make – at least 25.

Q: Each one has a different piece rate attached to it?

A: Yes.

Q: Are some piece rates better than others?

A: Yes.

Q: How do you determine which ones you are going to do?

A: You don't. Your supervisor assigns them.

Q: How much money did you make last year?

A: $53,000.

Q: Have you ever received any kind of award or citation?

A: No.

Q: Was your rating ever over 110?

A: Yes. For the past five years, probably, I made over 110 points.

Q: Is there any attempt to let the others know...?

A: The kind of points I get? No.

Q: Do you know what they are making?

A: No. There are some who might not be too happy with their points and they might make it known. The majority, though, do not make it a point of telling other employees.

Q: Would you be just as happy earning a little less money and working a little slower?

A: I don't think I would – not at this point. I have done piecework all these years, and the fast pace doesn't really bother me.

Q: Why do you think Lincoln productivity is so high? The incentive thing – the bonus distribution.

A: I think that would be the main reason. The pay check you get every two weeks is important too.

Q: Do you think Lincoln employees would ever join a union?

A: I don't think so. I have never heard anyone mention it.

Q: What is the most important advantage of working here?

A: Amount of money you make. I don't think I could make this type of money anywhere else, especially with only a high school education.

Q: As a black person, do you feel that Lincoln discriminates in any way against blacks?

A: No. I don't think any more so than any other job. Naturally, there is a certain amount of discrimination, regardless of where you are.

Interview 5

Joe Trahan, 58-year-old high school graduate who had been with Lincoln 39 years and who was employed as a working supervisor in the tool room at the time of the interview.

Q: Roughly what was your pay last year?

A: Over $56,000; salary, bonus, stock dividends.

Q: How much was your bonus?

A: About $26,000.

Q: Have you ever gotten a special award of any kind?

A: Not really.

Q: What have you done with your money?

A: My house is paid for – and my two cars. I also have some bonds and the Lincoln stock.

Q: What do you think of the executives at Lincoln?

A: They're really top notch.

Q: What is the major disadvantage of working at Lincoln Electric?

A: I don't know of any disadvantage at all.

Q: Do you think you produce more than most people in similar jobs with other companies?

A: I do believe that.

Q: Why is that? Why do you believe that?

A: We are on the incentive system. Everything we do, we try to improve to make a better product with a minimum of outlay. We try to improve the bonus.

Q: Would you be just as happy making a little less money and not working quite so hard?

A: I don't think so.

Q: Do you think Lincoln employees would ever join a union?

A: I don't think they would ever consider it.

Q: What is the most important advantage of working at Lincoln?

A: Compensation.

Q: Tell me something about Mr. James Lincoln, who died in 1965.

A: You are talking about Jimmy, Sr. He always strolled through the shop in his shirt sleeves. Big fellow. Always looked distinguished. Gray hair. Friendly sort of guy. I was a member of the advisory board one year. He was there each time.

Q: Did he strike you as really caring?

A: I think he always cared for people.

Q: Did you get any sensation of a religious nature from him?

A: No, not really.

Q: And religion is not part of the program now?

A: No.

Q: Do you think Mr. Lincoln was a very intelligent man, or was he just a nice guy?

A: I would say he was pretty well educated. A great talker – always right off the top of his head. He knew what he was talking about all the time.

Q: When were bonuses for beneficial suggestions done away with?

A: About 18 years ago.

Q: Did that hurt very much?

A: I don't think so, because suggestions are still rewarded through the merit rating system.

Q: Is there anything you would like to add?

A: It's a good place to work. The union kind of ties other places down. At other places, electricians only do electrical work, carpenters only do carpenter work. At Lincoln Electric we all pitch in and do whatever needs to be done. *> drive to learn*

Q: So a major advantage is not having a union?

A: That's right.

Mission and Values Statement

World's Leader in Welding and Cutting Products • Premier Manufacturer of Industrial Motors

The mission of The Lincoln Electric Company is to earn and retain global leadership as a total quality supplier of superior products and services.

Our Core Values

As a responsible and successful company in partnership with our customers, distributors, employees, shareholders, suppliers and our host communities, we pledge ourselves to conduct our business in accordance with these core values:

- Respond to our customers' needs and expectations with quality, integrity and value
- Recognize people as our most valuable asset
- Maintain and expand the Lincoln Incentive Management philosophy
- Practice prudent and responsible financial management
- Strive continually to be environmentally responsible
- Support communities where we operate and industries in which we participate

To Realize Our Mission and Support Our Core Values, We Have Established the Following Goals:

Respond to Our Customers' Needs and Expectations With Quality, Integrity and Value
- Assure value through innovative, functional and reliable products and services in all the markets we serve around the world.
- Exceed global standards for products and service quality.
- Provide our customers with personalized technical support that helps them achieve improvements in cost reduction, productivity and quality.
- Lead the industry in aggressive application of advanced technology to meet customer requirements.
- Invest constantly in creative research and development dedicated to maintaining our position of market leadership.
- Achieve and maintain the leading market share position in our major markets around the world.

Recognize People As Our Most Valuable Asset
- Maintain a safe, clean and healthy environment for our employees.
- Promote employee training, education and development, and broaden skills through multi-departmental and international assignments.
- Maintain an affirmative action program and provide all employees with opportunities for advancement commensurate with their abilities and performance regardless of race, religion, national origin, sex, age or disability.

- Maintain an environment that fosters ethical behavior, mutual trust, equal opportunity, open communication, personal growth and creativity.
- Demand integrity, discipline and professional conduct from our employees in every aspect of our business and conduct our operations ethically and in accordance with the law.
- Reward employees through recognition, "pay for performance," and by sharing our profits with incentive bonus compensation based on extraordinary achievement.

Maintain and Expand the Lincoln Incentive Management Philosophy

Promote dynamic teamwork and incentive as the most profitable and cost-effective way of achieving.

- A committed work ethic and positive employee attitudes throughout the Company.
- High quality, low-cost manufacturing.
- Efficient and innovative engineering.
- Customer-oriented operation and administration.
- A dedicated and knowledgeable sales and service force.
- A total organization responsive to the needs of our worldwide customers.

Practice Prudent and Responsible Financial Management

- Establish attainable goals, strategic planning and accountability for results that enhance shareholder value.
- Promote the process of employee involvement in cost reductions and quality improvements.
- Recognize profit as the resource that enables our Company to serve our customers.

Strive Continually To Be Environmentally Responsible

- Continue to pursue the most environmentally sound operating practices, processes and products to protect the global environment.
- Maintain a clean and healthy environment in our host communities.

Support Communities Where We Operate and Industries In Which We Participate

- Invest prudently in social, cultural, educational and charitable activities.
- Contribute to the industries we serve and society as a whole by continuing our leadership role in professional organizations and education.
- Encourage and support appropriate employee involvement in community activities.

To Our Shareholders:

Each of you is aware that your company faced enormous challenges in 1993. Those challenges required a focused, creative and positive leadership approach on the part of your management team. As I write this, first quarter 1994 results indicate that the domestic economy is continuing its upward surge. Because of the many tough decisions we had to make in 1993, we are now poised to take advantage of an improved economic climate. Even though much of my personal time has been devoted to overseeing the situation in Europe, excellent results are being achieved in the U.S.A. and Canada.

During 1993, a thorough strategic assessment of our foreign operations led to the conclusion that Lincoln Electric lacked the necessary financial resources to continue to support twenty-one manufacturing sites. We did not have the luxury of time to keep those plants operating while working to increase our sales and profitability. As a result, with the endorsement of our financial community, the Board of Directors approved management's recommendation to restructure operations in Europe, Latin America and Japan.

The restructuring included closing the Messer Lincoln operations in Germany; reducing employment throughout Lincoln Norweld, which operates plants in England, France, the Netherlands, Spain and Norway; and closing manufacturing plants in Venezuela, Brazil and Japan. The result was a workforce reduction totaling some 770 employees worldwide. We are not abandoning these markets by any means. Rather, the restructuring will allow us to retain and increase sales while relieving us of the high costs associated with excess manufacturing capacity. Now that the restructuring has been accomplished, we operate fifteen plants in ten countries. This capacity will be adequate to supply the inventory needed to support our customers and an increasingly aggressive marketing strategy. We are internationally recognized for outstanding products and service, and we have been certified to the international quality standard ISO-9002.

It was not easy for Lincoln Electric to eliminate manufacturing capacity and jobs. However, I must point out that the overseas companies were given repeated opportunities to turn their performance around. In all fairness, no one anticipated the depth of the recession that continues to devastate Europe, and particularly Germany. But we could not in good conscience, risk both the continuous erosion of shareholder value and the jobs of our dedicated U.S. employees, by retaining unprofitable manufacturing operations.

For the second year in the history of this company, it was necessary to take restructuring charges that resulted in a consolidated loss. The restructuring charge totaled $70,100,000 ($40,900,000 after tax), and contributed to a consolidated net loss for 1993 of $38,100,000, compared to a $45,800,000 consolidated loss in 1992. In 1993 our U.S. and Canadian operations achieved outstanding results with increased levels of sales and profitability and a significant gain in market share. We made a huge step forward by concentrating on the "Top Line" to meet one of our major goals – manufacturing and selling $2.1 million worth of product from our Ohio company each billing day from June 1 through the end of the year. Our

Canadian company also made significant contributions with a 38 percent increase in sales. The bottom line automatically moved into greater profitability.

These impressive gains were not made without sacrifice. Lincoln manufacturing people voluntary deferred 614 weeks of vacation, worked holidays, and many employees worked a seven day week schedule to fill the steady stream of orders brought in by the sales department as we capitalized on an emerging domestic economy that we felt was being largely ignored by our major competitors.

This remarkable achievement would never have been possible without the expert management of your President and Chief Operating Officer Frederick W. Mackenbach. His leadership consistently inspired our employees and management team alike. The U.S. company's extraordinary performance encouraged the Board of Directors to approve a gross bonus of $55 million, and to continue the regular quarterly dividend payment throughout the year. As you know, the usual course of action for a company reporting a consolidated loss is to cut or defer bonuses and dividends. That these were paid is a tribute to our Board and their steadfast belief in the long range, proven benefits of the Incentive Management System.

Thinking in the long term is critical to our progress in a world that too often seems to demand instant solutions to complex problems. Your Chairman, your Board, and your management team are determined to resist that impulse. Currently, Lincoln people around the world are working diligently to formulate a Strategic Plan that will carry this company into the next century. An important element of this business plan will be our new state-of-the-art motor manufacturing facility, which is on schedule. Furthermore, we have strengthened our international leadership with the addition of executives experienced in global management to our Board and to key management posts.

While your company is indeed emerging from a very challenging period in its history, we project excellent results for 1994, with strong sales, increased profits, and the benefits of those developments accruing to shareholders, customers and employees. As the year proceeds, we will be looking forward to our Centennial in 1995. I am confident that you and I will enjoy celebrating that event together.

Sincerely,
Donald F. Hastings
Chairman and Chief Executive Officer

1992 Annual Report

Consolidated Financial Statements

Financial Highlights (In thousands of dollars, except per share data)

	1992	1991	1990
Net Sales	$853,007	$833,892	$796,671
Net Income (Loss)	(45,800)	14,365	11,052
Earnings Per Share of Common Stock (Loss)	(42.42)	13.31	10.33
Cash Dividends Paid Per Share of Common Stock	7.20	11.45	12.60
Working Capital	172,651	203,479	184,341
Current Ratio (current assets to current liabilities)	2.2 to 1	2.3 to 1	2.3 to 1
Total Assets	$603, 347	$640,261	$572,230
Shareholders' Equity	198,723	264,136	254,290
Return on Shareholders' Equity	-19.8%	5.5%	4.4%

1993 Annual Report

Consolidated Financial Statements

Financial Highlights (In thousands of dollars, except per share data)

	1993	1992	1991
Net Sales	$845,999	$853,007	$833,892
Net Income (Loss)*	(38,068)	(45,800)	14,365
Earnings Per Share of Common Stock (Loss)*	(3.51)	(4.24)	1.33
Cash Dividends Paid Per Share of Common Stock*	.72	.72	1.15
Working Capital	149,853	172,651	203,479
Current Ratio (current assets to current liabilities)	1.9 to 1	2.2 to 1	2.3 to 1
Total Assets	$559,543	$603,347	$640,261
Shareholders' Equity	143,495	198,723	264,136
Return on Shareholders' Equity	-22.2%	-19.8%	5.5%

*Note: Net income (loss) and per share amounts for 1993 include the cumulative effect to January 1, 1993 of the change in method of accounting for income taxes of $2,468 and $.23 per share. Additionally, all per share amounts reported have been adjusted for the effects of the ten-for-one stock split in 1993.

1994 Annual Report

Consolidated Financial Statements
Financial Highlights (In millions of dollars, except per share data)

	1994	1993	1992
Net Sales	$907	$846	$853
Net Income (Loss)*	48	(38)	(46)
Earnings Per Share of Common Stock (Loss)*	4.38	(3.51)	(4.24)
Cash Dividends Paid Per Share of Common Stock*	.74	.72	.72
Working Capital	169	150	173
Current Ratio (current assets to current liabilities)	2.2 to 1	1.9 to 1	2.2 to 1
Total Assets	557	560	603
Shareholders' Equity	194	143	199
Return on Shareholders' Equity	28.4%	-22.2%	-19.8%

*Note: Net income (loss) and per share amounts for 1993 include the cumulative effect to January 1, 1993, of the change in method of accounting for income taxes of $2.5 million or $.23 per share.

34. Nordstrom*

In 1880, John W. Nordstrom left Sweden and sailed to the United States. Twenty one years later, with a $13,000 fortune struck in Klondike gold, he opened up a shoe store in Seattle. Today that small downtown store is a shoe and apparel empire with over fifty outlets across the nation.

Nordstrom is one of the most successful department stores with 1989 sales of $2.67 billion and net earnings of $114.9 million.[1] During the 1980's alone, the company doubled its size from 29 to 59 stores, opening outlets across California and eastward, in Virginia, Washington, DC and, most recently, in Paramus, New Jersey. Sales and net earnings grew comparably; 21% and 33% respectively in the fiscal year ending January 31, 1989.[2] The number of Nordstrom employees grew to 30,000.[3]

Despite its recent expansion, Nordstrom has remained a family operation. Grandsons John, Bruce and Jim are all co-chairmen and Jack McMillan, a Nordstrom by marriage, is the company's president. Nordstrom has no chief executive. The company prides itself on having cultivated a family orientation among its workers. All employees are made to feel like members of a family sharing in "the Nordstrom Way".

The Nordstrom Way is perhaps what has set the department store apart from its competition. It is customer service like no one else offers, service above and beyond the call of duty. At Nordstrom, service is an art form. The store hosts gala dinners and fashion shows, has valet parking, concierges for special requests stationed near every store's entrance and soothing ballads played on Steinways at every store accompanying eager smiles from salespeople ready and willing to go to great lengths to please the Nordstrom customer. Such amenities have won Nordstrom customer loyalty and affection. In Seattle, it is common to see bumper stickers that proclaim: "I'd rather be shopping at Nordstrom's." Bruce Nordstrom says of the company's customer service tradition: "We were raised sitting on a shoe stool on our knees in front of a customer. And that is both a literal and figurative posture...A born servant, if you will. There's nothing wrong with that. We're proud of it....and I think our people know that that's what we do."[4]

Nordstrom employees, 'Nordies' all have similar characteristics. They are upbeat, ambitious but, at the same time, selfless. The Nordstrom store directory describes the Nordie service expectation:

> "Our staff is genuinely interested in seeing that all your needs are met. They are professionals — will help you with everything from gift suggestions to wardrobe planning. They will even accompany you from department to department until you find exactly what you're looking for."[5]

Nordies keep personal books listing each of their customers and record every activity and correspondence. Thank you letters are sent to customers for purchases regardless of how small. One man was sent a thank you note for buying only a pair of socks.[6] Nordies will personally

---

*This case was prepared by Richard D. Freedman and Jill Vohr, Stern School of Business, New York University. Copyright 1991 by Professor Richard D. Freedman. Reprinted with permission.

deliver purchases as well; outside of work time and even on holidays, all to cultivate that special relationship and trust that has resulted in Nordstrom's faithful customer base and glowing sales record.

Thank you letters and personal deliveries only barely suggest what the Nordstrom Way entails. One employee spent over three hours on Easter Sunday finding a customer's house so he could deliver a stuffed rabbit to the customer's wife in person.[7] Another employee searched every store in the company to find a blue shirt with a white cuff and white collar that a customer had seen in an ad. Although the employee never found the shirt in his size, she personally delivered one to him at work the next morning. She had sewn a blue and white shirt together.[8]

What motivates Nordstrom employees to go to such personal trouble for their customers? High salaries for one. Nordstrom employees earn some of the highest salaries in the retail business. The average salesperson earns approximately $23,000 per year, while top salespeople make more than $50,000.[9] Pat McCarthy, a longtime Nordie, is one of them. Twenty years at Nordstrom has enabled him to cultivate a strong, loyal customer base that has brought him commissions of $80,000 plus a year.[10] "It's really a people job, which I love," says McCarthy. "Every year my sales have gotten progressively better."[11] Base pay rates are also high - as much as $9.50 an hour, which is well above the industry standard of $6 to $7.[12] High salaries have given Nordstrom a reputation that attracts good sales people. Company officials say as many as 2,000 employment applications are received when 100 new entry level openings are announced.[13]   *Contradicted by anecdotes*

All salespeople start "on the floor", and the company has a strict policy of promoting only from within. Potential managers are required to have at least two years experience selling, and are promoted after less time only under special circumstances. Promotions for all Nordies are based on three criteria: customer service, productivity and teamwork. If a salesperson has good team spirit, a solid record of fine customer service and high sales per hour (SPH), after an appropriate length of time with the company, that employee will likely be promoted to department manager. Similarly, a manager whose department goals have been successively reached or surpassed over his or her length of employment, has fine customer service skills and good relations with employees will rise to buyer or store manager positions.

Employees receive little formal training when they are hired or promoted to a new position. Most of the training is informally provided through on the job communication. What formal training they do receive is of a practical nature, e.g. scheduling procedures, salary and commission determinations, benefit opportunities. The three Nordstrom performance criteria (customer service, productivity and teamwork) are emphasized, although trainees are not told how these criteria are evaluated. Trainees are encouraged to seek information from co-workers and superiors who are described as friendly and accessible. Personal books are provided for use in keeping records of customers, sales, thank you letters and letters from customers. New employees are also given their own set of business cards to emphasize entrepreneurial opportunities and to encourage them to develop a solid customer base.

Not long ago, Nordstrom replaced its 20-page rule book with a one page sheet and a few words of wisdom: "Use your best judgement in all situations." and "Do whatever it takes to make the customer happy."[14] The company has since continued to maintain a decentralized approach to management. Managers are given significant freedom to operate their departments in the Nordstrom way. They are responsible for hiring, scheduling and evaluating their crew and receive little guidance in the form of written company policies. Nordstrom hires people that will create their own business and strict policy might stifle ingenuity and creativity. Therefore, most of the information guiding salespeople is received from their managers and not dictated from above. As described by regional personnel director, Molly Goe, each department manager runs his or her department like an individual boutique.[15]

Managers are solely responsible for evaluating their employees. According to Personnel Manager, Mary Kim Stuart, no specific, company-wide evaluation forms are used for salespeople and managers.[16] Rather, each manager designs his or her own evaluation system. If the manager considers an aspect of an employee's performance worth noting it is communicated to the store manager. The store manager, in turn, decides whether to note it in the employee's file.

Like their salespeople, managers are "on the floor" selling and receive a commission. However, their base salaries are much higher. Consequently, although commissions provide managers with an incentive to sell they are less critical for their income than for salespeople.

All Nordstrom salespeople are on a commission system called a draw. Hourly rates are determined based on the salesperson's abilities and length of employment with the company. Commission percentages for salespeople are strictly based on SPH. Employees receive either their commission percentage times their total sales for that pay period or their hourly rate times their total work hours depending on which is higher. For example, Joe Demarte, Nordstrom's vice president of personnel, explains that a salesperson with a 6.75% commission who works 40 hours for $10 an hour and sells $10,000 worth would earn $675 rather than $400. If he sold $1,000 worth, he would earn his hourly wage and no commission.[17] Consequently, only if an employee's sales are high relative to the hours they have worked, will they receive a commission. The higher the total dollar sales, the higher the commission. The incentive is to generate high pace and high dollar sales.

Although most of the training is implicit, Nordstrom's expectations of its employees are explicit. "The life of a Nordstrom salesperson is defined by goals. Daily, monthly, quarterly and annual goals, departmental, storewide and company goals, qualitative and quantitative."[18] These goals are formulated at the top by senior managers and trickle down through the hierarchy to departmental managers who are responsible for meeting designated sales quotas for their departments. Managers' salaries, commissions and bonuses depend on whether or not they attain these goals. Successive failure to reach targets can lead to dismissal. The same is true for salespeople. Managers encourage salespeople to reach high SPH levels. Some even set specific targets for their employees to ensure the attainment of their departments' sales quotas. Managers are free to implement their own approach to productivity as long as it achieves set targets and is consistent with the Nordstrom Way.

SPHs must be kept above a specified minimum level or a salesperson will not receive commission. Low SPHs reflect poor performance and can therefore be grounds for dismissal. Charts are displayed on bulletin boards in back rooms that rank employees by SPH. Ranking reflects an employee's sales ability on the floor. A red line across the chart designates the minimum SPH level necessary to receive a commission. Employees use these charts to keep tabs on their performance and see themselves in relation to their co-workers.

Everyone is formally and informally aware of their sales performance. In addition to the SPH chart, employees can keep track of their performance on computer printouts available in back offices that list their sales by employee identification number. Salespeople often know each other's number and can see how they stand in relation to one another. Numerous sales contests operate as incentives. For example, free dinners are given to employees who make the most multiple-item sales to individual customers. Often, within a department, a $20 bill is passed around throughout the day to the salesperson who has rung up the highest single sale. At the end of the day, the winner gets to keep the $20 bill. Top salespeople are named "Pacesetters", which carries with it roughly the status of a varsity letter on a high school athlete's jacket. Motivational skits are used to generate sales enthusiasm. Managers dress up as Kermit the Frog to get employees whipped into a selling frenzy, or a department's staff performs the Michael Jackson song "Beat it" with the words, "Charge it".[19] Nordstrom also offers a course on self-motivation encouraging salespeople to ask themselves what they want to accomplish each day to spur them to take responsibility for their own future. Many do, especially the successful ones. Employees seem to know precisely what they want and need to achieve. One top saleswomen stated, "The first year I consciously set quarterly goals to achieve the Pacesetter requirement. My second year my personal goal was $500,000, and I paced myself accordingly. My third year I wanted to achieve $1 million in total sales. To accomplish this I set monthly and quarterly quotas and closely monitored my progress."[20]

Managers are also encouraged to be self-motivated. "Every year the company's managers gather in meetings where they publicly state their store or departmental goals for the next 12 months. Then their bosses will reveal their own goals for the same manager, sometimes with a dramatic flourish." [21]

Good customer relations the Nordstrom Way are also important. Employees buzz with tales of extraordinary efforts made by salespeople. Peer competition and pressures to be a member of "the Nordstrom family" keep salespeople striving for a popularity that is based on their sales ability. Rewards for customer satisfaction are high. Bonuses up to $100 are awarded to salespeople with the best customer relations. Managers read letters received from pleased customers aloud at company meetings and over the loudspeaker. Whoops and cheers are heard from listeners. The salespeople who received the letters are honored as "Customer Service All Stars".[22] Their pictures are hung on the wall next to the customer service desk. They receive extra discounts on store merchandise and commendations on their personal records.

To check on the customer service provided by their employees, Nordstrom periodically dispatches "secret shoppers", people who pretend to be shoppers.[23] Salespeople are encouraged to be friendly and warm. Nordstrom does not tolerate rude behavior towards its customers. Smile contests are conducted to motivate courteous behavior. Pictures of smiling employees are taken and displayed in the lunchroom. Those that smile the most on the job receive the highest praise. "Recognition is the number one motivator," says Demarte with respect to Nordstrom contests. "We recognize our top performers constantly, as well as our customer service heroics."[24]

Most Nordstrom employees strongly uphold the Nordstrom philosophy of service. Some are almost religious about it, happily dedicating their lives to master "The Nordstrom Way". Yet, other employees feel the customers are catered to at the expense of their own working conditions, that systems meant to encourage employees actually oppress them, placing them in an environment of constant pressure, harassment and competition. Some employees began to accuse Nordstrom of unfair labor practices. The United Food and Commercial Workers Union, of which only 2,000 of the 30,000 Nordstrom work force are members, became involved.[25] Accusations of "off the clock" work and overbearing work pressures dominated complaints.

All employees are expected to contribute to stocking, delivering and picking up merchandise. Much of this work is done off the clock, past the end of a shift, on the weekends or through breaks and lunches. Also employees are expected to maintain close relations with their customers which implicitly entails thank you notes and sometimes personal deliveries. The Nordstrom practice is not to include the hours spent at these activities in the total hours worked for each employee's pay period. Union leader, Joe Peterson, in his fight against Nordstrom and what he feels is grossly unfair treatment of employees, continues to search for and encourage employees to hop on the bandwagon. Over 500 complaints were filed with the workers' union and as more complaints poured in, the union set up an 800 hotline to handle them. An article in *The Wall Street Journal Journal* included several stories told by Nordstrom employees themselves:

Taking Out The Trash

A divorced California homemaker who returned to the job market at 40, Patty Bemis joined Nordstrom in 1981, lured by the promise of a bigger income and the "status" of induction in the Nordie elite. She stayed for eight years. "They came to me", she recalls of the Nordstrom recruiters. "I was working at The Broadway as Estee Lauder's counter manager and they said they had heard I had wonderful sales figures." Ms. Bemis was thrilled. "We'd all heard Nordstrom was the place to work. They painted a great picture and I fell right into it." She found herself working progressively harder-for less money and amid more fear. "The managers were these little tin gods, always grilling you about your sales," she recalls. "You feel like your job was constantly in jeopardy. They'd write you up for anything, being sick, the way you dressed." Once, she had to get a doctor's note so she wouldn't get in trouble for wearing low-heel shoes to work. Sufficiently cowed, she reported to work even when she had strep throat. Worn down by pressure, "the girls around me were dropping like flies," she says. "Everyone was always in tears. You feel like an absolute nothing working for them."

Ms. Bemis was consistently one of her department's top sellers, but some years she only made $18,000, far below what she had expected she would earn. She won a company-wide sales contest, and received "a pair of PJs," she recalls. "Whoopie-doo!" And she logged many unpaid hours, delivering cosmetics to customers and unpacking hundreds of boxes of makeup...."Working off the clock was standard," crucial to elevating sales per hour. "In the end, really serving the customer, being an All-Star, meant nothing; if you had low sales per hour, you were forced out."

During a big Clinique sale, Ms. Bemis says she worked 12 to 15 hours shifts for a number of days without overtime pay or a day off. On the drive home at 10:30 on the tenth night, she passed out at the wheel and slammed into the freeway's center divider, she says. While she was at home recovering from head injuries, she recalls, "The manager kept calling me and saying, 'Patty, we can't hold your job much longer.'" Her doctor told her she should stay out a few weeks but she didn't dare. "Now, I know I have all these rights. But at the time all I knew was I had to have that job."

She finally left last Spring. "I just couldn't take it anymore – the constant demands, the grueling hours. I just said one day, life's too short." She took a sales post at Scandia Down Shops, where she says she makes $400 more a month than at Nordstrom. "And I can sleep at night."[26]

A Broken Clock

The first time Lori Lucas came to one of the many "mandatory" Saturday morning department meetings and saw the sign - "Do Not Punch the Clock." - she assumed the managers were telling the truth when they said the clock was temporarily out of order. But as weeks went by, she discovered the clock was always "broken" or the timecards were just missing.

Finally she and several other employees just marked the hours down on their timecard manually. She and another employee recall that their manager whited-out the hours and accused the two of not being "team players."

The department meetings "were unbelievable," Ms Lucas recalls. "There you'd be at seven in the morning and they had all these security guards dressed up like the California Raisins, with plastic garbage bags stuffed with M&Ms around their midriffs. And all you can hear is people chanting, 'We're number one!' and 'You want to do it for Nordstrom.' Finally I went up to the store manager and said, 'What is this all about?' and she said, 'You are here to learn the Nordstrom Way.' "

The Nordstrom Way involved an endless round of contests ("Who Looks More Nordstrom" was a popular one, intended to encourage employees to shop at the stores) and the daily recital of "affirmations" ("I only sell multiples," was one chanted by salespeople).

And the Nordstrom Way, Ms. Lucas discovered, meant working for free. "My manager would say, 'You go clock out and come down and we'll talk.' That was her little trick way of saying there's nonsell work to do."

Like most salesclerks at Nordstrom, Ms. Lucas also had daily quotas of thank you letters to write, and monthly customer-service "books" to generate - photo albums that are supposed to be filled with letters from grateful customers. ("People would get so desperate they would have their friends and relatives write fake letters for them." Petra Rousu, a 10-year salesclerk veteran, recalls.) Such duties, Ms. Lucas says, were supposed to be tackled only after hours. "I'd be up til 3 a.m., doing my letters, and doing my manager's books" she says. "Before you know it, your whole life is Nordstrom. But you couldn't complain, because then your manager would schedule you for the bad hours, your sales per hour would fall and next thing you know, you're out the door."

The pressure eventually gave Ms. Lucas and ulcer, she says. One day after working 22 days without a day off, she demanded a lunch break. On her hour off, she applied for and got a new job elsewhere and gave notice as soon as she returned. "I remember thinking, I'm making less than $20,000 a year. Why am I killing myself? Nordstrom was the most unfair place I ever worked."[27]

Staying On Top

For nearly two years, Cindy Nelson had stayed on top of the chart in one of the Bellevue, Wash., stores. She was on her way to making "Pacesetter" again....A clique of salesclerks on the floor - led by numbers two and three on the charts - held a pow-wow one day, decided that Ms. Nelson must be stealing their sales and vowed to have her "watched," according to court depositions that later became part of a suit filed by Ms. Nelson against Nordstrom in Bellevue, Wash..

How is teamwork rewarded? ←

On September 29, 1986, Cindy Nelson reported for work and was immediately whisked into the personnel office. The department manager had before her five notes of complaint from the salesclerks, all unsigned, which claimed Ms. Nelson had been stealing sales.

Ms. Nelson asked to inspect the sales receipts in question and confront her accusers, but the manager, Rhonda Eakes, refused. "I just didn't feel that it was any of her business," Ms. Eakes explained later in her deposition. Then she told Ms. Nelson that she was fired. (All of the managers and employees involved in Ms. Nelson's firing declined comment, referring queries to Mr. Nordstrom, who said, "That gal wasn't a good employee.")

"I was totally stunned," recalls Ms. Nelson, who had a stack of customer-service citations in her file and had been told she was about to make manager. She was also, up until then, "your 100-percent gung-ho Nordie. This whole time I thought I was going to be this great Nordstrom person and now I was nothing, a nobody. I became an emotional wreck."[28]

Other criticisms were made of Nordstrom. Allegedly employees were required to purchase and wear Nordstrom clothing while on the job.[30] The company was also accused of having discriminatory practices.[31] Part of becoming a Nordie, employees say, involves acquiring a certain look. Lupe Sakagawa, a top saleswoman, recalls that on her first day on the job, her manager strong-armed her into buying $1,400 of the "right" clothes - all from the department. But that wasn't enough: The store manager then called her in and told her: "Correct your accent." Ms. Sakagawa is Mexican. "It was very hard for me to prove myself," she says, "because of that image of the Nordstrom Girl - blond hair, young and cute."[32] Nordstrom has since hired a black human resources officer and the company reports that 25.6% of all its employees are minorities.[33]

Other sentiments are being brought to the attention of the media through Peterson, who feels employees are being exploited. Peterson specifically criticizes the SPH incentive. He believes that in order to keep SPH up, employees are encouraged to keep their work hours down. Consequently, they may not record hours spent doing certain non-selling chores (stock taking, personal deliveries, thank you notes) on their time sheets. Nordstrom's position is that the employees are compensated by commissions that actually pay them for doing extra tasks. Employees willingly donate their time. It is not explicitly required of them. Peterson argues that "...If one employee is donating a lot of time, it forces others to do the same or it creates an atmosphere where everyone is playing on an unequal playing field."[34] Because employees who log only sales times have higher SPH than co-workers who clock in all other business and support activities, employees are motivated to decrease their nonsales hours. They work off the clock to be awarded better shifts and more hours. In response, Demarte insists that because SPH is the objective performance evaluation factor...that's what people focus on."[35] Evaluation is not based just on SPH. People who perform the best are also best in giving the customer service and working as a team. Yet, Demarte does admit there is pressure. "People who perform the most effectively are the ones we need to have on the floor. Therefore, there's this pressure to be better."[36] Middle management encourages workers to get jobs done within certain time frames and if they can't meet the deadlines, exert "implied pressures" on their salespeople to get the job done after work hours. President Jack McMillan insists that "the system is as level a playing field as you can find for people to rise up quickly on their own merit. Everybody starts on the selling floor and the ones that show initiative, creativity and desire rise up in the system and become department managers. Those department managers that show the ability to make things happen rise up to be buyers or store managers or vice presidents. We think it's a great system, but it's obvious there are some glitches in it. One way to control selling costs - not the right way - is to encourage people to get the work done in a certain time frame. If they can't get it done, then there is implied pressure to work off the clock. We are responsible for the pressure from middle managers. There was no plan or scheme, but it happened. I guess you could say we were negligent for not knowing, but we are responsible for it."[37] Recently Nordstrom set aside $15 million to pay back employees who were victims of management glitches.[38]

Despite Nordstrom's promises of back pay, the union is still fighting them, pointing a finger at Nordstrom's high turnover rates, even for the retail industry. Nordstrom replies that although salespeople who regularly have trouble meeting sales quotas or coping with pressure to improve their performance are dismissed, these employees usually leave of their own volition. Having been made to feel uncomfortable or inadequate in the Nordstrom culture that celebrates accomplishment, they recognize that they do not belong. They leave before the company has cause to dismiss them. Nordstrom compensates by attempting to hire people who are innate Nordies. The company's hiring philosophy supports their decentralized management style. Bruce Nordstrom is quoted as saying "All we do is hire nice, motivated, hardworking people and then we leave them alone to do what they do best. The system is to have self-empowered people who have an entrepreneurial spirit, who feel that they're in this to better themselves and to feet good about themselves and to make more money and to be successful."[40] Jim Nordstrom adds, "There's expectations on our people. And when people apply for a job anyplace, they want to work hard and they want to do a good job. That's their intention. And our intention is to allow them the freedom to work as hard as they want to work."[41]

Although there have been several complaints, it seems that most Nordstrom employees also do not support their union leader's accusations. In December 1990, more than half of the 1,850 employees left the union after membership became optional.[42] And in July of 1991, employees consisting of sales people, office workers, clerks and display workers at five stores in Seattle voted by more than a 2-to-1 ratio to end union representation altogether.[43] Indeed, several employees speak in favor of Nordstrom stating that they love working for the company and do not want anything changed.[44]

> "It's a feeling, it's family," Ms. Sargent says enthusiastically. "Sure, during the busy seasons, you do work six to seven days a week, but being in the store with the Christmas tree here, you create your own memories." Ms. Sargent, who has

worked for Nordstrom in Seattle for seven years, says she doesn't mind working for free. "When I go home and do follow-ups or write thank-yous, I think it's inappropriate to be charging the company for that."

At the San Francisco store, another set of employees testify to the company's virtues. "Here at Nordstrom, I feel I can be the best that I can be," says Doris Quiros, a salesperson in the women's sportswear department. While other retailers "give you a big book of rules, when I came here, Nordstrom gave me one with only one rule: Use you best judgement. That's because they want me to be my own boss." In the women's shoes department, Tim Snow, a former waiter, says people are impressed now when they learn where he works. "You can be at the grocery store and you show them your ID card and they'll start right off on how much they love to shop there."[45]

If happy employees aren't enough to justify the existing Nordstrom system, the company's success and their numerous satisfied customers are. "They treat you with the most reverence you can imagine," one customer said after a salesperson offered her the option of either wearing a Nordstrom dress that had a run in it and returning it at her convenience for a full refund or taking $100 off the price. "It's so darn easy to go in there."[46] Betsy Sanders, the head of the company's Southern California division, sometimes stands at the store exit at night as the store closes and says good night to departing customers. One evening, as she bade some shoppers farewell, she heard one say: "What kind of drugs are these people on? Even the doormen are nice."[47]

Notes

1. Charlene Marmer Solomon, "Nightmare At Nordstrom," *Personnel Journal* September,1990: 77.
2. J.B.,"How Nordstrom Got There,"*Stores* January,1990: 68.
3. Charlene Marmer Solomon, "Nightmare At Nordstrom," *Personnel Journal* September,1990: 77.
4. Marti Galovic Palmer, Producer, "The Nordstrom Boys," *60 Minutes* Vol. XXII Num. 33, May 6, 1990: 8.
5. J.B.,"How Nordstrom Got There", *Stores* January 1990: 68.
6. Mary Kim Stuart, Nordstrom Personnel Director (Paramus, New Jersey) telephone conversation with author, November 9, 1990.
7. Marti Galovic Palmer, Producer, "The Nordstrom Boys,"*60 Minutes* Vol. XXII Num. 33, May 6, 1990: 8.
8. Ibid.
9. Ibid.10
10. Susan C. Faludi, "At Nordstrom Stores. Service Comes First - But at a Big Price," *The Wall Street Journal Journal* February 20, 1990.
11. Ibid.
12. Dori Jones Yang, "Will 'The Nordstrom Way' Travel Well?," *Business Week* September 3, 1990: 83.
13. Joyce Anne Oliver and Eric J.Johnson, "People Motive Redefines Customer Service," *HR Magazine* Vol. 35 Iss. 6, June 1990: 120.
14. Mary Kim Stuart, Nordstrom Personnel Director (Paramus, New Jersey) telephone conversation with author, November 9, 1990.
15. Charlene Marmer Solomon, "Nightmare At Nordstrom," *Personnel Journal* September 1990: 77.
16. Mary Kim Stuart, Nordstrom Personnel Director (Paramus, New Jersey) telephone conversation with author, November 9, 1990.
17. Charlene Marmer Solomon, "Nightmare At Nordstrom," *Personnel Journal* September 1990: 79.
18. Richard W. Stevenson, "Watch Out Macy's, Here Comes Nordstrom," *New York Times* August 27, 1989: 39.
19. Ibid.
20. Ibid.
21. Ibid.
22. Charlene Marmer Solomon, "Nightmare At Nordstrom," *Personnel Journal* September 1990: 83.
23. Susan C. Faludi, "At Nordstrom Stores, Service Comes First - But at a Big Price," *The Wall Street Journal Journal* February 20, 1990:
24. Charlene Marmer Solomon, "Nightmare At Nordstrom," *Personnel Journal* September 1990: 77.
25. Ibid: 78.
26. Susan C. Faludi, "At Nordstrom Stores, Service Comes First - But at a Big Price,"*The Wall Street Journal Journal* February 20, 1990:

27. Ibid

28. Ibid

29.

30. Charlene Marmer Solomon, "Nightmare At Nordstrom," *Personnel Journal* September 1990: 78.

31. Susan C. Faludi, "At Nordstrom Stores, Service Comes First - But at a Big Price," *The Wall Street Journal Journal* February 20, 1990.

32. Susan C. Faludi, "At Nordstrom Stores, Service Comes First - But at a Big Price,"*The Wall Street Journal Journal* February 20, 1990.

33. Charlene Marmer Solomon, "Nightmare At Nordstrom," *Personnel Journal* September 1990: 78.

34. Ibid: 80.

35. Ibid: 81.

36. Ibid: 81.

37. Robert Spector, "Nordstrom Discusses Its Problems," *Women's Wear Daily* March 27, 1990: 18.

38. Charlene Marmer Solomon, "Nightmare At Nordstrom," *Personnel Journal* September, 1990: 80.

39.

40. Marti Galovic Palmer, Producer, "The Nordstrom Boys," *60 Minutes* Vol. XXII Num. 33, May 6, 1990: 10.

41. Ibid.

42. "Nordstrom Workers in Seattle Reject Union", *The New York Times* July 20, 1991.

43. Ibid.

44. Charlene Marmer Solomon, "Nightmare At Nordstrom," *Personnel Journal* September, 1990: 77.

45. Susan C. Faludi, "At Nordstrom Stores, Service Comes First - But at a Big Price," *The Wall Street Journal Journal* February 20, 1990.

46. Richard W. Stevenson, "Watch Gut Macy's, Here Comes Nordstrom", *The New York Times* August 27, 1989: 38.

47. Ibid: 40.

35. General Motors*

"Above all [the automobile worker] wants a job in which he does not have to think."[1]

Henry Ford (1922)

"If you were 22 and had a job where you were treated like a machine and knew you had about 30 years to go, how would you feel?"[2]

GM Assembly line worker (1972)

"...the pace is so great that available assembly line equipment built for lower speeds is breaking down. The corporation is replacing the machines, but so far has not offered any consolation to the men who are being asked to meet the same killing pace."[3]

GM UAW 1112 representative (1972)

"GM workers actually prefer repetitive work. The workers feel that they are under less pressure, they do not have to think about their jobs and can let their minds wander to think about more important things."[4]

Edward N. Cole
President, GM (1972)

The Strike

After months of mounting worker resentment and increasing numbers of employee grievances, United Auto Workers (UAW) Local 1112 scheduled a strike vote against General Motors' Lordstown plant, for February 1, 1972. When the voting was over, more than 6,500 workers had decided by an overwhelming 97 percent to support a strike action at the GM Vega plant.[5] The workers went out on strike in early March.

The dispute between the workers and Lordstown management began in October 1971 when the General Motors Assembly Division (GMAD), a management team with a reputation for cutting costs and improving efficiency, took over.

This organizational change replaced a divided approach in which the Fisher Body Division and the Company's car division each managed different elements of automobile assembly. Upon their arrival, GMAD redesigned assembly-line jobs[6], and adopted "get tough" tactics to cope with high worker absenteeism and to boost productivity. The UAW charged that GMAD brought a return to the rigid sweatshop style of management "reminiscent of the 1930s."[7]

Dale

Dale, 27 years old, has worked in the Lordstown plant for three and a half years.

*This case was written by Richard D. Freedman and Velvet V. Mickens, Stern School of Business, New York University, 1992. Reprinted with permission.

Yeah, I voted for the strike. I mean, the way I see it, now we're nothing better than machines used to turn out profits. I'm willing to fight even if it means losing my job.

My first two years here at Lordstown, I took car doors off a pile and hung them on hooks on a moving, overhead monorail. I hated that job, so I asked for a transfer. This time I had to put two braces on a door. That was a real drag. You had to run along the car and put them in, then go back and start all over.

Now I have to place a hook under the body of each Vega to help lift it so that the welders and assemblers can see better. When the line is moving at top speed, I have 36 seconds to attach the hook. That's no problem – I can keep up. What I don't like is that when the line is movin' so fast it's impossible to talk to a buddy, stretch my arm, walk around a bit or take a few drags on my cigarette. What also bothers me is the fact that, no matter what the line speed is, I have nothing else to do on my eight-hour shift – aside from a half-hour lunch and two 23-minute breaks – except put that hook under the car body. That's about 650 times a day if the line is running right.

There's no way to beat the boredom on a job like this. You just try not to think about it or you can go insane. You just sort of go numb.[8]

General Motors Assembly Division (GMAD)

GMAD was set up in 1965, with initial jurisdiction over light assembly plants building Buicks, Oldsmobiles, Pontiacs, and Chevrolets, representing 27% of GM's domestic car and truck output.[9] Its assignment was to tighten and revamp assembly operations that senior GM management believed had become inefficient under divisional direction. The need for GMAD's belt-tightening role was underscored during the late 1960s when GM's profit margin dropped from 10% to 7%.[10] The new division engineered impressive cost reductions and quality improvements, and was subsequently given control of 10 more assembly plants formerly run by the Fisher Body and Chevrolet divisions.[11]

Prior to the creation of GMAD, most car bodies were built by Fisher in one operation, and assembled by a car division in another. In some cases, the two operations were miles apart and in others, in the same plant. But the profit squeeze and decreasing product quality suggested defects in the divided system.

As of the beginning of this year, GMAD controls 18 assembly plants – employing 91,000 workers and responsible for about 75 per cent of GM's production.[21] The division's policies have brought labor unrest to almost every plant it has taken over.

Whenever GMAD takes over a plant, the course is much the same. The two divisions – assembly and Fisher body — are merged into one, thereby eliminating duplicate white-collar positions.[12] But cuts are made also in production jobs, and these have generated much dissension.[13]

Union locals have long-term agreements, sometimes in writing and sometimes informal, that detail what a job entails and how many operations a worker must perform in a minute.[14] However, GMAD management takes the position that it can reorganize the job any way it wants in order to make it more efficient. "Within reason and without endangering their health, if we can occupy a man for 60 minutes, we've got that right,"[15] is the view held by Joseph

Godfrey, head of GMAD. According to Mr. Godfrey, a typical example would be to "rearrange a man's work area so that he no longer has to walk to get needed parts but can simply reach for them. With the time saved, the worker might be asked to put on an additional part."[16]

GMAD's mission, according to Godfrey, is to enable GM to "compete against the foreigner."[17] At the core of the division's system for meeting foreign competition, is a continuing, computerized system of grading and ranking. There is a highly sophisticated reporting network capable of giving Mr. Godfrey a daily performance rating for each plant. And at the end of each month, each plant is ranked according to efficiency and quality. Those in the lower third of the ranks get special attention – including a visit from the boss to talk things over – if no improvement is shown in succeeding months.[18] The ranking system is endless, since improvement in one plant pushes another down the scale; so, there are no final goals.[19] This open-endedness does put continuing pressure on management within each plant to reduce costs continually," Mr. Godfrey concedes, "however that's the name of the game if we want to be competitive."[20]

Irving Bluestone

Vice President, United Auto Workers

> The underlying assumption that auto plant management makes is that no worker wants to work. The plant is arranged so that employees can be controlled, checked, and supervised at every plant. The efficiency of an assembly line is not only its speed but in the fact that the workers are easily replaced. This allows the employer to cope with high turnover.
>
> But it's a vicious cycle. The job is so unpleasantly subdivided that men are constantly quitting and absenteeism is common. Even an accident is a welcome diversion. Because of the high turnover, management further simplifies the job, and more men quit. But the company has learned to cope with high turnover. So they don't have to worry if men quit or go crazy before they're forty.[22]

The Lordstown Complex

Originally built in 1966 on an 1,000 acre farm field near Lordstown, Ohio, the plant sits almost in the center of the heavy industrial triangle made up of Youngstown, with its steel plants; Akron, with its rubber industry, and Cleveland, a major center for heavy manufacturing.[23] The Lordstown complex – which was initially created to assemble Impalas – is composed of the Vega assembly plant, the van-truck assembly plant, and a Fisher Body metal fabricating plant.

In 1969, GM management redesigned the plant in order to transform it into the most modern, competitive and sophisticated assembly plant in America – a response to the challenge of imported autos turned out by low-wage labor in modern West German and Japanese factories. The Lordstown plant would produce the Vega 2300, a mini-car who's principal target was the Volkswagen Beetle, and, to a lesser extent, the Japanese entries, Toyota and Datsun.[24]

Developed to be the fastest-moving assembly line in the world, Lordstown is so automated that it has two dozen robot welding machines called Unimates, on each side of the line.[25] These robots are equipped to carry welding guns and "memorize" the motions they must go through on the job.[26]

The assembly line itself raises the car 14 to 72 inches to allow workers and machines easy access as the car body winds around a mile-and-a-quarter track.[27]

Through better design, a variety of new types of power tools and other automated devices, much of the heavy lifting and hard physical labor have been eliminated from the plant. These sophisticated techniques enable the assembly line to build 100 cars an hour; the majority of U.S. auto plants build 55 to 60 cars an hour. Interestingly enough, Japanese auto plants normally produced 120 to 140 cars per hour. Normal Vega output at Lordstown is 8,000 cars a week, on the basis of two 8-hour work shifts.[28]

As jobs in the Lordstown plant have become simplified because of increased automation, the rate at which these tasks can be performed can be increased. On a regular GM assembly line, a worker takes about a minute to perform a task, while workers at Lordstown need only about 36 seconds.

The Lordstown Workforce

General Motors purposely chose the small Ohio village of Lordstown as the sight for this plant, in hopes that it would provide a totally new workforce with none of the built-in prejudices of Detroit labor relations problems.[29] The plant draws its 6,400 workers from areas that have felt the sting of foreign competition and where unemployment and layoffs have been heavy.[30]

The workers in the plant are generally young, with the average age being 24 years old. This makes the workforce at Lordstown the second youngest among GM's 25 assembly plants in the United States. "With all the shoulder-length hair, beards, afros and mod clothing along the line, it looks for all the world like an industrial Woodstock."[31]

The educational profile of the Lordstown workers indicates that only 22.2 percent have less than a high school education. Nearly two-thirds or 62 percent are high school graduates, and 16 percent are either college graduates or have attended college. Another 26 percent have attended trade school. The average education of 13.2 years makes the Lordstown workers among the best educated in GM's assembly plants.[32]

As members of Local 1112, the workers command among the best wages and benefits in the industry. Certainly, there is no job in the Lordstown area whose terms compare with the high wages and fringe benefits that the GM workers enjoy. The wages are a tremendous initial attraction for workers and explain why many are reluctant to leave the plant.

Employees start out on the line at about $5.00 an hour, and get a 10 cents an hour increase within 30 days and another 10 cents after 90 days.[33] Benefits come to $2.50 an hour.[34] In addition, annual cost of living increases geared to the consumer price index had been incorporated into the labor contract.

The supplemental unemployment benefits virtually guarantee the worker's wages through-out the year; if the worker is laid off, he receives more than 90 percent of his wages for a period of one year. Employees are also eligible for up to six paid days to be used for holidays, excused absence or bereavement, and up to four weeks paid vacation.[35] Equally significant, GM is among the few places in the area still hiring a large number of employees. The steel mills, electrical plants, and retail trades offer lower wages to unskilled workers and less steady employment to low-seniority people. In contrast, Japanese automobile workers make an estimated $1.00 per hour, while West Germany workers earn approximately $2.00 per hour.[36]

Despite GM's attempt to choose a location whose workforce had no pre-disposed notions regarding the Corporation, Lordstown presents significant issues of its own. The mostly youthful workforce appears to have a rather cavalier work ethic, and little tolerance for the stringent discipline of the assembly line.[37] After an initial run of near perfect attendance, the absenteeism rate has steadily risen; in 1971 it averaged 7 percent.[38] The attitude of many Lordstown workers is summed up by one who customarily works four days a week on the assembly line and vanishes on the fifth. "How come you're working four days a week?' he was asked. 'Because I can't make enough money in three,' he shrugged."[39]

GM acknowledges that absenteeism, particularly on Mondays and Fridays, constitutes its most distressing discipline problem. Workers report line shutdowns "for as much as a half hour" on Mondays because there are simply not enough people to perform the operations. But many young people are prepared to sacrifice higher earnings for a respite from the hassles of assembly line work, even for one day. This is because the automation technology makes the work less creative and extremely boring to the workers. The better educated workers find the adjustment hard to make. The result is more absenteeism, a higher work force turnover, and less quality in the work turned out.[40]

Many of the fathers of the young auto workers are employed in steel and rubber factories and have watched their jobs dwindle because foreign products have undercut their industries.[41] As such, many of the elder workers do not sympathize with the issue of job-related boredom, that their offspring are raising. Reese Orlosky and his father, Tom, exemplify these opposing views.

Reese Orlosky

Reese is a 28 year old buffer, brazer and sealer at the Vega plant.

> I really hate my job. I can't stand the regimentation, and the lack of initiative and involvement needed for the work. Mostly, I can't stand the iron control. Miss a day and they'll question you. They're not paying you, but they'll question you.
>
> Look, I'm no stranger to hard work and I have a purpose in life. I have a degree in Psychology from Youngstown State University, and I used to teach in a school for the mentally retarded. But when I discovered that with my wife's and my salary combined we were only $600 a year above the poverty line, I went back to the assembly line. Now I make $4.78 an hour.
>
> The company just doesn't seem to understand why the young guys don't want a day's work plus overtime. We want 40 hours and that's it. Money is important to us, but it doesn't overwhelm.
>
> We want jobs where we can use our brains. Right now, a new guy can learn my job in half an hour. That's because our jobs are broken down into the simplest units. Our jobs are so subdivided that most of us don't even feel like we're making a car. GMAD made the work so much simpler that they removed the last traces of skill. Now we're nothing more than machines.

I guess our expectations are higher because most of us have high school diplomas. But is it too much to expect that we be treated as thinking beings?

It's going to take something, somewhere to change the status quo. Where a guy can take an interest in the job. GM can say to us 'You're crazy,' but a guy can't do the same thing 8 hours a day year after year. And it's got to be more than just saying to a guy 'Okay instead of 6 spots on the weld you'll do five spots.'

Even though we're on strike, I still don't think management truly understands why. The issue isn't money; it's the redefinition of work rules and some sort of solution to the dulling, repetitive and sometimes psychologically killing nature of the line. That's why alot of guys take Friday and Monday off. Anything to escape the monotony. The older workers in other plants took this treatment, but I've got 25 years ahead of me here – I'm going to fight.[42]

Tom Orlosky

Tom is a 68-year-old retired GM assembly line worker.

These kids who come up today want to sit on their fantails eight hours a day. They think the plant owes them a living. When I was young, you put in a day's work. No question about it. I figure that the trouble at Reese's plant is the younger generation of workers who just don't feel like working. They're spoiled. They act like having an education gives them the right to be lazy; they want to think, not do. Gee, I wish I had 24 minute breaks twice a day when I worked the line.

I'm an old GM man. Nobody offers better wages and working conditions then they do. I don't know how anybody who works for a living can do better than GM. Compared to my very first job at the steel mill, GM is not near as hard.

I realize that the line is monotonous, but I was willing to put up with it for the pay. I remember during the Depression when workers went in daily fear of hunger. Now these kids are striking because they're bored. I could see if they were striking because of dangerous conditions or something. I'm proud of the work I did for GM and I still drive a Chevrolet that came off my old line.[43]

GMAD At Lordstown

Upon arrival at Lordstown, GMAD launched an effort to improve production efficiency more in line with that of the other GM plants that the organization had taken over. This has included increasing job efficiency through reorganization and better coordination between the body and chassis assembly, and improving controls over product quality and worker absenteeism.

In seeking to improve job efficiency, GMAD has initiated changes in those work sequences and methods which were not well coordinated under the previous management. Although tasks were already simplified, GMAD further divided the work into the smallest possible units thereby creating narrow, repetitive tasks which do not allow the workers any flexibility. GMAD believes that efficiency is maximized and replacement costs minimized by this method. This reliance upon greater automation serves to minimize human effort and error.[44]

These improvements have resulted in savings in time and the number of workers required. In response, GMAD has laid off 5% of the Lordstown workforce (400 workers). However, the remaining workers are expected to produce as many cars as before. According to the union, "the understanding was that as GMAD merged the plants, none of the hourly workers would lose any benefits they enjoyed at the time of the merger."[45] But, GMAD has always held that when it takes over a plant, local agreements between the union and other GM divisions are no longer in force.[46] Additionally, management argues that every job on the Vega line has been engineered so that each worker is doing roughly as much work as his colleague on a line in a more conventional auto assembly plant.

The workers have resisted the manpower cuts by often continuing to work at the old pace. In addition, instances of sabotage, such as breaking windshields, breaking off rear-view mirrors, slashing upholstery and putting washers in carburetors have been reported.[47] So many defective Vegas have come off the line that repair shop employees were regularly putting in 60 hour weeks to repair the damage.[48] GMAD subsequently decreed that there would be no repair shop overtime. When work backed up in the repair shop, workers on the assembly line were sent home.

Workers are being penalized for not performing their jobs. GMAD's strategy is to increase employee compliance with the smaller pay checks that are issued when workers are sent home early and from foremen's disciplining workers by sending them home without pay. By the end of January, it was estimated that GM has lost the production of 12,000 cars and 4,000 trucks and that the workers have lost more than $3.3 million in wages.[49]

In addition, management imposed new, universally applicable rules which, in fact, were applied selectively. For example, on Mondays, when there are not many people on the line, the company tolerates lateness. This is because the foremen need as many workers as possible to maintain production schedules. However, on Tuesdays, when young workers come back from their long weekends, management strictly enforces their rules regarding lateness, and oftentimes many workers are sent home without pay.

The institution of these new rules has prompted a sharp change in the attitude of the plant foremen; fearful of losing their jobs in production quotas are not met, some have supported worker grievances, while others have pressured workers in order to impress their own new bosses. "I got sent home because I was one minute late," 23-year-old David Baily complained. "Before you could be two minutes late and they'd just say 'go to your job.'"[50] There are hundreds of discipline cases – men sent home because they could not meet the work standards.[51]

As the disciplinary controls have been increased, the number of worker grievances have also increased dramatically. Before GMAD took over, there were about 100 grievances in the plant. Since then, grievances increased to 5,000, about 1,000 of which are related to the claim that too much work has been added to the job. The workers complain that one has to shut off one's mind on the job and perform the same operation up to 800 times a day every 36 seconds at a pace set by computers.[52] "I no sooner get one job done than I have to do another," says a young woman worker, who claims that GMAD added two tasks to the three she was already doing. "I don't even have time to get a drink of water."[53]

In March 1972, the Lordstown workers went on strike.

Gary Bryner

Gary is the 29-year-old president of United Auto Workers Local 1112.

The bottom line is that because of the changes brought about by GMAD, fewer auto workers are now producing more cars, job descriptions have been changed, and men have been laid off.

I mean, look, 700 workers were laid off and there has been no appreciable decrease in the peak assembly line speed of 100 cars an hour. Call it what you want to, but those layoffs mean extra work for the remaining guys – around here that's known as a line speed-up. The extra work has been shifted to men who simply don't have enough time to do it.

That's the fastest line in the world. A guy has about 40 seconds to do his job. The company does some figuring and they say, "Look, we only added one thing to his job." On paper it looks like he's got time. But you've got 40 seconds to work with. You add one more thing and it can kill you. The guy can't get the stuff done on time and a car goes by. The company then blames us for sabotage and shoddy work.[54]

They come in here with their new system. Now, instead of having the guy bend over to pick something up, it's right at his waist level. They try to take every movement out of the guy's day, so he could conserve seconds in time, to make him more efficient, more productive, like a robot. They use stopwatches. They say, 'it takes so many seconds or hundredths of seconds to walk from here to there. We know it takes so many seconds to shoot a screw. We know the gun turns so fast, the screw's so long, the hole's so deep.' Our argument has always been: That's mechanical; that's not human.

What do the workers want? In general they want to reorganize the industry so that each guy plays a significant role in turning out a great product, without having to put up with degrading supervision. Do you know that there are a lot of guys who go through their assembly line routines without knowing what parts they're handling? More precisely, though, they want more time in each thirty-six-second cycle to sneeze or to scratch.[55]

Look, I don't give a damn what anybody says, it is boring, monotonous work. I was an inspector and I didn't actually shoot the screws or tighten the bolts or anything like that. A guy could be there eight hours and there was some other body doing the same job over and over, all day long, all week long, all year long. Years. If you thought about it, you'd go stir. Can you imagine squeezing the trigger of a gun while it's spotted so many times? You count the spots, the same count, the same job, job after job after job. It's got to drive a guy nuts.

Management must face the fact that the attitude that a guy goes to work and slaves to get his $4 an hour is passe. The guys want to feel like they're making real contributions. They don't want to feel like a part of the machinery.

Of course this attitude has to do with the fact that these guys are younger and better educated then before. The traditional concept that hard work is a virtue and a duty, which older workers adhered to, is not applicable to the younger workers. The young worker puts his personal life first.

Our struggle has raised a wider issue of how management can deal with a young worker who is determined to have a say as to how a job should be performed and is not so easily moved by management threats that there are plenty of others waiting in line if he does not want to do the job. The young guy believes he has something to say about what he does. He doesn't believe that when the foreman says it's right that it's right. Hell, he may be ten times more intelligent as this foreman. If he believes he's working too hard, he stands up and says so. He doesn't ask for more money. He says, 'I'll work at a normal pace, so I don't go home tired and sore, a physical wreck. I want to keep my job and keep my senses.'

The young people are seeking something more from their labor than high wages, pensions and job security. They are looking for a chance to use their brains, and a job where their education counts for something.[56]

Epilogue

The strike in the Lordstown plant was expected to affect other plants. The plants at Tonawanda, New York and Buffalo, New York were supplying parts for Vega. Despite the costly impact of the worker resistance and the strike, management felt that the job changes and cost reductions were essential if the Vega was to return a profit to the company. The plant had to be operating at about 90 percent capacity to break even. Not only had the highly automated plant cost twice as much as estimated, but also the Vega itself ended up weighing 10 percent more than had been planned.[57]

Despite the Lordstown walk-out there is a strong belief at General Motors that the issue of boredom has been exaggerated and that there is little evidence that workers do not like repetitive jobs.[58]

Notes

1. Russell W. Gibbons, "Showdown at Lordstown," Commonweal, March 3, 1972: 528
2. "The Spreading Lordstown Syndrome," Business Week, March 4, 1972: 69.
3. "Young Workers Disrupt Plant on Which GM Pins Its Hopes of Meeting Foreign Competition," The New York Times, January 23, 1972: 1.
4. "Trouble at GM," The New York Times, September 3, 1972: 3.
5. Russell W. Gibbons, "Showdown at Lordstown," Commonweal, March 3, 1972: 523.
6. "The GM Efficiency Move that Backfired," Business Week, March 25, 1972: 46.
7. Agis Salpukas, "Turn the Nut, Turn the Nut, Turn the ...," The New York Times, February 6, 1972: IV 5
8. Ibid.
9. "The GM Efficiency Move that Backfired," Business Week, March 25, 1972: 46.
10. Ibid.
11. Agis Salpukas, "GM's Toughest Division," April 16, 1972: III 4.
12. Ibid: III 1.
13. Ibid.
14. Ibid.
15. Ibid.
16. Ibid.
17. Ibid.
18. Ibid.
19. Ibid.
20. Ibid: III 4.
21. Barbara Garson, "Luddites in Lordstown," Harper's Magazine, June 1972: 73.
22. "What Next, GM?," The New York Times, January 23, 1972: 35N
23. "The Bullet Biters," Newsweek, February 7, 1972: 65.
24. Jerry M. Flint, "Auto Industry Struggling to Stop Lag in Productivity," The New York-Times, August 8, 1970: 10.
25. Ibid.
26. Ibid.
27. U.S. News and World Report, February 7, 1972: 45.
28. "The Bullet Biters," Newsweek, February 7, 1972: 65.
29. Ibid.
30. Ibid.
31. Ibid.
32. "Blue-Collar Blues: Just a Catch Phrase, or Real That?," U.S. News and World Report, December 25, 1972: 56.
33. Ibid.
34. Ibid.
35. "The Bullet Biters," Newsweek, February 7, 1972: 65.
36. "Autos 1: Both Sides Play It Cool In Strike," The New York Times, September 20, 1970:8E.
37. "The Bullet Biters," Newsweek, February 7, 1972: 65.
38. Ibid.

39. Ibid.
40. U.S. News, February 7, 1972: 45.
41. Ibid.42
42. Russell W. Gibbons, "Why One Worker Sticks With a Job He Finds Dull," Commonweal, March 3, 1972: 101.
43. Ibid: 103.44
44. Business Week, March 4, 1972: 70.
45. "The UAW Hits GM with Guerilla Tactics," Business Week, October 28, 1972: 39.
46. Business Week, March 25, 1972: 46.
47. Ibid: 47.
48. "GM Troubles," The New York Times, January 23, 1972: 35N.
49. Ibid.
50. Agis Salpukas, "Extra Work Prompts Vote to Strike at GM Plant," The New York Times, March 7, 1972: 38.
51. Ibid.
52. "The Spreading Lordstown Syndrome," Business Week, March 4, 1972: 69.
53. Ibid.
54. Agis Salpukas, "Extra Work Prompts Vote to Strike at GM Plant," The New York Times, March 7, 1972: 38.
55. Ibid.
56. Ibid.
57. Ibid.
58. Ibid.

36. Chiba International, Inc.*

Ken Morikawa, the general manager for administration of a Japanese manufacturing plant under construction in rural Georgia, was troubled. This morning his American personnel manager, John Sinclair, had walked eagerly across the temporary open-plan office and announced: "I've found a professor of Japanese at Georgia State University who is willing to help translate our corporate philosophy. I would like to hire him for the job."

Ken felt pressured. He thought that John Sinclair, like many Americans, was expecting too much of Japanese companies. The company philosophy that he, Ken, had learned to live by in Tokyo would continue to guide him, but he did not feel that Americans would welcome or even understand a Japanese company philosophy.

Ken had a very large task to do in supervising the building of a plant that might ultimately provide jobs for up to 2,000 employees in the area where very few workers had had any industrial experience. He wished to show that his was a company that cared about the welfare of its workers and their job security, and could be trusted to treat them fairly and not to lay them off. He believed that such a philosophy, if it could be properly explained to workers and carefully implemented, would help to build a high morale among the employees and consequently improve productivity.

Ken also wanted to ensure that high morale be maintained as the workforce expanded to full capacity. Indeed, aside from issues of ease of transportation and distribution, the characteristics of the local workforce, their "Japanese" work ethic, had been one of the primary reasons for establishing the plant here. He believed that the training costs involved in transforming very "green" workers were well worth it, to avoid people who had picked up "bad habits" or had had their morale lowered in prior industrial jobs. In Japan, teaching company philosophy is an important part of the company's introductory training program. But will it work here?

Ken wondered if his new administrative duties were lowering his concern for personnel matters. Ever since he had to read Alfred Sloan's *My Years with General Motors* during the company training program and had written a review that focused on human resource issues, he had held positions related to his field. Even though he had majored in mathematical economics in college, his first assignment had been in the personnel "design center," which controlled training and salary administration for white-collar employees. After two years he was sent to a district office as a salesman. He returned after thirteen months to the employee welfare section of the personnel department at the head office, administering such programs as house loans and recreational activities. Eight years with the company had passed by the time he was sent to an American college to study personnel-related subjects and improve his English.

After receiving his M.B.A. he returned to the head office. His most recent assignment before coming to Georgia was in personnel development research, planning new wages systems. It was expected that in his new job in Georgia he would eventually hand the reins over to an American general manager and remain only in an advisory capacity. However, he

---

*This case was written by Nina Hatvany and Vladimir Pucik for class discussion only. None of this material is to be quoted or reproduced without the permission of the authors.

felt that it was at this vital stage that the corporation depended on his human relations expertise to set the scene for future success. Was he neglecting an area in which he had been trained to be sensitive?

He brought the subject up at lunch with John Sinclair. "Let me tell you something, John. I have a hunch why the Japanese are more successful in achieving high quality and productivity than Americans have been recently. It has to do with application, rather than ideas. Many great ideas have come from the United States, but the Japanese concentrate on applying them very carefully. Americans emphasize creating something new and then moving on. The Japanese meticulously analyze a problem from all angles and see how a solution might be implemented.

"As they say, Rome wasn't built in a day. I'm not sure our American workers will understand what it really means to have a company philosophy. Let's take it slowly and see what kind of people we hire and then see what best meets their needs."

John, who had worked at a rather traditional U.S. company for 11 years and had become increasingly interested in how Japanese companies managed their U.S. employees, had been eager to join a Japanese company. He wanted to see in action such "Japanese" strategies as long-term employment, the expression of a company philosophy and careful attention to integrating the employees into the company. He answered comfortingly, "Ken, I know you hate conflict. But I also know that you think it important to gather information. One of our purchasing agents, Billy, told me about a Japanese company that he recently visited, Chiba International. Apparently, they already have a fully developed company philosophy and I understand that they're doing very well with it. Why don't we go out to California and talk with their management and try and understand how and why they concentrated on communicating their philosophy."

"And soak up some sun, too," beamed Ken. "You're on!"

The Company

Chiba International Inc. in San Jose, California, makes high-precision, sophisticated electronics parts used in the final assembly of customized and semi-customized integrated circuits – particularly the expensive memory chips used in computers and military hardware. In such products, reliability is everything, price a lesser consideration. The similar but cheaper parts that manufacturers use once a product reaches a high volume are left for others to make.

Chiba International is a subsidiary of Chiba Electronics Company. *Nihon Keizai Shimbun*, Japan's preeminent business paper, recently ranked Chiba Electronics as one of the foremost companies in Japan on the basis of its management earnings stability and performance, ahead of such better-known giants as Sony, Matshushita Electric and Toyota Motor. Chiba Electronics Co. has 70% of the $250 million-a-year world market for its products. Chiba International likewise has a 70% share of the $250 million-a-year U.S. market.

Chiba International started in the United States 12 years ago, with a small sales office. A manufacturing plant that had been losing $100,00 to $200,000 a month was acquired from an American competitor. The American management was terminated, and a team of Japanese, headed by a Canadian-born Japanese-reared executive, succeeded in turning it around within two years.

Today 14 out of the 24 top executives and 65 out of 70 salesmen at Chiba are Americans. All the employees in other categories are also American.

Chiba's Philosophy

"As the sun rises brilliantly in the sky,
Revealing the size of the mountain, the market,
Oh this is our goal.
With the highest degree of mission in our heart we serve our industry,
Meeting the strictest degree of customer requirement.
We are the leader in this industry and our future path
Is ever so bright and satisfying."

"That's a translation of our company song," said a high-ranking Japanese executive, one of the group of Japanese and American managers who had agreed to meet with Ken and John. "But we haven't introduced it to our employees yet. That's typical of the way we brought the company philosophy to our employees —slowly and carefully. Every line worker gets a leaflet explaining our company philosophy when he or she starts work. We don't have a specific training session on it and we don't force them to swallow it. It's up to them to digest and understand it."

"What about when you acquire a company as you have done over the past few years?" asked John.

"The same thing. It's very gradual. If we force it, it causes nothing but indigestion. Here it has been easy, the work is very labor intensive, repetitive, tedious assembly. In other places the soil is different. At one, for example, almost all the employees are exempts. They understand the philosophy but won't necessarily go by it. Engineers and technical people also seem to be less receptive than people in sales, personnel and administration. In other sites, though, where the technology is more similar to this, we have had no problem at all."

One of the other managers present in the group, this one American, interrupted to show Ken and John a copy of the leaflet. It was quite rhetorical in tone, a few paragraphs stuck them as particularly interesting.

Management Philosophy
Our goal is to strive toward both the material and spiritual fulfillment of all employees in the Company, and through this successful fulfillment, serve mankind in its progress and prosperity.

Management Policy
(...) Our purpose is to fully satisfy the needs of our customers and in return gain a just profit for ourselves. We are a family united in common bonds and singular goals. One of these bonds is the respect and support we feel for our fellow family coworkers.

Also, the following exhortation:

When there is a need, we all rally to meet it and consider no task too menial or demeaning; all that matters is that it should be done! We are all ready to sweep floors, sort parts, take inventory, clean machines, inspect parts, load trucks, carry boxes, wash windows, file papers, run furnaces, and do just about anything that has to be done.

Meetings

"Daily meetings at the beginning of each shift are held in the courtyard," explained the group. "All the workers stand in lines (indicated by metal dots in the asphalt). Each day, a different member of management speaks for about five minutes. On Mondays executives speak, on Tuesday, personnel and administration are represented, Wednesdays are about safety concerns, and on Thursdays and Fridays, members of production and sales speak. They are all free to say whatever they like. The shift workers tend to develop favorites, especially among the more extroverted sales managers.

"Then a personnel coordinator delivers news about sports events and so on, and perhaps a motivational message, and goes on to lead the group in exercises for one minute. These calisthenics are voluntary, but most of the employees join in. After that, the large group breaks up for brief departmental meetings.

"Again, in the departmental meetings, a speaker is chosen for the day and speaks for about five minutes. Even people at the lowest exempt level find themselves speaking. Then the department manager discusses yesterday's performance, today's schedule and any other messages, such as that housekeeping is inadequate or that certain raw materials are in short supply.

"Once a month, there is an announcement of total company performance versus plans. This is important, as all company employees share at the same rate in the annual company bonus, which is based on profitability and usually equals about one month's salary or wages."

Another Japanese manager continued, "Years ago, there were complaints about having so many meetings, but I haven't heard any for a long time now. The employees like to hear important announcements and even less important ones, such as who is selling theater tickets, bowling league reports, and tennis match dates."

The American personnel manager chimed in: "I was the one who came up with the idea of exercises. I saw it on my visit to Japan. They are just a part of the rituals and symbols that you need in order to get better mutual understanding. The atmosphere was right and the timing was good. Even so, because they weren't mandatory, it took about one-and-a-half years until everyone joined in. Now most people understand the meaning behind it. If we were to stop it now, we'd get complaints.

"Besides the morning meeting, we have several other meetings. On Mondays, we have a very large liaison meeting for information sharing. All the executives attend: sales managers and staff managers, the plant manager and the assistant plant manager. On Tuesdays, we have a production meeting attended by the production managers and any staff involved with their problems. On Monday at four o'clock every second week we have a supervisors' meeting mainly for one-way communication to them. On the alternating weeks we have a training meeting. The whole personnel department also meets every week.

"Less formally, we have many sales meetings about, for example, new products. We have combination sales and production meetings, which are called on an as-needed basis. Team meetings on the production line are also called whenever needed.

"All these formal meetings are supplemented by many company-sponsored activities. We have a company bowling league, tennis matches, softball, fishing, and skiing. We often organize discount tickets. We're planning the Christmas party. Each employee can bring a guest, so it costs us about $40,000. Our company picnic costs $29,000."

"It sounds very well worked out for the non-exempts," commented John. "How about for the exempts?"

Sales Force

They started with the largely American sales force.

"They're a very different species. They have tremendous professional pride. Most of the American sales engineers have a very arrogant take-or- leave-it attitude. Our attitude is almost the complete opposite. We try to serve our customer's needs, almost like a geisha girl, who makes her customer feel that he is the only one served by her.

"We try to communicate the following motto to them:

S	incerity
A	bility
L	ove
E	nergy
S	ervice

> Sincerity is the basic attitude you need to have, as well as the ability to convince the customer. You must love the products that you sell or you can't convince the customer. You must have energy because at the end of the day it's always the case that you could have done one more thing or made one more sales call. Finally, the mentality of serving the customer is the most important.

"We communicate that to our sales force and they like it, especially when they don't have to tell white lies to customers or put up with harassment from customers. We also want them to be honest with us, even about their mistakes. Quite often we depend on the salesmen's input for our understanding of customers, so an objective daily report by telex or phone is very important to us.

"No one in our company works on a commission basis, not even salesmen. We would lose market share for products that are difficult to promote. Also, the nature of different sales territories would make commissions unfair.

"Although we pay on straight salary only, we don't just have a unilateral sales quota. The salesman discusses his targets with his boss. They are purposely set high, so good performance against goals is grounds for a merit increase the next year.

"We don't really have a marketing department. We feel that it is an expensive luxury and while we have a Vice President in charge of marketing, his is almost a corporate sales staff function."

U.S. Management

John was curious about how American line managers reacted to working in a Japanese company.

A Japanese manager explained: "When Americans join us, they expect the usual great deal of internal politicking. They scan people in meetings, looking for those with real power, looking, to use our expression, for whose apple he should polish. It takes time for them to realize that it's unnecessary.

"When we interview American executives for a job, we do it collectively so 5 to 10 interviewers are present. This usually puzzles the interviewee. He wonders whom he will report to. We reply that he will be hired by the company, although he may report to one individual. As in Japan, the company will take care of him, so it does not depend on his loyalty to one individual."

What about your company criteria for hiring managers?

"His way of thinking, not necessarily his ability. Although a Harvard MBA is welcomed, it is not essential. In fact, no one here has one. We don't provide an elegant fit to his social elite. There are no private offices. Salary and benefits are up to par for the location (and industry) but not especially high. We work long hours.

"We're looking for devotion and dedication as well as an aggressive attitude. We conduct two or three long interviews for an important position. We ask questions like 'What is your shortcoming?' We're interested not in the answer itself but in the kind of thinking behind it. We do make mistakes sometimes, but our batting average is good.

"Sometimes there's a very deep communication gap between Japanese management and U.S. management because we believe in dedication and devotion to the company. They do, too, but only to a certain point. We often tell them that the joy of working for the company can be identical to personal happiness with the family. I ask my wife for her understanding of that, and I work six days a week, from seven o'clock to ten o'clock. Their wives place demands on them to come home at six o'clock. U.S. executives put personal and family happiness first. I'm not telling you which is right. But it is second nature for me to think about the future of the company. So long as I have challenging assignments and job opportunities, I will put the company before my personal happiness."

What do American interviewees feel about all this?

"One problem is that they ask, 'What's my real future? Can I be considered for President?' There's no real answer because it probably will be a Japanese. However, we don't like to close those doors to a really capable American.

"The issue of communication between Japanese and Americans is still a problem. After the Americans go home, the Japanese get together at seven or eight o'clock and talk in Japanese about problems and make decisions without the Americans present. Naturally this makes the Americans feel very apprehensive. We're trying to rectify it by asking the Japanese managers not to make decisions alone and asking the Americans to stay as late as possible.

"More important, if we could really have our philosophy permeate the American managers, we Japanese could all go back to Japan and not worry about it. Our mission is to expedite that day by education and training.

"So far, however, there is a gap. Americans are more interested in individual accomplishment, remuneration and power. When they are given more responsibility, they don't feel its heavy weight, rather they feel that it extends their sovereign area so that they have more of a whip. That creates power conflicts among U.S. managers."

"Let me tell you, though," summarized the American personnel manager, "I like it. I was recruited by a headhunter. Now, I've been with the company five years and the difference from my former employer is astounding. I don't have to get out there and be two-faced, fudging to keep the union out, hedging for the buck. In general, it's hard to find an American employer that really sincerely cares for the welfare of the low-level employee. This company went almost too far in the opposite direction at first. They wanted to do too much for the employees too quickly, without their earning it. That way, you don't get their respect."

Financial People

"Our financial people throughout the company are proud because of our impressive company performance. Only 20% of our financing is through debt, in contrast to many Japanese companies. We also have a rather unique way of treating some of our raw materials internally. We try to expense everything out. It's derived from our founder's very conservative management. We ask the question: 'If we closed down tomorrow, what would our liquid assets be?' In line with that, for example, internally we put our inventory at zero.

"We follow the 'noodle peddler theory.' The noodle peddler is an entrepreneur. He has to borrow his cart, his serving dishes and his pan to make ramen. He has to be a good marketer to know where to sell. He has to be a good purchasing director and not overbuy noodles, in case it rains. He could buy a fridge but he would need a lot of capital, the taste of noodles would deteriorate, and he would need additional manpower to keep an inventory of the contents of the fridge. The successful noodle peddler puts dollars aside at the end of the day for depreciation and raw materials for tomorrow. Only then does he count profits. That's also why we don't have a marketing department. The successful peddler doesn't have time to examine opportunities in the next town.

"This is the way a division manager has to operate. In order to maximize output with minimum expenditure, every effort is made to keep track on a daily basis of sales, returns, net shipment costs and expenses."

Open Communications

"I understand all that you've said so far," mused John, "but how exactly do you take all these abstract philosophical ideas and make them real?"

"Oh, open communications is the key. We have a fairly homogeneous workforce. Most are intelligent, some are even college graduates. Most are also very stable types with dependents or elderly parents they send money to.

"We're lucky, but of course it's not as homogeneous as in Japan where everyone has experienced one culture. So here, the philosophy has to be backed up by a great deal of communication.

"We mentioned the meetings. We also have a suggestion box and we answer all the suggestions in print in the company newspaper. Also, one person from personnel tours the plant all day, for all three shifts, once a week, just chatting and getting in touch with any potential problems as they arise. It's kind of a secondary grievance system. We're not unionized and I guess we'd rather stay that way as it helps us so much with flexibility and job changes among our workforce.

"In the fall, when work is slow, we have many kompas. You may not know about this, John. A kompa is a small gathering off-premises after work. Eight to eighteen people participate and the company pays for their time and for refreshments. They're rarely social, they have an objective. For example, if two departments don't get along and yet they need to work together, they might hold a kompa. A kompa can take place at all levels of the company. Those groups that do it more frequently tend to move on from talking about production problems to more philosophical issues."

Appraisal and Reward Systems

"It all sounds great," sighed Ken, "just as good as Japan. But tell me, how does it tie in with wages and salaries, because people here are used to such different systems."

"Well, we don't have lifetime employment, but we do have an explicit no-layoff commitment. We are responsible for our employees. This means that employees also have to take responsibility and have broad job categories so we don't have to redo paperwork all the time. We have tried to reduce the number of job classifications to the raw minimum, so we have two pay grades covering 700 workers. At the higher levels, we have three pay grades for craftsmen and two for technicians."

John ventured, "I guess an example of your job flexibility in action is the mechanic you mentioned when we toured the plant."

"Yes, the person you spoke with was a dry press mechanic. He's doing menial labor this week, but his pay hasn't been cut and he knows he wouldn't be taken off his job if it weren't important."

"We don't hire outside, if we can avoid it," added the personnel manager. "Only if the skill is not available in-house. The bulk of our training is on-the-job. We don't utilize job postings. We promote when a person's skills are ripe or when there is a need.

"The job of a 'lead' or team leader is the stepping-stone to supervisor. It's not a separate job status within our system, but the lead is given a few cents an hour extra and wears a pink, not a yellow, smock. The lead is carefully groomed for his or her position, and although a lead might be demoted because a specific need for them no longer existed, a lead would rarely be demoted for lack of skills or leadership ability.

"Rewards are for service and performance. Plant workers, unskilled and semiskilled, are reviewed every six months. The lead completes the evaluation form (see Exhibit 1). This is checked or confirmed by the supervisor and the overall point score translates into cents per hour. There are two copies, one for the supervisor and one for the employee. Depending on the supervisor, some employees get a copy, some don't.

"The office clerical staff are all reviewed on April 1st and October 1st. A similar review form for managers is used to determine overall letter scores. All the scores are posted on a spread sheet and compared across departments, through numerous meetings of managers and personnel people, until the scores are consistent with one another. Then the scores are tied to dollars. Some managers feed back, some don't.

"Exempt staff are reviewed on April 1st, and as a separate process, the spread sheet procedure just outlined is carried out. At least two managers review any exempt employee, but

Exhibit 1.

Emplyee's Name		Clock No.	Dept.	Shift	Over Last 6 Month Period			
					Days Absent	Number Tardies	Number Early Exit	Work Days Leave of Absences
Employee's Job Title		Anniversary						

Rate on Factors Below:		Numerical Score			
		L	S	M	F
1. LOYALTY/DEDICATION	Faithful to the company cause, ideals, philosophy, & customers; a devoting or setting aside for company purposes.				
2. SPIRIT/ZEAL	Amount of interest & enthusiasm shown in work; full of energy, animation & courage; eagerness & ardent interest in the pursuit of company goals.				
3. COOPERATION	A willingness & ability to work with leaders & fellow employees toward company goals.				
4. QUANTITY OF WORK	Volume of work regularly produced; speed & consistency of output.				
5. QUALITY OF WORK	Extent to which work produced meets quality requirements of accuracy, thoroughness & effectiveness.				
6. JOB KNOWLEDGE	The fact or condition of knowing the job with familiarity gained through experience, association & training.				
7. SAFETY ATTITUDE	The willingness & ability to perform work safely.				
8. CREATIVENESS	The ability to produce through imaginative skill.				
9. ATTENDANCE	Includes all types of absence (excused or unexcused), tardies, early exits, L.O.A.'s from scheduled work.				
10. LEADERSHIP	The ability to provide direction, guidance & training to others.				
OVERALL EVALUATION OF EMPLOYEE PERFORMANCE:					

Supervisor's Approval			Personnel Dept. Approval	

Do Not Write Below This Line - For Human Resource Department Use Only			
Present Base Rate	New Base Rate	Effective Date of Increase	Refer to instructions on the back side of this paper

feedback is usually minimal. The reason is that we encourage feedback all year. If there are no surprises for your subordinate at review time, then you've managed well.

"Agreements on reviews for exempt personnel take place in many meetings at various levels. The process is very thorough and exceptionally fair, and contributes to the levels of performance we get."

Quality and Service

A question from John as to how Chiba International was doing as a result of all this elicited much pride.

"Turnover is 2-1/2% a month, which is very satisfactory for our kind of labor given a transient society. We rarely have to advertise for new employees now. The community knows about us. But we do select carefully. The personnel department does the initial screening, and then the production managers and supervisors get together and interview people.

"The lack of available technically-trained people used to be a big problem, but over the years we've developed the expertise internally. Our productivity is now almost as high as in Japan."

Ken and John asked what other aspects of the company they had not yet discussed. They were told that quality and, hence, customer service, was another central part of the philosophy.

"Our founder, Mr. Amano, firmly believes in zero defect theory. Doctor Deming taught us the concept of quality control. Unfortunately, many American companies did not emphasize this. During World War II, the concept of acceptable quality level was developed in the United States. The idea was that with mass production there will be some defects. Rather than paying for more inspectors on the production line, real problems, for example, with cars, could be identified by the consumer in the field and repaired in the field.

"We don't allow that. We have 100% visual inspection of all our tiny parts. They only cost $50 per 1,000 units. We inspect every finished package under a microscope so we have 130 inspectors, which is about one sixth of our production staff.

"The company's founder, Amano, has said to us, 'We try to develop every item our customers want. Being latecomers, we never say no, we never say we can't.' Older ceramic manufacturers would evaluate a proposal on a cost basis and say no. Yet we have been profitable from the start."

As the interview drew to a close, one Japanese manager reflected Mr. Suzuki has a saying:

Ability x philosophy x zeal = performance.

If the philosophy is negative, performance is negative because it's a multiplicative relationship.

"But in our company, which now numbers 2,000, we must also start to have different kinds of thinking. The Japanese sword is strong because it is made of all different kinds of steel wrapped around one another. The Chinese sword is also very strong, but because it's all one material, it's vulnerable to a certain kind of shock. We must bear that in mind so that we have differences within a shared philosophy.

"We're thinking of writing a book on our philosophy, addressing such issues as what loyalty is, by piecing together events and stories from company history. This would be a book that would assist us in training."

Ken and John walked out into the parking lot. "Whew!" sighed John. "It's more complicated than I had thought."

"Oh, yes! You need a great deal of patience," responded Ken paternally.

"So we'd better get started quickly," enthused John. "Where shall we begin? Perhaps I should call the translator."

37. Are You Staying?*

During their traditional reunion on Cape Cod, Bob and Steve for the first time were contemplating their futures. Although only twenty-four years old, both were already wondering how to better manage their careers. Since graduating together three years ago, they already had attained some success, at least in their eyes. Both had passed the CPA exam the first time through and both had enjoyed significant pay increases the first two years. Their similarities ended here however, for while Bob was contemplating advancement in the same firm he joined two years ago, Steve was contemplating advancement in any firm except the firm he joined two years ago. In their discussion, each reflected on his career experiences thus far.

Bob Lemmon Gets Lucky

Whether it was lucky or not, Bob was mighty pleased about being at one of the more successful offices of the "Big Six" accounting firm he joined three years ago. It started even before he was hired. During the holiday break in December of his senior year he remembered going to a party thrown by the office for accounting students from schools the office typically recruited from. The party gave the students an informal opportunity to meet several partners, including the managing partner. It also gave the office an informal chance to look at the new crop of rookies. Bob couldn't help but be impressed by this party and the chance to meet the managing partner. He also got the chance to meet some of the other students who were eventually hired by the office.

Bob's first two years in the office were extremely gratifying. He worked on a variety of assignments, each one exposing him to different challenges, each one requiring slightly different skills. Any problems, personal or professional, were comfortably discussed with the senior "brother" he was assigned. He would have felt as comfortable, however, talking with a manager or even the managing partner. Managers, partners, and even the managing partner felt it was extremely important to have an open door policy with all employees, especially the new assistants. To facilitate this open door policy, the managing partner always made sure to hire for "anticipated growth" rather than to hire in order to catch up to the growth. Although this resulted in "excess hiring" until growth caught up, doing this helped ensure that managers and partners didn't exceed a 70 – 75% utilization rate. Year-end review time resulted in Bob being told exactly how well he was doing relative to the other assistants. His two pay increases were directly related to the performance appraisal results. As far as the office was concerned, this pay-for-performance policy and candor in telling folks where they stood resulted in enhanced loyalty and a low premature turnover rate. This was reinforced by the "excess hiring" that ensured that assistants were not overutilized. This in turn facilitated good leverage ratios and the manager and partner utilization rate of 70 – 75%. Thus Bob's pressing career question was whether he should stay in audit or transfer to tax in the next year or two.

---

*This case was prepared by Randall S. Schuler who expresses his appreciation for the assistance of Jim Clemence.

Steve Luck Gets a Lemon

As far as Steve was concerned he worked in an office of the same "Big Six" firm, but one that was on a different planet than Bob's. Because Steve lived on the West Coast, it hadn't been convenient for him to go to the holiday break party attended by Bob. Talk about being in the wrong place at the wrong time! Subsequently, Steve was hired by another office of the same firm in the following spring by someone he never saw again. Steve's first two years in the office were extremely frustrating and a bit dissatisfying. Although he had been given a variety of job assignments, his recollection of the experience was one of exhaustion rather than of the desired variety, growth and challenge. In each of his first two years he worked approximately 350 hours of overtime. He knew of three assistants who left because of the excessive overtime (excessive for them at least). What he didn't know, however, was that many of the managers and partners were working as much overtime as he was. Manager utilization rates had reached as high as 85%. As a consequence of this, the managers and partners really didn't have the time to sit down and be an "ear" for the assistants. While Steve knew that the "Big Six" accounting firms weren't in business to "coddle" people, he knew he would have appreciated a little pat on the back or word of encouragement. Because of this environment, he knew only the other assistants who stayed, the seniors, and some managers and partners by name. He was yet to meet the managing partner. Also because of this environment, performance review time was one filled with uncertainty. In part because managers and partners felt uncomfortable giving negative feedback, and in part because they thought it more motivating for assistants, assistants did not know how they were doing. Consequently, they relied on job assignments and pay raises to help them evaluate how well the firm thought they were doing. Thus, Steve's pressing career question was whether he should leave the firm now or stay through a third year. He couldn't think of any reason to stay, but he thought discussions with Bob could clarify his options along with increasing his level of envy.

Part 9 Communication and Group Dynamics

Cases Outline

38. Motor Parts Corporation

Bob Marvin, president of Motor Parts Corp (MPC), felt a great deal of conflict and frustration as he chaired the strategic planning meeting of his senior management team. Al Shepherd, his executive vice president, had just arose from the conference table and excused himself, saying:

> "I'm sorry but we have had a change in our chemotherapy appointment and I have to meet Ruth."

Ruth, Al's wife, had just recently learned that she had a recurrence of a malignant brain tumor. The prior bout, over only two years ago, had been difficult. Al was completely involved with his wife's fight against her illness. He had become about as expert as a layman could become on the disease, the many methods of fighting it and the best institutions and physicians. He had accompanied her to virtually all medical appointments and procedures. When asked about her condition he would report to colleagues at great length and in technical detail. He was consumed by her situation. It had been a year since she had been given a clean bill of health when they were devastated to learn about her relapse. Now, the odds were against her. The doctors suggested a variety of alternative treatments, but at best her chances of surviving two years were less than one in three.

Bob, with great self-restraint, did not want to react at the meeting, and as hard as it was he tried to work around some of the issues that most directly affected Al.

Bob couldn't help but notice increasing, and less subtle references by others in the meeting to problems they had working around Al. After all, the organization had to go on. They all had their jobs to do, and while none had problems as severe as Al many of them had their own serious problems. Jay Unger, VP Marketing had a son who had recently been expelled from college and was in rehabilitation with a drug dependency problem. Pete Arnell, was in the middle of a divorce. Bob himself, had his own problems, real problems.

At the end of the meeting he asked Mike Jones, who had happened to be at the meeting to return with him to his office. Mike is a management professor at the university and a consultant to MPC on planning issues.

> "What am I going to do about Al? As you know, after me, he has the most important job in this company. In fact, on a day-to-day basis he probably has the most critical job since all functions except for Finance, Legal and Public Relations report directly to him. For the past few months he has been out of the office as much as he has been in it. Even worse, numerous meetings have been set to coincide with his schedule only to be aborted at the last second because he had to leave to take his wife to a medical appointment.
>
> "Now I just heard that our national sales meeting which has to be set up months in advance can't be scheduled because he is not certain about a procedure she has scheduled for about that time period.

This case written by Richard D. Freedman, Stern School of Business, New Yory University. Copyright 1995 by Richard D. Freedman. Reprinted with permission.

"His job requires considerable travel to regional offices and he just has not been doing enough of it. We have a number of new regional managers who are not getting enough guidance. We have some regional managers who are not doing a good job. They require closer supervision, if not replacement. Instead of dealing with these issues directly he is delegating supervisory chores to the two senior staff people in his department. For example, I know Joe Roderick is a great planner and earlier in his career he was a regional manager at Major Parts, but he is not their boss. I don't want lines of authority confused. I told that to Al when we created those staff positions.

"You know that I try to keep in contact with our major customers. I have picked up hints that some of our regional people are just not performing adequately. He is not on top of things. Just look at how poor some of our regions are performing - Detroit and San Francisco are good examples. Our business is as dependent on service as price and quality. We can't afford not to be on top of things.

"Just think about today. Here we are under all of this pressure from our board to develop a new five year plan. Even though our performance has been, on a relative basis, the best in the industry they keep warning me that a company of our size has to do even better if it is going to avoid a takeover.

"And you know we haven't been cheap. Salaries have risen around here faster than any place in the industry. I think that is only fair given performance. No one has done better than Al in the eight years that he has been here. He started at a rather low pay level and now is the highest paid executive in a comparable position in the industry.

"Even though I have always had problems with his attention to detail, and some of the people he has hired, I have no complaint about overall results. But we have to continue to improve.

"By the way, you know that this is only part of the problem with Al. He's got to be one of the softest guys I've ever met. He stays home when he's got a bad cold, when there's a few inches of snow in his driveway. He was out a week last year with an ear infection. He is out about as much as any senior manager I've ever known.

"You really have to wonder sometimes about his commitment. Some Board members have picked this up. To be honest, if I something happened to me I don't think he would be a serious candidate for my job, even though they think he is very talented."

Mike couldn't help but think while Bob was talking. "If someone didn't know Bob they would think him quite callous if they overheard what he just said, but Bob is really a good person in his own way." He had known Bob for over twenty years. Their careers ran in parallels. Mike had been a consultant for three organizations that employed Bob, each watched the other move up their respective professions.

Bob was a rather shy person who frequently had to work in public. So he masked his shyness in formality. Although he encouraged subordinates to demonstrate initiative he tended to carefully scrutinize their work, even the work of those in whom he had developed considerable confidence. He wanted things done the "right" way. He was often characterized as a perfectionist. He was as meticulous in his dress as his work. Despite his success, he was quite insecure. He worried most of the time.

Bob held himself to the same standard as others. It was an unusual evening or weekend that he would not spend much of his time working on the thick pile of papers he would take home and dictating one of the dozen or so memos that he would send to subordinates every day. He tried to overcome his natural reticence in public by carefully developed presentations. There were times that he could spend half a day preparing a ten minute presentation to his board. One problem with the approach was that he came across to some as stiff and cold. People who did not know him well thought of him as a rather dry and formal person, even bureaucratic. Bob had few friends. Those few who managed to get close to him over the years know him as a caring and brilliant executive.

Bob said little to Al because he wanted to be supportive, and he certainly did not want to be perceived by Al as not caring or putting his job ahead of his family. After all, no one spent more time thinking about family issues than Bob. So what he did was constantly send Al reminders about unresolved issues, press him for dates and urge him to make trips in the field.

"Well what have you said to him?", asked Mike.

"I have stressed to him how important some of the meetings are and I have tried to alert him to some of the critical issues he has to handle."

"He has indicated that he has been working on many of the problems at home and over the phone. He says he is in constant contact with his people over the telephone and that there are very few problems that he is not able to deal with. But that is simply not true.

"You've known him for a long time. Why don't you talk to him and give me your assessment?"

The next week Mike asked Al out to lunch after they worked on the planning issues. Before lunch Mike couldn't help but review his impressions of Al. Al was like many people he had known who came up through sales. He was one of the most enjoyable people you could want to be around. He had an endless supply of the latest jokes - although he could be somewhat indiscreet as to who he told what joke. He was warm and friendly and showed great interest in the problems of the people he worked with - including his subordinates. He genuinely enjoyed helping his subordinates, although he was so busy that the lack of contact with him was a constant source of complaint. While this was a significant problem before the recurrence of Ruth's malignancy, now it was serious. Being liked was important to Al. His feelings would be hurt when he would hear about or sense the disapproval of a colleague. An ongoing source of conflict between Bob and Al was the fact the while Bob thought rules and regulations were meant to be followed, Al was inclined to overlook the rules, both for himself and others if the job was being done. Al was basically an optimistic person, he tended not to worry about the future, unless he had a specific problem he was forced to confront. He felt no need to control his subordinates if they were producing. After all, he had said to Mike many times what is the difference if he took time off if the job was being done?

After chatting for a while about issues that they were working on together Mike turned the conversation to Ruth's health. Al was quite hopeful about a new treatment available at the Morris Clinic. In fact, he had pulled strings with influential people and had a famous expert examine her. He advised an operation that would give her a one chance in three probability for surviving three years. Without the operation she had about a fifteen percent probability. The operation would be in two months and she would have to remain at the hospital for a month. Of course, he would stay with her.

Mike asked about other relatives who could share the load. Their two children were away at college and he did not think it would be right to ask them. They were under enough stress at school and with their mother's illness. She had one sister who had two young teenagers so she could not help. Of course, he would not even consider leaving her alone.

Mike then asked: "Given all of the important issues you are working on and the people who look to you for supervision, how will you deal with your work responsibilities?"

Al said. "No problem, I've thought it through. First, I will set up in the regional office. I will try to be available for three hours a day, when I can leave Ruth. When there are significant problems with regional managers I'll fly them in to see me. After all, what's the difference if I fly out to see them or they come in to see me? As you know we hired Joe Roderick to handle major staff responsibilities like planning and executive development. He's had many years of supervisory experience, so he can handle any other issues that come up. So you can see that we ought to be able to handle the problems.

"I guess I ought to tell you that this illness has been very troubling, very difficult for me to handle. I haven't been sleeping well for weeks. The same thing happened the last time. So I've been getting up at 3 or 4:00 a.m. every day. I have been using that time very productively. It is incredible how much work you can get done through the computer tie in to the office when everything is so quiet."

Mike had the feeling that there was a lot more to the story than he was getting from Al, so he responded that, "It is clear that you've given this a lot of thought. But don't tell me what your plans are, tell me how you feel about things. The fact that you are having trouble sleeping is understandable, but it's also suggestive of deeper issues."

Al replied that, "It is very difficult for me know. I know that I am not one hundred percent into my job. But let me remind you about what happened about a year-and-a-half ago. The presidency of Delta Corp, our major competitor, opened when Arnie Wyman had the sudden heart attack. Their Board hired that executive search firm to find candidates, and the partner managing the account knew me and wanted me to go on their short list. You'll surely remember that I came to you as a friend and discussed the situation with you. Everyone said I would be the prime candidate for the job."

"After thinking it over I decided not to interview with them. There were a lot of factors involved, of course. But in the end the determining factor was how MPC, and Bob in particular, treated me when we were having all those health problems. I felt, and I feel, part of a family. Families take care of their own in times of trouble. Mike, money can't buy that."

Mike later spoke to Bob about his lunch with Al. He tried to be descriptive and non-evaluative, urging Bob to speak to Al directly. Yet, after the discussion Bob seemed fixated on one point. He wondered whether Al's reference to being recruited away was a cryptic warning or a genuine statement of emotion. Or was it some combination?

Two weeks later Mike was in the office working with managers on some rather complex planning issues when he was called out of a meeting to take a long distance call from Al. Al was calling from Detroit where MPC had one of its most important regional offices and which happened to be his home town. While going over some of the planning issues Al interrupted the conversation, saying "Mike, I have to interrupt, I'm so excited, you'll never guess what happened last night. You know how long and hard we've been working on the Delta Corp account. Tim Reynolds, our Detroit regional manager, finally set things up and we met with Delta's senior management team. We got the account! It will be at least $15,000,000 this year - almost 2% of our sales goal! Don't tell Bob, I want to break the news to him. This account was a real high priority for him.

A few hours later, toward the end of the day, Mike was just completing a meeting with Bob, when Bob said to him:

"You'll never guess the latest with Al. He is in Detroit. I tried to get him in the office yesterday morning on a very important issue, but Tim Reynolds said that he hadn't been in. He said that Al was at his mother's house. You remember that his dad died last year and his mother is alone and is in the early stages of Alzheimer's. He didn't get back to me until the late afternoon. Then he told me that he had to cancel some important meetings back here because he had to spend Friday in Detroit. It's obvious that he is taking advantage again. On top of everything else. I'm really frustrated."

"Well", Mike said, "Why don't you think about discussing it with him in a more straightforward way?"

Bob replied, "What's the use? You heard what he said. He has us over a barrel. He is staying with us because we treat him like family."

"Bob, are you being sarcastic?"

39. Contract Negotiations in Western Africa: A Case of Mistaken Identity*

Peter Janes, a young member of Eurojet's Contracts Department, was on his way to Saheli in French-speaking West Africa to work on the complicated negotiations involved in selling a jet airliner to the Saheli government. He was not altogether thrilled with the assignment, and hoped it would be a quick deal, since financing seemed to be available for it. He had experience in contract negotiation in India, the Philippines, and Saudi Arabia, and most recently, Australia. At 27, he was one of the younger members of the department, but was seen as trustworthy with a high degree of motivation. If he succeeded, it would be the first deal he brought to closure on his own. But he had serious doubts about the project's feasibility or desirability. In addition, he had left behind what seemed to be the beginning of a great relationship in Australia, and he wanted to get back to his girlfriend. Furthermore, Janes had no desire to become a Francophone Africa expert within the company.

The Company

Eurojet was one of the larger diversified aircraft manufacturers. It had developed a particular jet for Third World operations, able to operate from hot and high airfields, including unprepared strips. Orders, however, were hard to come by because of the difficulties of Third World financing and the poor financial condition of regional airlines. The company was therefore delighted to learn that its regional sales executive in Saheli, Mr. Ali Osaju, had found a potential sale in the country's desire for a presidential aircraft, along with its need for reliable regional air transport.

The sale looked even more possible when it was discovered that the government Export Import Bank had a substantial budget available for Saheli, making financing of the multimillion dollar aircraft feasible. It would be necessary to arrange an international commercial bank loan for Saheli as well. The potential of the airliner to earn revenue through regional transport was considered important in securing the loan.

The Negotiating Team

In December 1987, the Saheli government announced that they were ready to begin detailed negotiations. According to company policy, negotiations were conducted by the Contracts Department in close cooperation with sales and internal specialist functions. Mr. Janes, having just spent a hard-working three months – he had had four days off in the last six months – based in Australia and working across southeast Asia on specialist leasing packages, was assigned to the team because of his Third World experience, and his ability to speak French. He had been with the company for about two years. He had no experience in Africa.

Mr. Osaju was a highly placed African of middle eastern origin, educated in Europe, with

*This case was prepared by Gordon Anderson, MBA graduate 1988, and Christine Mead, Research Assistant, under the supervision of Susan Schneider, associate professor, as a basis for class discussion rather than to illustrate either effective or ineffective handling of an administrative situation. Copyright © 1988, INSEAD/CEDEP.

a background in aviation. He had joined the company at about the same time as Mr. Janes. He had no previous experience in selling high tech capital goods, but had many good connections, and was seen as invaluable to the company because of his African cultural background, combined with his European education. He had been developing local contacts in Saheli by spending a week there every two or three months over the past two years.

The Negotiating Policy

The company's negotiating policy inevitably led to what was referred to as the "two-headed monster approach." The sales representative was responsible for initial discussions and for overall relations with the customer. The contracts representative was responsible for negotiating concrete offers and signing contracts and finance agreements on behalf of the company. This double approach led to varying degrees of tension between the members of particular teams as well as between the departments in general. Sales were particularly aggrieved that contracts operated on a worldwide rather than a regional basis.

Working in a team where both have important roles to play required considerable sensitivity. In his two years of working at Eurojet, Peter Janes was looked on by the sales people as a considerate and skilled negotiating partner. He was not likely to lose a contract which they had spent years developing because of cultural clumsiness. Nevertheless, he walked a very narrow line, as it was his role to say no to all the wishes of the customer which were not feasible from the company's perspective. As this was to be his first solo contract negotiation, and Ali Osaju's first sale with the company, they shared a certain personal enthusiasm for closing the deal.

The Negotiation: The Early Days

Eurojet was not the only company trying to sell a jetliner to Saheli. The Russians, who had had considerable influence over the country since its independence twenty years earlier, were very present, trying to sell their aircraft and to sabotage the deal with Eurojet. Mr. Janes and Mr. Osaju frequently received strange phone calls in their hotel rooms, and were aware that all their telephone calls were bugged. Once, Mr. Janes returned to his room to find that his briefcase had been tampered with. In addition, another European company with a number of contracts in surrounding countries was trying to arrange a deal.

The main negotiating point of the team to begin with was to have the Sahelis accept one airplane that could be converted from a regional airliner to a VIP presidential jet. The Sahelis originally wanted a specially designed VIP jet, which would have cost an extra ten million dollars and would never have been used other than for the president. The negotiations moved extremely slowly. Mr. Janes and Mr. Osaju spent hours waiting to see officials, chasing papers from one office to another. They became aware that no one official wanted to be responsible for making the decision, in case he would be blamed for it should things go wrong.

They spent many hours debating strategy in the bar of the hotel. Mr. Janes objected to Mr. Osaju telling him what to do. Mr. Osaju objected to Mr. Janes making issues too complicated for the client. The relationship was a very tense one. They both felt they were getting little support from the head office and that the circumstances they were working in were very difficult.

Mr. Janes began to feel he was in a no-win situation. He realized that the negotiating process could go on for months, and he knew that his colleague had already begun to take over his activities with multi-order prospects in Australia. Conditions at the hotel were not that comfortable, and both he and Mr. Osaju were paid on a salary only basis. There were no overseas allowances.

The lack of support from headquarters was a problem for both the negotiators. Communications were difficult, as they felt they could not talk freely over the telephone because of being bugged. Furthermore, they did not feel their contacts at headquarters would begin to understand the finer points of the negotiation difficulties. They did learn from headquarters that they were considered to be moving too slowly in making the deal.

There were constant discussions on finance, spares, configuration, certification, and training. All the legal and technical documents had to be translated from English to French, causing many minor but significant misunderstandings. In one case, the standard contract at home called for the Saheli government to waive its "sovereign immunity" and "contract in its private rather than its public capacity." Saheli had adopted the Napoleonic Code from France, and had no equivalent legal concepts. The courts in the home country have a very limited right to hear actions against the Crown, and they assume this element of the law holds true for all countries. The Saheli negotiators listened with polite disbelief to these explanations and sent a telegram to the president saying, "Sahelian sovereignty is being threatened."

Mr. Janes and Mr. Osaju decided on a very basic strategy of patience and a friendly, open manner. Establishing trust and preserving individual and corporate credibility were recognized as being vital. They placed great emphasis on simplifying the bureaucratic process. Two months of negotiating passed with no commitment in sight.

Eurojet management were beginning to show their lack of confidence in the deal. Peter Janes had committed them to one million dollars of expenditure on completing an airline to the Sahelis' expectations, so that it could be delivered on time, yet they saw no formalization of the contract, nor had they received any of the loan money. On the Saheli side, there was considerable nervousness about the commercial sovereign loans from the international banks.

Mr. Janes continued to make his daily round of visits to offices and homes, establishing himself as open and trustworthy and using his skill in expressing complex legal and technical terms in a simple way. He began to be aware of a warming of perceptions toward him. Up until then he had felt that the Sahelian officials were always guarded, on the defense in the presence of Eurojet's legal commercial representative. He thought that this was because it was his role to say "no" in the negotiations. In the third month of the negotiations, he received an extremely encouraging sign. A source close to the president had recently been quoted as saying, "He (Janes) doesn't say 'yes' very often, but when he says 'yes,' he means 'yes.'" This was the sign that they had been waiting for, that his credibility had been established and they could now begin to deal with some of the more sensitive issues in the negotiation.

Mr. Janes had adapted himself to local culture as much as he could. Although his natural inclination would have been to get things done quickly, deal with business first and make friends later, he was aware that this was not how business deals were made in Saheli. So he spent many hours making friends, going to people's houses, walking around their businesses and factories. On one such occasion, he was walking around a factory with one of his friends, holding his hand as was the custom for Sahelian male friends. To his horror, a group of foreign diplomats came toward them on their tour of the factory. Mr. Janes was aware of an almost super-human effort on his part not to let go of his friend's hand and keep it relaxed, even as he felt the rest of his body stiffen with tension.

On another occasion, one of Mr. Janes' acquaintances attributes to him the status of being a great football (soccer) player. Peter thinks this person is just kidding at first, so he just "plays along with it". Later, when Peter's friends begin introducing him around as an international soccer player, it begins to worry him. He was unwilling to embarrass people by saying they were wrong, but was equally uncomfortable not striking down the myth. Perhaps it served some purpose. His status as an international soccer player was apparently much greater than that of a young lawyer; perhaps he needed a little extra to justify his power in negotiating and signing the contract. It was relatively easy to give indirect answers to questions, thus saving his conscience and protecting his strangely acquired status. Nonetheless, alluding to his legal training, Mr. Janes had said to Mr. Osaju at this time, "I can put my hand on my heart and say, 'I have not told a lie,' but I don't feel comfortable. We have worked so hard for credibility I would hate a silly issue like this to backfire on us." At the time, they agreed to laugh off the issue, because so far the people involved were not main players in the negotiations.

Epilogue

Mr. Janes continued to make noncommittal replies and managed to avoid any further serious problems. Although greatly disturbing to him personally, it was a nonissue in terms of the negotiations. Fortunately for Peter Janes, he could discuss his feelings about the situation with Ali Osaju, and so relieve some of his own tension by laughing about the absurdity of it.

After ten months of intense negotiations, the deal was almost called off by the negotiating team at the last minute. They had spent days retranslating the French contract back into English, and then sitting by a Sahelian typist who did not speak English saying each word to her phonetically so that she could type it. They both had had very little sleep in order to get the contract finished on time. When they finally went with the attorney general to the president's office to sign the contract, they were as usual kept waiting for a few hours. During that time, the attorney general reread the French contract and discovered numerous spelling mistakes in it. He then declared that he could not give it to the president in its present condition, and that the signing would have to be delayed for another week.

Ali and Peter both hit the walls – literally. It was the last straw. While Ali threw books and papers at the walls, Peter strode around the room shouting that unless they signed immediately, he was withdrawing Eurojet's approval of the contract. The attorney general stood his ground, and Ali and Peter stormed off to the hotel. They could scarcely believe what they had done after almost a year's worth of friendly and meticulous negotiating. Peter went to sleep, exhausted after the last ten days of work and the loss of the contract.

He was woken four hours later to be informed that the attorney general was waiting to see him. He was escorted to an office across the road, where he found the attorney general in his shirtsleeves, sitting at a typewriter, carefully changing all the spelling mistakes himself. He wanted Peter to initial all the changes so that he would feel confident that no substantial changes were being made in the contract. The contract was signed the next day.

Despite Eurojet's advice, the aircraft was not handled by the national airlines but kept under the president's control, and so, rarely used. Debt servicing soon became a problem, and one year later, the aircraft was quietly and informally repossessed. Eurojet has offered to resell the aircraft, but the Saheli government balked at authorizing the sale.

Mr. Osaju spent one more year in Africa, and then was promoted to the Far East where he was made regional sales director. Mr. Janes was promoted to another program in early 1983, where he continued to work for the next four years.

40. *The Reporter**

The Reporter recently celebrated its thirteenth year as the student newspaper at State College. While it has experienced its share of ups and downs, it has always been published on time. In 1983 its staff was awarded the Red Key Student Organization of the Year Award for its outstanding performance and contribution to the college community. On October 20, 1985, *The Reporter* staff failed to print a weekly edition. This was the first time in its history that the paper had not met its deadline.

Background

Until 1964, the campus newspaper's banner read *Exec*. This title epitomized the college founder James D. Atherton's commitment to develop and educate affluent young men into wealthy business executives and leaders in the field.

With the advent of the 1970s, State College underwent drastic changes; it began admitting women into the school. At the same time, the newspaper underwent a major change. Now there are approximately 1,650 full-time undergraduate students pursuing the Bachelor of Science degree in management and about 2,000 graduate students pursuing the Master of Business Administration degree. Of the total enrollment, approximately 1,060 are women.

Traditionally, all student organizations receive operating funds by submitting annual budgets to the Student Government Executive Board. All budgets list the amount required to conduct operations as well as that necessary to sponsor student-related events. The Government Board must then allocate student activities fees (independent of college administration) as equitably as possible.

In 1973 the *Exec* assumed its current identity, *The Reporter*. Previously, the *Exec* had received insufficient operating funds whenever it had printed unfavorable information about student government. In order to operate efficiently and effectively, *The Reporter* had committed itself to accepting funds from the college treasurer directly. Today its management is completely responsible for its operations, future development, and all debts incurred.

Operations

The Reporter, a student newspaper for and by students, links 3,000 individuals on and off campus at all levels of State's hierarchy including students, college staff, administrators, corporation officers, and trustees. The newspaper is published every Thursday during the fall and spring semesters with the exception of vacations and final exam periods. Members of the staff, comprised solely of students and a faculty adviser, are responsible for financial operations and planning, editorial content and policy, production, layout design, and circulation. The staff controls and performs all operations except for printing; printing services are contracted with an offset printer.

Organized along functional lines (Exhibit 1), general operations are overseen by the

---

*Joseph J. Martocchio, University of Illinois. Printed with permission of the author. This case is based upon a real-life situation. It should serve as the basis for classroom discussion. Its purpose is not to convey what is effective or ineffective management. In this spirit, all proper names, dates, and vital information have been changed.

editor-in-chief. Each associate editor and all managers serve as the "movers" of the organization.

The editor-in-chief is elected by staff members to the post for a one-year period beginning in April; the transition month of May allows the newly elected editor-in-chief and staff members the opportunity to run the paper with the previous staff available to offer advice and support.

A successful candidate for the editor-in-chief position has made significant contributions to the organization by performing exceptionally in any functional area, has impeccable writing skills and command of grammar rules, and has a sincere commitment to task achievement.

Much like the student government president, *The Reporter* editor represents the entire student body. The editor acts as a liaison between the student body and college administration, faculty, and trustees. As part of the position, the editor serves as a member of the Trustee's Committee on Student Affairs which is comprised of both graduate and undergraduate student body presidents, one government-appointed student representative from each school, student judicial court chairperson, Greek Council President, the vice-president for student affairs, a faculty member, and the deans of students and student activities.

The editor's role on this committee is to summarize the issues that affect campus life. While the trustees may be aware of some issues, the editor relates the implication of any given policy or event, and the impact upon students' routines, morale, and attitudes. The editor also provides trustees with input through discussing letters to the editor. Letters, submitted by State community members, express attitudes, values, beliefs, and ways that a situation may be dealt with effectively.

Serving as a common bond between all persons affiliated with State College, from students to trustees, the newspaper is the student's formal mouthpiece. The newspaper enables students to get readers to know facts and feelings related to student concerns. The newspaper may be likened to a barometer that measures the general atmosphere of the student body.

Organizational Structure

Business Manager

Working closely with the editor is the business manager. Together they monitor the newspaper's financial affairs, allocating funds to support various functions. Only two variable sources of income beyond the student activities fees generate subscription revenue. They are alumni and parent readership and advertising revenue from local merchants (historically accounting for only 10 percent of operating funds). With approximately 90 percent of the newspaper's circulation confined to the campus, subscription and advertising revenue potential remains relatively low. Insightful planning is essential, otherwise spending more funds than available would result in the newspaper's shutdown. All debt incurred would be paid with funds from the following year's activities fees.

On the operations side, the business manager establishes the schedule for the collection of accounts receivable and the payment of accounts payable. At the editor's request, the business manager monitors the use of inventory and receives price quotes from various graphic supply houses. By comparing quotes and assessing the organization's needs, the business manager selects the most economical ones.

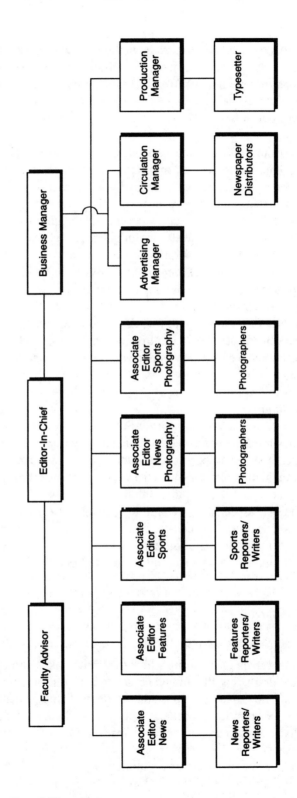

Exhibit 1. Organizational Structure

Finally, this position requires its incumbent to work closely with the college comptroller and treasurer in obtaining funds from the school when needed. Together they determine the optimum means of managing the funds for both short- and long-term requirements.

Associate Editors

Selected by the current editor, the associate editors are responsible for working with the editor frequently. Commitment to task completion, an affinity for writing, and adeptness in organizing people are the minimum requirements for a successful candidate. The news, features, and sports editors all determine their respective strategy, ensuring that each area complements the other style-wise. The associate editors coordinate the number of pages to be used by each.

Individually, each associate editor works with the editor to make certain that the information is objective, well-balanced, and of significance to the readers by answering how, what, why, when, who, and where. Key to any mission is that every story be followed up in subsequent issues, highlighting the impact upon the community, and the implications of both the short-run and the long-run.

Responsible for organizing, developing, and maintaining a staff of peers, each associate editor must establish source contacts from among students, college staff, faculty, and administration. The associate editor then works with each writer, providing support, information, and editorial assistance.

Advertising Manager

The advertising manager generates additional revenue by communicating with local merchants via telephone, letter, or in person. Accounts are won by eliciting a need in the advertiser's minds, communicating to them that a desire exists for the service or product, and convincing them that a handsome return on investments will follow.

Selling is one aspect of the advertising manager's position. Graphic layout is another. While some sponsors submit camera-ready mechanicals, others request that the advertising manager design the ad. Finally, both advertising manager and business manager work together to ensure that payment is received and that additional work is not provided for delinquent accounts.

Circulation Manager

Primary responsibilities of the circulation manager include delivering the mechanical (a mockup of a newspaper issue from which the printer takes photographs for offset printing) to the printer and delivering the printed copies to campus for distribution. With a staff of three or four students, newspapers are placed in students' campus mailboxes, handed to the campus mail center for distribution, to college faculty and administration, and dropped off at various high traffic locations on campus for public reading. For off-campus subscribers, the circulation manager prepares labels extracted from a computer program.

Soliciting for new subscriptions is limited. Feedback indicates that parents and alumni are not interested in day-to-day events on campus. Off-campus subscriptions equal a very small proportion of total circulation. The marginal revenue generated usually covers both fixed and variable expenses, contributing nothing to the newspaper's development.

State's Environment and Its Students

With approximately 30 percent of State's undergraduate students as commuters, the college is classified as a residence campus. Despite its heavy concentration of resident students, the college community, according to former editor (1984 – 1985) Jack Dolan, is far from cohesive:

> The students at State generally do not get very involved in community activities like the newspaper or government. For the most part, students have off-campus jobs and commitments that they feel are more instrumental to securing a lucrative job after graduation. I've asked many students why they have not gotten involved in community activities. Their feeling is that it is something a person does in high school as a means to present impressive credentials to admission committees of prestigious colleges and universities.

The typical *Reporter* staff member does not fit into the mold which Dolan perceives. Rather, the student displays a greater degree of curiosity and expresses a greater concern about issues affecting the college community as a whole. A staff member tends to possess a higher degree of motivation than others. Additionally, a staff member realizes the benefit of involvement with the newspaper; potential employers generally view extracurricular participation as a predictor of high motivation and a desire to learn varied tasks. The newspaper also provides students with the opportunity to express themselves in such ways as writing, photography, and designing the layout format. *The Reporter* is a learning ground for budding leaders, and allows students to integrate the academic side of management with the realities of running an organization.

Two Cases in Point

1984-1985

Led by Jack Dolan who served as editor during his junior year, *The Reporter* staff was comprised of forty active participants. Upon assuming the role of editor in April 1984, Dolan set out to build the remaining staff of twenty students to a greater size. During the previous year, much of the staff was doubling up in duties performed. For example, during the 1983 – 1984 administration, Dolan, who served as news editor, also assumed the responsibility for typesetting. Since most viewed this task as dull, volunteers were hard to come by.

Commenting on his decision to enlarge the staff, Dolan stated,

> With the pressure of academics, social concerns, and changing priorities, doubled responsibility just did not allow many of the staff enough room to breathe. In fact, morale suffered because of it. Not only was there a general lack of camaraderie, but the quality of the paper in comparison to previous editions also suffered. Bottom line, the lack of sufficient staffing made working on the paper unappealing. Staying

up until 5 a.m. (from noon of the previous day) to produce the mechanical took out all the fun and clouded any benefits to be gained.

Dolan involved himself in every aspect of the newspaper. By working closely with individuals, he sought not only to assist staff members in producing an informative vehicle of communication, but he also discussed the ways in which involvement benefited the individual.

Mindful of the entire staff, Dolan believed that exceptional work by individuals contributed nothing to the entire organization. Teamwork, Dolan felt was imperative. Standards and formats were not determined by any single person. By encouraging communication among each other, generally agreed upon standards and formats were devised. Given the staff members' raw ability and the available equipment with which to work, Dolan often worked in a particular functional area in order to realize realistic goals.

1985-1986

In the spring of 1985, Jean Beene, then a junior, assumed the responsibilities of *The Reporter* editorship. Having served as news editor in 1984 – 1985, Beene was a writer on the news staff in 1983 – 1984. A marketing major, Beene felt the role of editor would enable her to test lessons learned in class while accepting a management role in her area of interests.

Except for the news and sports photography editors and business manager, all other management positions were filled by students who had either never worked on the staff or who had worked as reporters/photographers under an associate editor. With the exception of the news and sports photography editor, business manager, advertising manager, and circulation manager, the other associate editors were entering their second year at the college. The 1985 – 1986 staff totaled twenty volunteers.

With the new staff's first issue just one week away, no attempt had been made to formulate strategies or policies. It was just expected that the functional areas would guess correctly the number of pages to be filled. No meeting had been called to set direction for the associate editors.

As the first issue was in production, the previous editors visited in order to answer any questions the new staff might have had. With production a few hours behind the pace kept during the previous year, Dolan asked Beene, "Jean, I know it is your first issue as editor. Perhaps I can help you out a little so that you (the staff) will not have to stay up all night. Do you mind?"

Beene responded, "Thanks for the offer, Jack. But, it'll be fine. We're new and we're learning." For the remaining few issues before the end of the semester, the staff had produced issues of quality above that of other new staffs in their respective initial periods.

During the summer there had been no contact between the new staff members, except for a note sent by Beene indicating that all associate editors and managers would return to campus three days before new student orientation. Normally, the early return was used by *The Reporter* management to compile an issue for new students that previewed fall sports, student organizations, the orientation program, and key college staff and administrators with whom new students might need to consult. Also included in the note was a time and place for a staffing meeting.

At the staff meeting, Beene welcomed everyone back. She stated that the format for the new issue would be the same as produced during previous years. She asked the editors to make plans for storywriting; the previous year's deadlines would apply. Without further specification, the meeting was adjourned.

As the semester progressed, there was no mention of the traditional *Reporter* open house, designed to have students meet with the management staff, and to afford students the opportunity to learn how they could contribute to the organization. While most reporters from the previous year had graduated, few of the underclass students continued with the paper in the fall of 1985. Contributors to the newspaper plummeted from forty students to twenty students.

Normally a twelve-page paper, eight pages seemed to become the norm (the mechanics of newspaper construction necessitate that an issue be done in increments of four pages). No longer was the production of an issue finished the day before publication at 11 p.m. The average time lapsed to about 3:30 a.m. the day of publication, just a few hours before the printer's 6 a.m. deadline. Students on campus stated that the paper was not as informative as it had been in the past. Clubs no longer sent messages about events and meetings. Traditionally, the newspaper had been the primary vehicle for such communication. The staff members' morale was on the decline.

A Critical Incident

On October 20, *The Reporter* was not published for the first time in its history. At 11 p.m. on its production night, Dolan had gone down to the newspaper's production office at the request of an associate editor. According to Dolan, "The associate editors were quite upset, stating that they were sick of the conditions." Due to understaffing, none of the typesetting had been done (typesetting for an eight-page paper requires about ten hours of labor). After that, layout normally takes four hours. The printer's deadline was only eight hours away.

Beene was determined to put out a paper that week. Even though production was at a standstill, she insisted that they would make it. Everyone knew it was physically impossible. And since the printer runs copy only on Thursday, the outcome was certain. An emergency meeting was held among *The Reporter* staff members.

Given the information presented in the case:

1. What do you expect had happened at the meeting? What considerations (i.e., to staff members, readers) might have been entertained?
2. If you were the editor of *The Reporter*, what would you have done to prevent the situation? As a reality, what would you do now?
3. What are the short- and long-term considerations?

41. The Luggers Versus the Butchers*

Food Merchandising Corporation had one of its warehouses in a small city in northern New Jersey. The main operation of the warehouse was to stock certain goods, and then ship them on order to various stores. The meat department handled packaged meats, and wholesale cuts of lamb, veal, and beef. Beef, by far the biggest and most expensive commodity, was generally bought from midwestern packers and shipped either by railroad or truck. On arrival at the warehouse, the beef was in the form of two hindquarters and two forequarters, each weighing close to two hundred pounds. The problem was to get these heavy pieces of meat off the trucks (or freight cars) and onto the intricate system of rails within the warehouse. Freight was paid by the shipper.

Company and union rules proscribed warehousemen from unloading trucks. It became the function of the general warehouseman (designated "lugger") to assist in the unloading of the trucks, but with no lifting. If, however, the beef was shipped by rail, it became his function to unload the freight cars. After the meat was placed on company rails, it was pushed through the doors into the 35° warehouse where it was placed in stock until it was butchered. The butchery process involved several men. First, the meat went to the sawman. While someone steadied the meat on the rail, the rib, plate, brisket, and shoulder bones were served. Then it was passed on to the cutters, who butchered it into several smaller wholesale cuts. After that the meat was again placed in stock to be shipped out by the night crews.

The "Luggers" Versus the "Butchers"

The operation of the warehouse involved two distinct functions: to unload and stock the beef, and then to butcher it. The unloading process was wholly different from the butchering. It required physical strength and coordination to lift 200 pounds of beef all day. Furthermore, when the workload slowed down, the luggers were given different tasks. There was a degree of variety in their work. But the butchering function was very different. The men were geographically confined to the cutting line and performed the same basic operations day after day.

When the warehouse was unionized eight years ago, the men who had most seniority were given first option as to the jobs they preferred. Since many of these men were on the older side, they gravitated away from the more laborious general warehouse work toward the higher-wage butcher jobs. Consequently, two different types of individuals became associated with the two different types of jobs.

The eight butchers were engaged in the skilled practice of butchering meat. Most of them had been with the company for many years. For the most part, they were family men with many off-the-job responsibilities, were by no means in union affairs, and probably had more loyalty to the company than to the union local. They had a high number of social activities off-the-job such as group picnics, bowling, golf, et cetera. The tedious boredom of their job was somewhat mitigated by these mutual activities, and an atmosphere of good humor usually prevailed in their corner of the warehouse.

*Robert E. C. Wegner and Leonard Sayles, *Cases in Organizational and Administrative Behavior*, 1972, pp. 42 – 48. Reprinted by permission of Prentice-Hall, Inc., Englewood Cliffs, New Jersey.

There were nine luggers, but two of these had been butchers until very recently. More will be said later about these men. A third man usually worked in another section. Thus the term "lugger" referred to a specific group of six general warehousemen. These men were younger and generally had less company time than the butchers, but this is not to say that they were young or new. Most of them were married, but treated their home responsibilities differently. For instance, the typical butcher would spend his night at home, and most of the luggers would spend their night working a part-time job.

Hank, Josh, and Mr. Abrams

Hank was the foreman. When he became foreman about ten years ago, the men considered him a walking terror but a good foreman. Now he was considered neither. There were several reasons for this change. First, the coming of the union had made Hank more careful in the way he handled the men. Second, Hank had lost control of the luggers. After several fiery confrontations, he more or less left them alone. When it was necessary to give them an order, great explanations and apologies often accompanied it. His relationship with butchers, however, remained fairly intact. In effect, Hank was afraid of the luggers but not of the butchers. Third, when Mr. Abrams became manager two years ago it was his policy to use close personal supervision of the men to ensure efficiency. Mr. Abrams, therefore, usurped considerable portions of Hank's responsibility.

Josh was the union representative. He had built up a great friendship with Carl, the shop steward, and the other luggers. His relationship with the butchers, however, was strictly on a business basis. Usually this meant that the butchers complained about the luggers, but nothing really important was done about it.

Mr. Abrams' assistant was Lyle, nicknamed "the Puppy." Lyle used to follow Mr. Abrams everywhere he went, to the great enjoyment of the men. Thus came the nickname "Puppy."

The butchers took the brunt of Mr. Abrams' close supervision, mainly because they were confined to one spot and were easy to observe. Also, this was where the real pressure had to be applied, for if the meat was not butchered, it could not be sent out and stores would run short. Mr. Abrams had the responsibility to ensure that stores were not short. He evidently felt that standing over the men (with the Puppy at his side) would cut down on the little games the men developed to break up their boring routine (talking, bathroom breaks, et cetera). The net effect was that the men, being old timers, took their breaks anyway but grumbled about being watched over. The luggers were harder to watch, being more spread out, and they also managed to gain some control over Mr. Abrams. He knew that an ill-timed remark or too much supervision would only result in later slowdowns by these men.

A Slow Change in Status

Six years ago the butcher's job was considered much more desirable than that of the luggers. At that time most of the meat was shipped by railroad. This necessitated a great deal of heavy work. Most of the men would have preferred the cold monotony of cutting meat to lugging 200 pounds of beef from a railroad car to a loading dock. It was at this point that two luggers, Brent and Terry, began to think of developing a system of portable rails that would be adaptable to the large variety of freight cars which came to the warehouse. The rails were successfully designed and developed by the two men. With the passage of time, skill in their use was achieved and the job of unloading freight cars became quite simple.

The ingenuity of two luggers was widely heralded about the warehouse and in the company, and recognition was given in due proportion. More importantly, a job that was undesirable before became quite attractive because the chief reason for its undesirability had ceased to exist. The main attractions of the butcher's job were reduced to the companionship of the group, the waning prestige of being a skilled workman, and the higher-wage-more-over-time benefits. This was quite sufficient to keep them satisfied, if not as happy as before.

Hank's foremanship also suffered. At this date, his position had already been dealt a few blows by the union and the men. Now an innovation was introduced that had no place in his way of doing things. He preferred to completely ignore the rails and allow the luggers to use them as they saw fit. From the company's point of view, the use of rails in freight cars meant very little. Four men were still required in each car. Efficiency remained about the same because it took time to assemble and disassemble the rail system.

If the use of the rails had resulted solely in physical advantages, it is probable that the situation would have gone along unchanged. But the luggers were quick to discover an economic value in their use. The trucks coming in on the front docks had to be unloaded. Since freight was paid by the shipper, the company and union had worked out an agreement in which the trucker was responsible for delivering the meat to the dock. The warehouse workers were only to assist peripherally, and were not permitted inside the trucks unless it was absolutely necessary.

The drivers were not happy with their lot of unloading up to 35,000 pounds of beef. Consequently, they often hired warehouse vagrants – men who sat around the warehouse waiting for such opportunities. The going rate was one dollar per 1,000 pounds: between $30.00 and $35.00 a truck. It generally took two hours to unload one truck. The enterprising luggers redesigned the rails for use on the trucks, and made it known that a tip of two dollars was in order for anyone who cared to use them. Since the railroad was making more and more use of piggyback services, the number of trucks as well as the amount of the tips began to increase.

A Dispute Develops

Last year, two butchers were given the option of working as luggers. They exercised the option, partly hoping to recuperate some of their wage losses by sharing in the tip money. It was not long before serious arguments developed between the old and new luggers. Beforehand, the luggers had worked out a one-for-you and one-for-me system with the trucks. Such an informal understanding was possible because this tightly cohesive group knew that petty bickering would soon take the problem out of their own hands. The two ex-butchers, however, had no desire to work with the old group. They were in no way amenable to tacit understandings that cut them out. Consequently, when the big trailers turned into the driveway, there began a jockeying for position.

Arguments developed, and other work suffered. When the two ex-butchers turned to the union, they found their upward paths of communication thoroughly blocked. Carl, the shop steward, was a lugger. It was to his disadvantage to press hard on behalf of the two ex-butchers. Josh, the union representative, was much too friendly with the luggers and no progress could be made here. Hank, the foreman, was worthless in this matter, and Mr. Abrams was too new at this stage to take action. For these reasons, and because of a normal reluctance to push grievances, little pressure was placed on the union.

Early last spring, following a series of flare-ups over equipment usage and truck tips, two "clubs" were formed: Club "Six" and Club "Three." Brent, one of the two rail designers, originated the idea of formalizing the two groups. Each club was given a separate locker for equipment. No exchanges were to take place. Members of Club Three (the two ex-butchers and a third who worked in a different part of the warehouse) were permitted to work a share of trucks proportional to club membership. Members of Club Six (the six original luggers) began a practice of pooling tips and dividing them equally.

At first the formalization of the two groups appeared to be a good solution. There were fewer arguments, and Club Three was reasonably satisfied. However, an unfortunate side effect developed. Previously, the distinctions between luggers and butchers were implicit and the warehouse as a whole was a friendly place. People knew who got along with whom, and friendships often crossed group lines. With the formalization, however, people began to class themselves as "in" or "out." Club Six members began to be more and more isolated among the twenty-five men who worked in this section of the warehouse. Butchers and luggers constantly complained about each other. Members of Club Six refused to work with members of Club Three, and much ill feeling was generated. But even so, had there been nothing else, these difficulties would probably not have caused any lasting problems. There was, however, something else – the piggyback development.

The railroads were making more and more use of piggyback trucking. This is a system whereby trailers are hauled part of the way by rail, and part of the way by road. As the number of freight cars decreased and the warehouse volume increased, more trucks began coming. These trucks had to be unloaded, and unloading was an expensive and time-consuming proposition. The use of rails on the trucks had cut down the time it took to unload. A good crew could "knock one off" in less than an hour, though the average time was about two hours. The luggers began to move into this very lucrative area. It became quite a steady thing for them to bring home an extra $30.00 or $40.00 per week. Occasionally, if things were slow enough, the luggers would work a truck on company time. Or they would begin setting it up about 3:30, so there would be no delay in getting it started at 4:00.

From a company viewpoint, there was no problem. Trucks were being emptied faster than ever before, even on the rare occasion when a truck came in purposely late. The more usual situation was either that there were too many trucks to unload in the normal day or that the truck was legitimately delayed. At any rate, the rails enabled the ordinary trucks to be unloaded much more rapidly and the experienced luggers often finished their after-hour trucks in half the normal time. Warehouse efficiency did not suffer.

The butchers, however, were not a happy group. They continued to work the same boring routine in the same 35°. Their income did not change. They watched the luggers develop into a very cohesive group and usurp their status position. They resented the different treatments meted out to the two groups. The luggers were given too much freedom, and the butchers were too closely supervised. The luggers quite often "couldn't" stay overtime, yet they could almost always work a truck. Nothing was ever said when luggers made excuses; but if the butchers did not want to stay, they were given a great deal of grief.

Pressure was applied, and it was not a rare thing to find butchers working three hours overtime for half the money the luggers made in an hour by working a truck. The obvious inequity was deeply resented. The luggers used company time to work trucks, or to set them up, and this violated the union contract. Yet nothing concrete was ever done to stop them. The butchers felt totally frustrated and disenchanted with what they had once considered as high-status jobs. Despite their innate conservatism and procompany attitude they seriously considered a massive walkout to get their grievances heard.

Part 10 Organizational Change and Transformation

Cases Outline

42. Organizational Change: Planning and Implementing Teams At AAL and IPS*

All across the United States millions of Americans buy a variety of insurance products each year. They buy them from insurers like Met Life and Prudential, the so-called commercial insurers, and from Aid Association for Lutherans (AAL) and Knights of Columbus, the so-called fraternal benefit societies. Unlike commercial insurers, the approximately 200 fraternal benefit societies that are exempt from certain taxes serve up a mix of financial products, good works, member services and sometimes social activities. Generally founded at the turn of the century by immigrants to provide for each other in tough times, the groups were among the first to offer insurance to working-class people. Although the societies account for less than 2 percent of the new life insurance policies written each year, about 10 million Americans buy life insurance and annuities – and sometimes health insurance, disability insurance and mutual funds – from them.

A key concern for anyone when buying life insurance is a company's financial soundness. In this regard, fraternal societies appear to be ahead of the pack. There have been no losses to policyholders in recent memory, said a spokesman for A. M. Best, an independent agency that reviews and rates the insurance industry on the basis of overall performance and financial strength. But a few societies have merged because of declining membership. Of the 42 fraternals rated by the agency, 30 fall in the top six of its 15 rating categories, and the six largest fraternals, after which size drops off considerably, are in that upper tier. The largest of these is Aid Association for Lutherans.[1]

Aid Association for Lutherans (AAL)

AAL is a fraternal benefit society which provides fraternal benefits and financial security for Lutherans and their families. Individuals who purchase financial products from AAL also become members of AAL and join one of over 8,600 local volunteer service chapters called branches. Through the volunteer efforts of 1.6 million members, branches are provided opportunities to help themselves, their churches and communities. Members also receive free educational materials on family and health topics. AAL also offers scholarship opportunities for members as well as grants to help Lutheran congregations and institutions. In total, nearly $62 million was spent on AAL's fraternal outreach last year.

AAL's financial products include individual life, disability income and long-term care insurance, and annuity products. Our subsidiary company, AAL Capital Management Corporation, offers mutual funds to our members. The AAL Member Credit Union is an affiliate which offers members federally insured savings accounts, a credit card and various types of loans and home mortgages.

AAL assets under management are over $12 billion. Total annual premium income is over $1.5 billion. AAL is among the top two percent of all U. S. life insurers and is the nation's

* This case was prepared by Jerome Laubenstein and his team members at IPS department of AAL. It is used here by permission. Reprinted from Randall S. Schuler, *Managing Human Resources*, 6th Edition, West Publishing Company, 1996.

largest fraternal benefit society in terms of assets and ordinary life insurance in force. AAL also maintains an A+ rating, the highest possible, from A. M. Best and also maintains a Duff & Phelps AAA rating and a Standard & Poors AAA rating, both the highest possible.

AAL markets its products and services in all 50 states and the District of Columbia through a sales staff of over 2,400 employees. Corporate headquarters are located in Appleton, Wisconsin, where over 1,400 are employed. (Note: Staffing numbers throughout this paper are in terms of "full time equivalents" or FTEs. Since a sizable number of regular part-time employees are utilized, the actual number of people employed is greater than stated.)

Organizational Change at AAL

AAL's organizational change, which was dubbed "Renewal" and "Transformation", officially began in December 1985 with the engagement of Roy Walters and Associates as consultants for a diagnostic process. But we can trace the beginnings of this change effort back years before that time.[2]

Some seeds were planted during the period of some very successful product introductions in 1982. The focus and energy level of the organization during that time was exciting, even though we were up to our ears trying to keep up with business due to the phenomenal success of our universal life product. We can remember saying that we should have one of these situations every two years or so, for the energizing effects it had on us and the organization.

With the introduction of these new products, we also ushered in a new awareness of the shrinking margins in financial services and our needs to rein in expenses in order to stay competitive. In addition, our president and CEO had announced his upcoming retirement, and our new president, Dick Gunderson, came in September 1985 from another life insurance organization. Studies of the insurance industry convinced Gunderson that the association had to cut costs by over $50 million over the next five years to stay competitive. In so many ways, the question on the minds of some senior managers was: What choices could be made now to position AAL for the future? Organizational change or transformation became the answer.

Positive Dissatisfaction

One of the hardest parts about the change effort was the fact that AAL was not in crisis. The good news is that this gave us the luxury of time to change and adjust; the bad news is that it's difficult to motivate oneself to go through the effort of change when things are going so well. Many of the concerns mentioned were like clouds out at the distant horizon; sales, financial and fraternal results were continuing to grow and seemingly there was nothing in the status quo that would point to the need for fundamental change. As our consultant Bob Janson pointed out, what we did need to discover and tap was the sense of what he termed "positive dissatisfaction" within the organization – the feeling that even if AAL was doing well, we have an even higher potential to reach.

Where are we? The first task of the change effort was an organizational diagnosis to seek out this positive dissatisfaction. A team of 12 managers was trained in a structured interview process, then went out and conducted over 200 interviews in a diagonal slice of the home office and field. The team asked people what AAL's strengths and weaknesses were in 10 categories: Control; Culture; Management Style; Marketing; Mission; Historic Strengths; Productivity; Quality; Structure; and Technology.

Those team interviews were a great experience; people in our organization did share their hopes and dreams for what AAL could become and their frustration that we weren't working as effectively as we could to reach those dreams. People identified many strengths on which to build: our members and market, financial strength, fraternal focus and reputation, dedicated employees - both home office and field. But as the team reported out to a larger management group in May 1986, there were areas that needed attention. Our consultant has often told us since this time that he had never seen an organization so "ripe" for change.

AAL's vision. In a process working in parallel with the diagnosis, 100 of AAL's managers also worked on the development of a vision statement[3] for the organization. The result was viewed as a reaffirmation of what AAL had become and what we stood for. It reads as follows:

> "AAL, the leader in fraternalism, brings Lutheran people together to pursue quality
> living through financial security, volunteer action and help for others."

So, six months from the start of the transformation process, AAL had both a vision statement and a current snapshot of the organization; when the two were compared, the gaps that needed to be addressed came into clearer focus. We were set to launch our efforts to close these gaps in order to position ourselves even more strongly for the future. The working theme at that time was "Touch Tomorrow Today."

Closing Gaps

The first gaps to be addressed were in the areas of: 1) organizational structure, 2) management style, and 3) marketing strategy. Efforts to study and recommend ways to close the gaps between our current situation and our vision in these three areas were launched anew, still employing participative methods. For example, for the structure study, a team of six managers was charged to develop alternative proposals for restructuring the organization through the two management levels below the president. The recommendations were developed by the team, with input from a larger circle of managers, then finally delivered to the president. He chose to reorganize AAL using many of the concepts recommended and the new organization was put into place late in November 1986. The reorganization was significant; 25 of the top 26 positions in the organization had changes in responsibility, including significant changes in senior management.

The efforts in other areas continue to this day. A new marketing strategy was completed in the fall of 1988. Work progressed this past year at defining a more precise vision of desired management style and assessing ourselves as managers (and having employees assess us) against that vision. We have also produced a technology strategy in response to a gap-closing need, and are now wrestling with ways to address the productivity and quality variables in a more direct way.

Organizational Change Results

Our corporate restructuring, just by its nature, has been the most visible result. Frankly, after restructuring at the top of the organization was over, it was hard to convince employees that the change process was not complete.

In response to our expense challenges, the organization also achieved its downsizing goal of 250 positions by 1990. This was primarily accomplished through an early retirement window offered in 1986, as well as through attrition.

Structure and personnel changes can always be disrupting, but were especially so in our organization. Not only were we a part of a very stable industry, we were one of the largest employers in a relatively small community, with very low turnover. One of the key elements of our change process, I feel, is the guarantee of continued employment that was built into our change effort. As Robert Waterman of In Search of Excellence fame terms it, there is a need to maintain "stability in motion" throughout renewal. We strive to give our managers and employees the freedom and courage to reorganize and try new ways of work by placing a safety net underneath them. Employees whose positions are eliminated during the change process, or who turn out to have a mismatch of skills for new ways of work become members of a program. The program helps assess skills, finds temporary work assignments, offers support and works to find them internal placements, field transfer or voluntary outplacement.

Now for the sharper focus on the planning and implementing of teams within a key service area of AAL. We'll tell you about the transition of a large service department set against the backdrop of this larger change effort.

Organizational Change of the Insurance Product Services Department: Planning and Implementing Teams

The Insurance Product Services Department (IPS) provides all services related to the individual life, long-term care and disability income insurance product lines, from the initial underwriting of contracts to the ultimate handling of claims. IPS currently consists of 426 employees, about 30 percent of the home office employees.

Phase I - "Identifying the Need"

The desire for a new organizational design for IPS had its roots in the corporate change study and subsequent corporate reorganization described above. As a result, the change efforts of IPS management were fully supported by Gunderson and top management in the spirit of corporate renewal. IPS management had the freedom to proceed with the restructuring of the department without the need for periodic presentations and approvals.

The major concerns that came out of the corporate change study regarding the "old" insurance product services environment were:

1. It was not considered to be truly customer oriented because of its functional rather than wholistic approach to service.
2. Most decisions were made very high in a hierarchical organization with as many as six levels of supervision. As a result decisions were made some distance from the problems which negatively impacted timeliness. They were also made by people other than those who knew most about the "problems." That had a negative impact on the quality of the decisions.
3. Skills and abilities of people were underutilized and many jobs tended to be boring because of their narrow scope.

4. Productivity was viewed from a functional perspective rather than from an integrated perspective.
5. Recent marketing successes had caused significant growth in staff and related expenses. Top management felt it was excessive growth.

Related to this last point, the change of IPS was addressed in an environment which called for the downsizing of the corporate staff by 250 over a five-year period. Corporate staff numbered 1,556 on Jan. 1, 1987.

As part of the corporate change action, a new IPS department head was put in place in December 1986. Jerome (Jerry) Laubenstein, a former marketing executive, was noted for his participative style. He was given the charge to "regionalize" the service function in an effort to get closer to the customer and to address the corporate downsizing goal as it related to the significant growth experienced by IPS in recent years.

Jerry then brought in a new senior level departmental management team in January 1987. This new senior management team consisted of five individuals to manage five geographic service regions. These people were selected for their action oriented management style, creativity, and their demonstrated willingness to take calculated risks – a contrast to the risk-averse former culture. They were also selected because of their management strengths and highly participative management style. Technical insurance knowledge, though desirable, was not felt to be essential.

Phase II - "Setting Broad Parameters"

The second week after selection, the new IPS management team (Jerry Laubenstein, the department head, and his five regional managers) came together in an off-site retreat to address the approach to be used for redesigning the department. The first step was to develop a vision for the new IPS organization. The result was a simple statement which read "regionalization plus 'one team' processing" and included the following list of "desired outcomes":

1. A "customer driven" organization. (Customers were identified as field staff and members.)
    Being customer driven was perceived to include:
    • Listening to customer for wants/needs.
    • Being responsive and pro-active to customer wants/needs.
    • Acknowledging that the customer's problem is the provider's problem.
    • Seeing the provider as problem solver rather than order taker.
    • Informing/educating the customer.
    • Using customer-informed measures on how we're meeting their needs.
2. A strong "team" relationship with the field staff and internal support units.
    The need for "networking" was heavily stressed.
3. A "flat" organization with fewer levels of supervision and fewer staff.
4. "One stop" processing as fully as possible to avoid the delays and lack of ownership associated with an assembly line approach.
5. A quality management team which would model participative management, more involvement of employees in deciding how work was to be accomplished, and more decision making authority for employees in carrying out their day to day assignments.

A very simple mission statement was also established for the new organization:

IPS Mission

"To enable the agent, the primary customer, to do an even better job of serving the policyholder, the ultimate customer."

Phase III - "Design and Development"

The design process did not begin with the self-managing team concept as a goal. However, the design process did begin with a strong desire to obtain "buy in" by employees to the need for restructuring. Therefore, one of the first major tasks of the new departmental management team was to communicate the reasons for pursuing a change in work design to every employee in the department. The reasons for change really were restatements of what individuals had related to the corporate change interview teams.

Communications. Because AAL had no facility to bring the entire IPS staff together at one time (484 people at that time), the first attempt at communication to all employees was through the existing functional management structure in IPS. They were asked to conduct unit meetings, explaining the reasons for and parameters around which a new organization would be developed. Information and support materials were provided to facilitate communication. This approach met with <u>limited</u> success.

More communications. A second effort was structured around large group meetings with approximately 100 employees per group. AAL CEO Richard Gunderson, and Jerry Laubenstein, IPS department head, also participated. This attempt met with more success. Periodic unit meetings, led by the new regional managers, were continued. A departmental newsletter was also established. The newsletter was distributed to all IPS employees to provide continuing communications as the process progressed through the planning and implementation stages of the redesign. As we look back we'd reaffirm the fact that good solid communication cannot be over-emphasized in a restructuring process such as AAL experienced.

Design teams. Because the "new" management team was committed to a highly participative team oriented management style, it involved a significant cross section of employees in the departmental "redesign". Ten teams (approximately 125 employees) were appointed from lists of employees nominated by managers, supervisors and employees. Team members consisted of employees from all levels within the organization. The teams and team charges were as follows:

- STRUCTURE TEAMS - Three of the 10 teams were charged to independently propose a new departmental structure, taking into account several "givens" such as regional organization, and a maximum of three levels of supervision.
- PHYSICAL RESOURCES - Was charged to address the physical resource issues that need to be dealt with in any organization.
- MANAGEMENT STYLE TEAM - Was charged to address management style and to propose a "culture" in which employees could grow and perform in the spirit of service excellence.
- MANAGEMENT INFORMATION TEAM - Was charged to evaluate the types of management information needed to manage the operation.

- FIELD INPUT TEAM - Was charged to gain agent (customer) input on our EDP support services. IPS is a highly mechanized operation and as a result the impact was quite significant.
- EDP RESOURCE TEAM - Was charged to look at the impact on our EDP support services. IPS was a highly mechanized operation and as a result the impact on EDP operations was quite significant.
- OPERATIONS TEAM - Was charged to look after ongoing operations during the renewal effort.
- CELEBRATION TEAM - Finally, a team was appointed to plan and administer appropriate and timely celebration events to highlight specific milestones and successes along the way.

The results produced by these teams in a very short, three-week period were phenomenal. It should be noted that these results were achieved while employees continued to handle normal work activities.

Role clarification. It was important during this time to clearly articulate the role of teams within a participative management decision-making process, especially when proposals required modification or rejection. It was IPS management's experience that employees tended to confuse the various teams' roles of providing input with management's accountability for making decisions. Managers, on the other hand, had to remember the need to explain why team decisions were modified or rejected. Looking back, it probably would have been better to label the approach as "high involvement" rather than "participative management." Doing so may have avoided some misunderstandings.

Decision Making and Implementation

Two of the three structure teams submitted organizational proposals that closely parallel our current design. These proposals, together with input from a variety of sources including a literature search which produced the self-managing team concept, provided the direction for our organizational model. This was followed by contacting some of the proponents of sociotechnical management. As a result, it was recognized that to attain the desired outcomes and accomplish our mission, we had to move away from a hierarchically arranged, functional, and highly specialized structure which extensively used rules, records, reports and precedents. Instead, we had to move toward a flat, full service, self-managing, self-regulating service team concept which would move decision making closer to the transaction and to the customer. Management then created a tentative model of the new organization. This model was worked with all employees, using the nominal group process, in an attempt to get their input into potential pitfalls.

Once the organizational concept was finalized, the number of service teams needed to serve our customers was determined by modeling service activity by region. The goal was to have as many teams (i. e., customer face-offs) as could be supported by existing staff capabilities. We concluded that the "critical mass" of knowledge and skills currently available in the department could support 16 service teams. Managers were then selected to lead these teams.

Implementation. The next step was to develop an implementation plan. Implementation teams were named, again using a significant cross section of employees. The charges to the implementation teams were to do everything necessary to ready the department for a physical move to the new organizational structure. In addition to continuing the EDP resource team, the physical resource team, and the celebration team, teams were formed around service functions of the "old" organization. They were to address the disbursement of the three functions of the insurance services: life, medical and disability.

Employee assignments. After decisions were reached on how the functions and staff should be disbursed and the timing of the moves was established, the new management team addressed the issue of employee assignments. After an initial "reallocation" of employees was agreed upon, employees were given the opportunity to request a change in tentative team assignment. However, because it was necessary to balance the existing knowledge among the teams, changes in assignments were not made unless exceptional reasons existed. This "assignment issue" was perhaps one of the biggest and least anticipated social issues of the renewal effort. Not since high school had adults had their social choices removed; choices of colleagues, work location, and work environment. As these new "groups" moved into the group formation stages of "forming, storming, norming and performing," much time and energy was spent in the storming and norming phases.

Security. The impact of organizational change – including downsizing – caused this to be a trying time for many employees, even though all employees were guaranteed employment (not positions). It was especially so for supervisors and managers. The organizational redesign reduced supervisory positions from 62 to 22. By the end of 1987, a total of 57.5 full-time equivalent positions were eliminated. To reduce the stress created by this downsizing and the impact of overall change, stress management sessions were made available to all employees through the medical department. Several hundred employees took advantage of this opportunity. A course on managing change was also made available to management through a local technical institute. A career counseling service was offered to employees whose jobs were eliminated. And finally, an existing corporate "Employee Placement Program" was strengthened to help employees cope with the loss of positions (not employment) as a result of the total corporate renewal effort.

The move. The physical move from a functional structure to one centered around self-managing teams was made in August 1987. This move was one of the first opportunities to demonstrate the power of "team problem solving." Our building services and space management units provided estimates of three to five months to move the 484 employees and associated equipment. Obviously IPS management could not live with that kind of time frame. The physical resources implementation team, led by their advisor, a newly appointed and creative regional manager, together with the building services people, synergistically arrived at an alternative which was to move people but not workstations. This required employees to accept the inadequacies of their new workstations until they could be modified at a later date. Our space management folks also had to accept something less than a "clean" move. The only change in equipment was to provide computer terminals on workstations where they had not been required earlier. Employees moved themselves by packing their belongings in boxes, putting boxes on their chairs and wheeling both to their new workstations. This was something never before done. An incentive was provided. The move began at noon on a Friday. As soon as the unit was moved, employees were given the rest of the day off. The move was completed in less than two hours. Terminals caught up the following Tuesday.

Self-Managing Work Teams at IPS

Teams within teams. There are four significant aspects of the IPS organizational team design:

1. It's a regional organization with each region providing all services to their designated customers. (These service regions paralleled the existing field distribution and management regions.)
2. Each region has four service teams, with each service team providing almost all services to a specific group of agencies. A few services were handled by such a small staff that it was difficult to spread them to service teams in the early stages of restructuring. The number of employees sufficient to constitute adequate "critical mass" to permit disbursement was a major point of discussion. Management tended to be more risk oriented than staff in this area.
3. Each service team was initially structured to have three self-managing work teams within it, one around the underwriting and issue functions, another around "service" functions such as loans, terminations, dividends, pre-authorized check handling, etc., and the third around the claims functions.
4. Our goal is to move to more wholistic self-managing teams by encouraging the integration of the three functional teams. Finally, IPS had a cadre of functional specialists with responsibility for establishing functional policy and for monitoring the appropriate administration of policy across regions and teams. These functional specialists are currently organized by line of business and report to the regional managers.

Self-managed teams defined. The focal point of our current organization is clearly the self-managing work team. The self-managing work team concept, as found in our literature search and adopted by AAL, is as follows:

*   Self-managing work teams are semi-autonomous groups of workers who share the responsibility for carrying out a significant piece of work and who run their own operations with almost no supervision. The group has the authority and the technical, interpersonal and managerial skills to make decisions about how the work should be done.
*   The team is accountable as a group for processing all work for which it's responsible. Members plan, do and control their work. The team decides who will do what work, and assigns members to tasks. The group has control over scheduling and coordinating its own work, formulating vacation schedules, monitoring quality, solving technical problems, and improving work methods. Employees have both responsibility and accountability for quantity, quality and costs. The team meets regularly to discuss goals, to identify, analyze and solve work-related problems and/or provide improvement ideas.
*   Employees typically possess a variety of skills and are encouraged to develop new skills to increase their flexibility. Workers typically learn second and third jobs. The team is responsible for motivating, training, coaching and developing its members. The team trains one another or arranges for their own training.

- The team is also responsible for employee evaluation and discipline. The group, as a whole, reviews overall team performance, conducts peer evaluation of individual members, and handles problems such as absenteeism and poor performance. Teams need to be skilled in handling the social system as well. This means being able to celebrate their success, recognize one another's efforts, thank one another for help, and in general reinforce positive behavior. As teams mature they hire new members or do final selection of new team members.
- Reward systems typically reward teamwork as well as the individual acquisition of skills and the individual's performance. For example, the team's results may determine the size of the compensation resource pool available to be distributed as increases and/or bonuses to individual members of the team. Team members then determine how the team's allocation is distributed to individual team members.

There are some aspects of the self-managing work team concept that have not been implemented at AAL. For example, peer appraisal is achieved by anonymous input and not by direct input and significant performance problems continue to be turned over to managers for disciplinary measures.

Benefits of the Self-Managing Team Concept

The benefits of the self-managing team concept to both management and employees are perhaps obvious. Nevertheless, we'll state a few of them. Fred Emery has identified six intrinsic factors that are motivators:

1. Variety and challenge   → drive + learn
2. Elbow room for decision making
3. Feedback and learning
4. Mutual support and respect   → drive to bond
5. Wholeness and meaning
6. Room to grow; a bright future

With respect to these motivators, Marvin Weisbord, in his book, <u>Productive Workplaces</u>, comments that "the first three must be optimal - not too much, which adds to stress and anxiety, nor too little, which produces stultifying tedium. The second trio are open ended. No one can have too much respect, growing room, or 'wholeness'- meaning a view of both the origin and the customer's use of your work." All of this assumes that in place are "satisfiers" identified by Emery and Trist, a list of six conditions of employment: fair and adequate pay, job security, benefits, safety, health and due process. As Weisbord comments, "Only in workplaces embodying both lists can the century-old dreams of labor-management cooperation ever come true."

It is our contention that the six motivational factors can be met far more effectively through the self-managing team structure as described above than through the traditional one person/one task, multi-level hierarchical management structure.

Joseph Boyett and Henry Conn suggest in their book, <u>Maximum Performance Management</u>, that excellence is a function of the knowledge and skills, motives and abilities of employees. However, they also suggest that we cannot directly change them and thus we are stuck with the internal traits and characteristics employees bring to the job. They further suggest that we can, however, adjust the work environment to compensate for weaknesses in knowledge and skills, motives, and/or abilities. The three leverages they propose for doing this are:

1. Information   Shared Values and Business Strategies
                        Linked Missions and Goals
                        Measures and Feedback
                        Identification of Critical Behaviors

2. Consequences   Social Reinforcement
                        Contingent Awards
                        Pay-for-Performance (Variable portion up to 40% of
                              total compensation)

3. Involvement   Non-Voluntary
                        Management Directed Teams
                        Cross-Functional Task Forces

We'd suggest that AAL's self-managing team approach supported by our pay-for-performance compensation system, which is anchored to team measures and results, takes full advantage of these areas of leverage far better and with far less effort than can be done in a traditional hierarchical structure.

Manager's Role in Self-Managing Team Environment   — *mgmt objectives*

The move to self-managing teams required a redefinition of the role of the team manager. The manager is still responsible and accountable for the bottom line results of the team, but these results are attained differently. In the new work environment, the creative abilities of all team members are used, not just those of the manager.

The redefined role requires managers to:

- set direction by creating and focusing the team's efforts toward a common vision;
- to coach and counsel, to ensure and support the development of team members;
- to lead the team in problem solving;
- to make sure the team has needed information and resources; and
- to encourage the team to make its own decisions on operating problems.

The new role requires managers to manage through use of "boundaries" or "parameters" rather than by directive. Key challenges are the need to create a motivating work environment and to remove barriers for team members. The latter is accomplished by managing relationships among teams and between the team and other areas of the organization.

Although the role of the manager in a self-managing team environment differs from the role of a manager in the traditional environment, research has shown that the profile of outstanding managers is very similar regardless of the environment. They are visionaries, use a participative management style, and they can deal with ambiguity and lack of structure. They share information and responsibility with employees and are committed both to the work and to the individuals on their team. And they deliver results!

Key Support Systems

Pay-for-Applied-Services for individuals and teams. Pay-for-Applied-Services (PAS) is the name selected for the compensation systems designed to support self-managing work teams. It offers maximum flexibility in order to support the unique job design needs of each team.

One of our more significant challenges during the development of PAS was to integrate it into a corporate culture firmly entrenched in the Hay system of job evaluation. Nevertheless, the task was uniquely and creatively accomplished by a team including individuals from the service areas and corporate compensation services.

Within IPS, individual position descriptions have been replaced by a team job description and individual personal assignments. The personal assignment is a listing of the services an individual performs to support the needs of the team and their own career interests. Employees have identified approximately 165 services which are being performed within the department.

Compensation is delivered through four components. The first is a "valued services" component. As new services are learned and applied, the value of the services learned and applied is added to the employee's ongoing compensation. The value of individual services is determined using the know-how portion of the Hay system. A matrix has been constructed using Hay know-how values. One axis of the matrix is absolute values representing the minimum AAL is willing to pay for a service if it were a stand-alone service. The other axis of the matrix is incremental values. The more an individual learns with the same base knowhow value, the less additional learning is worth.

The second component of pay delivery is the team incentive. Incentive dollars are tied to productivity measures. Allocation is based on a team's contribution to productivity. Distribution to individuals within the team is based on an individual's support of the team. Incentive dollars are distributed quarterly.

The third component is a market adjustment feature. In order to remain competitive within the market place and with comparable jobs within the organization, market adjustments are considered annually. These adjustments may be made to either the matrix or the incentive "pot". When made to the matrix, a recalculation of the value of individual personal assignments will result. Where appropriate, immediate adjustments are made to pay.

The fourth component is an individual-incentive program. IPS has added an incentive component that recognizes outstanding achievement by individual employees. This lump-sum incentive is paid once a year only to those employees who are already paid at market value. This incentive is worth as much as 6 percent of an individual's compensation.

This new compensation system encourages cross-training, enhances team flexibility and encourages team performance, but, very importantly, still permits compensation dollars to be managed and controlled. It was implemented on April 1, 1989, and underwent a degree of modification in 1991 to bring it into closer synchronization with a new incentive compensation plan introduced to the rest of the organization in 1991.

Training for self-managing work teams. A comprehensive training program continues to be developed for all employees working in a sociotechnical management environment within the organization. The entire program design and delivery to all employees was completed in 1990. Some of the topics covered include:

- Team self-management roles. Typical supervisory responsibilities which teams may take on in their own self-management includes:
  - Planning and scheduling own time schedules
  - Securing and allocating resources
  - Scheduling and coordinating work in team
  - Setting standards, rotating assignments
  - Providing performance data
  - Recruiting, selecting and fixing
  - Disciplining and rewarding
  - Celebrating successes
  - Motivating/training
  - Coaching/developing
  - Problem solving and conflict resolution

Management allocates these tasks to team members as the team is ready for them. A part of the preparation for this passing of responsibilities includes training and development activities relevant to each team's needs.

- Team manager's role. Service team managers must play a stronger coaching and counseling role than the traditional manager. They find themselves in the role of facilitator, empowerer and consultant, responsible for "managing the culture." Therefore, the training program developed for managers pays special attention to the development of these skills.

Performance appraisal

- Peer (individual) appraisal. Self-managing work teams require a new concept in performance appraisals. Members of the team use an anonymous peer appraisal concept. In addition, teams "certify" their members' skill levels.
- Group (team) appraisal. Teams are expected to function as teams and not just groups of individuals. Team members receive training in the skill areas required to enable groups of individuals to function as a team. The individual's ability to function as a team member is evaluated as part of the training process. However, managers assess the team's actual behavior in this area. Teams are able to assess their own progress against the standards and goals which contribute to bonus results.

Successes And Challenges of Change and Self-managed Teams at IPS

External Visibility

The self-managing work team concept initially found only a modest level of credibility within the rest of the organization because, in the minds of many, it still had to be proven. The attention given our efforts helped support the validity of the work team concept. Examples include an article about our efforts by John Hoerr in the July 10, 1989 issue of *Business Week*; several references by Tom Peters in his syndicated newspaper column; several other references in other national and local publications; requests for and subsequent site visits by many organizations; and invitations to make presentations about our team concept by organizations such as the Association for Quality and Participation and the Work in America Institute. Subsequently, demonstrated improvements in productivity and customer satisfaction made it more difficult to criticize the concept. However, the one soft spot that plagued us for some time was overall employee satisfaction. Employee satisfaction was probably impacted most significantly by the introduction of an incentive compensation system with pay at risk during a time when the rest of the organization remained on the traditional merit system.

Employee Successes and Challenges

Employee reactions to the redesigned organization are monitored by a number of approaches. First, monthly employee "feedback" sessions are sponsored and hosted by the department head. Employees are randomly selected from throughout the department and offered the opportunity to air their concerns, ask questions and suggest changes. This approach is also used by regional managers.

In addition, a survey instrument was introduced in July 1987, to monitor employee attitude as IPS moved through implementation of the redesigned organization. The survey continues to be used on a periodic basis. Results are evaluated on a regional and service team level as well as on a departmental level. Employee attitude goals are established for service teams and actual results against goals are used in evaluating managers' overall performance. The first reading was taken in July 1987, just prior to the physical move. A second was taken in October 1987, shortly after the physical move, followed by a third in May 1988, a fourth in September 1989 following the introduction of the Pay-for-Applied-Services compensation system, and the last in August of 1990. A few comparative readings from the old organization were available from several years before. Some results are shown in Exhibit 1.

The significant impact of change can be noted in the overall satisfaction of employees. A very stable "comfortably staffed" functional organization in 1983 resulted in a relatively high level of overall satisfaction. Surprisingly, the design phase and, not so surprisingly, the implementation phase of the new design resulted in a significant deterioration in overall employee satisfaction even though employees were heavily involved in developing and implementing the new design. However, it should be pointed out that employees, for the most

Exhibit 1. Percent Agreeing

	1983	7/87	10/87	5/88	9/89	8/90	8/91
Overall satisfaction	70%	56%	47%	41%	51%	58%	65%
Encouraged to innovate		58%	73%	69%	66%	70%	69%
Adequate training		60%	49%	51%	57%	58%	58%
Permitted to use judgment		81%	90%	88%	89%	89%	88%
Good communication between field and HO	30%	58%	66%	58%	54%	66%	68%
Familiar with measures for for doing good job		64%	38%	42%	45%	52%	57%

part, still respond that they would not want to go back to the old structure and organization, even though there are some things about the new they dislike.

The tough spots. Two specific "problem" areas identified by the survey were (1) lack of **advance** training for the new roles and duties employees were being asked to assume and (2) the employees' inability to measure how well they were doing in their new roles.

First, the training issue was an enormous challenge for both management and employees. Enlarging jobs put a tremendous strain on training capabilities during the early stages of transformation. That, together with not having a compensation system in place to support the cross-training concept, may have negatively impacted employee morale by not having adequate incentives in place. It's understandable that employees did not feel very good about this aspect of the renewal effort. Second, moving from individual standards to measuring and rewarding individuals on the basis of team results is a difficult change for some to accept in a culture in which "individuality" has been lauded and many prefer to be "fully" in control of their own destinies.

In addition, as previously mentioned, the approach used to assign employees to new work teams had a significant negative impact on the existing "social system". This was further compounded in January 1989 when the department moved from a five-region structure to a four-region structure to parallel a similar move in the field distribution system. The other major impact on employee satisfaction was the installation of a new compensation system that has the effect of putting a part of their compensation "at risk" based on performance. The aggregation of all of this change has had a negative impact on employees' overall satisfaction level. It's doubtful that the negative impact of change can be avoided, but what could be avoided ← is drawing it out over an extended period of time. In our case, we began the design in January 1987, and implemented the last piece, the compensation program, in 1989 and 1991. This is probably an excessive time frame.

Nevertheless, there are some really positive results. For example, communications between the employee and our customers has improved. The employee now feels challenged to innovate. And employees feel free to use their own rather than a supervisor's judgment. We also have a very large number of employees who favor the new compensation system because of the positive impact it has had on their ability to influence their earnings.

One of the most noteworthy results is the gain in productivity which as been accomplished and which will be addressed later. An additional "nice to see" is the rapidity with which the

Exhibit 2. Percent Agreeing

	8/85	9/87	10/88	9/89	9/90	10/91
IPS understands field	27%	47%	45%	48%	57%	60%
IPS wants to help field		83%	78%	79%	84%	89%
IPS will respond	*	84%	82%	85%	85%	89%
Satisfactory speed	61%	68%	61%	65%	77%	73%
Accuracy	76%	79%	74%	77%	85%	84%

* No survey-data, but focus of high level of complaints from field.

organization is moving from the concept of three functional self-managing work teams within a service team to a more integrated, functionally inclusive self-managing team. The latter was a longer range design goal but it is coming to realization much more quickly than anticipated.

Customer Successes and Challenges

Perhaps the most visible success thus far is the favorable impact the new self-managed design is having on IPS' customers, the field staff. Input gathered from them, as part of a field renewal effort and reported in March 1988, indicated that the field staff felt the new IPS organization was one of the four best things about AAL.

A survey instrument was implemented to measure the satisfaction of the field staff. The results are shown in Exhibit 2.

The improvement in customer attitude between August 1985 and March 1988 is probably primarily related to (1) the promise of "better" service, (2) the "face off" of specific service teams with specific customers (agencies), (3) field visits where members of service teams would attend agency meetings, and (4) an experimental "partnership program" in which specific IPS employees would "partner" with specific agents. The slight deterioration in October 1988 is probably somewhat related to the establishment of higher expectations and to field renewal activity that was taking place. Speed, for example, shows a fairly significant deterioration in level of satisfaction when, in fact, we've been providing better service than earlier in the renewal process. Other "anecdotal evidences" of customer satisfaction are numerous letters and other communications about how pleased individuals are with the support they're getting from their home office service team; flowers, candy and other "treats" received by service teams from their field customers; and customer hosted "celebrations" in conjunction with successful sales results.

Looking at the results of the survey instrument from the perspective of ignoring the "neutral" responses and focusing only on the "disagrees", would suggest even better results. For example:

	PERCENT DISAGREEING		
	9/89	9/90	10/91
IPS understands field	19%	12%	13%
IPS wants to help field	2%	2%	2%
IPS will respond	4%	5%	2%
Satisfactory speed	14%	8%	13%
Accuracy	6%	2%	4%

Productivity Successes and Challenges

Very tangible productivity gains have been realized. As previously indicated, the department was initially "right-sized" by 59 positions (12 percent) resulting in a savings of over one million dollars of salaries and benefits. Additional reallocation of employee resources has since occurred. On the other hand, business processed has continued to increase. A "macro" productivity model developed to monitor our progress shows a cumulative productivity increase of approximately 29 percent through 1990. This means that if we were operating at the same standard of productivity as we were in 1985 and 1986, we would require about 120 more positions than we had at the end of 1990.

We anticipate additional productivity gains as cross-training progresses and teams mature. However, the amount of time and energy it takes to cross-train while continuing to process business should not be underestimated. It is a significant commitment of time and resources.

Future Design Changes

The first phases of the sociotechnical design were implemented in IPS in August 1987. A review of the original design decisions, in view of the knowledge gained from a little over a year of operation, took place in December 1988. As a consequence, we implemented several modifications to the organization in March 1989 and introduced the individual-incentive modification to the compensation system (PAS) in 1991.

First, we've moved from a five region to a four region design to face off with a similar change that was made in the alignment of our field distribution organization effective January 1989. Second, we moved the reporting relationship of "specialists" from service team managers to the regional managers. This was done to recognize that specialists have a departmental role, not a service team role, and thus are a part of the departmental management team. We later reorganized the specialists by line of business with each regional manager taking responsibility for one of the major areas. Third, we moved from 16 service team managers to 15, further broadening the span of control of the managers. This was possible because of the progress made in the self-managing capabilities of employees.

It should be pointed out that this "fine-tuning" of the organization resulted in employee reassignments and as a result was followed by some deterioration in the morale of employees who were looking for stability.

And finally, as previously mentioned, a modification of the compensation system was implemented in 1991.

CEO Diagnostic Intervention

We contracted with the Center for Effective Organizations (CEO), University of Southern California, in October 1992, to learn how to better understand the effect of IPS structure and support systems on team performance and employee satisfaction. We felt we needed to understand the employee concerns voiced in the November 1991 corporate employee survey, and we needed to respond by addressing these concerns. Also it was five years since IPS had been reorganized into teams and the timing would indicate that it was time to reassess our direction. We selected CEO to do the research because they would be a neutral third-party, carried the prestige of being an internationally known organization in the study of teams and team work, and employed some of the leading thinkers on compensation, particularly skill-based pay.

As we began our research in the fall of 1992, we had four key objectives:

1. Assess the current status and design of the team-based IPS organization.
2. Specifically address the issue of why improvements in employee morale lagged improvements in productivity and customer satisfaction.

3. Suggest possible innovations in our team based design, which could be implemented and tested for their impact on the effectiveness of teams and the department as a whole.
4. Assist with the design, implementation and assessment of innovations related to new ways of doing business that were planned for at least some of the work teams.

Here's what we learned from a year of intensive self-scrutiny:

1. Despite our hypothesis that employee quality of work life (QWL) lagged improvements in productivity and customer satisfaction, QWL for IPS employees was in fact above average compared to other organizations.
2. Our efforts at empowerment were effective, but room for continued progress remained.
3. Employee quality of work life was not strongly related to either productivity or customer satisfaction.

In other words, changes in employee quality of work life were not likely to have major effects on either productivity or customer satisfaction. This was a surprising finding, but is consistent with findings from other CEO research into the relationship of QWL to organizational performance. It does not mean QWL is unimportant, but that we can't predict how changes in employee QWL might affect other business results.

4. The need for communication is strong.
5. Overall satisfaction with pay was high, but not all employees agreed with AAL's compensation system or the philosophy behind it. Most employees demonstrated a good understanding of the PAS compensation system (base pay, team incentives, individual incentives) and the corporate Success Share incentive program. However, they indicated some dissatisfaction with non-annuitized incentive compensation (they would prefer annual base salary increases over annual bonuses), and felt that the compensation system does not effectively reward good performers.
6. Service team director visibility was low; the supervisory style of the manager is not related to the team's performance.

Most employees reported that they did not see their managers frequently and would appreciate more contact. A second learning was that there was no correlation between management style and team results in employee QWL, productivity or customer satisfaction.

These findings led us to convene the department management team (regional managers, service team directors and lead specialists) so we could communicate the issues to them and involve them in developing a work plan for addressing areas for improvement. The work of "fine tuning" the organization based on the CEO findings was begun in August 1993.

SUMMARY

In summary, the primary driving forces for the redesign of IPS were a desire to get closer to the customer, a desire to enlarge jobs and empower employees and a need to "right-size" staff levels. The organizational concept utilized to accomplish our task was the self-managing work team. Although early results indicate customers are more satisfied, and corporate productivity goals are being met, employee satisfaction goals are not being fully achieved. If there is one point to really emphasize, it's that the transition from traditional hierarchical management to sociotechnical management has not been without a lot of "pain" for all involved. Thus, IPS management would be the first to emphasize that we are still heavily into change even though it's been going on for several years.

Some of the more significant conclusions we've reached may be worth sharing. The greatest value of restructuring is probably derived from the process of organizational diagnosis, establishing a vision, and participatively discovering the answer to the gap between the results of the diagnosis and the vision and creating the organizational response. We also feel that "unfreezing" needs to occur to give permission for change (creating positive dissatisfaction is healthy), preferably led by top management example. In AAL's case, this took place through the corporate change that preceded the IPS effort. We'd suggest that it's impossible to over-communicate to employees as the process unfolds, that participation by impacted employees is a must and that the impact of change on employees cannot be underestimated. It's helpful if support systems are implemented concurrently with the renewal efforts and if at all possible, it's probably best to implement all aspects of the change at one time to avoid prolonged "organizational instability" and the associated negative impact on employee morale.

Thus we'd suggest that some of the keys for success would include:

- Participation: Employee involvement at all levels will help ensure buy-in and the best results. The more "brain power" applied to the problem, the better chance the emerging solution will be successful.
- Vision: A clear energizing vision must be created to gain the commitment of staff and to motivate them through times of "pain."
- Commitment: Commitment of top management and support of other key corporate staff, such as human resource management, is critical. Employees have to know their efforts are part of a larger strategy.
- Patience: If the focus is on short-term results, the effort will probably not achieve the ultimate vision. If the goal is to avoid all "pain" in the organization, it's probably un-achievable. Change brings pain, but pain disappears with newfound stability.
- Time: Implementation and cultural change take time. Although some immediate benefits will occur, the ultimate payoff may not be realized for several years.

If the above conditions are not present, success is unlikely.

Notes

1. Scherreik, S. "Off the Beaten Path in the Insurance Field," *New York Times*, December 25, 1993, p. LA5.
2. Hoerr, J. "Work Teams Can Rev-Up Paper-Pushers, Too," *Business Week*, November 28, 1988, pp. 64-72.
3. This vision statement later became the organization's mission statement.

References

Boyett, J. H., and Henry P. Conn. *Maximum Performance Management.* Glenbridge Publishing Ltd., 1988.

Caudron, S. "Team Staffing Requires New HR Role." *Personnel Journal* (May 1994): 88-94.

Hoerr, J. "The Payoff From Teamwork." *Business Week* (July 10, 1989): 56-62.

Weisbord, M. R. *Productive Workplaces.* Jossey-Bass, Inc., 1987.

Wellins, R. S., W. C. Byham, and J. M. Wilson. *Empowered Teams.* Jossey-Bass, Inc., 1991.

43. Wang/Microsoft*

At the end of fiscal year 1989, Wang Laboratories announced that its entrepreneurial leader and founder, An Wang, had been diagnosed as having esophageal cancer. That following August, An Wang's son, Frederick A. Wang, resigned as president and chief operating officer. The company experienced an operating loss of $262 million.[1] It had a total deficit of $424 million for the year ending June 30th and its net worth had fallen below the level required by lenders, placing it in technical violation of its loan agreements worth $962 million.[2] Yet, only seven years before, the company had an unbroken string of 26 record growth quarters and was considered one of the fastest growing, most successful companies of the decade.[3]

An Wang and Wang Laboratories

An Wang came to America from Shanghai, China in 1946 and brought with him an "unusual blend of Confucian philosophy and American frontier ethics".[4] In 1951, after he received a doctorate in Physics from Harvard University, he invented the magnetic-core memory, a system to store data in computers, in his South End Boston loft apartment. He spent the next ten years at various consulting and custom manufacturing jobs. In 1965, he founded Wang Laboratories. His first invention for the company was a programmable desktop calculator, and it was followed by a string of brilliant product introductions that propelled the company to remarkable success. Revenues grew from 1.8 million in 1965 to $75 million in 1975.

Dr. Wang was considered a technical wizard.[6] He "...was always good at seeing what was on the leading edge of physics, in the semiconductor labs and what the implications would be in the marketplace."[7] In the early 1970s, for example, Wang decided to abandon his main business of programmable calculators when he foresaw that such semiconductor giants as Texas Instruments Inc. would dominate the calculator market.

An Wang was more than a technical wizard and entrepreneur, he was also a manager who had his own individual style. Sometimes called a "benevolent dictator"[8], he thrived on keeping his hands in every aspect of his business, and the company's management system developed around his style. A former engineer commented that "The Doctor (as he was affectionately referred to by his employees) had a whim of iron. He was into everything. He would come into the engineering department, head to the blackboard of a first-level engineer, and sketch out what he wanted. What Dr. Wang wanted then became the design."[9] Others described his management practices as "more akin to a Japanese than a U.S. company"; quoting Wang as having said "I'm here (at the company) to impart the philosophy I value, to serve a useful purpose to society at large, and to make sure the people we serve, stockholders, employees, and customers - get a fair return."[10] He had "entrepreneurial genius and ability to inspire messianic zeal and loyalty among his employees. 'He has done so much right for so long that you become a believer, a disciple,'" declared Wang Director Earnest F. Stockwell Jr.[11]

---

*This case was written by Richard D. Freedman and Jill Vohr, Leonard N. Stern School of Business, New York University. Copyright © 1991 by Professor Richard D. Freedman. Reprinted with permission.

Rapid Growth

By 1972 the company had grown to some 2,000 employees. An Wang maintained the centralized and highly personal management style that characterized the company's early days. He reserved final decision making power for himself and most decisions could be appealed to the top.

> "An organizational chart drawn up as late as 1972...showed no fewer than 136 people reporting to the chairman. His accessibility created a sense of participation among employees that earned An Wang their fierce personal loyalty. Wang Labs was a family, and the Doctor was the patriarch, bestowing rewards and punishments at will. His policy, explicitly stated, was never to hire top-level executives from outside. 'We have all the talent we need right here', he once told the board." [12]

Despite its first growth surge in 1973, Wang Labs was still considered "...a small entrepreneurial company ...(that)...was able to flourish under its one-man management style."[13]

Throughout the seventies and into the eighties, the company continued to experience success and growth. From 1973 to 1983, sales grew an average of 42% a year and revenues climbed to $1.5 billion.[14] The work force had increased nine-fold to 18,500.

The Changing Environment

The computer industry environment was changing. Technology was developing rapidly on many fronts and competition was increasing. IBM, AT&T, Digital Equipment Corporation and Data General Corporation were making a strong entrance into Wang Lab's traditional markets of word processing equipment and integrated office packages, offering systems similar to Wang's. IBM had recently introduced many new products aimed directly at Wang. These "me-too" products were less expensive than Wang's originals. Furthermore, the markets in which Wang was strongest - data processing, word processing and low end systems, no longer experienced growth. Consumer demand had shifted toward professional work stations, mini-computer based office systems and personal computers, none of which were in Wang's area of expertise. Sales of Wang's small business computers flattened out as customers chose to buy personal computers instead. "In the past eight months (since February, 1983), we've watched major end-user customers walk away from a Wang decision ...", commented Amy D. Wohl, president of Advanced Office Concepts Inc., an office automation consulting firm. Added Patricia B. Seybold, editor of the Seybold Report on Office Automation, "The perception is that Wang's product line is a little tired and expensive." [15]

In the process of trying to strengthen its competitive edge, Wang discovered marketing problems. The company's success in selling to end-user departments, as opposed to the large central sites had resulted in Wang's image as a word processing company even though more than 50% of its revenues came from data processing products.[16] Fred Wang had commented "...in some ways we are prisoners of our own success...But now we must communicate with and sell more to the center which is usually controlled by IBM." [17]

Growing Pains

Wang Lab's rapid growth resulted in certain financial problems, the balance sheet began to reflect the characteristics of "...an overachiever. High fixed costs, combined with swollen inventories and accounts receivable,...(had)...given the company a voracious appetite for cash. To satisfy that hunger, Wang...had to raise $465 million in the public markets, most of it through convertible debentures. This high debt position saddled the company with interest payments that...drained earnings. Said Sy Kaufman, a partner with Hambrecht and Quist in San Francisco, 'Wang has simply not done a good job managing its assets.'"[18]

Wang Lab's R&D department also began to evidence problems. The R&D group "...was once an efficient operation under the doctor's guiding hand, but as the company grew, an increasing lack of control and planning resulted in efforts that were often redundant or off the mark."[19] Analysts claimed that "Wang's R&D division (was)...extremely disorganized with engineers being shunted around from project to project"[20] "The lack of planning over-committed the company's resources"...(said)...one former executive.[21] *Business Week* described Wang's problems during this time:

> "There is little doubt that...(Wang Lab's)...blues have been aggravated by some Wang executives' lack of professional maturity in managing large groups of employees and in creating sophisticated systems to manage growth. As a result, such operations as manufacturing and product services have careened out of control. For example, Wang until recently had no system for tracking material usage during production. There was also little or no communication and coordination between functional groups in the company, and people often worked at cross-purposes. Wang engineers, for instance, never took into account how much it would cost to manufacture or service a product when they were designing it.

> Ironically, it was An Wang's centralized and highly personal management style - so important to the company's success - that exacerbated its growing pains. The company took longer to go through adolescence because of the tight control at the top." [22]

Poor management was at least partly responsible for the release of a data-base management software package that subsequently had to be recalled.[23] Also, Wang's voice-mail system and two-year old proprietary local area network for linking office equipment had technical problems and failed to take off.

Changes Within Wang Laboratories

Outside projects, such as advisory positions at colleges and the Massachusetts Board of Regents, were taking up an increasingly significant portion of An Wang's time.[24] In 1981, responding to his company's problems and the limited time he had to spend managing them. He began to transfer some of his responsibilities in hopes of strengthening control systems deeper within the organization.

The first change An Wang implemented was the establishment of an executive operating committee. The committee was formed to handle top management decision-making during Wang's frequent absences and to broaden top management's perspective. It included the four senior functional managers: John Cunningham, head of marketing and sales; Harry H.S. Chou, Executive Vice President; and Senior Vice President John F. Kopper. Each member continued to run his own division day-to-day. The group provided "...a good forum to air issues that cut across functional lines. Decisions once made during casual hallway conversations now (were)...brought before the committee through formal presentations. 'We are institutionalizing processes that were once informal.'" said Chou.[25] Decisions were also being made by consensus rather than by Wang himself. He remained uninvolved unless the other members could not reach a decision or if he felt that their judgment ran counter to his. The committee even began to issue orders on its own letterhead.[26] Decision-making was pushed further into the organization as well. A third tier of managers were hired and decision-making was delegated down to their level. "This has resulted in a badly needed infusion of fresh management blood into Wang's inbred hierarchy and the institution of formal systems for such jobs as material planning. Similarly, Chou has hired a comptroller to take over this function from himself. And Cunningham - who personally used to answer every inquiry from Wall Street - has turned over the day-to-day management of investor relations, marketing support, and U.S. sales to newly hired professionals. Product pricing and marketing plans, once settled over lunch by Chou and Cunningham, now are threshed out by committees."[27] Similarly, members of the committee began to hire new professionals to handle their day-to-day functions, leaving them time for more important duties.

In order to maintain the company's competitive edge, Wang Lab's R&D department was gearing up to introduce 14 new products. The objective was to broaden its product line significantly so that it could participate in the entire office automation field. It was hoped that this move would bring the company in close competition with IBM, Digital Equipment and Xerox .

Wang also brought his 30-year-old son, Frederick A. Wang, into the forefront of the company by promoting him to the position of director of R&D.

Frederick A. Wang

Fred Wang, graduate of Brown University and the Harvard Business School's 13 week Program for Management Development, started in his father's company when he was only 22. He began as a "technical grunt"[28]. He was considered technically competent and "...didn't pose any real threat to those whose ambitions included running Wang Laboratories - until 1980 when An Wang put him in charge of R&D."[29]

Fred's management style was very different from his father's. It was more deliberate and conciliatory. "Fred needed peace and concurrence. The Doctor thrived on chaos and confusion.", said Cunningham Fred did not approve of his father's unruly and impulsive management style. "An Wang had always advocated the earliest conceivable release of technology, which often proved to be too early for effective marketing and well ahead of what the company could realistically deliver."[30] His impulsiveness, however, was continually checked by his senior managers. If Harold Kaplow, Wang's prized engineer, was unable to slow things down,

"...at least Cunningham could minimize the damage to the bottom line by whipping the sales staff into a frenzy when the products did hit the market."[31]

At his new post, Fred reorganized the department in order to solve some of these problems. He redefined development goals to focus more heavily on innovation. He streamlined management, trimming the development staff by 10% and instituted a dual-career path for engineers that enabled those who were especially creative to earn management salaries without having any management responsibilities so they could concentrate on functions they were best suited for and be justly rewarded.[32] These changes, however, were met with resistance. Many employees were unhappy reporting to Fred Wang instead of his father. They felt Fred was "too green for (the)...job"[33] and "no match for the company's top engineers"[34] whom he was directing. According to Daniel Cohen, of *Business Month*, Fred's "...need for consensus seemed to stifle disagreements, leaving no faction satisfied and the company without an effective plan."[35] Many felt that he was "in over his head."[36]

These conflicts eventually resulted in company defections. The first to leave was Harold Kaplow. Kaplow was a most valued engineer, "...one of the few at Wang Labs to have command of both hardware and software..."[37] In 1983, John Cunningham also resigned. Cunningham was credited as having "...molded (the company's)...direct sales force into an exuberant and lavishly rewarded powerhouse and gave Wang products a more prominent identity in the marketplace." As the senior managers who would argue against An Wang's impulsiveness began to depart, "...there were few left who were willing to disagree with An Wang, and the company lurched from bad decision to bad decision. The result was a series of misguided product introductions and a deteriorating reputation for service."[38] Then, in 1983, Fred Wang

> "...presided over one of the company's most disastrous gambits. With great fanfare, he announced delivery dates for (the) 14 new products, provoking large customers to postpone purchases in expectation of the promised upgrades. When virtually every product missed its target delivery date by months and, in some cases, as much as four years, customers were left holding the bag. It was the kind of fiasco that, in a highly competitive, rapidly changing industry, can drive customers away forever.

> This time the devastating results couldn't be ignored and Fred Wang was...(taken)... out of his position as head of R&D. His new title was executive vice president/chief development officer, and observers hoped the new assignment in management, where most believed his talents lay, might signal a slowing of Fred Wang's rise to power. But not long after, he began to accumulate more titles: treasurer, head of worldwide manufacturing, and it became clear to any potential rivals that far from slowing Fred Wang's rise, An Wang was actually passing the mantle to his first-born."[39]

The Fall of Wang Laboratories

In the Autumn of 1984, An Wang announced that he intended to name his son president. Yet the company continued to be plagued by the same problems. "...In July, 1985, Wang Labs...suffered a $109 million quarterly loss - its worst to that time - and faced a hurricane of customer complaints for product breakdowns that servicers seemed unable to fix. In the period after Cunningham's departure - a sort of interregnum in which no new president was named - the defection of key executives escalated."[40]

Fred Wang was named president in 1986. The following two years were encouraging for the company. Fred seemed to making the right moves to restore the company's competitive edge."[41] Also, according to Cohen, he took on:

> "...one of the firm's most persistent - and alarming - management lacunae. Under the Doctor, there had never been a strong comptroller. The company had no reliable product-line earnings statements and often, in fact, did not know what return its various offerings brought. The firm's weaknesses in implementation – a by-product of its factionalism – remained intractable, however, and continued to erode confidence in Fred Wang. The honeymoon ended when the company posted a $70 million loss in his first year, only to have him press for sales to expand by 25 percent the next year. As expected, they fell short of that goal by an impressive 19 percent."[42]

After An Wang returned from his hospital surgery for esophageal cancer in July of 1989, he openly gave his evaluation of his son on page one of *The Wall Street Journal*. "While acknowledging the rough times in which Fred Wang became president, Wang opined: 'I would rate him at 75 percent. I can't rate him super.' Three weeks later, on the eve of Wang labs' default on its loan agreements, father and son conferred in private over the weekend and on Monday, August 8, 1989, announced Fred Wang's resignation." [43]

Microsoft

> Microsoft's wealth and power just grows and grows. On the day that Bill Gates turned 37, the stock closed at $88.50 a share. On paper, the value of his 30% stake reached $7.3 billion. He could buy out an entire year's production of his 99 nearest competitors, burn it, and still be worth more than Rupert Murdoch or Ted Turner. Microsoft's $25 billion dollar market value tops that of Ford, General Motors, 3M, Boeing, RJR Nabisco, General Mills, Anheuser-Busch or Eastman Kodak.
>
> *- Fortune*, December 28, 1992

In 1975, college-aged William H. Gates and Paul G. Allen worked freelance writing a version of the computer programming language, BASIC, for a small hobbyist's computer called Altair. When the program was a success, Gates, who was an undergraduate at Harvard, left school and with Allen set up a programming company in Boston. Five years later, IBM was looking to enter the personal computer market. Gates and Allen had moved their company, now called Microsoft, to Seattle. Over the five years, it had become "...primarily a language programming house, with a few computer games thrown in."[44] IBM wanted a programming company to write software that would run on the IBM personal computer and requested that Microsoft write versions of BASIC, four other languages and the operating system for their PC. Microsoft agreed and wrote MS-DOS. When the computer hit the market in the summer of 1981, MS-DOS was a huge success.

Since that time, Microsoft "...has grown nearly 50-fold without a blip."[45] *Fortune* magazine's Brenton Schlender said that "most high-tech companies make at least one major misstep on the way to becoming billion-dollar behemoths. That still hasn't happened to Microsoft."[46] With the announcement of the newest version of Microsoft Windows in May 1990, analysts "...predict that by mid 1991, Microsoft (will have) ...total revenues of about $1.2 billion (and) ... have sold over $500 million worth of Windows programs and Windows compatible applications."[47]

William H. Gates

Gates started working on computers in the seventh grade. The son of a Seattle lawyer, he went to private school. Bill was "...instantly hooked and made $4,200 that summer programming class schedules."[48] At 15, Gates and a friend ran a small company called Traf-O-Data. The company used a computer to track traffic patterns and sold it to municipalities across the northwest making $20,000. [49]

Today, "Gates is the only one of the personal computer entrepreneurs who surfaced in the 1970's who still runs his own company...he is known as the 'world's youngest billionaire' and the 'quintessential nerd.'"[50] "When you talk to him, he tends to put his elbows on his knees, lean forward and rock," said Jeff Raikes, Microsoft's director of applications marketing. "When he does this, his glasses tend to slide down to the end of his nose, and if you don't know the guy, it can be a little disarming. I mean, here's this very intense, very smart guy rocking away, and kind of looking at you - probably through glasses that aren't all that clean."[51]

Gates has proved to be that rare combination of technical visionary and pragmatic businessman[52] which has contributed to the staying power of the company. "There are few people who can play both sides of the street - managerial and technical - as well as he can,"[53] said an industry source.

A Visionary

John Dvorak, an industry watcher and columnist for *PC Magazine*, described Gates as having "...a real vision of what personal computing is all about. And he takes the perspective of the user-hacker, as opposed to the perspective of the businessman." Larry Michels, president of The Santa Cruz Operation, the outfit which co-authored with Microsoft the Unix-based Xenix operating system, called Gates "...the visionary...He looks at the present and blazes the future trail."[54] "Gates is always thinking and talking about the next ten years," said Teresa Lotzgesell, a software analyst with Cable, Howse & Ragen. "As a result, customers have a lot of confidence in Microsoft to prepare for their future needs."[55] Microsoft has clearly benefitted from Gates' approach to the business. The company made over $1 billion in revenues in 1990 and has the broadest array of products in the personal computer software business.[56]

A Pragmatic Manager

Gates' unique and versatile management style has also contributed to Microsoft's success. "Despite his company's swelling size, he has found an effective way to keep communicating (his visions) directly...His personal qualities have helped him keep the magic going after Microsoft's initial, spectacular success."[57]

"Gates' management style underscores his obsession with quality. A workaholic who routinely puts in 12 to 15 hour days and works weekends, he spends much of his time directing and driving...(his employees)...and motivating them through confrontation and challenge. He wants his people to strive to be as bright, thorough and forthright as he is," says Paul Allen, "...and he demands that they be prepared to defend their ideas."[58] "It's very challenging to work for him," says Stephen Wood, former general manager of Microsoft. "He's so bright that you really have to stay on your toes. If you can hang in there more than a couple of years, you probably have a lot of self confidence."[59] James A. Towne, a former Microsoft president adds, "Bill is a perfectionist who demands that his people move at his speed...Despite his intimidating manner, Gates inspires fierce loyalty among his employees, who get used to his ways. They respond to the high standard he sets and to the excitement of working in a trailblazing company."[60]

Gates also works his employees hard. Seventy five hour work weeks are not uncommon and many work until 3 or 4 in the morning.[61] Still, the turnover rate is low, 8% to 10% annually for marketing and administrative employees,[62] and less than 5% for programmers.[63] Microsoft hires carefully. The company can afford to be choosy. Less than 1% of those who apply for jobs are hired.[64] This is partly due to Gates' belief in conservative hiring. "Once you allow managers to think that it takes 100 people to do something when it should be 20, that's extremely hard to reverse."[65] Once programmers are hired, the promotion and compensation systems at Microsoft are rewarding:

> Each programmer is rated at one of six levels between 10 and 15, with architects at 15. "When you hit 13, it's like making partner," says Gates. "We have a big ceremony and everything," including awarding the programmer more stock op-

tions. While some programmers also perform some management chores, they don't have to be managers to climb the scale. A nifty piece of programming will do the trick. All this inspires tremendous loyalty.[66]

Managing Growth

With Microsoft's spectacular growth, managing the organization is a constant challenge. Gates realized that an executive was sorely needed. "When you looked at the company's organizational chart...it became clear that Bill Gates was the sole head of everything, with seven of his twenty-six employees nominally, and far more actually, reporting directly to him. Middle managers were nowhere to be seen."[67]

Gates called Steve Ballmer and told him he needed someone with business savvy to join the Microsoft team. Ballmer joined Microsoft in June 1980 to replace Steve Wood as assistant to the president. Ballmer was brought in to focus on business. He had worked at Proctor & Gamble in marketing and had attended the Stanford business school. He knew little about computers, but much about business. Upon his arrival, Ballmer set upon formalizing operations within Microsoft. For the first time, someone at Microsoft was charged with specifically addressing operational areas such as finance, legal and personnel.[68]

In the early 1980's, the focus of Microsoft's business was changing. Its major thrust had been to sell code to original equipment manufacturers (OEM's). That high-margin business was still essential, but now the company was also trying to sell products directly to the public via retail channels. Although the OEM sales force was experienced, the retail marketing department consisted of MBA's barely out of school.[69]

Gates faced a new managerial challenge in 1983 when Paul Allen was diagnosed as suffering from Hodgkin's disease and left Microsoft. Gates had the foresight to realize that he was going to need more help running his fast-growing, young company. He brought in Jon A. Shirley to manage day-to-day operations. This move was considered to be "a milestone in the young company's history... (because)...it gave Microsoft the business structure it needed to manage dynamic growth, and it freed Gates to concentrate on technology and planning."[70] Shirley was charged with managing Microsoft's retail business, where his years of experience would be put to good use. His experience meshed well with Microsoft's inexperienced marketing team. Manufacturing, merchandising and finance were also put under the new president's wing.[71]

In addition to Shirley and Ballmer, Gates has relied on other strong professional managers to the point where he has been able to remove himself so completely from routine operations that "...he checks the company's profit-and-loss statement only at the end of each quarter, and he confers with Shirley once a week, in a brief meeting on Saturday morning.[72] Consequently, Gates is free "...to develop long-range strategy, hang out with key industry leaders, travel and work on software."

"Usually companies as big as Microsoft don't react fast, but Gates is very much on top of everything," says Philippe Kahn, President, President and Chief Executive Officer of Borland International, a major competitor.[73] "The key to Gates' control and ability to spread himself around is that each of his technical strategies are broken down by his managers into concise business goals that are handled by small, independent business units of programmers and marketers. These units are easier to manage and foster more innovation and fewer crossed signals among managers. The groups are small enough so that Gates can sit around a table to chat with the members and inject his ideas personally. While he would prefer not to be bothered with operational details, he is quick to identify both organizational weaknesses and the management talent required to repair them."[74]

Despite announcing earnings of $100 million for 1984, (twice as much as the year before), the financial side of the business at Microsoft was experiencing serious problems. Frank Gaudette was hired as Chief Operating Officer (COO) to rectify the situation. He found "close to uncontrollable chaos in finance." Ironically, one thing that Microsoft needed most in its finance department was computers. Gaudette professionalized Microsoft's finance department by introducing financial controls.[75] Gaudette's controls included extension of profit-and-loss responsibilities to as many managers as possible.[76]

Meanwhile, Jon Shirley had reorganized the development, product marketing, user education and testing groups into two departments; systems software and applications. Gates was named to head the applications department until a successor could be found, after which he would "spend full time as chairman - representing the Company, selling to key customers, and, most importantly, formulating strategy, designing and providing design guidance and review."[77]

Product Development

Microsoft's R&D uses creative teams to develop new products. Gates and a select team of high-level managers brainstorm at Microsoft's weekend retreat, a hotel near company head-quarters. "On a weekend in October, 1983, for example, top personnel gathered 'to launch the world's greatest spreadsheet,'" as Shirley puts it. Three years later, the finished product, Excel, made its debut.

Usually, Gates refines the development process in two follow-up retreats, bringing along the team of programmers and marketers who will see the product though to fruition. He delegates full authority to a team once it gets started, allowing the members to set goals, split up to work and generally treat the project as their baby."[78] He also makes each responsible for its own profitability.

Because virtually all the company's projects are handled by individual groups, Gates is able to maintain personal contact involving direct communication, accessibility and involvement with every aspect of the business, from product development to programming. At meetings with his managers, "he is...likely to check the math in handouts and overhead slides for ... errors ... (and) critique fuzzy marketing strategies." He enjoys joining Microsoft programmers in the brainstorming sessions that give birth to new products.[79] He "...encourages employees to communicate with him directly through the company's electronic mail system, and dozens do it each day." He tries to respond to each message the same day he gets it. "That's a big deal," says William Sahlman, a Harvard business school management professor. "as a company gets larger and the charismatic figurehead gets further and further away from the bowels of the company, it's particularly useful for people to feel they have some direct access."[80] "It's very important to me and to the guys that work for us that Microsoft feel like a small company, even though it isn't one anymore," says Gates. "I remember how much fun it is to be small, and the business units help preserve that feeling."[81]

To save money, ease communication, and preserve the underdog spirit, Microsoft intentionally understaffs its product teams. Gates wants to have fewer spreadsheet programmers than Lotus. Microsoft is organized into small bands of "people who can pound, pound, pound," says sales head Steve Ballmer.[82]

The size of Microsoft's teams grew as Microsoft grew. Microsoft, however, is consciously trying to keep its work teams small. "Gates knows that big groups of programmers can create bad software more slowly than small ones can write good software. Teams are therefore kept to a maximum of 200 people. But this increases the company's managerial challenge. Not only must its managers keep information flowing smoothly across hundreds of small teams - despite rivalries and differences in focus - they must also choreograph the teams so that they can leap at new opportunities without landing on each other's toes."[83]

As Microsoft has grown, its number of business units have also increased. In 1986, the company had 1,000 employees. In two years, this number grew to 5,200 and Microsoft reacted by creating five business units to focus on such areas as spreadsheets or network systems software.[85] By 1990, the company grew to 8,000 employees and expanded to 12 business units.[86] This continual adjustment has allowed the company to stay nimble despite its large size. This means it can react quickly to the competition. In a rapidly developing industry, this is important.

Linking Mechanisms for Teams

Microsoft uses several tools to coordinate its teams. First, an e-mail system is used that keeps the information flowing between the organizational groups. A typical Microsoft executive receives about 100 messages a day from all parts of the firm on topics ranging from product strategy briefings to personal barbs.[87]

·Second, committees were created to promote uniformity across key issues such as marketing, development and program management. Within each functional area is a director that coordinates the function across the business units in a matrix-like structure. An employee from each functional area is assigned the director position, mostly on a part-time basis. In those cases where the director position became a full-time job, the responsibility is rotated among employees.[88]

To help keep Microsoft's "small" feel, Gates devised the Office of the President, consisting of Gates, Steve Ballmer and Mike Maples. The office of the president manages Gates' vision of the future. Maples is in charge of product development. He has split his division into five groups, each dealing with its own customers and technologies.[89]

Hiring and Personnel

"For its crucial line positions in programming and product management, Microsoft can still pick with extreme selectivity from the graduates of elite universities and business schools."[90] "Microsoft's personnel reviews 10,000 resumes per month, with more of an eye on raw talent rather than industry experience."[91] Gates follows a simple rule when hiring," I hire smart people that are pretty high bandwidth*, and I challenge them to think. I ask them to be pretty committed and work pretty hard."[92]

---

*High bandwidth- Gates-speak for the ability to quickly digest a lot of information.

"The chosen few get lots of responsibility right away. Gates earns high marks for pushing authority down through the ranks. He limits his one role largely to conceiving and spreading the vision, helping to sell key customers and keeping a close eye on R&D.[93] The training is on-the-job. Says Pete Higgins, a vice-president: 'throw them in and good-luck.' In return, recruits aren't saddled with a lot of rules and bureaucracy."[94]

Microsoft's Culture

The corporate culture at Microsoft is legendary. Dress is casual, the atmosphere informal, if not very much like a college campus. Much of this attitude stems from Microsoft's early days in Albuquerque as a start-up computer software firm.[95] "Some of the free form, improvisatory environment is unquestionably fostered to be a spur to creativity. Employees are not encumbered with a 'corporate' atmosphere, but are encouraged to personalize their office space."[96]

Microsoft is conscious of its culture and works to maintain it. Products chief Mike Maples goes on two dozen off-site retreats with younger managers each year to consider Microsoft's culture. The managers are asked to look at both the strengths and weaknesses that result from the culture. "We're smart - how not to be arrogant? We're aggressive - how to make sure we negotiate win-win contracts rather than going for all we can get?"[97]

Managing the Competition

The computer software industry is volatile and extremely competitive. Microsoft has been able to maintain a central role in the industry because of the dominance of MS-DOS. Yet, unless Gates had persuaded IBM to let him sell DOS to all comers in 1981, allowing other manufacturers to make PC clones, Microsoft's products would not be as successful and as prevalent as they are today. "IBM PC's and other clones dominate the business, with 74% of their market. Microsoft has sold more than 40 million copies of DOS. The preeminence lets Gates plug into a lot of other people's secrets, because throughout the PC industry anyone developing new programs or machines is virtually compelled to work with his products."[98]

There are other factors that contribute to Microsoft's competitive strength. The company has a near monopoly on operating systems software for IBM compatible PC's. Its "...after tax profit margins of 24% are the highest in the software industry, mainly because the company gets by with fewer programmers and marketers than its rivals."[99] Also, Gates involved Microsoft internationally before the competition. "Microsoft products predominate in nearly every foreign market they are in; they generate more sales and profits overseas than at home."[100] Larry Michels says, "what differentiates Microsoft from its competition is its proven ability to simultaneously work on all phases of the software product life cycle ranging from product development to distribution...Other software vendors have modeled themselves after the hardware business. Microsoft created its own model of how to do business."[101]

More than one manager would not survive Microsoft's rapid growth. Vern Raburn was president of the Consumer Products Division, responsible for developing retail markets for Microsoft's new applications. Penetrating the retail market required more than technical skills, it required a strong marketing and sales department as well. Raburn's strength, however, lay in his relationships with the pioneers in the computer industry. While this produced strong results early, a more formal and professional marketing approach was required as the market matured.[102]

Microsoft competes in nearly all factions of the computer industry: computer languages to build products, operating systems and networking software, spreadsheets and word-processing programs. It its introduction of Windows, the company hopes to expand into yet another market.

Some believe that Microsoft rode to the top on "...IBM's pinstriped coat tails."[103] Yet, although Microsoft is dependent on IBM, "...it is strong enough to survive on its own. The company is managed very conservatively and has virtually no debt and lots of cash. 'If IBM was unhappy with us, certainly it would damage us a great deal in terms of our growth and our ability to set new standards,' Gates says. "But going down the tubes is not one of the possibilities."

Helping to lessen its dependence on IBM, Microsoft has been churning out a steady stream of applications software and now has a lineup of nearly three dozen programs for MS-DOS based, UNIX based and Macintosh personal computers.[104]

Gates "...confers frequently with computer industry leaders about the directions they plan to take in product development. But he also follows his own instincts when he smells a promising new market."[105]

Some Problems

Microsoft does have its weaknesses. One is its tendency to rush a product to market too quickly. "Time after time the company has targeted a new market only to introduce a mediocre product the first time out."[106] Michael Swavely, president of Compaq computer's North American operations says "Microsoft is a very seat-of-the-pants operation in certain ways. In particular, their understanding of market research is only rudimentary. But that is typical of a fast growing company, and it's fixable."[107]

The Future

"For all of Microsoft's accomplishments so far, just about everybody in the company believes its best days are still ahead. Gates has his brain trust of architects developing lots of new technologies...Gates insists that all of the challenges only make his job more fascinating. 'I'd get bored if things just stayed the same.'"[108]

Things are not likely to stay the same. Microsoft has historically capitalized on the ideas of others rather than produced its own innovations. DOS, for example, was bought from another company.

Microsoft finds that it must speculate in new, ground-breaking technologies to ensure itself a central role in the future of computing.[109]

Microsoft's biggest problem today may well be much the same one as that ten years ago, itself. A 1984 *Fortune* article noted:

> In the course of its frantic growth the company has churned out a bewildering variety of products...seven languages...three operating systems...as well as several games...and miscellaneous pieces of hardware. That makes for management headaches, since each additional product can add exponentially to the complex task of maintaining compatibility across product lines. [110]

How well Microsoft will do in the future depends largely on how well its spectacular growth is managed. Says Microsoft's president, Hallman: "the big challenge for me will be how to deal with constant growth. We can't have a flat organization with all the business units on equal footing forever, and even with our e-mail system, communications could become a big problem."[111] Similarly, *The Economist* views Microsoft as "entering corporate middle age, with 10,000 employees in 1993, and new employees joining on at a rate of 2,000 per year. Microsoft is having to walk an increasingly difficult line between the stifling bureaucracy of a too-rigid management discipline and the chaos of being too loose."[112]

Endnotes

1. Daniel Cohen, "The Fall of the House of Wang" *Business Month*, February, 1990: 23.
2. Ibid.
3. "Wang Labs' Run For a Second Billion" *Business Week*, May 17, 1982: 100
4. Ibid: 103.
5. Daniel Cohen, "The Fall of the House of Wang" *Business Month*, February, 1990: 24.
6. Ibid.
7. Ibid.
8. "Wang Labs' Run For a Second Billion" *Business Week*, May 17, 1982: 100.
9. Ibid.
10. Ibid: 103.
11. Ibid. p. 104.
12. Daniel Cohen, "The Fall of the House of Wang" *Business Month*, February, 1990: 24.
13. "Wang Labs' Run For a Second Billion" *Business Week*, May 17, 1982: 101.
14. Ibid.
15. "The First Hint of Trouble at Wang" *Business Week*, October 17, 1983: 45.
16. Ralph Emmett, "Trouble in Paradise? Analysts wonder whether Wang laboratories' high-flying days are numbered," *Datamation*, April, 1983: 42.
17. Ibid.
18. "Wang Labs' Run For a Second Billion" *Business Week*, May 17, 1982: 101.
19. Ibid: 103.
20. Ralph Emmett, "Trouble in Paradise? Analysts wonder whether Wang laboratories' high-flying days are numbered," *Datamation*, April, 1983: 43.
21. Ibid.
22. "Wang Labs' Run For a Second Billion" *Business Week*, May 17, 1982: 102.
23. Ibid: 103.
24. Ibid: 102.
25. Ibid: 102.
26. Ibid.
27. Ibid.
28. Daniel Cohen, "The Fall of the House of Wang" *Business Month*, February, 1990: 25.
29. Ibid.
30. Ibid: 28.
31. Ibid.
32. "Wang Labs' Run For a Second Billion" *Business Week*, May 17, 1982: 104.
33. Daniel Cohen, "The Fall of the House of Wang" *Business Month*, February, 1990: 28.
34. Ibid: 26
35. Ibid: 28.
36. Ibid.
37. Ibid.
38. Ibid: 29.
39. Daniel Cohen, "The Fall of the House of Wang" *Business Month*, February, 1990: 29.
40. Ibid: 29.
41. Ibid: 30.

42. Ibid: 30.
43. Ibid: 30.
44. Thomas J. Murphy, "Management by Obsession" *Business Month*, April, 1988, p.58.
45. Brenton Schlender, "How Bill Gates Keeps the Magic Going" *Fortune*, June 18, 1990,p.84.
46. Ibid.
47. Ibid. p. 85.
48. Thomas J. Murphy, "Management by Obsession" *Business Month* April, 1988, p.58.
49. Ibid.
50. Ibid. p. 57.
51. Ibid. p. 60.
52. Ibid. p. 57.
53. Mary Jo Foley, "Boy Wonder Microsoft's Bill Gates," *Electronic Business*, August 15, 1988, p.55.
54. Ibid. p. 56.
55. Thomas J. Murphy, "Management by Obsession" *Business Month* April, 1988, p.59.
56. Brenton Schlender, "How Bill Gates Keeps the Magic Going" *Fortune*, June 18, 1990, p.83.
57. Ibid.
58. Thomas J. Murphy, "Management by Obsession" *Business Month* April, 1988, p.59.
59. Mary Jo Foley, "Boy Wonder Microsoft's Bill Gates," *Electronic Business*, August 15, 1988, p.56.
60. Thomas J. Murphy, "Management by Obsession" *Business Month* April, 1988, p.59.
61. Ibid.
62. Mary Jo Foley, "Boy Wonder Microsoft's Bill Gates," *Electronic Business*, August 15, 1988, p.56.
63. Thomas J. Murphy, "Management by Obsession" *Business Month* April, 1988, p.59.
64. Brenton Schlender, "How Bill Gates Keeps the Magic Going" *Fortune*, June 18, 1990, p.86.
65. Ibid.
66. Ibid. p. 84.
67. Stephen Manes and Paul Andrews, Gates: How Microsoft's mogul reinvented an industry -and made himself the richest man in America (New York: Doubleday, 1993), p. 145.
68. Ibid.
69. Stephen Manes and Paul Andrews, Gates: how Microsoft's mogul reinvented an industry -and made himself the richest man in America (New York: Doubleday, 1993), p. 236.
70. Thomas J. Murphy, "Management by Obsession" *Business Month* April, 1988, p.59.
71. Stephen Manes and Paul Andrews, Gates: how Microsoft's mogul reinvented an industry -and made himself the richest man in America (New York: Doubleday, 1993), p. 236.
72. Thomas J. Murphy, "Management by Obsession" *Business Month* April, 1988, p.59.
73. Ibid.
74. Brenton Schlender, "How Bill Gates Keeps the Magic Going" *Fortune*, June 18, 1990, p.86.
75. Stephen Manes and Paul Andrews, Gates: how Microsoft's mogul reinvented an industry -and made himself the richest man in America (New York: Doubleday, 1993), p. 272.

76. Philip M. Rosenzweig, "Bill Gates and the Management of Microsoft," Harvard Business School Case 9-392-019, (Boston: Publishing Division, Harvard Business School, 1991), p. 12.
77. Stephen Manes and Paul Andrews, Gates: how Microsoft's mogul reinvented an industry -and made himself the richest man in America (New York: Doubleday, 1993), p. 272.
78. Thomas J. Murphy, "Management by Obsession" *Business Month* April, 1988, p.59.
79. Brenton Schlender, "How Bill Gates Keeps the Magic Going" *Fortune*, June 18, 1990, p.86.
80. Ibid. p. 86.
81. Brenton Schlender, "How Bill Gates Keeps the Magic Going" *Fortune*, June 18, 1990, p.86.
82. Mark D. Fefer, "Bill Gates' Next Challenge," *Fortune*, December 28, 1992, p.36.
83. Anonymous, "Top of the World: Can anything stop its phenomenal growth?" The Economist, April 4, 1992.
84. "Microsoft Planning Bigger Work Force," *The New York Times*, June 16, 1990, 19(N), 29(L), Col. 2.
85. Ibid.
86. Brenton Schlender, "How Bill Gates Keeps the Magic Going" *Fortune*, June 18, 1990, p.84.
87. Anonymous, "Top of the World: Can anything stop its phenomenal growth?" *The Economist*, April 4, 1992.
88. Philip M. Rosenzweig, "Bill Gates and the Management of Microsoft," Harvard Business School Case 9-392-019, (Boston: Publishing Division, Harvard Business School, 1991), p. 12.
89. Anonymous, "Top of the World: Can anything stop its phenomenal growth?" *The Economist*, April 4, 1992.
90. Mark D. Fefer, "Bill Gates' Next Challenge," *Fortune*, December 28, 1992, p.36.
91. Kathy Rebello and Eran I. Schwartz, "Microsoft," *Business Week*, February 24, 1992, p. 62.
92. Ibid.
93. Mark D. Fefer, "Bill Gates' Next Challenge," *Fortune*, December 28, 1992, p.36.
94. Kathy Rebello and Eran I. Schwartz, "Microsoft," *Business Week*, February 24, 1992, p. 62.
95. Ibid
96. Stephen Manes and Paul Andrews, Gates: how Microsoft's mogul reinvented an industry -and made himself the richest man in America (New York: Doubleday, 1993), p. 197.
97. Mark D. Fefer, "Bill Gates Next Challenge," *Fortune*, December 28, 1992, p.36.
98. Brenton Schlender, "How Bill Gates Keeps the Magic Going" *Fortune*, June 18, 1990, p.83.
99. Ibid. p. 84.
100. Ibid.
101. Mary Jo Foley, "Boy Wonder Microsoft's Bill Gates," *Electronic Business*, August 15, 1988, p.55.
102. James Wallace and Jim Erickson, Hard Drive: Bill Gates and the Making of the Microsoft Empire (New York: HarperBusiness, 1993), p. 228-9.

103. Thomas J. Murphy, "Management by Obsession" *Business Month* April, 1988, p.59.

104. Ibid.

105. Ibid

106. .Brenton Schlender, "How Bill Gates Keeps the Magic Going" *Fortune*, June 18, 1990,p.86.

107. Ibid. p. 86.

108. Ibid. p. 89.

109. Mark D. Fefer, "Microsoft," *Fortune*,December 28, 1992, p. 31.

110. Peter D. Petre, "Microsoft's Drive to Dominate Software," *Fortune*, January 23, 1984, p.88-90.

111. Brenton Schlender, "How Bill Gates Keeps the Magic Going" *Fortune*, June 18, 1990, p.86.

112. Anonymous, "Top of the World: Can anything stop its phenomenal growth?" *The Economist*, April 4, 1992.

44. Using Leadership to Promote TQM*

Case Setting

The Tropical Export Company is a U.S. based multinational corporation with extensive production operations in Latin America that produce LITEP — an acronym for the labor intensive tropical export product grown and exported by the company – for industrialized markets, mainly North America and Europe. The company is one of the 3-4 major players in the industry. Several production divisions are located in the Central American country of Morazan. Each employs approximately 5,500-6,500 employees of whom around 500-550 are salaried; the rest are union members. The divisions are focused on exported volume of high quality LITEP. Quality is vital to the customer and export volume is the key to lowering costs and increasing productivity.

The village-like, relatively closed company towns created social situations where the distinction between one's work and social roles was blurred. The company was very figural in the gestalt of workers' lives in Playa Negra, the production division where the case occurred.

Adoption of TQM

Playa Negra was one of the first sites, within the company, where TQM was implemented, beginning with a training program. The objectives of the training program were to understand how to work within a TQM culture and learn the basic steps in beginning a TQM program to shift attention from inspecting the final product to analyzing the processes used to produce and ship LITEP. The transition from traditional quality inspection of the final product to TQM's continuous improvement of work processes involved the following changes:

1. include the internal customers in the analysis and revision of work processes;
2. focus on the prevention of quality problems rather than inspection;
3. manage the process rather than the results; managers were to work with subordinates in problem solving;
4. develop participative employees rather than passive subordinates;
5. provide basic analytical tools (e.g., Pareto charts, "fishbone" or cause-effect diagrams, control charts, histograms, and flow charts) to teams of subordinates who would analyze problems and make presentations to managers committed to listening rather than deciding based on intuition; and
6. assure continuous improvement of work processes that should ultimately be reflected in higher quality scores and customer satisfaction in the market rather than relying on a commodity-low cost producer approach.

There was no connection established between the TQM program and compensation; it was viewed as part of the participants' duties. However, executives did have bonuses tied to the

---

*Copyright Asbjorn Osland, George Fox College. Reprinted with permission.

achievement of TQM objectives.

The TQM process was housed in a structure parallel to the hierarchy and consisted of the following:

1. a quality council, made up of department heads and supervisors;
2. a full time TQM coordinator who had fairly extensive experience within operations; he had worked for the company in purchasing, the controller's office and operational roles for six years; and
3. the quality action, also called continuous improvement, teams, made up of a variety of people with particular expertise or involvement in a specific process that was designated for improvement by the quality council.

Such a parallel structure was necessary because the TQM process was not perceived as a replacement for the regular machine bureaucracy that had relentlessly met production targets for decades.

In Playa Negra, in addition to the introductory seminars given by the TQM coordinator, dozens of employees attended workshops conducted by external consultants. Topics covered included facilitation skills, leadership in participative workplaces, and statistical process control.

The General Manager's Questions

Armando, the general manager of Playa Negra, sat wondering how to proceed. He understood that TQM doctrine emphasized the importance of a relatively autonomous quality council and the need for cross-functional teams. Yet he was puzzled how to proceed in a culturally appropriate fashion. The dilemma was to strike a balance that would allow TQM to flourish while preserving enough continuity to maintain an organizational foundation that members found satisfying and consistent with their culturally determined expectations of the organization.

The quality council was to provide leadership to the TQM process. However, the council had done next to nothing for 18 months. Armando, the general manager, had quietly sat through the meetings as an observer. The controller, a relatively young expatriate, had led the council meetings.

Everyone, including Armando, was frustrated with the lack of progress. As Armando saw it, he had three alternatives:

1. He could continue within the council as he had for the past 18 months, basically an observer, in the hopes that the council would eventually coalesce around some high priority project.
2. He could aggressively push his TQM agenda within the council. A colleague in another production division, Karl, had done this and was pleased that the quality council was pursuing the projects that were high on his list of priorities. The general manager's control over the organization was extreme due to the power Latin society gives to heads of organizations and the role the company had carved out for the position in its century of neocolonialist domination of the Latino workforce. Karl, a European with long family

links to the company and extensive production experience and competence, observed that even if he asked a question, the Latino council members would try to infer what his desires were and would try to please him. Karl's view was that it would take too long for the council to become truly autonomous and he had decided to use the culturally acceptable role of strong leadership to use the council as a vehicle to achieve his ends. He once confided to Armando that the council was a "manager's council." Both Armando and Karl, as general managers in a very competitive industry, were pressured by their superiors to complete numerous specific projects. Their annual bonuses, of up to 30% of their base pay, depended on achievement of these objectives. Thus, it was understandable why Karl would feel compelled to do what he was doing. Plus, the general manager's role is so powerful that using it to achieve the ends of TQM seemed better to Karl than "sitting around" through endless meetings.

3. A subsidiary, Packing, Inc., that provided plastic and cardboard packaging materials to Playa Negra, had a different approach. The assistant manager, who reported to the general manager and was second-in-command, assumed leadership of the quality council. The general manager was only allowed to attend when the council had completed analyzing an issue and wanted to present their recommendations to him. The assistant manager found that when the general manager observed, the other executives were preoccupied with what they thought he might want rather than analyzing a problem independent of the general manager. Armando wondered if he would get too distant from the process with this method. He was accustomed to assuming strong leadership.

Based on the advice of the both the external and the corporate TQM consultants and his internal TQM coordinator, Armando had attempted to establish quality action teams with members from various functions who were to collaboratively problem solve and thereby improve interdepartmental communication. However, the department heads had resorted to "turf" conscious behaviors and were not allowing their subordinates, who were on the quality action teams, to cooperate with other departments without passing things up the hierarchy for review, thereby slowing the process down and involving the more turf conscious department heads. Armando saw three alternatives:

1. He knew he could order the department heads to do as he told them. In the past, when he led change efforts, he aggressively pursued what he wanted to accomplish by bringing his immediate subordinates along and disseminating the information associated with the change throughout the organization. He followed up with consistent monitoring and encouragement. However, if he aggressively pushed the concept of cross-functional teams, he was worried that if he was to be transferred, the department heads would abandon TQM as they would not have a sense of ownership of the process because they would not have internalized the TQM philosophy.

2. He could allow the department heads to revert back to functional teams and then later attempt to convince them of the utility of cross-functional teams and functional interdependence between departments.

3. He was also considering naming respected middle managers to head the teams who would then choose the members of the quality action teams from their own departments and

other departments, based the team leader's relationship with the prospective members and their perceived competence relating to the problem addressed.

The corporate TQM consultant, Bob, who had encouraged Armando to push the cross-functional teams and also to keep the quality council on track, was doing a training program that day. Armando invited him and the internal TQM coordinator, Francisco, to play a round of golf after work and discuss how they should proceed with the TQM process.

The Golf Game

Armando sat on the verandah of the club and watched Francisco and Bob walk toward him. Though they were not very good golfers, he enjoyed playing with them because it was a more relaxed way to discuss things with them. He had developed confidence in their ability to provide him with assistance but felt that they were mistaken by following TQM as though it were an ideology or an off-the-shelf recipe for the latest potion of managerial self-help. Armando had grown leery of such rigidity as he knew the extremely strong organizational culture of a 70 year old LITEP production division and the uniqueness of Latino culture forced him to modify managerial interventions developed in the U.S. Armando greeted them, "Well, are you ready to wager a few pesos on the game? I'll give you 2 to 1 odds and bet 300 pesos."

Francisco and Bob looked at one another and shrugged assent. They knew they would lose but were also familiar with the custom of wagering and losing to the general manager.

They played a few holes and exchanged small talk about families and politics. Armando began the discussion, "I read your report, Bob. I understand that I have the power and authority to kick the council in the rear and get it moving, or the TQM budget might be at risk given the austerity campaign our financial wizards have imposed on us due to the falling P/E ratio. I also agree that I could force the department heads to adopt the cross-functional approach we've discussed for the quality action teams. I know that you believe such teams are essential due to the need for interdependent groups and cross-functional communication. But, I worry about jamming things down their throats because I could be transferred at any time to another production division and my successor might simply throw out the whole process if it's not strongly entrenched and supported by the department heads and supervisors."

Bob responded, "Your position is such a powerful one that I think you can get away with it and I think there's enough support in corporate to lean on the incoming general manager to follow the playbook we've laid out."

Francisco and Armando exchanged furtive glances and smiles. They were continually amazed that the U.S. corporate offices believed they could simply order the Latin American production divisions to follow some policy. If they followed everything corporate said there would be no production. They would either be paralyzed by strikes or have on-going conflict with the local government. Armando understood how the company's neocolonialist past had fostered the arrogance that confused decision making but also understood that sometimes he had to be cautious in aggressively pushing things that didn't seem to fit with the peculiar culture of the LITEP production divisions.

Armando mused about Bob's reference to the power given the role of the general manager, "From a cultural standpoint, I know my Central American compatriots would accept my autocratic authority. I understand that the 'ingroup,' as you call my department heads and supervisors, will do as I say. However, this same bond also works within departments and creates a powerful 'in-group' feeling that works against cross-functional teams."

As Armando prepared to drive, Bob thought how struck he had been by the loyalty, commitment, and obedience that characterized the organizational culture. He had likened it to the military. People did as they are told. They hesitated to contradict their superiors. They expressed high levels of commitment to the company. Turnover was practically non-existent; people spend their lives working for LITEP, Inc.

Bob was also aware that the general managers, including Armando, enjoyed great power and respect because they had passed all the tests laid before them in their careers and deserved their designation as general manager. They had mastered various jobs and tasks over the 15 years or more that it usually took to become a general manager. When they attained the level of general manager, they were generally recognized as competent production and operations specialists who also had soundly developed managerial and political skills.

Armando drove within 25 yards of the hole. While walking up the fairway they continued chatting. Armando said, "We can't spell out everything. You seem to want to follow a recipe or some doctrine you heard from Deming, Juran or one of the other TQM gurus. It doesn't work that way. Aside from our culture being very different than where you saw TQM work in the U.S., things are in such an upheaval now that conditions are too unpredictable to spell every step out." Armando understood that this uncertainty allowed the general manager great power as there were no established rules and procedures to solve such nonroutine problems.

Francisco listened and thought about Armando. He believed that Armando had highly developed political skills and charismatic leadership qualities. As a large fit man, he struck an imposing image. During meetings, he frequently stood and walked around the room speaking with a thundering voice and waved his arms to emphasize a point. He combined an engaging manner with total authority; one could speak frankly with him and challenge him with solid arguments yet one was always aware of his authority. Francisco asked Armando, "What is it about TQM that you like?"

Armando thought for a few moments and replied, "I enjoy getting a large organization to do what I want it to do." I see TQM as an opportunity to try something new. "You learn from your bosses but you want to do more. TQM gave me that opportunity. I have nothing to fear from more employee participation or the involvement that comes with TQM. If you know the business, you can help people problem solve in a manner that enables them to develop. By giving people authority they will come to you and seek your input. This gives me more power than I would have had if I simply had told a passive work force what to do. I want a proactive group seeking answers. But I never submit anything to a group for their input when I already know the answer. You don't have to tell people you're in charge — they know it."

Francisco thought of all the conversations he had had with company colleagues about the power of the general manager. In one club in another LITEP producing country Francisco had visited, he saw a photo of a former American general manager (who later became the regional vice president) wearing two six-shooters, prominently displayed as part of the club's memorabilia. He also recalled the Spanish businessman who had said that many years ago he bought the first car owned by a "civilian" (i.e., non-company) in a geographically isolated division. When it was delivered on the company train, the general manager initially refused to allow it to be unloaded saying he hadn't given his authorization.

As though he sensed what Francisco was thinking about, Armando continued, "If you think I'm autocratic you should have seen the first American general manager I worked for. He had a boat called 'Solo Mio' ("only mine") that nobody touched, except to keep it ready for his personal and exclusive use. This was how company employees grew to feel a general manager should behave."

Armando continued, "You must recall that our employees are not professionally educated specialists with strong ties outside Playa Negra. Sure, there are professional engineers, accountants, and some college educated production specialists but most of the supervisors do not have much education. Instead they learned their jobs within the company. This made them heavily socialized within Playa Negra – an army of enlisted men, if you will. And I'm their general."

Bob thought about how power was most evident within hierarchical interaction with subordinates. He recalled how the need to dominate subordinates was commonly expressed by superiors. Once a subordinate threatened to quit if he did not receive a raise in his salary to increase it to a level comparable to that of others. His manager swore Bob to secrecy and said, "Julian is very good." Bob believed that, the correct inference was that subordinates should not be told by their superiors how valuable they were because such knowledge would give them power.

Bob thought also of how for one department head, hierarchy was more than simple power associated with a senior position. It had a raw element to it wherein his authority could not be questioned. He expressed the explicit desire that his subordinates fear him. His preference for primitive domination was extreme but such a desire for control over subordinates was not unusual in traditional LITEP culture. He actually asked Bob to do a survey feedback of his department to find out if his subordinates held a sufficient degree of fear for him.

They continued playing. Bob and Francisco were soundly beaten. They paid the obligatory "round fee" to Armando. As Armando walked to his car, Francisco said to Bob, "He'll do what he wants but I think he has a point about not pushing the council too hard. If he's replaced, the new general manager could throw everything out the window.

Also, I'm having a devil of a time getting the department heads to support the cross-functional teams."

Bob countered, "Yes but we know Armando could make things happen if he wanted to and also I strongly believe that the corporate offices won't allow any new general manager, in the event Armando is transferred, to regress to the bad old days and drop his support of TQM."

45. Peoples Trust Company*

The Peoples Trust Company first opened its doors to the public on June 1, 1875, with a total salaried staff of eight members: a treasurer; a secretary; and six assistants (three of whom held the positions of day watchman, night watchman, and messenger). Located in a large, midwestern city, the original company had occupied the basement floor of a new five-story office building with an electric-bell system, steam heat, and steam-driven elevator.

During its early years, the Trust Company had concentrated its activities on providing vault services to its customers for the safekeeping of tangible items and securities. Management had been able to develop the reputation of being a highly conservative trust company that concentrated on a relatively small and select market of wealthy individuals from the local area. In the years following, the vault service had been retained as an accommodation to its customers, but the company's emphasis had slowly shifted from vault service to a wider range of banking and trust services.

Until the early 1900s, banking services had overshadowed trust services in terms of asset volume. Following the turn of the century, trust assets had begun to grow at an increasing rate. Over the years, the company had been able to achieve an impressive record of sound and steady growth. According to a story often told in banking circles: "Peoples Trust was so conservative that they prospered even during the Depression!"

In 1963, with the appointment of a new president, a new era began for Peoples Trust Company. Between 1963 and 1978, trust assets under supervision rose by $145 million, while deposits increased by more than $20 million. The company entered 1983 with about $2 billion in trust assets and $90 million in savings deposits.

Accompanying this recent growth has been the company's desire to fashion a new image for itself. In 1979, Mr. Robert Toller assumed the presidency of Peoples Trust. In 1982, he remarked: "... it should be said that the old concept of a trust involving merely the regular payment of income and preservation of capital is largely obsolete." Accordingly, the Investment Division of the company had been expanded and strengthened. Similar changes had been effected in the Trust and Estate Administrative Group and other customer services. Among these were the improvement of accounting methods and procedures, the installation of electronic data processing systems, and complete renovation of the company's eight-floor building and facilities. Most recently, the company has extended its services into the field of management consulting. This had been acknowledged as a "pioneer" step for a banking institution. The president recently characterized the company as "an organization in the fiduciary business."

At the time these data were gathered, the company had a total of 602 employees. Of this number, 109 were in what is considered the "officer-group"[1] positions of the company. The company's relations with its employees over the years have been satisfactory. The Peoples Trust is generally recognized by city residents and those in suburban areas as a good place to work. The company hires most of its employees from the local area.

---

*This case was prepared by Hrach Bedrosian, New York University, and used here with his permission.

[1] Membership in the officer group is determined by an employee's being legally empowered to represent the company in a transaction.

In the period before 1980 Peoples Trust had provided satisfactory advancement opportunities for its employees, and it had been possible for a young, high-school graduate who showed promise on the job to work his way up gradually to officer status. Graduates of banking institutions were also sought for employment with the company. Ordinarily individuals were considered eligible for promotion to the jobs above them after they had thoroughly mastered the details of their present positions.

Prior to 1980 the total staff of the company was small enough so that there was no need to prepare official organization charts or job descriptions. Virtually all of the employees knew each other on a first-name basis, and they were generally familiar with each other's area of job responsibility. New employees were rapidly able to learn "whom you had to go to for what."

In 1980 the company management called in an outside consultant to appraise its organizational structure and operations and to confer on the rapid expansion and diversification of banking services that the company had planned. The presence of the consultants and the subsequent preparation of organization charts and job descriptions reportedly "shook up a lot of people" – many feared loss of their jobs or, at least, substantial changes in the nature of work and assignments. However, there was little overt reaction among the officer-level employees in terms of turnover and/or other indices of unrest.

Over the years it had been the policy of the company to pay wages that were at least average or a little above the average paid by comparable banking organizations in the area. This, combined with favorable employee relations and the stable and prestigious nature of the work, resulted in a low turnover of personnel. The bulk of employee turnover occurred among the younger employees who filled clerical positions throughout the company's various departments.

Since 1980, the personnel picture at Peoples Trust has been shifting. Several changes have taken place in the top management of the company. By adding several new customer services, the company has altered the very nature of its business. This has resulted in a trend toward "professionalism" of many of the officer-level positions in that these positions now require individuals with higher levels of education and broader abilities. The impact of these changes on current employees has been a matter of concern to several executives in the company, particularly to Mr. John Moore, Manager of the Organization Planning and Personnel Department. Mr. Moore described his picture of the situation to the researcher as follows.[2]

Interview with John Moore— V.P., Organization Planning and Personnel

Our problem here is one of a changing image and along with it the changing of people. As a trust company, we had no other ties with an individual's financial needs ... we could only talk in terms of death. We wanted to be able to talk in terms of life, we got active in the investment-advisory business.

The old wealth around here is pretty well locked up, so we wanted to provide services to new and growing organizations and to individuals who are accumulating wealth. Our problem is one of reorientation. We used to provide one service for one customer. We now want to enter

---

[2]Mr. Moore drew from his files a list of ten individuals who he felt were representative of the group whose lack of appropriate experience or qualifications created a road block to their future development and advancement with the company. These individuals are described in Exhibit 1.

Exhibit 1. Peoples Trust Company

Name	Age	Education	Date of Hire	Positions Held
Linda Horn	37	2-year technical institute of business administration	1975	Messenger Clearance clerk Accounting clerk Unit head (working supervisor) Section head (supervisor)
Richard Gaul*	30	2-year junior college program in 1977 in business administration	1977	Business machines operator Section head (supervisor) Operations officer
Fred James	35	B.A. degree, local university American Institute of Banking	1976	Loan clerk Teller Accounting unit head (working supervisor)
Fran Wilson*	35	1 year at a local university	1981	Methods analyst Operations unit head (working supervisor) Systems programmer Property accounting department head
Martin Pfieffer*	32	Prep school	1977	Messenger Accounting clerk Section head (supervisor) Department head
James Klinger	38	B.A. degree from local university 1972	1972	Messenger Accounting clerk Records clerk Unit head (working supervisor) Administrative specialist
Karen Kissler*	35	B.A. degree from local university 1974 co-op program	1974	Messenger Real property specialist Assistant estate officer
Charles Ferris	42	2-year junior college program in business administration American Institute of Banking	1962	Messenger Deposit accounting section head (supervisor) Unit head (working supervisor)
William Jagger	54	High school	1949	Messenger Trust liaison clerk Accounting clerk Bookkeeping section head
Thomas Geoghigan*	42	2-year junior college program in business administration	1969	Messenger Securities accountant Property custodian Office manager Assistant operations officer

*Officer

new ventures, offer new services, attract new customers. The problem has become one of how to make the change ... do we have the talent and the people to make the change?

We have a "band" of people (see Exhibits 1 and 2) in our organization ... in the thirty-five to fifty age group who came in under the old hiring practices and ground rules. Given the new directions in which our company is moving and the changing job requirements, it's clear that, considering their current qualifications and capabilities, these individuals have nowhere to go. Some have been able to accept this; and this acceptance includes watching others move past them. Others have difficulty accepting it ... a few have left ... and we haven't discouraged anyone from leaving. For those who can't accept it, there is the problem of integrating their career strategy with ours. We've articulated our objectives clearly; now individuals need clarification of their own strategies.

As I see it, change caught up with these individuals. They had on-the-job training in their own areas, but that doesn't help them much to cope with the new demands. New functional areas are being melded on top of old ones. For example, marketing is new; so is electronic data processing. They both require qualities that our existing employee staff didn't have.

To date, we have not approached any of these people in an individual way to discuss their problems with them. Our objectives are to further develop these people, but we'll first have to get the support of the department managers who supervise them.

We want to find ways to further develop personnel of the kind represented by this group through a variety of approaches. I am thinking here not only of formal job training in management development, but also of management techniques that would help individuals identify new kinds of qualifications or possible new standards of performance they must take into consideration in planning their own personal growth.

Exhibit 2. Peoples Trust Company Organization Chart (June 1983)

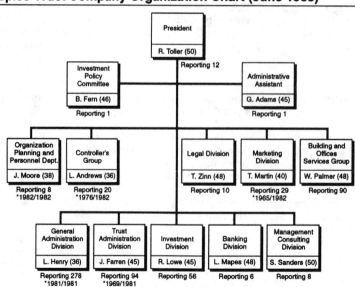

Note: Numbers in parentheses indicate manager's age. These are included for planning purposes only. Numbers below each position indicate number of subordinates.

*Indicates year in which manager joined the Company and year in which he assumed current position. For example, Mr. Larry Andrews joined Peoples Trust Company in 1976, and became Controller in 1982.

We also have to find ways to provide more opportunities for minorities and women in the organization, particularly at the officer level. Although Peoples Trust is not a federal contractor, we would like to be seen as and be an affirmative action employer and an organization where everyone has an equal chance for employment and promotion.

We have to change the conditioning of old times throughout the company. A recently hired MBA is now an officer. Years ago that couldn't have happened so rapidly. And not everyone here is in agreement that the appointment I just mentioned *should* have happened the way it did. We have to develop support in our company for the new recruiting image.

There are two things which really concern me most about this whole problem:

1. We have a problem in under-utilization of resources.
2. There is a problem which is presented to the growth and development of the company in having some of the individuals I have been discussing settled into key spots.

The company really bears the responsibility for the current situation as I described it. In addition, what this all means to me is that our personnel function may change considerably over the coming year.

After this interview with Mr. Moore, the researcher talked with other company executives to learn their views of the problems outlined by Mr. Moore. The findings from these interviews are presented below.

Interview with Fred Bellows – Human Resource Planning

Historically we have been conservatively managed ... you might say "ultra-conservatively." But now we want to change that image. Several years ago there was a revolution in top management. In 1979, Mr. Toller took over and brought in young people, many not from the banking field but from other types of business and consulting organizations. Our employment philosophy may be stated as follows: "We want above-average people ... for above-average pay ... and we want to give them a chance to learn and grow and move with the organization." This applies mainly to those in whom we see management-level potential.

They are told in their employment interview that if they don't see opportunity with us, then they should leave. This is in contrast to the old philosophy that this is a secure place to work, that you can stay here by keeping your nose clean, and that you can sit and wait for pot luck to become a trust officer.

Many people are caught in this changing philosophy. A case in the Trust Administration Division is a good example. There we have an employee in a Grade 10 job who has been with the bank eight years. We just hired a new person out of college who we put in that same Grade 10. Now they're both at the same level, but they're entirely different people in terms of education, social background, etc.

Now the Head of our Trust Division bucks this sort of thing. She argues that we don't need all "stars" in the company. Yet, the president wants young, dynamic individuals who can develop and be developed. So I'm trying to get the Trust Division to define: what does the job really require?

We have a number of people with two years of accounting training who have been with the company anywhere from six to nine years. Under our old system they'd be okay, but under the new system they're not. They're not realistic about their future. Our problem is that we're being honest, but few are getting the message.

We bring in a new individual ... ask others to train that person ... and then promote that person over their heads. We have people whose jobs we could get done for a lot less money. When, if ever, do we tell them to go elsewhere?

Interview with Larry Andrews – Controller

There is no question but that there has been a complete revolution around here. In the past, we were in business to serve the community; to handle small accounts; to help the small investor who needed investment service. Our motto was "help anyone who needs help." Our employees were geared to this kind of work orientation and felt at home with it. They could easily identify themselves with this sort of approach to doing business. Most people were quite comfortable; their personal goals coincided with the company goal.

But we found that we couldn't make money conducting this kind of business. So, we've had to extend our services to attract people who have money and can afford our service. Now the company goal has changed. For example, the Trust Department is now concerned with the management of property in general. The "dead man's bank" has become the "live people's service organization." So we've had to create a kind of snob appeal that too many of our people can't identify with or don't believe in.

Many problems have emerged from these changes. Before, individuals' knowledge of the details of their jobs was their greatest asset. They worked to develop that knowledge and protected it. Now – and I'm speaking of supervisory jobs – the important factor is to have some familiarity with the work but to be able to work with people; to get others to do the detail. Too many of our people still don't understand this....

The route to the top is no longer clear. Over a five-year period this organization has changed. There have been reorganizations, new functions created, and some realignment of existing functions. Many who felt they had a clear line to something higher in the organization now find that that "something" isn't there anymore.

We've had lots of hiring-in at higher levels. Many old-timers have been bypassed. In some cases, the new, outside hirees came into jobs that never existed before, or were hired into a job that had previously existed, but which is now a "cut" above what it was before. What used to be a top job is now a second or third spot.

What we need now are people who are "professional managers" – by that I mean a supervisor versus a technical specialist. Years ago supervision could be concentrated in a few key individuals ... but in the past five years we've grown 20 percent to 30 percent and have a management hierarchy. A person used to be able to grow up as a technical specialist and develop managerial skills secondarily.

To a small extent it's a matter of personality too. We have a new president, and what is acceptable to him differs from what was acceptable to his predecessor. There's a new mix of personal favoritism that goes along with the new vogue. Technical specialists are "low need" as far as the company is concerned. I estimate we now have about thirty people in this category in officer-level jobs.

Interview with Tom Martin – Marketing Division Head

There have been many changes over the past six years. Mr. Toller took a look at the entire organization ... and then hired a consultant to do an organization study. It was sort of an outside stamp of approval.

His hope was to move some of the dead wood ... the senior people who were past their peak and didn't represent what the company wanted anymore in its managerial and officer staff. Few of these individuals have the capacity to change, and for others it may already be too late to change. Many had leveled off in their development long before these changes came about, and the changes just made it more apparent. Early retirement has been given to some of those over sixty. Others remained as titular head of their departments, but in essence report to a younger person who is really running the department.

Banking used to be a soft industry ... you were hired and never fired. If you were a poor performer, you were given a lousy job that you could stay at. No one was ever called in and told to shape up. The pay was so poor it attracted people who wanted to work in a sheltered area, and they were satisfied to try and build a career in that area. So it was a job with low pay, high prestige, and some opportunity.

Our biggest problem is to convince people that they are not technicians anymore, that they are to supervise their subordinates and work to develop them. Apparently, for many older individuals, and younger ones too, this is an impossible assignment. They can do the jobs themselves, but having anyone else do it in any other way runs against their grain.

If our rate of personnel growth over the next ten years is as fast as the previous ten years, I'm afraid we can only absorb about 50 percent of our most promising people.

Interview with Jane Farren – Trust Administration Division Head

We have several people for whom there is very little opportunity anymore. We just don't see any potential in these people. There are about fifteen of them who are in their forties and are really not capable of making any independent decisions. We're trying to get them to see other opportunities ... both inside and outside the company. For example, our Real Estate group was big in the 1960s and 1970s. We're trying to make it important again, and there may be some opportunities in that area.

To give you an idea of the problem we're faced with: One individual is really a personality problem. He's an attorney but he can't get along with others. He wants people to come to him; he focuses on detail too much; and he has great difficulty in telling others what to do and how to do it. He has to do the job all by himself.

Another individual: We gave him a section to supervise but he really hasn't measured up. But, he was the president's pet. I suppose we'll let him continue on ... he's fifty-seven ... and then retire him early.

Interview with Mr. L. Henry – General Administration Division

The company has been undergoing basic change. In the past, if people demonstrated technical competence they were promoted, and that was fine while the company was a small, stable group, and everyone knew what the other was thinking. But then, many in the senior group began to retire. With this "changing of the guard" and the growth of the company, many of us have lost communication with our counterparts. Many of us are new in this field, new to this company, and, of course, new to each other. But we recognize this, so half the communication problem is solved. In a sense, we're not constrained by "how it was done before."

46. Seeing the Forest and the Trees*

The changing face of competition, both domestic and global, was looking directly into the window of the headquarters of the Forest Products Company (FPC) of the Weyerhaeuser Corporation in Seattle. It was a face that reflected the trend away from the large firm, commodity lumber business and toward the small mills that tailor-made products to meet the demands of their customers. Interestingly, these small mills owed their existence, in large part, to the sale of machinery by the larger firms when they were faced with the depressed housing market in the early 1980s. As a consequence of being able to buy this machinery at depressed prices, these small, nonunion, owner-operated, entrepreneurial, customer-oriented mills were able to not only be the most market-oriented but also the lowest cost operations.

Deciding that going out of business was not an alternative, Charley Bingham, the CEO of the FPC, suggested that something needed to he done, preferrably sooner than later. Together, the top dozen managers decided that a massive reorganization was called for, accompanied by a radical change in strategy. According to Bingham, the change in strategy went something like this:

> Approximately 80 percent of our sales dollars in 1982 represented products sold as commodities. By 1995 we resolved that we must reverse the proportions.

The massive reorganization mirrored that being done by the headquarters. The headquarters decided to decentralize dramatically. The three operating units, of which FPC was one, were given free reign on how to do their business. Given this scenario, Bingham and his top team decided it needed to create an organization capable of acting and responding just like their competitors. Thus, they created 200 profit centers with each center being largely responsible for its own bottom line.

This restructuring soon proved to be only a step in the right direction. The ability of the organization to implement, its new strategy was being undermined by the pervasive poor morale. In addition, many middle managers, those needed to actually carry out the change, were pessimistic about the possibility of sustained future success. Silently, they even questioned their own ability to operate the profit centers.

With insights from Horace Parker, director of executive development at FPC, the rest of the top team came to realize that there would have to be a total transformation of the organization: the corporate culture, knowledge base, skill levels, style of leadership and team orientation would all have to change, for all employees. With 18,000 employees across the U.S., Parker wasn't sure where to start. The others said they would help, but Horace had to tell them what to do. Horace, of course, is waiting to hear what you have to tell him.

Discussion Questions for "Seeing the Forest and the Trees"

In responding to this case, it would help students to refer to the reading, R.S. Schuler, "Strategic

---

Human Resource Management: Linking the People with the Strategic Needs of the Business."
Organizational Dynamics, (Summer 1992): 18-32. To narrow down your analysis, focus on
those aspects most closely related to management and executive development.

1. What are the business objectives here that Horace must use to focus his activities?
2. What are his new management and executive development objectives?
3. How should he go about addressing the implications of these objectives for management
   and executive development?
4. In addition to management and executive development, what other organizational changes
   are needed to support this transformation?